MIŁOSZ

A BIOGRAPHY

MIŁOSZ

Andrzej Franaszek

Edited and Translated by Aleksandra and Michael Parker

THE BELKNAP PRESS *of* HARVARD UNIVERSITY PRESS

Cambridge, Massachusetts & London, England | 2017

First printing

Library of Congress Cataloging-in-Publication Data

Names: Franaszek, Andrzej, author. | Parker, Aleksandra, editor, translator. | Parker, Michael, (Translator of Miłosz), editor, translator.
Title: Miłosz : a biography / Andrzej Franaszek ; edited and translated by Aleksandra and Michael Parker.
Other titles: Miłosz. English
Description: Cambridge, Massachusetts : The Belknap Press of Harvard University Press, 2017. | Includes bibliographical references and index.
Identifiers: LCCN 2016052061 | ISBN 9780674495043 (cloth : alk. paper)
Subjects: LCSH: Miłosz, Czesław. | Poets, Polish—20th century—Biography. | Poets, Polish—21st century—Biography.
Classification: LCC PG7158.M5532 F7313 2017 | DDC 891.8/58709 [B] —dc23
LC record available at https://lccn.loc.gov/2016052061

CONTENTS

Illustrations follow pages 128 and 224

All extracts with titles in Polish within the main text have been translated by Aleksandra and Michael Parker.

ABC   *Miłosz's ABC.* Trans. Madeline G. Levine. New York: Farrar, Straus and Giroux, 2002.

HPL   *History of Polish Literature.* Berkeley: University of California Press, 1983.

Issa   *The Issa Valley.* Trans. Louis Iribarne. First publ. Sidgwick and Jackson, 1981.

NCP   *New Collected Poems, 1931–2001.* New York: Ecco Press, 2003.

NR   *Native Realm.* Trans. Catherine S. Leach. London: Sidgwick and Jackson, 1981.

RD   *Road-Side Dog.* Trans. Czesław Miłosz and Robert Hass. Farrar, Straus and Giroux, 1998.

S&LP   *Selected and Last Poems 1931–2004.* Selected by Robert Hass and Anthony Miłosz. New York: Ecco, 2011.

SS   *Second Space.* Trans. Czesław Miłosz and Robert Hass. New York: Ecco, 2004.

Ulro   *The Land of Ulro.* Trans. Louis Iribarne. New York: Farrar, Straus and Giroux, 1984.

Visions   *Visions from San Francisco Bay.* Trans. Richard Lourie. New York: Farrar, Straus and Giroux, 1982.

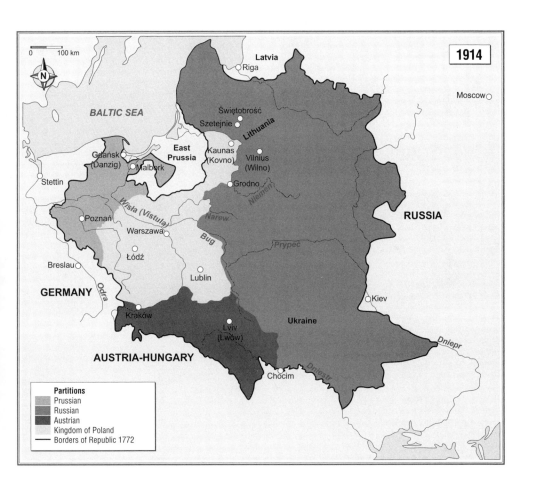

Partitioned Poland and its neighbours, 1914.

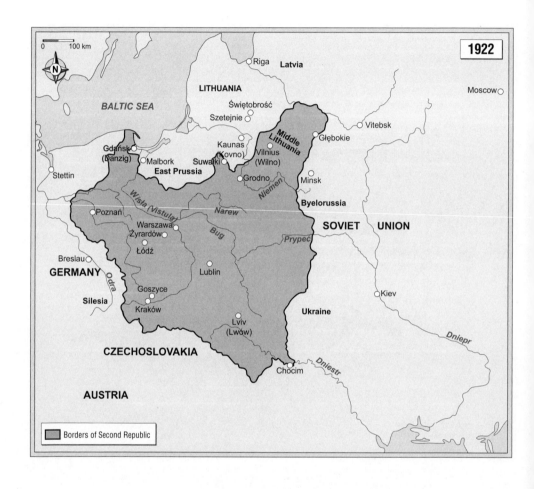

Second Polish Republic, 1922, and its neighbours following the Polish-Soviet War.

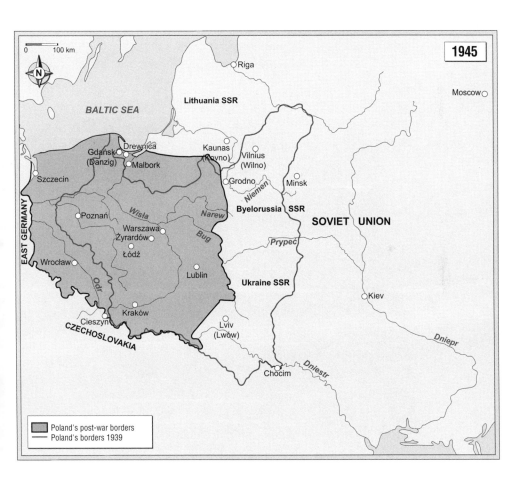

Poland's new borders, as ratified at Potsdam Conference, August 1945.

MIŁOSZ

INTRODUCTION

MICHAEL PARKER

What surrounds us, here and now, is not guaranteed. It could just as well not exist—
and so man constructs poetry out of the remnants found in ruins.

Czesław Miłosz, *The Witness of Poetry*

'I have no hesitation whatsoever in stating that Czesław Miłosz is one of the greatest poets of our time, perhaps the greatest'.[1] These were the words with which Joseph Brodsky began his encomium to the jury tasked with selecting the winner of the Neustadt Award in 1978. Two years later the Lithuanian-born Polish poet received the Nobel Prize for Literature, and with it the international acclaim which for decades Miłosz had thought impossible. In the official citation, the Swedish Academy emphasised the metaphysical and ethical dimensions of Miłosz's work, drawing attention to the 'uncompromising', 'unerring perspicacity' manifested in his texts, which embody a lifetime's resistance to the forces of 'evil and havoc',[2] and, they might have added, 'death and nothingness'.[3] What the two award committees recognised, and what consequently large numbers of readers, writers and critics worldwide would discover, was the exceptional scope, power, passion and compassion that suffuse Miłosz's writings.

Unlike many other contemporary poets living in North America and Europe whose perspective on the world reflects a scepticism, minimalism and distrust, Miłosz never displays 'a shyness in the face of great subjects' ('A Giant at My Shoulder'), as Seamus Heaney points out. What equipped him for his truth-telling role was the incomparable quality of his intellect and poetic skills, which enabled him to endure and, much later, process imaginatively experiences and sufferings which might well have destroyed a less driven individual.

From early childhood onwards, as Andrzej Franaszek, the author of this biography, reveals in his detailed account of the years from 1911 to 1945, Miłosz was repeatedly exposed to war and acts of appalling cruelty, which clearly left their impress on his psychological state, and also on his moral imagination and vision. 'For Miłosz,' as Helen Vendler succinctly notes, 'the person is irrevocably a person in history, and the interchange between external event and the individual life is the matrix of poetry' (Vendler, *The Music of What Happens* 210). During the first eleven years of his life, his family were caught up successively in the events of the First World War, the Russian Revolution, and the Russian-Polish war. Twice in the 1930s, in 1931 and 1934, he travelled to Paris, where he encountered Oskar Miłosz, an uncle, who would become an enduring literary and spiritual guide; a writer and mystic, Oskar predicted that 1939 would see the outbreak of another world war that would last five years, but which his nephew would survive (*NR* 172, 182). In his late twenties and early thirties, as his uncle foresaw, he witnessed the catastrophe of the Second World War, and lived through 'the hell of Nazi occupation' (Miłosz, *Conversation*). The 'liberation' and 'peace' saw the assimilation of Lithuania, Poland and most of the rest of Eastern Europe into the Soviet bloc, with the complicity of the British and American governments.[4]

Following the Second World War, Miłosz worked in the Polish diplomatic service for the new Polish Communist-dominated government, and was given postings first in Washington and subsequently in Paris. In the late 1940s, as the Cold War intensified, Poland's Communist regime lurched increasingly in a Stalinist direction. In order to ensure 'Poland's reliability in the looming international conflict',[5] the Polish-born Soviet marshal Konstanty Rokossowski was appointed Minister of Defence in November 1949; five years earlier he had been the very commander who had delayed the Soviet advance on Warsaw, thereby enabling the Nazis to crush the Warsaw Rising and subsequently raze the city to the ground.[6]

Since the Catholic Church constituted a major challenge to Communist authority and ideology, the Polish government introduced a range of measures designed to destroy its influence, confiscating Church lands and imprisoning over 500 clergy, amongst them Cardinal Stefan Wyszyński, the Primate of Poland. In addition the regime banned religious parades, ordered the removal of religious symbols from schools and other public buildings, and forced Catholic newspapers out of print. In state-run enterprises Sunday working was introduced, and activities were organised to discourage young people from attending mass (Craig 87). Individuals with middle-class origins or with relatives in the West were removed from public positions. Included in the purge was anyone who had seen service in the Allied forces or who had belonged to the resistance organisation Armia Krajowa (Home Army), loyal to the London-based Polish Government-in-Exile during the war (Ascherson 57–62). Pressures were exerted on those engaged in education, journalism and the arts. In 1950 members of the Polish Writers' Union were informed of an edict from the Politburo which required that all future literary works subscribe to the principles of 'socialist realism' (ibid., 59).

Franaszek provides a compelling and detailed account of the effect on Miłosz of the accelerating pace of repression in Poland. Miłosz's political masters started to doubt his loyalties, and in December 1950, on a return visit to Poland, his passport was confiscated by the authorities, effectively trapping him there. Only after appeals to President Bolesław Bierut from Zygmunt Modzelewski, his Foreign Minister, 'at the insistence of his wife' (Haven, *Czesław Miłosz*, xxvi), was Miłosz's passport restored, enabling him to return to France, where on 1 February 1951 he formally requested political asylum.

Over the next three decades, the poet struggled with life in exile, particularly during the period between September 1950 and July 1953 when he endured an enforced separation from his family, now living in the United States. Franaszek discloses how his survival in this intensely difficult period was made possible due to the efforts of the team at *Kultura* in Paris, led by its editor, Jerzy Giedroyc, and supported by Józef Czapski and Zygmunt and Zofia Hertz. Though Miłosz repeatedly made attempts to secure an American visa to rejoin his wife, Janka, and their two boys, Antoni and Piotr, the U.S. authorities decided against granting him one in the light of the substantial number of denunciations they received from émigrés who were suspicious of someone who until recently had worked for the Polish People's Republic. Polonia, the Polish-American community, particularly railed against his involvement in establishing in 1948 the first-ever endowed chair in Polish Literature at Columbia University, regarding the project as tainted by being funded with 'Bolshevik money' (*ABC* 31). Janka, meanwhile, was reluctant to join Miłosz in France, fearing that at some point the Soviets would march in triumph into Western Europe. Miłosz's anguish intensified as the months apart became years, since by his own admission he lacked 'the resilience necessary to oppose the corroding effects of isolation' (Miłosz, *To Begin Where I Am* 15). To the humiliation of being poor and dependent on others was added a fierce hostility from the Polish émigré communities in Britain, France and America. The animus only gradually abated long after the publication of *The Captive Mind* (1953).

Aimed at readers in the West, Miłosz's landmark book set out to explain the ideological allure of communism, and also to expose its effects in practice—cultural and economic poverty, psychological and spiritual servitude. In 'the so-called people's democracies' of Eastern Europe, the new Soviet-installed ruling elites were eager to present communism as *the* 'New Faith', which would over time deliver 'sublime ends' (*Captive Mind* xiii, 17).[7] Its sudden 'growth' convinced many of its disciples—some true believers, many cynical opportunists—that its triumph worldwide was inevitable, and dictated by 'historical necessity'. Conscious that their new political masters had no qualms about fabricating gross lies and committing terrible injustices in the service of that mighty First Cause, Miłosz argued, large sections of the masses in Soviet-occupied Europe masked their contempt for the Party line, while on the surface appearing to acquiesce. 'Ketman', the term Miłosz deploys to describe this ploy, is derived from a mid-nineteenth-century book on Central Asia and is not without its negative repercussions: 'Those who adopt the practice ... can live with the contradictions of saying one thing and believing another, adapting freely to each new requirement of their rulers while believing that they have preserved somewhere within themselves the autonomy of a free thinker' (Judt, 'Captive Minds').

It was *The Captive Mind,* not his poetry, which first brought Miłosz's name to the attention of American intellectuals. Susan Sontag recalled how as a student she initially had reservations about its argument and analysis, a response conditioned partly by the way the book was taken up by the right wing in America during 'the virulent anti-Communism of the McCarthy era'. Later, like others elsewhere, she credited Miłosz's achievement not just in revealing the levels of coercion operative in Central and Eastern Europe, but also in giving intellectuals like her the impetus 'to rethink our position' (*New York Times,* 27 February 1982). And yet, despite the international attention the book garnered, which often saw it bracketed with Koestler's *Darkness at Noon* (1940) and Orwell's *Nineteen Eighty-Four* (1949), there was a downside to its fame, as Miłosz informed an audience at Rutgers University in 1992:

> It elicited denunciations by Poles to the American Embassy in Paris (for being crypto-communist), which meant it wrecked my chances of getting a visa to America for nine years; it earned me the 'mark of a traitor' among the progressives; and also, something I didn't like at all, it meant I was considered a prose writer, a scholar in the field of political science.
> (Qtd. in Kurtzweil, *Partisan Review* 55)

One of the few French intellectuals to offer friendship and support throughout Miłosz's distressing early years in France was Albert Camus; others on the left regarded Miłosz as 'something of a leper or a sinner against "the future"' (Lottman 718). Meanwhile, back in Poland the Bierut regime co-ordinated attacks on him, using former colleagues and fellow writers as their mouthpieces (Grudzińska-Gross 63–69).

Miłosz's literary fortunes slowly began to change after he left France in 1960 to accept a lectureship in America in the Department of Slavic Languages at the University of California, Berkeley. Initially, as was the case in France, the early years exacerbated Miłosz's feelings of isolation and frustration. Peter Dale Scott recalled how, on his arrival at UC Berkeley in 1961, 'many in the local Polish community fervently advised me against meeting Miłosz', regarding the poet's years as a diplomat 'as a treason that could never be exculpated' (Haven, *An Invisible Rope* 65). He goes on to emphasise that Miłosz had very 'few friends outside the Slavic Department' and felt a strong distaste for the 'secular culture of America' (ibid.). Since his poetry was written in Polish, he had no audience in the United States, and, for all he knew, reached only a small number of people in Poland. In early 1962, he wrote in a letter to Thomas Merton, the Catholic writer and mystic based in Kentucky, 'I have no right to have any opinions on politics in this country as I am not even a resident but a guest' (*Striving towards Being* 139). Later in their correspondence, however, he alludes to the sympathy he feels for the civil rights movement and his hostility towards the war in Vietnam (ibid., 164, 174).

More so than in his exile in France, because of his familiarity with its culture and tongue, in America issues around language and identity became more problematic. Attempting to mitigate the disorientating effects of operating in a foreign language during his working, 'external' hours, he conducted his inner, creative and domestic life in Polish. In an interview from 1980, he explains that he adopted this strategy of linguistic bifurcation as a means of stabilising the self, believing that managing 'two personalities in one' (Mona Simpson, in Haven 9) might be preferable to having his identity fundamentally altered by the acquired language. Unlike many other migrants, Miłosz consciously sought to preserve a strong, foreign inflection in his English, in order to accentuate his distinctness. Rather than killing his creativity, as he initially feared it might, Miłosz's immersion in English proved salutary in the long term, as he later observed:

> A writer living among people who speak a language different from his own discovers after a while that he senses his native language in a new manner. It is not true that a long stay abroad leads to withering of styles . . . What is true, however, is that new aspects and tonalities of the native tongue are discovered, for they stand out against the background of the language spoken in the new milieu. ('Language', in *To Begin Where I Am* 19)

Though for a long time the feeling of being 'out of place' in America persisted, his intensive work as a translator of others' and his own poems introduced him to a circle of writers and admirers whose friendship sustained him both personally and artistically. W. S. Merwin is one of many who cites the massive impact on young American poets in the 1960s of the publication of Miłosz's anthology *Post-War Polish Poetry* in 1965, which

> appeared at the height of the timely, but noisy controversy over the differences, real and concocted, between 'academic' and the 'Beat' poets . . . I had been drawn to the poetry of other languages and traditions. Miłosz's book had been a talisman and had made most of the literary bickering among the various ideological encampments, then most audible among the poetic doctrines in English, seem frivolous and silly. (Haven, *An Invisible Rope* 75)

In 'The Unacknowledged Legislator's Dream', Clare Cavanagh provides a roll-call of distinguished American poets who were similarly drawn strongly to the challenge of Miłosz's 'densely historical',[8] deeply philosophical work. Her list includes 'Robert Pinsky, Edward Hirsch, Rosanna Warren, Robert Hass, Charles Simic, Mary Karr, Carolyn Forché, Mark Strand' (ibid., 236), but, for good measure, she also mentions four non-American heavyweights, Ted Hughes, Seamus Heaney, Joseph Brodsky and Derek Walcott. Her essay focuses specifically on the Polish poet's positive effect on American literature, enabling poets, in Jonathan Galassi's words, 'to exit from the labyrinth of the self and begin to grapple again with the larger problems of being in the world' (Qtd. in Cavanagh 243). Yet, in a useful corrective to what is sometimes presented as one way westbound traffic, she also points out how, for example, Miłosz's haunting depictions of wartime Warsaw bear traces of his engagement with T. S. Eliot's *The Waste Land*, which he had recently attempted to translate (ibid., 246–247).

Translation of the work of other writers played a large part in enriching and extending the scope of his work, by opening it up to new perspectives, 'models and traditions' (Grudzińska-Gross 246). Of course, the poet himself was not the sole beneficiary of this crucial form of cultural interchange. Readers of English worldwide, including readers of this book, owe a huge debt to the work of a succession of loyal, committed translators of Miłosz's poetry and prose—Jane Zielonko, Peter Dale Scott, Jan Darowski, Richard Lourie, Renata Gorczyński, Lillian Vallee, Celina Wieniewska, Lawrence Davis, Louis Iribarne, David Brooks, John Carpenter, Leonard Nathan, Madeline Levine, Robert Pinsky, Robert Hass and, most recently, the poet's older son, Tony Miłosz.

The Miłosz who emerges from Franaszek's pages is an intriguing, deeply complex, often contradictory being. Since his was such a protracted, anguished encounter with history, it is hardly surprising that he should often return in his writings to the horrors humankind inflicts on its own across the centuries. 'A Poor Christian Looks at the Ghetto' (1943) exhibits his consummate sensitivity and skill in responding to the experience of war. The poem offers an outsider's view of the Warsaw Ghetto after it was 'liquidated' in mid-May 1943, when the young Jewish fighters determined to resist further deportations to the death camps had finally run out of ammunition. Of the estimated 56,000 Jews the Germans captured after the Warsaw Ghetto Rising, 7,000 were immediately shot, 22,000 sent to extermination camps at Treblinka and Majdanek, and the remaining 27,000 to forced labour camps.[9]

From the outset, the poem's narrator places before the reader a world of chilling contrasts and reversals, in which the 'natural' hierarchy of species no longer applies. To the active, productive, humble insects now occupying the ghetto, human 'presence' there is merely an obstacle to be circumvented:

> Bees build around red liver,
> Ants build around black bone . . .
>
> Bees build around the honeycomb of lungs,
> Ants build around white bone.

These stark juxtapositions and repetitions recur in succeeding lines, which list materials and objects, natural and man-made, torn, broken and trampled upon in the course of the SS's ethnic cleansing programme. Certain items scattered in the rubble stand out, albeit not as shockingly as the body parts cited above; 'silks' and 'crystals', 'violin strings' and 'trumpets', evoke, respectively, elegance, delicacy and a harmony destroyed.

Numbed at its scale and extent, the poetic observer is capable of offering only a matter-of-fact account of the devastation, regarding it almost as a dramatic spectacle:

> Poof! Phosphorescent fire from yellow walls
> Engulfs animal and human hair.

What takes the reader aback initially is that exclamation, which sounds like something a child might say watching a fireworks' display. That is immediately followed up with a reminder of the catastrophic effects of phosphorus in incendiary devices, which do not discriminate between brick, hair or flesh (German forces had used flamethrowers to burn down buildings, forcing out those in hiding or still resisting). The force of the explosions sees 'wall and roof collapse', releasing an inferno which 'seizes the foundations'. A terrible irony is hinted at here by means of that personification, since a 'foundational' moment in the development of civilisation was, of course, humanity's discovery of the positive uses of fire.

At this, the poem's midway point, Miłosz depicts a landscape whose desolation exceeds, yet also anticipates, that of Beckett's *Waiting for Godot;* 'earth' and meaning have been 'trodden down', and all that exists above ground is 'one leafless tree'. Changes in perspective and mood occur from the third stanza onwards, initially through the introduction of another non-human figure, the solitary mole, whom Miłosz then proceeds to humanise. With the 'small red lamp fastened to his forehead', he resembles a miner. Encountering 'buried bodies' underground, he 'touches' and 'counts' them. A 'worthy pioner' (*Hamlet,* I: v, l.163), he 'distinguishes . . . the ashes of each man', significantly treating the dead as individuals, and as being of account, something the poet repeatedly will endeavour to do in his writings.

As the third stanza of 'A Poor Christian Looks at the Ghetto' ends and the fourth begins, the as yet unidentified speaker shifts from third to first person, alluding to the empty space 'my body' left, which the ants instantly encircle. He confesses to being unsettled by the 'guardian mole' *(strażnik-kret)*, whom he likens to a 'Patriarch', a word with strong associations with Judaism, and regularly applied to Abraham, Isaac and Jacob. The mole's 'swollen eyelids' he attributes to his intensive, late-night poring over the Bible, referred to as 'the great book of the species'. Crucially, the phrase the speaker deploys to define himself ('I, a Jew of the New Testament') acknowledges both affiliation and difference, in an attempt to differentiate himself from death's helpers, gentiles like him. Although he talks of his body as 'broken', it is rather, one suspects, his conscience that is afflicted. As one of the 'uncircumcised', he feels to some degree complicit in this and all the other despicable crimes carried out over the centuries against Jews and other races by poor specimens of humanity claiming to be Christians.

————————————

Crucial to any understanding of Miłosz's work is his complex relationship to Catholicism. During his adolescence and early manhood he frequently voiced his profound antipathy towards the Catholic Church as an institution, since it aligned itself so closely with right-wing, often anti-Semitic nationalists. His encounters and discussions with Oskar Miłosz in the 1930s, however, had a transformative effect on his attitude towards religion. Not least because of his direct experiences of war and occupation, metaphysical questions increasingly absorbed him, as he sought out answers to contradictions in himself, humanity and its relationship with the divine. As he grew older he came to accept the essential mysteries of the Catholic faith, and, significantly, in the late 1970s, embarked on translations of some key books from the Old and New Testaments. And as his death approached, he 'asked for confession and took the sacrament of the Eucharist' (Skwarnicki, in Haven, *An Invisible Rope* 38).

This deeply spiritual strain within his work manifests itself in recurring allusions to concepts, images, forms and figures from Jewish and Christian tradition, as well as in its preoccupations with evil, suffering and justice. Miłosz counters in his writings the Communist orthodoxy that human beings are solely products of blind historical forces and ideological conditioning, by re-asserting their status as beings possessed of a 'soul' and having the potential for free will.[10]

His sense of the individual as a being capable of transcendence, but equally prone to utter indifference to 'the Good',[11] can be glimpsed in his parable-poem 'The Master' (1959). Set in an indeterminate period of history, it is voiced by a composer, who represents the archetypal artist. Its opening stanzas convey the transfigurative power of music and its radical effects on all levels of the social hierarchy, from the Prince to ordinary 'men and women'. Aptly, the choir who perform his choral mass is named after Saint Cecilia, the patron saint of music:

> They say that my music is angelic.
> That when the Prince listens to it
> His face, hidden from sight, *turns* gentle.
> With a beggar he would share power.
> A fan of a lady-in-waiting *is immobile* . . .
>
> Everyone has heard in the cathedral my Missa Solemnis.
> I *changed* the throats of girls from the Saint Cecilia choir
> Into an instrument that *raises* us
> Above what we are. I know how *to free*
> Men and women from remembrances of their long lives
> *So they stand* in the smoke of the nave
> *Restored.* (*NCP* 167–168; my italics)

An immediate source of uncertainty for the reader is how to respond to this maestro. Is he justifiably proud of real achievements, or is he arrogantly over-stating his abilities? In a trope common in Romantic poetry, he pitches art's sublime, miraculous capacity to suspend time, and the artist's compulsion to impose form and structure, against the material world and its mutability. Whereas people diminish to mere sound and then disappear—note the Eliot-like use of the 'steps' metonym[12]—flute and violin as a result of the aural effects they generate in succeeding generations endure, and so the master's will is done:

> Over there a swallow
> Will pass away and return, changed in its slanting flight.
> Steps will be heard at the well but of other people.
> The ploughs will erase a forest. The flute and the violin
> Will always work as I have ordered them.

Though confident of his ability to orchestrate the future, he is at a loss when it comes to controlling perceptions in the present. Audiences lack any conception of the price an artist must pay for the gift of creativity, he complains. Some imagine that artistic achievement has its origin in an act of divine grace ('pierced by a ray', like Saint Teresa of Ávila), others, with more primitive imaginations, that it is the result of a compact made with the devil. The final stanzas intimate, rather, that the master's art emerges not from any other-worldly source but from a very human darkness, out of unspecified guilt and betrayals. A dream provides the first discomposing glimpse into his psyche:

> It comes back in the middle of the night. Who are those
> > holding torches,
> So that what is long past occurs in full light?

The torch-bearers here recall those sent to the Garden of Gethsemane to arrest Christ. The speaker's projection of himself into that narrative conveys not only the scale of his ego, but also a deep vulnerability and his fears of exposure. A far less dramatic scene from his waking life follows, a poignant moment of 'Regret, to no end'. Watching the elderly bless themselves as they file into church, the speaker brings to mind an absence, an unidentified 'she' who may well be his mother.[13] Both in the original Polish ('Zdaję mi się, że mogłaby być jedną z nich') and in translation, loss is voiced in the simplest of utterances:

> When old and white-haired under their laced shawls
> They dip their fingers in a basin at the entrance
> It seems to me she might have been one of them

That conditional 'might have been' gives way to the present continuous in the very next line, a line which makes present the landscape of Miłosz's childhood home: 'The same firs/Rustle and with a shallow wave sheens the lake'. In order to evoke the onomatopoeia in the Polish original (*szumią* is rendered by the English 'rustle'), Miłosz transfers the rippling sound from the trees to the water, hence the alliteration in '*sh*allow' and '*sh*eens'.

The deployment of those surface metaphors anticipates the poem's parting warning to superficial readers:

> A language of angels! Before you mention Grace
> Mind that you do not deceive yourself and others.
> What comes from my evil—that only is true.

This conclusion echoes remarks made by the protagonist in Thomas Mann's *Tonio Kröger*, who is scathing about the naivety of those who idealise the artist and the origins of art: 'In their innocence they assume that beautiful and uplifting results must have beautiful and uplifting causes, they never dream that the "gift" in question is a very dubious affair and rests upon extremely sinister foundations' (Mann 154).

Though vast in their temporal, spiritual, intellectual and spatial reach, Miłosz's poems maintain attachments to the local and individual, often in the form of elegies for lost family and friends and the places they shared, but also in lyric epiphanies which, in Heaney's words, make 'time stand still' (*A Giant at My Shoulder*). His ultimate goal, according to Stanislaw Barańczak, was to create an Art that would attest to and celebrate a world 'Incorrigibly plural' (Mac-Neice, 'Snow', 23) in its forms, features, peoples and perspectives, one in which the poet's own 'individual voice' would be subsumed into 'an all-encompassing polyphony' (Barańczak 177).

Reading Andrzej Franaszek's fine biography, with the *New and Collected Poems* and *The Witness of Poetry* close at hand, few could fail to be struck by the astonishing scope and range of Miłosz's achievements in the course of a long, arduous, often painful lifetime, and the knowledge and imaginative depth he accrued. The last thirty of his ninety-plus years, which were spent in the United States, were at times disorientating, confronting him with landscapes and a culture to which he found it difficult to adjust, but which in the longer term stretched him. Although he arrived with an impressive body of work in his native tongue, the fact that he was able to enhance greatly that store can be attributed not just to his own seemingly limitless imaginative and intellectual resources, but also to the friends, often writers, scholars and students, he encountered there.[14] What should not be underestimated is the impact teaching, translators and translation had on the continuing growth and maturation of his art, enabling him to draw renewed insights from the originary places, people, experiences and history that shaped him, and to offer up what he had gleaned and clarified in another language capable of reaching an audience worldwide. Among the poems that render gratitude for these gifts is 'Late Ripeness', from his last published collection, *Second Space* (2004). It is a poem that deserves quoting at length:

> Not soon, as late as the approach of my ninetieth year
> I felt a door opening in me and I entered
> the clarity of early morning.
>
> One after another my former lives were departing,
> like ships, together with their sorrow.
>
> And the countries, cities, gardens, the bays of seas
> assigned to my brush came closer,
> ready to be described better than they were before.
>
> I was not separated from people, grief and pity joined us.
> We forget—I kept saying—that we are all children of the King
> . . .
> Moments from yesterday and from centuries ago—
> a sword blow, the painting of eyelashes before a mirror
> of polished metal, a lethal musket shot . . .
> . . . they dwell in us
> waiting for a fulfillment.

I knew, always, that I would be a worker in the vineyard,
as are all men and women living at the same time,
whether they are aware of it or not. (*SS* 4)

What Miłosz the philosopher-poet hoped for from the end of the twentieth century and the start of the twenty-first was a far more developed historical
consciousness. In the closing lecture of *The Witness of Poetry,* he lamented how
'mass culture' and the education systems in many parts of the world made so little
effort to foster awareness of history, without which citizens have enormous difficulty making sense of the complexities and confusions of the times they are living
through. Though capable of reading and writing, Miłosz argues, too many are left
'unprepared to receive nourishment of a higher intellectual order. They are sustained artificially on a lower level by television, films and illustrated magazines—
media that are for the mind what too small slippers were for women's feet in old
China' (*The Witness of Poetry* 109). More positively, he detected that intellectual
curiosity about the shared human past had revived, with numbers visiting museums and galleries rising steeply. Though writing before the age of the World
Wide Web, he recognized what advances in technology had already achieved and
could potentially make in extending access, heightening our sensitivity to 'the
exceptionality, strangeness, and loneliness of that creature mysterious to itself', a
being as he was, 'incessantly transcending its own limits' (ibid., 110).

The Garden of Eden
1911–1920

'Darkness . . . split by distant flashes, illuminations'

What should we do with the child of a woman? Ask
The Powers above the earth. The barrel of a cannon
Leaps recoiling. Again. And a plain flares up
As far as the horizon. Thousands of them, running.
In the park on the lake shore tents of the Red Cross
Among hedges, flower beds, vegetable gardens.
Now, into a gallop: the nurse's veil, streaming.
A pitch black stallion rearing; stubble, ravines.
At the riverbank, red-bearded soldiers rowing.
Through the smoke, opening, a forest of broken firs.

Czesław Miłosz, *Personal Notebook*

At the beginning of this story there was once a child, for whom the world began in wonder: the buzzing of insects, a canopy of green trees, millions of sun-gleams on the ripples of the river, sharp grass-blades and the strong grasp of his nanny's hands. From the poet's autobiographical novel, *The Issa Valley*, we learn that his 'cradle stood in the old part of the house, facing the garden, and birdsongs were most likely the first sounds to greet him' (6). If life began with music and enchantment, then it was not long before fear made its presence known. 'As a baby, he was often placed on a bearskin, at which time a sacred peace descended on him . . . he would sit motionless, lifting his hands so as not to touch the shaggy beast' (*Issa* 76).

In spring 1911, Weronika Miłosz, happily married for over two years, returned from Riga in Latvia to Szetejnie in Lithuania, to her parents' estate near

Kiejdany, on the River Niewiaża. What no doubt dictated the timing was the fact that she was six months' pregnant and had decided to have the baby at home. On 30 June, under the sign of Cancer, a baby boy was born, and soon after given the name Czesław at his christening ceremony. Weronika must have been moved by a feeling of tenderness or regret when she named her son after an old admirer.

Her husband, Aleksander, was not present for the child's birth. He had remained behind in Riga, where he was finishing his studies in engineering at Riga University. Not long after graduating, he may well have visited his in-laws, Zygmunt Kunat and Józefa, neé Syruć, to see his firstborn, at a time when he would have been already seeking work and sending out letters of enquiry. No doubt he would have also asked the Kunats for photographs of the baby. This was a period when the tsarist empire that ruled over Lithuania was beginning to crumble, though in the Niewiaża valley nothing much had altered since the nineteenth century. Time was measured by the rhythm of harvesting, with Lithuanian peasants, Polish nobility, Jewish tradesmen and Russian civil servants bustling alongside each other and living in relative peace. That nothing in this world was likely to change turned out to be a naive illusion, not least because, in the words of W. H. Auden, Miłosz's near-contemporary,

> The night was full of wrong,
> ... all over Europe stood horrible nurses
> Itching to boil their children.
>
> ('Voltaire at Ferney')[1]

From very early childhood onwards Miłosz remembered his first encounter with fear, which he would later inflict on Thomas, the protagonist in *The Issa Valley*. The child is bathing in the river, beside a meadow, when a stray, dangerous dog appears, one which might well be afflicted with rabies. His mother grabbed Thomas,

> jumped out of the water and, stark naked, dashed uphill to the park. The hand towel she had snatched up on the run and that had fluttered behind her, the way her panic was transmitted to him, the mouth gasping for air, the wildly pounding heart ... Did he only imagine these things? He could even see the dog—reddish-brown, with hollow flanks—and hear it panting at their heels. Or were they from a dream?—he was haunted by such fleeing nightmares. Paralyzed, entirely at the mercy of her running, he was scared stiff that her legs would give out, that she would collapse from exhaustion. (*Issa* 210)

Years later, the adults will tell him how, at eighteen months, he contracted diphtheria. He was so close to death that, filled with despair, 'his mother had butted the wall and crawled about the room on her knees, wailing and imploring God's mercy. With hands prayerfully raised, she had vowed that if her son recovered she would make a pilgrimage on foot to Wilno, to the shrine of Our Lady of Ostrabrama. Recovery came quickly' (*Issa* 210). In Lithuania over the centuries, many similar promises must have been made, followed by miraculous recoveries. In the opening verses of Adam Mickiewicz's epic poem, *Pan Tadeusz*, a work with which Miłosz was extremely familiar, the poetic speaker alludes to his own unexpected return to good health, following his mother's prayer to the Madonna of Ostrabrama to intercede on his behalf.[2]

Weronika did not keep her promise, yet the boy still grew up hale and hearty. In a surviving photograph from the summer of 1913, taken in the park in Szetejnie, the happy mother is leaning against the back of a bench built around a clump of trees, holding a strong two year-old. A studio portrait from the same period finds him on his own, sitting on a rug holding a toy, while another shows him standing alone, dressed in a white smock, according to the fashion of the time, with features which already prefigure the adult face of Czesław Miłosz.

The boy was clearly robust enough to accompany his mother on a journey of over three thousand miles to join her husband, Aleksander, in Krasnoyarsk, Siberia, where he was working on a government contract. Together with a nanny, they started their trip via Riga, then St Petersburg, where the little boy encountered a car for the first time in his life:

> Clinging to the door handle, my foot on the running-board, I yelled and screamed; they could not tear me away, and the uniformed chauffeur laughed. It seems improbable that something that happened so early in one's life can be remembered, yet I would swear that I can still see the curb, the shiny black paint, or, rather, that I carry the aura of that experience within myself. (*NR* 37)

Mother and son spent many days cooped up in a wagon of the Trans-Siberian Railway, travelling through Moscow, Nizhny Novgorod and Omsk. The long journey must have left the impression that the empire of the Romanovs was without end. In order to exploit its rich resources fully, Russia invested heavily in Siberia, bringing in farm machinery, setting up factories and building roads. The young engineer, Aleksander Miłosz, was busy making drawings of bridges, and was involved in various construction projects, including plans for the routes future railroads would take.

While in Krasnoyarsk, Aleksander also found time to hunt deer in the Sayan Mountains, which stretch from Altai to Baikal. He travelled far into the Arctic Circle, going by boat down the Yenisei River, and venturing deep into the tundra on sledges pulled by dogs. He shot wild ducks, and in 'thick black notebooks' which his son would later examine, he wrote 'hymns in honor of the wild north' (*NR* 38). At the mouth of Yenisei, he came across a ship belonging to the famous explorer Fridtjöf Nansen (1861–1930). In 1913, Nansen was commissioned by Norwegian traders to explore the possibility of creating regular sea-links between the northern shores of Russia and Europe. A photograph commemorating Aleksander's meeting with Nansen and his crew was proudly displayed in the family's home in Podgorna Street, Wilno (and subsequently beside the poet's desk in his apartment in Kraków, where it still can be seen):

> I recognize them. They stand on the deck
> Of the steamer *Correct* when it entered Yenisei estuary.
> The swarthy one, in the leather jacket of an automobilist
> Is Loris-Melikov, diplomat. The fat one, Vostrotin,
> Owner of a gold mine and a deputy to the Duma.
> Beside him, a lean blond man, is my father. And the bony Nansen.
>
> ('The Northern Route', *NCP* 480)

While Weronika Miłosz's recollections of the journey to Krasnoyarsk would always be stirred by the sight of a Mongol ring an archaeologist presented to her on a train, the little boy's lasting memory was of the train itself, in particular one of its more surreal features—a 'urinal' which hung precariously from a wall.

In 1914 the whole family arrived back at the estate in Szetejnie, where, according to ancestral custom among the landowning classes, a dinner was given in their honour. During the meal little Czesław's eyes remained constantly focused on his beautiful young aunt, Gabriela Kunat, an early indication of how frequently and intensely he would be attracted to the female face and form.

All too soon, a succession of major historical events would irreversibly alter their lives and those of millions of other people. On 28 June 1914, in Sarajevo, Gavril Princip, a Bosnian Serb nationalist, assassinated Archduke Franz Ferdinand, heir to the Austro-Hungarian crown, which ruled over a large swathe of the Balkans. On 1 August, Germany declared war on Russia, Serbia's ally. Almost immediately Aleksander Miłosz was conscripted into the Russian armed forces and tasked again with building bridges, though this time to allow soldiers and military vehicles to cross. For most Lithuanians life did not change immediately, but when folk in the countryside held up soot-darkened pieces of glass to the sun during the total solar eclipse of 21 August 1914, they couldn't entirely dismiss the idea that what they were witnessing was an evil omen.

By 1915 the Germans had made huge advances on the eastern front, forcing Russian units to withdraw with heavy casualties. One of little Czesław's contemporaries, living on a neighbouring estate, recorded his memories of this period:

'Some days we could hear loud thuds of heavy artillery . . . People began to dig shelters in case the fighting spread here . . . In mid-July, when the front was getting closer, a decision was made by our family to flee' (Stomma 18). Miłosz himself remembered low-flying planes with black crosses passing over Niewiaża; he tried to escape them by burying himself in the safe warmth of Grandma Syruć's body: 'Peeping out from under my grandmother's cloak, I discovered horror: the bellow of cattle being driven off, the panic, the dust-laden air, the rumbling and flashing on a darkened horizon' (*NR* 40). Whereas Grandfather Kunat probably stayed behind to watch over the estate, the women and children sought shelter in the towns, as was often the case in times of crisis.

It is not possible to reconstruct exactly the chronology of the family's subsequent wartime wanderings. All that exists are the flashes of memory Miłosz recovered for *Native Realm,* starting with an incident on an estate near a small [village] called Rukla, located beside the sandy River Wilia. He recalls

> sitting on a bench with a young good-looking Cossack, whom I like a lot. He is slim-waisted and black-haired. On strips, criss-crossed over his chest, there are cartridges. He twists a bullet out and empties the powder grains onto the bench. Then a tragedy occurs. I was very attached to a little white lamb. Now, the Cossacks are running him into the green, heading him off. To slaughter him. My Cossack tears off to help them. My desperate cry, the inability to bear irrevocable unhappiness, was my first protest against necessity. (*NR* 40–41)

Later he witnessed the arrival of masses of other refugees fleeing to Wilno, and a stay with the Romer family in Bakszta Street, where Barbara, a severe and godfearing Lithuanian woman and former housekeeper in Szetejnie, ruled the roost.

In the autumn of that year the Germans captured the Lithuanian capital. Grandma Syruć was not inclined to take to the roads, however, and when anxieties over the occupation abated, she returned to Szetejnie. Weronika, along with her son, opted to follow her husband's detachment, a brave but also reckless decision. For months they wandered behind the front line, living in a horse-drawn cart or on a troop train wagon. Miłosz, as always, recalled in sharp detail much of what he saw during what must have seemed to him at the time an exciting odyssey:

> A chaos of fascinating and colorful images streamed over me: guns of various caliber, rifles, tents, locomotives (one looked like a gigantic green wasp and for [a] long time inhabited my drowsy fantasies), sailors wearing daggers, which bounced on their hips as they walked, Kirghiz in smocks that reached to the ground, Chinese with their pigtails. Near some depot, I gaped at a maze of cloth surfaces and ropes that

was supposed to be an airplane. The presents I received were always games about battleships and war. All my scribblings and drawings were of soldiers running to attack and shells bursting . . . With my friend, Pavlushka (he was the son of an old bearded believer) . . . I sneaked into the rooms where uniformed men were writing and calculating on abacuses. We made ourselves comfortable at an empty table and I called out in a severe voice: *'Pavlushka, davay bumagu!'* ('Pavlushka, hand over the papers!'). Brow furrowed, I scrawled something illegible that was supposed to be a signature—the movement of the pencil filled me with a feeling of power—and handed it to Pavlushka for further processing. (*NR* 41–42)

At one point, they stopped at a castle in Druya, in Byelorussia, where one set of relatives lived, and then at Imbrody, the estate of the Mohl family, from whom Aleksander's mother was descended. Eventually, they reached as far as Vitebsk, an area at one time Polish territory, but contested at different times between the Poles, the Russians and the Swedes:

He remembers tents of the Red Cross on the shore of a lake at a place called Wyszki. He remembers water scooped out of the boat, big grey waves and a bulb-like Orthodox church which seems to emerge from them. He thinks about that year, 1916, and of his beautiful cousin, Ela, in the uniform of an army nurse, of her riding through hundreds of versts along the front with a handsome officer, whom she has just married. Mama, covered in a shawl, is sitting by the fireplace at dusk with Mr Niekrasz, whom she knows from her student days at Riga, and his epaulets glitter. He had disturbed their conversation, but now he sits quietly and looks intently at the bluish flames, for she has told him that if he looks long enough he would see a funny little man with a pipe in there, riding around. ('Pages Concerning the Years of Independence', *NCP* 386)

Perhaps it was then that the most beautiful photograph of Miłosz's childhood was taken: with soft features and a pageboy haircut, he is sitting on his mother's lap, his slender hands around her neck.

There was an extended halt in Lucyn, Latvia, where a colony of Polish refugees gathered, and where for the first time little Czesław met his paternal grandmother, Stanisława Miłosz. Smoking cigarette after cigarette, elegantly using a holder, she gave vent to her deep anxieties about her younger son, Czesław's Uncle Witold. He had been taken by the Germans to a prisoner of war camp, and to ease his distress, she forwarded him regular parcels with sugar, chocolate, tea and rice.

Czesław is indebted to Grandmother Stanisława for introducing him to literature, when she read to him the tale of a cat called Psik, who 'stopped the hands of a clock in order to have more time with his grandmother'. She dipped next into a book of Japanese fairy tales. Nearly ninety years later, a few months before his death, in the last article he ever dictated, Miłosz reminisced about those exotic tales: 'I remember kimonos, which I liked a lot. In any case, Japan had a special place in my imagination. My future wife had to be Japanese' (CM, in *Tygodnik Powszechny* 25, 2004).

The story which created the greatest impression on him, however, was a very different one, with subject matter much closer to home:

> I was in floods of tears when I heard it. It was about a boy returning to his village, which had been burnt down. He is looking for his mother's grave. The place is overgrown with weeds and wild raspberry bushes. He wanders through the space where the village stood. Suddenly, he is grabbed by thorny brambles which wrap themselves around him, and that's where his mother's grave is. This was his mother's sign to show him where she was buried. Holy Father!' (CM, in Fiut 57)

He listened intently to the talk of the adults, drew ships, airplanes and soldiers running to attack, and sketched the ruins of a castle belonging to the Teutonic knights. But, in addition, he discovered the power and importance of companionship:

> Still today I can feel the intense emotion that was stirred in me by a family, who were also Polish refugees, who lived on the other side of the river. I longed for 'there', because there everything was different, tempting, wonderful, if only the children wanted to play with me. I screamed every time grandmother forcibly dragged me away to take me home. ('Lucyn', *Abecadło* 203)

Countless numbers of the tsar's subjects fell in the trenches, were taken prisoner, and suffered terrible privation. From 18 February 1917 onwards, strikes and civil unrest spread throughout St Petersburg and grew in momentum, and, in contrast to what happened in 1905, soldiers disobeyed orders to fire on civilians. In March, Tsar Nicholas II was forced to abdicate, and an interim government formed; however, it failed to stabilise the situation. As the country was sliding into chaos, the Bolsheviks' position increasingly gained ground, and Russians started to be seen wearing red armbands.

Meanwhile, Poles escaping from the rapidly advancing German Army were forced further eastward. Weronika Miłosz and her six year-old son found refuge next at Jermołowka manor house on the Volga, near Rżew, not far from Moscow, where, on 18 September 1917, a second son, Andrzej, was born. For Czesław, a distraction from this development came in the form of a shy infatuation with twelve year-old Lena, the daughter of their hosts, whose name to his ears resembled 'Lenin', the mysterious name on everyone's lips. By now he had acquired sufficient skill to communicate easily with people around him, not realising that he had learnt Russian:

> The Russian soldiers were my best friends. Their reddish beards tickled softly like the little monkey that had been sewn for me from rags. I assisted at all their meals downstairs in the kitchen, perched on one of the bearded men's laps. They would thrust a spoon into my hand and order me to eat. I treated that activity as a boring duty, which, for some unknown reason, had to be fulfilled in order to win the privilege of their company. (NR 43)

In the course of early childhood Czesław developed an adeptness for languages, speaking Polish at home, but outside it Russian, Byelorussian, Lithuanian, and a Wilno dialect. There was a downside, however, as the rich regional vocabularies he so effortlessly acquired would in the long term cause him considerable difficulties at school.

When reports of the October Revolution reached Rżew, soldiers turned on their officers and murdered them, and after a distillery was stormed, spirits coursed through the gutters. One soldier killed his comrade and hid in the loft of the manor house: 'I was lying in bed. Opening my eyes, I saw one of my bearded friends in front of me. His army shirt was spattered all over with blood ... Then he vanished. Immediately afterward my parents rushed in, thinking that I might have taken fright. "Seryozha's slaughtered a rooster", I said in answer, and rolled over and fell asleep' (NR 44). It was also around that time that Czesław's father turned up with a delegation of soldiers, wearing the fashionable new red armbands, who reassured the family that 'nothing wrong will happen to our dear engineer' (Andrzej Miłosz, 'O starszym bracie', 26).

It was probably then that Aleksander was issued orders that would necessitate the family's relocation hundreds of miles north to Dorpat in Estonia, where, about a century before, one of Aleksander's forefathers had set up a student co-operative. A fond, memorable experience from this time was watching a friend perform magic tricks, though Miłosz's principal recollections of winter 1917–18 were dark and full of fear:

> Our flat had shabby wooden stairs; the courtyard was dreary. Talk about hunger never ceased. One could get bread that contained more sawdust than flour, saccharin and potatoes, but no sugar or meat. At night I

would be awakened by battering at the door, stamping of feet and loud voices. Men in leather jackets and high boots would come in and, by the light of a smoking kerosene lamp, dump the contents of cupboards and drawers onto the floor. My father did not figure on the list of suspects . . . house searches were no doubt a matter of routine. The terror-stricken faces of the women, my brother's screams from his cradle, the whole miserable family sanctuary, or rather den, turned topsy-turvy—all that was not healthy for the heart of a child. (*NR* 45)

In February 1918 the Kaiser's army captured Dorpat. As a consequence Grandmother Stanisława Miłosz's knowledge of German became an important asset to the family. A grimmer consequence, however, was the sight of corpses of leather-jacketed commissars, left unburied, strewn over the snow. To the six year-old, however, this was a time associated with music, with marches played by a military orchestra mixed in with the waltz tunes he once heard in a cinema, a piano accompaniment to documentary footage from the victorious front line.

At the beginning of March 1918, the newly-installed Bolshevik government signed a cease-fire with Germany and the Austro-Hungarian Empire. Eight months later, on 11 November, the war ended, two days after Germany opened negotiations for an armistice with the Allies, following the Kaiser's abdication. Within a short period of time the map of Europe was radically redrawn, studded with newly independent states, including Estonia, Latvia, Lithuania and Poland. As a result, Aleksander was at last able to head home to his in-laws' estate, now with a larger family in tow. The packed locomotives bearing them back moved at a snail's pace, with some travellers precariously seated on any available space on the carriage roofs; the only way to get inside the trains was through the windows. Due to all this turmoil and desperation, little Czesław became separated from the rest of the family at one point at a station which had recently fallen into Bolshevik hands:

Orsha is a bad station. In Orsha a train risks stopping for days.
Thus perhaps in Orsha, I, six years old, got lost
And the repatriation train was starting, about to leave me behind,
Forever. As if I grasped that I would have been somebody else,
A poet of another language, of a different fate.
As if I guessed my end at the shores of Kolyma
Where the bottom of the sea is white with human skulls.
And a great dread visited me then,
The one destined to be the mother of all my fears.

A trembling of the small before the great. Before the Empire.
Which constantly marches westward, armed with bows, lariats, rifles,

Riding in a troika, pummeling the driver's back,
Or in a jeep, wearing fur hats, with a file full of conquered countries.
And I just flee, for a hundred, three hundred years,
On the ice, swimming across, by day, by night, on and on.
Abandoning by my river a punctured cuirass and a coffer with king's
    grants.
Beyond the Dnieper, then the Niemen, then the Bug and the Vistula.

                                                    ('Fear-Dream', *NCP* 487)

At the very last moment he was restored to his parents by unknown hands. The poem above, written almost seventy years later, conjoins an individual child's memory with an archetypal Polish nightmare, expressing as it does the urgent need to avoid falling prey to Russian expansionism from the east. Miłosz never became a typical exile, and, luckily, he never had to experience prison or transportation. A primary motive behind his numerous future relocations would be his desire to get as far away as possible from the aggressive imperium alluded to here.

When in *Native Realm* he reflected on what shaped his world-view during childhood, he stressed his early awareness of the impermanence of state and social formations, the fragility of buildings and of history, which becomes 'equated with ceaseless wandering' (*NR* 41). But the formula is too bland, too tame, since what must have made the deepest impression on the little boy's psyche was not so much an emerging consciousness of the changeability of things, but rather an overwhelming dread, an awareness that for the vast majority of human beings the reality of existence is 'hard and ruthless' (*Szukanie ojczyzny* 224).

In 'War', an unpublished poem from 1953, he recalled the experience of flight in 1915:

And memory returned, the first remembrance from childhood.

Night and darkness are split by distant flashes, illuminations,
A horse's rump is glimpsed, a whip and strap, wheels clatter and rustle,
But I fall asleep again, snug in the warmth of a protective arm.

Darkness without a name, roughed-up by thunder and light without a
    name,
Just that and nothing more defined the face of earth.

                                                    (Beinecke Library Archive)

In Russia he observed the outset of the bloody, hellish terror which every revolution unleashes. He looked on as savagery broke loose, hacking away the thin layer of culture and civilisation, exposing brute instincts underneath. Though only par-

tially conscious of what he was witnessing, Miłosz learnt early the folly of delusions about human nature. No wonder that for him the matrix for fear was not so
much the city of Warsaw under Nazi occupation during the Second World War,
appalling though that was, but childhood memories of revolutionary Russia. In
'O Rzeczywistość' ('On Reality'), an unpublished, unfinished poem dating from
1964, he alludes to how, beneath surfaces, the unspeakable persists:

> The blackness and awfulness of this Volga River
> Which I take in at dusk from the path of a chill park,
> Holding on tightly to adults' hands, hearing dry leaves woosh-woosh.
> Now I know I was six; it happened in nineteen seventeen. And I also
>   know
> That the blackness and awfulness of this Volga river
> Are everywhere. What an embarrassment to be small
> And that everyone around you pretends that it isn't so.
>   (Beinecke Library Archive)

Nightmares about escape from imminent lethal danger would prove an enduring
legacy of his childhood years, seeping their way, like that black river water, into
and between the lines of his poetry.

The Earthly Paradise

> In reward for all this, when I arrived at the end of the journey I found an
> earthly paradise . . . I entered into a stunning greenness, into choruses of
> birds, into orchards bent low with the weight of fruit, into the enchant-
> ment of my native river, so unlike the boundless, dreary rivers of the Eastern
> plains. (*NR* 47)

Czesław's seventh birthday, spent in Szetejnie, would always remain in the writer's memory—a sunny June day, the orchard, his small chair decorated with a
garland of peonies and jasmine, flaxen-haired village girls clapping and singing
songs. He sensed the love and inclusion so necessary in childhood, and also realised how different the world can be from barren, frozen greyness. It could be a
homely place, blessed by human toil and care: 'That country revealed to me
something not named, what might be called today a peaceful husbandry of man
on the earth: the smoke of villages, cattle coming back from pasture, mowers with
their scythes cutting oats and after-grasses, here and there a rowboat near the
shore, rocked gently by a wave' ('Kazia' *NCP* 570).

In Samogitia, nature is lush. The valley drowns in flowers and grasses, and under dazzling blue skies estates and rich Lithuanian villages sprang up. On one side of the river, there was the Ginejty estate, which belonged to relations of Józef Piłsudski, who served as Poland's first chief of state (1918–1922) and as Minister of Defence until 1935.

On the other side of the Niewiaża River was another property with a manor house, where as young ladies Miłosz's mother, Weronika, and her sister were regularly invited. It had belonged to the progressive Prime Minister of Russia, Piotr Stolypin, who initiated land reform, but was assassinated in 1911 in mysterious circumstances.[3] Nearby was the village of Kiejdany, which contained many small shops run by Jews, selling paraffin, soap and herrings, amongst other goods. And close to Kiejdany was a happy spot accessible only by means of muddy lanes, a three days' journey away from Wilno.

The construction of the manor house in Szetejnie began in the eighteenth century. It was given an upgrade at the start of the next century, when Miłosz's grandfather, Szymon Syruć, fitted out and furnished the house, assembled an impressive range of books for his big library, and installed avenues of lime and oak trees. The house was badly built, however, and was frequently damp and cold; on frosty days a whole wing had to be closed, because it was impossible to heat. At its front was a porch with columns, which stood in front of a vestibule, latterly used as a drying room for seeds, and then a hallway. The two reception rooms, with their waxed wooden floors and a grand piano, were used only when receiving guests. As a child, Czesław sometimes would peer in at the covered furniture, but felt uncomfortable in the silence and emptiness of the rooms. The opposite side of the building consisted of a dining room with an oilcloth-covered sofa, on which the boy curled up to read his books, as well as a kitchen, guest room and library. With its colour scheme, lights and shiny pots, detailed in *The Issa Valley* and 'The World'—one of his finest lyric sequences—the living area would not have been out of place in a seventeenth-century painting by a Dutch master. What appealed most to the acutely receptive child was the larder, which the family referred to as 'the pharmacy',

> a magical space on whose shelves 'stood various copper, red and beautifully golden pots, and in drawers diverse ingredients and aromas. Ginger and such like. Those vermillion coloured pots, in combination with the smells, were Chardin in itself. Chardin and Dutch paintings. Here is the key to my attraction to Dutch still life and Chardin . . . Good God! I think that my whole poetry came from that pharmacy'. (CM, in Fiut 154)

Significantly, the last book he ever published was entitled *Spiżarnia literacka* (A Literary Larder).

Rather than staying in the damp, chill manor house, Weronika lived with her sons in a farmhouse she had inherited, roughly two miles away. Warm, made of wood, but rustling with cockroaches in the winter months, this house was referred to as the grange, and was where the boy often took his books to read by candlelight. The family lived upstairs, and farm-workers downstairs,

> a room for each of the four families
> I pronounce the names with surprise:
> Tomaszunas, Sagatis, Osipowicz and Vackonis, the manager,
> Though I felt embarrassed at being the young master.
> ('Do Natury', *Wiersze* V 281)

On the upper floor Polish was spoken, on the lower, Lithuanian. Despite the class division between landowners and the local Lithuanian people, which caused Miłosz anxieties and sometimes nightmares, relations between the two were amicable. The Lithuanians regarded Zygmunt Kunat as congenial and supportive. Although at times he was involved in disputes over the rights to pastures and forests, his tolerance and respect towards others earned him considerable esteem. Weronika ran a school for the village children where they learnt to read and write in Polish, which was a standard practice in those days. As a child, Czesław often accompanied his mother to visit people in their cottages:

> Your former pupils, now farmers, entertained us with talks of crops,
>   women showed their looms and deliberated with you about colors
>   of the warp and the woof.
> On the table slices of ham and sausage, a honeycomb in a clay bowl,
>   and I was drinking *kvas* from a tin cup.
> ('In Szetejnie', *NCP* 641)

Szetejnie, Ginejty, and Peiksva were prosperous villages, where farms were run ethically and in accordance with Lithuanian culture and good practice: 'People loved trees there, and they also loved whittling away at wood: carved window shutters, symbols and letters chiseled into beams, stools of a prescribed shape, frequent roadside crosses linked with the radiant symbol of the sun and an inverted crescent moon, or little chapels, in which sat a mournful Jesus' (*ABC* 280). Retained in the boy's memory were the voices of women singing Lithuanian airs, carried from afar across the water, and also the bells tolling in the nearby wooden church where he had been christened, sounding out for the inhabitants of the manor and cottages alike.

The estate of Szetejnie was well managed. The owners did not go in for hunting or employ other means to parade their aristocratic credentials, such as swanning around in the old family carriage; instead it gathered dust in the carriage

house. The estate brought in good earnings and remained self-sufficient, as it
had throughout its history. Good crops were guaranteed by the black, fertile soil.
The folk who worked their masters' fields were supervised by a manager named
Sypniewski, and, along with their very basic accommodation, received payment
in the form of corn or potatoes. Those in service at the manor were supervised
by Paulina, the manager's wife, whose stern features were not uncommon among
Lithuanian peasant women.

In the estate's workshop linen cloth was woven, while the sheep in its pastures supplied plenty of wool and hides, which were niftily turned into coats by
Jewish tailors in Kiejdany. All the household furniture was made by family employees, and, when need arose, mended by the Kunats' blacksmith.

I liked the bellows operated by rope.
A hand or foot pedal—I don't remember which.
But that blowing, and the blazing of the fire!
And a piece of iron in the fire, held there by tongs,
Red, softened for the anvil,
Beaten with a hammer, bent into a horseshoe,
Thrown in a bucket of water, sizzle, steam.

('Blacksmith Shop', *NCP* 503)

Part of the yearly cycle involved collecting various types of edible mushrooms from the forests and turning vegetables and fruit into homemade preserves,
while in the cellars were stored apples and pears, and, under a cover of straw, ice.
In a pantry next to the kitchen they kept a range of different cheeses, cream and
butter produced in a special dairy room, its walls dotted by a mobile community
of black flies. During the major religious festivals, such as Christmas and Easter,
traditional Polish and local dishes were prepared and old customs observed. Easter
celebrations included the trial of Judas outside the church, and on All Souls Day
(31 October), as on Halloween in the West, pumpkin lamps were carved to frighten
people. Folk superstition led women on St Andrew's Day (30 November) to pour
hot wax into water to determine what the future might hold.

Unlike most Polish poets of later generations, who were usually raised in
urban surroundings, Miłosz was brought up in communion with country life, and
was familiar with its riches in the form of flavours, aromas, colours and sounds.
Its delights were accessible, tangible—not cordoned off by counters and glass, foil
and polythene. His imagination expanded as a result of immediate contact with
nature and immersion in rural culture.[4] At the ages of seven and eight he was
in a state of ecstasy never repeated later in life, in an Edenic world replete with
plenty. He ran now with a child's lightness through oak- and lime-lined avenues,
stopping to reflect awhile by the Black Pond, or cutting hazel branches with a

pocket-knife to make bows and arrows, carving boats out of bark, breathing in the smells of 'marshes, wet linen in the autumn, wood shavings, tree resin and wet dog's hair' (*Piesek przydrożny* 207), absorbing it all with an innate responsiveness and insight. Happy the child, he rhapsodises in *The Issa Valley*, who

> wakes on a summer morning to the oriole's song outside his window, to a chorus of quacks, cackling, and gaggling from the barnyard, to a steady stream of voices bathed in never-ending light, to appreciate the futility of such musical exertions. Touch was also a kind of ecstasy—the feel of naked feet racing over smooth boards on to the cool of a corridor's tiled floor, over a garden path's circular flagstones still wet with dew . . .
>
> As soon as the peonies were in bloom, Antonina would cut a bunch for church. Thomas loved to immerse his gaze in them, straining his whole body to enter their rose-colored palace, as the sun filtered through their petal walls and little bugs wallowed in the yellow pollen—once, when he sniffed too hard, a bug ran up his nose . . .
>
> Hidden in the bushes, Thomas would shinny up a willow and while away the hours, listening and staring down at the water—at the water spiders, their legs ringed by little pools, engaging in their endless pursuit: at the beetles, those drops of metal so smooth the water never clung to them as they danced their continuous round, always a round. Sunbeams revealed whole forests at the bottom, traversed by schools of fish that darted helter-skelter, only to band together again with a flick of the tail, a scattering motion, then another flick . . . Now and then, a larger fish meandered from the deep into the light, and Thomas's heart throbbed with excitement. (*Issa* 13–14)

These were such powerful sensations that they erased or at least consigned to the depths of his psyche the terror and suffering he had so lately experienced in the course of the family's wartime wanderings. Neither the inevitable village cruelty—he witnessed animals being slaughtered—nor the headless body of a cockerel bizarrely flapping around the garden, or even the instance when he himself inflicted pain by putting a hook through a perch to use it as bait for pike, disturbed his joy or stirred his instinct or consciousness to protest. Retrospectively, one of his fictional characters speculated whether 'the pessimism in my later life had its origins in those moments of my childhood, this pessimism, which was entrenched so deeply, that as an adult, I only appreciated one philosopher—sardonic Schopenhauer' (*O podróżach w czasie* 264). He will become acutely aware of evil some years later, but for the present senses only uncertain forebodings, as if among the sunny splashes on the river the devil's grimace flashed: 'For Thomas, one St Andrew's Eve augured genuine horror. Only girls were permitted to look into the mirror, and at midnight, with a solemn air, to shut themselves up in their rooms. Once, as a joke, he tried to mimic them, but when the mirror reflected a pair of red horns, it ended in tears' (*Issa* 17). To come face to face with the Devil was not uncommon. As late as 1923 local peasants came to the cemetery at night to stab with an axle the corpse of a young woman. They were convinced that she was haunting the presbytery, after having committed suicide out of love for a priest. 'From my childhood in Lithuania, I know what is forbidden: it is forbidden to spit on a fire, it is forbidden to place a loaf of bread upside down, it is forbidden to throw bread into the garbage, it is forbidden to walk backward, because that means that you are measuring your mother's grave' (*ABC* 223).

Remnants of pagan prejudices and Christian beliefs jostled in his head with contemporary knowledge, which increasingly achieved mastery when he learnt to read and write. He did not attend school, however. Instead his mother took charge of his early education. On occasion he would hide from her to ensure that his hand did not join together the letters 'n' and 'u', or introduce a gap between 'r' and 'z': 'I remember the garden table (round?) in what I think was a shady bower of lilacs and spirea, where I formed my letters under my mother's watchful eye. It cost her a lot of effort to catch hold of me in the garden, because I hated those writing lessons, I wriggled, sobbed, and screamed that I would never learn' (*ABC* 219). Reading came much more easily to him, and before long the time came when he began to explore the swathes of material gathered in Szetejnie's library, which was packed with 'books, vellum, scrolls and illustrations' (CM, in Fiut 154). It was a room full of treasures from antiquity. After brushing aside the cobwebs, the young Miłosz unearthed a number of French geographic journals to which his great-grandfather had subscribed at the start of the nineteenth century, shortly after the fall of Napoleon, and an atlas which pictured the middle of Africa as a white patch, since it had been drawn before David Livingstone's explorations bore fruit. Next to the journals were compendia on gardening, and a magazine, *Wiadomości Brukowe* (News from the Streets) for which Mickiewicz wrote, along with a first edition of his *Ballads and Romances,* dating from 1822. The illustrations to Shakespeare's works he encountered, which depicted soldiers dressed in short tunics, with swords drawn, he dismissed as uninteresting; the story of a boy stowaway was far more exciting.

Not unsurprisingly, his favourite books were concerned with faraway travel. One of these depicted naked black men, standing armed with bows in boats made of reeds; in another picture they were shown using ropes to tow a hippopotamus ashore (*Issa* 47). He often dreamt of joining them in the water, or of building a shelter for himself among reeds taller than a man, where no strangers could find him. Nestled on the sofa, breathing on his hands to keep them warm, as the dining room was often so cold that a sheepskin coat was necessary, he browsed through innumerable copies of magazines edited in Warsaw, making his first contact with contemporary literature. He would later claim that these first literary encounters strengthened his aversion to societies divided by class.

On the same sofa he listened attentively to his cousin Maria Pawlikowska as she read him the *Trilogy* by Henryk Sienkiewicz (1846–1916), the Nobel Prize–winning Polish novelist and author of *Quo Vadis*. Over time, he would come to view Sienkiewicz as a symbol of the naive, conservative form of the Polish nationalist spirit, but as a child he was probably thrilled by the adventures and incidents. The concept of victory in itself would have held no enchantment for him, as instinctively he felt an affinity with the conquered—the early Christians persecuted by the Emperor Nero, the Lithuanians slaughtered by the Teutonic Knights, the twelfth-century Milanese murdered on the orders of the Holy Roman Emperor, Frederick Barbarossa.

Of the many books he devoured in his early years, the two which made the biggest impression on him belonged to the genre of children's fantasy fiction: Zofia Urbanowska's *Gucio Zaczarowany* (Little Gustav's Metamorphosis) and Selma Lagerlöf's *The Wonderful Adventures of Nils*. Both present a similar scenario, in which a self-centred, selfish child is magically reduced in size and interacts with the world of insects and animals. Through contact with nature, the protagonist learns to respect others, and discovers altruism and friendship. Spoilt, lazy Gucio metamorphoses and becomes a fly, and finds himself in a meadow where he meets its various inhabitants—a mole, a sparrow, a spider, beetles and bees. Over time he starts feeling ashamed of his indolence, an emotion which may well have resonated in the mind of the busy, industrious young Miłosz. He may well have appreciated how cleverly Gucio's initiation into the natural world was interwoven with the story's moral and religious dimensions, but also would have been intrigued, like any child, with the magical switch in perspective: 'Gucio was very surprised that he could see everything much better, clearer than when he was human; it was as if he had put on magnifying glasses. It was not the glasses, but different eyes, a fly's eyes, consisting of a multitude of hexagonal little eyes, which saw everything with exceptional clarity' (Urbanowska 46). Years later Miłosz would deploy this metamorphosis as a metaphor for the poet's necessary detachment from the concerns of the mediocre, and his own strategy of pretending to be a 'normal' adult member of society:

> Bobo,[5] a nasty boy, was changed into a fly
>
> . . .
>
> Later on, when he had pressed trousers and a trimmed moustache
> He always thought, holding a glass of liquor, that he was cheating
>   them
> For a fly should not discuss the nation and productivity.
>
> ('Bobo's Metamorphosis', *NCP* 196)

Another prompt for Miłosz's later reflections on the poet's calling came from the story of little Nils Holgersson, the principal character in Selma Lagerlöf's wonderful book. The punishment visited on Nils for his slothfulness and mindless cruelty is to be reduced to the size of an elf. Along with his diminished stature, he acquires the capacity to understand the language of animals, and hears their bitter reproaches. Traversing the world with a flock of wild geese, Nils is like an artist, 'one who flies above the Earth and looks at it *from above* but at the same time sees it in every detail' (Nobel Lecture 11). This ability to assimilate every aspect of the world, its people, its history and nature, while acknowledging the uniqueness of each single being, was given considerable prominence in Miłosz's Nobel speech:

> What is this enigmatic impulse that does not allow one to settle down in the achieved, the finished? I think it is a quest for reality. I give to this word its naive and solemn meaning, a meaning having nothing to do with the philosophical debates of the last few centuries. It is the Earth as seen by Nils from the back of the gander and by the author of the Latin ode from the back of Pegasus. (Nobel Lecture 11)

Looking back in old age, Miłosz declared that he had no regrets about his upbringing and how his consciousness had been shaped equally by 'the Bible, fairy tales and a scientific outlook on the world'. The books he read between the ages of seven and ten 'fired his imagination', provided a key to understanding the culture of his 'native surroundings', and implanted a belief that telluric forces were at work in certain locales. It is partly due to these influences that Miłosz retained in his writing traces of the pantheistic strain within Lithuanian folk culture, which had little doubt that the divine was dispersed among old trees, burial mounds, caves, rocks, rivers and even some animals. Indeed, as he knelt on the cold floor of the church at Świętobrość,[6] watching light flicker against the vibrant colours of the stained glass, and repeated trustingly the 'Our Father', he may well have sensed also something more primal, an ancient, nameless, sacred Presence.

The intensity with which he then apprehended the world revealed itself in other childhood fascinations. Objects as diverse as a coloured pencil, a black ink tablet, a stamp from Borneo, a rag toy monkey, a cardboard cut-out squirrel, a botanical atlas, a picture of the Virgin Mary given to him by a priest, in which the combination of the dark blue of her dress and the bronze of her face, framed in real gold, entranced him, all these triggered profound, conflicting emotions in him, in which desire and wonder are tainted by shame, since he is conscious of a strong urge to lock them away so that they remain solely his.

An early manifestation of this secretive, hoarding instinct was a ban he imposed on himself: 'No sooner would he commence sketching a bow than he stopped and tore up the drawing. Bows were his great passion, and somehow he had formed the idea that one should avoid showing the things one loved, that they should be guarded in absolute privacy' (*Issa* 48).

Already at that age, as has been noted in regard to Gabriela and Lena, he was strongly affected by the sight of the beauty, delicacy and gentleness of a woman's body. Another instance of arousal occurred when he met up with a neighbour's daughter:

> We walked along the paths, crossed some little bridges, which had railings made of birch poles—I remember that well. Then it happened. I looked at her thin bare shoulders, the narrowness of her arms above the elbow, and an emotion I had never experienced, a tenderness, a rapture, unnameable, welled up in my throat. I had no idea that this is called love'. (*ABC* 186)

This sense of wonderment will be strengthened by the realisation that beauty lessens with the passing of time. A cluster of interrelated concerns began to knit together within his conscious and unconscious mind, which would in time force their way into his lines: beauty, frailty, transience, mortality awakened in him, as in Keats, a prevailing, overpowering sadness.

An incident which illustrates his disquiet at the intimate contiguity of *eros* and *thanatos* took place when, at the age of ten, he was on his way to his aunt's estate. He suddenly came upon a shrine set beside a crossroads:

> There was a structure made of bricks and a blocked entrance, but I managed to scramble in. Inside I saw a smashed coffin, a satin dress, and small shoes belonging to a young lady, who was buried there. Later that night I had nightmares about her. I sensed the strange ephemerality of things . . . In my head, I called her 'princess'. (*Podróżny świata* 131)

———

> Enchantment at a very young age is a sacrament, an experience whose memory acts upon us throughout our life. Having been wounded, I ought to have become a complete pessimist; my ecstatic praises of existence can be explained by that early gift I received through my five senses. ('Nature', *ABC* 209)

Although the time Miłosz spent in the 'earthly paradise' lasted just over a year, it is imperative not to underestimate its importance. The account presented above of an idyllic, Rousseauesque childhood, played out in an enchanted garden, learning without pressure, sheltered in a mother's tender care, may seem the stuff of cliché, yet it reflects precisely what this particular phase of his life was like and, equally importantly, how it *seemed* in retrospect. The child's happiness sprang from the fact that there were no rivals to compete with, no-one who could have bested him. Free from being appraised or judged—as he would observe many years later—he retained an innocence, as Adam and Eve had before the Fall: 'Guilt arises from the awareness of the eyes of others who are watching us ... Innocence is due in no small measure due to the fact that I do not have to take exams. I do not have to think that he is better than me and that I am weaker' (*Podróżny świata* 129). No other places he subsequently lived, not Wilno, Warsaw, Montgeron, Berkeley, would displace Szetejnie as the name which embodied 'home' in the deepest meaning of the word. It persisted in his memory as the still point of the world, the spot on earth he considered wholly his own. When during years of painful loneliness in Paris he struggled to regain his creative powers, what generated an Antaeus-like revival was renewed contact, albeit metaphorically, with the ground of his being. Writing *The Issa Valley*, he sought to re-capture childhood. When towards the end of his life he was able to make the pilgrimage back to his natal realm, the result was a series of epiphanies and affirmations almost without parallel:

> It was a riverside meadow, lush, from before the hay harvest,
> On an immaculate day in the sun of June.
> I searched for it, found it, recognized it.
> Grasses and flowers grew there familiar in my childhood.
> With half-closed eyelids I absorbed luminescence.
> And the scent garnered me, all knowing ceased.
> Suddenly I felt I was disappearing and weeping with joy.
>
> ('A Meadow', *NCP* 597)

Good and Bad Blood

For Thomas she was almost too beautiful to be real, and he gulped with love at the sight of her. His father was practically a stranger to him. (*Issa* 9)

Or were the devils attracted to the Issa because of its water? It is said that it possesses properties affecting the personalities of those born along its shores who are inclined to be eccentric, are far from being at peace with themselves, and whose blue eyes, blond hair, and somewhat sturdy build only give a semblance of Nordic health. (*Issa* 4–5)

'As I ranged over the past, for some obscure reason it was my mother's family, when I recognized its importance, that stimulated my imagination the most. Its women were made of tougher fiber' (*NR* 65). Even a fleeting perusal of Czesław Miłosz's forays into autobiography reveals that the key figures in his childhood were invariably women, starting with his mother, Weronika, then her mother, Józefa Syruć, whose unique personality could not fail to hold his attention. Next in line in terms of impact was Grandma Stanisława, and then Grandfather Kunat. Contrastingly, at the periphery, always, was his father.

The emotional map altered, however, once the family moved to Wilno. Alongside the marked difference between his mother and father—the one close and accessible, the other distant and weak—an equally important and distinct opposition came into play within the young Miłosz's emerging personality. He attributed this tension within himself to the two competing strains. As he saw it, the thick, healthy, hard-working blood of the Syruć and Kunat[7] families had conjoined with the insipid, unstable, impressionable blood of the Miłoszes, who were prone to depression and other troubling psychological conditions. Out of this complex mix arose his own tendency to low spirits and despair, which co-existed with an extraordinary robustness of temperament and an instinct to survive. In formulating this self-analysis Czesław was not just indulging in a rhetorical exercise. During the early period in Wilno, the two figures closest to the boy turned out to be the indomitable Józefa Syruć and Witold Miłosz, his father's brother, a fragile wreck of a man:

> At the age when children begin to look critically at the adult world and wonder who might be worth emulating, I quickly made a decision which was detrimental with regard to my father's family and privileged my mother's . . . I was ambitious as a child, as well as secretive and thoughtful, and I viewed (half consciously) as virtues persistence, stubbornness, an inward focus, along with the adoption of an outer mask . . . by that means, the centre remains intact. I regarded openness as unforgivable . . . and indicative of a lack of strong will . . . a sign of being too easily influenced by others. Naturally, I did not share these observations verbally, just recognized examples in actual people. ('Ze wszystkich możliwych pobudek do pisania', 1951, an unpublished autobiographical sketch, held in the Beinecke Library Archive)

Of all his relatives, his maternal grandmother, Józefa, was one of those who merited the greatest respect. There was a wiliness about her, and a depth which adversity never seemed to penetrate. Slim, tall, with a long face like 'an old Indian woman', she was referred to as 'Lisia'[8] by her grandson, because 'she resembled . . . a forest creature, perhaps a fox' ('Ze wszystkich możliwych'). Kinship with animals, to his way of thinking, meant strength, independence, the rejection of convention.

Her reluctance to display hospitality, her distaste for convention and good manners, such as the ritual involved in sitting down at table, seemed to suggest, at least to him, that at some point she had opted for a more primal life, in accordance with the rules of nature. Her counterpart in *The Issa Valley* would in late May start

> the first of her expeditions to the river; in summer she took several baths
> daily, and in autumn she broke the ice with her foot . . . If she had a yen
> to eat, she would duck into the kitchen for a crock of buttermilk, a snack
> of salted cucumbers or pickled cabbage (she had a positive weakness for
> anything sour or salty) . . . She wore no jerkins, woolen underwear, or
> corsets. In winter, her favorite pastime was to stand by the tiled stove, skirt
> hiked, and warm her posterior—a pose that meant that she was ready to
> engage in conversation. (*Issa* 11–12)

His life would probably have taken a very different turn had he spent his early childhood solely with his father's family. He might not have developed a complex about his separateness, which is attributable to his isolated upbringing in Szetejnie, where rituals associated with 'class' were hardly ever observed. The boy grew up without being drilled in good manners, and so was at a disadvantage when it came to later social interactions. Yet there was more to it than that. Whereas many of his contemporaries in the Polish gentry in Lithuania adhered to the hierarchical values and convictions of their class, as his grandparents did, he had no time for such conventions and no inclination to vaunt the supposed cultural superiority of his family over others.

When it came to their religious affiliations, there was also a degree of 'unorthodoxy' in both of his ancestral lines. During the Reformation the Kunats had been members of the Calvinist gentry, and the family faith endured right through to the beginning of the nineteenth century. Although Miłosz's grandfather was nominally a Catholic, he did not attend mass. In *The Issa Valley* Thomas learns about an Arian forefather. During the Swedish invasion, this man had to choose between remaining steadfast to his Protestant convictions and loyalty to the Catholic Polish king. Thomas becomes aware of the huge significance of national and religious affiliations, because had history turned out differently, he himself would have belonged to a Protestant family in Lithuania.

Czesław's grandmother, Józefa, seemed to manifest great piety, as she spent hours in prayer, locked up in a room. However, it later emerges that her religious stance was not typical either.

> Her ruling passion was magic, the world of spirits and the hereafter . . .
> At news that someone had been visited by a devil, that a house was feared

to be uninhabitable owing to reports of clanking chains and rolling barrels, she was all smiles. Any sign from the other world—a proof that man was never alone on this earth but always in company—was enough to brighten her spirits. She divined the clues and admonitions of various Powers in the most trivial events. (*Issa* 12)

Pride in their status was a given among the Polish gentry, even when their economic fortunes plunged into decline. The Syruć family were of Lithuanian origin, and were mentioned in a sixteenth-century chronicle. Szymon Syruć had his portrait painted when, at the beginning of eighteenth century, he attended the court of Stanisław I, the King of Poland and Grand Duke of Lithuania. The high point of his career came with his appointment as a personal secretary to the king. In addition he was given the title of senator, made a member of the Order of the White Eagle (established in 1705, and the highest decoration that Poland gives to its citizens), and handed responsibility for managing Kasztelania Witebska, a region in the northeast of Lithuania.

Almost seventy years after Poland ceased to exist as an independent kingdom, an antecedent of Szymon Syruć, another Szymon, took part in the 1863 rising against Russian rule and was imprisoned for several months once it was crushed. When he died in a train crash in Germany a decade later, he left behind a daughter, Józefa (the grandmother whom Miłosz so admired). Her choice of husband was the handsome and sensible Zygmunt Kunat, a descendant of a family whose line could be traced back to the thirteenth century. At the turn of the nineteenth century the Kunats owned an estate at Suwalszczyzna. Two of Zygmunt's uncles brought up there fought in the 1830 uprising against Russia. Its violent suppression resulted in the elder, Stanisław, having to flee the country before settling in Paris, where he became a professor at the Polish Batignol School.

Zygmunt's father was Teofil, the third and youngest of the three Kunat brothers. In the early 1850s, Teofil bought an estate in Krasnogruda, near Sejny, which was where Zygmunt and his elder brother, Bronisław, were raised. After studying agriculture in Warsaw, however, Zygmunt moved northward and, after marrying Józefa Syruć, settled in Szetejnie. In temperament and mindset, Miłosz's maternal grandfather was totally unlike most of Lithuania's Polish nobility. Intelligent, gentle and peaceful, Zygmunt was reluctant to get involved in local politics or other kinds of confrontation. Charming and polite towards everyone, including the local peasants and Jewish merchants, he was remembered by his neighbours as a learned, enlightened man, '*un gentilhomme du dix-huitième siècle*', as Oskar Miłosz called him (*NCP* 669). And when he finally died in the mid-1930s, an estimated five thousand people from the surrounding area attended the funeral. Although as a youngster Miłosz took no interest in Zygmunt Kunat's preoccupations with farming and ancestral history—'all my attention was directed towards the future'— he would write years later with great affection about his grandfather: 'This external polish did not tell the whole story; underneath he was hiding wisdom and genuine goodness. Meditating on my hereditary flaws, I have moments of relief any time I think of my grandfather; I had to have taken something from him, so I cannot be completely worthless' ('My Grandfather Sigismund Kunat', *NCP* 669).

Józefa and Zygmunt Kunat had two daughters, Maria and Weronika, Miłosz's mother, who was born in 1887. For Józefa, Kraków represented the apex of Polish culture and learning, and so her daughters were sent there to be educated in a private school run by nuns. Weronika 'was spontaneous, impulsive, and got into trouble with her teachers, but her minor acts of mischief were immediately forgiven'. Blessed with 'a rich imagination', when she was very young she used to stage little plays, creating in effect 'a children's theatre'. As an adult, she enjoyed company and parties, and 'was a very good dancer' (Janina Hajdasz, letter to AF, 14 September 2005). Weronika ran into Aleksander Miłosz, who was four years her senior, during a holiday visit he was making to relatives near Szetejnie. He must have been smitten by her charm and joviality, because, judging from photographs of the time, she could not be regarded as conventionally beautiful. Their wedding on 14 July 1909 in a church in Opitołoki was followed by a reception at the manor in Szetejnie. A friend of Aleksander's later noted in his diary that the festivities lasted until morning:

We danced to the music of a Jewish orchestra from Kiejdany, who were pretty good. They played waltzes, quadrille, mazurkas, polkas and krakowiak dances with verve and we danced till we were drenched in sweat, changing our stiff collars every hour and drinking lemonade, diluted fruit juice and yeast drink, as well as wine and vodka, though in moderation. Ladies did not drink alcohol at all—unlike women these days. I remember that the marriage ceremony was performed by a clergyman who was part-Lithuanian and spoke Polish badly. In a rather pathetic voice, he made a speech during the wedding feast and raised a toast to the newly-married couple, comparing the groom to the Sun and his bride to the Moon, that revolves round the Sun. He ended by reminding her about her duty to care for her husband ... 'When a tired husband, covered in sweat, sits down to table—wipe his forehead with the tablecloth!' ... Naturally, we burst out laughing and, for a long time afterwards, asked Wecia Miłosz whether she had wiped her husband's forehead with the cloth. (Qtd. in Fałtynowicz, 31)

The couple moved to Riga, where Aleksander continued his studies at the Department of Roads and Bridges and both of them enjoyed the benefits of living in a university city. In particular they liked frequenting the local restaurants. In photographs from that time Weronika can be seen alongside a man who still looks young, with delicate facial features, a figure slighter than his wife, who perhaps sought support from her.

'Both of us loved her very much', Miłosz's younger brother Andrzej remarked in an autobiographical piece for the journal *Jaćwież* in 2001. In Czesław's eyes his mother was a wise person, multidimensional, tolerant, interested in others, and with a keen desire to do good. As a young, serious child, however, he resented how she liked to party and indulge in innocent flirting, going 'doe-eyed'. During his student years, his criticisms were even more scathing, when he castigated her 'simplicity almost bordering on vulgarity' and her 'total lack of self-restraint, style, and knowing when to stay silent in certain situations. Peasants feel very comfortable in her presence. I detest that' (CM to Jarosław Iwaszkiewicz, 20 December 1930).

Nevertheless, he felt a strong bond with his mother. He recalled as a child how he once had to fight to defend her good reputation: 'Children were chanting silly skipping rhymes. When I said *'Matka, matka'* ('Mummy, mummy'), they began to chant *'Matka, szmatka'* ('Mummy, hussy'). I threw myself at a small boy, kicking him' (*Podróżny świata* 134). As his life was drawing to a close, his thoughts seem often to have returned to her: 'You were my beginning and again I am with you' ('In Szetejnie', *NCP* 642). He respected her religious faith, which did not take the form of moralistic commands or rigid binarisms, but was put into practice in her everyday life. Towards the end of her days she suffered from arthritis, contracted when, straight after a ball, she went to church one morning and during prayers took off her shoes to cool her tired feet:

> Seemingly weak and frivolous, she used superficiality as a mask and delighted in playing a role as it led people off the track. Her relationships were formed at the least cost to herself, and showed her not as she really was but as others expected her to be. Doubtless this mimicry was the result of a disbelief in her own worth and a complete inability to take command, or, possibly, of pride: 'What I know is not for others'. Under the surface was stubbornness, gravity, and the strong conviction that suffering is sent by God and that it should be borne cheerfully'. (*NR* 64–65)

No such sacred aura surrounded his estimation of his father, however. A graduate of a high school in Wilno and an admirer of Gogol, Aleksander had a nickname within the family, 'Psiapsiulewicz', whose meaning is uncertain, but suggests someone who is spineless and rather ridiculous. He had a great sense of humour and loved jokes, which he delivered mainly in Russian. A good singer and dancer, he was often the life and soul of the party. Lacking such skills himself, his first-born son never held him in high esteem. In the 1930s, Miłosz informed Iwaszkiewicz that his father was

> as a matter of fact, a big baby, a nervy type, who dreams about journeys, but is totally lacking when it comes to everyday life. At the same time, however, he has inexhaustible energy and zest for his professional work (he is an engineer). His weakness is the result of trusting people too much, and allowing people to take advantage of him. (CM to Jarosław Iwaszkiewicz, 20 December 1930)

Decades later he adopted a change of tone:

> He could never have a successful career or make money . . . he had no ammunition to fight with people, and apart from that, any plan or stratagem devised to achieve personal gain he condemned as base self-interest. Whenever he encountered deception or cunning, he simply parted company with the offender and looked for work elsewhere. On the other hand, battling the elements excited and delighted him, because that involved adventure. ('Ze wszystkich możliwych')

The propensity for wandering was something that affected two generations of Miłoszes, the father and the sons. Even before the expedition to Siberia, Aleksander had travelled to Sweden, and almost certainly to Denmark and Holland. Some years later he travelled to Brazil. But there was a more troubled side to Aleksander's character. He had been traumatised by the loss of his father at a very young age, which forced him into adulthood far too quickly, since he had to take on responsibility for his mother and brother. What pained him also was the recognition that his younger brother, Witold, who often caused him embarrassment, was in fact his mother's favourite.

Born in Riga, in 1883, Aleksander Miłosz inherited from preceding generations of his noble family a coat of arms and fine traditions, but no money. The Miłoszes had been living in Lithuania since at least the sixteenth century, as a signed document from 1578 proved. Their family estate was not far from Szetejnie, in Serbiny. That last place-name suggests the possibility that the family might have originated in Serbia; a hillock near Serbiny, perhaps an old burial mound, was called the Serbian Cemetery by the locals. At one time a Serb tribe, expelled by Germans from areas around Berlin and Frankfurt-on-Oder, had settled in Lithuania. A cuirassier called Andrzej Miłosz was wounded near Kircholm in 1605. Two centuries later, Józef Miłosz left all his wealth to his brothers and headed east to the Dnieper River, where he was given a lucrative post administering the huge financial resources of the Sapieha dynasty.[9] When the estate stood in danger of confiscation by the Russians, his Sapieha masters transferred to Józef Miłosz two rich estates, at Druja and Czereja. As a consequence, around the year 1825, a new branch of the family appeared, which, in contrast to the middle-class nobility in Niewiaża, was extremely wealthy. Józef had two sons, Eugeniusz and Artur, thus adding two branches to the family tree, with lands at Dźwina on the border between the Courland, Witebsk and Wilno regions, and near Czereja, a huge forested area in Mohylewska Province.

While living in Druja, Eugeniusz studied medicine in Dorpat, now Tartu, in Estonia, where he became one of the founders of the first Polish student organisation, Polonia. He possessed a trait which appears to be a characteristic of the family, absentmindedness. On one occasion, when setting off on a hunting expedition, he locked his wife in a pantry, and only remembered about it a few days later.

> Eccentrics and visionaries deserve a special place. My cousins from the Dnieper excelled in this sphere. No doubt they were trying to vanquish the boredom that comes with prosperity. After one of them died, five rooms of his house were discovered to be filled to the ceiling by hats and galoshes—as good a collection as any other. The family was also sensitive to aristocratic splendor and could not, for example, bear the idea that someone would be capable of thinking them related to the then famous Serbian dynasty of Miłosz Obrenowicz. One of them even wrote to a high czarist official in Petersburg: 'We were granted the coat of arms of Lubicz by His Highness Leshek V and we have nothing in common with those Serbian shepherds, the Miłoszes'. (*NR* 25)

His son, also Eugeniusz, gave up a career in the Russian Army because he did not want to change his religion. Most of his life thereafter was spent in almost total isolation in his castle, where he spent hours playing the piano. It was said that after his death there was evidence that his ghost haunted the place. The money inherited by the second son, Józef, disappeared, an indication of his lack of prudence in managing the family estates. This state of affairs compelled his two children, Emilia and Adam, to move to Warsaw. Czesław Miłosz met with these relations, the heirs of Oskar Miłosz, and later commented on the looseness of the ties between them: 'My family did not keep in touch with [the] Miłosz family from Druja . . . They used to refer to Emilia and Adam as "those rightwing nationalists"' (*Szukanie ojczyzny* 140).

The poet's branch of the family, which did not condone chauvinism, felt a greater affinity with their relations from Czereja, which began with Artur Miłosz. He had fought in the November 1830 Polish uprising against the occupying Russian Empire, for which he was awarded the most prestigious military decoration, the Virtuti Militari. In the battle of Ostrołęka he lost a leg, but that caused no diminution in his fighting spirit. Once, when a Russian general bumped into him while passing him on the stairs in a Warsaw hotel and walked on without an apology, Artur hit the offender with his crutch, causing the Russian to tumble all the way down. Like many others in the Miłosz clan, Artur was fond of travel and tended to make quick decisions. One of them was to marry an Italian singer, Natalia Tassistro, the daughter of an orchestral conductor at La Scala, Milan. Although from a good background, she was not considered a sufficiently worthy match by her new Polish relations. As a result, instead of settling in Czereja, the couple chose to live in Wilno. Their son, Władysław, whose parents died when he was still young, surpassed his father when it came to eccentricity and colourful adventures. His marriage to a Jewish woman from Warsaw resulted in a son, Oskar, a poet, mystic and highly regarded diplomat for the newly independent Lithuania, and one of the foremost enduring artistic and spiritual influences on Czesław Miłosz.

Aleksander's distant forebears, who had settled near Niewiaża, led a less spectacular life. The lives of later generations of the family, however, were not without turbulence. Czesław's grandfather, Artur, was another who took part in the struggle for Polish independence in January 1861. After the uprising was crushed, he was saved from certain death by Orthodox believers, who broke their religious commandment and gave false testimony that the master of Serbiny had not left home during the hostilities. Artur later married a doctor's daughter from Riga; her mother was a von Mohl, a German family that by the second half of the nineteenth century was more Polish than German. She was related to Countess Emilia Plater, a revolutionary in 1830, who came from the lands of the partitioned Polish-Lithuanian Commonwealth. As a child Czesław would hear tales about the von Mohl estate in Imbrody, where his grandmother was born, about old Hanseatic Riga, where rich city-dwellers lived and operas were performed, and about Majorenhof, where the wealthy went for their sea spa holidays. Artur, as noted earlier, had two boys, Aleksander and Witold, but died when they were small. His widow, who was neither resourceful nor competent when it came to managing the family's affairs, was quickly forced to sell the estate to pay off their debts.

The burden of supporting the impoverished family fell on Czesław's father, Aleksander, while the spoilt wunderkind, Witold, failed utterly to fulfil the hopes invested in him. Having been expelled from school, he joined the army. After demobilisation, he could not find a place for himself and, always prepared to lie and cheat, he started forging Aleksander's signature on cheques:

Among many disastrous career choices, before he died of tuberculosis at
the age of thirty-six, was a period serving in the border forces, and a share
in a Jewish company trading in furs . . . There was also an attempt to
open a cabaret-revue. I attended the opening night at *Helios*, when I was
fourteen and could not find any criteria that might justify the lewd vulgarity of the show . . . Embarrassment from the fact that its author was a
member of our family and also that my parents even laughed continued
to spread within me like a greasy stain'. (*Zaczynając od moich ulic* 34)

In Czesław's later adolescent years, this embarrassment with Uncle Witold's an-
tics took a darker turn, becoming almost a revulsion, quickened by a deep anxiety
as to whether he himself had 'bad blood' flowing in his veins.

Accounts, an autobiographical novella written mainly in 1938, explores how,
from the perspective of a young boy, social roles and adult behavior involve the
donning of masks in order to conceal weaknesses of the flesh, hidden fears and
the absence of self-assurance. An adolescent scrutinises with a deeply unforgiving gaze a protagonist almost certainly modelled on Witold: 'I experienced
my first bitter taste of domination over a man when I penetrated the frailty
and insecurity of his character, and could smile ironically at his quick, ungainly
gestures.' That his uncle came to represent for Miłosz an exemplum and a dire
warning is evident from the space devoted to him years later, when the author
started work on a memoir intended for a future biographer:

I thought about his fate my whole life, until this very day. Sometimes,
when my mother and I spent holidays at Dobkiewicz's house by Lake
Gaładuś, Witold came to stay with us there. He had no money and nowhere to go. It may not have been advisable considering the well-being
of others around him, because he had tuberculosis and died a year later,
but what can a family do in the circumstances? With no work, no profession and not a living soul who would look after him, he grew thinner
and weaker . . . Sometimes all he did was to take a boat and go fishing.
In addition, he had a very strong influence on my youthful sensitivities.
He entrenched in me a fear of failure, almost a kind of horror, and, as a
result, I developed my hyper-emphasis on exactitude and diligence. Also
my determination to cultivate the virtues of reliability and perseverance.
Fear of being a loser made it impossible for me to become a bohemian,
and drove me to maximise my income by working in the offices of the
Polish Radio and later in America at the university. Poor Witold was
responsible for so many of the distinctions and rewards I received, including the Nobel Prize . . .

And one more thing. If, despite all the weakness that afflicted him as a tuberculosis sufferer, he distinguished himself by having strong convictions, enthusiasms of any kind, depths of philosophical or religious knowledge, my sympathy would not have been tinged with contempt. But his mind was unbelievably banal, and his opinions reflected what others said. He was also the only member of my family who was willing to repeat the sloganising of Polish nationalism. His sufferings, for which I felt sympathy, seemed to me empty; he had nothing to cling on to. He suffered like a sick animal. I came to the conclusion that passing judgment on him was unfair, because who can really know what goes on inside another human being. However, looking at Witold, I felt anxiety of a different kind—a fear of the paralysis of the mind which affects adults, perhaps all adults . . . in particular those in whom the zest of youth has been extinguished. I resolved not to succumb to that and to remain intellectually active for as long as possible, which I managed to achieve until now, when I have reached the age of eighty-nine. Thinking of Witold, I came to the conclusion that I was genetically shaped by the Miłosz family and have had to, as a result, compensate for that by strenuous acts of will. ('Materiały do mojej biografii')

Burdened by guilt, Witold's mother blamed herself for her son's failures. In young Czesław's eyes, his paternal grandmother was the polar opposite of Grandma Lisia. Like her younger son, Stanisława Miłosz would be allocated a representative status in his compendium of types, as an illustration of deficiency, particularly the lack of get-up-and-go. She can be glimpsed in a beautiful but telling photograph, between her two grandsons, frail, elderly, dressed in black, with a noble but joyless face. Hers were the first attempts to 'civilise' Czesław, teaching him religion and history, trying to instil in him resentment at the defeat of the Polish uprising of 1863 and the need to continue the struggle against their Russian oppressors. Despite all her kindness, he backed away from her, maintaining a distance: 'Peeking into her room at five or six o'clock in the morning, he found her sitting up in bed, saying her prayers in a loud, keening voice, a vacant stare in her eyes, her cheeks bearing traces of two little wet streams' (*Issa* 52).

At a later date, when living with his grandmother in Wilno, the energetic but mischievous boy would be angry and embarrassed at having to accompany her on her lugubrious constitutionals. His grandmother's mournfulness aroused sympathy, but also the temptation to torment her:

'Kostuś will end up in prison', I hissed doggedly. 'It would be better, if Kostuś went to prison. At least he would have something to eat there'.

Grandmother then ... would turn red and her hands trembled. 'I know that Kostuś forged daddy's cheques', I shouted[,] leaving the room. Through a gap in the door I could see her sitting in her armchair, small, round, with a handkerchief close to her face, intoning her prayers aloud, almost shouting them'. (*Przygody młodego umysłu* 321)

It is impossible to establish how true this story might be. There is no doubt, however, that on 9 September 1930, when Stanisława Miłosz died in Suwałki, her grandson was racked with guilt and self-disgust, as is testified by his diary: 'My dear grandma, I told you, when you were lying on the catafalque, that I was mean. Mean, mean. My God, this striking of poses. Constant tacking between a huge desire for truth and rhythm, rhythm, rhythm ... And always this aesthetising and scenes constantly ordered, even here' (CM to Jarosław Iwaszkiewicz, 20 December 1930). Craving strength, he fled from weakness. Despite his protestations to the contrary, like his grandmother he too was vulnerable and sensitive to the cruelties of the world, and easily hurt: 'I was not made to live anywhere except in Paradise. Such, simply, was my genetic inadaptation. Here on earth every prick of a rose-thorn changed into a wound, whenever the sun hid behind a cloud, I grieved' ('Nonadaptation', *SS* 23).

A Grenade under the Bed

'I was born in the very centre of Lithuania and so have a greater right than my great forebear, Mickiewicz, to write '*O Lithuania, my country*'[10] ('Do przyjaciół Litwinów', *Gazeta Wyborcza*). Miłosz affirmed this in an article from 7–8 October 2000, which offers a reminder that his map of where Polishness begins and ends extends beyond the confines of national boundaries. He spent his formative years in Wilno, in a multi-ethnic cauldron open to the East, where Catholics, Russian Orthodox believers, Jews and descendants of the Tartars lived alongside each other. He was born a subject of the tsar, in a part of Europe which for over a century was a part of the Russian Empire, and so, rather than faraway Kraków, Warsaw and Poznań, the major cities of his forebears were Wilno, Riga and Dorpat. His family thought of themselves as Polish, though they also aligned themselves with the Grand Duchy of Lithuania, thinking in terms of co-existence, not separation, when it came to the political relationship between Lithuania and the Polish crown. Feelings that dated back to the Union of Lublin in 1569, when a single unified state was created, had not vanished:

My family practised a cult of separatism—much as the Scots, the Welsh or the Bretons did. Our Grand Duchy of Lithuania was 'better' and

Poland was 'worse', for what would she have accomplished without our kings, poets and politicians? In that local pride which was very widespread in our corner, the memories of a fame long past persisted. Poles from 'over there' (that is from the ethnic center) had a reputation for being shallow, irresponsible, and, what is more, impostors ... My family defined virtue as stubbornness and perseverance, the reverse of 'their' short-lived enthusiasm. (*NR* 96–97)

Miłosz came to wonder how much of his determination, trustworthiness and work ethic he owed to an anxiety at being branded a Polish weakling, or, to use a Polish-Lithuanian phrase, 'a crowner' (CM, in Fiut 157). This tradition was very strong on his mother's side, as his forefathers, like the majority of the nobility and landowners in the duchy, took on Polish nationality centuries earlier, while retaining a sense of allegiance to Lithuania. They also were very attached to their 'little homeland' in the Niewiaża valley. Although they travelled extensively by choice, at times because of historical turmoil, most of their lives were spent there, punctuated by sowings and harvests, weddings and christenings. They thought in terms that reached back further than the nineteenth-century concept of the nation-state, and would have been at ease with the idea of the multinational, multicultural entity dreamt of by the architects of Poland's first republic (1569–1795). Above all, one was a local inhabitant, attached to Polish culture and language, yet Lithuanian in culture and spirit. Miłosz recalled a remark made in the course of one particular journey from his youth. They were 'travelling in a light carriage and the conversation was in Polish. We were in independent Lithuania, close to the Polish border, and they used to say: "Our people are here, and over there the Poles"' (CM, in Fiut 148).

On the threshold of modernity, in the early twentieth century, it turned out that the idea inculcated in him by his mother—that two or more peoples *could* co-exist within a shared patriarchal structure—was anachronistic from a political point of view, doomed to fail, like Józef Piłsudski's dream of re-creating a Polish-Lithuanian union. The majority of Poles had no desire to see their supremacy constrained by having to make an accommodation with other national minorities, while Lithuanians hoping to achieve their independence did not wish to be accommodated. Weronika would retain two passports throughout her life, while Czesław, as a child, had only Lithuanian citizenship.

In November 1918, in line with decisions incorporated in the Treaty of Versailles, Poland was granted independence, and in Wilno, volunteers in the Samoobrona (a self-defence militia) became absorbed into the regular Polish Army. Aleksander Miłosz probably enlisted initially as a captain in one of those volunteer units, and later became a major in a sapper regiment. Although both Poles and Lithuanians were alert to the grave danger the new Bolshevik regime in Russia posed, negotiations between the two political entities failed. The main reason for the disagreement was the fact that after the Russians withdrew, Wilno was seized by the Poles in April 1919. Supported by a secret Polish military group, plans were set in motion to mount a rising in Kaunas, in one last attempt to impose the concept of federation on Lithuania. Its aim was to establish a new government which would dutifully proclaim Lithuania's incorporation into Poland. Unfortunately, the coup was thwarted when the Lithuanian Secret Service arrested its leaders. Listed among the 369 members of this secret organisation bent on forcing Lithuania to join the new Polish Republic was one Aleksander Miłosz. As a consequence, the new provisional Lithuanian government declared him a persona non grata and banned him from entering the country, thereby denying him all access to the Miłosz family's estates.

At this juncture, however, Aleksander was stationed with his troops in Wilno, which led to Weronika's decision once more to join her husband. In the spring of 1920, like westward-bound American settlers, she and her sons set off on a cloth-covered cart, taking with them a nanny and, as a source of milk for the younger son, a goat:

> I remember the sight of my mother's back as she sat in the opening of that cloth tunnel. We, too, forded rivers, stopped in the middle and whistled at the horses to get them to drink . . . Nights were spent in barns on the hay or around bonfires in the forest. The flash of hatchets chopping up kindling, a teapot hanging on a stick over the fire, wind blowing in the pines. (*NR* 48)

On arriving safely in Wilno, they rented a flat on Nadbrzeżna Street, close to St James Church. The poet's memories of this period include a painful operation to have his tonsils removed and his first experience of schooling. Since he had hitherto been taught at home, he had great difficulty understanding and adjusting to a host of new rules and practices.

> It was hard to visualize the wafer stuck to his palate—and which his tongue would shyly peel off—as the body of Jesus. But he was noticeably changed by it: for one whole day he was actually quiet and well-behaved. What appealed most to his imagination were the priest's words comparing the soul to a room that had to be cleaned and made worthy of receiving its Guest. He imagined that, after the wafer had melted, it was later healed in the soul, returning to its place in the chalice that stood among the greenery on the altar. (*Issa* 33)

In June, the eight year-old took his first communion, experiencing 'the ecstasy of the sinless' ('Capri', *NCP* 585), followed by cocoa and sweet rolls at a party for the communicants. He must have been conscious at this time of his father's important responsibilities and the possibility of military action, recalling as he did his uniform with its 'zigzag silver on the collar', the gun 'batteries painted that special olive-green', and, next to vegetable allotments, 'the sappers . . . stationed on the banks of the river' ('Pages Concerning the Years of Independence', *NCP* 378).

More and more the optimistic atmosphere was marred by adults talking in hushed, troubled voices. War had broken out between Poland and Bolshevik Russia, and in July 1920 the Red Army advanced for a second time closer and closer to Wilno. Polish forces had to retreat again, and with them a substantial number of people from the surrounding area who remembered all too well the terror of the recent Bolshevik occupation. Just as he had five years before, the young Czesław witnessed the panic of those fleeing and remembered the loud chanting of the Litany to the Virgin Mary, but above all 'dusty roads under the glow of artillery fire, military trains, wandering, panics. The very idea of defeat will always be for him a scorched highway leading to Niemenczyn, packed with carts, wagons, britzkas . . . when he looks back, the city is dark' ('Pages Concerning the Years of Independence', *NCP* 379). He also remembered a broken-down tank with terrified soldiers bustling around it, which he would later put in a poem:

> In the suburbs, where houses with bolted doors kept silent,
> a tank halted. Helmets on the heads of the entire crew slid with blood
>   and sweat.
> If they don't manage to fix the engine within an hour—
> And so they kneel, hands trembling in the heat. Brown oil drips slowly
>   into
> the snow.
> Measuring time.
>
>   (*Wiersze* I, 18)

Yet again the family became dispersed by war. Weronika headed back to Szetejnie with her sons, and on the way their cart came under fire from an armoured Polish train. Czesław's later recollection of the incident demonstrates his artist's eye, and how his observational skills continued to function despite the peril into which he had been plunged:

> . . . she noticed the danger first, pricking up her ears at the whizz of bullets, which sounded like bees' lightning-fast maneuvers during honey-gathering . . . I was two people at once: along with the rest of the living contents of our wagon, I spilled into the ditch and crouched there in the sticky mud, praying and sobbing; but at the same time, I did not stop

being curious, nor did my senses cease to collect impressions as keenly
as ever . . . A slight rise in the terrain protected the horses. On the bank
leading down into the ditch was a tree with protruding roots. I grabbed
onto them, wanting to see what was going on. (*NR* 49–50)

The Soviets meanwhile signed a treaty with the Lithuanians which gave
them control over the city, while at the same time attempting to incite a revolt
which would enable them to seize power in Lithuania. The Lithuanians gained
military control in Wilno only after what came to be referred to as 'the miracle
on the Vistula' of August 1920. Despite being hugely outnumbered and close to
total defeat, the Polish Army first repulsed, then defeated, the Red Army in the
Battle of Warsaw.

On 9 October, under pressure from the League of Nations, an interim
peace treaty was signed which ceded Wilno to the Lithuanians. At the beginning
of 1922, however, a breakaway group in the government of Middle Lithuania,
represented by boycotting Lithuanians, Jews and Byelorussians, passed a decree
which formally united the area with Poland. The new, now-truncated Lithuanian
state recognised Kaunas as its temporary capital and did not maintain diplomatic
relations with Poland until the ultimatum of March 1938, as the threat from Nazi
Germany intensified.

The outcome of this sequence of dramatic events had a huge impact on the
family in Szetejnie, forcing them into life-changing decisions. Weronika could
no longer risk staying with her parents on an estate which at any moment might
be subject to confiscation. Like the majority of Poles in their area, she opted to
settle in Wilno. The only possibility for former Polish inhabitants to re-visit their
families and home region was by crossing the border illegally.

In the course of Miłosz's summer breaks from secondary school, the family
several times returned to Lithuania by means of illegal crossings, an activity fraught
with danger:

Because diplomatic relations between Poland and Lithuania had been
broken off, it was impossible, legally, to get there. But such obstacles, like
other political stupidities, seemed to my mother quite unimportant . . .
The first task was to reach the settlement where proper smugglers lived,
usually deep in the forest. In their hut we decided on a plan of action;
either to bribe the frontier guards or to avoid their posts entirely. For
a certain period of time, the two countries shared a so-called neutral
zone, which meant that everyone shot at everyone else. Those who accompanied us, specialists in border crossings, carried a gun for doing
away, if need be, with any inconvenient figures. Once the peasant who

was leading us dropped down suddenly on one knee and raked through
the bushes with his rifle. Our moment of fear ended after he muttered,
'A doe'. I had many another scare, though. When you are ten years old,
it is especially unpleasant to be caught by Lithuanian guards and made
to sit in a pigsty all day as a lone prisoner . . . I learned to value the forest
even more; one is safe there and invisible. (*NR* 65–66)

Over time the number of border patrol guards increased, and the only way to travel
was to use two passports. Polish documents allowed entry into Latvia and, from
there, using different documentation, into Lithuania. Although the Miłosz family
chose allegiance to Poland, they remained hostile to the narrow nationalism of
either side. For a young man growing up in Wilno, Polish culture, though predominant, was not the sole point of reference. Summer crossings from one state to
another engendered great excitement because of the danger, but they also demonstrated the restrictiveness of political conventions with their borders and barriers.
They complicated the picture of the world, and made the young man recognise the
demonic aspects of history, which translated the Grand Duchy of Lithuania, the
land where Byelorussians, Lithuanians and Jews co-existed peacefully for centuries,
into a cauldron of hatred, which eventually saw those nations swallowed up and
subject to totalitarian rule from Moscow, the capital of the Soviet Empire.

Miłosz would later rail against the way he and his contemporaries were 'in-
doctrinated in Polish patriotism', taught 'hatred towards those who pose a threat,
that is Bolsheviks, Lithuanian plebs, and Jews because they welcomed Bolsheviks
and on 1 May hanged red banners on telegraph wires'. He soon started to develop
the suspicion that causes other than just Polish causes exist, and that 'the term
our people can include Lithuanians and Jews, who can regard Poles as outsiders'
(*RM* 80).

Childhood was moving towards its conclusion, with increasing, unstoppable momentum:

Awakened by a chill early one morning, Thomas curled into a ball,
but there was no escaping the draft . . . The pane was punctured by a
hole the size of two fists, its jagged outline shaped like a star. He ran
immediately to Misia's room, yelling that someone had thrown a rock
from the garden. It turned out he was mistaken. They searched high
and low, until finally, under Thomas's bed, in the very corner, Grandfather flushed out a black object which . . . had the shape of a large
egg, only heavier, with a notched flange wrapped around the middle.
In the orchard, below the window, they found boot tracks and a grenade pin.' (*Issa* 57)

History had the capacity to penetrate even his earthly paradise. A grenade thrust by a Lithuanian hand into a Polish manor house marked the symbolic end of the idyll. While Zygmunt Kunat was regarded in the surrounding villages as 'a local man', his son-in-law was viewed as an invader. The safest option for the Miłosz family was to leave, again thanking the Mother of God for saving them. That grenade was intended to kill, and only by some miracle failed to explode. Astonishingly, there would be many subsequent moments in Miłosz's life when it must have seemed that some benign divine protector was indeed watching over him.

The Young Man and the Mysteries
1921–1929

The Apartment with Fig-Plants

I could never leave you, my city.
A mile was long, but there was something that pulled me back,
Like a pawn on a chessboard.
I was running away on the earth which turned faster and faster,
And was always there: with books in my linen schoolbag,
Staring at brown hillocks behind the towers of St James,
Where a slight horse moves, with a slight man behind the plough,
Most likely both perished long, long ago.
Yes, it's true, nobody could understand the people or the city,
The Lux and Helios cinemas, signs for Halpern and Segal,
A promenade in Świętojerska called Mickiewicz.
No, no-one could. No-one did.
And when one day there is clarity and lucidity,
Then, very often it is pity.

Czesław Miłosz, 'Never from you, city' (Wiersze III, 15)

Once the Miłosz family had settled in Wilno in 1921, the dizzying period of repeated changes which constituted the first decade of the poet's life temporarily came to a halt.

> It takes no small amount of energy simply to plant one's feet on solid ground without falling . . . Where I grew up, there was no uniform gesture, no social code, no clear rules for behavior at table. Practically every

person I met was different, not because of his own special self, but as a
representative of some group, class, or nation. One lived in the twentieth
century, another in the nineteenth, a third in the fourteenth. When I
reached adolescence, I carried inside me a museum of mobile and gri-
macing images. (*NR* 67–68)

So he would judge years later. But as a teenager he was still immune to this strong
sense of otherness. Instead he was content simply to absorb the world in which
he now found himself, and to hare about with a bag full of books up and around
the steep but pleasant city streets.

Beautifully located amongst hills where two rivers converged, the Grand
Duchy of Lithuania's capital, Wilno, was a Baroque pearl hidden amidst vast
northern forests. Besides having a celebrated sixteenth-century university, the
city possessed a fine classical cathedral with origins dating back to the thirteenth
century, which in the early 1920s enabled it to retain an almost medieval character. In Wilno, there was so much for the country boy to see, hear and relish: the
dense labyrinth of winding streets and narrow alleyways; the rich façades of the
barons' palaces; the simultaneous tolling of multiple church bells; the surviving
remains of the old city walls; the monastery cell where Adam Mickiewicz and
his literary friends gathered; the shrine to Our Lady of Ostrabrama, with the
venerable city gates close by; a Jewish quarter; the necropolis on Rossa. Here was
a city with a distinct history written into its architecture, but also a city content
with its own lazy, laid-back, provincial rhythms.

At dawn, horse-drawn carts trundled by, taking away excrement in long
containers, the drivers shabbily dressed, sitting aslant the vehicle. Soon after,
servant girls would emerge to buy the morning milk, as would dog-catchers with
their lariats. Passers-by would stop and shout to warn the dogs what was coming
in a gesture of inter-species solidarity. However, evenings in the sleepy city centre
were filled with 'country noises'—birdsong, the crowing of cocks, the barking of
dogs—along with the far-off 'whistles of trains . . . announcing that somewhere
there is a different, distant world' (Dunin-Horkawicz 12).

With 120,000 inhabitants at the end of the First World War, Wilno lay
at the heart of a vast, thinly populated agricultural region, which primarily produced food, wood and paper. The pavements young Czesław used on his way to
school were made of wooden planks, which sagged like piano keys and splashed
mud on his trousers. Sometimes, without asking, he hitched rides on the backs
of carriages and had to escape the coachmen's whips. He would also have looked
out for the small, old-fashioned buses and Wilno's sole fuel-powered tram. A
favourite place to stand and stare was the window of the toy shop belonging to the
Jabłkowski brothers, where the clockwork toys on display left him mesmerised.

Another, albeit at times mixed delight, was the bookshop where he bought schoolbooks for the coming year, and a stationery shop owned by Puchaczewski, where he liked to look at paints which were far too expensive for him to afford. At Antokolska landing point, he admired the boats taking visitors to Werki and the rafts used to float timber down to the sawmills.

Often he would stop to take a drink of cold water from a sacred well belonging to the Bonifrater Church, and on spring market days feasted on bagels. Adjoining the family home were wooden sheds and outbuildings where he played with Yashka and Sonka, Jewish siblings, shouting out together the magic spell, 'Chur-churra'. In winter he slid down the sloping streets on his sled, lying on his stomach and steering with his legs. In the summer there would be class excursions outside town. These always had some romantic element to them, such as the time they visited the Puttkamer estate, where Mickiewicz held trysts with Maryla, a girl he loved.

> Provincial quaintness should not be exaggerated, however. The Jewish commercial districts looked like their counterparts all over the world and used the same kind of advertising. Façades were decorated with all sorts of colored signboards on which artists had drawn lions and tigers seemingly taken straight from the paintings of Rousseau Le Douanier, gloves, stockings and brassières. Movies were publicized by rows of electric lights and lurid billboards of love scenes placed at the entrances to the theatres'. (*NR* 58–59)

The cinema belonged in the vanguard of modernity, 'purred and projected fantasies/of Greta Garbo, Rudolf Valentino' ('In a Garrison Town', *S&LP* 311), making a huge impression on the imagination of the future poet. There were six working picture-houses immediately after the 1914–1918 war, with Cinema-Theatre Helios, which showed talkies, being the largest. The Lux, Hollywood and Eden cinemas tried to attract customers by presenting 'blockbusters depicting the sweetness of erotic life' or 'the biggest, most erotic Polish films' (Mikonis, *Życie filmowe Wilna*), but in the 1920s viewers could see Fritz Lang's *Doctor Mabuse* and *Die Nibelungen*, Cecil de Mille's *Ten Commandments, White Shadows*, or *Ben-Hur*. Like his European and American contemporaries, Miłosz laughed at the comedies with Charlie Chaplin, Harold Lloyd and Buster Keaton, was thrilled by the adventures of Douglas Fairbanks, and admired Mary Pickford, Lillian Gish and an actress less famous these days, Sylvia Sidney. Needless to say, like millions of other men, young and old, he was infatuated with Greta Garbo. He was now discovering distant parts of the world, not just from pictures in magazines, but also from shorts by the major studios, as well as educational films with titles such as *Inhabitants of the Deep, Fishing in the Baltic* and *India: Land of Tales and*

Wonders, which were shown in the rooms of the Municipal Cultural-Educational Cinematograph. 'There would be total pandemonium because all middle schools attended those. Countless crowds' (CM, in Fiut 203).

In spring 1921 Aleksander Miłosz rented a first-floor apartment in a house surrounded by a garden. The household would have consisted of the family and Grandma Stanisława Miłosz, along with, probably, a nanny and a servant, since there would have had to be someone to bring in wood, keep the stove burning and cook. In the youngster's eyes, however, it was just 'an ugly apartment with rubber plants' ('Overseas Song', *NCP* 301).

Wilno was the obvious place in which to settle, as it contained high-quality schools and a university and offered employment possibilities, and because members of the extended family already lived there. To Czesław, initially visiting relatives' houses and listening to conversations about coats of arms, estates and family trees was a tedious business. Bragging about aristocratic ancestry he found simply revolting: 'I did not want to belong to my caste . . . I avoided admitting that I belonged to the nobility' (*Szukanie ojczyzny* 63).

The family's financial situation was difficult, given that they relied solely on his father's modest earnings and his grandmother's meagre pension as a widow of an insurrectionist. There was enough to make ends meet, and, compared to the generally low standard of living at the time, they were not particularly badly off. Czesław, now a pupil at the gymnasium, still wore shirts of coarse linen manufactured locally, but other clothes were bought in sizes that were at first far too big for him, so that they would last longer.

There were many houses in Wilno without running water, so that buckets had to be carried from a well in the yard. Matters of the most basic hygiene were problematic as a result: 'I lived amidst filth and stench, without being aware of it . . . True, our apartment had a tin bathtub, but heating water for it was a major operation since we burned wood' ('Automobile', *ABC* 46). It was easier to go with his father at the end of the week to the baths in Tatarska Street, where 'one would fill a wooden bucket with cold water from a tap for dousing one's head, and carry it up to the highest shelf . . . among the roars of naked males lashing themselves with birch rods' ('Plato's Dialogues', *NCP* 618):

> My 'place' did not correspond in the least to what is generally known as the *bourgeois* way of life. Along with my feeling that one should know who one is went a pinched pocket book and an enforced curtailment of my personal needs. My material existence was so primitive that it would have startled proletarians in Western countries. The impoverishment of rural property holders, a certain incompetence in practical affairs, a contempt for 'elbowing one's way up' (because social standing clearly did

not depend on wealth), and, finally, the widespread economic difficulties after the First World War, all spelled one thing. (*NR* 32)

This section of *Native Realm* discloses an important feature of his character: though throughout his life he craved recognition from and popularity with women, he was totally without ambition or hunger when it came to wealth or social advancement.

Now demobbed, Aleksander first found work in a building firm in Lida and later started a bridge-building enterprise with his partners. Unfortunately, soon after the business began to take off, an accountant employed by the firm misappropriated a considerable amount of money and ran off to Argentina. Suddenly bankrupted, Miłosz's father decided to try his luck on a different continent, and in the mid-1920s set off for Brazil, believing that there must be substantial economic benefits from working abroad. An experienced engineer, he hoped that in a large, exotic country his career would flourish and that he would experience the further thrill of being an adventurer. Sadly, the whole enterprise turned out to be a fiasco, as he could not cope with loneliness and the separation from his family. He swiftly returned to Poland, presumably with some savings, since he was able to purchase a small piece of land outside Wilno. To the teenage son, the father seemed to have slipped into the shadows. This was a man of boundless ambition, an adventurer and a hunter, who, having reached forty, had lapsed into the role of a weary bureaucrat, who now kept company with defeat.

Tomcat

'A small pugnacious boy arrives from distant Szetejnie. Grandma buys him a new suit made of worsted fabric—probably made by a Jewish tailor in Kiejdany', he writes in *The Issa Valley*. According to one of the local children depicted in the novel, the character who embodies Miłosz's younger self had 'a face like a Tartar's ass' (*Issa* 75). An actual school friend, Bohdan Urbanowicz, recalled his impressions of the ten year-old Miłosz for posterity: 'I see him always as a tomcat, constantly tense and grumpy. A tomcat, even when stroked and purring, conceals its strength and identity' (Urbanowicz 142).

In a photograph of Czesław from this period, a rather round-faced child emanates tension and seriousness; there is no trace of a beaming smile or a cheeky expression. It may be that the camera lens intimidated him. The boy has short hair and is wearing a dark jacket, part of the school uniform, buttoned up to his neck:

School was, of course, a great turning point for me, because until then I had not known the bitter taste of social conventions. Learning had been a strictly individual activity. My mother had taught me reading, writing and figuring during our journeys. In the spring, a few months of daily going through the little gate into the verdant garden where my tutor lived sufficed to prepare me for my entrance examination'. (*NR* 62)

Czesław took the entrance examination for the King Sigismund Augustus Boys' State Gymnasium Number 1 on 20 June 1921, and passed. His academic preferences and interests were reflected in his marks: top grade for religious studies, a slightly lower grade for reading and writing in Polish, and close to a failure for algebra. As Wilno was so compact, with all its principal buildings clustered together, the walk between the apartment and school was a short one, though the streets tended to be on steep inclines. Miłosz had to run in order to get to school by eight o'clock, before the janitor closed the entrance doors. Every day classes started with the hymn 'When the Dawn Breaks'. Today the substantial two-storey building, with large windows, still exists, its origins dating back to the time of the tsars. It forms part of a complex, which also includes a dormitory built in the 1930s where Miłosz boarded.

In the 1920s the area outside school was an open space with grassy and clay slopes, which offered space for ritual fights over the lunch-break between classes. The break also allowed opportunities for pupils to drop in at a small shop where 'an old Jewish woman sold various sweets. I am moved every time I remember how she saved the meagre earnings for her children and grandchildren . . . There we used to buy buns, some seeds or sweets' (CM, in Fiut 198).

The earthly paradise of Szetejnie had become more and more a distant memory. Days were now passed monotonously learning Latin grammar by heart and struggling with mathematics. At the beginning Miłosz recollected how difficult it was to function among his fellow pupils, so different was he from the majority of his friends, and so preoccupied with his own inner experiences. In both a real and a symbolic sense he constructed a different world for himself. Like the cat Bohdan imagined him as, he inhabited his own space, maintained a secret life. This often took the form of 'drawing magical places, countries and plants' (CM, in Fiut 197).

'I was always very isolated and distant from the rest of my class' (*Podróżny świata* 112), he told Renata Gorczyńska in an interview. During his adolescent years the reason for this was Miłosz's intellectual distinctiveness, which often led him to enter into discussions with older boys such as Teodor Bujnicki and Stanisław Stomma. Initially, however, he experienced shock at having to face and interact with so many children after years of being alone with parents, grandparents and other adults. Suddenly he now seemed to lose his way and struggled to find a place within the new environment. He carried within him a pre-existing sense of otherness, as well as complexes, which included excessive pride and high expectations of other people. In the course of the eight years he spent at the gymnasium, the extent and intensity of this disconnection must have varied considerably.

From his later hazy memories of the time, there were about a dozen names that came to mind, amongst which those of four close friends stood out in particular. The first of these was Leon Szreder, who was later, along with Miłosz, involved in Żagary, a university poetry group. Its magazine, Żagary, promoted the idea of poetry's social function, and orientated politically to the left. Another friend was Stefan Zagórski, who was later Miłosz's companion on his 1934 journey to Paris. He was also the only pupil apart from Miłosz who read the progressive journal *Wiadomości Literackie* (Literary News). The son of a lawyer and a Jewish physician, Stefan was once a member of a Russian social democratic movement. Another schoolmate, Stanisław Kownacki, was totally committed to one activity—constructing shortwave radios and staying in touch with other enthusiasts worldwide (*ABC* 167–171). Miłosz would later meet him in America, with another longtime friend, Ignacy Święcicki. It was in Święcicki's house that Janina Miłosz, the poet's wife, and their two sons would stay in the 1950s, when, as a result of Czesław's defection to France and inability to obtain a U.S. visa, the family were separated for several years.

The dull regularity of school life was interrupted by group visits to church, in a procession headed by the school orchestra. On rare occasions, distinguished guests were invited to address the pupils; they included Władysław Mickiewicz, who was the son of the great Polish Romantic poet, and Stanisław Wojciechowski, the second ever President of Poland. Given the huge popularity in Wilno of Poland's chief of state, Józef Piłsudski, where the Miłosz family were among his admirers, Czesław was most impressed by the statesman's visit to the school in April 1922 during his first year there. It was not only Piłsudski's big moustache and grey army uniform that the schoolboy would remember, but also the fact that he pinched his cheek.

There can be little doubt that the individual behind Piłsudski's visit to the King Sigismund Augustus Gymnasium was its headmaster, Zygmunt Fedorowicz, who was a marshal of Middle Lithuania and the man who carried the motion proposing the unification of Lithuania with Poland. His staff included a number of particularly impressive characters and gifted teachers who helped shape Miłosz's intellectual development, most notably a priest, Father Leopold Chomski, Adolf Rożek, who taught him Latin, and Henryk Burhardt, who taught French. The poet would later claim that the inspiration for his own early creative work came from a textbook in French. It was Burhardt who also made clear to Miłosz that involvement in anti-Semitism was a sign of inferior intelligence:

> In our city, people called the first of May the 'Jewish' holiday. There was a big parade with banners and flags ... Our French teacher (we called him Sock, because he once pulled a dirty sock out of his pocket instead of a handkerchief) looks at me suspiciously. He beckons me to him with his finger. I go up to the table, my hair is unkempt, I am twelve years old. 'What do you have there?' Sticking out of my pocket are the forks of a slingshot [a catapult] 'What are you going to do with that?' I try to give my voice a hard, masculine ring. 'Beat Jews'. He narrows his eyes in a cold reflex, as if he were looking at an animal. I feel hot, I feel as if I had turned beet-red'. (*NR* 95–96)

The boy felt ashamed of his pitiful comment and realised that he was merely echoing Uncle Witold, the only one in the family whose nationalist views contained a marked anti-Semitic strain.

Polish lessons in the first two years began with an attempt to raise all the students to the same level of competence before introducing them to the history of Polish literature. For Miłosz, the most inspiring teacher of Polish was Maria Stabińska-Przybytko, with whom he had long discussions. In the final years at school he was taught by Stanisław Cywiński, a specialist in Norwegian studies from the University of Wilno. Cywiński also gave introductory classes in philosophy, and became a good friend to Miłosz when he started his degree course at the university. Cywiński's daughter recalled how very highly her father rated the young man for his intelligence and his inquisitive mind, which were demonstrated during sessions of a literary circle he had established.

In his 1979 essay collection *Ogród nauk* (The Garden of Science), Miłosz offered a picture of his psychological state in the course of his school years:

> A child with a highly-developed *ego* wants to excel in everything, and at once. Because it is difficult to achieve that in games and sports, the fear of not coming first is paralysing, and results in the child coming last. Then a child withdraws and creates for himself a closed, other world, a substitute world ... The complexity of what was happening inside me, when a traumatic pattern to my life was evolving between the tenth and fifteenth years of my life, terrified me. Although the child involved himself in many school activities, membership of scout groups, and Nature Club ... [he also displayed] strong signs of autistic behavior,

combined with incredible skill in masking his true self and pretending normality . . . My substitute world . . . was a world with fixed laws, a painless and safe world . . . My flights of imagination were a necessity and a flaw, because I would have given anything to be like the others, equal to the others. (17–18)

Here the youngster comes across as sensitive, easily hurt, and yet at the same time proud. He strives to make up for his actual and imagined failings and misdemeanours by being first in all subjects at school and the teachers' favourite, later by exhibiting a rebellious arrogance, and finally through art, a reaction against 'playground brutality'. A response to the sadistic cruelty that he associated with physical education and games lessons was the fervour with which he pursued his main preoccupation—nature.

Doctor Catchfly

The lament of a slaughtered hare fills the forest.
It fills the forest and disturbs nothing there.
For the dying of a particular being is its own private business
And everyone has to cope with it in whatever way he can . . .
If the wax in our ears could melt, a moth on pine needles,
A beetle half-eaten by a bird, a wounded lizard
Would all lie at the center of the expanding circles
Of their vibrating agony.

                                                            'Diary of a Naturalist', *NCP 285*

In his early years at the gymnasium, Miłosz read with great enthusiasm Maria Rodziewiczówna's novel *The Summer of Forest People* (1920). He began filling the pages of his exercise books with detailed maps of an ideal country, separated from the rest of the world by thick forests, where 'there were no fields or roads and the only permissible means of communication were boats on the rivers and canals' ('Automobile', *ABC 47*). There were separate areas for bison, moose and bears, to which only adults who were passionate about nature were allowed access. He studied different atlases, works on ornithology and textbooks on botany, along with articles about saving endangered species and the battle with poachers which he encountered in *Polish Hunter*, a journal to which his father subscribed. He collected and meticulously prepared dried plants, excelled in making sketches of nature, and revelled in Latin names for birds, such as *Emberiza citrinella* (the yellowhammer) and *Turdus musicus* (the redwing, a bird in the thrush family).

Discoveries about birds became miniature epiphanies which remained with him right through to the last years of his life, when he could still recall with ease the Linnaean classification of creatures. In his room there were fish tanks by the wall and various cages in which he kept noisy birds and busy mice. In a big glass jar swam newts brought from a pond in the suburbs, over which circled a huge eagle owl with red and golden eyes: "A soundless flight, a rush of air—when suddenly, in mid-flight, he would drop a pile, splattering the floor (which indiscretion Thomas immediately cleaned up, to avoid angering the grown-ups) and then from the top of the tiled stove, let out a real owl hoot' (*Issa* 78).

The first book on his school reading list was Adam Mickiewicz's great classic *Pan Tadeusz,* which he had reservations about because of its inaccurate descriptions of nature. The young Czesław was convinced at this time that he would become a botanist, or perhaps an ornithologist, and, in order to prepare for that, together with a schoolmate he read and re-read Włodzimierz Korsak's popular books *In the Footsteps of Nature* and *A Year of the Hunter.* From these books he also discovered the art of taxidermy, the better to preserve his finds.

His relationship with his father strengthened as a result of a shared fascination with hunting. He treasured the single-barrelled shotgun sported by Aleksander, cleaning it with cloths dipped in olive oil, and also helped prepare the cartridges with which they would bring down hares and ducks. In *Native Realm* he describes how the small house they lived in, located about ten miles outside Wilno, was surrounded by lakes and dense forests, and so fostered the feeling that they were in constant touch with nature. From there the family visited nearby villages to get food supplies, though what young Czesław primarily enjoyed doing was exploring the forest often to seek out game. Years later he recorded a particular instance of his wanderings in one of his most beautiful poems, 'Encounter':

> We were riding through frozen fields in a wagon at dawn.
> A redwing rose in the darkness.
>
> And suddenly a hare across the road.
> One of us pointed to it with his hand.
>
> That was long ago. Today neither of them is alive,
> Not the hare, nor the man who made the gesture.
>
> O my love, where are they, where are they going
> The flash of a hand, streak of movement, rustle of pebbles.
> I ask not out of sorrow, but in wonder.
>
> (*NCP* 27)

In *O podróżach w czasie* (About Journeys through Time), he reflected again on the anxieties of his adolescent years and their longer-term effects on his thinking:

> My father was good at shooting and I was poor and perhaps it was my inferiority that made me invent myths about myself. I began to lose interest in nature for other reasons too. I delivered brilliant talks at school about Darwin and the theory of evolution, and gradually the realm of nature appeared to me like one big slaughter house, *natura devorans et natura devorata* [devouring nature and devoured nature]. (260)

Disappointments during the hunting sessions, which crop up in *The Issa Valley*, made him realise that he was not wholly at ease in a man's world and so should not follow in his father's footsteps. His engagement with Darwin's theories of natural selection and the struggle for survival led to the painful conclusion that he was a collaborator in the boundless cruelty which permeates the world of nature. From then on he experienced two types of feelings: the entrancing joy at the sight of a flash on a bird's wing or the eyes of a deer would always be accompanied by a recognition of the stern laws on which the realm of nature is founded. This in turn prompted questions concerning the Author of this order. If the intelligence behind creation allowed such carnage to occur, then that intelligence must be totally heartless.

Another text that helped shape his changing responses to the universe was a book for young readers by the archaeologist, naturalist and philosopher, Erazm Majewski; this was entitled *Doctor Flycatcher: Fantastic Adventures in the World of Insects* (1890). Its cleverly constructed story line provides profound insights into the worlds of insects, plants and animals. In the beautiful, richly illustrated edition he came upon, the young Miłosz followed the thrilling adventures of an entomologist who, after taking a potion, finds himself reduced to the size of an ant.[1] As a consequence, a blade of grass in the Tatra mountains seems as huge as a tree, and a spider a dangerous opponent. Subsequently, the protagonist comes to the aid of another magically miniaturised traveller, a sign of his ethical awareness.

In the early 1970s Miłosz would later return to the good doctor while working on his narrative poem 'From the Rising of the Sun', in which a small boy dreams of hunting trophies and of achieving manhood, and so values above all else steadiness of hand. The stanzas that follow become an adieu and, at the same time, a homage to the characters in these children's books:

> To the masters of our youth, greetings.
> To you, my teacher, Mr Life Science,

Spleeny Bagiński in checkered knickers,
The ruler of *infusoria* and amoebas.
. . .

And to you, Doctor Catchfly,
Who are free from destruction, the hero
Of a historic expedition to the land of insects.
You live as always on Miodowa in Warsaw,
. . . you set off on your old bachelor's walk
Through the park, the place of your victory
Over all things subject to ruin and change.
. . .

You infected me with your pity for computers
Dressed in chitin cloaks, in transparent armor.
And in my child's imagination
I still bear your mark, O philosopher of pain.

    ('Diary of a Naturalist', *NCP* 286, 288–289)

By now, Miłosz must have reached fourteen or fifteen. Majewski's re-markable fiction prompted the teenage Miłosz to reflect deeply on the vi-ciousness at large in the world, as well as the origins of evil. At the sight of the ruins of a burnt anthill, Catchfly stands helpless and speechless—as indeed the young Miłosz must have when he had what he later described as 'my first encounter with God's cruelty'. This happened when his good friend Alik Protasewicz was robbed of his youth and future by the sudden onset of paralysis, probably as a result of poliomyelitis: 'I was fond of him and used to visit him . . . Alik, vigorous and sturdily built, bore his helplessness badly, was profoundly depressed'. Miłosz recalled vividly in later years how in his sick-room it was almost possible to hear the unspoken question reverberate: 'Why me?' (*ABC* 19).

Manichean Poisons

All of us, in our flesh and in the affairs of daily life, are subject to the devil and are guests in a world in which he is a master and a god. That is why the bread we eat, the clothes we wear, even the air, everything by which we live is under his power.

    Martin Luther, Commentary on Galatians 3,
    used as the epigraph to 'Gardener', *NCP* 731

A period of what may have been merely outward conformity to the rules of the school and its general ethos came to an end. What followed was adolescent rebellion whose origins lay in a crisis in how he perceived the world and which was explosive in its effects. At around sixteen and seventeen, Miłosz switched from being a model pupil and turned into one of the gymnasium's worst students. The fistfights and setting fire to papers were a sure sign that he and his emotions were in revolt, which soon manifested itself in the revulsion he displayed towards power and authority.

Half-way through his high school years, Miłosz ceased attending scout meetings, suggesting an awakening self-awareness and a desire to make decisions for himself. Like the majority of his companions, he had acquired various skills through scouts, learning to tie knots and to keep fires going, and had enjoyed spending time camping; one of his proudest achievements was receiving a Golden Lily, one of the most prestigious awards in Polish scouting. At the same time, however, he felt a constant distaste for other aspects of scouting, an instinctive dislike of worn phrases about God and homeland, the emphasis on group discipline, all those roll calls, and having to line up and be counted off one by one: 'I knew that I had to behave in a certain way and no other way, but why? There were various orders, oaths . . . I can more or less understand the feelings of people who are Catholics without comprehending why. Because that is what is expected. Yet while accepting, "well, that's how it is", I was haunted by the question—why?' (CM, in Fiut 180). Although, as he later remarked to a mentor, by the third and fourth grade, he felt 'sick with disgust at having to endure that regimentation' (CM to Iwaszkiewicz, 22 April 1932), for a long time he had deferred confronting that question. In the end, however, he opted not to conform. Evidence of his growing intellectual autonomy was his open scorn in the classroom for Henryk Sienkiewicz's *With Fire and Sword*.[2]

A factor in his adoption of a more independent line at this juncture may well have been that he had just begun to live alone. Towards the end of 1926 his family relocated to Suwałki in Poland, leaving Czesław behind to continue his studies in Wilno. He was placed in a pension with a family whose host held far-right nationalist views. From this point onwards his parents' influence waned, and the two individuals who did most to enable him to forge his own sense of the world were Father Chomski and his Latin teacher, Adolf Rożek, a humanist: 'When I read Thomas Mann's *The Magic Mountain* at university, I saw that it was really a book about these two' (*NR* 71).

Classical studies were a compulsory component in the gymnasium curriculum, with the result that all pupils undertook an extensive course in Latin. After a dour grounding in the basics of the language, they moved on to a more comprehensive course in the fifth grade, delivered by Mr Rożek. Lessons resembled translation seminars, in which hours were devoted to polishing chosen textual extracts. Such classes not only provided an in-depth introduction to classical literature, but also instilled in Miłosz a respect for the translator's art, as well as recognition of the importance of total concentration on any task. These sessions influenced his own future writing, increasing his distrust of Romantic verbal excess, strengthening his conviction that the artist's goal must be *claritas*.

Most importantly, this was a period in which his questioning of religious practice and the theology that underpinned it reached a new intensity. He began to clash with Father Chomski over aspects of Catholic dogma, asserting, with some courage, that if a confession had to be certified by a priest as a pre-requisite for receiving the eucharist, then it ceased to be a voluntary spiritual act and became a sign of mere conformity. In a situation where freedom of conscience was violated, he would not take communion. The priest came to regard the young Miłosz as the 'black sheep' in his flock who 'contaminated the rest with his insolence'. On occasion, Miłosz recalled how Chomski

> became so touchy that even if I was sitting quietly, he would interrupt himself in the middle of a word to shout at me: 'You have an unseemly look on your face, leave the room!' If it had depended on him alone, he would probably have expelled me from the school, but a group of teachers, who might be called 'Rożek's party', protected me as a 'capable student'. (*NR* 82)

Years later, in *Native Realm,* the poet represented the school catechist as embodying aspects of Polish Catholicism which had done so much to alienate him. Instead of fostering an intimate connection with God and emphasising human beings' moral responsibilities for each other, in Miłosz's view the Polish Church was over-concerned with the social arena and notions of 'the Homeland'. Inner personal experience was relegated to the margins. The insistence on regular weekly church attendance meant that the 'faith' became something to be exhibited, rather than an energising moral force:

> Owing to various circumstances, pupils of the higher classes did not go to Sunday Mass at the school chapel. Instead we went to St. George's Church in town. St. George's was attended by 'good society' who, after Mass was over, would parade down the front walk: officers saluted, lawyers and doctors dispensed bows, women displayed their smiles, furs, and hats. As I moved out with this crowd or watched them from the nearby square, I was nearly bursting with hatred. A man, in my opinion, was only worth his passion for nature, hunting, literature, or whatever,

so long as he put into it everything he had. But these people were apes. What meaning had they? What did they exist for? I was soaring at some divine height, poised over them as if they were specimens under a microscope, which are born, last a second, and die without leaving a trace. Just look at their coquetting, their little intrigues, their showing off, their mutual favours, their bustling for money: they have nothing more to them . . . Taking part in rituals along with apes humiliated me. Religion was a sacred thing: how could their God be mine at the same time? . . . In the face of clearly inferior creatures, it would be better to proclaim oneself an atheist in order to remove oneself from the circles of the unworthy. Religion, insofar as it was a social convention and a constraint, ought to be destroyed. In my battle [with the catechist], it is apparent that the best and the worst motives converged. A taste for independence, a loathing for all hypocrisy, a defence of freedom of conscience joined with intellectual arrogance, an obsession with purity, and the conviction that I understood more than anybody else. (*NR* 80–81)

Like Thomas Mann's protagonist in *The Magic Mountain*, the young Miłosz felt torn between competing mentors, discourses and positions. Although subsequently the choice between Rożek and Chomski seemed finely balanced, in actuality he was much closer to the world-view of the priest. The humanist's trust in reason he regarded as naive; it provided no explanation as to the origin of evil which suffuses the natural world. Although at times Chomski appeared to him ridiculous and superficial, his antithetical stance towards a callous, amoral nature held a strong appeal: 'He proclaimed another law, battled with the enemy, the Prince of This World. Like the rest of our class, I snickered at [his] foolish performances and at his suspiciousness. Yet his old cassock, his tormented face, and his inner tension aroused my pity and created something like a feeling of kinship' (*NR* 79). What became the motor of Miłosz's spiritual transformation was the break from tainted nature, and his conception of literary culture as a refuge or haven where the individual could rise above matter:

In my last year before graduation, a sort of cool politeness grew up between us. He realized, no doubt, that force would never break me. When he stopped pressuring me, I went to Confession. But because the act of humbling oneself before Existence ought to be a strictly voluntary, personal thing, beyond social convention, I swore never to form an alliance with Polish Catholicism—I did not necessarily use those terms. In other words, I would not submit to apes. (*NR* 88)

Although Father Chomski suspected that the young man would become an atheist, Miłosz writes that that was not the path he would ever have taken 'because I lived in a state of constant wonder, as if before a curtain which I knew had to rise someday . . . Moreover, nothing at home could have induced a religious revolt' (*NR* 85). His upbringing had taken place within a largely broad-minded, tolerant family. Whereas his father seemed 'indifferent' when it came to religion, his mother remained 'a practising Catholic, without making a big issue of it'. A phrase often on her lips was that 'everyone praises God in their own way'. Miłosz reflects that 'it would have been difficult, I think, for her to have accepted it as certain that Catholicism is the only true religion. The stern categories of Heaven and Hell were dismissed with a shrug of the shoulders: "What do we know?" My bickering with the school authorities did not upset her at all' (*NR* 85–86). Where in others the quest to achieve a profounder faith and understanding could result in mental illness and a cruel end, for Miłosz it was invigorating. One can imagine how he might have relished living through periods of intense theological dispute, such as when Christianity began taking shape or during the Reformation period, rather than the time allotted to him, a century of lukewarm religion and scepticism.

Among his school peers, he felt something of an oddball, searching, as he did, so much more rigorously for intellectual confirmation for his perceptions. After a phase of poring over biology textbooks, he turned to esoteric, philosophic and religious texts. He was drawn to the mysticism of the Belgian author Maurice Maeterlinck (1862–1949), who had been awarded the Nobel Prize in the year of his birth and was very popular in Poland in the 1920s. Another writer whose work he looked into was the Danish Nobel Prize winner of 1917, Karl Adolph Gjellerup (1857–1919), whose interests included 'Hinduism, Occultism and Reincarnation' (*Podróżny świata* 58). After that he studied Schopenhauer, William James's *The Varieties of Religious Experience* and Saint Augustine's *Confessions,* where he found meditations on the nature of time and reflections on the depth of human contamination, from which the only means to be saved was God's grace. Undoubtedly Miłosz must have sensed a particular affinity with Augustine, the lust-filled ex-Manichean, whose examinations of conscience were undertaken with such extraordinary intensity.

Thus the crisis in his faith thrust Miłosz outside the safety zone occupied by so many Polish Catholics, whose clerics encouraged religiosity but not much in the way of reflection. The individual stance he came to adopt might be seen as not unlike a Protestant one, since it was fired mainly by a conviction that faith is deeply personal and that talking to God need not be an undertaking carried out in the presence of others. Far better to grow quietly and develop a hidden self than to join the 'apes'. The conflict, Miłosz would later state, 'increased my inborn secretiveness, my rebelliousness and my propensity for false poses' which were 'assumed either to deceive myself or to make the game more complicated' (*NR* 89).

The most significant turning point in his spiritual life occurred after meeting Oskar Miłosz in Paris in 1931. That encounter enabled him gradually to find a place for himself within the Church, while maintaining his fierce opposition to its politically right-wing sympathies. The convictions and positions identified above remained constants throughout his career, making him a unique figure in twentieth-century Polish literature.

Early Literary Tastes (and Russian Roulette)

As for so many other writers during childhood, imaginative literature promised Miłosz a measure of security, space and independence. While in his early years at school he collected books published by the Biblioteka Groszowa (Penny Library), and frequently popped into a nearby young people's library, where he encountered books by Thomas Mayne Reid, Jules Verne, Rudyard Kipling, Jack London and James Fenimore Cooper. In less interesting classes, he used to bury himself in adventure and detective stories. His desk was often covered with textbooks picked up in the secondhand school bookshop and other bookstores.

A particular favourite among these was a geography atlas, which opened possibilities of embarking on imaginary journeys all round the world. As Miłosz grew older, Jack London gave way to Joseph Conrad, whose novels he would come across in the reading rooms of the Tomasz Zan Library, which also held issues of Warsaw literary journals. Alongside the classics and romantic fiction in Wilno's well-stocked bookshops, he encountered contemporary literature, translations by Ilya Ehrenburg, Boris Pilnyak, Isaac Babel, Upton Sinclair, Stefan Zweig and Thomas Mann, whose *Tonio Kröger* resonated strongly with him because of its concerns with otherness, division and the artist as exile.

At school, Miłosz's Polish teacher had little appreciation of his talents and awarded him very low marks for his essays, and gave no additional support to enable him to improve his performance. Her expectations extended no further than that he should follow the course requirements and write with a degree of fluency. Miłosz realised at some point that poor marks would not help him in a future career as a clerk or a diplomat. Accepting the premise that test papers were simply exercises in rhetoric, he altered his attitude to school assignments and began to achieve the highest marks. In another sign of the caution and reserve that were now becoming second nature, he made sure that his real opinions about certain writers and their work did not stray into papers submitted for assessment.

———————

Miłosz must have experienced a degree of detachment, when, full of emotion and deeply immersed in his thoughts, he journeyed on an overnight train to visit his family in Suwałki. Barely awake in the early hours, standing at the station, he felt like a character in a story, the young man, empty inside, making his way back to the family home, where his rejoicing mother awaited him with open arms, while his father looked up as he sipped quietly from his glass. In a letter to his first-ever literary mentor he complains that

> my parents accuse me of falseness, secretiveness, and say that I don't care for them, that I am cold and don't love them. My behaviour is very rarely natural, and is characterised by a lot of posing, obstinacy, and contrariness. But there is no way in which I can discuss the purity of poetic form with them. As regards their mundane conversation and their friends—they really bore me. (CM to Jarosław Iwaszkiewicz, 20 December 1930)

By this time, Aleksander Miłosz was beginning to accept his limited career options, though with some sadness, which he tried to suppress by drinking. In December 1926 he had accepted an engineering post as manager in the Roads Department at Suwałki's Regional Office. He headed a committee tasked with building an airport near the town, and was a member of another group responsible for supervising school building projects. He also worked briefly as an architect. For these contributions to civic life he was awarded a Silver Cross for Merit in 1934. However, most of his working days were confined to inspecting roads and supervising their maintenance, which was a far cry from how he had imagined his career would pan out. In leather cap and goggles, his face reddened by wind, he spent long hours driving round the local roads in his Ford or on his Harley-Davidson, which had a sidecar. On occasion he would take one of his sons with him to Sejny to sample the delicious fish in a Jewish inn, or roam further into Eastern Prussia, where a home brew called Hindenburg could be sampled. Czesław's first contact with the West saw him accompanying his father to a trade exhibition in Poznań, and in addition there were sorties into Prussia and visits to the Kunat family in Krasnogruda, close to the Lithuanian border.

The Krasnogruda estate belonged to Bronisław Kunat, Czesław's grandfather's brother, who was the father of two daughters, Gabriela and Janina. A decline in earnings from farm production combined with higher taxation forced this branch of the Kunat family to try to generate income through other means. It was decided that twenty rooms in the house would be let in summer months to visitors, mainly people from Warsaw's intellectual elite. The seventeenth-century mansion stood close to a large pine forest, opposite which was a park containing three-hundred-year-old lime trees. Beautifully situated though it was, the house now functioned less as a residence, more as a focal point around which cows, sheep and pigs were reared. Relations with the local people were cordial on the whole, since the owners showed respect towards them and did not behave in a high-handed manner. Gabriela's son, Zaza, gave peasant children lifts sometimes, and often the family placed a radio on a windowsill so that the children's parents could listen to the news. Next to the main house, the family added a one-storey building with guest rooms and an avenue lined with chestnut trees which led to Lake Hołny, where visitors could swim and enjoy boat trips. In the evenings, the guests came to the house to play bridge and other card games, ate excellent fresh-water fish dishes, and danced to piano music which the master of the house pro-vided by means of a screeching gramophone. And, occasionally, holiday romances developed in these idyllic, relaxing surroundings.

Young Czesław visited the house a number of times. The place was often bursting at the seams in summer due to the sheer numbers of paying guests and visiting relatives. During his school years, he came with his parents, but also sometimes on his own when he lodged in an attic room and spent days roaming through the forests and around the lake, hunting wild ducks and grebe.

One summer, in July or August 1926 or 1927, the painfully shy teenager found himself surrounded by holidaymakers. From references to this stay in his later writings, one deduces that it proved particularly dramatic. No-one initially took any notice of him, though from time to time a condescending smile was directed towards him, which alternately made him feel a lesser being and then a far superior one in many ways. Among those holidaying in Krasnogruda was a red-haired lady called Irena, who arrived without her husband. In an approach which appears to have left Czesław at first speechless and in a state of shock, she took it upon herself to teach him how to dance the tango. A poem from the early 1990s recalls how she led him round the floor, 'with that smirk of a mature woman/Who initiates a young man' ('House in Krasnogruda', *NCP* 615). From his account of the incident it would appear that she was not simply paying him attention, but irresponsibly angling for a stronger response. Whatever her motives, as a consequence of her actions he fell head over heels in love.

Not long after the dancing lesson, probably that evening, three students from Warsaw turned up at the house, all of them two or three years older than him. The following morning, after rising early, the besotted teenager went outside with the intention of walking in the forest, perhaps to ease the intense longing he felt. Wandering in the direction of Irena's room, he spotted a figure making his exit through her window; this was Edward, one of the students who had struck lucky.[3] Not only did he feel betrayed; it was as if the utter vileness of life had been exposed before him. Sick with despair, he closeted himself in his attic room and after swallowing a quantity of vodka took out a revolver. He loaded it with a single bullet, spun the barrel, put it against his head and pulled the trigger (CM, in Fiut 164).

It would be difficult to evoke the emotions of the moment, although one can imagine the tension of the split second between 'is' and 'was', between the time when the finger of his trembling hand felt the trigger ease back and when he heard the metal click as the firing pin hit an empty chamber, a sound half-muted by the thumping of his terrified heart. The revolver did not go off. By a ghastly irony of fate, many years later, Irena's lover, Edward, committed suicide; he and his wife gassed themselves, feeling unable to see any future for themselves in stifling Stalinist Poland.

This episode from the mid-1920s continued to surface in Miłosz's later poetry and prose. *The Mountains of Parnassus,* an unfinished dystopian science fiction novel from the 1970s, includes an adolescent character called Oti who develops a passion for an older woman, partly driven by the need for a mother substitute. Within the narrative, in which autobiographical traces are clearly apparent, are elements that have much in common with the marriage of his aunt, Gabriela Kunat. Referring to Gabriela in an interview as his *'première passion d'amour'* (CM, in Fiut 153), he recalled vividly the time when he first saw her in Szetejnie. In opting for the French phrase, was Miłosz expecting readers to interpret *'passion'* and *'amour'* in a platonic sense? Might they have been lovers? What was she to him when in 1934 he wrote and dedicated 'The Song' (*NCP* 7) to her, and did the poem contain an intimate portrait?

When in 1962 Gabriela Kunat died in Sopot, a spa town not far from Gdańsk, Czesław Miłosz bade her farewell in 'Elegy for N. N.', which is dated 'Berkeley 1963'. It concludes:

> Guilt, yours and mine? Not a great guilt.
> Secrets, yours and mine? Not great secrets.
> Not when they bind the jaw with a kerchief, put a little cross
>   between the fingers,
> and somewhere a dog barks, and the first star flares up.
>
> No, it was not because it was too far
> You failed to visit me that day or night.
> From year to year it grows in us until it takes hold,
> I understood it as you did: indifference.

(NCP 267)

Inside the Lodge

Miłosz's intellectual isolation and his acutely painful feeling of alienation from both his family and most of his classmates were lessened by his links to a clandestine confraternity. From biographical hints dispersed in different texts in which characters probe the arcane mysteries of the twentieth century, it appears that he had joined a Masonic lodge. This particular organisation, called PET, had its roots in the nineteenth-century Union of Polish Youth (ZET), which brought together student members from all parts of partitioned Poland. After Poland achieved independence in 1918, ZET's underground activities were abandoned in favour of an ambitious educational mission, focused on developing future elites. However, the cultish secrecy surrounding the group was maintained, since exclusivity was an important part of its *raison d'être*. Although ZET at the outset had been a nationalist movement, by the 1920s and 1930s the various lodges differed in their political leanings. Interestingly, some of its members had close connections with a progressive, liberal group, Catholic Renaissance, and gave outstanding service to the Church. The PET chapter in Wilno maintained a progressive, tolerant outlook on most issues and was hostile to nationalist fanaticism. Its members did not regard themselves as part of a political group, but rather as a union of intellectuals who drew to their ranks only the most outstanding of their contemporaries.

The individual who invited Miłosz to join the group was Stanisław Stomma, who was three years his senior. They had met several times in the past, as their estates were close to each other and their families sometimes paid visits to one another. In Wilno, they attended the same school, getting together at break times and at the Stommas' place in the city. In PET, Miłosz encountered like-minded people, facing similar problems and sharing many of the same passions. The warmth he experienced meant a great deal to him because of the solitariness of his life as a lodger at pensions and in boarding houses and because of his desperate need to be accepted, particularly in these adolescent years.

In his memoir, Stomma recalls the intensity of the intellectual stimulus he and Miłosz enjoyed as youngsters: 'We had to read a lot, experience a lot and digest it all ... We were engrossed in endless discussions which only helped cement our friendship' (*Trudne Lekcje Historii* 48). Between 1925 and 1929 the Wilno theatre scene thrived. Talented directors and actors arrived in the city, and put on plays by Polish and foreign writers, often applying avant-garde techniques in stage design and technique. Along with works by Juliusz Słowacki, Stefan Żeromski and Stanisław Wyspiański, the friends encountered dramas by William Shakespeare, Pierre Corneille, Henrik Ibsen and Luigi Pirandello.

PET group meetings took place regularly, with members delivering papers presenting their thoughts and thinking processes; these writings were then incorporated into what was referred to as *The Green Book*. A diverse range of beliefs and opinions were represented within the group, which included Catholics, atheists and believers in pantheism—not surprisingly, given that freedom of opinion was prized. They sought ways of escaping the moral and cultural crises of the present, turning to different ideological options, ranging from conservative ones to the more popular leftist ones. The kinds of subjects explored included honesty and deceit, the nature of evil, rationality and the emotions, and the value of youth, though what above all engaged their interest were issues around beauty and art.

One member who became an exemplar for young Czesław was Teodor Bujnicki. Mature for his age, he studied history, had a passion for literature and wrote poetry. He became Miłosz's first master, the first link in a long chain of inspiring friendships which advanced his intellectual understanding, stimulated creativity and strengthened emotional ties. Although Miłosz liked having many casual acquaintances, he especially cherished close friends with whom he built strong bonds, undoubtedly because of his now very loose ties with the members of his family. His very strong sense of self required that companions prove their commitment and loyalty, though, it should be added, he was always a devoted friend himself.

The Rushing Heraclitean River

In my childhood, I was ecstatically devout and prayed to God often and heartily to give me the most impoverished life—so that I would be despised throughout my whole life—and only to give me undying fame after my death.

Juliusz Słowacki, letter to his mother

My generation was lost. Cities too. And nations.
But all this a little later. Meanwhile, in the window, a swallow
Performs its rite of the second. That boy, does he already suspect
That beauty is always elsewhere and always delusive?
Now he sees his homeland. At the time of the second mowing.
Roads winding uphill and down. Pine groves. Lakes.
An overcast sky with one slanting ray.
And everywhere men with scythes, in shirts of unbleached linen

And the dark-blue trousers that were common in the province.
He sees what I see even now. Oh but he was clever,
Attentive, as if things were instantly changed by memory.
Riding in a cart, he looked back to retain as much as possible.
Which means he knew what was needed for some ultimate moment
When he would compose from fragments a world perfect at last.

'Diary of a Naturalist', NCP 284

As the crises of the preceding years began to recede, Miłosz found fulfilment in
discussions, became a voracious reader, and began to contemplate the possibility
of a poetic calling. He remembered the last year at school as a time of reconciliation and hope: 'It was a year of great expectations . . . I remembered vividly
wooden walkways in the streets close to my house and how I wandered round the
city with some intoxicating promise of a vague future' (*Podróżny świata* 11). He
was beginning to develop an extraordinary sense of destiny: 'I had this certainty,
not based on anything, and so I did not admit to anyone at all that I would become a great poet' (*Powinien byłbym napisać* 79).

At about the age of thirteen, around his third year in the gymnasium, he
embarked on his first attempts to write when he co-authored a small satirical magazine containing prose and poems. The real breakthrough moment came in 1928–
1929, during the period when he belonged to PET. The friendship with Bujnicki
was a source of great pleasure, and living proof that secret passions such as poetic
composition could be acted upon. Unlike the majority of young would-be poets,
Miłosz looked to classical forms when composing his poetry. In line with Latin
authors, he was less preoccupied with expressing his emotions than with tirelessly
trying to attain formal perfection. He constructed sonnets as an exercise to develop
this skill, and for one on the subject of threshing he won an award in a school
competition. He was inspired by the work of the sixteenth-century French poet
Joachim du Bellay (1522–1560), who was a member of Pierre Ronsard's circle. He
particularly liked the poem 'Happy he who like Ulysses'. As he tapped the rhythm
with his fingers, counted syllables and spotted rhymes, he undoubtedly had no idea
what lay ahead, and how he would experience the fate of Odysseus, a life of exile:

Happy, the man who finds sweet journey's end,
Like Ulysses, or he of the Golden Fleece,
Returning home, well-travelled, wise, to Greece:
To live life out, among his own again!

Alas, when will I see the soft smoke rise
From my own village, in what far season

Shall I gaze on my poor house and garden,
Which are my province, and the greater prize?[4]

Miłosz did not have any future 'greater prize' on his mind at this particular juncture, however. It was May 1929, and he was preoccupied with his final school exams, which made him feel so stressed that he experienced nightmares. His fears were mostly unfounded, since he attained top marks in humanities subjects, but did not do well in mathematics. The high-quality education he had received at school would serve as sufficient preparation for him to give lectures in Polish literature at one of the best American universities, UC Berkeley. After the exams he and his friends went on a camping holiday in the primeval forest at Puszcza Rudnicka.

It was his passionate desire to resist the passing of time that led Miłosz to literature, art and the world of the imagination. On a return visit to Wilno from Szetejnie, he was overcome with nostalgia:

> When I was still at school, influenced by reading the fourth part of Mickiewicz's *Forefathers' Eve* (Gustav's tale about returning to the family home) and Słowacki's *An Hour of Thought*, my discovery was to imagine the sweet melancholy with which I would recall something that was happening at the present time. Or, to be more precise, I stumbled across that idea before my reading of the Romantics took hold, possessing an innate predisposition towards melancholy, which, according to Edgar Poe, provides the most fitting note for poetry. Walking to school every day, I looked at the hills on the other side of the River Wilia and I travelled in my mind to the lost paradise of Szetejnie. Who would have thought that already then, I had turned to the past, not fully conscious of the increasing power of my attachment to the place. (*Rok myśliwego* 114)

It was also the realisation that in order to avoid defeat he had to seek shelter from the oppressive adult world. 'Literature, and, through it[,] a discovery of motion, gave me sufficient ammunition to combat inertia, made me believe that I could stay perpetually young' (*Sunday in Brunnen* 33).

Indeed, over time, he would be given unusual vigour, constant movement, seemingly unending youthfulness, though written into the script after the page headed 'guilt' were 'loneliness', 'exile' and 'suffering'.

Life was impossible, but it was endured.
Whose life? Mine, but what does that mean?

During recess, biting into a sandwich wrapped in paper,
I stand under the wall in chubby meditation.

. . .

And if they say that all I heard was the rushing of the Heraclitean
   river,
That will be enough, for the mere listening to it wore me down.

('A Short Recess', *NCP* 314)

Black Ariel

1930–1934

'I devote too little time to study'

Having graduated from Wilno's King Sigismund Augustus Gymnasium, Miłosz had to decide on how to extend his education further. He had no intention of managing the Szetejnie estate and could not rely on his parents' connections to help him move up in the world. Among the career choices open to him were finding a job in the civil service, taking on freelance work or undertaking degree-level study. Without taking into account his parents' hopes or expectations, he settled on the third of these options, and embarked on the Polish language and literature programme in the Humanities Department of Wilno University. A driving factor in this was undoubtedly his keenness to develop his burgeoning literary talents, in an era in which poetry-writing courses did not exist.

A common perception about those drawn to Polish studies was that they were 'either young women who were looking for husbands or budding poets. Female students outnumbered male students by far' (Putrament 145). In no time Miłosz developed an allergic reaction to the 'matrimonial department', and quickly realised that he did not want to become a specialist in the history of literature or, worse still, a schoolteacher. What made him particularly uneasy was an anxiety about getting stuck in a rut: 'I was straight out of school, still full of keenness for pranks and jokes and making fun of our teachers, so the thought of joining those ranks was unbearable. I was filled with boundless ambition . . . so, two weeks later I made up my mind to study law' (Fiut 212). The evidence showing that he had switched subjects exists in a signed student's book with his signature, dated 29 October 1929. On the second page of the dark-pink booklet is a picture of a youth with hair combed back, sensuous lips and a resolute gaze. These defined features give the face an aura of intensive vitality, which ensured that

Miłosz appeared to female students as an intriguing young man; however, his male friends—a source only of derogatory and scathing comments—described him as resembling a gorilla. Most law students were men, but the relatively few women were very intelligent, as the poet described later. There were many poor Jewish students for whom the law was one of the few accessible subject areas, and a source of much-sought-after careers. A significant number of students who entered law studies, however, had yet to make any firm or final commitments regarding their future careers.

Wilno University's four-year law course was eclectic in its content and far exceeded Miłosz's expectations. 'Criminal law changed into anthropology and sociology, the history of philosophy of law into philosophy, statistics into higher mathematics torturing my antimathematical brain' (*NR* 112). One of the alumni commented that the lecturers endeavoured to equip future lawyers with a grasp of a wide range of social, political and psychological issues. In answer to a question in a survey conducted by the Wilno Vagabonds' Club, first-year law student Czesław Miłosz reported that he was attending lectures and seminars in philosophy, and added with an earnestness that was typical of him, 'I devote too little time to study, but I am going to improve that' (Vagabonds' Club Archive).

Law studies proved far from easy; there was a shortage of books, and lecture theatres were always filled to capacity, which made the acoustics so bad that it was often difficult to hear the lecturers. At the end of the academic year, there was an oral exam in which students were quizzed on the material they had covered in the course; preparations for that meant rote learning from the lecturers' handouts. As the fee for first-year students was very low, it meant that the numbers enrolled were very high, so at the year's close a high proportion of students were failed. Miłosz was one of those, having failed to meet the required standard in Roman law, which was the downfall of many. When he repeated the exam after the summer holiday, he passed.

During the second year, he had to face Church law, political law and economic policy, while in the third year he faced the terrible ordeal of exams in statistics and the philosophy of law. His lecturer for the latter course, Wiktor Sukiennicki, an expert in Soviet studies and subsequently a professor at Oxford and Stanford, recalled the young student as a skilled practitioner in the art of improvisation:

Miłosz announced that he wanted to discuss [John] Austin and Anglo-Saxon theorists. They were not particularly popular in Poland at the time and were not included in the courses. After hearing an argument, which was put together very well, and then questions and answers, I gave the candidate the highest mark possible and remembered the

exam as outstanding. Only many years later I learnt from Miłosz that
he couldn't remember the exam, and that he did not speak English well
enough then to dip into various sources and had no real interest in
Austin. (Sukiennicki 42)[1]

The most interesting lectures on criminal law for Miłosz were those delivered by Bronisław Wróblewski. He insisted that students learn the judicial code
by heart, and incorporated philosophy and sociology into his sessions, in which
the history of penal institutions became the history of societies. Looking into sociology and anthropology in depth played a very important part in Miłosz's intellectual development. While legal science bored him, the mechanisms governing
social behaviour interested him greatly. He was fascinated with human beings,
and also with the development of different theories about the world and their
application. Sociology appealed strongly to young people like him, fascinated
by and involved in politics, and who felt the need to have a direct influence on
reality. It was not by chance that members of the literary group, Żagary, in which
he first made his name, were mainly young lawyers. 'Although I didn't like my
training in legal science, I must admit that it proved helpful', wrote Miłosz years
later to Zbigniew Herbert, urging the younger poet to adopt regular, ordered
work habits (CM to Herbert, n.d. 1959 or 1960). He appreciated how law studies
had instilled in him a respect for precision of thought, though he acknowledged
that it might have been better had he opted for classical studies. If he had pursued that path, would Miłosz's poetry have been engaged to the same extent in
the key ethical, spiritual, political and social concerns of our times? Perhaps it
is not mere coincidence that Miłosz, Gombrowicz and Herbert all studied law,
conscious that twentieth-century artists should not confine themselves to literary
matters and milieux alone.

On completing his degree in the School of Law, the young poet had no plans
to take his legal education further. True, he belonged to the University Circle of
Lawyers, though membership of that body was commonplace among law students.
It came with some useful perks, such as access to reading rooms with journals and
handbooks, containing lecture notes and exercises from the current academic year,
which served as important resources for less affluent students. Theoretically, higher
education was free, but universities imposed various fees, covering administrative
costs, library membership and the expense of wear and tear on books. These sums
all added up, hitting the students' pockets or those of their parents. Sometimes
their finances could be boosted by offering private tuition, though those opportunities could be hard to come by.

Throughout his university years Miłosz managed on very little, minimising
his costs by attending lectures, sitting in heated library rooms, and distracting his

hungry stomach by voraciously acquiring knowledge. He was the happy owner of one pair of socks, which he repeatedly darned and washed, and he added to his monthly budget by writing. He was too proud to request financial aid, but managed to gain concessions in the student fees he had to pay. He also applied for a repayable stipend in the fourth year of his studies, but was rejected. From the application forms it appears that his father's income was 'around 400 złoty a month', but that level of remuneration was 'not regular'. Miłosz received 20 złoty from his parents each month, which he supplemented with his own earnings of 50 złoty by writing articles for journals. Given that his monthly expenses were 80 złoty, he was repeatedly obliged to ask for credit.

Students were expected to meet the costs of food and board themselves. In cheap eateries, it was possible to buy dinner for 50–60 groszy.[2] An alternative to that was a meal in an old dormitory or the new canteen in a students' hall of residence. A photograph that has survived shows a hall filled with young men in suits, interspersed with women here and there, and on the tables, next to glasses and soup plates, bread, the staple means of satisfying young stomachs. Students' modest finances hardly ever stretched to buying alcohol, and so, as a result, in the Vagabonds' Club milk was more popular than beer. While it must have been very rare for Miłosz to spend money on drink, his memoirs do mention occasional jaunts to Jewish backstreets for a glass of vodka and a herring. As to how often he indulged in other risky pleasures the city had to offer, there is no way of knowing. Miłosz alludes to visits to a brothel in his correspondence (CM to Iwaszkiewicz, 1 February 1931), and in one unpublished text refers to a district close to the river, and 'a prostitute called Helcia, who was very cheap and therefore affordable to workers and to us, students' (Beinecke Library Archive).

The student population at Wilno University in the 1920s and 1930s reached 3,110. Their diverse interests were catered to by seventy-one different groups, membership of which came with significant long-term career benefits. The organisation with the most members was Bratnia Pomoc (Brotherly Support), which charged membership fees. Income from these, along with donations from other sources, was used to fund a canteen as well as a loan scheme. Many student groups were formed with specific ideological agendas—some with far-right views, others linked to the Catholic Church or to rival youth organisations, such as the nationalist Młodzież Wszechpolska (All Polish Youth), chaired by Roman Dmowski, and the Akademicki Legion Młodych, whose loyalties lay with the statesman Józef Piłsudski.

At some point Konwent Polonia (Convention Polonia), a student association whose history dated back to 1828, approached Miłosz with a view to inducting him into their ranks. Several factors deterred him from accepting this invitation, not least their nationalist and anti-Semitic tendencies and the pomposity of the young people in the group. He did submit his name as a candidate in leadership elections to Bratnia Pomoc, though temperamentally he was disinclined to involve himself in organised camaraderie. Where he felt most at ease was with the Vagabonds' Club, since he shared their enjoyment of outdoor pursuits.

Egg-Man

'I never had any propensity to become a leader. Never. I always was a rank-and-file soldier. That was my ideal' (Fiut 229). Miłosz must have instinctively grasped that to take on a prominent role within a group or organisation necessitated a near-total commitment, leaving him no time for the arduous craft of text-making. What he did do, however, was join an association without a hierarchy, which, during the inter-war period in Wilno and the post-war period in Warsaw, performed very important work.

The Vagabonds' Club operated according to democratic rules, and appointed one person to liaise with the university authorities. What its members had in common was their oppositional stance and mind-set, or, as Miłosz put it, their penchant for 'sticking out their tongues'. The Vagabonds tended not to attack the small-town mentality or the lifestyle of beer-drinking members of the student honour society, but rather shrugged their shoulders and smiled condescendingly at them. In contrast to the majority of other groups, they seemed a bit of an enigma. Some people viewed them as the offshoot of a 'profligate masonic group', while for others they were little more than a band of worthy scouts (Jasienica 107).

A characteristic shared by the Vagabonds was their playfulness. During one meeting they tied together short pieces of parcel string and set off for a stroll together, each one holding the line. They walked down streets, stopping traffic once or twice, and at one point mounted a horse-drawn carriage in which Wilno's chief of police was a passenger. Braided yellow and dark-red string came to be adopted as the Vagabonds' emblem, whose colours symbolised sunrise and sunset. New members were admitted after a ritual that had echoes of masonic initiation rites. Candidates had to seek out lights in a dark forest, with green lights representing hope, red passionate love, and blue the luminosity of the spirit. Finally, the tied and hooded initiate was led to a cottage, where a 'christening' (Korabiewicz 226) of sorts was performed.

Group meetings were held in a place referred to as 'the cave', with most incorporating a strong educational element. Papers, debates and lectures delivered by older club members featured regularly in the group's programmes, as well as discussions about new books and films. Their marches were the most impressive, distinctive form of public activity they engaged in, and often were wryly humorous in tone. Their 'Week of National Produce' march parodied an official campaign to persuade people to buy Polish goods. On another occasion, they organised a street performance in which a giant dragon received its comeuppance.

The majority of the Vagabonds' time, however, was devoted to outings, expeditions and sport, thereby keeping faith with a motto coined by their liveliest, most health-conscious members: 'Not a Single Sunday Wasted'. In winter they went skiing, and in summer they organised hikes round Wilno and camped in places with strong literary associations from years past. They were generally one-day trips, but some members went on walks across Poland which lasted weeks. Kayaking on rivers and lakes was very popular, and one major trip took members as far as Istanbul.

Everyone in the Vagabonds had a nickname. Interestingly, Miłosz's was 'Ja', which means 'I' in Polish, but which is also the first syllable of 'Jajo' (pronounced 'yayo'), the Polish word for 'egg'. Different theories have been put forward as to how or why he acquired this name. It may have been to draw attention to the oval shape of his head, which was how he was depicted in caricatures during the early 1930s. Instructions for one of the group's Christmas shows specified that a large egg was required for the head and a raisin for the nose of the Miłosz puppet. Another, more interesting explanation was that when Miłosz volunteered to do something, he shouted out 'Ja, Ja', which in Polish means 'eggs'. Late in life the writer conceded that he talked about himself rather too much and overused the word 'Ja', another reason he might have been named Egg, an abbreviated version of 'ego'.

At first, Teodor Bujnicki seems to have been Miłosz's closest friend, and they regularly attended book club meetings together. Bujnicki loved poetry and had a very active social life, attending parties and taking part in plays and cabarets. Later he was replaced by Stefan Jędrychowski, who instilled in young Miłosz a fascination with politics. They participated in discussions at the Intellectuals' Club and co-wrote an article, 'A Personal Chronicle', which, though it lacked maturity and style, documented the turbulent mental state affecting young men, torn between erotic impulses and the need to impose discipline on the mind.

Miłosz's keen appetite for adventure led to the greatest expedition of his youth, in which he was accompanied by Jędrychowski and Stefan Zagórski during the summer vacation after his second year at university. In May 1931, at Vincennes, near Paris, an international exhibition showcasing France's extensive colonial empire was mounted, which included a zoological garden, a Buddhist pagoda and an exact replica of the famous Cambodian temple at Angkor Wat. Around eight million visitors attended this exhibition, so it is no wonder that it attracted three students from Wilno. To keep costs to a minimum, they decided to reach Vincennes by following water routes for most of the journey.

Although years later Miłosz referred to this bold enterprise in *Native Realm,* he withheld some details. Initially Miłosz, Jędrychowski and Zagórski set off by train to Warsaw, then travelled southwards through Poland to Prague, whose beauty and festive atmosphere they found captivating. As sporting goods in Poland were extremely expensive, Miłosz was tasked with buying a Canadian canoe in Czechoslovakia, which he then shipped to Lindau in Bavaria, beside Lake Constance, from which the water-borne phase of their journey would begin:

> The ensuing days of our trip took us from ecstasy to ecstasy. The lake as it narrowed changed into a taut sheet, almost bulging from the pressure of a current that was already the Rhine. With every thrust of the paddle our canoe fairly leaped into the air. And our physical joy was undiminished by the almost constant downpour . . . Every bend of the river concealed a secret which, when disclosed, took away our breath. If anywhere, it was here we could have said that we had penetrated into an enchanted land. (*NR* 153–154)

The speed with which they moved exhilarated them, that is, until they came within six hundred feet of being hurled down a steep precipice by the fierce waters of the Schaffhausen falls. Unfortunately, not long after that lucky escape, their adventure on the Rhine came to an abrupt end near the Swiss town of Koblenz. In a very difficult stretch of the river notorious for accidents, a rock lurking just beneath the surface of the water gouged a hole 'the size of a fist' in their canoe. Seeing this, one of Miłosz's companions remarked in a stoic voice: 'This is the end, gentlemen'. Seconds later they found themselves 'spitting water' before struggling to escape the mid-river current and reach 'the grasses on the shore' (*NR* 155).

River police from the nearby town of Waldshut came to the unlucky travellers' aid, and managed to retrieve two of their knapsacks. The most important one, containing their passports and money—a substantial part of which had been a gift from Iwaszkiewicz to Miłosz—sank to the bottom of the Rhine, along with a lot of their clothes. As a result, they had to borrow money from the police to enable them to return to the Swiss side of the river, from where they made their way to the Polish consulate in Zurich. While the formalities for acquiring new documents were in progress, they ate the cheapest foodstuff they could find— cheese—and drank water from fountains in the city's squares. And at night they sought shelter in the local woods. On receiving new passports and another loan to enable them to reach France, they travelled back to Waldshut. After discovering the time it would take to repair their canoe or to sell it, they abandoned it outside the police station, in lieu of the debt they owed. Slipping guiltily away at the crack of dawn, they set off on foot across Germany through the Black Forest. During their stays in youth hostels, they frequently encountered young Germans in twos and threes, all of them belonging to the Nazi youth movement. All attempts to communicate with them came to nothing. Miłosz observed that their 'overly polite' demeanour masked a 'contemptuous and hostile' attitude towards foreigners (*NR* 157).

Their first major stop in France was in Strasbourg, where Miłosz was left awestruck by the magnificence of the cathedral. While there, they came across large numbers of Polish labourers seeking work who possessed the same lowly 'status that was later to devolve on North Africans'; they were regularly deployed as a labour force 'for the heaviest jobs', but received 'the least pay' (*NR* 159). The three quickly came to share mixed feelings about France. Its beauty inspired 'the greatest tenderness', Miłosz would observe, and one could experience there a degree of freedom available 'nowhere else'. And yet, as he tellingly added, 'the price of this freedom is often indifference to the fate of the silent and the humiliated' (*NR* 160). Although they were shabbily dressed, the students still sensed that they belonged to a more privileged stratum of society. The Lithuanian consul treated them courteously, invited them to dinner and provided money. To Miłosz's relief, he discovered that his mother had already forwarded a cheque to the Lithuanian consulate in Paris. Nevertheless, when they left by train for Paris it was in a third-class compartment, sleeping on wooden seats.

They arrived at dawn at Gare Saint-Lazare and started to walk towards the Latin Quarter, taking in the legendary beauty of the city.

> On the deserted Place de la Concorde, the sight of the pearl-gray expanse between the Arc de Triomphe and the trees in the park made us want to draw deep breaths. Branches of trees emerged like huge feathers from the fog. There was not a soul in the Tuileries except for one pair on a stone bench . . . Further on, through the mist, the river already shone in the sun. (*NR* 161)

They stayed overnight at the Palais de Peuple, near Place d'Italie, in a Salvation Army shelter, which provided a cheap breakfast and a free dinner on condition that the visitors attended evening service. From there they journeyed to Vincennes, where, with a mixture of curiosity and embarrassment, they witnessed native inhabitants of French colonies being exhibited like monkeys and giraffes in the neighboring zoo.

The most memorable aspect of the trip for the young poet, however, was his meeting with Oskar Miłosz. He remembered in his later years how he saw that name for the first time on the cover of Oskar's *Selected Poems,* lying in the salon of the flat in Wilno. Although the book in Bronisława Ostrowska's translation seemed not to have been opened very often, it had been nice for Miłosz to boast to people that his family had a relative living in Paris who wrote in French. At some point before the expedition, a correspondence had begun, and his relative from Paris sent him replies and books. On hearing of his nephew's misfortunes, he sent a letter along with a money order, thanks to which the tramp was able to purchase 'a cheap suit from the Samaritaine department store' (*NR* 164). Having changed into that, the young Miłosz set off for Fontainebleau.

On his arrival at the Hotel de l'Aigle Noir, he noted from the way the staff behaved that he was visiting 'a person who was highly esteemed' (*NR* 165). From outside, the room to which he was directed seemed filled with birdsong, and once inside he discovered its source: cage after cage of African birds, their wings rustling and flapping as they flew to and fro. Oskar Miłosz turned out to have thick eyebrows, a high forehead and arresting deep-set eyes. His eyelids resembled those of 'a tired bird of prey' and 'disclosed hot, black lava . . . smouldering coals; there was an aura of the desert, which suggested an image from the pages of the Bible' (*NR* 166). In late December 2003, close to the end of his own life, Miłosz's thoughts repeatedly circled back to that inspirational presence who did so much to shape his dream of a future as a poet:

> Beneath the flawless manners of a worldly gentleman he hid
> His compassion for all that is living.
> Some people perhaps could sense it, but it was certainly known,
> In ways mysterious to us, to the small birds
> That would perch on his head and hands when he stopped
> In a park alley.
>
> ('Goodness', *S&LP* 325)

What did a barbarian from the furthest corners of Europe feel, having reached its mythical heart? The young man experienced the sensation of having walked into a different order of reality, one held together by rigorous form, a somewhere so different from what he knew, a world of birches and muddy roads, which seemed woven from mist. At the same time, however, he felt the weight of a knowledge and experience of which citizens from the opulent West had no idea. When reporting back to the writer Jarosław Iwaszkiewicz, Miłosz said that after their stay in Switzerland he and his companions developed a condescending attitude towards 'Emmental freedom'. While western Europe might be superior in some respects, he realised that cultures there experienced 'no tensions or struggle—which are a prerequisite for confronting so many crucial issues' (CM to Iwaszkiewicz, 12 September 1931).

In the same letter he also wrote what good friends he was now with his uncle, who was an extremely wise man who urged him to return to Lithuania:

'I must admit the legitimacy of many of his arguments. Though it is not 100% through and through, he thinks my "Polishness" would diminish by dozens of percentage points were I to live abroad'. Later, back in Wilno, Miłosz said little about his contacts with his uncle. For one thing, Oskar backed independent Lithuania's rights to the city, and secondly, contact with a rich aristocrat living in Paris hardly fitted the image of a left-wing poet.

Meanwhile, back in Fontainebleau, writing to friends, Oskar Miłosz spoke of how highly impressed he had been with his visitor, concluding his letter by prophesying great things for his future:

> I met my nephew, who is an immediate descendant of my great-grandfather. I expected to meet a fright, a monster resembling the rest of my family, who are terribly bourgeois, and in times gone by were noblemen and knights. What a great surprise it was to see before me a nineteen-year-old young man, of pleasant appearance, a poet, who, at the same time, was unusually enthusiastic and clear-minded, showed respect for and appreciation of my work. He is very devoted to the intel- ligent and honorable sides of the monarchic, Catholic traditions of the gentry, a little inclined towards communism—possesses just those at- tributes which are necessary to carry out useful work in our improbable times—in short, a young knight whom I regard a little like my son . . . Despite the distaste that I have towards my family, I am glad that the line stretching back to the thirteenth century is assured relative conti- nuity thanks to the existence of this young man, who will certainly bring it (at long last) honour. (Letter to Leon and Mme Grumbach-Vogt, 11 November 1931)

What benefits did the expedition to Paris bring to Miłosz? Adventure, curiosity satisfied, perhaps pleasure from following the vagabond spirit he had inherited from his father. Another profitable experience was his confrontation with the Western world, and the way it treated newcomers: 'The sign prohibited Gypsies, Poles, Rumanians and Bulgarians from entering the country' (*NR* 158).

And what happened as regards the Vagabonds' Club? Like PET previously, the club provided him with friendship and a lesson in ironic non-conformism. It soon became apparent, however, that that was not enough for him. In mid-October 1930, Bujnicki and Jędrychowski left. When asked why, they replied, 'Nothing in par- ticular. We simply cannot see any point in participating any longer. We have other social tasks to perform'. Miłosz quitted soon after: the wanderer metamorphosed into an intellectual.

The Cezary Baryka Complex

The deteriorating political and economic situation in Europe in the 1930s helped young men in Lithuania during that period to mature more quickly. As they saw little point in confining themselves to criticising the older generations, in Wilno a number of young men, including Bujnicki, Jędrychowski, Zagórski and Miłosz, whose political opinions varied widely, decided to found the Intellectuals' Club in order to voice and exchange views. Not long afterwards a sub-group emerged from the club, known as Żagary, similarly consisting of a diverse mix of progressive Catholics, Liberals, Piłsudski supporters and socialists, most of whom shifted ideologically in the course of the decade towards the left of the political arena.

The poet's university years had passed in the shadow of a major economic crisis, which was especially severe in the region around Wilno, the poorest area in Poland at the time. On walking trips the Vagabonds passed cottages whose inhabitants cooked stinging nettle soup, while in the city itself they witnessed mass evictions and observed large numbers of beggars. In *Miesięcznik Literacki*, a literary monthly edited by Aleksander Wat, they read reports about poverty in Poland and articles about socially-engaged American novels, such as Upton Sinclair's *The Jungle.*

Amongst the privileged within the student population, the extreme social stratification in their country triggered a guilt complex, as it did in Cezary Baryka, a character in Stefan Żeromski's 1925 novel *Przedwiośnie* (The Coming Spring), which depicted the social and political difficulties newly-independent Poland faced after the First World War. The Polish government attempted to channel the wave of leftist sympathies that arose by creating, for example, Legion Młodych (The Legion of the Young), whose ranks included Bujnicki, Jędrychowski and Jerzy Zagórski. Members were free to publish magazines and were often sent overseas on scholarships or given work experience in the hope that their political fervour would wane.

In practice, however, the scheme backfired. Extreme factions, such as the Communists and the National Democrats, simply grew stronger. Within the latter, far-right activists gained even more power, forming organisations copying the Nazi model. All efforts based on parliamentary control and free-market economic mechanisms proved useless in quelling the growing polarisation in opinion and stance. Different propositions were put forward, ranging from anarchism to autocratic rule, and for many young people each seemed preferable to the rotten democracy they lived under. In his third year at university Miłosz read Thomas Mann's *The Magic Mountain* and identified strongly with the main character, Hans Castorp. In a letter to Iwaszkiewicz from this period, he wrote about the reservations he had about communism, but also stressed his distaste for the moderate parliamentary left: 'Theoretically, we are tired of the whole morass of capitalism, but we cannot be communists, nor, needless to say, members of any silly socialist movements' (CM to Iwaszkiewicz, 11 February 1931). The Communist propaganda machine was on the offensive, demanding spectacular changes in line with those taking place in Soviet Russia. Many of his contemporaries were shocked by the contrast between the steep decline in the Polish economy and the dynamic development of 'the first socialist state', where the electrification of the entire country was taking place, heavy industry developed, steelworks and factories built, huge electric dams constructed and canals dug across vast tracts of land. The *human* cost of those gigantic enterprises—some of which were pointless—was unknown or largely ignored. It was easier to believe that however high the price, these experiments could produce astonishing results, which might also be extended to the cultural sphere. The Warsaw periodical *Wiadomości Literackie* (Literary News) published a special edition devoted to the Soviets; many people explored the work of Russian writers such as Ilya Ehrenburg, Boris Pilnyak and Isaac Babel. Vsevolod Pudovkin's film *Storm over Asia* appeared in the cinemas and made a great impression on Miłosz, who commended its verve and spirit, but also its catastrophic vision of history: 'Perhaps one day I will be able to write poems like that, or maybe live like that' (CM to Iwaszkiewicz, 2 January 1931). As elsewhere in the world, many writers in Lithuania and Poland were highly impressed by the Communist regime's efforts to eradicate illiteracy in the Soviet Union and by the exceptionally high number of books published there compared to Poland. In an article entitled 'Brotherhood of Nations', Miłosz commented on a temporary thaw in Polish-Soviet relationships, but displayed a certain scepticism over the possibilities of forging closer links. As much as he shared his friends' leftist views, he had no illusions about the Soviet Union. Miłosz owed his knowledge about Stalin's savage regime to his Lithuanian friend, Franciszek Ancewicz. During seminars in his first year of studies, he recalled the interventions made by 'a massive lanky figure sitting in the last row' who 'tried to express himself in a mixture of Russian and German' (*Podróżny świata* 43). Ancewicz had left Lithuania, moving to Riga, then Vienna, before finally settling in Poland, in the wake of a military coup in December 1926, which installed an authoritarian government.

Miłosz and Ancewicz became steadfast friends, revising together for exams, going out for drinks, and meeting young Lithuanians, Byelorussians and Jews. Ancewicz was a promising literary critic and the president of a socialist students' union. At the time he was friends with Antanas Venclova (the father of Tomas), who would later compose the words to the Lithuanian Socialist Republic's anthem. Ancewicz was a radical, not an orthodox Marxist, and a fierce opponent of Soviet totalitarianism. He revealed to Miłosz what he had learned about the

Moscow Purges,[3] and persuaded him of the necessity of adopting a Marxist interpretation of the human condition and of recognising economic and historic determinism.

In December 1934, Miłosz expressed relief at being intellectually detached from Ancewicz: 'How many things have now become clear, now that my blindness—which I was aware of—has gone. You must understand that I am a barbarian and for some years I was a friend of an even greater barbarian, a Lithuanian peasant, to whom I was drawn by his similar nature' (CM to Iwaszkiewicz, 19 December 1934). An enduring, highly positive outcome of their relationship, however, was Ancewicz's instrumental role in alerting Miłosz to the importance of the Jewish community living in Jeruszalaim de Lite, Lithuanian Jerusalem. *Kurier Wileński*, a local daily newspaper, felt obliged to inform its readers on 17 April 1929 that 'Wilno is one of the most important centres of Jewish literary and scientific life, not just for Poland or just for Europe. Unfortunately, the least aware of this fact are the inhabitants of Wilno, the non-Jewish majority'.

Each of the different nationalities and ethnicities inhabiting the former capital of the Grand Duchy of Lithuania had only the most superficial contact with the others. To Polish eyes, a Jew must be a shopkeeper or a communist, in other words, a source of economic competition or a political threat. Intercommunal communications were very rare, and 'mixed' marriages almost unheard of. Czesław Miłosz wrote that he only came to fully understand the importance of the religious and intellectual life of Wilno after the war, when reading books in New York that arrived from publishing houses in the narrow streets of Wilno's Jewish quarter. As a child he used to buy stamps in little shops where tins with a blue Star of David hung from the walls. These were used to collect donations raised to bring about the creation of a Jewish state. The reason he never dropped his small change into the tins was because for him the Jews belonged to a totally alien, almost unreal reality. In his final year at school all the students were from Christian backgrounds, while at Wilno University Jewish students segregated themselves in separate unions. In the mind of an average young Catholic, the word 'Jew' conjured merely a set of stereotypes. Yet Miłosz was no ordinary Catholic, and from his words and actions it is evident that he was devoid of any anti-Semitic prejudices and utterly impervious to ideological influences from the far right.

During the 1920s and 1930s issues around nationality and race had a major influence on the choice of political allegiance. For young Lithuanian Jews keen to distance themselves from their Orthodox families, and antagonistic towards Polish society, the vision of a new social order promised by communism made it seem a natural choice. Whereas in 1930s the majority of Polish students veered towards National Democracy policies, small liberal and leftist groups recognised how important it was to open up lines of communication with their Jewish peers. Consequently, people in Miłosz's circle were dubbed 'Jewish lackeys'. This did not necessarily mean that the members of the Intellectuals' Club or Żagary were actually *close* to Jewish groups; given the substantial obstacles between them, it must have seemed far easier to confront anti-Semitic Poles than to engage in dialogue with their Jewish brethren. Nevertheless, contacts were made. One such example was the Poetry of Protest meeting organised on Sunday, 5 February 1933, six days after Adolf Hitler was installed as the new German Chancellor. During the evening, there were readings of poems by the Lithuanian poet Kazys Boruta, the Polish poet Władysław Broniewski, the Russian poet Vladimir Mayakovsky, and a less-well-known twenty-one year-old, Czesław Miłosz, along with contributions from Lithuanian, Byelorussian, Jewish and Polish poets who read from their own work. One participant, 'a small tailor, literally magnetized the whole hall, packed as never before, by turning one Yiddish poem of Ernst Toller's into a rhythmic dance' (*NR* 101). Among the poets belonging to the Jewish literary group, Jung Wilne, whom Miłosz met were Chaim Grade, who went on to become one of Wilno's most acclaimed writers, and Abraham Suckewer, later a close friend of Marc Chagall. The atmosphere in which these timid attempts to approach one another grew is evoked in a letter sent years later by Miłosz's friend:

> I am writing my recollections of you. A ramp in Śniadecki Hall, you running at the head of a group of workers and students, chasing a National Democrat mob who wanted to disperse people attending a poetry evening in which different nations were represented. Your expression resembles a werewolf's . . . teeth bared, eyes wide open and in your hand, pieces of a broken chair'. (*Rok myśliwego* 243)

Although during Miłosz's time at Wilno University segregation in seating arrangements had not yet been introduced, a wave of anti-Jewish feeling was on the rise. Between 8 and 9 November 1931 a serious conflict about 'Jewish corpses' broke out in Wilno.[4] In dissecting rooms, medical students practised on bodies received from the city morgue. These belonged to people who had no-one to bury them and were always 'Aryan' corpses, since the Jewish community always bore the cost of funerals of anyone of Jewish origin. This became a pretext for an attack carried out by the right-wing nationalists of Młodzież Wszechpolska (the All-Polish Youth Movement), which beat and kicked Jewish students when they tried to enter the university. The attackers included Jerzy Putrament, armed with a heavy cane, who latterly would achieve notoriety in Miłosz's *The Captive Mind* as 'Gamma, the Slave of History', due to his craven support for those who became masters of post-war Poland. Among the few defending the Jewish students was Czesław Miłosz, who found himself surrounded by angry nationalists. When he appealed to their humanity and better judgment, they responded, 'Tell that to your grandma'. Jewish butchers and porters came to the aid of the encircled students, and stones began to be thrown. One struck Stanisław Wacławski, a National Democracy supporter, in the head, causing his death. This triggered a reaction not far removed from a pogrom when a mob of around two thousand Polish students set about smashing the windows of Jewish shops and looting their contents, broke into a synagogue, and attacked the headquarters of the Jewish Students Union. In the resultant skirmishes nearly two hundred people were injured.

In the latter half of the 1930s the situation at the university worsened further. An extreme-right group, Obóz Narodowo-Radykalny (the National-Radical Camp), who had broken away from the Nationalist Party, began attacking 'disloyal' professors. 'Smoke bombs, knuckle dusters and other blunt objects' became commonplace on the campuses in Wilno, Warsaw and Lwów. In Wilno 'eight Jewish students were seriously injured, two of whom were professorial assistants'. 'The rector's windows were broken, because he refused to accept demands from young nationalists' groups (unpublished novel, Beinecke Library). The combination of religious fervour and hatred was appalling. The anti-Semitic zeal of the right had the effect of crystallising views among the left-leaning young in Wilno, who were very conscious of the increasing persecution of Jews in Nazi Germany. As polarisation in political opinion grew apace, and as measured thinking vanished at the university, there was a pressing need for wiser counsels to prevail. The figure who attempted to fulfil that heroic role was a philosophy and law student, Henryk Dembiński (1908–1941).

Extremely intelligent, a great orator, and a born leader, Dembiński began his journey with Odrodzenie (Catholic Renaissance, the Association of Catholic Academic Youth). In Poland the organisation was linked with Chrześcijańska Demokracja (Christian Democracy) and promoted nationalist views, whereas in Wilno it was run by students, many of whom were former members of PET and committed to bringing together Catholicism, social awareness and, importantly, social action. In the academic year 1929–30, Dembiński, now the president of Wilno Catholic Renaissance, managed to create a new bloc whose mission was to support underprivileged students; he achieved this by assembling a broad coalition consisting of pro-Piłsudski organisations, leftists, liberal Catholics belonging to Odrodzenie and Vagabonds' Club members. In addition he was elected to high office in the student welfare body, Bratnia Pomoc, or Bratniak, as it was often called.[5] At a rally in November 1931, during the anti-Semitic disturbances referred to above, Dembiński demonstrated his courage by appealing at a rally for Jewish students to be welcomed into Bratniak. This made him and the groups he represented unpopular, and when the next round of elections took place in March 1933, they were won by a nationalist bloc; Miłosz was one of the losing progressive candidates in that election. Dembiński gradually shifted leftwards politically, turning from socially-engaged Catholicism to orthodox Communism.

With regard to his political activism and his poetry from this period, Miłosz found himself swayed at times by the collective emotion of the moment, attracted as he was towards the limelight. In his latter years he felt relief at having escaped Soviet-occupied Wilno and then Soviet-controlled Poland, where he would have been compelled to compose some kind of hymn to Stalin as proof of his 'commitment' to the Great Cause. As an individual he valued privacy, and as a poet he increasingly defended the artist's independence against attempts to be drawn into doctrinaire political positions. His interests in Marxism and the Hegelian vision of the rational, purposeful flow of history were only partially shaped by his sensitivity to social injustice and his outrage at anti-Semitism. He protested against and felt disgust at the very idea that the order of the world was subject to the laws of nature and 'the survival of the fittest':

> What if we were to test the political leanings of individual people, looking into their innate features and character? Then my constant distaste for capitalism would turn out to be my dislike of Nature ... And the reason is the feeling of threat both create, my aversion to brutality, and my sense of pity, which are mixed together, and difficult to separate.
> (*Rok myśliwego* 58)

From a certain perspective, the idea of communism would be a response to these fears—the fulfilling of a dream to conquer the world by reason and step outside the laws of nature. Leon Naphta, a Jewish activist who glorified terror and fascinated young Miłosz, considered communism as a revolution of the mind against nature; to a man who experienced the chaos of the world, Marxism provided a tool, enabling him to recognise a structure within the chaos.

A revulsion for Darwinian nature could lead to the desire for revolution, which constituted a rejection of the law of the jungle and democratic order. In their place, revolution might result in a rational distribution of wealth and tasks, together with enlightened dictatorship, which would lead the people, even against their will, to a wonderful tomorrow. Often the few who regarded themselves as destined to lead mankind had to endure rejection by this contemptuous majority. Miłosz regarded himself as a similarly rejected figure and also saw the same trait in Gombrowicz and, most of all, in Oskar Miłosz. Amongst the attributes that afflicted certain artists, he concluded, were a tendency to consider oneself wiser and more sensitive than others, and, at the same time, to long to be simpler so that one 'fitted in' and seemed a better, less egocentric person. At some level, however, he derived a certain wry satisfaction from being perceived as a defector from his class, having no sense of affiliation with the precious little sons of manor houses, who paradoxically *also* regarded gentry life as unbearable and outmoded. The need to find lines of communication with those who stood out from the rest, and the desire to free himself from his background, inclined him to choose the left. His difficulties were not dissimilar to those of young Jews trying to escape Jewishness: 'Somewhere in the depths glimmered the thought that my Leftism and theirs was a disguise for our otherness. As they repudiated the ghetto, so I hid away the Grand Duchy of Lithuania among dusty souvenirs' (*NR* 102). More potent than the Cezary Baryka complex, Ancewicz's exhortations, or compassion for the conditions and fate of weavers in Żyrardów was Miłosz's loathing for the reactionary, bigoted mindset of the Polish nationalist majority. 'The choices made by my friends stemmed from a background of resentments and personal circum-stances that diverged from the accepted norms of behavior, so that our Left was something like a league of sufferers' (*NR* 101). Among the members of this league, Miłosz attained a lofty position both as a publicist and as 'the black Ariel of social engagement poetry' (Stanisław Bereś 226).

Friday Seminars, Literary Wednesdays

As they come closer and closer, down Castle Street
And then suddenly nothing, only a white puff of cloud
Over the Humanities Students Club,
Division of Creative Writing.
Czesław Miłosz, 'City without a Name' (*NCP* 215)

Intellectual circles in Wilno were not over-subscribed at this period. Poring over the lists of members of the Vagabonds' Club, or participants in the Intellectuals' Club meetings, or the editorial staff of *Żagary*, we encounter the same names, all of them ambitious for a new direction in their lives. Miłosz involved himself not only in the twice-weekly activities of the Law Department, but also with a group styling itself the Circle of Scholars of Polish Literature, which consumed a lot of his time and energies, not least because he managed their radio and press relations. The chair of this circle was Manfred Kridl, an academic whom Miłosz regarded very highly. Kridl had opened up Polish studies to research focused on the structure of literary works. He generously provided the introduction to Miłosz and Zbigniew Folejewski's *Anthology of Social Poetry,* and subsequently headed the jury which in 1934 presented the Philomaths Award to Miłosz for *A Poem on Frozen Time*.

The poet regularly looked in at the buildings which housed the Humanities Department and the Circle of Scholars, making a beeline for a sub-section of the group devoted to original creative work. Productivity amongst the writing fraternity reached its zenith once Teodor Bujnicki became section president, since he drew in many local rising stars, such as Miłosz, Jerzy and Stefan Zagórski and Aleksander Rymkiewicz. Often in their writing they adopted a provocative stance, challenging established figures and exercising their literary muscles to drive off the stifling provincial air.

Each Friday Bujnicki's apartment served as their meeting point, but they also met at a tavern, Pod Dwunastką, frequented by carters and prostitutes. There they consumed *irsha*, a beverage that consisted of vodka and beer in equal proportions. Women students interested in poems and poets attended the sessions in the flat, at which Teodor's ever-hospitable mother dispensed tea and sandwiches. Discussions, which often became heated, centred on articles in the literary press and on the latest publications, but the group also put on poetry events and their own plays, taking them to different towns. While Bujnicki wrote the first play, many others between 1930 and 1933 were co-written, and usually contained a strong political component, including one from 1932 that depicted the anti-Jewish riots in Wilno and the struggle for power within Bratniak.

A question Jerzy Zagórski posed was whether Miłosz had a sense of humour in those days. Certainly he did explode with laughter at times, yet not like Bujnicki or Konstanty Gałczyński. He treated the world with a certain gravity, as well as the artist's duty within it. In his vast output one finds no light verse, limericks or any other literary trivia. Although he had a great sense of humour, when it came to certain matters he was deeply serious, valuing words too highly to treat them as material for playfulness. He did not possess a flair for writing on any given subject on call. It would have been a dangerous trait because it could have led him to abuse his talents for ideological purposes, as happened with Bujnicki and Gałczyński.

> He was a young man, quite able to learn, but without talent.
> Others were talented, his friend, the poet Theodore, for example

he wrote in 'From the Rising of the Sun' (*NCP* 301), and even tried to convince the dumbfounded Aleksander Fiut[6] of his shortcomings: 'I have no talent ... I never had talent ... Only hard work' (Fiut 223).

It is easy to imagine the fullness of hope and frustration in this group of young men. Their section of the Circle of Scholars did, after all, publish three books of poems, but the contents were mostly juvenilia and leant excessively on books and movements they had encountered at the gymnasium—the Romantic tradition, sentimentalism and pathos, the futuristic cult of physical strength, life-lust, poems that followed 'fashion in bringing in motifs from science, technology, sport, the exotic' (Bujnicki 136). There was nothing to indicate that truly exceptional personalities might emerge from this company which generated poetry with such ease. The turning point occurred when two new members joined, Jerzy Zagórski, who came from Warsaw and was familiar with the avant-garde movement, and Czesław Miłosz. Together with Bujnicki, the three soon stepped beyond the hith-erto tight framework that had held back the section.

The fourth question in the Vagabonds' survey mentioned previously asked members to list their 'interests and natural abilities'. Miłosz's reply was 'literary criticism and philosophy', to which he appended, with a mixture of accuracy and irony, 'arguing'. In writing this he probably had no intention of being self-critical, but rather highlighting the fervour with which customarily he defended his points of view. It *was* his tendency to get involved in arguments with his contemporaries, and to turn to polemic in order to critique the entrenched positions they adopted. One Vagabond member, present at a meeting of the Circle of Scholars in early 1930, recalled how Miłosz accused some other members of 'adolescence, egotism, and an obsessive concern with form'. He demanded that the poetry under discus-sion should face up to social issues. It must be a 'poetry with a wide, social, or even global focus, poetry full of moral impetus and power that would break aesthetic ties' (qtd. in Tarnowska 121).

Gradually it became evident that Bujnicki had ceased being an irrefutable au-thority for Miłosz. Theirs had been a close bond, founded on mutual attraction, strengthened by common interests, deepened by shared disappointments. At the outset companionship with a man respected city-wide had provided Miłosz with a pass into the literary world: 'My desperate hunger for recognition manifested itself in wanting to sit next to him. No, let me correct that, perhaps it was a desire to sit alongside more people from journalistic circles. For me, as a student, being in a café and next to writers, lifted my spirits' (Fiut 275). It was Bujnicki, as literary director of the students' magazine *Alma Mater Vilnensis,* who launched Miłosz's poetic career when he accepted two poems, 'Composition' and 'A Journey'.

In the eyes of audiences invited to literary evenings, Bujnicki was at first the more popular figure, though over time the regard in which the two were held began to level out. When Bujnicki chanted his famous poem 'Mayakovsky', the power and resonance his voice generated were always enthusiastically applauded. A turning point occurred in 1931, however, when the verse of the younger poet achieved pre-eminence because of its distinctiveness and absolute originality, as several observers instantly recognised: 'When Miłosz read in a calm, non-declamatory manner his short poem "Homeland"—a "hard", condensed composition, lacking all trace of avant-garde extravagance—it became apparent from the slightly shocked, but concentrated faces that they had witnessed and heard something really "new"' (Folejewski, *Poezja* 5/6). Jerzy Putrament's reaction to the poem was identical: 'His poem, "Homeland", the first one I ever heard, seemed wonderful to me' (25). This success led directly to the formation of the literary group Żagary and to Bujnicki's reluctant acceptance that his role might now be peripheral to the newly formed society (*Kurier Wileński*, 6 December 1937).

Another factor in the cooling of their friendship was Bujnicki's decision to get married, which seemed in Miłosz's eyes almost an act of betrayal, an over-reaction which illustrates how much emotional investment he poured into certain of his closest contacts. Bujnicki wrote in a poem dedicated to Miłosz that he had 'placed his heart in someone else's hands'; it did not mean that links with his apprentice had been curtailed completely. Until 1937, when Miłosz left Wilno, they met often, though the relationship never recaptured its first intensity.

Quickly the new cluster of poets in Żagary established themselves at the forefront of literary life in Wilno. What in due course came to be regarded as their legendary gatherings took place in a building belonging to the Basilian monastery, a site steeped in cultural significance, since Adam Mickiewicz had been imprisoned there in 1823–1824. During 'Literary Wednesdays', books and theatrical premieres were discussed, poems read aloud and up-and-coming writers given a chance to shine. The hall where the meetings took place accommodated around forty people at most, and was furnished with heavy oak chairs and benches. During breaks tea and cakes from the local bakery were served.

Amongst the many distinguished guest speakers at these events were the poet Julian Tuwim, the novelist and playwright Maria Dąbrowska, the composer Karol Szymanowski, the film and theatre director Leon Schiller and the English poet, philosopher, journalist and literary critic, G. K. Chesterton.

On Ostrobramska Street, in Konrad's cell,[7] on 31 January 1931, Miłosz took the stage alongside Bujnicki, Jerzy Zagórski and Kazimierz Hałaburda, in a satirical seasonal performance using puppetry. Their script had been composed with the intention of portraying themselves as the latest stars on Wilno's literary scene. In effect this young generation of poets were declaring war on their predecessors. One puppet, who represented Zagórski, threw down a challenge to the old guard in Skamander:[8]

Lechoń, Wierzyński, Słonimski, Kaden,
Let them write, let them write, we will surpass them.

Leviathan's Wardens

At a Wednesday evening meeting held on 28 January 1931, Miłosz and Zagórski were invited by Bujnicki to be guest speakers. Stefan Jędrychowski was tasked with the opening address, in which he made the point that although a bond inevitably existed between members of the group, not only were they without a particular programme, they repudiated the very idea of one:

> We have not chosen to use a banner, because we are afraid of being com-
> partmentalised, as each one of us works and writes individually. There is
> a spiritual affinity between us and common ground because of our links
> to the University . . . We look, grasp, absorb everything that surrounds
> us, to experience it fully and convert it into art.

Similar sentiments, albeit slightly muted, appeared in the first issue of *Żagary*, which was published soon after.

And what was the audience reaction to the 28 January event? The *Kurier Wileński* of 30 January 1931 was fairly complimentary: 'The crowd left the room feeling that they heard something new and refreshing, and stimulating in its origi-nality'. The newspaper also implied that Miłosz had not done very well and that 'his poems were more complicated, unnaturally constructed, and deployed strange ex-pressions'. However, it added, his poems depicted 'an interesting context' and con-fronted head-on 'brutal and horrible visions'. A reviewer from *Dziennik Wileński* was more critical, and on 31 January declared that 'the poems of Mr Miłosz, who was striving for novelty and originality, seemed rather insipid'. It is easy to imagine the principal participants in the event leafing speedily through the papers the next morning, wondering, 'Have they written? Is there anything about me?' One won-ders how Miłosz responded to the word 'insipid'. In his correspondence he adopted a show of indifference: 'There was our reading evening at the Writers Association . . . they did not seem to understand my poems at all—they were mainly old codgers, or worse, old hags' (CM to Iwaszkiewicz, 1 February 1931).

The budding young poets attracted the attention of Stanisław Cat-Mackiewicz, a publicist and editor of a conservative Wilno daily, *Słowo* (Word). After attending that first Wednesday event he concluded that it might be worthwhile meeting up with the group to offer them support, though it initially transpired that the regional authority's cultural budget had no funding available for that purpose. In the meantime, on 1 February, Miłosz divulged to Iwaszkie-wicz his plans for developing a new poetry magazine and its initial programme:

1. highlight ethnic diversity—re-write our culture, taking into
    account our hybrid heritage as half-Poles, half-Lithuanians, half-
    Ukrainians=delve into borderland elements generally;

2. promote the expansion of Polish culture to the east, as well as the mutual penetration of cultures;

3. fight the psychosis generated by National Democracy.

As late as March 1931 *Słowo*'s editor turned to Bujnicki with a proposal to introduce a literary supplement into the newspaper. As a result Bujnicki contacted Miłosz, Stefan Jędrychowski, Jerzy Zagórski and Tadeusz Byrski, among others, to gauge their views. In a private meeting held in his apartment, the writers talked through the possibility of launching a paper as an independent ensemble of artists. Then, one Sunday evening, 29 March, the entire group were invited to meet Cat-Mackiewicz at his home *'na herbatce'* (for a cup of tea), which, when they arrived, turned out to be a sumptuous meal, after which the editor remarked, 'Now we need to discuss the title of the monthly'.

On 1 April the proposed editorial team gathered for an official meeting. Bujnicki put forward different possible titles, including *Żagary,* a word which carried a strong local emphasis, as it was used only in the Wilno region.[9] To Cat-Mackiewicz's ear the title had a 'swaggering sound' and feel. It was intriguing, evoked the exotic, the earthy and organic, and so represented something far removed from the usual dull-as-dishwater titles such as *Literary News,* or the more technical-sounding *Switch-Point.* But what did the word actually mean? Lithuanians in the Wilno area used it to denote dry twigs and branches, kindling material. It also meant 'smouldering', 'half-burnt sticks', which could be used to poke a fire or light a fire. 'It is something like a burning torch, sticks used to transfer fire! So, in a symbolic sense, it resembles a candle, a torch or a spark from which a flame will burn' (*Pół Wieku* 178), explained Putrament. 'Żagary' could also refer to dry pine branches, which could scratch a rambler walking through a thick forest. Whether the journal's founders wanted to affirm that they would rake up a dying fire to make it flare up again, or to allow the flames to burn away 'old' poetry, or that no one could stroll past and ignore them matters little. The fact was that the name functioned like a 'literary trumpet', the name originally suggested for the supplement, and played louder than Mackiewicz could ever have expected.

At the outset, however, there were no indications that the journal would be a success. In April 1931 the readers of *Słowo* found the first edition of the literary supplement, whose full title was *Żagary: A Monthly Reflecting Wilno on the Move, Devoted to Art.* Its editors placed a declaration on the opening page stating that

> Wilno on the Move is a generation, which is only starting. It is
> starting on its chosen course.

> We do not constitute a group, school or direction. What keeps us together is a common effort, rather than a character. It is true that we write or paint, but not that we write or paint in this way or that.
>
> By 'moving' we pass by, we encounter a whole number of issues, which we have to address . . .
>
> We are not a closed group. We anticipate working with people we have not heard of before. You are welcome to join us as we set off.

The editorial team received no salary for their work, and it is not clear whether they were paid by the page or were simply happy to have a platform provided which would enable them to gain the attention of readers. Miłosz was involved in editing the work from the start, but was only officially listed in the editorial staff in late winter 1933 and early 1934, when *Żagary* began to come out as an independent publication. At that point the team included Miłosz, Bujnicki, Zagórski and Jędrychowski, as well as Józef Maśliński, a poet and a critic, who would become editor of Kraków's foremost literary magazine, *Życie Literackie*. Other members who should be mentioned are Tadeusz Byrski and Antoni Bohdziewicz, both of whom later worked for Polish Radio in Wilno with Miłosz and were respectively involved in directing plays for the radio and theatre. And finally there was Jerzy Putrament.

Putrament performed a secondary role within Żagary. In meetings when deliberations about publishing his short stories took place, the main editors were usually very reluctant to use them. On one occasion when they did include a piece of his writing, they appended a disclaimer distancing themselves from it. He was treated as a prospective contributor, but never taken seriously. Years later, when he became a very powerful figure in the Polish People's Republic, many of his former colleagues found themselves in precarious situations when they approached him for support.

Out of the whole group, it was Miłosz who was most susceptible to the revolutionary atmosphere, Bujnicki used to quip, with his tongue firmly in his cheek. Whereas Bujnicki was a man of moderation, and Jędrychowski and Dembiński invested a great deal in their political activity based on their analysis of the social and economic reality, Miłosz saw things from the perspective of an impassioned artist who wanted to destroy the old order, but had no proposals to put forward as to what an altered, improved social structure might look like. It was that which prompted colleagues to reproach him. Possibly for him, social issues were of secondary importance, and deep down there were other problems that preoccupied his mind.

In one of his early articles Miłosz wrote scathingly: 'Designating love with a capital "L" as the *raison d'être* of one's life, [and] succumbing to the cult of

impetuous emotions are most typical symptoms of bourgeois art and culture'
(*Przygody młodego umysłu* 29). Writing at this time to a regular confidant, he
averred: 'I have lost interest in the matter of sex. I have more important things to
write about than trivia. Something I share with many other people is a sense of
the apocalyptic state of our times and I am conscious of the utter ridiculousness
of particular individual crises' (CM to Iwaszkiewicz, 15 October 1931). Five days
later his focus turned to 'a dream about a literary school, which would introduce
a tangible rule, a poetry founded on organising intellect, which would definitely
eliminate moments of elation'. Ten days later, the next letter brought an unequivocal declaration: 'The only criterion for evaluating a piece of art is its social role . . .
Enough of this liberal equality in everything. We need to rehabilitate fanaticism'
(CM to Iwaszkiewicz, 20 October and 1 November 1931).

The lure of fanaticism reached its culmination in a piece for *Żagary* from
December 1931. This began with a claim that Polish literary figures were spineless and that 'their attitude to social issues was woolly. Completely emotional'.
Given that people were living through apocalyptic times, it was imperative that a
principled stand was adopted: 'The artist affects how people are reared . . . Word
order, the choice of lexis, the deployment of certain metaphors and of rhythm
and rhyme, all these have a great influence on the audience's mindset and make a
deep imprint upon it, and influence even their political views' (*Bulion z gwóździ*,
Żagary, December 1931). An artwork ought to be assessed on the basis of its
political ramifications, as art should be a 'tool in a society's fight for better forms
of existence. A provider of artistic merchandise must have a clear and definite
objective. This objective ought to be creating the type of person society will most
need in the near future' (ibid.).

These pronouncements may well seem crudely utilitarian, but they reflect
a very important phase in Miłosz's artistic development. His brief, heady flirta-
tion with the left sprang not so much from firmly-held political beliefs as from
an inner compulsion to give literature a high status, to make it matter. The poet
then went on to ponder: 'When is art going to be a structure which has the earth
as its base? Until now, it has been a colourful balloon, floating high up above
the admiring, opened-mouthed crowd'. Instead of arousing a fleeting delight, the
artist ought to forge reality, prioritising 'instead of emotions—dictatorship of
the intellect', 'instead of biology—sociology'. Such statements at first appear to
resemble sound-bites from a social-realist manifesto, but Miłosz's primary concern was with the intellectual formation of the audience.

Żagary members seem to have egged each other on to move things a step
further. Successive issues of the journal carried critical readings of recent literary trends and traditions. Its younger writers reproached their elders for getting
stuck in a rut, accusing the Skamander group from the previous generation of a

lack of creative seriousness and of representing the avant-garde of superficiality. For Jędrychowski, contemporary poetry had a duty to be responsive to the blood pulsating in the veins of the industrial workshops.

A contention reiterated in *Żagary* was that an artist could not run away from politics or economics, and that art should be subjected to social verification. Did Miłosz's new poems such as 'Opowieść' (A Story) and 'Sprawca' (The Guilty Man) meet these criteria? References to 'a militarised country', the revolt of the proletariat, 'when the wind tore to shreds the emblem of the state', and a flag the colour of 'a romantic rose' rang out like portents of a revolution. A protagonist around whom the poet's feeling at the time centred was not a fighter, but an out-sider posing philosophical questions, who would become one of the accidental victims of the revolution.

In the wake of Wilno's anti-Semitic riots of November 1931 and the relative indifference of the majority of the intelligentsia to them, Miłosz felt compelled to confront the right-wing, nationalist strain in Polish society and gaze into the dark void of future historical events. In *Piony* (Divisions), a supplement to *Kurier Wileński*, he depicted two communities equally alien to him: on the one hand, the nationalistic middle class, and on the other, the naive liberal bourgeoisie. He voiced his view that young people ought to oppose both, but what this early ex-ample of his journalism revealed more strongly than anything was his unusually intense dislike of the middle classes. However, he made no attempt to engage with the social experimentation being carried out to the east of Poland's borders. All of the representative types Miłosz portrayed seemed anachronistic, individ-uals whom history would soon consign to the rubbish dump. The future, it would appear, belonged to a different class altogether: the proletariat, the young, radical intelligentsia, the budding artists who would bring fresh air into the musty mu-seum halls of literature, and breathe into them truth and life.

> While I was at the university, I did not call myself a Marxist out of modesty, because I had not read *Das Kapital*. I was governed less by reason than by a sense of smell ... and this, in turn, put me on guard against any 'ism' as a temporary construction bearing the imprint of the nineteenth century ... I condemned the capitalist system, but was sus-picious of becoming enmeshed in philosophical intricacies. Sacred texts, such as Feuerbach's *The Essence of Christianity,* Engels's *Anti-Dühring,* Lenin's *Materialism and Empirio-Criticism,* I read as literature, unable to prevent humorous images of beards, moustaches and frockcoats from creeping into my thoughts. (*NR* 115)

The Marxist author who influenced Miłosz most was Stanisław Brzozowski (1878–1911),[10] a Polish philosopher and literary critic who drew some of his ideas from Marxism, but rejected deterministic readings of historical materialism. Brzozowski's insistence on literature's engagement in social life made him an ideal intellectual patron for the *Żagary* team, and three decades later Miłosz wrote a biography about this figure, who, like himself, had experienced persecution from 'the forces of conformism' (Grudzińska-Gross 69).

The group's need to signal their authenticity as committed activists in the cause of radical transformative change was clearly visible in an article published under a pseudonym by Dembiński, which presented the case in a rhetorically convincing way:

> The intelligentsia, if they do not want their historical role as low-paid lackeys to end in infamy . . . must alter their social stance and come to some clear, unequivocal decisions [about their role]. Either as Leviathan's wardens . . . [or giving service] in the headquarters of the workers, organising groups to fight for a better future of the whole nation.

Leviathan's wardens? Although Dembiński belonged to Leviata (the Society of Polish Industrialists), it is clear that he is also alluding to the biblical Leviathan. In articulating their leftist sympathies and their opposition to unjust social policies being implemented in 1930s Poland, Dembiński and Miłosz often deployed religious, and even occasionally gnostic motifs. It gradually became apparent that there was a rift among Żagary members between ideologues, pragmatists and poets who were perhaps rather lost. As Dembiński endeavoured to introduce and enforce a rigorous discipline on the group, Miłosz, who treasured his independence, found the situation increasingly difficult. He was reluctant to accede to demands to make political declarations and to pressures to align himself with one position or another within the group.

At this particular juncture, Miłosz was working on *An Anthology of Social Poetry*, a book which aimed to demonstrate that the literary and political convictions driving young writers in Wilno were shared by their peers in Lublin, Kraków, Łódź and Cieszyn. The poets whose work was featured in the anthology displayed a certain reticence when it came to defining their social status: thus, Józef Czechowicz 'comes from an old bourgeois family, which now belongs to the proletariat', while Stefan Flukowski's origins lay in 'a family of craftsmen'. When it came to Bujnicki, Zagórski and Miłosz, their roots apparently lay in the 'working intelligentsia'.

In order to invest the anthology with 'greater authority', Professor Manfred Kridl was approached by Miłosz and Folejewski to write the introduction. In it Kridl sought to balance critical distance with the friendly disposition he felt towards the young poets. The anthology, he declared, constituted 'an interesting and thought-provoking document of our times', a view not without continuing validity, since the majority of poems selected retain considerable historical value.

In late 1933 Miłosz was ready to shed the mask of 'revolutionary poet', which provoked a hostile reception from some of his colleagues. The pressure they exerted proved counter-productive and served to strengthen his conviction about the need to strike out on his own. An indication of what lay ahead came in a talk given during a Literary Wednesday in March 1934. He defended himself against a number of accusations directed at him and attempted to persuade his opponents that modernity in poetry did not necessitate the deployment of certain gimmicky effects: 'If anyone wishes to be a truly contemporary poet, they must give due attention to the quality of their technical skills. They have to master a range of techniques and not cling dogmatically to ones regarded as avant-garde. One has to develop one's own technique from amongst the diverse ones available' (qtd. in *Kurier Wileński*, 23 March 1934). A letter written four weeks later provides confirmation that he had adopted a new, unequivocal position:

> I am entering a completely new period, and feel total indifference towards doctrinarian poses. I am not interested in so-called radical attitudes and other such nonsense. I have had enough of sucking up to plebs, by telling myself that we occupy the same level. I hate these primitive people, as well as the plebeian traits within myself. (CM to Iwaszkiewicz, 18 April 1934)

The definitive breakup of Żagary as a poetic group occurred at around this time. The journal's printer was owed money, but was prepared to write off the remainder after the editors paid a portion of the debt out of their own funds. Financial troubles represented one of the major reasons for the publication's demise. Others included intellectual and ideological differences amongst its members, who had been drifting apart anyway. Besides, their careers were starting to get underway, taking them to positions scattered throughout Europe.

In March 1934 *Żagary*'s final issue appeared. It was devoted to an examination of Lithuanian culture, and included 'A Discussion about Literature', a co-written contribution from Miłosz and Ancewicz, which, surprisingly, possessed a definite religious accent:

> This Lithuanian revolutionary trend is an interesting phenomenon, since what it most resembles is a purely religious revolt. An intrinsic accessory to so much of the so-called social writing is the Cross. The predominant emblem of your literature is *smutkelis*, the sorrowful Christ at the crossroads. Religion is like a chalk-circle, outside of which you

cannot step. You are incapable of escaping from the problem of a Christian conscience. (*Przygody młodego umysłu* 84)

These words accord with others penned elsewhere. To accompany his translation of Oskar Miłosz's 'Talita cumi', Miłosz had composed a note which can hardly be said to provide a lucid account of his uncle's work. Nevertheless, it reflects how after the tempestuous period from 1931 to 1932, he was beginning to seek new outlets for his restless energies:

> I am not brave enough to claim that I understand the works of the author of *Miguel Mañara:* my lack of faith prevents me. But what one can feel is awe, a revelation of truth, like the experience of seeing high mountains. What compassion one feels … for millions of people who have the courage to call themselves Catholics! Compassion and sympathy for those believers, who draw solace and joy from repeating Catholic words. They utter them while thinking about eating, sleeping and love-making. What would the lives of such people akin to animals be like were they to confront [the] terrifying core of Catholicism?[11] It would be better if such Catholic mystics as Oskar V. de L. Miłosz taught … a few revolutionary poets. To a journalist the idea of a link between the concepts of revolution and mysticism may well seem amusing. But what if the two address the same wish for gratification, the needs of the heart, which reach beyond the limits of time, and borders of places? … It is possible to be at a distance from mysticism, but still appreciate and revere it. One only has to know about brotherhood, which binds those who cannot be bought off. (*Przygody młodego umysłu* 87)

A Bridge Suspended in Mid-Air

This image appears in a Miłosz poem shortly before a liminal moment in his life and poetry, his second meeting with Oskar Miłosz during a few months' stay in Paris. In Europe in the early to mid-1930s, the worsening social and political situation made young rebels of those who, in different circumstances, might have been content with 'mystic revelations'. Such converts to the left, or 'fellow travellers', were regarded with suspicion by the real revolutionary left, especially the Communists, who kept them at arm's length. For an oversensitive poet-turned-revolutionary the hope was that if his work was received with indifference by the bourgeoisie, it might find a warmer reception from the masses.

Decades later Miłosz revisited the complex predicament in which he had found himself:

In 1928–29 I sensed the fervour in the air rather than the tragic nature of what was unfolding. The years that followed were difficult years for me, and perhaps I was looking for a way out. The result of those youthful experiences and dramas was [that] my attention turned to society in the collection *A Poem on Frozen Time*. The title itself gestured towards iciness and cold. (*Podróżny świata* 12)

The volume's fifth poem pictures how

Poverty is rife here. There is the cry of starving masses.
There is despair, which sears the heart.
. . . In tenebrous smoke, at a dangerous time
    Żyrardów
       Roared
          Day and night.
('Against Them', Wiersze I, 14)

Was Miłosz's professed concern with the masses merely a fashionable suit that he donned? The young graduate in Wilno certainly did not travel to Łódź or Żyrardów to learn first-hand about the hardships of women working in the textile mills; he relied solely on a written account in *Wiadomości Literackie*. A sceptical observer might detect a certain lack of authenticity in the indignation he expressed about the 'plight of the masses'. At a reading, he knew that working one's way through a list of indictments against capitalism, arranged in a format copied from Mayakovsky, prompted a strong audience reaction. It did not necessarily mean that the young poet was simply playing to the gallery.

In retrospect, Miłosz came to the conclusion that 'the so-called poetry of social protest had no connection with the living springs' of his art. Rather, 'it was journalism, which I wrote to redeem myself for not taking part in the workers' clashes with the police' (*NR* 121). Conscious that history was inexorably heading towards a terrible crisis, he was beset with feelings of helplessness and frustration, knowing that poetry could neither address nor cope with what was to come. Belonging to the literary avant-garde in itself was a source of embarrassment. 'We began to press the social, left pedal' and so experienced 'a sense of relief', he explained. The feelings of mortification arose from

a guilty conscience. Why should we offer a peasant . . . who has no need for it, a jumble of less or more noble gestures: excessive ambition, a craving for recognition, love of equality and justice . . . The main merit of the second avant-garde wave in Poland in the 1930s was this anxiety, this strong apprehension, which would not allow [us] to settle for any of the tricks and motifs once used. I don't like 'literature'. It ought to be broken, defeated and rid of its habits, so that in the end it could be *literature* and not a companionable toy. ('O wstydzie i agresji' [On Shame and Aggression], *Kultura:* 7–8, 1962)

It was the discord within himself, the contradictions, that gave his poetry power. He was a writer drawn to the esoteric and arcane, yet, at the same time, driven by other imperatives—a need to participate, to contribute, to make a stand on behalf of culture. When his friend the poet Józef Czechowicz threatened to stop writing, Miłosz's response was a telling rhetorical question: 'Isn't the determination to act . . . by any chance, the moral duty of an artist?' ('Chcieć więcej' [To Want More], *Kurier Wileński:* 81, 1936).

————————————

The place where Miłosz had made his literary debut was the academic almanac *Alma Mater Vilnensis*, which published articles by professors and students of Wilno University. The poems 'Kompozycja' (Composition) and 'Podróż' (A Journey) appeared in its ninth issue of the year 1930, and documented how the nineteen year-old saw the world, presenting a striking starting point for his poetic odyssey and the spiritual changes it prompted. Whereas at the end of his life, he felt in harmony with the parish community, united in shared troubles and prayers, as *Treatise on Theology* shows, 'Composition' depicts the mass as a theatrical show, which fails to engage the speaker, making him feel stranded, peripheral:

> Bells bells burst out
> *pons Christi pons Christi*
>   *pons pons Chriiisti*
>
> Curtains tore open with a crash
> Look—we are in a theatre.
>
> (*Wiersze* I, 31)

Christ's bridge (*pons Christi*), the means by which we are able to cross safely over the abyss of death, appears no longer intact. Below it a chasm, a space, a nothing. These images make up the elements of a recurring vision, as a letter from late 1930 reveals: 'I would love to be a true, believing Catholic. This suspended bridge impresses me enormously. It is a separate structure, self-sufficient; it is not tempted to seek after the truth of the external [physical] world, as the Gothic does. If only one could write even one poem so self-enclosed, so objective!!!' (CM to Iwaszkiewicz, 11 December 1930). Many years passed before Miłosz was able to accept the rites of the Catholic mass as a means to enable humankind to transcend their imperfections, their sinfulness and silliness, to be lifted up to spiritual reality, to some kind of, though perhaps uncertain, recognition of God.

'A Journey' is a highly self-reflexive, oblique lyric, which at one point asserts that 'all ideas of the soul's elevation are lies / emptiness reigns above us' (*Wiersze* I, 32). The poem concludes with its speaker acknowledging a 'great impulse' propelling him towards 'distant fates'. The tone is nihilistic, negating the possibility of stepping outside gravity, to employ Simone Weil's metaphor:

> One Sunday morning, 1931, knowing that the first issue of *Żagary* came out with my poems in it my feeling was not pride, but a deep shame. Naturally, I got up early and ran out to get a copy. But the sight of those who were buying it: poor women leaving St. James' Church, men with moustaches, carrying the aura of their small wooden huts, made me feel ashamed even more . . . I was fully aware of what poetry meant to me: healing lack, hurt, a need for self-defence. But to expose oneself publicly? Publicly, by which I mean, not before people like myself, but before a wider public, who, in my view, had no need of that. (*Mój wileński opiekun* 67)

Miłosz did not expect much publicity when his first small volume of poetry, *A Poem on Frozen Time,* was dispatched from the printers in the spring of 1933. Three hundred copies of this thin, light-brown booklet were produced, an average run for those times, and usually sufficient. There was no expectation that any income might be derived from sales, but the book did gain attention. Significantly, it received awards from the Union of Polish Writers in Wilno and the Ministry of Religious Faith and Education, and a substantial sum of money. Manfred Kridl, who was one of the judges, declared that 'Miłosz is one of the genuine, fresh and clearly defined talents that make up the new generation'. Kridl noted that in Miłosz's poetical world 'the social element' is very pronounced and that his work often displays 'a very noble kind of outrage and revolt against the horrors of today'. Patently, 'compassion and pain' are what compel him 'to look and listen' (*Mój wileński opiekun* 67).

Compassion and pain. Only to a certain extent were they connected to politics and sensitivity to social problems. There were other, more profound reasons for their inclusion in the poems, whose protagonist lived in a chaotic, imperilled world, looking for support in what was closest, most intimate to him: his own body, pulse rate, heartbeat: he felt the surrounding world as a physical, tangible dimension. In the poem 'Morning', looking at the world, he could not see any hidden dimension, only the alarming whirling of galaxies, a counterpoint to birth and death. There was no special dispensation which would enable humanity to rise above the fate of animals, plants or stones—no word, promise or hope. Dying, as in the poem 'Death of a Young Man', was not felt as a transition, but as an irreversible ending.

The protagonist's gaze could not penetrate the surface of the earth, and reality was hard and impermeable, the sky like a metal carapace. There was a significant section in 'A Story' (*Żagary*: 2, 1931) where socio-political concerns were suffused with elements of existential philosophy. The poem ends in revolution, a reminder of the uncertain, precarious structure of the world: 'The sky cracked at dawn, revealing shamelessly the flesh of the sun'. The crack resembles a wound, a tear in the skin, and uncovers muscles and blood; above the world a huge chunk of meat steamed, and the light was not so much personified as materialised—flesh a body devoid of spiritual secrets. Even if the man portrayed by Miłosz managed to find some crack in the stone or lead crust of the world, he would not come upon 'one bright point' ('Eyes', *SS* 31), which many decades later the old man going blind manages to detect. Through the gap darkness gapes, a frightening emptiness, nothingness. The sense of threat did not relate to his own death; it was the entire world that was heading towards collapse and catastrophe. 'Spring 1932' talked about the humiliation of 'those who sleep in railway stations', and also about the fact that reality itself was subject to destruction. In what was to all intents and purposes a propaganda poem, 'The Reverence for Money', human life is bound up not only with class struggle, but also with a wider struggle against restriction affecting everyone. The truth about human fate cannot be rationally grasped, since it is 'illogical', an experience of passing time. In one poem the apprehension of cosmic nothingness is juxtaposed with the vacancy of the capitalist system, dominated as it is by the 'ruthlessly aggressive' but 'perpetually dissatisfying' (Bond vii) pursuit of money. For that reason, sometimes instead of eliciting expressions of fear, the coming catastrophe is embraced from the conviction that the world is so corrupt that the Last Judgment should take place now.

What could anaesthetise us from fear? The poem 'Razors' provides one answer. Love, or specifically sex. Orgasm can block out for a moment the emptiness and ominousness of the sky, performing a role similar to the curtain in a church ritual. Love for the poetic personae in Miłosz's earlier poems was, in fact, impossible, demanding complete commitment, an unusual measure of grace. Typically, he was conscious of a radical tension between 'me' and other people, which took the form of the full spectrum of emotions: from relatively neutral detachment through dislike to outright hatred. A core reason for his distrust was a conviction that others give up their freedom of thought, the need to question, the search for meaning in the world and in human fate. The origins of this aversion undoubtedly lay in Miłosz's own childhood. Here was an innocent boy, disgusted by guffawing adults whose notion of human reality was limited to food, sex and a lust for money.

Doesn't that sound rather like hubris? The speaker in 'Verses of the Possessed' admits to his lover:

> While I have no belief in God, who out of mercy
> Shields with his hands our eyes,
> I certainly believe in Satan, whose sharp thorns
> Press against one's temples . . .
>
> I know he awaits me, and when at dawn
> I will slip away quietly
> He swishes behind me amongst the rye
> And punishes me with pride.
>
> (Wiersze I, 59–60)

Miłosz's ferocity, fury and irresistible will, not surprisingly, made Satan an intriguing figure, inciting him to offer up 'blasphemous prayers'. His devil, 'dark-skinned and livid', resembled to some extent Milton's fallen archangel from *Paradise Lost*, but in this poem appears as 'a good brother'. The excessive pride for which he is punished arises out of a desire for individuality. When competing with Satan and his enchantments, the girl who wants to win over her lover is powerless. Several of these first lyrics address, like Coleridge's 'Christabel' or Keats's 'Lamia', the seductiveness of evil and the pitfalls of pride and complacency.

Life dominated by biology condemned humankind to ultimate emptiness. If the theological concept of eschatology is set aside, time becomes a trap, its end merely destruction. If God did not exist, then there was no one to blame for this cruel state of affairs, and protestation was out of the question. Post-Darwin, human society seemed largely to have succumbed to spiritual indifference. A life without spiritual ambitions meant nothing better than a bestial existence, and for Miłosz personally could end only in existential and artistic failure. Did hope remain? To answer the question it is necessary to study the figure of the child, who re-emerges time and again in his later poetry, in works such as 'Treatise on Theology'.

'Land', which pictures children playing and breaking ice on the river, freeing the waters, bore traces of hope. Though failure is acknowledged, for the personae in the poems life continues and does not constitute a source of additional suffering. The existence of the world itself, the renewal of joy in living—these were liberating to a certain degree and eased disquiet. Struggling with his proud soul, Miłosz longed for security, simplicity and faith. To free himself from torment, even for a moment, proved possible, if self-love could be overcome. To grow meant stepping outside the 'I', reaching out to the other, towards the world. The earliest testimony that he could achieve that better state arrived in a poem composed in Paris in 1934:

What I had written, seemed suddenly
Buffoonery. I could not find words.
I looked at the enormous, pulsating world
With elbows lodged on a marble balustrade.
Rivers flowed, sails tore through a cloud,
Sunsets fainted. Every beautiful land,
Every being that I desired,
Rose into the sky like huge moons.
Staring into these stirring lamps,
Counting their astrological arcs,
I whispered: O world, vanish, be merciful, I am sinking!
No fine speech will suffice.
I saw in myself vast valleys,
And with a foot winged with bronze I could
Traverse above them on stilts of air.
But then all faded, forgotten night.

('To co pisałem' [What I Had Written], *Wiersze* I, 51)

The Devil's See-Saw

As will have become apparent, Miłosz had an extremely strong bond with a much older poet, Jarosław Iwaszkiewicz (1894–1980), who served as both mentor and confidant. His literary reputation was at its height in the inter-war period, not least because of his role as a co-founder with Julian Tuwim and Antoni Słonimski of Skamander, the highly influential poetry group formed following Independence. Despite the fifteen year age-gap between them, Iwaszkiewicz was one of the few people to whom Miłosz could reveal his hurt. In each of his first publications, *A Poem on Frozen Time* (1933), *An Anthology of Social Poetry* (1933) and *Three Winters* (1936), the young apprentice inscribed a dedicatory note: 'Asking you to forgive many things', 'To a pure poet from one of the less pure youths', and one in which he dismissively referred to his latest work as 'this exercise book'.

For Miłosz, Iwaszkiewicz's poetry offered a crash course in modernity, possessing as it did a Dionysian sensuality, an intensity of experience, literary and erotic: 'To me Iwaszkiewicz's small volumes, with their greyish though good quality paper and rough covers were not books, but cult objects. And so they occupied a place previously reserved for my colourful botanical and ornithological atlases' (*Rok myśliwego* 203). Towards the close of his life, Miłosz wrote, 'It is possible that I attributed to his poems something that was not there, projecting onto them my own eroticism, greed, and feel for music' (ibid., 218). When he was sixteen and seventeen, as we have seen, he was subject to such overwhelming emotions that they nearly cost him his life. Miłosz first encountered Iwaszkiewicz in school at an evening reading which had attracted a disappointingly small audience. A good while later, on 30 November 1930, he sent a letter to the author. Latterly, Iwaszkiewicz recalled:

> I found the letter interesting, intense and intelligent, which is why I responded to it. Several weeks later the young man sat by the dining table in our family home, Stawisko, near Warsaw. Then our friendship began, this correspondence and the mutual disappointment, that's how the painful relationship started, which until this day sits like a thorn, if not in my heart, then in my hand. (*Portrety na Marginesach* 94)

The letter was indeed intense, and above all, extremely complimentary about the older writer's work and worth:

> Dear Sir,
>
> I adore you. Your every poem is a revelation to me. This is why I turn to you to ask your opinion about my poems. I have no idea whether they are good, or derivative of literary trends.
>
> My friends say that they are good. How could I know whether they are just saying that out of politeness?
>
> Please tell me, you are my dearest friend and master. To me your assessment will be conclusive and will decide whether I ought to take my literary work seriously. I am a student in the second year of my law degree, I am nineteen and I come from Lithuania—that's all I can say about myself.
>
> Oskar Miłosz, whose mystery play, *Miguel Mañara,* was translated by Bronisława Ostrowska, is my uncle. You can understand how that feeds my happy dreams.
>
> I am hardly ever overcome by ecstatic feelings. My mind is never clouded by emotions when I write and that troubles me. I get out of breath and the only thing left for me is to humble myself before the tension in your *Dionizje.*
>
> The poems I enclose, 'Composition' and 'A Journey[,]' will soon be published in *Alma Mater Vilnensis.* But it is all nothing and until you give me your verdict, I will not know anything about my poems.
>
> Yours faithfully.
> Yours always.
> Czesław Miłosz

No wonder that Iwaszkiewicz's reply was sent as early as 3 December and included an invitation to Stawisko. When the student from Wilno wrote back that sadly the visit could not occur because of his meagre funds, Iwaszkiewicz proposed a loan. And, as a consequence, in January 1931 Miłosz visited Warsaw for the first time, though the meeting was not a success.

To the youngster from the provinces, the sheer size of the capital city probably felt intimidating. Another Wilno inhabitant, Jerzy Putrament, described his first impressions after arriving in Warsaw on an overnight train at around five in the morning.

> Darkness everywhere, but the place was already very busy. After a sleepless night . . . all the traffic, sparks flying from overhead tram lines, cars, bustle, passers-by with their spiteful jokes, repulsive and alien. And instead of snow, some horrible slush, pavements full of melting snow, always close to thawing, and strong winds from River Vistula. (*Pół Wieku* 238)

The Iwaszkiewicz family residence was a rich estate in a huge park, which must have dazzled the student more used to rented rooms. There was also the matter of his host's homosexuality, his only part-covert relationship with his chauffeur, which added an ambiguous, uncomfortable atmosphere. The crucial point was that this was a young, high-minded student who was exposed for the first time to the sophisticated, blasé, ironic world of the salons, where eloquence, witty quips and highly-developed social networks, as well as fluency in etiquette, were the order of the day. The religious and literary preoccupations of Anna Iwaszkiewicz, a keen reader of Proust, Miłosz also found overbearing. In short, the meeting merely reinforced his pre-existing 'sense of inferiority' and feelings of inadequacy (*Rok myśliwego* 208).

A few days later Miłosz returned to Wilno, stricken by failure; the fact that he was now on first-name terms with his favourite writer was no compensation. He confessed later in a letter sent to Iwaszkiewicz on 3 February 1931: 'The stay in Warsaw was a humiliation for me. All the time I tried to convince myself that your attention was not dictated by pity for me'. Not that long afterwards, however, the older poet visited Wilno to watch a mystery play, and met up with Miłosz again. The relationship soon became more relaxed, which produced an uplift in the young poet's mood: 'I feel a strength in me. Ideas and logical structures keep coming, images race through my mind, and I am happy that I have a lifetime ahead of me to realise them' (CM to Iwaszkiewicz, 8 March 1931). And in a letter just over five weeks later, he requested his friend's help in placing a poem in one of the prestigious magazines.

An entry in Iwaszkiewicz's diary from January 1955 remarks that

> each epoch has its own style, even down to minute details and it is not
> possible to appreciate certain things at any other time. In May 1936 I
> could have had Czesio Miłosz in the Basilian monastery cell, where one
> of Mickiewicz's characters, Konrad, stayed. It was a wonderful night
> with moonlight and nightingales. Something that couldn't have hap-
> pened in 1824 or in 1954. (*Dzienniki 1911–1955* 450)

Some years later, having read *Native Realm,* he felt hurt and jotted down a few
critical notes about the author, adding:

> Luckily I have kept letters from him and from them it will be clear
> what the meaning of his first visit to Stawisko in the autumn of 1930
> was ('I adore you!'), whose money it was that ended up at the bottom
> of the Rhine, who helped Jędrychowski, why the Consul in Stras-
> bourg was so friendly (after my telegram from the Office of Foreign
> Affairs)—under whose vigilant eye the expedition took place, what
> was the meaning of the two weeks spent in Brussels at my place, with a
> weekend in Zout, my visit to Wilno in May 1936, and so on. (*Dzienniki
> 1956–1963* 422)

Not just the spectacular sentence 'I could have had Czesio', but also several other
facts revealed that Iwaszkiewicz took special care of Miłosz, which might lead to
speculation as to whether the two poets could have had a homosexual relationship. Certainly the earliest of the frequent letters Miłosz wrote display considerable emotion, bordering on hysteria at times, and a tone close to lovesickness: 'I
do not know how to express my gratitude and love for you . . . If I could, I would
write a book about you and entitle it *J'adore'*, he wrote on 11 December 1930; nine
days later, he declared that 'correspondence between us gives meaning to my
existence'; 'He [Iwaszkiewicz] was complimentary because they were my first attempts . . . good for a nineteen-year-old (I am not Rimbaud). To tell the truth, I
never felt so happy as I am now. The state of intoxication and some expectation';
'You know, you are dear to me, that's why I cursed myself all that time—I will
always have to stay lonely—it is funny—I constantly look for friendship, but the
moment I know I could find a friend, I feel I will be overcome by guilt because
of my coldness, dream-like state, scepticism, bitterness, and this horrible stoni-
ness' (1 February 1931); 'I think about you and imagine you in the office, home, in
the street, or in a queue' (11 February 1931); 'Where are you now? Still in Paris? I
received your letter. Write to me if you can—it is the best thing you can give me.
Your letters have a calming effect on me for quite a while' (3 April 1931). And lastly:

Too many inhibitions—and that's why my dreams reveal a lot . . . One was particularly fantastic. You were in it, once as you, and then the second time when certain of your traits entered a woman's body. This dream, full of horror, made me shiver, contained strange images—this creature kissed me and caressed me—it was that You in a woman's body—and in another part of that dream, I had sex with a man, who was a man turned into a woman, with whom I spent a few nights. The first dream was delightful and the other—horrible—an ideal subject for Freud's followers. (CM to Iwaszkiewicz, 8 March 1931)

It was not until the spring of 1931 that the intensity of Miłosz's emotions cooled, and critical observations about his mentor began to surface in letters. Tellingly, these coincided with the launch of Żagary.

During a later, extended stay in Warsaw, Miłosz wrote how Iwaszkiewicz used to take him to meetings in literary circles, which instead of being an opportunity to advance his career intensified his sense of isolation and humiliation, as everyone instantly assumed they must be lovers. Homosexual relationships were commonplace among artistic circles at the time, and in some quarters regarded as *de rigueur*. Maria Iwaszkiewicz, a daughter of the writer, in an interview with the author of this book, was convinced that there was a love-hate relationship between her father and Miłosz, which, though highly charged emotionally, lacked any strictly erotic element. Miłosz himself stated, 'I am not a homosexual, although I have had gay friends, who said that I am one of them, though not "initiated". And the fact that I did not "initiate" never stood in the way of our frank conversations' (*Zaczynając od moich ulic* 279).

The above-quoted fragments from his letters ought to be read in the context of Miłosz's spiritual and emotional state at the time, which was often characterised by periods of tension, torment, self-doubt, guilt and pain.

In the volume *Verses for the Possessed*, published a few months later, the young man grappled with the—actual or imagined?—coldness of his heart. 'I cannot have anything, not even a genuine feeling. This is horrible especially because it seems immature' (11 December 1930). Was there a shard of the Devil's mirror in the poet's heart? Concentrating on self, feeling that all experiences and relationships were just fuel for his creativity, he wrote after his second wife's death, 'Lyric poets / Usually have—as he knew—cold hearts' ('Orpheus and Eurydice', *SS* 99). One of the most interesting self-portraits in Miłosz's work appeared in a novella entitled *Tryton*, written just before the war. Its protagonist, Theodore, a schoolboy, dreams of having some unusual quality which will make him stand out above his peers. He invests all his passion in biology; but despite the wonderment generated by silkworms, stick insects and the molluscs called tritons, what the boy in fact loves is not so much the creatures themselves as the experience of loving, how the beauty of creatures could arouse in him an almost erotic passion. In tones reminiscent of those we find in his early letters to Iwaszkiewicz, the writer speaks of the merciless nature of Eros, where the pursuit after new beauty meant abandoning previous lovers. As they had lost the charm of novelty, Theodore half-consciously wished that his tritons would die and create space for a new fascination. He allowed them to perish, despite the guilt that aroused: 'guilty, guilty, you cruel creature . . . Sunlight, which slid down the bannisters, table legs which were, despite everything, jolly. The chirping swallows flew high up in the bright, golden sky. To run in the fields, to run along the earth in order to come upon a new gift, a new delight' (*Przygody młodego umysłu* 324–334). The story was a parable about cruelty, with a clear sexual subtext. The young poet seems to have had a strong need to analyse and assess his emotions and actions: 'I have what they refer to in dogmatics as "a meticulous conscience" and forever reproach myself for telling lies' (11 December 1930). This stayed with him until the end of his life:

> My nature and my character were to blame, a complaint called in moral theology 'a meticulous conscience', and also inclination to *delectatio morosa,* the negative tendency to mull over a bowl of one's sins. My life was full of joy and despair, reason and madness, good and bad. This would be sufficient material for a bearable biography, if it wasn't for the fact that each pin-prick turned into a knife-wound, a wound that would not heal. (*Ulro* 34)

To Iwaszkiewicz, he talked frankly of his low self-esteem and uninhibited pride and also of the masochistic pleasure he derived from thinking about his sinful nature:

> It is perhaps pathological. I think, that if am to continue living . . . then I will end up as a neo-Catholic, because with a make-up like mine, sustaining a questioning attitude to life is torture. Oh, this Christian masochism. I only feel right when I commit a sin or can talk about my insignificance in simple terms. I used to visit a brothel in order to cultivate bitterness—that opens a way. (CM to Iwaszkiewicz, 1 February 1931)

Meeting Iwaszkiewicz happened at an extremely difficult time for Miłosz, when he desperately needed friendship, intellectual guidance and confirmation in literary ambitions, which neither his parents nor his friends could provide. Was there anything more between the two poets than a close, intimate, tangled friendship? Of course, the unusual see-saw of tension between them might indicate that they stepped outside the ramifications of friendship.

In an introduction to a reading by Iwaszkiewicz on 20 May 1936, Miłosz referred to 'a new generation of writers, uncertain about their political convictions and looking to the past for support from such artists as Jarosław Iwaszkiewicz [who] will find what they are looking for: not politics, not ideology, but literature' (Hernik-Spalińska 258). From this one might deduce that Miłosz now felt on an equal footing with his erstwhile master. What precipitated his first critical remarks about the poet may well have been the involvement in *Żagary*. Its intellectually inferior passion was preferable to sweet nothingness, a subject about which he wrote decades later in the snappily titled 'Selecting Iwaszkiewicz's Poems for an Evening of his Poetry at the National Theater in Warsaw':

> Your poems, beautifully made, carry within them
> Contents so funereal they can hardly be read
> Without harming their admirers. Unfortunately it's so.
> Isn't it the case that you succumbed to the temptation,
> Deeply sweet, of relief through nonexistence,
> Of escape into nothingness? Even if it's true
> That after the dream of our species is done with,
> Only the immense laughter of the void remains,
> Even if we are nothing, lumps of mucus on a beach
> Without limit, even then some glory is due
> To the brave who raised a protest to the end
> Against death, the destroyer of faith.
>
> (*NCP* 708)

Letters exchanged between the two poets testify to years of friendship in the terrible times to come, but the bond was severed following Miłosz's defection to the West in 1951. In the 1970s the warmth of the relationship was revived and continued until Iwaszkiewicz's death in 1980.

What was particularly striking about Miłosz's exchanges with Iwaszkiewicz was their openness and frankness. For so much of his life Miłosz felt as if he were hiding under a mask, not least in his struggle to achieve a higher social status. He regarded disguise as a necessary part of the game he had to play in order to be accepted, for example, by the post-war Polish Communist authorities. The mask features prominently in the title poem to one of his late collections, where he refers to

> my ecstatic praises of being
> Might just have been exercises in the high style.
> Underneath was this, which I do not dare to name.
>
> 				(*NCP* 663)

He posed the question as to whether a poet had to share his knowledge with others. And if he camouflaged his feelings, then what was it that dictated that manoeuvre? The concern of a wise man who wanted to save others from falling prey to despair? A conviction that others were not capable of recognising the horror with their own eyes and enduring it? Perhaps it was a dread of becoming an object of ridicule? He lived for many years in America disguised as a 'normal', psychologically sound person, content with his bourgeois life. A mask served particularly as a means of helping him manage his internal chaos, of preventing him from meeting the ill fate that befell his relatives. At times, as Hamlet knew, it made sense to imitate madness, or, as Oskar Miłosz phrased it, to act 'Miłosz-style'.

'If early love had lasted . . .'

> And like an unfortunate stone at the bottom of a dark lake,
> Hurled by a hand from a beautiful cruel heart,
> So, in the darkest corners of the heart, amid
> Dreamy silt, rests love's heavy memory.
>
> 			Oskar Miłosz, 'September Symphony'

In the undated 'Materiały do mojej biografii' (Material for My Biography), Miłosz identifies another critical, testing juncture in his life, one of many moments so painful that he found it impossible to speak directly about it years later:

> Summer 1936. Intoxication with the summer and life . . . I ought to have felt happy. I had a job, enough money for my own needs and to share with a glamorous lover. In a word, things were just as they should be. And yet, I felt that it was an interim time, a period, as if set aside after my suffering, my grievous sin and guilt, but before an unforeseeable complication, which drew me towards it, like a moth to a flame.

In a letter from 24 September 1984, Miłosz reflected on the dynamic that initially had brought him and its addressee together: 'The basis of a relationship between a man and a woman ought to be through the power of physical attraction, primitive magnetism, and not something dreamt up in the head. If possible this should be love at first sight, such as happened, when on a rainy day in Wilno ... I took you back home in a carriage'. Its recipient was Jadwiga Waszkiewicz, perhaps the most 'true and tragic love' (*NR* 216) of his life. She was born on 11 July 1910. Her mother, Izabela, was a housewife, and her father, Antoni, was a gynaecologist. Initially, he co-owned a private clinic, but later became a director of St James' Hospital and the first doctor in Wilno to perform a caesarean section. The Waszkiewiczes must have been very affluent, because they could afford a big house with a huge garden at 10 Portowa Street, as well as a sixty-hectare estate in the suburbs at Barcie. There had been plans to receive paying guests on the estate in the summer to generate additional income, but for the time being, they used it to entertain friends from Wilno, who swam, played with Jadwiga's favourite dog and picked mushrooms in the beautiful nearby forest. The younger of their two daughters, Jadwiga, after taking her final exams in a gymnasium managed by nuns of the Nazareth order, followed by a year-long course preparing her for married life, decided to enrol for a law degree in 1929. She frequently clashed with her father over his nationalistic stance, which was indicative of her character, as she was resolute and intelligent, and, above all, had a mind of her own.

During her studies at Wilno University's Law Department she lived with her parents in Portowa (which in 'A Short Recess' is rendered Harbour Street), next to the student dormitory. Years later, on 1 December 1983, she sent Miłosz a postcard in which she suggested that he make 'one more visit to Portowa, enter our rooms with high ceilings, stop by the fireplace and remember the times of innocence'. What prompted the card was a poem she came across in *Tygodnik Powszechny*:

> Dreams visit me year after year,
> They are expendable, J.W.
> What might have been is just thin air,
> A loss we long ago outgrew.
> So why do we talk and why do we care?

> (In Salem', *NCP* 423)

Her relationship with Miłosz probably began in 1931, when they both had to repeat exams after the first year. Following his return from the expedition to Paris, Anna Jędrychowska remembered how 'Czesław boasted that he was descended from the Jadźwing family ... I think, however, that he said that because he was then deeply in love with a certain girl called Jadwiga' (*Zygzakiem i po prostu* 40). It seems very likely that the girl referred to in a letter from early summer 1931 was Jadwiga: 'It is a funny thing that a great adventurer and a rebel like me should be head-over-heels in love with a girl and entangled in an erotic relationship' (CM to Iwaszkiewicz, 21 May 1931). He was reading *The Magic Mountain* at that time, and, as he later revealed in *A Year of the Hunter,* 'identified myself with Hans Castorp and Jadwiga with Klaudia Chauchat' (134).

Amongst the few photographs that have survived is one in an *indeks,* a book recording student achievement, probably from the final year at law school; it displays a very young, child-like face, which has something compelling, even magnetic, about it. Another picture, unfortunately without a date, shows the couple standing, embracing, beside a wooden fence. Whereas he is talking animatedly and gesticulating, she looks attentively towards the camera, as if composing herself to look good in the picture. There is a beautiful portrait taken in about 1938 of Jadwiga as a mature woman at the height of her beauty. That was sent to Miłosz on 2 April 1986. It was probably to her that the following words were addressed in 'A Certain Neighbourhood':

> The glitter of a small lake, but its shores lack the rushes
> Through which we struggled forward, swimming,
> To dry ourselves afterwards, I and Miss X, and one towel, dancing

And from 'A Naiad':

> The only proof of the existence of Miss X
> Is my writing. As long as I am here
> She lives not far from the places she loved.
>
> Her hair was dark blond, nearly chestnut,
> Of a tint common among the girls of our gentry
> Her eyes were gray, rarely blue,
> More often greenish, the cut of her eyelids
> Somewhat oriental.
>
> (From 'Lithuania, after Fifty-Two Years', *NCP* 593–594)

In his autobiographical novel *Człowiek przemieniony w wilka* (The Man Who Changed into a Wolf), Sergiusz Piasecki, who later married Jadwiga, describes a character, Helena, who was

> a Cinderella in the family. Her older sister, Lidia, knew how to win her father. When she married, she bore a son and became the queen of the house. Her husband, Karol, with the support of Lidia, knew how to push her sister into a secondary position in the family. Helena's ultimate goal was to lead an independent life.

One day, two intellectuals came to stay with Karol. One of them, whom Helena named Narcissus in the story, began to try to win her heart. He made her feel adored, wrote poems for her and letters filled with tenderness. He assured her that he would love her 'until death'. She became his lover, after he had assured her of his honourable intentions . . .

After a while, she found out that she was pregnant. Narcissus was then in Wilno. She informed him of her predicament and asked him to keep his promise and marry her as soon as possible. Narcissus ignored her letters. When she demanded that he meet her and suggested a date, he left for Warsaw. She went to Wilno and got his address in Warsaw. She travelled there and managed, with difficulty, to arrange a meeting at the railway station. She begged him to help her find a way out of her tragic situation. He promised he would help and again assured her about his love for her. When she got back to Wilno, however, he sent a cruel letter, in which he wrote that he did not intend to ruin his future by marrying her, that he did not know who could have made her pregnant, because she used to flirt even with his friends. He added that he was going abroad.

Helena was driven to despair. She even considered committing suicide. In the end, with the help of an older friend, she found a midwife, who aborted the foetus. At home the same day, she developed [a] high temperature and was taken ill. She was rushed to hospital and underwent an operation. Her life was saved, but the situation in the family became terrible. She was treated like a criminal. She then left the city and took on clerical work in some provincial town. When war broke out, she returned to Wilno. Her return was welcome, because they needed someone to work on the estate, which had been abandoned by the farmhand and his wife. Helena wasn't spared and was made to do the hardest work. When the Bolsheviks began a mass transportation of people out of the area, everyone hid and Helena was left at the farm to guard it. (Piasecki 206)

To what degree might Piasecki's narrative give an accurate account of what happened? Certainly some facts fit what is known. Miłosz used to visit the estate outside Wilno, initially with Jędrychowski. He later left for Warsaw and then Paris, while Jadwiga went to work in a small town after graduation, although not until after 1937. And finally, it cannot be denied that there was a great deal of Narcissus in Miłosz at the time.

Who was the Anielka mentioned in a letter to Jadwiga? Is it possible that there was a child? Could this be 'the grievous sin and guilt' Miłosz alludes to in 'Material for My Biography'? Piasecki wrote his novel in the 1960s, at a time when there were venomous attacks on Miłosz's reputation, so he might have embellished or largely invented the story. Letters sent between Waszkiewicz and Miłosz offer no shred of confirmation. It is beyond doubt, however, that Miłosz's abandonment of Jadwiga, whatever the circumstances, had traumatic repercussions which affected him for the rest of his life.

Their relationship seems to have lasted until their graduation in July 1934, though on 7 August 1934, Miłosz mentioned that he had just spent time on Jadwiga's estate. Half a century later, he confessed to Jadwiga:

> When I look back, I do not understand my life. Even that Jadwiga, who was a source of such despair because of Anielka, and the Jadwiga changed in my memories and the real you could not merge into one now . . . Summer at the estate in Barcie. And the constant questions, why did I behave the way I did. Did it have to be that way? You have been so courageous, and nowadays I can see that mutual understanding between a man and a woman could be so different from what I, unfortunately, was capable of achieving in my youth. (CM to Jadwiga Waszkiewicz, 18 August 1982)

One surmises that he was fleeing from 'normality', fearing that marriage, and family, and regular employment would diminish or destroy his poetic gift. That is certainly how he felt in May 1931, when he wrote to his regular confidant:

> I believe in Satan, I really do—he is beside me at all times . . . He displays to me on the mountain-top, the way he did with Christ, all the treasures of the world, the most beautiful rhythm in verses, the most beautiful images in prose, and then . . . opens up the future and shows me as a bourgeois who can think of nothing else but bills. (CM to Iwaszkiewicz, 1 May 1931)

Four years on, he returned to the same theme:

> I am far away from thinking about marriage and could not imagine myself being a part of a society preoccupied just with earning a living—I am not interested in either—it's disgusting, horrible—I notice in myself the disappearance of almost all instincts, other than survival and perhaps metaphysical and other related passions. (CM to Iwaszkiewicz, 7 December 1935)

And even later, when it came to choosing his future wife, Janina Cękalska, above all he sought a spiritual affinity; he was unconcerned with material advantages.

A fast-paced life and change was also what he craved, like Doctor Catchfly, who, on the way to his wedding, came upon an unusual insect in the park and began to chase after it to catch it with his top hat, forgetting altogether his waiting fiancée. Miłosz caused intense grief by rejecting love, and then for a long period had sexual relationships without emotional involvement, so resolute was he about achieving his literary goals.

One route to escaping the role of husband and father was to travel to Paris, where he again became engrossed in the lofty spiritual deliberations emanating from the master, Oskar Miłosz. But demons still haunted him:

> My intelligence remained disturbingly disproportionate to my develop-
> ment as a man, to the formation of character. I was like a child, in love
> with myself, yet enough aware so that my conscience bothered me in-
> cessantly. Despair over my monstrous egoism—which I did not want to
> renounce—reached extremes of tension in Paris. It was not only adoles-
> cent *Weltschmertz*. My sins, after all, were not imagined. Who knows if
> it was not precisely this impossibility of bringing order to my personal
> problems that caused me to nourish myself so passionately for several
> years on catastrophic visions, borrowing from the Marxists little more
> than their belief in a spasm of history? The impending annihilation was
> sweet: it would resolve everything; individual destiny lost its significance,
> all would become equal. So my relative's predictions fell on fertile ground.
> I was thrown into a near-trance by my dread and intoxication with the in-
> evitable disaster, and this made me forget my private despair. (*NR* 172–173)

Even after his return, in autumn 1935, he confided to his friend: 'You know in Wilno and on the estate outside the city, some kind of dust settled on me and I was descending into madness brought on . . . by Gide-like remorse. Who would have expected me to be like that?' (CM to Iwaszkiewicz, 13 September 1935). In old age he acknowledged that 'my crazy love for Jadwiga W. was my main ca-lamity, causing every inner torment . . . And I think that refusal to accept fate, a lack of Christian love for W., you might say, was the greatest sin of my life' (CM to Jadwiga Tomaszewicz née Waszkiewicz, 17 September 1935).

Eventually, she forgave him, and wrote in a letter of 15 April 1986: 'I would only like you to know that you were never a bad person, but very immature . . . too young'. She had previously observed: 'After your return from Paris, I believe you chose the only appropriate way—since it took you to where you are now' (Jadwiga Tomaszewicz née Waszkiewicz to CM, 29 July 1982). Their last meeting perhaps took place in 1935, when Miłosz wrote 'A Statue of a Couple':

Where are you, living in what depths of time,
love, stepping down into what waters,
now, when the frost of our voiceless lips
cannot fend off the divine flames?

(Wiersze I, 96)

As Renata Gorczyńska astutely observes, 'In reality, it was not so much a statue,
more a tombstone of a couple' (*Podróżny świata* 26). But Jadwiga's son, Władysław,
informed the author of this book that he was positive that his mother travelled
to Warsaw no earlier than 1937 to meet Miłosz, wearing a dress especially made
for the occasion.

An exact chronology may not be crucial here. What was important then
was the intensity of the emotion and the moment they chose, because it is likely
that had they married they would have remained in Wilno until the outbreak of
war. In that scenario in all probability forced transportation to the east would
have been his fate and nothing of his would ever have been published after *Three
Winters*. In Wilno's Basilian monastery walls, whispering ghosts, who proffer
everyone a portion of bitterness, decided otherwise:

And you with them, Claudine, who once wrote to me this:
'You are for me a man of a somewhat childish character (perhaps poets
remain so all their lives), all of whose transgressions one forgives,
    whom
one loves in spite of everything'

That man, who was myself, now sees suddenly a birch forest and both
of us in the house of our neighbors, on a bench at a table eating a
    supper

not unlike a wedding feast, but it is too late to tell the story of our
    lives.

('Persons', NCP 738–739)

And Jadwiga's life after that? She finished her university course and applied
for work at the Regional Court in Wilno. Subsequently, she found a job in Łuck
as the official running the Department for Farming and Farm Reforms for the
Wołyń region. When the Second World War broke out on 1 September 1939, she
returned to Wilno and Barcie, where her sister and other members of her family
ran the estate. In June 1941, when she heard of Soviet plans to repatriate Poles
from the area, she travelled to Wilno to warn her family. Without finishing their
dinner, they left the table and ran and hid in the nearby marshes for two weeks,
returning home only after the German Army marched into Lithuania.

She was quick. She shouted: 'Now!
No time to lose!'—and they grabbed the children,
They ran that path, from the house, by the alders, into the swamp.
The soldiers came out of the birch grove, were surrounding the house,
They had left their truck in the woods, so as not to scare people away.
'They did not think to let the dog loose,
It would have certainly led them to us'.
Thus our country was ending, still generously
Protective with its osiers, mosses, wild rosemaries.
Long trains were moving eastwards towards Asia,
With the laments of those who knew they would not return.

('Far Away', NCP 552)

Not long after that moment of crisis, she met Sergiusz Piasecki, who was a leading commander in the Armia Krajowa (Home Army), whose duties included executing collaborators and monitoring the activities of a group who prepared false documents. At the time he was masquerading under a different name, Makarewicz, and hiding on an estate neighboring Barcie. They became lovers, and when he left for Wilno, she joined him. What might have been a forged marriage certificate between Jadwiga Krystyna Waszkiewicz and Józef Makarewicz, written in Lithuanian, survived the war. In her later letters to Miłosz, Jadwiga remarked that she had not wanted to marry Piasecki and that the marriage was never legalised. In any case, on 17 June 1944, their son, Władysław, was born, and was christened in the cellar of the house in Portowa Street during a Soviet bombardment. In February of the following year, Piasecki, now using the name Jan Tomaszewicz, received permission to leave Wilno and travel to Poland together with his wife and son. Before long, however, he escaped to the West, hidden in a lorry belonging to the UNRRA (United Nations Relief and Rehabilitation Administration), while Jadwiga and her son remained, settling in with her parents in Giżycko. Following her father's death, she took on sole responsibility for her mother's well-being, as well as her son's. In a postcard sent to Miłosz on 29 July 1982, she described how 'there were times when I really learnt what hunger was, true Hamsun-esque hunger, and what it was like not being able to cope, and what shortages were and denial'. In order to make ends meet, she sold jewellery as well as a portrait of Piasecki painted by one of Poland's most celebrated artists, Stanisław Ignacy Witkiewicz. Due to her fear of imprisonment, because of her relationship with an 'enemy' Home Army officer, she disclosed to no-one her wartime experiences, which her son learnt about only after her death. Her granddaughter wrote a book about women in the life and work of Sergiusz Piasecki.

Did she ever hear Miłosz's voice on the radio she bought with her first salary? Did she buy a copy of his *Rescue* (1945)? Of course, she heard about the defection of her former lover, or, as the Polish Communist authorities then termed it, his 'desertion'. And she must have also been aware of the scathing articles about him written by the father of her son. Jadwiga's and Miłosz's correspondence resumed after he won the Nobel Prize and visited Poland. He admitted to her in a letter on 24 October 1981 that 'for many, many years there was not a single day that I did not think about you,' and he planned to meet her in Yugoslavia. The rendezvous did not take place, however, because she suffered a stroke; it is possible that anxiety at the prospective meeting had brought it on. From her letters she comes across as an impressive, intelligent, independent, well-read and ambitious woman, who might well have proved a good life partner for the writer, since she would not have balked at giving her honest opinion about his poems and his work in general. In a card sent in autumn 1987, she wrote:

> I am angry with you and you annoy me with talk of this *delectatio morosa* of yours. It is surely a delusion, something unreal ... There are so many people in the world that read your work and love you, but still you are not satisfied. Besides, you have not yet lived your whole life. You write and you publish and what your work will leave is the power of beauty and wisdom. Keep in good health and happy—those are a must. J. (Jadwiga Tomaszewicz to CM, 22 September 1987)

Jadwiga died on 11 September 1989 in a hospital in Gdańsk. In a letter to Miłosz, one of her relatives, Izabela Lejwoda, wrote, 'She was very brave, she did not complain, she endured her pain in silence'.

Jadwiga Waszkiewicz is now, in poems like those that follow, only a painful presence, and reminder of what might have been:

> If only my early love had come true.
> If only I had been happy walking down Harbor Street
> (Which, anyway, did not lead to a harbor
> But only to wet logs beyond the sawmills).
> Had I been counted among the elders of our city,
> And travelled abroad on an assignment.
> Had we concluded an alliance with Ferrara.
>
> ('A Short Recess', *NCP* 314)

> To see from the window the street you once took going to school.
> (On the wall sharply delineated zones of sun and shadow.)
> Canoeing together on the lakes.
> Romantic outings to islands overgrown with osiers.

Betrothal, and the wedding at St George's.
. . .
Would it were true. But I was blown away,
Beyond oceans and seas. Farewell, lost destiny.
Farewell, city of my sorrow, farewell, farewell.

('In a City', *NCP* 675)

'To the left, to the right'

Your unhappy and silly youth.
Your arrival from the provinces to the city.
Misted-over windowpanes of streetcars,
Restless misery of the crowd.
Your dread when you entered a place too expensive.
But everything was too expensive. Too high.
Those people must have noticed your crude manners,
Your outmoded clothes, and your awkwardness.

Czesław Miłosz, 'Youth' (*NCP* 532)

At the start of the New Year, 1931, Miłosz told Iwaszkiewicz of his frustration at the prospect of being back in harness in a provincial backwater:

It is hard, one always longs to be somewhere else, and as for me, stuck up to my neck in the atmosphere of dead Wilno, I will have to dream of the hustle and bustle of a big city, of the noisy background to quiet, modest experiences; perhaps it is an indication of some malaise, the need for my poor little deadened soul to be fired up. (CM to Iwaszkiewicz, 2 January 1931)

Despite the disastrousness of his first visit to Stawisko, the young man could not stop thinking about the exhilaration of living and working in a major urban centre.

Amongst the subjects students were examined on after the third year in Wilno University was Statistics, a nightmare for the majority of them. Miłosz shared their dread, and, probably with Iwaszkiewicz's encouragement, contemplated a move to Warsaw to continue his studies there. In that way, he would circumvent a number of tricky issues ahead of him, such as a tough exam and amatory complications, and possibly give fresh impetus to his life and career. However, as things panned out later that year, a transfer to Warsaw University became an utter impossibility because of his family's parlous financial situation; his father had recently been made redundant (CM to Iwaszkiewicz, 20 October 1931). Miłosz bowed to the inevitable, and resolved to remain in Wilno, rejecting his mentor's latest generous offer of help:

> Your letter terrified me and put me off moving to Warsaw. You mention an award of some kind which you could set up for me. You must understand that agreeing to something like that is out of the question … My opinion of myself is not so high that I would be comfortable entering into an obligation by accepting a scholarship from a private source. (CM to Iwaszkiewicz, 1 November 1931)

There must have been a sudden turnaround in the situation, because Miłosz withdrew his documents from Stefan Batory University, Wilno, on 11 December, and four days later filed an application to join the Department of Law and Political Studies at Warsaw University.

After only three months, Miłosz's studies in Warsaw were curtailed when he took a break in order to travel to Suwałki to stay with his family. While there, he sent a letter on 30 March 1932 to Władysław Sebyła, the editor of *ZET,* a bi-weekly literary magazine, submitting some of his poems:

> On leaving Warsaw, I bought a copy of *Z* and I liked it so much that I would seriously like to be published in your magazine. It may seem ill-mannered to thrust my poems before you and bother you with them. They won't take up too much of your attention, and despite my innate modesty, I consider my poems as far superior to a whole gamut of work from other, albeit pleasant, pricks, which will probably soon arrive like a deluge in your in-tray. (CM to Sebyła, 30 March 1932)

In April, he wrote to Iwaszkiewicz from Wilno, using as his address the Polish Radio station, which indicated that he was back working in Wilno. The same month, he wrote a letter to the Dean of Warsaw University asking permission to defer his exams. The reasons he gave for his absence from lectures were financial difficulties, which forced him to leave the city, along with health problems. In the autumn, he was summoned to appear before a National Service committee, but had to postpone the meeting because of appendicitis.

It was not possible to determine whether his illness was a coincidence or an excuse to extend his studies. He chose to pass the summer months without getting down to any serious revision, working instead on a translation by Oskar Miłosz of Lithuanian fairy tales. In October, he failed an exam in a subject taught by the 'disreputable', 'notorious' Professor Jarra, who 'forced students to memorise his handbook on the theory of law . . . [and] failed students who responded "in their own words'" (CM in Venclova 114). This was a rare occasion when Miłosz's excellent memory let him down, and he was obliged to leave Warsaw University.

How could this happen when he coped perfectly well at university in Wilno? It seems that he felt intimidated and insecure in the bigger, unfamiliar city, studying alongside a crowd of self-assured law students, who in most cases came from privileged backgrounds. At a much later date, he admitted to having succumbed to

> a period of depression. That year in Warsaw was a shameful period in my life. Failing exams seemed such a tragedy and terrible humiliation that I never alluded to it in my books, although it was not a disgrace that one cannot overcome *(laughter)*. Now I can talk calmly about that year in Warsaw. I was simply at a very low point, utterly penniless, incredibly poor. (*Podróżny świata* 22)

This claim perhaps should be taken with a pinch of salt. He had sufficient funds to rent a room with an old school friend for a few months, and then to stay in a dormitory. The truth was that he much preferred socialising in circles similar to those in Wilno—left-wing, literary and partly Jewish. While Miłosz had not stayed long enough in Warsaw to take an active part in its literary and political life, the time was not totally wasted.

> To the left, to the right,
> a little up and a little down,
> politics is a game,
> and poetry half the life.
> Let Thursdays applaud me
> Michalski is giving me a sign,
> to the left, to the right
> How else can we survive?

These were the words of a song in a Wilno students' Christmas pantomime from 1933. The Thursdays referred to meetings of the Intellectuals' Club, while the (Stanisław) Michalski mentioned in the next line was the director of the National Culture Fund, an institution which awarded scholarships to artists and scientists. Miłosz had qualms about having double standards for, on the one hand, associating with leftist groups, and, on the other, seeking funds from an institution dedicated to promoting national culture. The individual who enabled him to navigate these choppy waters and stay on course was Mieczysław Kotarbiński, a professor in the Academy of Fine Arts:

To his support I was indebted for all my scholarships—including the scholarship to Paris—my contacts in artistic-academic circles, and my room and board in their home whenever I came to Warsaw. That he had taken a liking to me when we met in the country at my relative's home was not strange, because he helped many young people using his personal influence with the stubborn and somewhat eccentric director of the Foundation for National Culture; that director, though a Rightist conservative, had succumbed to the charm of the freethinking and liberal Kotarbiński clan. (*NR* 196)

In 1943 this kindly, 'radiant' man was 'incarcerated in Pawiak prison and executed' (*ABC* 167) by the Gestapo. A year later, 'almost everything he painted' was 'burned up along with the city' (*NR* 196).

Journeying between Warsaw, Suwałki and Wilno in 1932, Miłosz avoided being conscripted into a then-militarized country. On 30 May he was identified as Category A by a recruitment committee in Suwałki and earmarked to join the infantry or cavalry. In the confusion caused by his departure from Warsaw University, the conscription letter went to his address in Warsaw. There the police received confirmation from neighbours that no-one called Miłosz lived at that address. By opting to resume his studies at Wilno University, he was able to defer joining up until after graduation. When, in 1934, he received a summons to join the unit, he appealed to the Ministry of Military Affairs for a further postponement. The reason he cited was that he had a scholarship abroad, in Paris, and so the matter was temporarily shelved. On his return, however, he learnt that the army was oversubscribed, due to a large influx of recruits younger than him, which resulted in his being relegated to the reserves.

He suspected that his known leftist sympathies may have been a factor in that decision. As a result, instead of being drafted into regular service, he spent a few days carrying out supplementary service, digging ditches and clearing paths. Most auxiliary troops given similar minor duties were drawn from the Warsaw and Jewish working classes.

Miłosz went on to take his final exams and on 2 July 1934 received an MA degree in law. At the beginning of the academic year he had forewarned his mentor that "when I finally leave university this year . . . perhaps I could fly off on a trip abroad, but for that I would need Iwaszkiewicz to put in a word for me. Most probably, I will be staying in the country and growing up listening to the boom of drums during national holidays and watching marching fusiliers' (CM to Iwaszkiewicz, 9 September 1933). It was likely that, following Iwaszkiewicz's suggestion, he contacted the Ministry of Foreign Affairs to request an opportunity to undertake consular training. In the meantime he submitted an application for an overseas scholarship, and Kridl wrote a covering letter on his behalf. The response was positive, and Miłosz started making plans for a trip to Paris.

1 Weronika Miłosz (née Kunat) and Aleksander Miłosz, the poet's parents.

2 Aleksander Miłosz *(fifth from left)* on board the ship of the explorer Fridtjöf Nansen *(centre)* in 1913.

3 In Szetejnie: Weronika Miłosz *(left)*, baby Czesław *(centre)* in the nurse's arms.

4 Weronika with the two-year-old Czesław.

5 Czesław, aged two.

6 Stanisława Miłosz, CM's paternal
   grandmother, with Czesław *(left)*
   and his brother, Andrzej *(right).*

7 Józefa Kunat, CM's maternal grandmother,
   with her daughter, Weronika (Miłosz).

8 Czesław at the start of his time at the King Sigismund Augustus Boys' State Gymnasium.

9 Czesław's Aunt Gabriela.

10 Czesław *(back row, far left)* towards the end of his time at the Gymnasium. Father Leopold Chomski is in the front row, third from left.

11 A view of Wilno (Vilnius) from Castle Hill, 1912.

12 Members of PET. Czesław is in the back row, centre.

13 Czesław smoking in the
Café Rudnicki, Wilno.

14 Czesław Miłosz in the 1930s.

15 Oskar Miłosz. © Collections de la Bibliothèque littéraire Jacques Doucet (Chancellerie des Universités de Paris), 2016.

16 Jadwiga Waszkiewicz with Czesław Miłosz on the Barcie estate, on the outskirts of Wilno.

17 Janina (Janka) Cękalska's identity card, 1935.

18 Czesław Miłosz, 1942.

19 A group of Jews being led away by German soldiers during the Warsaw Ghetto Rising, 1943.

20 General Dwight D. Eisenhower surveys Warsaw's Old Town in ruins after the conclusion of the war, 1946.

21 Czesław Miłosz *(standing)* in the Polish embassy, Washington, DC. Janka is seated on the sofa *(second from right)*.

22 Poster for a talk on the 1943 Ghetto Rising, during Miłosz's time as cultural attaché in the Polish consulate, New York, 1946.

23 Czesław Miłosz *(centre)* with Józefa Winiewicz, the Polish Ambassador's wife, and Natalia Modzelewska, the Foreign Minister's wife, in Club Cairo, Washington, DC, 1947.

The Country of the First Emigration
1935–1939

'A certain student in the city of Paris'

Bypassing Rue Descartes
I descended toward the Seine, shy, a traveller,
A young barbarian just come to the capital of the world.

We were many, from Jassy and Koloshvar, Wilno and Bucharest,
Saigon and Marrakesh,
Ashamed to remember the customs of our homes,
About which nobody here should ever be told:

I had left the cloudy provinces behind,
I entered the universal, dazzled and desiring.

Czesław Miłosz, 'Bypassing Rue Descartes' (*NCP* 393)

After his graduation, in the summer of 1934 Miłosz paid visits to his family, relatives and friends. He travelled to Kraków for the first time and found the city enchanting. What he anticipated with great keenness was his trip to Paris at the start of October. After settling in, he updated Iwaszkiewicz with his news, informing him how he was supplementing his stipend by giving lessons in Polish and sending reports to the *Kurier Wileński* (CM to Iwaszkiewicz, 7 November 1934). The additional income enabled him to eat better meals in Russian restaurants.

The academic year he spent in Paris was full of novel experiences. In fresh surroundings he reviewed his position on a number of fronts. Having breathing space enabled him to put into perspective the problems left behind in Wilno, though not entirely: 'Spring 1935 was a time when I could begin to relax. Nevertheless I should add that various complications in my personal life prior to the visit brought on sadness and depression' (Fiut 279).

That autumn Miłosz spent at 11–15 rue Lamandé, in the Batignolles district of the seventeenth arrondissement. His accommodation was in a building that in the nineteenth century had housed a Polish school, among whose former professors was his maternal ancestor, Stanisław Kunat. The school included a dormitory which regularly resounded with the loud noise of a trumpet played by one of the lodgers. It often reeked of smoke, evidence of a sustained attempt to rid the place of bedbugs. Overall, however, there was a convivial atmosphere to the place, enhanced at times by soirées devoted to the consumption of wine. A fellow resident at the school was Roman Maciejewski (1910–1998), a young composer who later wrote *Missa pro defunctis*, *Requiem* and scores for Ingmar Bergman's productions.

At the beginning of 1935, Miłosz found a new place to stay, in the Latin Quarter, a location more befitting an ambitious young writer. This was a pension at 21 rue Valette run by a woman from Martinique, and was close to the Panthéon and the beautiful church of Saint-Étienne du Mont, whose cemetery contains the grave of St Geneviève, the patron of Paris, along with those of Racine, Pascal and Marat. Every morning he entered the Place du Panthéon and encountered the watchful eye of Corneille's statue, the warm stone of the Sorbonne and the Bibliothèque Sainte-Geneviève, which today holds Oskar Miłosz's archive. These locations and the associations they carried left him feeling that he was now living at the heart of European culture. Even after many years living far away in America, he thought of Paris with considerable nostalgia, and wrote to his friend there:

> Send my regards to the Paris streets
> And the fountain in the Luxembourg Gardens,
> Also the Seine, where I can still see to this day
> Buttresses of the cathedral and sleepy boats.

('Central Park', Wiersze II, 50–51)

The boarding house itself resembled one of those familiar from French novels, complete with a miserly landlady, who measured out exact portions of lentil soup to a group of colourful lodgers. Among the guests were Antoni Potocki (1867–1939), the author of a history of early twentieth-century Polish literature, and a young émigré from Russia who looked after him, Wanda Chodasiewicz-Grabowska. Miłosz engaged in many political discussions with her, as they held polar opposite views. She was a Communist and a founder of a Suprematist[1] circle in Smoleńsk. She later became the editor of *L'Art Contemporain*, a Paris-run art magazine, and was a life companion of the painter Fernand Léger.

In February 1935, on the walls of the university buildings, next to the communists' hammer and sickle and the royalists' 'Vive le roi' (often changed by Parisians to 'Vive le roti!'—Long live roast!), more and more often a far-right slogan started to appear—'Aux chiottes les métèques', which meant 'Flush away the shitty foreigners'. When a student strike broke out near Montagne Sainte-Geneviève and crowds began chanting slogans against 'les métèques', Miłosz was reminded of the anti-Semitic disturbances back home in Wilno during November 1931; the difference was that in sweet France protests were carried out in a much calmer atmosphere, without skirmishes and broken windows. 'As a *"métèque"* myself, I was a hunted animal, but despite that, I allowed myself to write an insolent mocking piece about the Parisian racists for the *Kurier Wileński*' (24 February 1935). He made notes about his sociological observations not only during gatherings in cafés, but also at literary evenings in the Café de la Paix and dance cafés frequented by the working class. He drew comparisons between the French and the Polish mentality, noting that having a good time did not necessitate—surprise!, surprise!—heavy drinking and fighting.

On many occasions he visited a sheltered area for unemployed Poles in Levallois-Perret, where another scholarship recipient was working as a clerical assistant. This was Włodzimierz Lewik, a Polish literature specialist, who, in due course, became the editor of the biggest publishing house in post-war Poland, PIW (Państwowy Instytut Wydawniczy). 'It Is Possible to Breathe the Homeland Here' was the sarcastic title of another article Miłosz penned for *Kurier Wileński* on 7 July 1935:

> Sweltering weather, the horrible smell of smoke and petrol, a green coating on the barracks' wall, artificial, paper trees—all repellent. Levallois has changed. When it was autumn and winter here, one got used to the symmetrical, dark hell of garages and factories, gas street lamps, and the yawning patronesses of empty cafés. Now we have summer and the grime of a Parisian sky. Only the wall and the iron gate remain the same, the familiar sign *'Asile polonais'* and the same unshaven faces of the unemployed.

This extract illustrates his technique, juxtaposing the directness of journalistic observation with poetic touches such as the use of metaphors. He proceeds to reveal that he has no delusions regarding the fate of the migrant Polish peasants and labourers, who are hopeless, drunken and filled with animosity towards the French.

He rediscovered within himself the fiery excess of a Red commissar on his return from his perambulations:

The streets that led to it were a sterile hell of industrial civilization, a place of sojourn for souls who were born into degradation and who would die in degradation. The very thought of immortality was an outrage there. In this camp (high fence, narrow gate, like the doors of an armored train) one of my colleagues worked as both manager and clerk, earning the pittance of a salary. (*NR* 176)

Only a few stops away by metro, indifferent to the fate of the degraded, lay another world,

the luxury of the Champs-Elysées. For all I cared, that whole world could have fallen into the chastising fires, and I consoled myself that it certainly would fall. If it had been possible to drag those pomaded females from their limousines, kick them in the bottom and make them crawl on all fours, I could have taken revenge for those in the camp (or maybe for myself under a mask of justice). The setting up of machine guns aimed at the Café de la Paix I also would not have looked upon as an immoral act. (*NR* 176–177)

In *Native Realm* he pointed out that he did not dream about Soviet tanks on Haussmann's boulevards, but rather of a vague 'theocratic communism', like that established by the Jesuits in seventeenth-century Paraguay. His moral indignation echoes throughout 'Ballad of Levallois':

Oh God, have mercy on Levallois,
Look under these chestnut trees poisoned with smoke,
Give a moment of joy to the weak and the drunk,
Oh God, have mercy on Levallois.

All day long they stole and cursed,
Now they lie in their bunks and lick their wounds,
And while the darkness thickens over Paris
They hide their faces in their thieving hands.
Oh God, have mercy on Levallois ...

Darkness. Silence. A bridge hums in the distance.
The wind streams through Cain's trees.
On the void of the earth, on the human tribe
No mercy, no mercy on Levallois.

(*NCP* 25–26)

The ballad was not published until the time of the German occupation of Poland, in an underground edition of his poems that appeared in 1940, as if the author

until then did not want to be accused of poetic politicisation or naivete. It combined humanitarian passion and religious fervour, pointing an accusatory finger
at the Creator for the inequity of the world.

In spring 1935, Miłosz moved again, this time to Hôtel Central Laplace, by
rue Laplace, opposite the École Polytechnique. It was a cheap hotel in a narrow
street from the Middle Ages, mainly inhabited by Polish Jews studying medicine.
In the windows washing hung out to dry, and throughout the building there was
always a strong smell of cooking. 'I study, fry beef steaks and practise swimming the
breast-stroke. But I struggle to write anything, even a letter', he told Iwaszkiewicz,
adding, 'I regret that I allowed other loudmouths to indoctrinate me in my early
youth, but I only wanted things to be better'. On learning of Józef Piłsudski's recent
death, he remarked that despite everything 'it moved me' (CM to Iwaszkiewicz,
27 May 1935).

A neighbour at the hotel, Bolesław Bochwic, who was preparing for his
doctoral exam in chemistry, was fascinated by Miłosz and introduced him to a
large circle of interesting Poles living in Paris. Through his good offices, the poet
met the talented young musician Zygmunt Mycielski, who later composed music
for Miłosz's poems, and also the famous and feted composer, Karol Szymanowski.
He resumed his acquaintance with Roman Maciejewski, who provided Miłosz
with access to a host of major Polish figures from the musical and artistic world.

Another new contact was the Polish poet and co-founder of Skamander,
Jan Lechoń, who occupied the position of cultural attaché at the Polish embassy
in Paris. Although in his youth Miłosz had regarded him as embodying the very
concept of 'poet', in the flesh he exemplified narrow-mindedness and stupidity: 'I
was horrified by his snobbishness, and spotted from the outset the falseness there'
(Fiut 278). Hearing of Miłosz's repeated critical comments about a certain 'poet-
snob', Lechoń developed an obsessive hatred for him, wreaking revenge in the
post-war years by slandering him in his *Diaries* and in private correspondence. In
his New York apartment, he always kept a copy of *Three Winters*, with its fulsome
dedication: 'To Mr Jan Lechoń, as an expression of homage and gratitude for
friendly support' (Janta 272).

Miłosz also gained entry through his uncle into non-Polish artistic circles,
which were often inaccessible to his peers. Certain of these individuals appeared
distinctly exotic: 'I was walking down the Boulevard St Germain with Oskar
when we saw a man walking towards us, dressed in an ancient Greek traditional
cloak with sandals on his bare feet . . . This ancient Greek greeted my cousin
warmly and turned out to be Raymond Duncan, the brother of the ballet dancer,
Isadora' (*ABC* 121). Oskar Miłosz remembered Isadora as a lover of the Russian
poet Yesenin, a man whom later generations might well have seen as a poetic
James Dean, but who to Oskar was a repulsive barbarian.

Gradually, young Miłosz became immersed in this thick mélange of European culture, becoming acquainted with a Belgian mystic poet, Jean de Boschère, and the highly cosmopolitan Edouardo Roditi, who moved in the same circles as T. S. Eliot, James Joyce and André Breton. Roditi was a Sephardic Jew, a poet and a translator; he later became Miłosz's friend in Berkeley, and translated his work into English. Miłosz became acquainted with Carlos Larronde, a French poet with leftist views who was the creator and director of the Théâtre Idéaliste, where his uncle's play *Méphiboseth* was staged.

Another European artist Miłosz came across was a friend of Iwaszkiewicz's, Günther Eten, a young German writer and literature researcher, who believed in the possibility that Slavs and Germans might complement one another. In the first half of the 1930s it was still not clear how the rising political tension might be calmed, and artists from different cultural backgrounds often felt obliged to seek out common intellectual and spiritual terrain. However, from early on, Miłosz was conscious that this 'acquaintance with Günther disturbed me. In spite of the mutual distrust between us, there was a disquieting affinity. Günther, a young Nazi, used to recite his poems to me. They celebrated the age of chivalry, sacrifices and blood, and they had the sound of clanking swords' (*NR* 177). What they had in common was a scepticism about the democratic order of things and a conviction about the weakness of those who accepted its humanistic axioms.

Minutes away from the Piscine Pontoise where Miłosz regularly went swimming was the Maison de la Mutualité, which between 21 and 25 June 1935 served as the venue for the International Congress for the Defence of Culture in Paris. The previous month's French municipal elections had seen 'a marked swing to the Left' (Gilbert 71), paving the way for the election victory of the Popular Front—an alliance of Socialists, Radical Socialists and Communists—the following year.

Miłosz decided that he really ought to attend this 'convention of Anti-Fascists', having already 'written poems announcing Germany as the fuse of tomorrow's historical bomb' (*NR* 178). To his dismay, shortly before the congress began, Günther Eten announced his intention to come too, and they ended up sitting together in the gallery of the hall, listening as one distinguished international speaker after another—Aldous Huxley, André Gide, André Malraux, Louis Aragon, Isaac Babel, Ilya Ehrenburg, Boris Pasternak—denounced the Nazi regime. To Miłosz it was very obvious what the ulterior motives of the Soviet Union were in allowing some of their foremost writers to offer up 'lofty sentences about freedom, peace and respect for man' (*NR* 178) at the very time Stalin's secret police had been given the green light by their master 'to eliminate every trace of political opposition or potential opposition' (Gilbert 63). Their aim in allying themselves with the 'defence of culture', supposedly under threat *solely* from fascism, was to encourage western European leftist parties and organisations to join their ranks under the leadership of the Comintern.

In a report for a Wilno periodical, Miłosz remarked acerbically that 'the congress was a lot of smoke, resolutions, applause, dazzling bursts of charisma from time to time, and depressing heat. For those who believed salvation lay neither in communism nor in any other form of totalitarianism . . . it provided yet another moment of bitter thought' (*Bunt Młodych* [The Revolt of the Young], 20 July 1935). Many of the speeches defending humanitarian values emanating from André Gide and Aldous Huxley, and from the Soviet writers, sounded banal, weak and false. In the hall, however, delegates were swept up 'in a transport of pacifist enthusiasm'. Sitting alongside him, his German companion, Günther,

> hid an ugly leer behind his hand. His gesture reminded me of those other meetings I had attended in Poland with my Marxist colleagues and our scoffing at the speakers' old-maidish phraseology. Here, too, the toothless whinings, the smoke screen of 'declarations' and 'resolutions' aroused my anger and drove me into solidarity with Günther. In the final analysis, Günther's anger was the same—anger at weakness adorned with words. He preferred what he thought was more honest: naked violence. (*NR* 178)

The months in Paris kept bringing intimations of the catastrophe to come. Writing to Miłosz in 1964, a friend from Wilno recalled

> your letters which came from Paris . . . of course, we read them aloud together, Dorek, Jerzy and me. In one of those addressed to me, Dorek nearly choked reading one sentence: 'and despite all this metaphysics', you wrote, 'a man's penis still gets big, and stays that way'. We came to the conclusion that you had mixed up addresses, because a letter to Zagórski was almost idyllic. (Nika Kłosowska to CM, 9 September 1964)

Delightful girls sauntered down the Boulevard Saint-Michel. 'Where are they now, the seventy-year-old women?' (*Rok myśliwego* 315), he mused in old age. The twenty-something poet possessed by carnal demons was not as shy as he had been in Prague a few years earlier. Walking through the Latin Quarter, did he meet anyone who could satisfy his sensuous hunger? In an unfinished essay, he relived 'a memory of my foolishness and miseries . . . by a café stands a bench facing the Luxembourg Gardens. Since then hundreds of thousands of couples have sat on it, where she and I kissed. To me she was not one of those anonymous ones' ('It is a matter of our present', Beinecke Library Archive).

The Luxembourg Gardens feature again in a poem from 1952:

Look,
Here, in this garden I held her hand,
Her body was like a swallow's body
Fluttering in my palm. Death.
And I don't even know whether it could be said,
That she was taken away into darkness by Charon's boat,
Because of barbed wire, abomination, blood.

('Faust Warszawski'/'A Warsaw Faust', *Wiersze* II, 137)

Traces are faint like birds' footprints scattered in the snow, or a sketch on frosted glass. It may be that the shadow of a Jewish girl occupies these lines, one who met her end in a concentration camp. A notebook from 1934 captures both the flippancy and the fatalism with which he approached his many sexual encounters: 'Whom should I fuck, I don't care / there will be grief left afterwards anyway' ('Oh, how sad love-games are', Beinecke Library Archive).

The method he employed to 'subdue his inner chaos' (*NR* 177) was a fixed routine which he retained until the end of his life. Living at Hôtel Central Laplace, he would regularly go swimming, walk along rue Cujas, Boulevard Saint-Michel and the Luxembourg Gardens to the Alliance Française on Boulevard Raspail. It was there that he perfected his French, wrote essays, took exams, attended lectures in Thomist philosophy, and was finally awarded *un diplôme Supérieur d'études françaises modernes.*

Occasionally he went to concerts, although music never meant much to him. In *Native Realm* he recorded some of his impressions of concert evenings with Roman Maciejewski:

> I only pretended that I listened to music. At the Châtelet Theater, my attention was completely absorbed by the stage, which I looked down upon from my seat in the top row as into a well. Down there at the bottom a strange ritual was being enacted, and sound had value only insofar as it set two fields of bows in motion, like wheat bent in the wind. (*NR* 180)

Theatre definitely held more meaning for him, although his scholarship funds did not stretch to frequent visits. However, he also comments on how he easily became 'bored by the gestures and talk enclosed in a three-sided box of the stage. I liked various kinds of masques and interludes, things on the borderline between theater and ballet' (*NR* 180).

In Paris, Miłosz saw at least one play which continued to resonate in his memory. Georges Pitoëff, a Russian actor and the director of Théâtre des Mathurins, put on a performance of a play by Pirandello entitled *Ce soir on im-*

provise (Tonight We Improvise). In it, Ludmila Pitoëff, one of the greatest actresses of her day,

> changed from a young girl into an old woman within a quarter of an
> hour. She sat on her chair in front of the footlights, and her companions,
> the goddesses of time, applied wrinkles to her face, erased rouge from
> her lips, and scattered grey in her hair. Never before had the horror and
> pity of tragedy so deeply penetrated to me. My own regular subject of
> contemplation was the same: the devastating process of change—in individuals, in countries and in systems. Perhaps all poetry is simply this.
> (*NR* 180)

What is art if not an attempt to gainsay this destruction, the erasure of beauty by time? At the beginning of 1935 Miłosz attended an exhibition at the Louvre devoted to *'les peintres de la réalité'*, which illustrated the influence of Caravaggio and Dutch painters on seventeenth-century French artists. The phrase 'a painter of reality' might be applied to Miłosz's own work, which constantly endeavours to capture and salvage as much as possible of the visible world.

After his return to Wilno in December 1935, Miłosz wrote a review of two exhibitions, one in Paris and the other in Brussels. The most disturbing of all the pictures he saw was Brueghel's *The Fall of Icarus,* which W. H. Auden famously invokes in one of his greatest poems, 'Musée des Beaux Arts' (*Collected Shorter Poems* 123), and which, decades later, William Carlos Williams also turned his attention to.[2] The works which particularly spoke to his imagination were the Dutch masters' marine pictures, which he described as conveying a 'sobering and clear mysticism ... a realism transfigured by a totally free imagination' (*Pion,* 21 December 1935). For two reasons he drew attention to a canvas in which a young, lofty artist rises above the waters with the help of birds' wings. He identified in it a possible lesson in self-awareness he might absorb, while at the same time he attempted to view it from a religious perspective, which was untarnished by political considerations or primitive mystic associations. For him, as for Oskar Miłosz, mysticism was by no means antithetical to realism.

After the war, in 1946, Miłosz gave an interview in which he affirmed that 'as a poet I owe as much to paintings as to literature'. He went on to explain that

> the texture of paintings, colour, light, drawing, expresses a certain attitude to human reality, something which is intangible in poetry; ... a
> subject and its treatment is very meaningful and specific to a painter,
> symptomatic of his spiritual and artistic essence ... my favorite painters
> are Manet and Degas, because they are, for me, deeply human. In their
> pictures, one feels their desire to carry out a study of the human body

against a moral and contemporary background, and this expresses something very human, and encompasses a certain specific, ironic attitude to
the physiological rhythm of life … Degas' way of seeing things is particularly close to me … His dancers and ladies ironing clothes say so much
about the artist's attitude to humankind—an attitude containing an
infinite irony and pity at the same time, objectivity and subjectivity.
(Rzepińska, *Przegląd Artystyczny*)

That shoulder. An erotic thing submerged in duration.
Her hands are entangled in undone plaits of red hair
So dense that, combed, it pulls the head down,
A thigh, and under it the foot of another leg.
For she is sitting, her bent knees open,
And the movement of her arm reveals the shape of a breast.
. . .

Our human communion has a bitter taste
Because of the familiarity of touch, of avid lips,
The shape of loins, and talk of an immortal soul.
It flows and recedes. A wave, a sighing of surf.
And only a red mane flickered in the abyss.

('Pastels by Degas', *NCP* 723)

St Thomas Aquinas's ideas, discussed during morning classes delivered by Father
Lallemant at the Institute Catholique, conjoined perfectly with a sacred vision of
the world, which was how Miłosz responded to canvases of some old masters. He
began to draw from Thomism the philosophical underpinning of his essays about
art, which were about something more than evaluating creativity; his attentiveness to art was absolutely central to the battle against nothingness.

It is worth acquiring a smattering of Thomism, even superficially. It helps
one grasp what a joyous acceptance of the world could be like—and what
Bach or Mozart, for example, drew on for support. In the building trade,
there is a procedure, which involves injecting cement into the ground, if it
is sandy, to strengthen the foundations. St Thomas's system is this cement. ('Niedziela w Brunnen', *Kultura:* 3, 1954)

During this selfsame period, Miłosz wrote a very significant letter to Iwaszkiewicz:

So many things get discovered, when blindness, which I was conscious
of, stops … And Marxism and this reverence for all that can be measured on the outside … the greatness of life is immeasurable, and it is

right to give thanks to the hand that guides us. There are times when I am unhappy, periods of darkness, but the sense of it still is there, a true sense. I do not begin to like the French, or admire them—but what they have been given, which they are not conscious of, for me becomes a force . . . apart from lectures, museums and books, there is something at work inside me, which, as always, is not something one owns, but rather is something given. (CM to Iwaszkiewicz, 19 December 1934)

Indeed, work was continuing apace. Miłosz kept a notebook, which he used in Paris, and which makes it possible to dip into his literary labours of the time. There are sketches of unfinished works, along with words from folk songs, quotations from the Bible and notes probably taken at Father Lallemant's lectures, which are juxtaposed with the beginning of a story inspired by life on the Krasnogruda estate. There were consecutive versions of poems, almost certainly reflecting his preparation for the volume that became *Three Winters*.

By looking through the notebook, the letters to Iwaszkiewicz and later autobiographical memoirs, it is possible to discern that the months spent in Paris were a time of unremitting activity, which consisted of intensive, challenging reading and excursions to important places. Above all, what one detects in the notebook are fundamental changes within. The anxiety and guilt which emanated from his relationship with Jadwiga Waszkiewicz abated to a certain extent, and it was there that he decided definitely to end it. Gradually, the uncertainties that plagued him left, and he became a poet whose aims and values were more fully defined and clarified. The provincial boy began to feel more anchored in the Western world, sought out a place for himself there and developed new acquaintances, many of whom displayed their worth when Miłosz returned to Paris after the war. That he was gaining in confidence is visible from his later articles on French subjects. A city full of history, splendour, injustice and beauty, Paris helped him shed many of his complexes and to mature and widen his horizons. His uncle's insights and often sceptical outlook prevented him from conforming to current literary fads. The contrast between Wilno, held back in time, and Paris, with its eyes turned towards modernity, was extremely invigorating for him:

> Their big names, which Eastern Europe also uttered with a pious sigh, Oskar Miłosz dismissed with one snap of his fingers, and I see now that he was correct. The whole Eastern European attitude towards 'centers of culture' is false; it comes from timidity. They imitate instead of opposing; they reflect instead of being themselves. Through this very existence, my relative worked a cure in me, and fortified my contempt for the shrines of the vanguard back home, where ears strained to catch the latest novelties from Paris. (*NR* 181)

'The whole cosmos revolves within us'

Conversations with his Parisian uncle brought more to Miłosz's life than just a critical distance towards his youthful preoccupation with keeping up with the times and the latest news. Many years later he likened meeting Oskar Miłosz to the situation of a man who 'found treasure in a field and kept it buried in a pot, because the riches he had come upon could not be turned into something useful' (*Ulro* 86).

A recipient of a government grant ought to have considered it polite to show his face from time to time at the Polish Embassy, but Miłosz's visits were infrequent because to him the atmosphere there seemed pompous and false. He much preferred the Lithuanian Embassy in the Hôtel Fournier at 14 Place Malesherbes, which he later refrained from mentioning, as no diplomatic relations existed between Poland and Lithuania, and his benefactors in Warsaw might have taken a dim view of his socialising with the enemy. He met a number of Lithuanian dignitaries in the embassy while visiting his uncle in his office.

Another respect in which Miłosz experienced good fortune was gaining access to stories from his uncle, who often frequented cafés and salons where many of the literary colossi of the late nineteenth and early twentieth centuries used to visit, including Jules Laforgue, Alfred Jarry and Alain-Fournier, author of the brilliant novel *Le Grand Meaulnes,* not to mention Ezra Pound, T. S. Eliot and James Joyce. Around 1895 Oskar had engaged in an argument with Jean Moréas and Oscar Wilde about Byron, Shelley and what constituted 'pure poetry'. From time to time, Miłosz must have pinched himself, finding it hard to believe that here he was in Paris passing time with such a widely known, respected relative, and taking part in long discussions about matters that meant so much to him. Oskar was deeply convinced about the decadence of the epoch he lived in, which seemed unlikely to produce a truly great poet. Only exceptional interpreters of the collective imagination, intermediaries between men and God, like Homer, Dante, Goethe and Shakespeare, deserved to be called *real* poets. His anti-modernist stance originated in his belief that hierarchy, mystery and metaphysical sensitivity were fundamental to great art, whose function it was to enrich the human spirit and mind. Art had meaning when it reached back to its roots in religion, and turned its back on a solely materialistic vision of the world. Baudelaire's and Mallarmé's poetry seemed to him limited to the emotions of a single individual, and overly concerned with aesthetic experiments. Modernist dogma at this period eschewed religion, but also philosophy, science, politics and what Oskar termed 'pure poetry', with the result that contemporary poets were detached from 'the big human family'. Poets these days were mediocre, and 'we all belong to that category without exception, and so do not even bother to read each other's work' (Oskar Miłosz, 'Kilka słów o poezji'/'A Few Words on Poetry', 35).

These opinions were clearly in accord with the intuitions of the budding young poet from Wilno and helped shape his future artistic direction. In a later fight 'against incomprehensible poetry', in recommending 'useful books' to readers, and mainly in his own work, Miłosz sought a model of poetry which would enable him to escape the trap of subjectivism, and place poetry anew at the centre of the human world, restoring its long-forgotten dignity. Following the huge catastrophe that would shortly envelop the world, Oskar Miłosz was far more optimistic about the new age than his protégé.

This new age would bring a renaissance of spirituality and produce 'a great, inspiring poet, a modern Homer, Shakespeare or Dante, initiated through the renunciation of the paltry, often empty and always narrow ego, reaching into the most profound truths of the masses who were more than ever alive, receptive, but tortured' ('Kilka słów o poezji', 30). This hope could also be discerned in the post-war enthusiasm about the gradual creation of a new society in Poland, where books of poetry would be sold out within hours. Conversations with Oskar Miłosz generated or reinforced in his nephew a pre-existing conviction about the lofty significance of the poetic calling, but also, surprisingly, sharpened the younger man's ideas about Marxism's growing power and validity:

> Marxists touched the most essential problems of our century, which is why one should not bypass their theories with indifference. One should not, however, trust them too much, for often they draw the wrong conclusions from the correct premises, always yielding to the pressure of their own doctrines and bending the facts to them. (*The Witness of Poetry* 35)

The young poet, aware that he delved into the most burning issues of the time, had no means, nor anyone with whom to share these insights. He considered himself to be an initiate, but, after his return to Wilno, was forced to adopt a mask; if he had not done so, his friends would simply have thought that he had lost his mind. Oskar Miłosz had resigned from the pursuit of literary laurels, yet had the fervour of a prophet or evangelising disciple, having left everything to follow God's call. The younger Miłosz, whose achievements as a writer were far superior, would not go to that extreme; he always retained a measure of reserve towards his uncle's convictions. Ultimately, Czesław Miłosz was too much a child of his own epoch to accept that it was completely doomed. So, 'Worldly and sinful, I could only go forward with my own time, working in, at the most, one or two strands of a promise that something more was to come' (*NR* 184).

Towards the end of his life, Miłosz wrote a homage to his uncle in the poem 'Czeladnik' (An Apprentice):

The biography of this man is, in my opinion, as important
As the lives of saints and prophets are,
For it goes well beyond merely literary interest.

(SS 68)

Oskar Władysław Miłosz was born in 1877 on the Czereja estate, near Witebsk. His father, Władysław, was one of the greatest eccentrics of his epoch. He was an impulsive libertine who flew in a balloon, boasted about owning a carriage pulled by tame bears, kidnapped a nun from a Paris convent, and towards the end of his life suffered from paranoia, which caused him to sit for days on end with an axe on his lap waiting for his enemies. He fell in love with Miriam Rosenthal, the young daughter of a teacher of Hebrew, and carried her away to Czereja, where she presented him with one son. Oskar's parents travelled widely, leaving their sensitive, lonely boy behind. Starved of affection, he would wander round the estate's vast park, feeling an acute sense of exclusion and inferiority. Happily, his apprentice's childhood was different, and contained an idyllic spell, though Czesław was obliged to seek compensation in dreams and art for its darker moments. Oskar was Lithuanian by choice, but nevertheless like Czesław felt an outsider, and rejected the normative political positions of their social class. Tensions within Oskar were intensified by his half-Jewish parentage, while in Czesław they sprang from a superiority complex and exaggerated sensitivity. His uncle's dismissive attitude towards the Polish nobility enhanced the young man's propensity for social transgression. Oskar famously advised him, 'Remember, in Europe there is nothing more stupid or more brutal in its petty hatreds than the Polish gentry' (*NR* 28).

At the age of eleven, Oskar was sent to the prestigious Lycée Janson-de-Sailly in Paris and then continued his education at L'École du Louvre and L'École des Langues Orientales, where he read Hebrew texts and studied ancient Egypt and Assyria. He never returned to Poland, but sold his estate there and bought shares in the tsar's investment schemes, which were confiscated in 1917 when the revolution began. Until then he enjoyed a very comfortable life, travelling extensively round Europe and North Africa, and writing decadent poems, tinged with despair and melancholy. His verses revealed a sensuous, impulsive, but unhappy predisposition, and a hatred for his Hebrew heritage as well as for the 'Nazarene'. Often they also contained outbursts of mockery about the absurdity of existence.

On 1 January 1901, in a calculated gesture, and with a cigarette in his mouth, Oskar shot himself in the heart. The surgeon who was summoned refused to operate, thinking that the patient would very shortly die, but, strangely, against his own volition or in obedience to some higher force, Oskar survived. In his later writings, he recalled observing, through half-closed eyes, layers of dust on surfaces within the hospital, part of a world he no longer wished to see.

On the night of 14–15 December 1914, according to his account, a 'spiritual light' appeared before him, a mystic encounter which could be compared to Blaise Pascal's famous vision. Oskar interpreted this experience as a sign of his appointment as a prophet, as God's servant or, more precisely, a successor to Emanuel Swedenborg, and a founder of the Sixth Church.

During the First World War Oskar worked in an administrative capacity at Maison de la Presse, beside the Quai d'Orsay. He supported the Lithuanian struggle for independence, and joined the ranks of the Lithuanian delegation in the League of Nations, which affirmed their rights to the capital, Wilno. His diplomatic service quickened his will to serve and fostered a love for humanity, thereby initiating the great spiritual turning point in his life.

Did his nephew inform him about his own suicide attempt? And how did the young man react to his uncle's assertions about the forthcoming Apocalypse, how in the late 1930s a war would break out which would bring destruction to Russia and England by fire and water, and to America through fire. In 1944 a *conflagration universelle* would occur, he affirmed, bringing an end to reality. In due course, after years of contemplation and the dropping of the first atom bombs on Hiroshima and Nagasaki, Czesław felt that the prophecies were coming true, and placed his uncle next to Swedenborg, Blake and Mickiewicz as a member of a constellation of artists and mystics. Each of them rebelled against the post-Renaissance demythologisation of the world, and mankind's total submission to the forces of biology and physics.

In the final chapter of Oskar Miłosz's life, he returned to his exegesis of the Apocalypse to come. Earlier he had published two lengthy metaphysical poems, *Ars Magna* (1924) and *Les Arcanes* (1927), which he presented to his nephew in 1931. Czesław read them a few times, tried to understand them, and, albeit with a certain reluctance, admitted many years later that they were a decisive factor in his whole development; the constant questioning they provoked affected the direction he took. Oskar Miłosz preceded Einstein's thinking, due to his conviction about the falsity of Newton's concept, and because of his belief in the fundamental unity of matter, time and space, and the concurrent existence of past, present and future. Through blood, the living cosmic matter, we partake in the universal Movement; 'the whole cosmos revolves within us' (*Storge* 52), he declared. This is the basic spiritual principle of the world, and it is in the blood that our ancient memories are retained, traces of our experience and participation in a higher reality before the Fall and the fatal parting that caused.

According to Oskar Miłosz, the central element in the Movement, the *Axis mundi,* was love and eroticism; lust was merely a step on the path towards transcendence. Human love could be so powerful, said Miguel Mañara,[3] that an individual being talking to God face to face would be enough to scare the angels. In another lyrical poem, one of Oskar's characters experiences an absolute love in his relationship with a woman, yet in the end abandons her, because 'a human being is just a medium in great adoration. A true love yearns for reality; but there is no reality apart from God' ('The Initiation into Love', 164).

> I read *Miguel Mañara* in Bronisława Ostrowska's translation
> At the age of fourteen. It had to be so.
> I was spellbound by the beauty of Girolama. Which did me no good,
> Since it encouraged my search for a perfect love,
> That romantic mirroring of souls
> That proves to be a safe venture for very few people.
>
> I see, in this absolutizing of love
> The fruit of misogyny,
> The habit of opposing an ideal woman to real ones.
>
> ('Apprentice', *SS* 76, 78)

This poem mirrors something Miłosz confessed, with a surprising openness, to Jadwiga Waszkiewicz, an indirect victim of Oskar Miłosz's view of love: 'He was instrumental in my achievements in literature, and let's be frank, in spoiling my life by filling me with exaggerated spiritual yearnings' (CM to Jadwiga Tomaszewicz, 18 August 1982). In Miłosz's soul, a bitter mixture formed, a blend of intense sensuousness and unhappy romantic idealisation, resulting in superficial, almost casual, uncommitted relationships, which 'failed' because they could not fulfil an impossible ideal.

His uncle's teaching would continue to have an impact on Miłosz throughout his life. In 'Father Ch., Many Years Later', he depicts the spiritual journey he undertook, a route marked by uncertainty, constant temptation, and, most of all, a seeking after God in the earthly, the tangible, the corporeal:

> And yet I could not distinguish Him from the rhythm of my blood
> And felt false reaching beyond it in my prayer.
>
> I was not a spiritual man but flesh-enraptured,
> Called to celebrate Dionysian dances.
>
> And disobedient, curious, on the first step to Hell,
> Easily enticed by the newest idea.

Hearing all around me: it is good to experience,
It is good to feel, be bold, free yourself from guilt.

Wanting to absorb everything, comprehend everything,
And darkness proved to be forebearing toward me.

(NCP 436–437)

The road from revolutionary fire to a mystic hunger for God proved very short, as if the same stormy energy had found a fresh outlet; it left the converted sinner with a murky, unstable faith. From the mid-1930s a religious perspective began to permeate his work, enabling him to transcend his earlier anti-clerical and anti-bourgeois prejudices. What is more, he became—at times overtly, at others covertly—a defender of belief in the existence of a higher order, in the hope that the world we know is not the only one, that billions of unique human lives do not simply sink into the dark waters of nothingness, that their immortal elements dwell on the other side of time, waiting for an ultimate return. He realised, thanks to his uncle, that it was possible to be a Catholic, without succumbing to superficial ritual or to the characteristic Polish national trait—doggedness.

Oskar Miłosz's belief in the future rebirth of humanity remained a source of hope pervading his pupil's poems, a light which shone through *A Treatise on Poetry*, bearing 'a gift, more durable than Nature is, or Death' (*NCP* 130). The older writer died on 2 March 1939, lucky, unlike his apprentice, not to have lived to see his prophesies fulfilled:

I read 'The Letter to Storge' like a revelation,
Learning that time and space had a beginning,
That they appeared in a flash, together with so-called matter,
Just as medieval scholars from Oxford to Chartres had guessed,
Through a *transmutatio* of divine light into light merely physical.

(SS 83)

'On black meadows'

But I,
Body and soul, am like a line,

That rings. What is this thing that vibrates inside me,
Oh, what is that, that vibrates and groans inside me
Like lines on a winch on boats that are sailing away?

Oskar Miłosz, 'H'.

The Parisian months ought to be described from yet another perspective, and not through words, but in camera images, capturing hundreds of pictures put together in a kaleidoscopic combination. These might comprise a statue in the Luxembourg Gardens, the wind rippling the waters of a lake in Poland, the wing of a bird darkened by smoke—a changeable, unclear vision, although not accidental or chaotic. This is the way they appeared in the mind of a man, half conscious, as he wandered the Tuileries Gardens:

> I had such an extreme receptivity to external stimuli that every detail engraved itself in my memory with all its color and solidity; at the same time, like a lunatic, I was a passive instrument of another power that operated from somewhere inside, that was at once me and not me. There was nothing to do but submit. It transformed all my experiences into magic spells that were much too strong to be broken by putting them on paper. I wrote little, but I passed whole weeks in the power of one rhythmic phrase, which did not really leave much room for conscious aims—either good or evil. I acted like a medium at a spiritualist séance. (*NR* 179)

Never before and never again did he experience anything comparable. The way he composed his poems was by a slow process of writing stanzas, which were added—one or two lines at a time—over the course of several days, creating layers of consciousness. At the time when poems 'almost surrealistic in technique' were written, such as 'The Gates of the Arsenal' (*NCP* 10), he used to walk 'swollen as if at bursting point, repeating one line day after day, unable to progress any further, because [what he had in mind] was . . . so impossible to capture. The pressure was such, that it . . . almost choked him' (*Podróżny świata* 15), until the whole dense matter of emotions, images, rhythmic phrases drawn up from deep inside his soul poured onto paper, setting like lava.

He found exposing his deepest emotional experiences almost shameful. He was probably referring to the sexual directness in 'Hymn', when he mentions how 'I have just written a substantial piece, but would not like to publish it in *Pion,* but perhaps rather straight away in French in *Cahiers du Sud* or in another magazine, because I feel uneasy placing it in a Polish journal' (CM to Iwaszkiewicz, 19 December 1934). Despite his reservations, the poem appeared in *Pion* in January 1935.

Not all the poems in *Trzy Zimy* (Three Winters), his second book, were composed during his stay in Paris. Among pieces in the collection were some written in the spring of 1934, including 'The Song', and others immediately after his return, such as 'A Statue of a Couple'. It was the period of contact with Oskar and the incredible artistic pressure that Czesław was under that lent uniqueness to the collection, which laid the foundations for so much of his future work. Readers of *Three Winters* at first experienced a degree of confusion, sensing that they understood each of its polyphonic fragments, yet missed the overall drift of the volume, getting lost in the multiplicity of images and allusions. In 'The Gates of the Arsenal', robbed of her beautiful body, and now a mere 'handful of gathered ash', a dead woman moves through the 'lunar gardens, dominions of forlorn dreams' (*NCP* 11). The ageing heroine of 'Dawns' looks with horror at her image in a mirror, evoking a pity and tenderness so strong that it becomes one of the most moving invocations in the collection:

> Not enough. One life is not enough.
> I'd like to live twice on this sad planet,
> In lonely cities, in starved villages,
> To look at all evil, at the decay of bodies,
> And probe the laws to which the time was subject,
> Time that howled above us like a wind.
>
> ('Dawns', *NCP* 16)

In *Three Winters* things in this world are both present and constantly passing away; they disappear in the void, or reappear in another time. Ryszard Przybylski was perhaps right when he came up with this insightful summary: 'In Miłosz's early poetry iciness reigns ... The way frost freezes a stream of water, eternity stops and solidifies a stream of moments. Frost does not destroy water, and eternity does not destroy time or existence. It only changes their state. It halts a flowing stream in eternal immobility' ('O młodszym bracie', 88). People whose bodies turn cold are, after all, 'short lived'. In the vicinity of the visionary the living are fewer than the shadows of the dead, who are awaiting the next generation. Reading 'Elegy', we touch on what the writer himself would subsequently consider the core of his poetry: 'the mystery of death, that is, the possibility or not of mingling among innumerable crowds of bygone beings and gone generations' ('Nad Wigrami', *Kultura*: 10, 1984).

Stretches of time merge together; the joyless city dawn begins, as it does in Philip Larkin's poems, and, a few pages later, the world reawakens after its seeming end, everything having reached completion, passed. The concluding poem of the collection is 'To Father Ch.', in which a young man proffers an apology to a cleric who had seemed possessed, who detested the human senses and wanted to rid the contemporary world of the sulphurous stench of hell. Having tasted 'the forbidden fruit', the speaker now rejects 'the nothingness of alluring forms' (*Wiersze* I, 50).

What primarily pains the speaker in these poems? Time, which destroys us and smothers us in nothingness? Is the ever-present consciousness of sin so strong that, when experiencing *delectatio morosa,* condemnation is what is sought? He might repeat in a hot whisper St Paul's confession:

> I am carnal, sold to the slavery of sin. But I do not understand what I do, because I don't do what I am willing to do, but what I abhor—I do exactly that because the man within me likes things according to God's Law. In my body, I notice a different law, in conflict with my mind, which takes me into captivity, into submission to the law of sin living in my body. Poor me! Who could free me from the body, which leads to death? (Romans 7:14–24)

It is impossible to rid ourselves of the thoughts of the deep contamination within us, the stigma like that borne by Hanno Buddenbrook in Thomas Mann's novel, who himself 'became an artist, which was a stain on his family' (*Podróżny świata* 21), but also memories of more tangible guilt. After 'A Statue of a Couple', a memorial to lost love, comes 'Obłoki' (Clouds), a wonderful poem, full of regret and self-loathing, whose original title was 'Awakening', as if the hero had emerged from a stifling dream, and examined himself and his actions with a pitilessly critical eye.

Amongst Miłosz's reflections from the 1980s are these from his interview with Renata Gorczyńska:

> Isolation from people is important. Naturally, it is articulated in the whole collection [*Three Winters*], which illustrates the personal drama which I was undergoing at the time. I think that I was headed in the direction of overcoming my isolation as I evolved, although it took me decades. I am much warmer in my poetry now and more at ease in interpersonal contacts. (*Podróżny świata* 14)

An excessive preoccupation with the self and one's sins does not foster relationships with other human beings. Nor does simply following a female guide, as he does in *Unattainable Earth.* In *Three Winters,* prominence is given to the senses, the body and blood, and in poems like 'Hymn' it appears as if the cosmos really circulated in his veins, and transported him beyond time and restrictions of closed space. He seems to experience union with God:

> There is no one between you and me
> And to me strength is given.

> (*NCP* 13)

Miłosz explained to Gorczyńska, '"Hymn" is really a prayer, a request to be taken into heaven. And heaven is the whole concrete, material, sensual world, which, in some way, is translated into a different dimension' (*Podróżny świata* 18).

This pantheistic reading of the world did not re-surface for many years. A different strand within *Three Winters* received greater attention, resonating with readers' fears and reflecting unfolding historical events, and conferred on him the label 'catastrophist'. Indeed, the world in the poems was awaiting the imminent Holocaust. A forewarning of this comes in moments from his childhood in the First World War, along with images from the Russian Revolution, from the Russo-Polish War of 1920, as well as in dystopian echoes from Aldous Huxley's and Stanisław Witkiewicz's books. It required considerable intuition to deduce with certainty that war was looming from the behaviour of the German football supporters, whom he describes in *Native Realm* as almost like automatons, as they raised their arms in unison making the 'Heil Hitler' salute: 'During that period I often dreamt about light, which chased after me and pierced me. It was a kind of lethal ray, laser, which killed me. It was a leitmotif of my nightmares: running away and being chased by light, fires, rays, which stabbed like a sword' (*Podróżny świata* 20).

A letter to Jerzy Andrzejewski from the early 1960s offers further insight into the basis of Miłosz's acute sensitivity in the period running up to the war.

My attitude to Poland. I had a kind of horror, some basic dread, a complex about escaping before 1939. What was it?—I try to find an answer, but cannot. Much of it fed into my catastrophism. What were the answers? An intellectual longing to go to Europe? I don't think so. A sense of being stifled, in my career? Not that either. Today and in the past anyway, beginning from my early stay in Paris, the business of reputation and flying high are not great concerns of mine ... So it was very negative, let's say, it was simply fear, but so disturbing that some evenings in Byelorussia, the light in the fields seemed totally infernal (though beautiful in perspective), a Sunday in a village near the River Bug—all that and more moments of terror I could recall, which still live in my memory— perhaps others did not feel that at all ... Warsaw, which for me was always horrible, provincial, stale ... or a teachers' ball in Święciny which I attended and those red coarse hands and ugly, common faces, and this Gogolian world multiplied, haunting me. My biography. After all the only key to it was my fleeing Poland in 1934 for Paris, terrible, probably what touched me most deeply. Outwardly, it was just an ordinary trip, supported by National Culture funding (CM to Andrzrejewski, n.d. 1962).

That escape had a strange outcome, an unusual mix of pain, fear, sin, vision and ecstasy, which turned into a book of poems. The poet covered the cost of the publication with his own money, and a volume with a grey cover and rust-coloured lettering was published in three hundred volumes by the Union of Polish Writers on 1 December 1936.

> Immediately around the volume, a legend began to grow, and to a certain extent it had to do with the political climate, although there was nothing political in the book. Some intelligent critics from young circles uncovered in the poems an apocalyptic code and, under it, a protest, a foreboding of the end, which suited the Polish Communists perfectly. For example, there was an intelligent review by Severyn Pollak in *Nowa Kwadryga*—that it contained coded allusions to the approaching apocalypse. And it was he, really, who disseminated the notion that I was a catastrophist. (*Podróżny świata* 35)

And indeed *Three Winters* gave him prominence, drawing the attention of critics from a wide range of standpoints, seeing, or sensing at least, that they had encountered something that was not simply run of the mill. Pollak declared that

> Miłosz stands at the crossroads, if I may say so, on a step facing a crossroads. Lost in the senselessness of the world, oppressed by reality which blocks his path, he transforms the issues which concern him today into universal issues of life, death, love, and he escapes from the actual world into a world of abstractions and ideas. He is tormented by fear at the passing of time, and by death, and by the insignificance of humankind in the cosmic system, and the senselessness of any undertakings. (Pollak, *Nowa Kwadryga*)

Władysław Sebyła, speaking on Polish Radio, was unequivocal in his estimation of the collection. Because of its 'beauty, novelty and a new use of imagery allow me to call *Three Winters* the most outstanding of lyrical collections in recent times'. Kazimierz Wyka underlined the antitheses within the collection, and stated that it was evident that a new strain of Polish verse was being created (*Pion* 21, 1937). As late as 1939, Gustaw Herling-Grudziński wrote: 'Our times! ... When they turn for the better, Czesław Miłosz's poetry will offer a beautiful and moving documentation of their hardships and obstacles' (*Pion* 8, 1939). But perhaps the most telling, intuitive evaluation, in Miłosz's eyes, was penned by his friend Józef Czechowicz:

> The sheer gulf which divides Miłosz's poetry from everything else that appears from young Polish poets is a result of his intellectual stand towards two worlds: the tangible and the invisible. A great struggle to discover the essence of these categories lies behind *Three Winters*. The poet is sad, mature, bitter, full of understanding of the burdens of the

world, its coldness, terror and cruelty. Existence appears to him like
early but severe winters. We know that the earth is alluring with its
beautiful colors and voices, but what does existence weigh in the scale of
things? . . . It was once said that if God did not exist, he would have to
have been invented. That is true. Poets have no other option but to create
before God. If one does not write as if one was alone in the presence of
God, then there would be no point in writing. Any other writing is an
idle game. A game all the more terrible, because it would ring out in a
void'. (*Pion* 3, 1937)

Among the readers of *Three Winters* there was at least one who fully understood
it. Around 1938, a young critic, Ludwik Fryde, told a friend of his, Stefan
Kisielewski, that 'Czesław Miłosz is the greatest living Polish poet, one whose
level of talent could be compared to that of Mickiewicz' (Kisielewski, in *Trzy
Zimy: Głosy o wierszach*, 71).

Publican

The last time I saw Oskar Miłosz he was standing on the steps of the Opéra
Métro station, the day before my departure . . . Shaking hands in farewell, I
asked: 'Who will survive this war, if, as you say, it will begin in 1939 and last five
years?' 'You will survive'. Running down the steps, I turned around once more;
then, with the image of his narrow silhouette against the sky imprinted in my
memory, I presented my ticket to be punched.

(*NR* 182)

An academic year spent in Paris must have been for Czesław Miłosz a kind
of reprieve, a period of convalescence, almost a season on 'the magic mountain',
allowing him to detach himself from his problems. Getting into a rhythm and
routine, having an income, albeit a meagre one, with the constant cultural possibilities the metropolis offered, this was a time of happy change and self-development.
In Wilno, uncertainty awaited him, obligations to make decisions, including
searching for work. Added to all that was a sense of the looming catastrophe,
which might perhaps have been easier to survive in western Europe. Was he not
tempted to stay in Paris, and cope somehow, as many others managed to? He
admitted later that that proposition had occurred to him, but was he by nature
too passive, too reluctant to think practically? Hot summer days passed very
quickly, and it was time to get back: 'I was returning to Wilno with heavy heart . . .

as a catastrophist with visions of cosmic annihilation' (Gorczyńska, *Portrety paryskie* 225).

He did try, however, to delay his return. In June he mentioned to Iwaszkiewicz that he would like to visit him in Brussels, where the latter held the position of Secretary in the Polish Embassy. The suggestion received a positive response, and in July 1935 Miłosz spent about two weeks in Belgium. With Iwaszkiewicz, he attended an international exhibition, paying close attention to Dutch paintings, returning to Brueghel's canvases, and responding to them as he had before.

At the beginning of August he was back in Poland, visiting his family in Suwałki. Not long afterwards they moved to Głębokie, where his father had been offered the post of district engineer. In Wilno, Czesław moved into a dormitory, one of many addresses that academic year. In winter 1935–36 he stayed in a house not far from St Michael's Church, next to the building where Mickiewicz wrote his narrative poem *Grażyna*. In the spring of 1936, after being caught spending the night with a girl called Nika, he had to move into guest rooms at the Writers' Union. In the summer, he rented a room in a leafy part of Wilno in a house belonging to the wife of a biology professor.

That year saw numerous changes in Wilno circles and within Miłosz himself. Nevertheless, he renewed several friendships and found himself in the group working for a satirical supplement to *Kurier Wileński*. Paid commissioned assignments were insufficient to survive on even in a provincial town like Wilno, and he was under pressure to find a sustainable source of income. After Paris, a 'pleasant town' on the River Wilia must have appeared to him quite unreal, and for many months that strong feeling stayed with him. Letters written to Iwaszkiewicz the previous autumn were bitter in tone: 'Neither my talents nor qualifications are of interest to anyone here. At my age, I am not supposed to earn more than 100 złoty a month' (CM to Iwaszkiewicz, ca. 13–17 September 1935). Soon he asked for letters to be posted to him at the address of his friends Mieczysław Kotarbiński and his wife, Julia, who lived in Warsaw. He tried finding employment in the capital at the National Museum, the Institute for Promoting Art and Polish Radio. By December, not having found any interesting opening, he decided to work for *Pion*, although he was critical about the way its editors ingratiated themselves with right-wing and nationalist sympathisers. In the meantime, he received an offer from the Wilno radio station in 1936 to become a commentator. The radio station was one of a very few institutions supplying opportunities for interesting work with decent earnings. While he was still studying, Miłosz had received 75 złoty for a five-page text, which was broadcast nationally; that made a considerable contribution to his budget. Now, the poet became a full-time employee, a reporter on literary affairs, and secretary to Tadeusz Byrski (1906–1987). Thus began a chapter in his career which was to last until the outbreak of the war in

September 1939. In order to avoid the uncertainty a career as a professional writer posed, he undertook clerical duties, spending the best hours of the day on an office treadmill, dreaming about being elsewhere. Throughout the mornings of summer 1936, in his now constant self-disciplined manner, he laboured away on verse after verse of his poem 'Slow River', and prepared a translation of *The Balcony* by Charles Baudelaire.

The poet tried to rise early so as to avoid being late for work at the radio station, which moved into new premises on 22 Mickiewicz Street. For the first time in his life he enjoyed the comfort and security of a healthy income, not as high as Byrski's, but enough to put money away each month. On the other hand, he felt riven, not much better than a bureaucrat, or an evangelical publican, or a minor functionary in an immoral profession. Days were measured by the rhythm of tables outlining the duration and recording times of broadcasting programmes, correspondence with authors who were late submitting their work, and, of course, the ritual reports to Warsaw HQ, composed in the jargon of the time.

Along with the tedious clerical tasks, he also worked closely with Byrski, preparing radio plays for the Theatre of the Imagination. Out of seventeen dramatisations, two were even produced by Miłosz. On 6 January 1936 Wilno radio broadcast a play he had translated and edited, *High Stakes* by Henri Lefebvre, a French philosopher and writer with Marxist leanings, and on 15 October the station broadcast *The People's House* by Louis Guilloux, author of a famous novel, *Bitter Victory*, which Miłosz had reviewed for *Pion*. A particularly enjoyable memory from that time was meeting Konstanty Gałczyński, who lived in Wilno from 1934 to 1936, worked for the radio, and kept up friendly contact with Teodor Bujnicki. Gałczyński was always behind with his assignments, and on one occasion Miłosz, the programme secretary, dressed very formally in suit and tie, went to see him in person at his home. He was greeted by Gałczyński, who was lying naked on a sofa-bed with a volume of Horace in his hands. The next day, Gałczyński turned up at the radio station, found Byrski, handed him a letter and left. The letter said: 'Dear Sir, Unfortunately I am not able to write a script for a talk, which was commissioned and paid for by Polish Radio, because I have been confined to bed with a serious illness, as your secretary, Miłosz, who you sent to my apartment, observed' (Byrski, *Teatr-radio—Wspomnienia*/'Theatre-Radio Memoirs' 178).

Miłosz suffered psychologically not so much as a result of the daily monotony of his work as from the need to tailor his ambitions to the economic realities of his situation: 'I had to become a clerk here in this provincial city, and it suffocated me … And I had no real friends anymore' (*NR* 188–189). When one considers his life's trajectory, it is difficult not to see it as containing extended periods of suffering, much of the time self-inflicted. That the period after his return from Paris was extremely difficult, and involved frequent clenching of teeth, can be seen from a letter written to Iwaszkiewicz in the autumn of 1935:

> You know I need friendship and love . . . I am in a quandary—there is this girl, to whom I am physically attracted—but I can sense her aversion to the ever-present tumult inside me. She thinks that it is a mere pose and exaggeration . . . It is terrifying trying to determine what is worth sustaining, what is true. Doesn't what we took for a metaphysical whirlwind turn out to be a sob-story sung at a cheap cabaret? She could well be right in her suspicions about my emotional excesses. (CM to Iwaszkiewicz, 27 September 1935)

As the year 1935 approached its end, he wrote again of 'this great sense of isolation, and craving for friendship'. He was dispirited also by the state of Polish politics, the monstrousness of the military regime, and how those who opposed it seemed to him 'devoid of any elements of humanity . . . If only there was at least one group worth joining in the hope of some radical change. But there is none' (CM to Iwaszkiewicz, 7 December 1935). The letters to Iwaszkiewicz were—as can be seen—unique, intimate records, a substitute for the diary which Miłosz never kept, apart from briefly in his early youth. All his complexities are displayed in the correspondence, the different aspects of his perceptive intelligence, his various weaknesses and—in many periods of his life—his profound insecurities.

The summer months of 1936 were probably divided between work on *Three Winters* and a relationship with a new woman in his life, Irena Górska. In the autumn the poet's consuming doubts resurfaced and found release once more in a note to Iwaszkiewicz: 'I blame myself for cowardice. This staying put in Wilno, because I have a job here, may be a sign of how low my horizons have become. I cannot write here. I do not like self-abuse. One can read and produce rubbish for the radio, which as an institution is rightly ridiculed' (CM to Iwaszkiewicz, 3 November 1936). In November he went to Święciany to deliver a reading and to talk to schoolchildren, an experience he enjoyed. It had been organized by writers from Żagary. A longer meeting with the newly-married Jerzy Putrament provided the pretext for more reflections about himself. He describes his companion as 'a good and pleasant lad, and marriage seems to have had a positive influence on him. In this respect, I begin to feel acute loneliness since I have almost fallen into the habits of an old bachelor' (CM to Iwaszkiewicz, 24 November 1936).

Christmas was spent with his family in Głębokie, and the moment in which the traditional Christmas communion wafer was shared intensified his unhappiness at living alone. In another letter, sent on 13 January, he reported that since returning to Wilno, I suffered a minor crisis, the result of the cold and dirt in a small empty flat, as well as loneliness and so on. What I wrote was stuck in some mush of hopelessness. It was as if I had been placed in the stocks, a regret . . . at this overwhelming lack of freedom, so banal and so very familiar to Madame Bovary and also millions of other people trapped by circumstances—this has turned me into a hater . . . Now I feel that I would like to be someone with private means. I begin to envy those people. (CM to Iwaszkiewicz, 13 January 1937)

A lack of free time, as well as a disenchantment with his personal situation, stood in the way of his own poetry, though he was attempting to produce a substantial work in prose, which may have been the promising Krasnogruda story that he began in Paris. These bouts of frustration seem to have coincided with another emotional and erotic entanglement, a relationship with a young actress from a theatre in Wilno. 'I wanted to be capable of loving and sustaining friendship, but I doubted whether I was capable of either, and I despaired because of that . . . This is closely connected with a feeling of provisionality. Perhaps because my life itself is provisional, and because that other life, true life, is somewhere else' (*Rok myśliwego* 88). A life was somewhere else, definitely not at a desk at Wilno Radio. Byrski and his wife were by this time probably the only people with whom he had close regular contact. He sought comfort and fellow-feeling from them, manifested by sitting at a table for a meal together, enjoying conversation and warmth: 'If Thaddeus and his wife granted me their friendship, or, rather, their care, I ascribe it exclusively to my literary talents, not to any personal qualities. I paid them back with respect and affection, but their tranquility and balance were not for me in the state I was in at that time' (*NR* 189).

Tadeusz Byrski was an actor, director, teacher and a person with a strong social conscience. He expended considerable effort and energy in creating the Theatre of the Imagination and making it a success. Productions such as *The Defence of Socrates, Prometheus Bound, Faust* and *The Mystery of the Resurrection* served as proof that the radio was not such a ridiculous institution after all. His wife, Irena, meanwhile held down a high-profile position in the Wilno theatre. The couple were gracious, shining figures on the post-war theatre scene, and in the future brought considerable impetus to provincial theatres throughout Poland, as well as acting as mentors to the young Lwów-born poet, Zbigniew Herbert.

Their spiritual stability may have meant that they were not able to respond fully to the tortuous self-questioning and self-doubt that beset Miłosz. Whether that was the case or not, the strong sense of affinity he shared with the couple in relation to art, politics and religion certainly must have had positive effects. What

Miłosz especially appreciated was the careful attention with which Tadeusz read his poetry and grasped its artistic value. He must have derived much satisfaction from the enthusiasm with which Byrski reacted to his uncle's play *Miguel Mañara*, since he went on to direct a production of it for Wilno Radio. Miłosz's affection for the pair can be seen in the adjectival string with which he began his account of them in *Abecadło:* 'Byrski, Tadeusz and Irena. Magnificent. Wise, decent, noble. I idolised them' (*ABC* 74).

'A handful of unearthly truths'

My clear-eyed companions glanced distractedly
As I passed their table, a naïve lute player.
And while they sat at their chess games (the winner was to
execute the verdict)
I believed they were taking part in the tournaments for fun.

Czesław Miłosz, 'From the Rising of the Sun:
A Short Recess' (*NCP* 318)

That painful year in Wilno, 1936, was accompanied by a sense of powerlessness in the unrelenting logic of political events: rocks were tumbling, gathering speed, starting an unstoppable avalanche. This stony image haunted Miłosz throughout his life. He already had a phase of curiosity about the Soviet Union behind him, and unlike many of his contemporaries, did not believe that France had sufficient military power to resist Hitler. When it came to the western democracies, he often felt mistrustful of their abilities to withstand the totalitarian threat:

> On one side were the Germans—Hitler and the Four Horses of the Apocalypse. On the other was Russia. In the middle was the nauseating Polish Right, which, in the perspective of time, was doomed to failure. The groupings of the Center—Populists and Socialists undermined by Communist sympathies—were difficult to take seriously. Parliamentary methods were discredited in the eyes of my generation. I do not claim that I foresaw clearly the dilemma that part of Europe would have to face: either Hitler's victory or Stalin's . . . My state of mind in those days could be described as the same dream over and over: we want to run, but cannot because our legs are made of lead. (*NR* 120)

He felt like a chess player who could not make a move, and found himself in a stalemate as regards his life and his political outlook. Despite that, he wrote a number of articles in which he defended the independence of art, most forcibly in 'A Letter to Defenders of Culture', which was a resounding call of protest.

Miłosz moved away from ideological groups. He and Gałczyński had diametrically different opinions about politics, and he felt equally detached from Dembiński and Jędrychowski, with whom he had had such a close understanding until recently. He sensed that they had arrived at certain conclusions

> from their reading of Lenin; they were courageous and pure-hearted. The somnolence and passivity of a country of thatched roofs called out for a revolution . . . Caught between the devil and the deep, I reacted emotionally, and out of habits of friendship sought a place among those whom I looked upon as my intimates—only they were becoming less and less so. (*NR* 118)

This situation ought not to be interpreted as just a conflict between the artist and the activists, or a contrast between the sagacity of the one and brainwashing of the other. His actions were a constellation of small moves, dictated by emotions or incidents, rather than the realisation of a conscious plan. Another thing was that in a period when bright, shiny uniforms and talk of triumph were *de rigueur*, his civil, refined outlook on the world was doomed to find itself in a weak position. He stayed on the fringes, but in a group of people belonging to the Intellectuals' Club. No longer was there a happy consensus of opinions and goals:

> They read and commented on the so-called classics of Marxism; knowing smirks appeared on their faces; a hierarchy was established which could be felt in a wink, a sudden lowering of eyes, a sentence broken off in the middle. They sang revolutionary songs, and an atmosphere of sweetness and demonism, which I came to know well later on, was created. (*NR* 119)

From among the members of some official organisations, such as the Legion of Youth, the Union of Polish Democratic Youth, the Federation of Independent Socialist Youth and the so-called second Intellectuals' Club, young people who wanted to create a new reality developed a group which was unambiguously Communist—the Union of the Academic Left, which was referred to as 'Front'. Much earlier, in 1933, its future members made contact with the Communist Party of Poland, which was illegal. This was subordinate to dictates from Moscow, which meant that members agreed to follow party discipline and, what was more, proclaimed that they were prepared to fight the nation of their birth.

Miłosz's stay in Paris was a lucky coincidence, which enabled him to keep a safe distance and maintain the unspecified status of a 'friend'. As a result he was not included in the list of people arrested in 1935. The court charged the 'Front' leaders with engaging in attempts to change the political system of the Polish state by

force. Those who found themselves in the dock and subsequently arraigned in another anti-'Front' court case were Stefan Jędrychowski, Jerzy Sztachelski, Kazimierz Petrusewicz and the Dziewicka sisters, Maria and Irena. Following the first set
of proceedings, most were freed, but the case became a famous affair, polarising
public opinion. People with liberal views, unaware of the accused's links to the
Communist Party of Poland, defended the group and their right to have their own
political opinions. Despite the case that had been levelled against them by the authorities, Jędrychowski, Sztachelski and Petrusewicz remained employees of Wilno
University, a turn of events that was not uncommon and lasted until war broke out.
Henryk Dembiński, who was not among the accused, started publishing a new
paper, the leftist bi-weekly *Poprostu* (Simply), which within a short time reached a
circulation of twenty thousand issues; many of its contributors were members of
'Front'. Censorship halted publication of some items, and before long the Wilno
authorities closed down the paper. In response the editors immediately launched
another paper, *Karta*. Miłosz appeared in the list of contributors and admitted that
he was invited to a meeting during which the name of the periodical was decided
upon. He was in fact the one who came up with its ambiguous title, which in Lithuanian meant 'a generation', and not 'a card', which was the Polish meaning of the
word. The publication was banned after its first three issues. In the meantime the
court cases against 'Front' continued, concluding with four-year prison sentences for
Jerzy Putrament, Stefan Jędrychowski and Anna Żeromska. In an undated memoir,
Miłosz recalled that the failure to arrest him too

> worried me a little, but as a matter of fact, I didn't have such close con-
> tacts with the group and I expressed my unorthodox attitude towards
> them in 'A Letter to Defenders of Culture'. I sat at the hearings in the
> courtroom, clenched my fists in anger at the existing political system
> and also felt ashamed of my role as an outsider, who was never involved
> in organisational aspects. I was not aware of their involvement with the
> Communists, but suspected it. ('Materiały do mojej biografii')

Miłosz's 'Letter' was a crowning piece amongst his newspaper articles, which
had begun with a sketch published in August 1935, a defence of Iwaszkiewicz's
book *Red Shields*. In this, Miłosz had emphasised the fact that a literary writer was
not a journalist, and that a poem, a short story or a novel reflecting on the deep
structure of contemporary reality could not be treated as identical to a journalist's
report or a snatch of political polemic.

The mid-1930s were a period when many people joined ranks. Even those
who were known to have leftist leanings were urged by party publicists and more-
involved colleagues to choose between the proletariat and the fascists. The year 1935

saw the creation of the People's Front in Europe, a group strategically supported by Stalin with the aim of encouraging those without right-wing leanings to give up their neutrality and unequivocally align themselves in opposition to fascism. Using leftist publications like *Poprostu* as a forum, a declaration was issued, signed by Dembiński, Jędrychowski, Putrament, as well as Władysław Broniewski, Marian Czuchnowski, Andrzej Strug, Lucjan Szenwald, Wanda Wasilewska, Adam Ważyk and Aleksander Wat, appealing to all independent artists and writers to join in solidarity to defend progress, peace and culture, claiming that literature which lacked social 'involvement' passively contributed to the Nazification of culture.

One writer who felt obliged to respond to their plea was Miłosz. 'A Letter to Defenders of Culture', published on 20 January 1936, closed with a declaration of support, because he recognised 'the need for a common move against dangers which fascism posed to culture' (*Poprostu* 147–154). The overall tone of the article, however, was different. With hindsight, it is clear to see—although the author himself did not fully realise it—that 'A Letter to Defenders of Culture' was saying goodbye to that part of the left which uncritically submitted to Communist orthodoxy. His courage in speaking out against opinions considered politically 'correct' in progressive circles could be compared with his later stand as a defector in *Nie* (No) in 1951, which turned the majority of Polish émigrés against him. The 'Letter' contained the voice and views of a twenty-five year-old for whom being true to his ideals was more important than playing tactical games. It also demonstrated that he was already capable of self-criticism: 'I managed a few times to write a poem in which artistic values were secondary to the need to strike the right note with the public mood. With a bit of craftiness, that [kind of manoeuvre] is not difficult at all'. He continued:

> Here I have in mind only one aspect of the activities of the left, namely that aspect where attitudes to matters of culture are stated. No one will convince me that things are the way they ought to be. That view is barbarian—I will repeat it even if my colleagues on the left call me a lousy, anarchist intellectual, forgetting that so are Gide, Malraux, Guilloux and Guéhenno, along with many others whose names I will not mention ... Reading articles by young Polish Marxists, one suspects that they really wish for this period to herald a future which sees the total demise of art and artistry. They are preoccupied solely with sniffing out betrayal and class desertion, and are so zealous in poking around to establish whether someone had written 'God' with a capital 'g'. In this great revisionist utopia, there will be nothing left to read except a few books by Wanda Wasilewska.[4] (Ibid.)

The diagnosis was painful. Although Miłosz did not question the validity of making future changes to the political system, he condemned 'distortions' rather than the new directions put forward. He continued to declare himself as someone who opposed the bourgeois lifestyle and existence, and made critical remarks not as someone who feared for democratic freedom, but as an artist who saw the threats posed to *artistic* freedoms.

> From humanists who might want to speak out against fascism, it is demanded that their motives do not cross the agreed norm for a peasant with a small holding or a worker . . . What a humanist loves is in today's reality neglected or threatened with extinction. Education for all is, allegedly, a fiction, and art is of no interest to anyone. Millions of people have no access to what, for a humanist, is the essence of existence. And so, he enters a new path with Mickiewicz and Dante under his arm, not suspecting that he will encounter faithful, but dumb believers who will accuse him of being too classical and that he is rather too fond of . . . Pushkin. And that is how the tragic journey begins 'between lips and the edge of the chalice'. Everything that might provide a mystical vision into the future is taken from him. (Ibid.)

There is also here a forewarning of the post-war stalemate, when it appears that outstanding literature, even if progressive, may not be deemed as conforming to the 'standards' of social realism. It was Putrament in all probability, then running the literature office at *Poprostu*, who stated without hesitation that 'the world was becoming increasingly divided into two camps: on one side, there was the world of progress and culture and on the opposite side, reaction and ignorance. All good people, in his opinion, should transfer to the camp of change' (*Poprostu*, 5 March 1936). Unfortunately, Miłosz did not feature amongst the 'good' on the grounds that he was guilty of walking away from the proletariat. In order to justify his position, he created the concept of the classless poet and humanist, which provoked a great deal of criticism. Two types of accusation, political and aesthetic, were hurled in his direction. He was charged with betraying avant-garde ideals, taking the opportunists' option for pecuniary gain, and returning to the classicist mainstream. Any favourable references to Mickiewicz or Latin verse forms prompted vehement denunciation. Accepting an official literary prize in 1934, being published in the experimental poets' publication *Skamander*, and being praised by Antoni Słonimski in *Wiadomości* that year did not make him popular with some younger 'revolutionsts'. Anatol Mikułko wrote bluntly that 'no-one would call Miłosz a revolutionary poet, and that while Kapała went to prison, Miłosz, after dabbling in "vulgar Marxism", discovered himself and "moved on"' (Zaleski 143).

Not surprisingly, in January 1936, Miłosz ostentatiously refused to attend a reading in Wilno to listen to Marian Czuchnowski, a writer aligned with the radical peasant movement. In a letter to Iwaszkiewicz, he complained:

> Here in Wilno, they besieged me and I can see with dread that keeping a commendable position of isolation in Polish society is impossible. 'Miłosz, a fascist lackey', 'Miłosz, a pseudo-classic writer', 'Miłosz plunged into mysticism and classical forms', these are the most tender descriptions. And what's worse, looking at the muddy streets, the poverty, the idiocy of the government's farcical actions, there is no heart or courage to talk about pure art, there aren't sufficiently moral laws . . . I find myself overcome by fear when I contemplate my peers. Have I left them so far behind me? . . . I then think that my errors—my emotive language, my boring classical verses—are a result of a hunger of which those people have no conception. (CM to Iwaszkiewicz, 21 January 1936)

The return from seclusion in Paris to the Polish whirl left a strong, unpleasant aftertaste. He learnt from Józef Pankiewicz (1866–1940) that, when asked what he did during the Franco-Prussian War, Cézanne remembered only the intensity of his painting at the time. Conscious that the artist's true mission was to capture the light of the morning star, a moment later the great French master recalled being hassled by ideological corporals. Immediately he understood that society was anticipating a poster, and a few simple words which could easily be stitched onto a military banner. To follow one's own inner truth demanded sacrifices, Miłosz realised, thinking about Antony Pollaiuolo's *Tobias and the Angel*, a picture Iwaszkiewicz had informed him about. He had that in mind when writing 'A Statue of a Couple', and was soon to discover it for himself during his trip to Italy. 'It will be a fairly difficult effort to save from the general conflagration this handful of unearthly truths, and even wearing a Russian shirt to follow Pollaiuolo's angel' (ibid.).

'Siena descends into gleams'

Journeying in the footsteps of the angel of art and truth also became increasingly difficult for practical reasons. Miłosz was hesitant about leaving his post, given that until now it had given him financial security, though it was coming increasingly under threat. Accusations were made against the radio station that it was harbouring a Communist cell. The source of these allegations probably came from within the station itself, and clear proof of this were the invitations to Jews and Byelorussians to participate in programmes. According to Miłosz, Wiktor Trościanko was the most likely culprit ('Materiały do mojej biografii').

Trościanko, a graduate of the same gymnasium as Miłosz, had also gained a place in Wilno University's Law Department, and belonged to the Vagabonds' Club. In the 1930s he had an eventful future ahead of him, not untypical of Poles in this period. A writer and a soldier, he escaped an NKVD (Soviet Secret Police) prison during the war. Later he became an active member of the underground, an émigré, a right-wing National Party member, and an officer in the Armia Krajowa (Home Army), and took part in the Warsaw Rising of August 1944, after which he was imprisoned. After its defeat, he fled post-war Communist Poland and worked for Radio Free Europe in Munich. His dislike of Miłosz may well have been the cause of a difficult situation in which the latter found himself in 1936 and 1937, and in later years had a negative impact on the poet's relationship with Radio Free Europe. Its roots lay in their very different political standpoints, but also in past personal conflicts. Miłosz did not rate Trościanko's writing highly, and opposed publishing it in the papers he edited. A report found in the General Office of the Home Army represents a more serious example of the likely informer's handiwork. It stated:

> Polish Radio has false ideological policies, as they are liberal and intellectual in character and support tendencies which aim at hindering progress towards a healthy, energetic national expansion . . . it is controlled by a group of people who are connected by race or organisational membership . . . It is imperative that changes take place immediately and it is necessary to carry out a thorough analysis of Aryan [racial origins] and patriotic [beliefs]. (Maciej Kwiatkowski 13)

Miłosz was branded as a left-wing sympathiser and also a 'Byrski man'. Byrski, the station's programme manager, a definite liberal, was abhorred in expansionist, nationalistic and religious circles. Actions such as inviting a Jewish speaker to deliver a talk on religious topics, asking a Byelorussian choir to sing a song which became a favourite tune throughout Wilno, and allowing the editors of *Poprostu* to participate in programmes aroused deep reservations within the radio's management; for some, Byrski's trip to the Soviet Union to attend a theatre festival was the last straw. In his memoirs Byrski mentions how

> sometime in January 1937, after returning from the festival together with my wife, we organised a meeting of friends at my office to report on our impressions of the Soviet Union. Miłosz did not come to it and afterwards invited me to another office where he informed me with a sour expression that there were black clouds gathering over us. Someone was

turning the senior management in the local station against us. Miłosz
had a credible source . . . The director invited me and announced that
Colonel Ludwik Bociański, the regional governor, prohibited my name
from appearing in any radio programme. (Byrski 191)

Byrski refused to work under a pseudonym, and after he was offered a post as general director of Polish Radio Warsaw, he promptly left Wilno. Acting on information from 'credible sources', Miłosz himself began to seek a post in the capital. The appointment of Bociański to the most powerful position in the multicultural Wilno region in 1935 immediately resulted in the closure of the Byelorussian Cultural Society and the Byelorussian Institute of Economy and Culture, as well as a few hundred Russian Orthodox churches and chapels, and the expulsion of troublesome activists representing the Byelorussian and Lithuanian minorities. He pursued a policy of drastically limiting the freedoms of the Lithuanian minority, closing all schools, and introducing the most stringent possible controls on the Wilno press. He was the man responsible for Miłosz's dismissal from his post in Wilno Radio. Halina Sosnowska, a director at the Warsaw studios, who was a keen observer of Miłosz's interesting contributions, proffered a helping hand at this juncture and helped him secure a position at Warsaw Radio.

Having some free time, and wanting to take a break after the recent unpleasant turn of events in Wilno, Miłosz applied for a passport and then moved with his few belongings to Warsaw. In April 1937, he travelled by train to Venice via Vienna, each hour bearing him nearer to the Mediterranean, and further from stuffy, provincial Poland. On arrival in Venice

I recollected the high bridge over the Niemen
As the train wound out of an Alpine pass.
And I woke up by the waters, grayish blue,
In the radiance of the pearly lagoon,
In the city where a traveler forgets who he is.
By the waters of Lethe I saw the future.

('1913', *NCP* 424)

In this poem from *Unattainable Earth,* his aim was not to capture Venice in stanzas, but to ponder the mystery of each individual fate and the continuity of human generations. His intention was to avoid becoming yet another in an endless line of artists who visited the city in pursuit of beauty, and who duly came to regard it as a cultural paradise. Venice must have made its mark on Miłosz, a faithful reader of Thomas Mann, but what remained fixed in his memory was not the shimmering surface of the Grand Canal, where space is forever changing, but the most physical and sensual of experiences.

> My thirst for brotherhood, for being a part of the human throng, an equal
> among equals, also remained unsatisfied ... Arms gesticulating on the
> Campo dei Fiori, shouts, glances, a collective warmth such as I had not
> felt since those moments in Prague, aroused desires impossible to name. I
> remember a man named Francesco Ficello. Francesco sat across from me
> in a third class railway compartment and drank wine from a bottle. He
> wiped it with his sleeve and stretched it out to me without a word. Then
> he cut a piece of cheese and gave it to me. So began our short friendship.
> He was a railroad watchman in Maestre. His home in the workers' suburb
> of Venice harbored an unheard-of number of bedbugs, which I verified
> for myself when he invited me to his house. (*NR* 194)

With Francesco as his guide, he toured the taverns, learnt how to prepare *frutti
di mare,* came to tell the differences between wines, and also visited a cheap
brothel. On the Lido, he also experienced one of the greatest sights of his life to
date when he observed a slender young German girl, a Diana with Titian hair,
who was so beautiful that her image stayed with him for many years.

At the beginning of May he sent a postcard to Iwaszkiewicz from Florence
reporting that he had arrived there after trips to Padua and Bologna, and that the
next place he planned to visit was Assisi. Seeing Florence and the Uffizi 'was
perhaps the highlight of all' his experiences.

> In Assisi I did not give a single thought to the Franciscan Fathers. Besides
> St Francis was like air, impossible to imagine. I was interested in the
> villages in the valley of Umbria, seen from above, and in the Lake of
> Trasimeno—I looked for a boat, the shape of a boat, because wood, more
> than stone, always provides a tangible contact with the past. The land
> where I was born, after all, was a land of wood. (*NR* 193)

This note has a symbolic meaning, because Miłosz, as a matter of fact, was never
attracted to architecture or paintings as pure disciplines in themselves—he always looked for signs of human presence in them, a trace of those who paced the
'unattainable earth' before us.

Tirelessly his eyes took in shapes and colours and landscapes, and he continu-
ously and laboriously filled his notebook with impressions of the consecutive galleries he visited: 'In the rectangular courtyard of the university in Padua there was a
plaque that I read attentively. It bore names of students who had studied there during
the Renaissance. I felt a certain pride finding many Polish names on it' (*NR* 193).

It was the Italian paintings that made the biggest impression on him. He saw
Pollaiuolo's *Tobias and the Angel,* which for him represented a symbol of the bond

between master and apprentice. The works of the old masters in Siena (Duccio, Simone Martini or Sassetta) he found so moving that they 'pulled the ground from under my feet' (*NR* 193). The most significant appeared to be frescoes by Luca Signorelli in Orvieto, which he visited at Iwaszkiewicz's urging. Of the many pictures he saw, *The Arrival of the Antichrist* seemed to Miłosz almost contemporary, a symbolic portrayal of the omnipotent lie, evil dressed in robes of the good:

> The fresco shows the antichrist in the form of Christ. He is pointing at his heart, from which flames are bursting. His smile of kindness seems to contain a flicker of irony, but that may be just an illusion of the viewer. What goes on at the edges of the picture reveals his true identity: torturers kneel on the chests of their victims; they are choking them with rope nooses and their knives are raised to strike. (*NR* 194)

Behind the back of the false Christ, who gives the illusion of compassion, peers Satan. This was an image of the contemporary messiah unusual in its precision. Signorelli also depicted the helplessness of the artist, who could only look on at scenes of brutal violence.

The breathtaking beauty of Siena did not, however, soothe or calm Miłosz's ever-present anxieties. He saw Italy as the realisation of a dream, one which we ourselves would be incapable of dreaming. Though he rejected aspects of what he saw, because he did not want to rest in the eternal space its artworks evoked, it served also as an inspiration, enabling him to turn inwards to the pangs he was enduring. His poem 'Siena' is as evocative and mysterious as its stone prototype:

> Siena descends into gleams, as if dew shaken
> Into streams flowing down from mountains.
> And Siena descends into gleams and eyes fail to recall
> Its colours, its stone feathers.
> The clamour of phantoms dies, gates of war open.
> Star, save us—from happiness and peace
>
> (*Wiersze* I, 146–147)

'In my homeland, to which I will not return'

> It is neither Sunset, nor Sunrise here
> Something, as if someone stood in the door . . .
>
> Jerzy Liebert, 'A Song to Warsaw'

In summer 1937 Miłosz moved to Warsaw for good. He remembered instances of humiliation he had suffered while staying there on previous occasions, but now he was strong enough to make his way in the city.

> I rose in my career with a staggering speed that was directly propor-
> tional to the boredom and sarcasm I began to manifest after my initial
> timidity had worn off. A combination of hard work and impudence is
> perhaps the best formula for anyone who wants to get ahead. But I was
> not counting my steps forward; I cared only about getting another day
> behind me. With surprise I noticed after a year that I had made a lot of
> money. (*NR* 196)

He lived in an apartment vacated by Bolesław Miciński and Halina Micińska, who had been awarded scholarships to study in France. Their rooms up in a loft in an attractive district, Saska Kępa, were comfortable enough for an overworked single man. 'On our return we found our place clean and tidy, except for my desk where the veneer was damaged, because Czesio kept putting a metal mug on it with hot water to shave, which was something I found unforgivable', said Halina in her unpublished memoirs. Every day Miłosz ate at the same restaurant in Hoża Street, which served home-cooked meals; he also visited bars where they served vodka and attended concerts at the Philharmonic Hall, pretending to Iwaszkie-wicz, Bolesław and Halina that he had become a music connoisseur. He swam at the municipal swimming pool, where he did the breast stroke, often overtaking noted poets and literary figures who used it too. He had little free time, as he was busy writing in the mornings, then started work at the station at eleven, finishing at around eight or nine in the evening, totally exhausted and bored.

Polish Radio was enjoying a golden age, building new stations. In 1939, the number of subscribers reached one million, which made it a blessed cash-cow for many writers, aspiring and established. Miłosz was initially brought in to send international telegrams, and later moved to the Department of Programme Planning. Once again, his duties were largely clerical, reviewing existing pro-grammes and proposing new ones, trying to promote ambitious projects. He worked hard preparing lengthy monthly reports, which reflected the wide range of the programmes broadcast by the stations. His department had to sum up 256 programmes released in one day by all the regional radio stations and in Warsaw, compiling data on over 330 sheets. His immediate boss was Halina Sosnowska, who was a liberal, intelligent woman with a degree in philosophy. A former ac-tivist during the struggle for independence and a supporter of Piłsudski, she joined Polish Radio in the 1930s. Of her, Miłosz wrote: 'Sosnowska embodied patriotism, honesty, a lack of political imagination, iron energy, but also a gift for leadership and a great management style. No wonder that she had all the men working at the station under her thumb' (*Kontynenty* 338). He spent hours at meetings with her and other programme contributors, listening to the monotonous voices of people presenting their proposals.

Miłosz's financial situation was gradually improving, and he began furnishing a place for himself and dressing smartly. He was a conscientious employee, but appeared ironic and at times rather arrogant. Sosnowska regarded him highly and had a good rapport with him; she was the only person with whom he could have honest political discussions. In Wilno he could barely make ends meet, but here he was successful, although at times he did consider leaving because of the dullness of the work at the radio station. The prospect of sliding back into poverty, however, filled him with dread.

He regarded that period as a time of artistic impasse, of carrying the burden of 'problematic knowledge' which he could not share, due to fear it would be misinterpreted. In *Beginning with My Streets,* Miłosz wrote: 'My years of emigration probably date from 1937, when I left Wilno, and acclimatising to Warsaw was not necessarily easier than getting used to living in France or America' (*Zaczynając od moich ulic* 161). He called the city a 'Babylon of depravity', where the profligate nouveau riche lived in close proximity to districts of poverty. Antoni Słonimski wrote in an article in 1934: 'The place we live in resembles a parody of Greece. A handful of people dressed lightly, saying wise and subtle things, every other one a homosexual; Byelorussians dressed in leather from Apfelbaum; fetishists, nationalists, army people, Jews, quack doctors and millions of peasants multiplying like grains of sand in a desert' (*Wyprawa w Dwudziestolecie* 319). *Poems 1937* presents a God-forsaken, barren, sulphurous land, devoid of love, full of people who stir feelings of pity and other uneasy emotions. Published after the war, and read by some as Miłosz's farewell to Poland, 'In My Homeland' reflects on a life left far behind, but the guilt it voices relates to the Middle Lithuania homeland he had left behind:

> In my homeland, to which I will never return,
> There is a vast forest lake,
> Broad clouds, ripped, wonderful
> I remember, when I glance back.
>
> . . .
>
> This lake of briars sleeps in my heaven.
> I bend over and see there at the bottom
> A flash from my life. And what frightens me
> Is there, before death takes my body forever.
>
> ('W mojej ojczyźnie'/'In My Homeland', *Wiersze* I, 142)

Warsaw Friendships

Be good to him, you birds and trees. Guard him,
From ravaging time protect his grave in Lublin.
Czesław Miłosz, From *A Treatise on Poetry*, II (*NCP* 123)

In *A Year of the Hunter* Miłosz returned to his years in the capital in the late 1930s, which he contrasted with happier times with Żagary:

> It was much harder in Warsaw, where finally I was acknowledged as one of the most gifted young poets. In addition, I was on bad terms with *Wiadomości Literackie,* and I was not greeted as a celebrity when I entered cafés frequented by people from literary circles ... My fractious nature, that is, my bristly reaction whenever anyone wanted to stroke me, as well as my various mannerisms, appear funny to me now, though it is strange to think that all the famous people from those cafés and streets faded, and I, the shy, arrogant one, remained. (*Rok myśliwego* 180)

As often is the case with artists, the feeling of being misunderstood and undervalued reflects the scale of the individual's emotional needs, although following the publication of *Three Winters*, he had become a very highly regarded writer.

During the time he joined the Union of Polish Writers, his work appeared in major publications, such as *Ateneum, Marchołt, Verbum, Zaczyn* and *Pion,* which awarded him a prize for his novella *Obrachunki* (Reckonings). In addition, he was a serious contender for a major literary prize for young writers. Frequently he developed contacts and literary alliances in circles outside the mainstream. He was pursuing poetic forms capable of bearing more metaphysical weight, yet would avoid excessive elaboration.

Thanks to the establishment of diplomatic relations between Lithuania and Poland, Miłosz paid a short visit to Kaunas (Kowno) in August 1938, where he became acquainted with a circle of artists around *Naujoji Romuva,* a weekly magazine, and its chief editor and essayist, Juozas Keliuotis. The artists were interested in combining contemporary art with Christian tradition, referring to such thinkers as Søren Kierkegaard, Nikolai Berdyaev and Jacques Maritain. Miłosz and Keliuotis shared similar views when it came to aesthetics and politics. While visiting museums, they conducted long discussions in French, both expressing a fascination with Mickiewicz, whose ideological heir Miłosz considered himself to be. Keliuotis drew up plans for their cultural partnership, which he refers to in his memoirs. He applauded the fact that Miłosz 'was free from Polish nationalist and imperialist tendencies' (Keliuotis 516). Keliuotis paid a reciprocal visit to Warsaw and later published Miłosz's poems in his periodical. The friendship between them would prove vital to the poet's survival during the war.

In the months preceding the war, two people, Bolesław Miciński and Józef Czechowicz, played a crucial role in Miłosz's life. Miciński was the same age as Miłosz, and, like him, a philosopher, poet and author. In the mid-1930s he had published *Journeys to Hell,* a volume of innovative essays, with an introduction written by Czechowicz. Popular in artistic and intellectual circles in Warsaw, Miciński was endowed with a sharp intellect and a gift for making friends. Initially this extremely erudite philosopher, who could read Plato in the original, made the newcomer from Wilno feel inferior. What brought the two together, however, were common political and artistic ideals and a comparable outlook on the most important challenges of the times posed by the rival totalitarian ideologies. By increasingly alluding to Christianity and classical tradition in his writings, Miłosz sought in part to remind readers of the existence of older, alternative value systems. Just as Miłosz had been back in Wilno, Miciński was appalled when he witnessed a spate of anti-Semitic brawls at Warsaw University. The previous year he had severed his links with *Prosto z Mostu* (Speaking Directly), the radical literary magazine he wrote for, when it had published a series of virulently racist pieces. These were the work of extreme anti-Semitic nationalists who were outraged at news that a small number of their fellow Polish writers, Miciński included, had raised money and made donations in support of Jewish expatriates expelled from Germany. The break with *Prosto z Mostu* left Miciński in very difficult financial circumstances. Realising this, Miłosz asked Halina Sosnowska to employ his friend at Polish Radio. Up until the outbreak of war, he and Miciński, along with Jerzy Andrzejewski and Władysław Sebyła, continued to explore the possibility of setting up their own journal, which would cover philosophical and literary subjects and be funded largely by a rich aristocrat, Jan Tarnowski.

Miłosz's friendship with Józef Czechowicz was different, as it was much more cordial and direct. Miłosz had been drawn to his poetry from his school years onward and became acquainted with the poet at an avant-garde festival in 1934. Czechowicz's poetry had a strong influence on Miłosz's style, loosening its metric structure. They shared common perspectives on the challenges and mission of art, and attributed to culture the highest aims. Fittingly, around this time Miłosz started reading and translating T. S. Eliot, and developed a fascination for William Blake, Emanuel Swedenborg and Joachim Boehme.

> One morning in 1938 I told Czechowicz about a dream I had had. I saw a house, which had one wall made of glass. The Mongol behind the glass played the violin, and it was Czechowicz. The music did not reach my

ears. I avoided telling my friend that the house was called the House of the Dead, and that the face of the player was marked with signs of decay. My restraint was excused by the fact that I was aware of an acute obsession he had that his own death was imminent. (*Kontynenty* 341)

On 9 September 1939, Czechowicz perished during the Nazi bombing of Lublin. Until the end of his life, Miłosz treasured the memory of his friend and admonished people from Lublin: 'Remember Józek's grave, because the city that does not remember its poet fades.' He also composed a beautiful record of his faithfulness in a poem from *Hymn of the Pearl* published in 1981:

Therefore I try to describe how you appear now, on this other continent, in the sudden lightning of your afterlife.

A dark-haired young boy in a blue infantry uniform, a cap with a little white eagle, and puttees.

Because you were a soldier for two weeks in the Nineteen Twenty, and wrote about it, and the actors in your play were dressed in the same uniform.

That play which Horzyca succeeded in putting on stage, before our desks in that creaky office on Dąbrowski Square disintegrated.

Before you perished from a bomb, Szulc in Auschwitz, Szpak from a bullet because he refused to be closed in a ghetto, Janina Włodarkiewicz from a heart attack in New York.

So I am not surprised at your being dressed that way as you circle around me, when I record your poems in the Language Lab or play them back from a tape.

Lives taken away, lands defiled, sins: and your note, pure above the abyss.

('To Józef Czechowicz', *NCP* 382)

Janka

I searched
For you, my love, for a very, very long time, so that
In you, as in a mirror, white-frosted,
I could see the world without those wreaths the muses weave.

Czesław Miłosz, 'Like the Rulers'

As the young poet inched closer to his thirtieth birthday, his mood veered from dejection to melancholic indifference. At least that is how he put it in *Poems 1937*, where he speaks of wasted years, of emotions which waned 'like a flame' ('Komin'/'Chimney', *Wiersze* I, 149). They portray a man lost, tormented by guilt on account of his coldness and lack of tenderness. He little knew that he was soon to meet his life companion.

Two years his senior, Janina Dłuska—or Janka, as everyone called her—was born in the village of Zuzela,[5] in the Mazovian region near Warsaw. Like her husband-to-be, Janka was employed at Polish Radio, combining her work in the personnel department with studies on an MA course in law at Warsaw University. She was of slight build, blonde, and had grey eyes. The picture on her identity card gave the impression of a woman who was decisive, energetic and, as her family always thought of her, ambitious and persevering.

She was interested in theatre and cinema, and regularly mixed with young filmmakers who combined avant-garde tendencies with leftist and Communist sympathies. A co-founder of Start, the Society of Artistic Film Enthusiasts, she also set up Krąg (Circle), a film agency, to promote socially-engaged films, as a protest against the commercialisation of Polish cinematography. In 1934 she married a film director, Eugeniusz Cękalski (1906–1952), and the following year accompanied him on his scholarship trip to London, where they were involved in an agency promoting experimental cinema.

Although the couple shared the same passions and interests, the marriage became a strictly formal arrangement, and never seemed happy, according to Miłosz. He ran into Janka at the radio station in the course of the winter of 1937–38, and much later commented:

> She was a rational person, but made a mistake choosing me. My *Three Winters* collection made me well-known in poetic circles, but my susceptibility to the paranormal and my mood swings posed the question as to whether the quality of my poems came at a price. The reality was that I was a man of short-term passions, illusions and dreams, not at all material to be a husband and father. ('Materiały do mojej biografii')

Undoubtedly, as her family recalled, Janka was deeply in love with Miłosz, and continued to be until the end of her life. For him, in turn, 'Janka was the focus of my thoughts, and also my tentative efforts to find out what it was in her that grasped and held me' (*Rok myśliwego* 263). At the outset he appeared to treat the relationship as strictly spiritual, nonphysical, a meeting of two minds above the normal human passions. He was still wary of being dragged into so-called normality, which could have threatened his poetic calling. It may well be that he wished to do penance for earlier physical relationships, particularly with Jadwiga Waszkiewicz.

He was driven not only by his emotions, but also by what he subsequently termed a risky 'moral engagement', in which the humble rural origins of the woman he had chosen played a part. The key factor, though, was the need to grow in humility and goodness in accordance with the Maritain[6] version of Catholicism he then espoused. Janka was anti-clerical, and also, it would seem, a non-believer, which for Miłosz at that time must have been a real problem. Marriage inside the Church was impossible, as Janka was separated from her husband. The prospective couple made an appointment with a priest, Father Korniłowicz, to discuss their difficult situation, but the meeting failed to resolve any issues.

Regardless of these complications, having received her parents' consent and having met with no objections from Cękalski, Janka and Miłosz began to live together, moving into her new flat. Through the relationship the poet was introduced to new film circles, began writing film reviews and even considered penning a script for a film about the Polish-born novelist Joseph Conrad, whose real name was Józef Teodor Konrad Korzeniowski. Miłosz's précis for the project includes these telling comments which shed light not just on Conrad: 'He is leaving Poland and will never come back . . . From the mist of a tradition of martyrs' uprisings, plots, and dreams about an independent homeland, he travels to Europe and there begins his existence as an active and free man' ('Sea Is My Destination', Beinecke Library Archive). Janka had dreams of becoming a film director, but so deeply convinced was she of Miłosz's rare talent, she set those aside and prioritised her partner's needs. Throughout their lives together she performed a valuable service as the first, and often critical, reader of his poems.

To some of his friends it was a mystery as to why this often gregarious, open-hearted man, who was so keen to be accepted, had entered into a relationship with a woman who, in their eyes, seemed rather cold. Janka's common sense and clear-headedness put a brake on his incredible vitality, his pursuit of other women, his partying, singing and alcohol consumption. Beautiful, very intelligent, but domineering, she tried keeping him on a short leash, and could be at times uncompromising. She was perhaps not so much jealous—he gave her no grounds to be—as terrified by his volcanic energy. At times slightly caustic, and perhaps afraid of being hurt, she maintained a distance from those who surrounded them. Exceptions to this rule were Józef Czechowicz and Jerzy Andrzejewski, with whom she had very close and warm relationships.

While as a couple they seem not to have been fully compatible, Miłosz and Janka spent nearly half a century together, which included years of total devotion, but also periods when they inflicted pain on each other.

Coming Down to Earth

Art and poetry are more necessary to human beings than bread. They prepare them
for the life of the spirit.

Jacques Maritain, *Réponse à Jean Cocteau*

Taking into account the amount of time that he had to set aside on paperwork
for his radio job and the difficulties in his personal life, it is surprising how much
Miłosz wrote during his Warsaw years. There were superb lyrics such as 'Encounter', 'Siena' and 'Ballad of Levallois', but the artist expressed himself most
often in prose. Along with two novellas, he wrote extensively about Oskar Miłosz
and published several essays voicing his opposition to the exploitation of art as a
tool to promote ideology, and how that resulted in its impoverishment.

   In retrospect, he had a clear view, which perhaps unnecessarily he wove
into his texts, that he ought to have 'shouted' more, warned of the coming war
and the demonic totalitarian threat, instead of musing on the symbiotic links
between religion and poetry. All too vividly he remembered Oskar's premoni-
tions of the dangers ahead, of the caterpillar treads of tanks crossing the Mazovian plain, but at the same time he wanted to suppress these terrible visions. He
could not see any feasible political solutions opening up, and was alarmed at the
empty jabberings of the right while communism advanced remorselessly: 'In open
discussions with Sosnowska, I used to say that Poland exists in an ideological
vacuum, because there is nothing apart from fascist nationalism—and on the
other side—Marxism' ('Materiały do mojej biografii'). Before the November 1938
elections, Obóz Zjednoczenia Narodowego (Camp of National Unity), which
won 164 out of 218 seats in the Polish Parliament, employed this slogan: 'Jeśli
Polski chcesz bez Żyda/To twój głos się w urnie przyda'. A rough translation into
English might read:

   If you want a Poland without Jews
   Then a ballot in the box you must surely use.

(Dąbrowska 91)

Amongst the ranks of this fiercely nationalist coalition were many who were
convinced that were they simply to mobilise the Polish cavalry, it would conquer
Berlin.

   What characterises the texts Miłosz wrote at this juncture was their heightened intensity and anxiety, and their pathos, and, as so often, their preoccupation
with the personal dilemmas he faced. The idea of abandoning his ivory tower, of

fleeing from 'selfish art', which meant accepting the collective fate, dominated his imagination. He seemed to revert to the state of mind in which he had written some of the early poems, depicting humanity reduced to the status of beasts, harnessed, trapped in their stinking lairs, in the 'damp of sperm and juices' (*Przygody młodego umysłu* 218). The key issue for him was not an aesthetic but a spiritual one, how an individual soul was lost in a system which changed citizens into cogs in a machine. He reflects on 'small souls that are ridiculed, kicked with boots, harangued with slogans, silent, unable to find words, to express things that offend and hurt. Punishment by exile, concentration camps, armies of spies stalk their movements' (ibid., 221). Those were risky sentences. Coming down to earth was a painful transition. If a prospect of hope remained, it lay in Oskar Miłosz's words: 'Loving humankind is not demeaning, but [releases] the power of developing one's personality and the art of seeing in every passer-by you meet someone equally important, similar, and at the same time different . . . We need to love people with "old love, worn by pity, solitude and anger"' (ibid., 224).

It was exactly that difficult love that was the basis of Miłosz's attack on art for art's sake. In an article from March 1938, 'Almost the Dusk of Gods', the poet put forward the thesis that contemporary writers lacked the courage to reveal their own inner selves, to reach for the most important issues, that they got lost in allusions and ambiguities, which led to 'the unprecedented sterilisation of art' (ibid., 211). A few months later, he elaborated on these comments in a sketch, 'The Lie of Today's Poetry', urging poets: 'Before you print a poem, you should reflect on whether this verse could be of use to at least one person in the struggle with himself and the world' (ibid., 241). In the autumn of that year, in a reply to critics, he explained that he was not arguing for didactic art, but for a restoration to people of their cultural heritage, giving them the opportunity to enter into dialogue with their predecessors, and freeing them from the pressure of constant innovation. Art cannot be reduced to a series of ethical recommendations or social tasks, but it also cannot be self-serving, because, if it tries, it destroys itself ('Obrona rzeczy nieuznanych', 242–250).

Miłosz was tormented by the omnipresence of the lie—both in the world of ideology and in the work and conscience of a writer, who had no right to reduce literary art to an exercise in style. At the core of his work was a need to defend, openly and with consistency, the religious perspective in contemplating humanity and the sense of art it created. One of his most important essays at this time began with a clarion call:

> No more remaining silent. No more constant silence, no more deep
> sleep without dreaming in the midst of meanness, doing without every-
> thing that is human, apart from scoffing food, making love and resting,

apart from artistic creation even, which does not encompass everything, and which deceives when unable to bear the burden of wrong. (*Przygody młodego umysłu* 199)

He noticed around him, especially in himself, a religious hunger, a need for belief, a desire for experiences that were too easy, too quick, and did not satisfy. The Church had lost its role as a guide and comforter, while artists wasted the gift of prophecy, locking themselves in towers, helpless in the face of people's needs.

The poet dreamt of a return to the status quo, in which faith, ethics and art were not at odds with, but rather complemented, each other. To demonstrate that the supreme aim of art was to serve the truth, and not to satisfy self-love, Miłosz referred to Thomistic aesthetics, whose modern interpretation was derived from Maritain. He asked for the gift of humility and carried out self-examination: 'I inflict pain on myself with every word and that is my inner suffering, to be plagued by phantoms of my weakness, with the unkept promise of deeds, which fade before they were thought through' (ibid., 207). In these declarations of artistic humility, these renunciations of self-love, and in the devoted commitment to serve higher goals can be detected a compulsion to make amends. We can see a spiritual vehemence, a gulf between an extreme longing for fame and the submissive quietness of the heart, observing things from above and falling on one's knees with awe. Undeniable, though, was the spiritual passion he voiced, the understanding of religion as a continuous drama, something Miłosz expressed in his review of George Bernanos's *A Diary of a Country Priest*. In the poet's interpretation, the novel confronted 'the problem of holiness, which, despite the promises of cheerful purists, is borne in torment, and borders on darkness and abyss' (ibid., 182). Its protagonist, though, is a man whose psyche 'demands tumultuous ecstasy, complete devotion, sacrifices, total achievements'. From a very personal perspective, the author added, 'greed and impatience drive us, contemporary people, from doctrine to doctrine, from truth to truth, we who cannot accept the sordidness today which is our doing. Could it be possible that in this there is a seed of hope, a seed of forgiveness?' (ibid., 185).

In the second half of the 1930s, the poet was experiencing a spiritual evolution and sought guidance from the philosopher Jacques Maritain. The Frenchman's vision of a human being bound for transcendence, possessing an immortal soul, did not involve a negation of biology, history, economy, or one's individual psyche. Rather, it strongly emphasised the importance of the spiritual element, and humankind's inability to submit to any deterministic system—whether the laws of biology, or those of a state and its ideology, which, of course, resonated powerfully in that era when totalitarian systems bloomed. From the perspective of the theologian, civilisation was worthy of its name only when combined with

culture; the artist's task was to attempt to capture the intense light of transcen-
dental mystery, and, at the same time, to present a singularity and uniqueness of
an individual being; and the basis of poetical energy was love for people and love
of the world. The poet himself was to be 'above all and primarily a person who
reached into greater depths than others and who discovers in reality the radiance
of the spirit' (Maritain 86). Miłosz expected poets to find a love for the world
within themselves which yields words that are true and that denote reality, and that
allows them like a child 'to name a tree, a tree; a man, a man; a star, a star'.

A Blood-Red Star

> In a night train, completely empty, clattering through fields
> and woods, a young man, my ancient self, incomprehensibly
> identical with me, tucks up his legs on a hard bench—it
> is cold in the wagon—and in his slumber hears the clap of
> level crossings, echo of bridges, thrum of spans, the whistle
> of the locomotive. He wakes up, rubs his eyes, and above
> the tossed-back scarecrows of the pines he sees a dark blue
> expanse in which, on the low horizon, one blood-red star is
> glowing.
>
> Czesław Miłosz, 'The Wormwood Star' (*NCP* 391)

There was less and less time, and the events of the last year before the war accrued
a symbolic dimension. In February 1939 Miłosz saw Józef Czechowicz's play *Czasu
jutrzennego* (Of Tomorrow's Time), in which the main protagonist, a boy-soldier, is
tormented by a dream foretelling his early death. It seems not to have met the audience's expectations and received crushing reviews. In the same month, he attended
the opening night of a production of Thornton Wilder's *Our Town*, ascetically
staged by Leon Schiller. The multiple voices of Grover's Corners, the village where
Wilder's play is set, offered a meditation about the fate and frailty of human life.

At the start of the summer holiday, 10 July, Miłosz was suffering from severe flu. He recuperated at his parents' place in Głębokie, among Baroque churches,
shtetl houses and endless market stalls. In a letter to Iwaszkiewicz the following
month, he wrote:

> Even Jews speak Byelorussian there, typhus is rife and peasants walk
> around in woven footwear and have pots full of golden roubles, a very
> prosperous area—linen. As soon as the political situation worsens—they

get rid of Polish currency and buy up everything possible: old horse-mills, bicycles, gramophones, motorcycles, vodka. (CM to Iwaszkiewicz, 14 August 1939)

The rest of the summer was spent in eastern Poland with Janka at a friend's estate, in what today is Belarus. In a letter dated the same day he informed his friend:

I feel comfortable here, it is already 14 August, and war hasn't started. But, really, no one believes it is going to happen ... I have not felt so relaxed for a long time—there is an air here of carefreeness, of secure plenty—so unfamiliar and unusual in Poland. A vast forest, and a comfortable house in the middle of it, made of brick, two storeys, with a bathroom, a telephone and in the garden wonderful fruit and roses and right behind it a wall of spruce trees. What a relief, so few people, a sense of space, fish and game.

The poet seemed happy, bursting with energy, and had many plans. In the autumn he expected to publish a new volume of poetry, along with translations of Oskar Miłosz's poetry, and a collection of essays with Miciński and Andrzejewski. 'All of the above mentioned projects were almost ready' (CM to Iwaszkiewicz, 14 August 1939).

Under the blazing light of fire-red Mars, Janka Dłuska and Czesław Miłosz were returning from Baranowicze by train, passing wagons full of laughing recruits. They spent the last Sunday before war broke out on 1 September 1939 at Iwaszkiewicz's house, partying and relaxing.

Miłosz was not conscripted. During the first nights of September, he was on guard duty on the roof of their house, supplied with sand and water in case of fire. The setting impressed itself deeply in his mind. Years later he described it in *A Treatise on Poetry,* giving proof that the source of poetic energy could be in fact, as Jacques Maritain asserted, love for people and the world and that the sentence written to Iwaszkiewicz, his final letter before the Apocalypse began, was true: 'I began to get damned interested in matters relating to people, and human problems, and listening to stories about them and observing people gives me great pleasure' (ibid.). Three verses convey this tenderness:

A beautiful night. A huge, lambent moon
Pours down a light that only happens
In September. In the hours before dawn
The air above Warsaw is utterly silent.
Barrage balloons hang like ripened fruit
In a sky just grown silvery with dawn.

On Tamka Street a girl's heels click.
She calls in half a whisper. They go together
To an empty lot overgrown with weeds.
A watchman on duty, hidden in the shadows,
Hears their soft voices in the bedding dark.
I do not know how to bear my pity.

Or how to find words for our common plight.
A little whore and a worker from Tamka.
Before them, the terror of the rising sun.
Later I would ask myself more than once
What became of them in the coming years and ages.

(*A Treatise on Poetry*, II, *NCP* 126)

F I V E

Voices of Poor People
1939–1945

Medals in the Suitcase

We pass by a procession of children,
Women with traces of rouge not yet washed off their faces
And so, with one lip red and the other white.
Rattle, rattle of the guns.
Once the killing started, killing is what there is left
And everyone lies, everyone lies.

Czesław Miłosz, 'September Poem'

The opening salvos of the Second World War were fired at 4:45 a.m. on 1 September 1939, when a German battleship shelled Polish positions at the Westerplatte Fort in Danzig, present-day Gdańsk. Concurrently, over sixty divisions of German troops with aircraft support invaded Poland from the west and the south, and at 6:00 a.m. the first bombs rained down on Warsaw. Elsewhere towns and villages were particularly targeted 'to create a fleeing mass of terror-stricken civilians to block the roads and hamper the flow of [Polish troop] reinforcements'[1] sent to halt the invasion. In an autobiographical piece from the mid-1990s, the poet conceded that 'I would not know how to recreate . . . 1 September, when we did not identify the explosions as bombing at first. The fire service was on standby, eager to receive orders from somebody. So traumatic was it to accept defeat that we are still unwilling to make room for it in our memories' (*Rok myśliwego* 266). Oskar Miłosz's prophecy and Czesław Miłosz's intuitions and fears were soon being realised, but the first days of the war were still a massive shock, before the obvious outcome of the invasion came to be reluctantly accepted. Briefly, the mood in

Warsaw lightened, particularly when Britain and France declared war on Germany on 3 September. Outside the British Embassy, a crowd broke into cheers.

Meanwhile, Poland's Second Republic was collapsing like a house of cards. On the night of 4 September 1939 a number of government institutions were evacuated. Soon after, the newly-appointed Minister for Propaganda announced the evacuation of further departments, amongst them Polish Radio, which was described as a source of 'important spiritual ammunition'. Radio employees were instructed to head towards Lublin and Lwów, hoping that in the eastern town of Baranowicze they also would manage to set up a radio station from which Poland's Commander-in-Chief, Marshal Edward Rydz-Śmigły, could broadcast to the nation.

Evacuation from Polish Radio's Warsaw HQ was ordered to take place at 4:00 p.m. from Dąbrowski Square, where a long column of busses, lorries and cars, as well as outside broadcast and propaganda vehicles with loudspeakers on their roofs, had been assembled. Supervising the move was the station's Secretary General, a retired lieutenant colonel, Zygmunt Karaffa-Kraueterkraft, who wore an army uniform for the occasion, and whose sword, stirrups and chestful of medals jingled as he issued instructions. One individual, repelled by this ostentatious display, shouted out at Karaffa-Kraueterkraft, 'Since you are fleeing, you might as well put your medals in the suitcase' (Maciej Kwiatkowski 75). As the unholy exodus of government officials gathered apace, the population of Warsaw felt that they were being abandoned by their leaders. On 6 September, Rydz-Śmigły left Warsaw, and Colonel Roman Umiastowski triggered a panic by calling for all men of conscription age to march eastwards.

Outside the radio building personal dramas began to unfold. Tadeusz Byrski, who was ordered to leave his wife and children behind, refused to join the evacuation, and there were many other similar cases involving radio staff. The core group who set off for the southeast consisted of Halina Sosnowska, Józef Czechowicz and Czesław Miłosz. His partner, Janina, however, was not with them.

What had happened? On the day of Polish Radio's departure, Janka was staying with her parents outside Warsaw, perhaps along with her husband, Cękalski; she was still formally his wife, though it was not clear what the relationship between them was now like. On returning to Warsaw, she could not find Miłosz and decided to wait for him, declining the opportunity to travel to Hungary with a relative of her husband.

Miłosz, in the meantime, had reached Lublin after travelling through the night on busy roads full of people fleeing south. One of the vehicles fitted with loudspeakers needed to be taken to the front line. Miłosz volunteered to take on this task, only to find, not long after setting out, that it was impossible to fulfil. The incredibly rapid advance of German troops in the area forced Miłosz and those with him to halt and hide the vehicle. By way of minor roads, they made their way back to Lublin on 9 September, a few hours after a heavy bombardment in which Józef Czechowicz was killed. The radio authorities made the decision that Miłosz should go to Lwów, Antoni Bohdziewicz to Wilno, and Bolesław Miciński to Baranowicze. The three set off in different directions at around the time the Blitzkrieg on Polish cities was at its height; no sooner did Miłosz reach the outskirts of Lwów than he realised that there was no hope of reaching the centre alive.

In the not so distant past he had written about propagandist lies. Now he experienced the sensation, while 'crawling into ditches, looking for cover . . . catching up on sleep between long stretches of bombing', that before his eyes the fancy theatrical facade had disintegrated and the costumes vanished in flames, revealing the nakedness and helplessness of the cast. The weakness of the over-proud nation had been suddenly exposed; ministers and departmental directors who fought over priceless, escape-enabling fuel, the elites who deserted en masse, all awoke feelings of fury in him, yet also relief that 'the nonsense had ended', that the long-expected catastrophe had 'freed us from the self-reassuring lies, illusions, subterfuges' (*NR* 204). In *Native Realm* he also mentions that, like most Poles, he did not believe that ultimately the Nazis would triumph in the war. However, in contrast to his fellow countrymen, Miłosz knew all too well the irreversibility of historical processes, and that the fate of eastern Europe would be changed dramatically. In the midst of fear and uncertainty, he experienced, curiously, a sense of liberation from the shackles of office life. Unexpectedly, life suddenly became simpler, limited to obeying orders and answering the most basic needs. His great friend Jerzy Andrzejewski (1909–1983) reacted similarly to news of the outbreak of war, describing it as a moment of 'purification': 'in the first months of the occupation he experienced something until then unknown to him, peace, concentration and equipoise'. In the space of a few days and months, 'life on a cerebral, spiritual and moral level ceased to exist, and there was only the life of reflex reactions and impulses to which one succumbed' (Synoradzka 44).

In Lwów, Miłosz stumbled upon *la caravane Potocki*, a long line of cars filled with fleeing aristocrats, among whom he found Jan Tarnowski, the wealthy philanthropist who had been keen to back his recent journal project. A descendant of a famous hetman, a keen traveller and a rich collector, he probably, like Miłosz, had no intention of escaping Poland. As Tarnowski had his own car and a supply of fuel, Miłosz joined him with the aim of getting back to Warsaw. To achieve that they thought the best plan would be to drive directly north first, then follow the eastern border before veering westwards.

They were thwarted, however. In accordance with the terms of the Molotov-Ribbentrop Pact, the Soviet Union invaded Poland on 17 September. It was the first stage in a process that would see the USSR's borders shifted over two hundred kilometres to the west, and the disappearance of Poland as a state. On their journey north, Miłosz and Tarnowski chanced upon early evidence of Stalin's cynical, opportunistic, callous plans to annex large swathes of Poland and all of the Baltic states: 'A large number of low-flying planes resembling bats convinced us that something was happening. Soon we were informed that Soviet tanks were on their way. We did not speak to one another. Jaś [Tarnowski] turned back' (*Rok myśliwego* 267).

Conscious that this meant Poland's utter defeat, they drove south through villages where the Ukrainians welcomed the arriving troops from the Red Army, before they eventually reached the border at Zaleszczyki, in western Ukraine. Not long afterwards, their fuel ran out, but then they struck it lucky when a young Romanian man came to their aid. He had spent time in Poland on a sailing course, and it transpired that his instructor had been Miłosz's brother, Andrzej. Keeping to minor roads to avoid being stopped by the police, and after a spell in a refugee camp, they reached Bucharest.

In Romania they learnt that they were far from alone. About twenty-five thousand Polish soldiers and twice as many fleeing civilians had preceded them, as well as the Polish President, Ignacy Mościcki, Marshal Rydz-Śmigły, dozens of generals and members of the cabinet. Under diplomatic pressure from the Germans, the French and the Soviets, the Romanian authorities interned them, refusing to allow them an onward passage to France. In that situation President Mościcki resigned, and his position was taken by Władysław Raczkiewicz, who was already in France. He in turn appointed General Władysław Sikorski as Prime Minister and Commander-in-Chief, thereby beginning the formation of the Polish Government-in-Exile. Both soldiers and civilians left the camps en masse to travel west to France, with the silent agreement of the Romanian guards. From the latter part of 1939 to the beginning of 1940, Bucharest was 'one of the most interesting cities on earth' (Żebrowski). Émigré life thrived there, and more than a dozen periodicals were published, thanks to financial support from the American Commission for Polish Relief.

Miłosz's memories about his stay in Bucharest are sketchy, and the poet made a point of saying that he did not want to dwell too much on that particular time in his life. The reason for that must have been his feelings of humiliation, as, faced with danger, he had connected himself with a privileged elite whom he had previously lambasted from his leftist standpoint. Thanks to Tarnowski and his acquaintances, Miłosz was allowed to stay in a large house belonging to a high-ranking officer and lived in relative luxury for a while. Not surprisingly, given his make-up, history and recent past, accepting these kindnesses seemed like an act of betrayal.

Miłosz also suffered constant bouts of guilt for having abandoned Janka. He managed to get in touch with her by mail and discovered that she had given up the opportunity to escape Poland, believing that he was still in the country. He longed to meet her at whatever cost, but did not plan to get back to Warsaw; the far more sensible option was to flee together to the West.

Tarnowski, who was heading next for Zagreb, offered Miłosz a seat in his car; around the same time, a radio crew setting off for France said he could have a place with them. He declined both offers, but arranged for Aniela Micińska, the sister of his friend, Bolesław Miciński, to travel with the radio crew, so that she could join her brother in Paris, which they hoped to reach via Wilno and Sweden. On hearing about that route to France, Miłosz resolved on a plan to meet up with Janka in Wilno, which by this time had been handed over to the Lithuanians by its Soviet conquerors.

He wrote immediately to Juozas Keliuotis, the *Naujoji Romuva* editor whom he had met just over twelve months before in Kaunas, asking for his assistance in getting permission to come to Lithuania. Keliuotis approached a contact of his, Juozas Urbšys, who worked at the Lithuanian consulate in Paris, and whom Czesław knew through Uncle Oskar. Urbšys, who was born in Szetejnie and knew Czesław's grandfather, Zygmunt Kunat, played a key role in arranging for some form of Lithuanian identity card to be prepared for Miłosz. According to Kelioutis, the documentation stated that Miłosz was Lithuanian and a Lithuanian citizen; according to Miłosz, however, the type of document he received simply guaranteed safety within the borders of the country issuing it. He stressed that travelling through the Soviet Union without a proper passport posed a massive risk, as he could be removed from a train at any time and then perish without trace. There is no official record in the archives to confirm either account.

Whatever document he possessed, he was still required to obtain a transit visa from the Soviet authorities. That took a few weeks before he was ready to travel eastwards, while his radio colleagues were en route to France. In those days 'farewells meant saying goodbye to the pre-war Poland ... I made a big mistake showing my travel documents to one of my radio colleagues, Wagner. He later made it public. The deduction was made that I had approached the Soviets in order to get into Lithuania' ('Materiały do mojej biografii').

That episode was the first link in a series of events which for many years prompted attacks on Miłosz for accepting a Lithuanian passport to avoid sharing the fate of the Poles during the war. In the minds of his accusers, it all fitted in with his membership in a circle which included Jędrychowski and Putrament, who soon displayed their zeal in giving full support to the new Soviet authorities. At the beginning of 1940, Lithuania was still an independent country, and entering its territory certainly could not be construed as an act of treachery. It was a different matter that, while he had been staying in Bucharest, Miłosz showed no interest in joining the Polish army to help restore Polish independence.

From a letter he wrote to Miciński, it appears that Miłosz was granted a Soviet visa in December 1939, and in January set off on a long journey which took him through Kiev, Orsha and Vitebsk, and was marked by traumatic experiences. These consisted of constant anxiety that he might be arrested; crowds of people filling railway stations for days and nights, and his having to fight for a place on a train; painful flashbacks of travelling through revolutionary Russia as a child; and then two episodes at the railway station at Kiev, where he was interrogated by an NKVD officer, and observed the poignancy of a fearful family, trying to hold things together, to keep going for their children's sakes:

> A peasant family—husband, wife and two children—had settled down by the wall. They were sitting on baskets and bundles. The wife was feeding the younger child; the husband, who had a dark, wrinkled face and a black drooping moustache, was pouring tea out of a kettle into a cup for the older boy. They were whispering to each other in Polish in muted voices. I gazed at them until I felt moved to the point of tears . . . This was a human group, an island in a crowd, that lacked something proper to humble, ordinary human life. The gesture of a hand pouring tea, the careful, delicate handing of the cup to the child, the worried words I guessed from the movement of their lips, their isolation, their privacy in the midst of the crowd—that is what moved me. (*Captive Mind* 248–249)

In a note to Iwaszkiewicz, Miłosz likened these encounters in Kiev to entering 'the last Dantean circle' of hell, and also reiterated what a massive gulf separated him from the Polish Communists and their sympathisers, which had increased after September's Soviet invasion:

> In order to understand the utter revulsion, the cold misery of this hell in which people are reduced to insects, one has to experience it in person. Only Zdziechowski and a few decent Catholic writers grasped the meaning of these occurrences. And perhaps, Céline. That's why I cannot find an ounce of pity for those home-grown enthusiasts [for communism] . . . the European tragedy will be horrific. (CM to Iwaszkiewicz, 28 May 1940)

He wrote later that 'the greatest calamity which could happen to anyone was to become a Soviet citizen' ('Materiały do mojej biografii'). That conviction would determine his actions when he fled Wilno following its annexation by the Soviet Union. Memories of Kiev quickened more subtle feelings within him: greater compassion and respect for other human beings, and a counter-discourse to that of the cynical ideologues of the far right and far left who viewed people simply as a malleable mass.

Reflections on the Inferno

'The poet, Czesław Miłosz, well known to the inhabitants of Wilno, arrived a few days ago in Kowno [Kaunas], following a journey from Romania, via Kiev and Leningrad', wrote Teodor Bujnicki in a Wilno daily, *Gazeta Codzienna*, on 7 February 1940. Before reaching Kaunas, Miłosz had stayed with his parents in Podkomorzynek, where life was largely unchanged from pre-war times, though it was by pure chance that they were still there.

Shortly before the outbreak of war, his brother, Andrzej, had turned up in Głębokie, eager to join the Polish Army, but the officer in charge at the chaotic station could not assign him to any posting. He waited until 17 September for news, when

> at five in the morning we were woken up by loud knocking on the window shutters of the wooden house where my parents lived. Someone sent from the district office shouted: 'Sir! The prefect says to flee immediately! The Bolsheviks are coming!' We heard the roar of tanks on a cobbled road coming from the east into town. We jumped out of bed: father—in his pyjamas, mother in her night-dress, me in my sports shorts. We ran straight for the car in the garage just as we were ... We ran leaving everything behind, as the tanks were already entering town. (Andrzej Miłosz, *Jaćwież*)

They escaped in an old Ford, along with a chest with the family silver in the trunk, getting to Wilno first, where they stayed overnight with relatives, and then on to Szetejnie. Despite Aleksander's status as a persona non grata, they were allowed to cross the border, where, on the other side, Lithuanian women welcomed fleeing people with bread and butter and tea. It was probably thanks to that hair-raising escape that Aleksander avoided summary execution or transportation, which is what happened to the majority of educated Poles in the Wilno region.

Andrzej looked after his parents, who were not well, and together with his friend from Suwałki set up an organisation to help Polish officers escape from Lithuanian internment camps before sending them on through Sweden to France. One of the links in the escape route was the manor house in Krasnogruda. In Wilno, they were in contact with a priest, Kazimierz Kucharski, at whose workshop false documents were produced; it was perhaps from this source that Czesław acquired passes for his further travel. During the period of Nazi occupation Andrzej

Miłosz established a transit point for Jews escaping from the Wilno ghetto to the Rudnicka Forests. Amongst those who escaped were Seweryn Trossa and his wife, for whom Czesław found a safe hiding place in Warsaw. These and similar acts would earn both brothers the title 'Righteous among the Nations,' issued by the Yad Vashem Institute in Israel.

On arrival in Kaunas, the Miłosz family arranged to meet Keliuotis to thank him in person for his help. Two pieces by the poet, 'Reflections on the Times of the Inferno' and, in another issue, 'The Ideas of Oskar Miłosz', appeared soon after in *Naujoji Romuva* in Lithuanian translations. In April 1940 Miłosz, Maśliński and Bujnicki joined a discussion forum of politicians, journalists, writers and scientists centred round Keliuotis's journal. With the takeover of Wilno by Lithuania, the new authorities entered into discussions with the Polish inhabitants of the city and its environs, who regarded the presence of the Lithuanian army and administration as temporary. This was the only area within the Poland of the Second Republic which continued to lead a fairly normal life; as it had good food provisions and active Polish organisations, it drew thousands of refugees. The Lithuanians, fearing too great an influx of Polish nationals into the Wilno enclave, considered transferring a portion of them elsewhere, and old antagonisms were heightened with the introduction of Lithuanian into schools and public life. Gradually, violent incidents began to occur, including attacks on Polish people leaving church after mass. Groups trying to reach a compromise by accepting Wilno's historical association with Polish culture were in a minority. While papers like *Gazeta Codzienna,* managed by Józef Mackiewicz and Teodor Bujnicki, harshly criticised Poland's right-wing, nationalist record, others, such as the circle around *Naujoji Romuva,* hoped that through a well-thought-out integration of the Wilno region within Lithuania there was a strong chance that the city could emerge as a tolerant space where different cultures and traditions received equal respect. Keliuotis saw Czesław Miłosz as someone who would be an ideal mediator between *Gazeta Codzienna* and *Naujoji Romuva* since he was related to the pro-Lithuanian Oskar Miłosz, held sound, inclusive political opinions and had a history of valuable public service.

In the early months of 1940, Miłosz submitted articles for both papers, introduced Keliuotis to Polish authors, and, according to Keliuotis's account, lived in the Lithuanian paper's publishing house. These were tense times, however, conducive to strengthening stereotypes and disagreements between the two communities. In Wilno, Lithuanian-Polish relations were deteriorating, with refugees from Poland regarded by the majority of Lithuanians as representing a 'colonist' threat and unwelcome competition when it came to jobs. Consequently, an act was passed in November 1939 concerning citizenship rights of the inhabitants of Wilno and its surroundings. It contained many conditions which made citizenship harder to secure even for Wilno residents of long standing. Many Poles, not surprisingly, felt threatened by being designated as 'foreigners', which could mean losing employment, or even repatriation into the Lithuanian countryside.

Miłosz passed most of his time in Wilno in the company of writers and thinkers who spent much of the day consuming vodka provided by a very rich Jew, Feliks Ferber:

> The drinking usually began at eleven in the morning . . . The poets J. and S., who set the pace, were too much the seasoned drunkards to fall into oblivion. They sipped vodka from large tumblers, continually refilling them to the brim, and carried on a ceaseless palaver throughout the entire day and far into the night. Next morning the hangover had to be cured, so the whole thing started all over again. Thus time, meaningless and hopeless, was experienced differently than in naked reality; it was transformed by alcohol. (*NR* 207–208)

Life was lived as on the *Titanic,* except that they had foreknowledge of the inevitable end—German or Soviet troops marching into Wilno. The alcohol had little impact on Miłosz, failing to allow him to forget his longing and his dread.

Much of his attention was concentrated on trying to bring Janka from Warsaw, so that they could leave for France together. This seemingly unattainable outcome received a boost when Miłosz faced a Polish military committee in Kaunas and was declared fit for military service. He was given a French visa and a plane ticket from Riga to Stockholm, and then from neutral Sweden to Brussels and Paris. Did he really plan to join the army and part with his love again? He had to buy a separate ticket for her, which cost several hundred dollars. The plan required Janka's determination to make the trip to Wilno with the aid of people traffickers, then pick a way through 'green borders'. With the plane to Stockholm due to leave at the beginning of April 1940, Janka decided not to come. The Germans had uncovered the escape route and stopped the flights, leaving Miłosz trapped and alone.

In the meantime, Wilno, which until then had been a relatively safe place, became itself a trap when, on 15 June 1940, the Red Army marched in, putting an end to Lithuania's brief independence. If his autobiographical description is accurate, Miłosz was sitting in the Rudnicki café at the moment the invaders appeared:

> A sudden heavy scrape of metal on the pavement roused my curiosity, as it did everybody's. People got up from their tables only to freeze in their tracks as they watched the large, dusty tanks with their little turrets from which Soviet officers waved amicably . . .

To the uninitiated observer, nothing special happened that day. Only
toward evening, megaphones began to blare and patrols of Asiatic soldiers paced up and down ... But the population, thanks to the proximity
of the Polish counties that had already been occupied, was initiated—
except for a few hundred naïve Communist enthusiasts. The fear, as it
mounted from hour to hour, seemed to become almost a physical, tangible presence. (*NR* 211)

In mid-July, in an atmosphere of terror, an election was arranged, accompanied
by the customary Stalinist practice of rigging the results beforehand.[2] The outcome was that a new, so-called people's parliament was created, which promptly
passed an act whereby Lithuania was incorporated into the Soviet Union.

Retrospectively, over many years, Miłosz reflected on the dilemma of
making the choice between collaboration and deportation, which the new ruling
powers in Lithuania would have insisted upon. In the ranks of those who worked
for the aggressors were Stefan Jędrychowski and Irena Sztachelska, who, a few
years later, along with Dembiński and Bujnicki, were given death sentences by
the tribunal of the Polish underground army for their collaboration with the
Soviet Union. Only one sentence was carried out, when Bujnicki was shot dead
in his apartment in November 1944. Miłosz's knowledge of what becoming a Soviet citizen would entail and his desperate need to get to Janka compelled him to
quit Wilno. Known in the city for having had a close association with some of the
Communist activists, he pretended to welcome the change in Lithuania's status
while, in secret, planning an escape. He found a guide from among a group of socialist activists, who were also looking at various means of leaving the occupied
zone through a 'green border'. There were incidents where so-called guides took
money from people, then led them straight into traps set by the Soviets. Miłosz was
more fortunate in choosing Zofia Rogowicz, an energetic and brave fifty year-old
socialist, who acted as a courier between Warsaw and Wilno, carrying documents
and money and subsidising her income by smuggling people fleeing Lithuania.
Miłosz had false documents allowing two inhabitants of Suwałki to travel to
areas of Poland occupied by the new Nazi regime whose official title was the
'General Government'. The plans got complicated when Rogowicz brought in a
rich pharmacist from Częstochowa in order to be able to cover the cost of guides
on the way. His appearance itself put them in danger:

Sophia, in a kerchief and carrying an old knapsack, looked like a country
schoolteacher; nor did I, with my homespun bag and the face of a native,
stand out. But the pharmacist—a greyish, bloated face, faded-blue little
eyes sneaking fearful and suspicious glances in our direction. The slug-

gishness of a hippopotamus, the very caricature of a bourgeois. He was dragging a huge suitcase tied round with a leather strap. (*NR* 216)

The inclusion of an additional traveller, who did not possess forged papers, forced the group to cross the Lithuanian border on foot.

They set off on their journey in July 1940, travelling by train westwards to a small town, Kalwaria. From there they started walking, bypassing an NKVD camp, to a village near the border which itself ran through marshland. They hid in a loft for two days, watching from a window a soldier patrolling the streets. At last, an opportune moment arose, a Sunday evening when country dancing was scheduled, which they hoped would act as a distraction to the guards. Wading for several hours through the marsh, they successfully reached the other side, where in the next village they found a peasant who took them by cart to the town of Suwałki, where they found shelter in a house on the outskirts: 'The fullness of being human is difficult to achieve; but to this day the inhabitants of that little house, a young droshky driver and his wife, who was suckling an infant, are proof to me that it is possible. Their fear struggled with a sense of duty toward their neighbor' (*NR* 221). Not realising that the majority of Suwałki's male population had already been sent to forced labour in Germany or murdered, Miłosz decided to take a walk in the town which was so familiar to him. He then discovered its new face: 'It was an appalling place. In a pharmacy owned by Szwejkowski, his son, dressed in a white overall, waved his hands when I entered the shop as if he had seen a ghost' (CM to Zbigniew Fałtynowicz, 21 September 1988), he recalled to a friend long after. He did not know then that his cousin Zaza, from Krasnogruda, had recently been arrested. Two years later he perished in Sachsenhausen concentration camp.

The driver from Suwałki gave them considerable assistance over the next part of their journey. They crossed the border with Eastern Prussia at night, close to a place called Raczki, and were met, as prearranged, by a Polish peasant working for a German farmer, who took them in his cart to Ortelsburg (now Szczytno). From there they took a train to Willenberg (now Wielbark), where the false passes suddenly came in useful when Miłosz and the pharmacist were stopped. After they showed their passes, they were allowed to move on. The next contact they were introduced to turned out to be an informer who handed them over to the military police. On the way to the police station, Miłosz ate his Lithuanian passport, because the data in it did not match the data on their passes. Luck was on their side. The commandant, a 'fat Bavarian' (*NR* 225), not only did not order them to be searched, but, perhaps through laziness or a bribe, let them go free. Soon they crossed another border and found themselves in the German

Reich. The next stage of the journey took them through villages where they found shelter with local people each night they stopped. In another town, Ostrołęka, Miłosz was struck in the face by a Gestapo officer. He had not known that when passing a German, one was always supposed to remove one's cap and step off the pavement. Yet again he was lucky, because the man in the black overcoat did not think to ask for documents. This left one last crossing to make.

> Never in my life had I crossed a 'green border' like this one, although I had seen a good many since my childhood. The theory went that the best time to cross was at noon, because all the guards ate lunch then; the theory . . . was known to everyone, including the guards. Through a forest of pines heated by the sun, groups of men and women, bent over by the load of their sacks and bundles, advanced in extended battle order, crouching behind trees, crawling along the moss, then making a run for it to the accompaniments of shots from all sides. These men and women were peasant smugglers carrying food products to be sold in Warsaw . . . That whole horde then crammed onto the train, hens cackled from baskets, geese honked, piglets squealed under the benches, people talked about prices and policemen, the coach smelled of cheap tobacco. We were in the Government-General. (*NR* 227)

After ten months, and having covered thousands of miles, Miłosz was again in Warsaw, faithful to Janka, but also to the pursuit of poetry.

The Theory of the Last Złoty

However shocking it may sound, the next few years brought personal happiness to Miłosz's life, despite its unspeakable horrors. He was in the prime of life, and uplifted by the company of the woman he loved. In some sense, he experienced a measure of freedom by not having to struggle to keep up a material position. The challenges that faced the couple involved fulfilling the most immediate needs, and the situation gave him the opportunity to concentrate on the most important things to him, poetry, poems and thinking. To the Nazis he was little more than an animal they could crush at will, which made him afraid, though the fear did not paralyse him. He learnt a new language, English, and began to translate, to read extensively, and to put together an anthology. He also wrote a play and essays, and enjoyed a breakthrough in his lyric work.

Miłosz finally made it to Warsaw at the end of July or the beginning of August 1940, and found Janka at their old address. Soon afterwards they were forced to find new lodgings, because the Germans continually sought out

Warsaw's best streets, expelling the Poles already living there. Miłosz and Janka, with a sole piece of furniture, an ottoman bed, moved in with Antoni Bohdziewicz on Mazowiecka Street and took one of his rooms. He had a job as a barman in one of the popular city cafés where actors performed and met.

When, in June 1941, Hitler launched Operation Barbarossa, his invasion of the Soviet Union, a considerable number of German officers were sent to the eastern front, freeing up many apartments and houses. Miłosz managed to get a spacious three-room apartment with a kitchen in Niepodległości Street, which also offered sufficient space for Janka's parents. The area was not at all built up, and the few individual houses stood next to small factories and wooden shacks. On the outskirts of the city, they could take walks in the fields. Miłosz learnt 'to live in a community, sharing fear, joy, poverty and hope' ('Na skraju Warszawy', *Przekrój* 16, 1945), as the poet wrote at the end of the occupation: 'They were inhabitants of the house and people from the neighbourhood with whom they went to collect rations of usually frozen potatoes, those with whom they stood in a queue for cigarettes and a hairdresser who was constantly in fear of being one of those picked up at random from the street' (ibid.) and either shot on the spot or taken to a concentration camp. 'A part of their community were smokers, who at first were young boys, but then springs, summers, falls and winters came and went and the little boys turned into beanpoles who played cards all day long' (ibid.).

In the vicinity of their apartment, as it was not a locale excluded from the nightmare, graves of people executed in the street began to appear, and a janitor threatened to denounce anyone he saw feeding Jewish children. In an article entitled 'On the Fringes of Warsaw', Miłosz wrote of

> a twelve year-old leader and his eight year-old sidekick who carried out his orders. They did their rounds, begging in the neighborhood exactly at the same time each day . . . We cheered inwardly when the younger one, grabbed by a passing German officer, used the moment when he was struggling with his holster, and to avoid execution ran into the yard, jumped inside a metal bin, putting the lid back on. The German was furious, went round the whole house, but could not find him. ('Na skaju Warszawy', *Przekrój:* 16, 1945)

In an unpublished sketch, 'Children of Europe', Miłosz wrote how, in an apartment one floor above them, someone installed a printing machine, which did not allow them to sleep in peace. He had nothing to do with the activities upstairs, which served a different political orientation, but was furious at the thought that he could have been killed by the Germans because someone else was producing a publication which was full of rubbish. Another story was about young Karol, one of the smokers, whom he saw just after the outbreak of the 1944 Warsaw Rising as he ran past wearing an old French helmet and was struck down immediately.

Former radio employees like Czesław and Janka could not return to work, of course, and had to find other sources of income, like so many others from the intelligentsia. Meagre earnings did not suffice to survive on, and tiny rations had to be supplemented by produce bought on the black market. Thanks to a system which involved smuggling, bazaars and bribes, the market functioned perfectly well, with the merchandise available in Warsaw sometimes surprising the buyers. An instance of this was the time when wagons of produce bought from the Germans turned out to be full of turtles. Writers found themselves in difficult circumstances, having to choose between collaboration, an option taken by very few, or finding new ways of earning money. Some put up their libraries for sale, worked as waiters, opened shops, drove rickshaws, or simply, like everyone else, sold anything they could. 'Living conditions are difficult to describe—generally, things are not as some people may imagine—the whole economic side does not look too bad—and I personally have not experienced poverty,' Miłosz assured his friends, now safe in France (CM to Aniela and Halina Micińska, n.d, but probably early 1944). In a poem written in 1944, 'A Book in the Ruins', he described a place which provided his first earning opportunity:

> A dark building. Crossed boards, nailed up, create
> A barrier at the entrance, or a gate
> When you go in. Here, in the gutted foyer,
> The ivy snaking down the walls is wire
> Dangling. And over there the twisted metal
> Columns rising from the undergrowth of rubble
> Are tattered tree trunks . . .
> . . .
> Now walk carefully. You see whole blocks
> Of ceiling caved in by a recent blast.
> And above, through jagged tiers of plaster,
> A patch of blue . . .

> (*NCP* 28)

During the fighting in September 1939, a building which housed the Polish Academy of Sciences was bombed, and a great number of books from the French Institute were buried under the rubble, among other collections. The library of Warsaw University began trying to salvage this material and offered badly paid but legal employment. Together with Stanisław Dygat, Miłosz pulled books from under the rubble and loaded them onto carts: 'I warmed myself in the sun, stretching out on the packing cases; I felt as if I were melting into a fascinating city-jungle

with its waves of panic and intermittent bursts of gunfire. In winter we sometimes made a detour to one of the employee's houses, where we warmed up with
a shot of pure alcohol' (*NR* 234). Sometimes alcohol made them reckless. On
one occasion, for example, on Puławska Street, a major street in the city, a Gestapo officer walking on his own looked uneasy when two drunk men staggered
towards him and a collision almost occurred. The first man, Miłosz, was belting
out 'The Internationale' in Russian at the time, and his companion 'The Marseillaise', out of tune, in French (Toporowski 340).

In the first months of occupation the Warsaw University Library became a
haven for Miłosz. The library retained some of its personnel, with whom he made
friends. The transporting of books from one site to another seemed to have no
end. The Germans decided to combine collections from the National Library
with the University Library to create Staatsbibliothek Warschau. The originator
of the move and his deputy set out to work on the gigantic project, reorganising
books according to different criteria, relocating them to different buildings, probably with the hope that the material would remain in Warsaw and not be sent off
to some eastern destination. The project was utopian, and, unbeknownst to them,
sabotaged by Polish workers, who were worried that the collections would become dispersed and destroyed. The German authorities halted the merger plan
before it could be completed, but it provided fairly long-term employment to
Miłosz. Watery carrot soup and potatoes, baked on the rings of electric cookers,
helped fill empty stomachs, and in the library buildings the poet could satisfy
another hunger, as he had access to heaps of books. Two decades later, he commented to a friend: 'Humanity, or civilisation, felt like a huge piece of cheese, and
I was inside that cheese. What a feast!' (CM to Jan Błoński, 3 April 1963). His
extensive reading, much of it in French literature, was reflected in essays in which
Miłosz made reference to a range of works by Roger Caillois, the French poly-
math, Max Scheler, the German philosopher, and Johan Huizinga, the Dutch
historian, as well as books about Nietzsche and Gide.

Hungry, overworked librarians laboured with great commitment to save
books, but also tried to collect material from the unofficial press. Some were involved in underground activities, and behind rows of ancient books in folio copies
they sometimes kept guns. Those who died in the Warsaw Rising, like 'Miss
Jadwiga', were remembered in one of the 'Six Lectures in Verse', with these famous
words:

Reality, what can we do with it? Where is it in words?
Just as it flickers, it vanishes. Innumerable lives
Unremembered.

. . .

While here, I, an instructor in forgetting,
Teach that pain passes (for it's the pain of others),
Still in my mind trying to save Miss Jadwiga,
A little hunchback, librarian by profession,
Who perished in the shelter of an apartment house
That was considered safe, but toppled down
And no one was able to dig through the slabs of wall,
Though knocking and voices were heard for many days.
. . .
The true enemy of man is generalization.
The true enemy of man, so-called History,
Attracts and terrifies with its plural number.
. . .
The little skeleton of Miss Jadwiga, the spot
Where her heart was pulsating. This only
I set against necessity, law, theory.

('Six Lectures in Verse', IV, *NCP* 497)

Miłosz's earnings from the library were not enough to sustain the couple. Janka found a job in a café bar, which after the autumn of 1939 was turned into the Sportmen's Inn, employing, among others, the athlete Jan Kusociński, winner of the ten thousand metres at the 1932 Olympics. At the time he was also secretly a member of the Polish resistance, and was killed by the Gestapo in 1940. Janka and Czesław also engaged in trading. After the retreat at Dunkirk, Players and Woodbine cigarettes and whiskey appeared on the market, along with less attractive merchandise to sell, including black pudding. Trading in gold was a much more profitable activity, and Janka worked as a buyer for an acquaintance who had opened a jewellery shop. Pieces of jewellery were melted and made into bracelets. The months preceding winter were often the hardest, when they had to buy in supplies of coal and potatoes. Jerzy Andrzejewski had a theory that the moment only one złoty was left, something positive had to turn up. More often than not, however, they had to borrow money, but in order to receive support from the Communal Bank, they had to find someone who would endorse them. The loan they secured was considerable, but enabled them to survive for over a year. Miłosz also received financial support from the clandestine Polskie Państwo Podziemne (the Polish Underground State), financed by the London-based Polish Government-in-Exile, for whom Iwaszkiewicz helped distribute funds.

An improvement in the writers' situation began in 1943, when editors began to buy manuscripts in anticipation of future publications. One such energetic individual was Zbigniew Mitzner, a pre-war socialist, journalist, satirist and creator of a satirical magazine, *Szpilki*, someone Miłosz knew from Wilno and a fellow member of the underground movement Wolność (Freedom) during the war. He planned to found a new publishing house, Wisła (Vistula) after the war. Many writers and scientists had their work published by him, for which they were well paid. Under the pseudonyms Edward Malisz and B. B. Kózka, Miłosz signed a contract to issue a collection of essays, 'Legends of the Present', a cycle of poems, 'The World', and a volume of poems published previously by the author himself.

———————————

A colourful individual with whom Miłosz became reacquainted during the war was Władysław Ryńca, who had shared a room with him at Wilno University. When they were students, Ryńca was a tall, thin-looking young man who always seemed very calm and collected, and spoke very little. As Miłosz observes in *Native Realm*, 'No-one ... could have foreseen his later [wartime] metamorphosis into a trader worthy of the Wild West' (*NR* 238). Acting on instructions from the Polish underground authorities, in 1941 Ryńca set up a transport company, known as 'The Firm', in occupied Wilno. It quickly proved unbelievably profitable, conducting business transactions among Wilno, Minsk and Warsaw. By bribing individuals from the German authorities and co-operating with partisans of different orientations, The Firm was able to trade in currency, smuggled guns and secret documents, and help Jews escape from Wilno. In Warsaw, Ryńca invested part of his colossal income in books. Miłosz, acting as his intermediary, signed contracts with, among others, Jan Brzechwa, Jarosław Iwaszkiewicz and Stanisław Dygat. The poet also conducted negotiations between Mitzner and Ryńca relating to a slightly surreal project, 'a merger between two non-existent publishing houses, both of which relied on the black market for income ... Negotiations were protracted, as they usually are when what is at stake is a treasure on a non-existent island' (*NR* 240).

Living under Nazi occupation meant constantly being stopped by German soldiers and having to produce valid personal documents. There were different, sometimes conflicting reports about the origin of Miłosz's papers, and accusations circulated that he was hiding behind a Lithuanian passport, which in reality would not have given him extra protection. In a letter to the editor of *Kultura* in 1956, in response to allegations coming from Poland regarding his allegiances during the war, he wrote:

> Wilno and the surrounding areas were re-integrated into Lithuania at the beginning of the war. When new passports were being issued to the

inhabitants in the spring of 1940, in the 'nationality' box I had *Polish* written in. Later, in Warsaw, I kept Lithuanian papers at the request of 'The Chief', who was then involved in transferring microfilms to London, and today belongs to the Polish United Workers Party (PZPR). I, however, did not even once show the [Lithuanian] passport to the Germans and cannot say whether the allegation that it saved me from being picked up and taken away by the Germans during round-ups in the streets was justified. (CM, letter to *Kultura:* 2, 1956)

Miranda's Island

And yet still we lived and because we were writers, we tried to write. Admittedly one of us disappeared from time to time, taken away to concentration camps or shot. We couldn't help it. We were like people on an ice floe, which was melting.

Czesław Miłosz, *The Captive Mind*

During the occupation years cultural life did not merely survive; on the contrary, it strengthened in importance, manifesting how vital its role was within society and Polish identity. Through the courage of creative artists and with the support of the well-structured Underground State, cultural events continued on an impressive scale. Examples of this are the series of thirteen poetry readings which were held, drawing an audience of over seven thousand, and the clandestine training course for filmmakers, who were later to document both German atrocities and the acts of defiance with which Poles responded. The organisers of the film course were Antoni Bohdziewicz and Jerzy Zarzycki, who were later joined by Janka Cękalska, whose pseudonym in the AK (the underground Home Army) was Joanna. Bohdziewicz and Zarzycki later documented on film the Warsaw Rising of 1944.

Cinemas and theatres which were officially sanctioned by the occupying General Government were almost entirely boycotted by the Poles, and so it was with the 'unofficial' theatre that Miłosz developed a strong bond. In April 1941, he attended group readings of *Miguel Mañara* organised by Byrski, and, later that year, Iwaszkiewicz's new translation of Giraudoux's *Electra,* as well as other adaptations of classical Polish and foreign literature. These events brought poetry, relaxation and laughter to people's lives, helping them forget, if only for a few hours, the horror of the occupation. In January 1943, Miłosz, Janka and Jerzy

Andrzejewski attended a performance of Leon Schiller's *Pastorale*, a Christmas play, in a home run by nuns for underage girls who had been rescued from prostitution:

> This was something else. The Mother of God, played by a girl from Powiśle or Grochów, was more human, more serene in her pain than any Italian Madonnas. Joseph, with his head shaved after typhoid, had a face which bore the marks of many years of poverty and hunger. The audience were school children with runny noses. The frantic manner with which those girls performed the shepherds' dance. ('Na Fantazym')

Miłosz went on to describe the experience at greater length in *Rok myśliwego* (A Year of the Hunter). A child-like, innocent Madonna with a mousy voice, who not that long ago had sold herself to German soldiers, appeared to him the essence of what theatre should be, 'a celebration of multi-faceted human character and adaptability, as a result of which everyone carries a whole range of experiences and gifts, from the highest virtue to the commonest evil' (*Rok myśliwego* 368). A few pages earlier he affirms, 'No Greek tragedy, no piece of work by Shakespeare, no Romantic drama gave me the greatest theatrical experience of my life, but rather a folk nativity play, acted out by poor girls from the Warsaw suburbs' (ibid., 366).

In 1942, Miłosz spent a few months translating *As You Like It*, using a French version and a nineteenth-century Polish translation, as well as his own modest knowledge of English. He had begun to learn English in the late 1930s, and during the war attended lessons regularly with Janka, initially taught by Jerzy Toeplitz (later the co-founder of the Polish Film School in Łódź), and subsequently with an Englishwoman, Mary Skryżalin, who came to their flat several times a week. From the library he borrowed books by Robert Browning, Edgar Lee Masters, William Blake, John Milton and T. S. Eliot, who had a considerable impact on his work, though Miłosz insists 'this did not mean imitating, for the disparity in experience was too great: T. S. Eliot's *The Waste Land*, for example, made somewhat weird reading as the glow from the burning ghetto illuminated the city skyline' (*NR* 238). Nevertheless, over the winter of 1943 he translated Eliot's famous poem, struck by how the 'unreal city' *The Waste Land*'s narrator describes mirrored the desolation beyond his windows, causing him to reflect, 'so many,/I had not thought death had undone so many' (Eliot, 'The Burial of the Dead', in *The Poems of T. S. Eliot* 58).

Over the four years he endured in occupied Warsaw, Miłosz took part in numerous meetings, held in the Pen Club, with authors representing different generations who would gather there to exchange opinions. Regular gatherings took place at the salon of Kazimiera Morawska, the widow of Professor Marian Morawski, rector at the Jagiellonian University in Kraków, who, following his

arrest in November 1939, perished in Auschwitz in September 1940. As an antidote to Nazi barbarism, those attending listened, for example, to translations
from German of poems by Rainer Maria Rilke (1875–1926). Apart from readings,
there were competitions, lectures and discussions, and also a number of organisational meetings involving what Jerzy Zagórski refers to as the 'poetry section': 'I
remember from these events Miłosz, Anna Świrszczyńska, Krzysztof Baczyński.
It was important to make contact with people from Kraków, like Jerzy Turowicz,
Kazimierz Wyka and Wojciech Żukrowski' (Zagórski, *Poezja* 1981, 5–6).

Miłosz had by this time moved far away from the mode he had deployed in
Three Winters, and began adopting the sparer style of poets ten years his junior.
Closer to him now was the work of writers such as Tadeusz Borowski (1922–1951),
whose 1942 volume *Gdziekolwiek Ziemia* (Wherever Earth) contains the reflection
'What will be left of us is scrap iron / and the muffled sneer of generations'. He also
admired greatly the poetry of Krzysztof Kamil Baczyński (1921–1944), recognising
in him a rare artistic talent.[3] Like Wilfred Owen, Edward Thomas and Siegfried
Sassoon, a poet-soldier and soldier-poet, he died fighting in the Warsaw Rising
in early August 1944.

During these literary encounters new work was presented. Although
sometimes heated discussions followed, generally the atmosphere was of mutual
support and camaraderie. As Miłosz remarks in *The Captive Mind,* their lives
were passed on a melting floe, from which people disappeared one after another,
arrested, sent to a concentration camp or killed. In order to numb fear, far more
vodka and moonshine were drunk than before the war. Small, 'thimble' glasses
were replaced by ones double the size. As drinking at evening social gatherings
was not possible or, indeed, sensible, sessions took place in the afternoons so that
everyone could get back home before the curfew.

Because of their similar sense of ironic humour and their increasing criticism
of the predominant stance within the Underground State, Miłosz, Janka and Jerzy
Andrzejewski became almost inseparable. They would read Balzac together and
discuss their periodical, which was either the first or amongst the first to appear in
occupied Warsaw. A small, hand-typed issue of a dozen copies appeared in 1940,
bearing the unstartling title *Magazyn Literacki* (Literary Magazine). It contained
articles and short stories mostly written by Miłosz and Andrzejewski under assumed names. Andrzejewski, the future author of *Ashes and Diamonds* (1948), was
particularly keen to develop a wider circle of friends and acquaintances and over
time became a very well-known figure. In his relationship with the occupiers, he
showed courage, and when under the influence of alcohol, he recklessly ignored
danger. Miłosz recalled a particular drunken incident when, while travelling in the
carriage of a suburban train, Andrejewski broke into song, 'Je suis Goebbels, /

je déclare la guerre totalle' (I am Goebbels and I declare total war): 'The situation began to look dangerous, because the carriage had a compartment for Germans, so I grabbed him and pushed him out at the very next stop, when we both fell on all fours in the snow' (*Zaczynając od moich ulic* 467).

Andrzejewski was habitually lucky, and his presence seemed to guarantee safety. Another illustration of this was the occasion when he and Miłosz were returning from Iwaszkiewicz's estate outside Warsaw on a morning train on 19 September 1940. Carefree, they got off at a station not far from Miłosz's apartment. They strolled casually along the street, unaware that a roundup was taking place not far behind them. When the poet reached home and opened his front door, he heard noises downstairs, and when he looked out his window he spotted the Germans taking away the janitor, who had been standing at the gate. That same day, the Germans arrested two thousand men: 'They became the men who built Auschwitz. If I was there then, I don't think I would have survived' (*Rok myśliwego* 349).

Miłosz accompanied Andrzejewski on at least one trip far outside Warsaw in August 1941 to deliver relief money to Józef Morton:

> In Jędrychów, we had to wait throughout the night for the next connec-
> tion, on a narrow-gauge train to Pińczów. The waiting room was for the
> benefit of Germans only and we were sent to a small building behind the
> station building. When we opened the door, we were hit by stuffy air and
> snoring. People slept on the floor and in layers. Here, Jerzy, always neat
> and picky, discovered my Samogitian indifference to a lack of comfort, to
> which he reacted with distaste. I lay down on this tangle of bodies and
> fell asleep immediately. I woke up rested while he spent the night sitting
> somewhere on a bench. (*Beginning with My Streets* 462–463)

On another narrow-gauge train they reached a station some distance from Kraków and travelled on to the city by foot. That hot summer day, walking along the fields, Miłosz remembered as one of the happiest in his life, as there was no sign of a black uniform. Kraków then seemed calm and safe, as if seemingly cordoned off from the horror of the war. They got to Łobzowska, and in an almost Parisian-style artists' garden café, they recognised with great astonishment the Jewish wife of Adam Ważyk. After Andrzejewski had attended a few meetings, in the evening he and Miłosz got drunk in a bar at the station, yet managed to catch a train to their next destination, Krzeszowice, where supper awaited them at the home of Kazimierz Wyka.

A photograph survives of the visit there, showing the three writers sitting on a heap of wooden planks by a sawmill. Wyka, who had reviewed *Three Winters,* shared Miłosz's desire to enhance intellectual life and his longing to see work that went far deeper than the writing appearing in the underground press, which largely offered reports on recent events and pieces to lift people's spirits, as well as propaganda. In a prose essay entitled 'With Coloured Ink', Miłosz recalled how

> in the first year of the war, I read the underground press with great enthusiasm, in the second with interest, but later I hardly ever touched it. The immensity of nonsense which anonymous journalists wrote was depressing for the reader and even today the thought of it comes back as sad memories, especially when one thinks how many human lives were lost because of those 'bulletins'. ('Kolorowym atramentem', *Przekrój*)

Both writers dreamt of book publications and mature discussion about the national myths, unafraid that they might be accused of 'blasphemy'. There was no platform for polemics and, as an alternative, they resorted to writing long letters.

At a later date the three men visited Kraków again, when 'because of some Nazi celebrations their red and black flags were everywhere'. Andrzejewski perhaps spoke for all three in remembering how 'we walked from Grodzka up to Skałka, and it was very quiet there, mildewy, with the breath of death. I understood then why the very young Conrad Korzeniowski fled from the graves and heavy atmosphere induced by signs of national martyrdom' (*Z dnia na dzień* 335).

The most important meeting place for Miłosz was at Stawisko. He wrote to his friends in France in the summer of 1942: 'Jaros [Iwaszkiewicz] gives us our feelgood factor: their hospitality (good alcohol, plenty of food, servants, fine conversations ... coffee in the study and memories of the fates of close friends)—are a respite, an escape from the reality of war, are unreal, like a film from a bygone era' (CM to Aniela Micińska and Jan Ulanowski, 28 June 1942). As the Iwaszkiewiczes were able to sell off plots of land, they managed to maintain a quality of life unattainable by the majority of writers. At times they had to improvise, however, with such intriguing dishes as chicken *à la literary style* (in other words, tough old birds), beans *à la Stawisko* and asparagus *à la Iwaszkiewicz*. They could still afford to invite fifty guests to celebrate their daughter's birthday in February 1942. Guests were taken back to the station in a sleigh pulled by horses which had bells in their harness: 'Miłosz, Andrzejewski and Roman Jasiński left singing and jingling' (Iwaskiewicz, *Dzienniki 1911–55* 196). Snow-white tablecloths, china, a glass of wine, a boat trip on the Vistula to Kazimierz, these were something more than 'bourgeois' pleasures; they offered a reminder or a sign of an almost forgotten normality. Situated off the beaten track and never bothered by the Gestapo, the manor house at Stawisko provided a refuge to many runaways, and moments of relief to a larger number. Reading evenings and concerts were organised there, and amongst the most frequent guests were Andrzejewski, Baczyński, Dygat, Witold Lutosławski, Andrzej Panufnik, and, arriving almost every Sunday, Miłosz. He later wrote:

> Here events of the Warsaw underground were discussed and rated, underground publications evaluated, as well as their anonymous authors whose names were really known, as well as what was happening to writers, actors, musicians, museums and libraries. Here Iwaszkiewicz read his latest work to a small audience and so did others, including me. (*Rok myśliwego* 212)

Iwaszkiewicz, ten years later, found a neatly hand-written poem, which Miłosz had presented to his wife, Anna, on her name-day, and noted in his journal: 'What a splendid poet, whose wonder is impossible to define, one of the greatest poets of this brow-beaten world' (Iwaskiewicz, *Dzienniki 1911–55*, 185). In July 1943, in the bowels of hell, his words of beauty and joy rang out:

> Miranda descends in glare. The dark ringlets of her hair
> Fall on a long dress coloured by her flesh.
> The guests come up the steps, and she leads them
> To the rooms and calls out clapping, hey, Artemis,
> Bring wine, take the one on the right.
>
> ('Sicilia sive insula Miranda', *Wiersze* V, 142)

Gniewosz

> Pruszyński in his book about Spain talks about a young Basque poet, who translates Sophocles' *Antigone* while on the front line. That poet understood that crossing out a year from a nation's culture will not go unpunished. Future generations will forget about the state of people's nerves [in war-time], but they certainly will not forget about a good translation of *Antigone*.
>
> Czesław Miłosz, 'Seeing Things at a Distance'

> A tough life cutting a sheet of the world with a diamond!
> If I died young, I would die in a dream of thoughts
> Not knowing that nimble one, who rules the world.
> Hence, the moral, one should not die too soon.
>
> Czesław Miłosz, 'A Moral', *Wiersze wszystkie*, 137

On 28 June 1942, Miłosz wrote to Aniela Micińska, 'I have been getting closer to getting a laurel wreath (I'd rather it was not awarded posthumously) and I have been learning, and the years pass so fast'. He was half-joking, hinting at the dangers in Warsaw, but also quite seriously acknowledging his rising position, and the fact that more and more often he was being rated as an outstanding poet of his generation. Already in September 1940 he had been at work preparing a new collection of poetry. He typed out and then copied *Poems,* a twenty-eight-page booklet. It had a black card cover emblazoned with his grandfather's name, 'Jan Syruć', and a note, 'From the Library of Manuscripts of the "Brzask" Publishing House, Lwów 1939'. This may well have been the first clandestine book published in occupied Warsaw. Forty-six copies were made, a portion of which were probably given out gratis and the rest sold directly by Miłosz himself or with the help of friendly booksellers. This is how Andrzejewski, the co-founder, remembered setting up the fictional publishing house:

> Antoni Bohdziewicz came to our aid. He had a copying machine and paper ... Miłosz used an ordinary cobbler's needle to punch holes in the paper, while I cut the black sheets and Janka sewed the copies together with ornamental chenille ... From a safety point of view, the room was a death-trap. On the table, the couch, the desk and the floor, everywhere lay white, treacherous pages. Miłosz struggled with the cheap needle, and Janka stabbed her fingers, while I, using a razor blade, did not always manage to get the sheets to the required size. And that is perhaps why we experienced during those days some of the most joyous and brightest days of the whole occupation. We were creating a small and modest thing, with our own hands, and against the nightmare of reality. (*Gra z cieniem* 145)

A year later, in autumn 1941, 'Jan Syruć' was visited by Zenon Skierski, an old acquaintance from the radio, a prose writer, a journalist, and the editor of *Jutro* (Tomorrow), a *Free Poland* publication. He had decided to set up an underground publishing house and was looking for materials. Miłosz told him about a Jacques Maritain essay he had read, *A travers le désastre,* which offered an analysis of the reasons for the French defeat in June 1940 and voiced his vehement opposition to the puppet Vichy government which was collaborating with the Nazis. Having emigrated to the United States, Maritain published this piece in New York in 1941 under the title *France My Country, through the Disaster.* A copy was brought to Poland by a Dutch merchant, and then forwarded to the literary historian and essayist Maria Czapska. Miłosz wanted to translate the book for two reasons: firstly, because he wanted to introduce the author to Polish readers, and secondly, to improve Polish opinions about the French, as they had been gravely shaken by the French collapse. Skierski accepted Miłosz's proposal, fast-tracked its printing and 'waved the proof-sheets triumphantly in the middle of a street with many Germans around' (*Ogród nauk* 172). At the beginning of 1942 the first publication of the Polish Publishing House appeared. Astonishingly, *Drogami klęski*, to give it its Polish title, was printed in a run of 1,640 copies, of which 1,300 were sold in six weeks. In his introduction Miłosz claimed that

> Maritain's importance lies not only in his explanation about the mechanism of the French defeat, but also in putting forward a sensible mode of thinking about the current situation in the world. A most difficult task at present is to take a sober, hard-headed look at the failings and vices of one's own nation and not begin to doubt its worth. ('Poszukiwania' 29)

This 'sober tone' was not easily adopted in the circumstances in which Poland currently found itself, especially by the artists, who might have had the capacity to plumb the state of its soul. Miłosz must have been aware of that when working on the translation, as well as when he assembled for Skierski an anthology titled *Invincible Song: Polish Poetry of War Time*, which also came out in 1942, in 1,600 copies. It was later regarded as one of the greatest achievements of wartime typography and had a colourful cover which depicted a lyre, a scroll, a symbolic dried-up branch and a sword, although Miłosz had not been keen on this imagery. In a volume of 120-plus pages, Miłosz included poems by both established and lesser-known authors, such as Julian Tuwim, Antoni Słonimski, Władysław Broniewski, Anna Świerszczyńska, Jerzy Zagórski and Krzysztof Kamil Baczyński. It was a comprehensive collection representing different trends and voices that did, however, omit some of the youngest poets.

Part One, 'The Omens of a Storm', identified a number of pre-war lyrics which foretold the catastrophe. Later, in an introduction to 'Human Lament', Miłosz wrote that 'only human suffering is a measure of the world', and pointed to the impossibility of capturing war's reality in words. In another section, 'A Calm Glance', Baczyński's poem beginning with the words 'Oh city, city— Jerusalem of woe' stressed the necessity for affirmative ethical values countering the triumph of nihilism, as well as the need for a global perspective and a global reckoning.

In the final section, 'The Road to Poland', Miłosz discussed the position of Polish émigrés and the kind of society now existing in the country, stating emphatically that 'all crucial changes affecting the future of Poland will be determined by the large masses of people still living in the country, rather than by those who emigrated, whose role must not be overstated' (*Pieśń niepodległa* 94). *Invincible Song* was not merely a collection of poems about the war, but an anthology realised with a conscious intention. Miłosz estimated that the book ranked amongst the best of underground publications, and at the same time that it was the least 'useful', because poems had been selected on the basis of their artistic merit, and not for their rhetorical quality.

A poem he wrote two years later, 'A Journey', asked questions about the meaning of war experiences, the possibility of finding in them something more than fear. At the same time, it enabled the poet, who pictures rubble and children shivering among ruins, to walk 'in calm brightness', when

> Outside Warsaw stood dazzling seas,
> The warm ocean turned into pearls the Mazovian sands
> And in the open background of clouds
> The fire of a rising sun burst through.
>
> (*Wiersze* I, 173)

Poems from that time often invoked motifs from songs, as if a lullaby could offer an escape from fear. Having translated Shakespeare, he was able to combine elements from the great dramatist's oeuvre with traces from his own past poetry into the new work. What Miłosz sought was a magic wand, like Prospero's, enabling him to conjure an island—and a new beginning—far from the horrors of the occupation. Metaphors generate epiphanies, like that moment when God created the world: 'let the poem open up like a golden sphere, / and in a blaze a light a different earth is born' ('Morning', *Wiersze* I, 185).

In a note to Kazimierz Wyka, responding to a critique of his poems, Miłosz confessed:

> My ability to feel pity for my situation in the world lessens, which perhaps is a necessity for the lyrics ... I do not have the capacity to empathise with the wider community either. Instead my whole effort is directed towards an intellectual structure, towards thesis and antithesis of thought ... Times of great crisis are not conducive to lament and elegies. A cry sounds then like the buzz of a mosquito.

The poet's task is to employ

> language as a means of rendering some mental representation of reality, taking great care to use the widest possible range of imagery and diction, creating an overgrown garden rather than beautiful stone flowers. (CM to Wyka, 29 November 1941)

The poet was engaged in a testing intellectual journey. Together with Janka and Stanisław Dygat, he attended clandestine philosophy seminars delivered by Władysław Tatarkiewicz (1886–1980), one of Warsaw's most eminent professors.

In August 1942 Miłosz began a lengthy, highly cerebral correspondence with Andrzejewski. Its principal aims, they decided, would be totally candid, to distance themselves from any kind of myths, using 'different means than the measure of patriotic exultation' (*Legends of Modernity* 195). At times of great cultural catastrophe, an intellectual's task was not to offer consolation, but to secure the foundations of humanity endangered by ideological lies, to find anew 'seeds of good sense' (ibid., 184), ethical norms with which to resist despondency. He stressed the undeniability of the religious dimension, challenging humanist claims about the total freedom of the individual, which paradoxically carried in itself the germs of totalitarian thinking. He was carrying out research reading at this juncture for *Legends of Modernity*, a collection of essays exploring the trends in thought which had nurtured the European culture of totalitarianism. The book was completed in 1944, expressing a conviction that the developments of these philosophical, political and social ideas had produced two distinct but contrary outcomes: 'terrible wars, exploitation and degradation', but also 'the concept of a common humanity', which had led to the growth of 'workers' unions and security schemes and education for all' (ibid., 157). That it was easier for Miłosz to demythologise than to identify the sources of hope was picked up on by Anna Kowalska (*1903–1969*), an exceptional writer and intellectual from Lwów, who was one of *Legends of Modernity*'s first readers:

> Miłosz's essays made a great impression on me. His almost hawk-like clarity in observing various issues. But this book also emanated frostiness. His own favourite ways of thinking, values, sense of how the world of spirit was ordered—it is all in tatters, everyone who wants to live must start afresh. No alternative, no easier solutions. (Kowalska 78)

Irrationality, according to Miłosz, marked the starting point for the loss of moral values. In an effort to capture 'the experience of war', he also pointed out that a society that loses faith in civilisation, human values and democratic order might well end up fixating on its own myths to oppose those of the invaders, instead of challenging them with reason and truth.

These reflections and warnings set Miłosz in opposition to the views held by large numbers of people at the time. Reconstructing his life during the occupation period reveals further instances when he diverged from the mainstream of underground thinking. He was frequently moved to anger by publications filled with Romantic political fantasies aimed at supporting resistance activity, but which at times led to the totally needless loss of life. For Miłosz wisdom should not shy away from expressing anger, nor should it ignore stupidity which generates evil. Sources from the occupation period refer to Miłosz being vivacious and often bursting into song, but also exploding with rage. That happened, for example, at a reading event, because of what he sensed as the emotionally overcharged, Romantic 'nationalist' atmosphere prevalent amongst the audience. Subsequently, he wrote to the organiser to apologise for his outburst and his unacceptable behaviour, which was caused, he admitted, by his extreme, intensely felt opinions. Such incidents lay behind the nickname he acquired, 'Gniewosz', from *gniew*, meaning 'anger', which was grafted onto his actual name.

A crucial debate in which Miłosz participated in those years centred around democracy, which, in part, was blamed for enabling Hitler to gain power. Others concerned what might justify the use of violence, and the effects of Romantic mythology. Often his adversaries were the young poets who wrote for the periodical *Sztuka i naród* (Art and Nation). Miłosz remembered how 'conversations with those young people were difficult. To them we were "gentlemen humanists" and the word "democracy" sounded *passé*, something spoken about by the old and toothless' (*Zaraz po wojnie*, Kraków, 1998). Miłosz's attitude towards involvement in the resistance movement diverged strikingly from theirs. The risk of ending up in Auschwitz had not deterred him from attending discussion group meetings or publishing books. Like many of his friends, including Iwaszkiewicz, he drew the line at participating in sabotage and propagandist activities, since he considered these as irresponsibly playing with too many human lives. Amongst Warsaw's young, where the cult of patriotic bravery was nourished, readiness for martyrdom in the service of Poland was lauded. Miłosz's stand made him unpopular, and he was accused of remaining on the sidelines, a spectator, a poetic commentator neutral on the great struggle. In May 1943, the twenty-one year-old Wacław Bojarski, whose poems appeared in *Art and Nation*, was shot and mortally wounded by the Germans for placing flowers on Copernicus's monument on the four-hundredth anniversary of his death. In the early days of the Warsaw Rising, two twenty-two year-old poets, Tadeusz Gajcy and Zdzisław Stroiński, who were arrested for accompanying Bojarski on his fateful mission, perished on the barricades. On the fourth day of the Rising, a bullet from a German sniper destroyed the life of the greatest hope of Polish poetry, Krzysztof Kamil Baczyński.

It is difficult even today to look dispassionately from a distance at these acts of blood-letting. While honouring the courage these young men showed, it is hard not to see a tinge of recklessness in their deeds and to feel that those deaths ought to have been prevented. 'Although many will die,/ perhaps me, perhaps you among them/ the nation will not perish', Anna Świrszczyńska had written in the *Invincible Song* anthology. Miłosz did not want to be one of those who died, and had the honesty to admit it; in an interview with the author in May 2005, Marian Brandys remembered the poet's tirade against what he termed 'a compost generation'. Miłosz himself wrote later: 'I carried terror around inside me like a bullet ready to explode (*ABC* 285). In the occupation years, he lost nearly half his friends, and observed a terrible incident near his house when the Gestapo drove up to a couple walking with a pram to arrest the man and a Jewish woman of about twenty:

> Her body was full, splendid, exultant. She was running along the street, her hands raised, her chest thrust forward. She cried piercingly 'No! No! No!'. The necessity to die was beyond her comprehension—a necessity that came from outside, having nothing in common with her unprepared body. The bullets of the SS guards' automatic pistols reached her in her cry. (*Captive Mind* 184)

Miłosz believed that he had been given a different fate, that he was an instrument of powers stronger than himself. He believed also that if he had not completed the work he was destined to do, then he must remain alive to carry it through. He did not want to be a stone thrown into a trench. His continuing ambivalence about the sacrifices others made pervades 'The Spirit of History', from his volume *A Treatise on Poetry* (1957):

> The twenty-year-old poets of Warsaw
> Did not want to know that something in this century
> Submits to thought, not to Davids with their slings.
> . . .
> Copernicus: the statue of a German or a Pole?
> Leaving a spray of flowers, Bojarski perished:
> A sacrifice should be pure, unreasoned.
> Trzebiński, the new Polish Nietzsche,
> Had his mouth plastered shut before he died.
> He took with him the view of a wall, low clouds
> His black eyes had just a moment to absorb.
> Baczyński's head fell against his rifle.
> The uprising scared up flocks of pigeons.
> Gajcy, Stroiński were raised to the sky,
> A red sky, on the shield of an explosion.
>
> (*NCP* 130, 131)

Miłosz admitted to Aniela Micińska in a letter written in 1942 that he had become less mystical, but more sceptical. He mentioned how much he enjoyed the company of Tadeusz Kroński, who called himself 'Tiger' because of his intellectual rapacity. They had met before the war, and later, with Bolesław Miciński and Jan Kott, attended Professor Tatarkiewicz's seminars on philosophy together. Kroński and his wife, Irena, a philosopher and classical linguist, lived in Warsaw during the occupation, earning money by producing cigarettes for the black market. Because she was Jewish and he was half-Jewish, they rarely left their apartment.[4] Despite the potential risks, they maintained their pre-war contacts. After Kroński's essay 'Fascism and European Tradition' appeared in one of Skierski's clandestine publications, he and Miłosz met more often, and before long Irena, Tadeusz, Janka and Czesław became firm friends. As so often, a connecting factor was their shared interest in leftist idealism in pre-war Poland, and the fact that they all dreaded what Communism might bring. Undoubtedly Tiger was full of private complexes and phobias; he loathed nationalism and anti-Semitism, and was closest in spirit to eighteenth-century Enlightenment rationalism. He believed in reason, which, in his eyes, took the form of a Power governing the earth, according to whose rule one ought to live in order to avoid misfortune. A wise and moral person who in occupied Warsaw read the Gospel and Plato in Greek, he never criticised Russia, because then it had the victorious Ghost of History on its side.

Those who came to know Kroński well used to say that his thoughts sparkled in jokes and mockery, but on paper they faded and were boring, as if he were not a philosopher, but lived philosophy. Under Tiger's influence, Miłosz became interested in the ideas of Pierre Benjamin Cornichon, who championed the intellect, the concrete, the truth, and deplored irrationality, naive vitality and abstract dreams, which led inexorably to misfortune. In a short essay titled 'Political Imagination', written in 1943, Kroński argued that the second set of characteristics had been prevalent within Germany's Weimar Republic, and had rendered it helpless in preventing Hitler from coming to power. However, it is highly likely that he also had in mind the leaders of Poland's underground movement, who imagined that an eventual victory would herald the restoration of Poland's pre-war borders. Miłosz recalled Kroński's defining

> hatred for people who live badly. Hatred not only for the Nazis ... but also for most of their adversaries, the Polish patriots. During great catastrophes one should try to live well: that, for him, was the only guarantee of salvation. What does that mean? It means not sinning in thought against the structure of the universe, which is meaningful. One sins by falling into hallucinations, by absolutizing impermanent values, by despising our mind, which leads us towards a mathematical ordering of cause and effect ... Poland's underground was self-sacrificing as perhaps no other in Europe. But just for that reason, Tiger watched it with horror and pity, realizing the full extent of the tragedy. (*NR* 244, 245)

Politicians in the London Government-in-Exile, officers in the AK (Home Army) and its dedicated soldiers did not know how to be 'wise', that is, how to understand the shape of History, which resulted in the extensive loss of life in the Warsaw Rising. For Kroński, Marxism provided the tools of reason—and here began the most risky part of his analysis—which, in his view, pointed to the objective inevitability of Communist Russia's eventual triumph. On an intellectual level, Miłosz seemed to accept this conclusion, but disagreed strongly with Kroński's failure to apply any ethical evaluation to actions taken by the Soviet Union. Whereas Miłosz was left with no illusions about Stalinism, not just due to his personal experiences, but also because of the reliable information provided by the weekly *Novoye Slovo,* published by White Russian émigrés in Berlin, Kroński refused to acknowledge the validity of this evidence. They would be at odds after the war, arguing whether the new political reality was 'real', but also 'good'. For the moment, Kroński was an important factor in, or perhaps only a catalyst for, the change in Miłosz's poetry. He himself called it a liberation, a conscious realisation that the world of pre-war Poland was finished completely, and also that, as an artist, he had the right not to submit to the pressure of society or his environment. He also felt that his duty as a poet was not to conform to his readers' expectations by giving them the answers they wanted, but rather to display sovereignty, clear vision and wisdom, even if the wisdom was to cause pain. This is what led to the emergence of a new poetry, where

> pity, sympathy and anger gave that poetry directness. Despite the circumstances, and despite images of ruins and destruction taken from my surroundings, it was a triumphal poetry. It celebrated the holiday of my coming into health, for the first time in my life. A recovery from that powerlessness when everything, both in the world and in us, is so obscure and tied up in knots that we lack the courage to be sharp, like a diamond cutting glass. I had written poems on 'social' themes and had been bothered by their artificiality. I had practiced 'pure' poetry and had been no less irritated. Only now had the contradiction vanished. Now even the most personal poem translated a human situation and contained a streak of irony that made it objective. Something had gone on inside me after I admitted a brutal truth to myself: Poland's pre-war society, which had shackled me with its subtle collective censorship, meant absolutely nothing to me, and I was indifferent to its latest pathetic and messianic embodiment. Virtue had gagged me up to then: one had to throw it off and proclaim that what appeared to be the end was not the end of either tradition or literature or art. (*NR* 247)

'A Poor Christian Looks at the Ghetto'

Someone lies under machine gun crossfire in a city where fierce battle is taking place. He looks at the block paving-stones and observes an amusing spectacle: the paving blocks start standing up like a hedgehog's bristles—the bullets hitting their sides

displace them and shift them sideways. Such a moment puts to the test poets and
philosophers.

Czesław Miłosz, Zniewolony umysł / Captive Mind

In the spring of 1943, Miłosz wrote a cycle of twenty short poems entitled 'The
World: Naive Poems', which, when read out loud, must have shocked his listeners.
With the sounds of shooting and terrified cries still ringing in their ears, they heard
verses composed in regular eleven-syllable lines, rhymed *abab cdcd*, depicting scenes
totally at variance with the familiar hellish reality they faced daily. 'The World' presented them with a sequence of little cameos from childhood, images which would
not be out of place if hung above a tiny bed, showing a guardian angel watching
over a child and its night-time journeying.

Here is the world in which a brother and a sister walk home from school
through 'an oak wood': there is a picket-gate, its top painted white, next to which
'yellow jasmine' flashes like 'a tiny lantern' ('The Gate', *NCP* 37); and there again,
a wooden handle that remembers thousands of touches, and a porch from which
a view 'of forests, rivers, fields and tree-lined lanes' stretches on and on. Here,
Mother pours out soup, and Father studies 'a book drawn by thought from nothingness', which provides him with peace-giving wisdom. From this he can show
them Europe, since

> On sunny days you can see it all clearly.
> Now it is smoking after many floods,
> A home for people, dogs, cats, and horses.

('From the Window', NCP 44)

Surrounding the home are 'the trees so huge you can't see treetops', and high
above them 'the bird kingdom'. War exists only as illustrations to *The Iliad*, death
will only take away a moth hiding in a book ('Pictures', *NCP* 41), and even devils
smile happily—from sculptured heads in the dining room (*NCP* 39). When the
little hearts get frightened by the stuffed head of a boar, Mother will calm them
with a lit candle; and when the girl and the boy get caught outside by night in
a forest, Father will disappear from their eyes, and fear suggests that the 'darkness will last forever' ('Fear', *NCP* 53), soon the black will yield before the beloved voice.

> 'Here I am—why this senseless fear?
> The night is over, the day will soon arise.
> You hear. The shepherds' horns already sound,
> And stars grow pale over the rosy glow.

'The path is straight. We are at the edge.
Down in the village the little bell chimes.
Roosters on the fences greet the light
And the earth steams, fertile and happy.

'Here it is still dark. Fog like a river flood
Swaddles the black clumps of bilberries.
But the dawn on bright stilts wades in from the shore
And the ball of the sun, ringing, rolls.'

('Recovery', *NCP* 54)

Here we have the world, discovered with the eyes of a child and, at the same time, as it ought to be, given to human beings to live in—a world filled with sacred order, as if the poet raised a building of sense in spite of the nightmare surrounding him, setting existence against nothingness. It is possible that the idea for 'The World' was influenced by the Oriental poetry Miłosz read, or by a translation from the English poet Thomas Traherne (1636–1674), aged six at the outbreak of the bloody English Civil War, in whose poetry childhood is paradisal, and the brutal world of adulthood is suspended in time. Another, later, obvious model must have been William Blake's *Songs of Innocence and Experience,* whose composition coincided, respectively, with the start of the French Revolution and the time of the Reign of Terror. The principal resource Miłosz drew upon in 'The World' was rooted in childhood memory, that brief spell in Szetejnie when as a young boy he knew the meaning of security, trust and delight, onto which was grafted his early intellectual journeying in Thomistic philosophy, in which the world is presented as it is in reality, independent of our perception, and at the same time allowing access to a higher, divine reality. The poet himself pointed out that 'the "naïve poems" I wrote then have a somewhat deceptive simplicity; they are really a metaphysical tract, an equivalent, in colors and shapes, of the school blackboard on the Rue d'Assas where Father Lallemant drew his Thomistic circles' (*NR* 248). In the cycle he also included poems outside a child's perspective, dedicated to three divine virtues—love, faith and hope:

Hope is with you when you believe
The earth is not a dream but living flesh,
That sight, touch, and hearing do not lie
. . .

Some people say we should not trust our eyes,
That there is nothing, just a seeming,
These are the ones who have no hope.
They think that the moment we turn away,

The world, behind our backs, ceases to exist,
As if snatched up by the hands of thieves.

('Hope', *NCP* 49)

The concluding poem in the sequence, 'The Sun', introduces in seemingly naive words the dilemma over whether art should be 'pure or engaged'. It speaks of the necessity of never losing the capacity 'to credit marvels' (Seamus Heaney, 'Fosterling', *Opened Ground* 357), responding to the inexhaustible variousness of the physical universe with due humility:

Whoever wants to paint the variegated world
Let him never look straight up at the sun
Or he will lose the memory of things he has seen.
Only burning tears will stay in his eyes.

Let him kneel down, lower his face to the grass,
And look at light reflected by the ground.
There he will find everything we have lost:
The stars and the roses, the dusks and the dawns.

('The Sun', *NCP* 55)

In order to kneel before the world, seek in it the divine reflection, and claim that this world is more important than the ego, there needs to be love, and

Love means to learn to look at yourself
The one looks at distant things
For you are only one thing among many.
And whoever sees that way heals his heart,

Without knowing it, from various ills—
A bird and a tree say to him: Friend.

('Love', *NCP* 50)

As the distinguished American critic Helen Vendler noted in an essay presented at the International Czesław Miłosz Festival at Claremont-McKenna College in April 1998:

'The World' could have been *The Waste Land*. Both spring from the devastation of a world war; but where Eliot shows what was, Miłosz shows what-ought-to-be as an 'is'. And yet Miłosz's '*ought-to-be* seen as *is*' does not inhabit the Absolute. To the contrary: it inhabits the actual. (Vendler, *Partisan Review* 133)

Miłosz's *The Waste Land* or Miłosz's *Songs of Experience* became *Voices of Poor People,* but both 'The World' and the deliberately chosen subtitle, *Naïve Poems,* must be read as wholly ironic, a quality the reality of the time bestowed on the poems. While seemingly stepping outside of the current moment, the lyrics became a means of not just facing, but universalising it. It was with this poem that irony began to be a recurring feature in Miłosz's poetry, undoubtedly as a result of Kroński's influence. His experience as the translator of Eliot's many-voiced poem and of Shakespeare's plays, along with his reading of Robert Browning's dramatic monologues and his observation of Tiger's ability to don multiple personae, may have all contributed to Miłosz's success. The use of 'personae' opened the possibility of giving voice to many characters, some of whom were completely distinct from him, and allowed the author to avoid having to proffer his own commentary.

The *Voices of Poor People* sequence was written in a radically different style. There is no earlier melody, no poetic tone; the words are bare, like the earth given over to human cruelty, and simple, not giving room to pathos. With its light, ironic tone, which resembles that with which Auden's 'Musée des Beaux Arts' closes, 'A Song on the End of the World' records the non-drama of daily life, but also how menace and catastrophe wait in the wings. 'Song of a Citizen' invites the reader to witness its speaker's unmasking, torn between his former self and a desire to embrace the world and the present; living in fear, conforming cynically, he wishes simply to survive. 'The Poor Poet' combines reflections on the imperfections of the word and the world, and the bitter fate of human beings and their lost, hopeless wandering:

> Some take refuge in despair, which is sweet
> Like strong tobacco, like a glass of vodka drunk in the hour of
>   annihilation.
> Others have the hope of fools, rosy as erotic dreams.
>
> Still others find peace in the idolatry of country,
> Which can last for a long time,
> Although little longer than the nineteenth century lasts.
>
> (*NCP* 59)

It may be that once more the memory of Witkiewicz's[5] suicide surfaced in Miłosz's mind, and how it portended malign approaching years of abandoned metaphysics, of animal-like existence.

The six poems that make up 'Songs of Adrian Zieliński' are the monologue of a coward, but also 'one of us', desperate to survive. This is a world without consolation, with no sign of reality other than the murder zone, where people perish like trodden ants. The moving poem 'Outskirts' presents what seems at first merely a journalistic image of the fringes of a city, or more precisely, areas closely familiar to Miłosz. At the same time, without the journalist's commentary distancing it, and through the power of minimalistic description, its narrator uncovers the macabre apathy of 'dogged and fertile' humanity, which appalled Witkiewicz. Thistle and couch-grass stay forever in the parched field of Warsaw, a site even more barren than Eliot's *The Waste Land*:

> A hand with cards drops down
> on the hot sand.
> The sun turned white drops down
> on the hot sand.
> Ted holds the bank. Now Ted is dealing.
> The glare stabs through the sticky pack
> into hot sand.
>
> A broken shadow of a chimney. Thin grass.
> Farther on, the city torn into red brick.
> Brown heaps, barbed wire tangled at stations.
> Dry rib of a rusty automobile.
> A claypit glitters.
> . . .
> Frank holds the bank. Now Frank is dealing.
> We play, Julys and Mays go by.
> We play one year, we play a fourth.
> The glare pours through our blackened cards
> into hot sand.
>
> Farther on, the city torn into red brick.
> A lone pine tree behind a Jewish house.
> Loose footprints and the plain up to the horizon.
> The dust of quicklime, wagons rolling,
> and in the wagons a whining lament.
>
> ('Outskirts', *NCP* 65)

———————————

Shortly after the war ended in 1945, Miłosz published in a national periodical a vivid account of how he learnt of the Warsaw Ghetto Rising:

In the spring of 1943, on a beautiful quiet night, a country night in the outskirts of Warsaw, standing on the balcony, we could hear screaming from the ghetto . . . This screaming gave us goose pimples. They were the screams of thousands of people being murdered. It travelled through the silent spaces of the city from among a red glow of fires, under indifferent stars, into the benevolent silence of gardens in which plants laboriously emitted oxygen, the air was fragrant, and a man felt that it was good to be alive. There was something particularly cruel in this peace of the night, whose beauty and human crime struck the heart simultaneously. We did not look each other in the eye. ('Na skraju Warszawy', *Przekrój*: 16, 1945)

The Rising broke out on 19 April. Six days later, on Easter Sunday, Miłosz and Janka went to visit Andrzejewski, who lived on the other side of the city. At one of the stops at Krasiński Square, they saw a merry-go-round, its seats ascending high above the ghetto walls, and a crowd of people watching. There were many pages written on the subject, whether it stood there or not, whether it was switched on, and why the Germans chose to place a fairground there and not elsewhere, and particularly whether the crowd did, in fact, laugh as they watched the Jews being murdered. It seems more likely that there were a handful of people having fun, while in close proximity a passive crowd stood, stunned, because they were watching those in the merry-go-round seats going up towards the flakes of soot and scorched fragments of burnt clothes, amidst the cries of the dying. The Holocaust did not eliminate Polish anti-Semitism.

Perhaps on that same day Miłosz composed 'Campo dei Fiori', which begins by recalling the martyr's death of Giordano Bruno, watched by a self-absorbed, indifferent Roman crowd, then segues into the barbaric present:

I thought of the Campo dei Fiori
in Warsaw by the sky-carousel
one clear spring evening
to the strains of a carnival tune.
The bright melody drowned
the salvos from the ghetto wall,
and couples were flying
high in the cloudless sky.

At times wind from the burning
would drift dark kites along
and riders on the carousel

caught petals in midair.
That same hot wind
blew open the skirts of the girls
and the crowds were laughing
on that beautiful Warsaw Sunday.

. . .

But that day I thought only
of the loneliness of the dying,

('Campo dei Fiori', NCP 33)

This poem was included a year later in the anthology *From the Chasm,* published as the result of an initiative from Żegota, the Polish Council to Aid Jews, and became the best-known Polish poem to voice protest at the destruction of the ghetto. Years later Miłosz termed the poem immoral, as it was written from the point of view of a bystander. Certainly, there are flaws in this remarkable, compassionate poem, especially in its final stanzas, which could be accused of aestheticising the horror.

Until, when all is legend
and many years have passed,
on a new Campo dei Fiori
rage will kindle at a poet's word.

(Ibid., NCP 35)

Someone passes by, looks, feels empathy, but at the same time is also detached, innocent, pure. To penetrate to the crux of how human beings jointly participate in evil, even through passivity, the language deployed in 'Voices of Poor People' is needed. 'A Poor Christian Looks at the Ghetto' is the most significant poem in the cycle, an obsessive study of dehumanization which carries us into the heart of darkness. In the poem the narrator is already dead, his body shattered, decomposed.

Bees build around the honeycomb of lungs,
Ants build around white bone.
Torn is paper, rubber, linen, leather, flax,
Fiber, fabrics, cellulose, snakeskin, wire.
The roof and the wall collapse in flame and heat seizes the
    foundations.
Now there is only the earth, sandy, trodden down,
With one leafless tree.

Slowly, boring a tunnel, a guardian mole makes his way,
With a small red lamp fastened to his forehead.
He touches buried bodies, counts them, pushes on
. . .

I am afraid, so afraid of the guardian mole.
He has swollen eyelids, like a Patriarch
Who has sat much in the light of candles
Reading the great book of the species.

What will I tell him, I, a Jew of the New Testament,
Waiting two thousand years for the second coming of Jesus?
My broken body will deliver me to his sight
And he will count me among the helpers of death:
The uncircumcised.

('A Poor Christian Looks at the Ghetto', NCP 63)

Nearly a quarter of a century later, these words were taken up again by Jan
Błoński in his famous essay *Poor Poles Look at the Ghetto,* raising the question of
the shared responsibility of the Poles for the Holocaust that took place on their
land. It prompted the start of a discussion which initiated works of remembrance
that continue to this day. Miłosz knew all too well how anti-Semitism permeated
pre-war Poland:

> Can we rid ourselves of it? Can we prevent it? I don't think so, because
> it is—to be truthful—within us. We are afraid of the mole that gnaws at
> our conscience. And I also believe that we cannot push it away. As long
> as we forget about the past, or adopt a defensive position about it, we
> will not be able to rid ourselves of the mole. We have to answer openly
> and honestly questions about shared responsibility.
>
> Was it instrumental in the genocide? No. When one reads now what
> was written about Jews before the war, when it is revealed how much ha-
> tred there was in the Polish society—it is a wonder that the words were
> not followed by actions. But they weren't (or rarely). God held that hand
> back. Yes, God, because if we didn't take part in this crime, it is because
> we were Christians to some extent, and understood in the last moment
> how diabolical that was . . . But it does not release us from shared guilt.
> Contamination and violation of Polish land did take place and we still
> have the duty to clean it up. Although—at this cemetery—it leads to one
> thing: to a duty of seeing our past in its true colours. (Błoński, *Tygodnik
> Powszechny:* 2, 1987)

Noah's Ark

When we were fleeing the burning city
And looked back from the first field path,
I said: 'Let the grass grow over our footprints,
Let the harsh prophets fall silent in the fire,
Let the dead explain to the dead what happened.
We are fated to beget a new and violent tribe
Free from the evil and the happiness that drowsed there.
Let us go'—and the earth was opened for us by a sword of flames.

Czesław Miłosz, 'Flight' (NCP 74)

On 1 August 1944, having just eaten a dinner cooked by Janka's mother, the Miłoszes were walking to a tram stop at the corner of Rakowiecka and Aleja Niepodległości. They were on their way to visit Tadeusz and Irena Kroński. Miłosz was carrying Eliot's *Collected Poems*, because he wanted to discuss details of his translation of *The Waste Land* with Tiger. They only realised that the Warsaw Rising[6] had started in Rakowiecka when they had to evade a barrage of machine gun fire by throwing themselves flat on the ground. They crawled, trying to find shelter, and only managed to come upon a safe place at dawn. It was a house just a few hundred metres away where their friends lived and where they had attended literary meetings. Thereafter it served as a shelter for them and for Janka's mother, since her father at that time was in Wołomin, outside Warsaw.

> Yet during our two weeks of forced internment we did not run out of groats or potatoes or even coffee. From our host's bookcase I dug out a volume of sociological essays about pre-war Poland, *The Young Generation of Peasants,* and plunged into its sorry reckoning of my own and my country's past, from time to time dropping flat on the floor as bullets traced long patterns across the plaster.
>
> A kind of well in the cellar, which was connected to the fire hydrant, figured in one humiliating experience. The well was big enough for two to stand in comfortably, but there were eleven of us—all the men in the house. We hid in it when the rumble of huge S.S. tanks sounded in the vicinity. The women closed the metal cover over us, and inside we immediately began to suffocate ... One of us was picked up by the S.S. one day. He died running with upraised arms in front of a tank, along with a group of unlucky people like himself who were used as human shields in an attack on the insurrectionists' barricades. (*NR* 250)

When the Germans began to torch surrounding houses, on 13 August, some of the inhabitants of the tenement house decided to get away through allotments and fields, reaching Okęcie airport, and finding shelter in an unfinished storehouse, where seeds were kept. They hid on the top floor, between sacks. From there they could see the panorama of the burning city, while downstairs, very close, they could see a detachment of Russian soldiers who fought alongside the Germans against the Soviet Union. Between intervals in the fighting, murder and rape, they passed their time learning how to ride bicycles.

> Among the companions in the group one person who stuck in my mind was a friend of the Zyga couple, Mr Okulicz. His name was an indication of his noble descent and that he came from the eastern part of Poland. He worked as a clerk. He said: 'I have spent all my life running away from them. I remember, I was seven when wearing a cape I ran across the ice near Minsk'. Imagine this surprising phenomenon, from which a far-reaching conclusion could be drawn. Here are the Germans, the most immediate danger, and he ... knows only one thing: the Bolsheviks are coming. (*Rok myśliwego* 50)

It seemed that it would be easy to escape from the outskirts of the city. However, Czesław, Janka and her mother were caught and taken to an interim camp in Okęcie, before the Germans sent the prisoners on to Pruszków, which was a few kilometres away. Miłosz scribbled notes asking for help on pieces of paper, and handed them through a fence to children playing nearby. One of them carried out the task of delivering a message to the building where Okulicz and his wife were staying. They organised a rescue, sending in a nun, who, after spending a long time pleading with the Germans, managed to persuade them to let Miłosz, Janka and her mother go.

They moved further west by foot and stopped at a villa belonging to Władysław Ryński, in Piastów, where others had found refuge. There they fell victim to robbers who seized what money and valuables they had with them; the modest belongings and most of the useful things Janka had managed to bring from home were of no great interest to the thieves. The whole area was dangerous, and so they moved further west towards Skierniewice, where at the beginning of September they ended up in the village of Janisławice. There they obtained lodgings and work, digging potatoes for a farmer, whom Miłosz called 'Kijo' in *Native Realm*.

Miłosz thought then about the peasants attached to their land for hundreds of years, who had a similar attitude to partisans, Soviet runaways from captivity and Jews, their former neighbors, who were then hiding in bunkers in the forests—and who quietly hoped for the manor houses' era to end.

Not having access to a library was the least of the problems faced by the refugees from Warsaw. A village could act only as a temporary place to stay, and so it was necessary to find somewhere more comfortable and safer. Miłosz then remembered about his friend Kazimierz Wyka, who had recently introduced him to a Catholic publicist and faithful reader of poetry. Jerzy Turowicz and his wife, Anna, lived in Goszyce, near Kraków. The couple had visited Miłosz during the occupation and even taken away with them copies of his unpublished poems. They had a beautiful manor house, set off the beaten track. Miłosz had reservations about pleading for help because Turowicz was a Catholic. Despite this, at the end of September he started sending postcards to Wyka and Turowicz in the hope that they might reach one or the other of them:

Dear Sirs,

My wife and I are staying in the countryside in not too desperate circumstances as we have some most necessary things with us. If things go according to plan, we are hoping to travel to an area near Kraków or Zakopane for the winter. In this eventuality, it would necessitate imposing ourselves on you . . . I would welcome your reply saying

> i) whether the situation and conditions are reasonable
> ii) is there any hope of finding accommodation there?

We realise that surviving here without books and in very primitive conditions would be difficult. (CM to Jerzy Turowicz, 23 or 25 September 1944)

The letter took a long time to reach the addressees, or perhaps their reply got lost. The fact was that Miłosz sent another missive on 5 October: 'The situation is deteriorating, because there is no opportunity to get money or clothes—we left Warsaw in what we stood in and tried to carry food rather than clothes'. On 9 October he followed this up with: 'We are staying in a village which so far is quiet, but from here there is no chance of getting anywhere to earn money or acquire provisions enabling us to stay for much longer—and winter is not long off and the prospects for travelling unknown'. Happily, in the end, an invitation did arrive. Miłosz and Janka set off southwards and reached their destination, probably by the end of October. He received an Ausweis—an ID document issued by the Germans—provided by helpful contacts of their hosts. It was dated 1 November 1944, and on it his profession was stated as a book-keeper.

Eventually Miłosz and Janka arrived safely in Goszyce, where they joined many other 'lodgers' taken in by the couple. The estate belonged to Jerzy's wife and had two houses alongside each other—a relatively modern nineteenth-century building called Noah's Ark, and a seventeenth-century manor house built from larch wood. Their host, Turowicz, held anti-nationalist views and was a student of philosophy, and, like Miłosz, was fascinated by Jacques Maritain. Turowicz took part in stage productions of the underground theatre run by Tadeusz Kantor. He was a journalist on a daily, and at the end of the war planned to edit a Catholic weekly, which would act as a forum to discuss social and cultural issues.

Not just family and friends of the Turowiczes found refuge on their estate, but also people who were in hiding: partisans, Jews and even an Australian paratrooper. After the Warsaw Rising many people from the capital were made welcome, and every free space in both buildings was utilised. Sometimes there were thirty people of all ages at the dining table. The guests of the manor were entertained by Turowicz in the dining room by the light of an oil lamp; often he read the poems of his guest, and sometimes Miłosz read his own work. He composed many poems during the time there, and a sole copy of a booklet comprising ten handwritten poems was produced and presented to Jerzy. In the poems 'Pearl', 'Star' and 'The World', Miłosz sought an antidote to human pain, and to the uncertainty of tomorrow. He advocated suppressing the ego and replacing it with awe for the beauty of the world, which could be observed in even the most minute created forms. Humanity stood at the threshold of great changes, he felt, and there was no use looking back. In 'Farewell', the flight from burning Warsaw resembled scenes from the fall of Troy. The refugees knew perfectly well that there was no return and that the pages of the past had to be closed forever. Two poems devoted to Janka, 'Good Night' and 'A Wish', are beautifully tender, and articulate a joyous certainty after the bonds between them were strengthened by their travails in what were the last days of the war; 'we survived, we can now enter new, certainly better times', they seemed to say.

One guest who spent a considerable period of time with the Turowiczes was Father Adam Boniecki, who recalled an episode from his stay in Goszyce, where

> one day, a friend of the lady of the house arrived, Jan Józef Szczepański, a partisan, Anna remembered an argument between him and Miłosz, who explained to Jan with great conviction that he had no intention of fighting, because it was essential for him survive the war: his duty was to write, not to fight. The possible loss of his life would be of no use, but his writing was very important to the country. (*Czesław Miłosz: In Memoriam* 76)

The heated discussion with Szczepański—a soldier, and later a writer and the author of *The Polish Autumn*, a bitter account of the defeat in 1939—addressed the issue of the way an artist could be useful to the homeland and society. The argument centered upon the future of Poland and the word 'honour', which was difficult to explain rationally.

As New Year's Eve 1945 approached, Miłosz started once again to feel trapped. He advised the owners of the Goszyce estate to sell the land very quickly and take all their valuables to Kraków. Instead of heeding his prediction that the old order would be swept away very soon, the Turowizes bought more land. That special celebratory night in Goszyce had a profound importance in contemporary Polish history. Noah's Ark was still carried on the strong currents of history, but before long waves would hurl the broken vessel onto a hostile shore, forcing the survivors of the flood to rush away in different directions.

Reconcilation between Miłosz and Szczepański occurred only towards the end of their lives. When it came to Miłosz's relationship with Turowicz, however, political choices and historical changes affected but ultimately did not stop the warmth of their friendship. Turowicz went on to found *Tygodnik Powszechny*, the only official publication which managed to maintain its independence in the entire Communist bloc. Miłosz refused to write for the paper, fearing how a 'Catholic' writer might fare in the new Polish People's Republic, but also how it might lead to his being ostracised in certain circles. He did, however, entrust Turowicz with the task of proofreading poems from his *Ocalenie* ('Rescue') collection before its publication, because the author could not do it himself due to his imminent departure for America. They corresponded and met regularly over the course of the next five decades, Turowicz being one of his closest friends and one of the most receptive readers of his poems. When the political thaw finally came in the 1980s, Miłosz became one of the most important contributors to *Tygodnik Powszechny*, and appeared alongside Szczepański. Turowicz's sagacity and generosity were well documented in 'Caffe Greco':

> In the eighties of the twentieth century, in Rome, via Condotti
> We were sitting with Turowicz in Caffe Greco
> And I spoke in, more or less, these words
>
> —We have seen much, comprehended much.
> States were falling, countries passed away,
> Chimeras of the human mind besieged us,
> And made people perish or sink into slavery.
> . . .
> By what can literature redeem itself,
> If not by melopoeia of praise, a hymn
> Even unintended? And you have my admiration,
> For you accomplished more than did my companions,
> Who once sat here, the proud geniuses.
> Why they grieved over their lack of virtue,
> Why they felt such pangs of conscience, I now understand.

With age and with the waning of this age
One learns to value wisdom, and simple goodness.

(NCP 466)

On 17 January 1945 the inhabitants of Goszyce saw a troop of soldiers approaching from a distance. Before they could recognise the uniforms, they tried to discern the language the soldiers were speaking. Were they still Germans, or had the Russians arrived already? Everyone thought they heard German. Only Miłosz declared, 'No, it sounds like a Slavonic language to me'. It turned out that his ears did not fail him, and he acted as an interpreter. One of the officers nearly had him shot, asking him suspiciously beforehand: 'How come your Russian is so good? You must be a spy!' The advance of the Red Army through Polish territory left large estates, humble fields, modest-sized towns and small villages devastated. Plunder, arson, rape and murder were commonplace. Miłosz shared a cigarette with one of the few remaining Wehrmacht soldiers, a tank commander, who must have been fearful as to the treatment he might receive as a German prisoner of war held by Russian captors. In *Native Realm*, Miłosz evokes just such a scene as the one he witnessed in January 1945:

> In the largest room of a country house, a dozen or so Soviet soldiers and non-coms are seated on benches next to the walls. On my knees, which are pressing through my threadbare civilian trousers, I hold a tin of tobacco and I roll up a pinch of the crumbly leaves in cigarette paper ... Our gazes converge toward the center of the room, where a man is standing who could not have been much over thirty. He wears a long white sheepskin coat and has the type of attractive face often met in the Rhine country. The man is a German prisoner of war; a conquistador now in their power.
>
> ... Behind him he had left tidy houses, bathrooms, Christmas trees with colored ornaments, vineyards cultivated for generations, and the music of Johann Sebastian Bach ... He looked stupid there, or, if one prefers, naïve. Because it was more than just his standing alone in front of all of them, one against many; more than his being weaponless and they armed. No, it was the psychic density of that silent Areopagus[7] that overwhelmed him. With his own people he had never created such tension; it was almost a telepathy, going around without words or signs, welding individuals into a whole bigger than themselves. He had always needed speech, a shout, or a song. But these men, perhaps semi-literate, emanated some kind of monumental knowledge of resignation ...
>
> ... But I found no hate in myself ... They did not hate him either. Because, like a caged animal, he was afraid of the unknown, one of them

got up and gave him a cigarette; that movement of the hand meant reconciliation. Another clapped him on the back. Then an officer went up to him and slowly, distinctly, pronounced a long speech . . . The pity, even cordiality in the voice, the mild, grave tone of authority quieted the prisoner and he smiled timidly: gratitude. Though no command had been given, one of the soldiers sleepily picked himself up from his bench and took the prisoner from the room. The rest fell back into their previous apathy of physically exhausted human beings. In a few minutes the soldier returned alone, dragging the white sheepskin coat that he threw next to his duffel bag. He sat down and rolled a cigarette. The melancholy way he inhaled his smoke and spat on the floor expressed the thoughts of all of them in that room on the frailty of human life: 'That's fate'. (*NR* 140–142)

It only took a few days for all the supplies in Goszyce to be plundered. It was time to say goodbyes. Miłosz remembered all too well the drunken Cossacks from the time of the Russian Revolution. The estate's inhabitants recognised that it was imperative that vodka had to be hidden; as a result, there was no alcohol available even for their parting drink. According to the recollections of Danuta Szczepańska, Janka 'invited all the young people to her room and said: "We are all going our own ways, but to make it nice for you, since it will be some time before Czesław gets his Nobel Prize, let's drink to it now"' (Szczepańska 157).

On a January morning they set off for Kraków. They had twenty kilometres ahead of them; in the fields snow was covering corpses in green uniforms and buckles with the inscription 'Gott mit uns'. Miłosz was walking in army boots borrowed from Turowicz. A month later, the owners of Goszyce were thrown off their property, but the Ghost of History was merciful: no-one got shot, and in order for them to gather their things, they were generously given twenty-four hours.

24 Andrzej and Czesław Miłosz in Sopot, on the Baltic Coast, 1949.

25 Janka in the United States in the late 1940s.

26 Czesław Miłosz relaxing in Rehoboth Beach, Delaware.

27 Kultura's main office and its staff: Jerzy Giedroyc, James Burnham, Zygmunt Hertz, Józef Czapski, Zofia Hertz, Maria Czapska, Czesław Miłosz, 1951.

28 Janina Miłosz with her sons, Antoni *(standing, left)* and Piotr *(sitting, right)*.

29 The Miłosz family at Montgeron, near Paris, 1957.

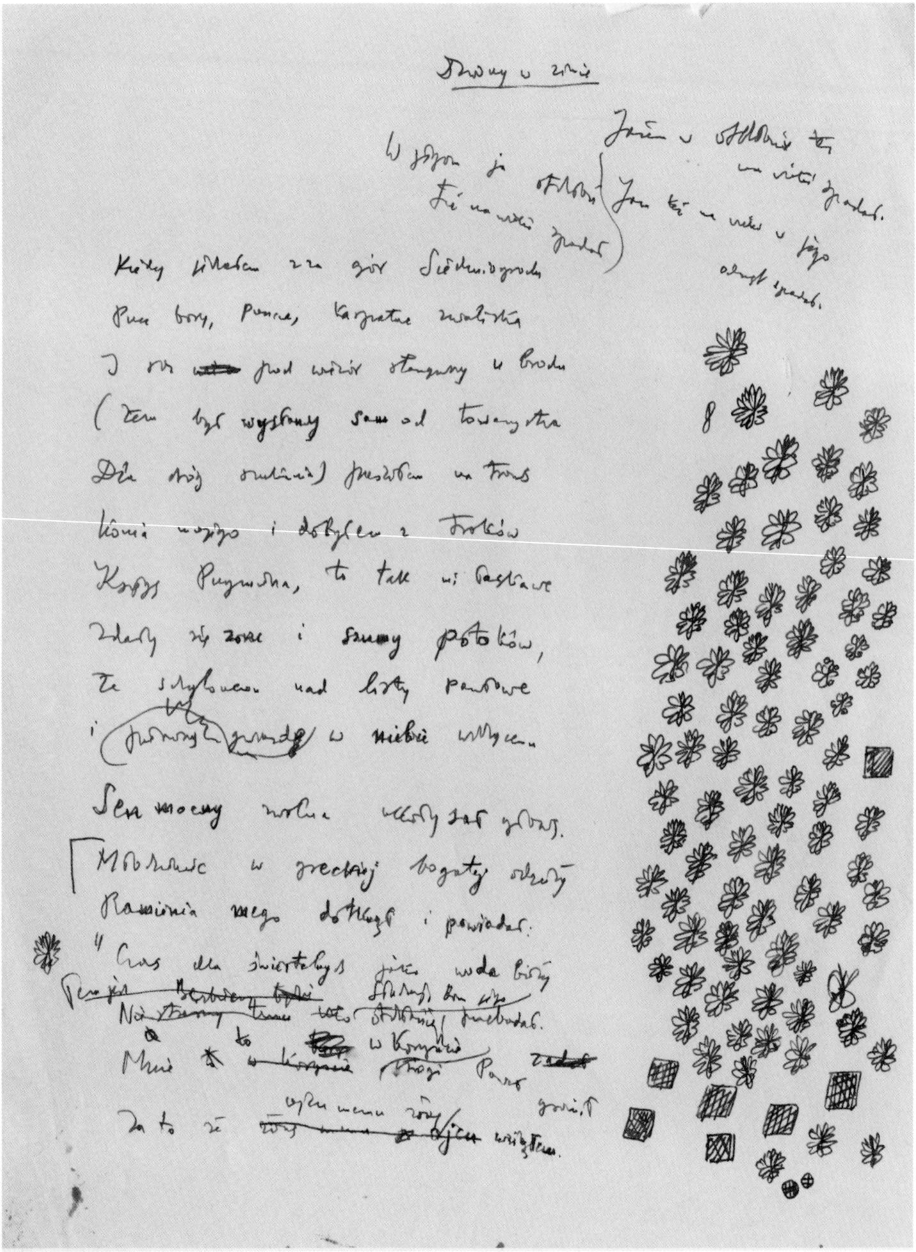

30 Manuscript of the poem 'From the Rising of the Sun'.

31 Piotr, Janina, and Czesław Miłosz, with Zbigniew Herbert, on board a ship taking them to America. Taken by Antoni Miłosz, 8 January 1964.

32 Witold Gombrowicz with
Czesław Miłosz, Vence, May 1967.

33 Czesław Miłosz at the University of
California, Berkeley in 1980, holding
a copy of *Utwory poetyckie*.

34 Czesław Miłosz receiving the Nobel Prize for Literature from King Carl Gustaf XVI of Sweden, 10 December 1980.

35 Antoni and Czesław Miłosz visiting Zuzela, the birthplace of Janina Miłosz (née Dłuska) in 1981.

36 Lech Wałęsa, addressing crowds following attacks on Solidarity members in Bydgoszcz, 21 March 1981.

37 Lech Wałęsa and Czesław Miłosz, during the poet's return visit to Poland, June 1981.

38 Czesław Miłosz addressing staff at NOWA, an underground publishing house,
   June 1981. Adam Michnik is seated at the front left of the photo.

39 Czesław Miłosz and Carol Thigpen on holiday in Yugoslavia, 1985.

40 Czesław Miłosz in his homeland, beside the River Niewiaża, Lithuania.

41 Czesław and Carol Miłosz in the composer Zbigniew Preisner's house, October 2001.

In Partibus Daemonis
1945–1951

'We are from Lublin'

You, the last Polish poet! A drunk hugged me
A friend from the avant-garde, wearing a long army coat,
One who survived the war in the east and understood things there.

. . .

I did not know that I would speak the language of the conquered,
No more lasting than remains, family customs,
Christmas decorations, yearly heart-warming carols.

Czesław Miłosz, 'Rok 1945', *Wiersze wszystkie*, 962

Kraków was spared major devastation, so when the war ended, crowds of refugees flocked to the city. The first wave included people who fled bombed and razed Warsaw and was then followed by prisoners from nearby liberated concentration camps. At the Yalta Conference of February 1945, Roosevelt, Churchill and Stalin agreed that a Provisional Government of National Unity should be set up in Poland, in which Communists and non-Communists would be represented. The Soviet Union's annexation of eastern areas of Poland was accepted as a fait accompli by America and Britain, and in compensation for those losses Poles from these regions were resettled in territories stripped from Germany. Kraków was the first major city on these displaced people's journey westwards. The last group that headed for Kraków were prisoners of war and people seized to carry out forced labour in Germany during the war.

As a consequence of all these factors, the number of inhabitants in the city swelled from a pre-war figure of two hundred thousand to half a million. A steep

decline in moral standards was observed in the early post-war period; it manifested itself in cruel and ruthless behaviour and in the ease with which people
would commit murder. Incidents of theft and rape were daily occurrences, and
animosity towards the surviving Jewish population was often overt. Shops and
apartments formerly owned by Jews were taken over by new owners, and in August 1945 riots broke out and a pogrom started. For months soldiers had to be
stationed in the city centre; there, too, very high hoardings were erected, from
which peered gigantic portraits of Soviet marshals Zhukov, Konyev and Rokossowski. Not long after that, shocked inhabitants of Kraków saw posters depicting
the Armia Krajowa as 'repulsive reactionary dwarves'. The AK had been formed by
the Polish Government-in-Exile in 1942 and remained the dominant resistance
movement in German-occupied areas of Poland until the end of the war.

The scale of assaults and arrests carried out by Soviet 'liberators' on the
orders of the NKVD (the Soviet secret police and the forerunners of the KGB)
was such that the Polish Communist authorities began to encourage Polish soldiers to defend the local population from the Russians. The fact that the NKVD's
headquarters were located in the Old Town's magnificent marketplace added
insult to injury. For most of Kraków's inhabitants this 'peace' must have seemed
much harder to live through than the occupation.

> The purest of nations on earth when it's judged by a flash of lightning,
> But thoughtless and sly in everyday toil.
>
> Pitiless to its widows and orphans, pitiless to its old people,
> Stealing a crust of bread from a child's hand.
> . . .
> A nation in crumpled caps, carrying all they own,
> They go west and south searching for a place to live.
>
> It has no cities, or monuments, no painting or sculpture,
> Only the word passed from mouth to mouth and prophecy of poets.
>
> ('A Nation', *NCP* 89–90)

After the first days in Kraków, Miłosz by some coincidence ran into the
writer Tadeusz Breza and his wife, Zofia, whom he knew from Wilno. From a
friend of his, a dermatologist who lectured at the Jagiellonian University, Breza
learnt of an apartment recently vacated by Germans. To move in there, the two
couples had to obtain a permit from the local administration. On the way there,
by chance, they encountered another figure from the past:

> I came across a Polish officer who had arrived from the east. He was a
> small man and had a massive revolver bashing about his calves. Adam

Ważyk! We threw ourselves into each other's arms. We headed over to the Housing Office, which was easily recognisable, because crowds of people were trying to enter the building. A civilian wearing a white and red armband fired in the air from time to time to regain order. Ważyk walked first and waded through the crowd, declaring, 'We are from Lublin'. That was enough to get us into the building, up the stairs and into the office. (*Zaraz po wojnie* 464)

Previously, Ważyk had been an avant-garde poet, but now he served as a political officer in the Soviet-created Armia Ludowa, and as a representative of the new authority the clerks would not dare refuse him anything. He himself used to say with irony that he felt like 'the king of Kraków'.

As a result of this new king's timely appearance, Miłosz, Janka, Tadeusz and Zofia came to share a four-room apartment at St Thomas Street, a three-minute walk from the Old Town. They lived frugally. On the bookshelf Miłosz placed a solitary book, Berthold Brecht's *Threepenny Opera*, bought after the Rising. Yet material difficulties seemed a minor matter compared to what the new political system might bring.

Immediately after the liberation, Czesław Miłosz joined the Writers' Union. A fellow member recalled that 'he cut a handsome figure and with it he had a low, sexy voice. Women were crazy about him. Tall, with broad shoulders, he resembled a teddy bear with his charming smile which helped him win everyone's heart' (Kwiatkowski, *Panopticum* 264). On 29 January the Inaugural General Meeting of the Kraków branch of the Writers' Union took place in the unheated auditorium of Teatr Stary (Old Theatre). It was filled to capacity by people dressed in the most curious clothes, mostly hungry writers who had survived the wartime slaughter. They recalled the names of those who had perished, and, with pain and a sense of guilt, they shared joy at having made it through, along with an overwhelming desire to resume the semblance of a normal life. In the evening a select group from their ranks went to the Hotel Francuski to meet with top representatives of the new government. These included Bolesław Bierut, Edward Osóbka-Morawski (Premier of the Provisional Government of National Unity), Jan Karol Wend (Deputy Minister of Culture and Arts), and, last but not least, a Russian general, Vasily Shatilov. Sandwiches were ready on the table, but first they had to listen to speeches. Finally, Miłosz's companion recalled that Prime Minister Osóbka-Morawski stood up and said: '"And now gentlemen, to the bottles." We reached for glasses and sandwiches. A number of those invited made speeches, which were neither toasts nor announcements' (Breza 92). This was how the new regime's wooing of the artistic community began. A weekly paper from Lublin, *Odrodzenie* (Resurrection), transferred its headquarters to Kraków, while a newly established newspaper, *Dziennik Polski* (Poland Daily), commenced publication there; after a few months, it moved to Warsaw under its editor, Jerzy Putrament.

On the morning of 31 January at the Teatr Stary, the first post-war poetry reading took place. The auditorium was filled with avid listeners, who loudly applauded the poets, asked for autographs, showered them with kisses and gave them flowers (potted plants because of the shortage of cut flowers). Wisława Szymborska remembered the occasion vividly:

> I was most taken with Czesław Miłosz. Most of the poets read badly, made mistakes, stammered ... And then, all of a sudden, out comes Miłosz, looking like an angry cherub, with this distinguished voice. I remember thinking to myself, 'This is a great poet'. (Bikont and Szczęsna)

Angry this cherub might have been, but he threw himself zealously into efforts to try to rebuild Poland's cultural life. In the spring, he participated in a meeting to set up a new literary magazine, *Twórczość*, and in due course became one of its editors.

In the summer of 1945 he gave a reading of the 'Voices of Poor People' sequence and sections from 'The World' in Krupnicza Street, Kraków, and an introductory talk at a meeting with the Polish writer, literary historian and critic, Artur Sandauer. At the end of August, during the opening of the National Convention of the Polish Writers Union, he voted for Jarosław Iwaszkiewicz for the top position. During the convention, he voiced his support for freedom of speech and for forging cultural links with the West. Around the same period, Miłosz visited an exhibition of the work of young painters and attended several theatre productions, including one by Tadeusz Kantor. He seemed to be less than impressed with what he saw, commenting that he was 'a great fan of clarity of style and that is why I dislike overacted interpretation of classical drama, in grotesque artistic settings' (CM, in *Odrodzenie:* 37, 1945).

This insistence on upholding certain basic standards can be seen in an article in which he criticised lamentable aspects of behaviour in some of those he happened to work alongside:

> In Poland there are many people who are over-partial to drinking, mumbling and cackling. Amongst this group are those who oppose the printing of a diverse range of interesting, enchanting and inspiring books ... They are editors who curtail humorous and absorbing discussions popular with readers and it is all done in the name of seriousness. ('Kolorowym atramentem')

In the 'times of re-building', activism was the answer, he affirmed: 'I am not teetotal and I do not refuse a drink. As it happens, since the last German soldier left

Warsaw and Kraków, I have not been drunk once. There simply isn't time for it. Life is short, and the task substantial' (ibid).

Robinson Crusoe from Warsaw

When, in the occupied capital, Miłosz was working on *Prologue,* his only play, presciently he imagined as its backdrop a Warsaw utterly devastated, with ghosts of fighters 'in plain clothes' as the inhabitants of the city. In the post-war period, he imagined a clash between a politician and a poet who sets against the need to forge a unified nation, born from carnage and a terrible struggle for survival, another necessity, the necessity to remember the fallen. To remember is to acknowledge a basic defining element that makes us human:

> spurned word, forgotten word! . . .
> Do not let it be ill-treated! Do not!
> Because it will spring from the earth like a pillar of fire
> An accusation from the dead that we betrayed them.
>
> ('Prolog', in *Pamiętnik Teatralny*, 1–2)

It now appeared that those who died on the barricades in the Warsaw Rising were to be erased from memory, buried beneath a layer of obscurity. Miłosz's conclusion was that under this newly-installed regime one would be compelled to play a double game:

> If someone had no illusions regarding the nature of the Soviet state, the only moral stand they could take was not to support them. I looked critically at my leftist friends who involved themselves actively in working with the Soviets after 1940 . . . In 1945 they showed up in Poland with the Red Army as the influential 'Wilno group'. The unfolding course of events supported the validity of their pre-war convictions, I had to admit, but it did not mean that I could afford to talk to them openly . . . I was prepared to use my connections, but kept back my Jesuit *reservatio mentalis* (mental objections). In no circumstances would I join the Polish Workers' Party, although I shared their hostility and paranoia about the right, so in fact, I did not have to lie. (*Zaraz po wojnie* 8)

The game of pretence was really linked to a growing wish to leave Poland, but it was also crucial for Miłosz to maintain an active position in the literary field. To be marginalised, especially now, when he felt at the height of his creative potential, would be too much to bear. He paid a visit to Jerzy Putrament, then chief editor of the *Dziennik Polski,* who received him in his office dressed in his army uniform. Soon afterwards, in the 11 February 1945 issue of the paper, a poem appeared that began with the words 'They fell into the darkness of contempt', a line from the chorus in *Prologue*. As Miłosz admitted later, the poem, when taken out of its dramatic context in a paper sponsored by the new authorities, unexpectedly began to acquire a secondary meaning. Whereas initially the 'they' referred to were the Nazi occupiers, following Poland's 'liberation' by the Red Army the pronoun might equally be applied to its new masters:

> They fell into the darkness of contempt
> . . .
> Those displaying deceit and arrogance,
> Envoys of unlawful intention,
> Leaving behind them burning cities,
> Above their heads a crown of cinders.
> . . .
> Humble people trample on the ashes.
> The mission of violence is now complete,
> The most horrific of all undertakings.

> (*Wiersze* I, 226)

It would be interesting to know which of the two at that meeting—the editor or his visitor—came up with the idea of the latter contributing a regular column. Why did Miłosz agree? To secure an additional source of income? To make a small political gesture? To consolidate his position as a writer? The outcome of the visit was two series of opinion pieces, *Jaunts* and *Literary Jaunts*, which together added up to over thirty articles. In one of these he described a wartime hecatomb of books and appealed to readers: 'When you see books in an abandoned house, immediately hand them over to the library authorities, so that they don't end up as mats placed under saucepans' (*Dziennik Polski*, 17). In another, he addressed writers directly, reminding them that given all that their readers had experienced in the last five years, they were able to discern truth in literature, and its absence. He observed that there were now 'swarms of thieves in Poland. There were those who stole money, public property, awards, time, rights and entitlements' (*Dziennik Polski*, 34), and said that if there was no other weapon to fight those who ceased being true to themselves in the recent past, then poking fun at them might be a harmless punishment. He expressed contentment at the annexation of Pomerania by Poland, since it gave the country a large stretch of the Baltic coastline. It meant that a friend of his, 'a thirteen-year-old shepherd from a small village, who longed to be a sailor, will now be able to realise that dream' (*Dziennik Polski*, 68). Endeavouring to maintain a balance, he assessed the position of Polish émigrés. More contentiously, later in the piece, he alluded to those who declined to join in the process of rebuilding the country. 'We wish for the particles of golden sand to find their place here, so that they stop being unhappy, but not for the dry leaves and garbage, who know how to fight, but not how to build' (*Dziennik Polski,* 21).

Generally speaking, Miłosz expressed opinions on subjects close to his heart, which two years earlier he would have had to defend in underground meetings. Now some of his pronouncements began to sound like propaganda, since he was writing for a newspaper funded by the regime. There were those who found it disturbing that he could criticise civil servants, yet not express his opinions on the wholesale arrests of wartime underground fighters. Later, he reconsidered his opinions and regretted using bitter words about those who emigrated, because although there was some truth in them, they unnecessarily hurt people's feelings. That he became quickly aware of how his involvement was being manipulated may be sensed in his choice of the following quotation: 'Why did Mickiewicz call adulthood a time of defeat? Because when we reach maturity, we realise the price we have to pay for all our actions' (*Dziennik Polski,* 41).

Miłosz entered into a polemical debate with those who, long before the imposition of social realism, wanted to subject literature to dogmatic rules. He protested against central planning in the editing process, saying that it would stifle initiative and radically reduce the number of new titles:

> I would gather all those who have any editorial plans and would shout to them: get on with it, publish and reprint—even those books which I would regard as less significant . . . I want the minds of young generations to develop in knowledge and not in ignorance. I want them to be able to declare that an author is an idiot, but *after* reading him, not as a result of being told so. (*Dziennik Polski,* 36)

He opposed policies aimed at limiting people's access to great art and plans to replace outstanding authors with third-rate but 'correct' ones. 'We own Shakespeare, Mickiewicz, Velasquez and Titian', he affirmed, and after suffering appallingly in recent years people deserved to be granted 'their full rights to art' (*Przekrój:* 18, 1945).

At the end of February 1945, Miłosz completed a project entitled 'Accounts of Losses in Poland's Sciences and Arts', which was intended as 'an indictment. It would document for the benefit of the rest of the world our losses and would find a place on the table at the peace conference' (*Dziennik Polski,* 29). It would feature pictures of artists and scientists who had perished as a result of the war and the German occupation. In the spring, together with Breza, he drafted a memorandum, 'On the Full Use of the Creative and Social Potential of the Writer', which reflected his leftist sympathies and a strong conviction that, after the war's end, it would be impossible to return to a totally liberal model of society, and that it would be essential to leave the regulation of cultural life to the state, on condition that it is enlightened and strongly democratic.

> The writer's status has been elevated considerably . . . everyone is of the opinion that he has to become a healer for all the psychological disorders caused by the occupation and a moral legislator for building the future. Writers welcome statements from government representatives which honour them, but they do not much care about being praised for performing useful roles. What roles? By writing, which is their profession, and what they are best at. The authors called on the government to create conditions most conducive to producing good work, so that they would not be compelled to supplement their income by additional undertakings, like journalism. Society ought to look upon the writer as a person who has a predisposition to carry out a kind of production work, which would make a necessary contribution to society. (Qtd. in Kornacki 186–189)

Around this time, Miłosz was responsible for penning a beautiful polemic against Jan Kott, who nonchalantly had drawn up a new literary canon, from which almost all twentieth-century literature had been excised. He also wanted to ban Dante, and argued for a condensed version of the Bible. Kott had identified 'two books without which I cannot imagine a library. One of them is the Bible, even a version with selected fragments, and the other one, *Tales of a Thousand and One Nights*' (Kott, 'Sprawa Książki'). In response to this, Miłosz remarked:

> If one is seeking 'good' books, I would not recommend the Bible—it is a horrific book, bloody and depressing. And it is not a book, as such. It is the world. You can hear a cry of longing by the waters of Babylon, thunderous sounds of joy in a Jerusalem temple. It contains the history of one of the most fascinating nations in the world, which first understood the notion of what we call history. This suffering nation's journey can only be explained perhaps by their status as a chosen people. For centuries they prepared for the coming of Christ. On Babylonian roads, Egyptian sands, through the fortifications of Jerusalem, and at Treblinka, the nation poured out copious amounts of blood in atonement.
>
> I wonder how Kott imagines the Bible in selected form. He, Jan Kott, will sit down and censor Solomon's Proverbs, abbreviate Jeremiah, improve Ezekiel. It is so easy, almost as easy as putting together the Bible and *Tales of a Thousand and One Nights*, composed a long time ago in a sultan's harem, as a joke. ('Lekkie umysły', *Dziennik Polski*, 56)

When Satan is expelled from Heaven in Milton's *Paradise Lost,* he cries out:

> Farewell, happy fields
> Where joy forever dwells: hail horrors, hail
> Infernal world, and thou profoundest hell
> Receive thy new possessor.

'There was pleasure in translating Milton in the summer of 1945 in Kraków ... we were *in patribus daemonis* [in the provinces of demons], and tied to our fate. Milton's cosmic visions seemed apt, I would say, offering the key to survival' (*Kontynenty* 16), explained Miłosz, revealing how complicated were his motivations then, in which artistic pride mingled with the fear of being in league with the defeated. Driving him on was also the desire to save the culture while it was still possible, and a strong sense that he was participating in events of an apocalyptic character, a period comparable to that which witnessed the fall of the Roman Empire.

Fragments of Milton's poem came from Miłosz's anthology of English and American poetry. It was supposed to represent a political gesture, a presentation of the culture of the West in the face of approaching barbarity, and also suggested an attempt on Miłosz's part to re-orient Polish culture away from its strong traditional ties with France towards the Anglo-Saxon countries. At this period Miłosz began to treat translation as a constant element in his work. In the first months after the war he translated, among others, Blake, Milton, Wordsworth and Browning. He chose as co-author and co-editor Aleksander Messing-Mierzejewski, a poet, translator, painter and former underground fighter, and, more latterly, an announcer on Polish Radio and a future Minister of Foreign Affairs who later worked for various international organisations based in the United States. Together they collected materials in libraries and, in a gesture to help her out financially, invited Witkacy's widow, Jadwiga Witkiewicz, to type the texts out for them. The Warsaw publisher Czytelnik accepted the book, but due to the rapidly deteriorating political atmosphere between the USSR and the West, it never appeared.

In early spring 1945, Miłosz and Jerzy Andrzejewski travelled back to Warsaw to see what was left of the city. They entered a sea of burnt-out ruins, above which hung the red dust of crumbled bricks. He wrote down the outline of a poem, 'In Warsaw', with which the collection *Ocalenie* ('Rescue') would end. The poet scribbled it on small pages pulled from a notebook, and at the top of one of them he added and underlined this disturbing sentence: 'God is just'. They had difficulty finding the ruined house in Aleja Niepodległości where he lived during the war: 'The house was damaged by artillery shells. A page from André Gide flapped ironically in the wind. There were other book covers that feet had stamped on ... Rimbaud, French surrealists, Kafka, Proust. It looked a little stupid in the background of the ruins ... What was the point in looking for the rest of my books? I felt revulsion at the sight' ('Odczyt o literaturze', 1949, Beinecke Library). From among the remains he dug out a pierced copy of his book, *Three Winters*. Shrapnel had left a gaping hole, a wound in which one could fit a small finger. It had also damaged, among others, the beginning of the poem 'About a Book', which contains the line 'above our heads the bullets sang'. It was then that the two writers met the celebrated pianist Władysław Szpilman,[1] whom Miłosz remembered from the radio. After the failure of the Rising in October 1944, Szpilman hid in Warsaw to avoid joining thousands of its remaining inhabitants who were being forcibly marched out of the city by the Germans, and was there when the Soviet troops entered. As he and Andrzejewski listened to his Robinson Crusoe–like story with incredulity, Miłosz began to think about a film script about 'a lonely animal hunted in Warsaw'. His intention was to use the landscape of the totally ruined city and 'place in it a lonely man, who begins to live as if civilisation had ceased to exist and he found himself on a desert island' (Fiut 104). They took the idea back to Kraków and started working on a script.

The proposed treatment was avant-garde and experimental, but the dramatic requirements forced them to introduce other characters; in the final version there were seven of them, representatives of post-war society, including intellectuals and bandits, as well as a young couple introduced as love-interest. The writers took the script to Łódź to Wytwórnia Filmowa Wojska Polskiego (Polish Army Film Producers), hoping that it might be directed by Jerzy Zarzycki and co-directed by Janka Cękalska. Unfortunately, Zarzycki fell ill. Tensions between his replacement, Antoni Bohdziewicz, and Janka, who had a very clear vision of what the film should be, hindered the production. It can be inferred from letters exchanged between Andrzejewski and Miłosz that they became disappointed and disillusioned with the film industry, which turned out to be full of intrigue and turf wars. What was worse, not much remained of the first concept of the script after so many changes were introduced. In accordance with the brave new spirit of the times, the entire spectrum of society had to be represented, and so someone inserted in the middle of the script a Soviet parachutist who used a radio to direct artillery. The introduction of such an intrusive propagandist element prevented the two writers from completing their experiment.

The project ended up on the shelf until in 1948 work began on Andrzejewski's new version. Miłosz removed his name and the Defoe allusion, and a new title was chosen. Directed by Zarzycki, *The Unvanquished City* was released in 1950, and was an artistic disaster.

A Pact with the Devil

Everything is like a new volume of Balzac's—perhaps *The Last Incarnation of Vautrin*—and the aura of it resembles endings of two novels by Witkacy, who was a genius in that respect.

CM to Aniela Micińska, n.d. [1946]

The windows of the Young People's Film Workshop, where Andrzejewski and Miłosz worked on the *Robinson Crusoe* screenplay looked out on the regional offices of Urząd Bezpieczeństwa Publicznego, or Public Security.

> We saw scores of young men behind the barred windows on the ground floor. Some had thrust their faces in the sun in an effort to get a tan. Others were fishing with wire hooks for bits of paper which had been tossed out on the sand from neighbouring cells. Standing in the window, we observed them in silence.
>
> It was easy to guess that these were soldiers of the Underground Army [the AK]. If the London Government-in-Exile returned to Poland, these soldiers of the 'underground state' would have been honored and feted as heroes. (*Captive Mind* 101)

Of the two writers silently watching these caged, innocent men, one, Andrzejewski, would shortly write a distorted story about them,[2] while the other, Miłosz, would not protest openly about their fate until six years had passed. Instead his focus would be to fight to get out of the trap Poland had become.

It seems highly likely that Miłosz's eagerness to obtain a diplomatic post was prompted by a desire to have the opportunity of staying in the West. Neither he nor Janka had any illusions about the quality of life citizens enjoyed under Soviet rule; in childhood both had acquired prejudices against the Russians. These feelings resurfaced in Janka, who, immediately after watching in horror as the Red Army flooded into Goszyce, urged Czesław to leave while it was still possible. 'Do you think that I did not want to defect in 1946 immediately after I left for America?', he would ask Melchior Wańkowicz, while to Renata Gorczyńska he said: 'I had no illusions, because what 1945 exposed was horrific. It really was an occupation, and then appointing a marionette to govern . . . All I wanted was to get out, and see what would happen next. Anything but being strangled' (*Podróżny świata* 81). Retrospectively, he reiterated that 'going abroad was a camouflaged lie from the start, because my only wish was to leave. And then we would see what would happen. My mother, before she died, urged me to leave' (*Rok myśliwego* 278). He probably was in a much worse state than was apparent from his active professional work or the majority of letters he sent to people. One could talk about real feelings only with people one could trust completely. Proof of that was a letter written in haste to Iwaszkiewicz in the autumn of 1945: 'Please do not attempt to interpret my reticence, but it is a fact that things are difficult and life is hard at present. I cannot communicate, I suffer from nightmares and horrible visions, horror at one's nature unfolds' (*Zaraz po wojnie* 137). Going to America would be a gift tinged with the devil's irony. He would discover a country totally alien to him, and the prospect of settling down there filled him with dismay.

He had not expected that when in 1945 he was looking for someone to nominate him for an overseas post in the diplomatic service. At the time these were particularly sought-after career opportunities, perhaps for the very reason that the majority of newly appointed diplomats chose not to return to Poland. One of the few people who could issue a letter of support for him was Jerzy Putrament, who no longer was the 'harmless young man' Miłosz had known before the war, but a political officer, a major in the Polish Army, and a member of the new elite with connections in high circles, possibly even within the NKVD. When he approached him this time, Miłosz was hoping for the old respect and fascination with which Putrament had regarded him in the early 1930s. His colleague, however, described their encounter with the meanest of similes, alleging that 'he fawned upon me like a dog' (Marx, *Poezja:* 5–6). Nevertheless, the sentiments from youth still meant something, because the 'Wilno group' supported their old members and maintained solidarity. Many Communists from Wilno now held prominent positions in the Polish government. Miłosz's candidature for the diplomatic service appointment was submitted by Putrament, Dembińska and Jerzy Borejsza to the upper echelons of the Party, where decisions regarding the awarding of passports were made. Borejsza and Dembińska were strengthening their position within Czytelnik, the former becoming its director when it started publishing in 1944. Borejsza, in particular, was gifted with managerial skills and seemed liberal at the time, believing—or at least appearing to believe—in Poland's separate road to communism. He thought he knew how to persuade 'as yet politically undecided émigrés' to return to Poland without waiting for declarations about their change of heart. On his desk he had a telephone with a direct line to Jakub Berman, one of the three most powerful Communists in Poland after the war. People with such telephones were maliciously called 'Dobermans', and if it happened that they were decent people, as some were, their acquaintance was undoubtedly useful in these times of increasing terror.

During preparations for publishing Mickiewicz's works, someone high up suggested that a sentence in his play *Forefathers' Eve*—'Terrible is

freedom from the hands of a Muscovite'—was not suitable for the reality
of the 1940s ... Borejsza moved every lever he could think of to persuade
decision-makers of the necessity of retaining the integrity of the work.
(Szymańska 43)

A person who was more sceptical in her assessment of Borejsza was the writer
Maria Dąbrowska:

> As a director, he is a skillful operator, presenting his views as liberal, and
> demonstrating a genial, and I would say, benevolent attitude to people ...
> He created a huge machinery of editorial-journalistic-bookshop-
> readership elements with almost American-like flair. But the intention of
> this activity was a clear, gradual and slow sovietisation and russification
> of the Polish culture. (Dąbrowska 197)

Perhaps Miłosz took to Borejsza's joviality, or maybe they grew to like each other,
because once Miłosz became an employee of the embassy in Washington he used
to send him letters that went beyond what was professionally necessary.

In summer 1945, Miłosz paid another visit to Warsaw. He used the opportunity on 19 August to visit Dąbrowska and told her that he had been promised
work in Switzerland or Italy. A day later he submitted an application to the
Ministry of Foreign Affairs: 'I am putting forward my candidacy to become an
employee of the Ministry in a post at the Polish Embassy in Switzerland' (Miłosz
Archives). The choice of Berne was not accidental: Putrament was soon to take
charge of the legation there and wanted Miłosz close by in order to keep an eye
on him. The future envoy wrote on 22 August:

> Honourable Comrade Minister! I would like to ask your permission to
> allocate to the Swiss embassy Czesław Miłosz, whom I know well ... I
> think that he could take on the post of deputy attaché. He is undoubt-
> edly a very able man, and having him at the embassy will be just a case
> of managing his talents. (Ibid.)

Three days later, Miłosz's personnel data sheet was created, which shows, among
other things, that in the box 'membership of any political parties and social organisations until 1939', he entered 'Polish Writers Union' and, added to strengthen
his application, '*Front* in Wilno (illegal)' (ibid.). In the box where references' details were required, the list of names included Jędrychowski, Borejsza, Sztachelski, and a roommate from Bucharest, Zygmunt Młynarski, Director of Polish
Radio. Two months later a decision was made, and although the Swiss plan did
not pan out, a contract signed on 22 November stated that Czesław Miłosz would
be fulfilling his duties as 'a contracted employee in service to the Ministry of

Foreign Affairs, in the General Consulate in Chicago' (ibid.). 'Miłosz then spent a lot of time at the ministry, which he described as "a terrible institution. First of all, it was located in Aleja Szucha, the former Gestapo headquarters, and secondly, there was a system of background checks which included ten levels of suspicions"' (*Podróżny świata* 82). Years later, in his fiction, he would describe how

> in the averted eyes of the new civil servants, in their shifty looks, was the same expression as there was in the eyes of the strangely dressed individuals who waited for an interview for hours on end; they walked nervously along the dirty corridors, cracking their fingers. Fear. All of them were desperately playing, each in his own way, for the stake of release of the trap. (*Seizure of Power* 231)

The recommendations from Putrament and Borejsza and even well-wishing signs of interest from the Minister of Foreign Affairs, Zygmunt Modzelewski, did not guarantee a passport. Jakub Berman, who belonged to a small group of very influential people in the country, mentioned later: 'There were some serious reservations about his departure, because he was outspoken ... and voiced opposition views' (Pasierski). In the autumn, not long after the date of his outbound flight from Poland had been decided upon, something terrible happened. Maria Dąbrowska recorded in her diary on 27 November: 'Miłosz. We drank vodka together, but hardly spoke. He was very sad. Someone had informed on him, saying that he had sent pessimistic letters abroad—the departure for Chicago was postponed. He is resigned and penniless, because he has spent all his money' (Dąbrowska 174). The situation is mentioned again in a number of letters Miłosz sent to Andrzejewski: 'Road lined with thorns ... I have seen so much of the highest calibre meanness ... that I feel sick' (*Zaraz po wojnie* 29); and to Turowicz: 'Someone denounced me and there are now endless tensions' (CM to Turowicz, 13 November 1945). What did the denunciation concern? Who was responsible? Could it have anything to do with monitoring carried out at the Polish Film Studios, which Janka mentioned in a letter she and Miłosz wrote to Andrzejewski: 'We are waiting for a flight, but still not sure whether we will definitely go' (*Zaraz po wojnie* 29). Is it perhaps that the poet confided to someone in America that he had no intention of returning to Poland? To whom did he have to pay backhanders?

He himself recalled the events slightly differently: 'I was about to be sent to New York, and suddenly someone withheld my passport. Then I gave Borejsza a good telling-off. Borejsza in front of me picked up the phone, rang Modzelewski and that's how the matter got resolved' (*Podróżny świata* 27). We ought to take this account with a pinch of salt and be sceptical about the poet's supposed boldness. Though it was an uncontrolled, risky, emotional outburst, Miłosz could not have afforded to make a scene. What was required and expected then were patience, continuing pressure and, unavoidably, a significant dose of humility.

The poet recalled a conversation with Putrament prior to his departure in a series of prose pieces entitled *Podróżny świata* (A World Traveller): 'Putrament said to me: "Have it if you want it. But remember, you are signing a pact with the devil. Do you understand? A pact with the devil"' (*Podróżny świata* 80). What did his patron really have in mind? The impossibility of withdrawing from the contract, which he had to vouch for with his word of honour? Or did it mean that for the privilege of leaving the Polish hell, he would have to give up his soul? In any case, Miłosz many times recalled the satanic nature of the commitment he had taken on:

> Undoubtedly it was a pact with the devil, bearing in mind what was hap-
> pening ... Millions of people in gulags, deportations after 1939, Katyń, the
> Warsaw Rising in 1944, terror in Poland—I was fully aware of all that.
> And at the same time the existence of the legitimate Polish army in the
> West, which was just being demobilised, and of a legitimate government
> in London. And against it, me, with this crowning argument, that they
> had lost and had no hope of winning. To break off the pact, join them,
> because they were noble and faithful to something that might yet come
> to pass? It is only today after many years of People's Poland that we
> praise the steadfastness of the émigrés. Then, it looked different. Janusz
> Minkiewicz wrote a few stanzas in which he said about the London
> government: 'With the devil, but not with you', and many of us writers
> shared the sentiment ... I suffered and accused myself of prostituting
> myself. (*Rok myśliwego* 155)

This analysis was mercilessly honest. Today, when we mainly remember the splendid history of the journal *Kultura* in Paris, and books by Gombrowicz, Bobkowski or Herling, it is difficult to empathise with this deep aversion to those who had emigrated. They were the heirs of pre-war Poland, a country full of injustices and which in 1939 had lost the war. It was not just Miłosz who felt like that. It seemed that the chessboard offered no possibility for any other move. Émigrés were waiting for a new war, in which the West, having the upper hand thanks to the atom bomb, would defeat the Soviet Union and restore Poland's pre-war borders. Those who did not believe in war and could observe from close proximity the strength of the Red Army were deeply convinced about the fatalistic course of history, and that communism was an uncontrollable force of nature. The divisions in Europe, from that perspective, were inevitable, as was the subordination of Poland to the So-viets. For many the conclusion seemed clear: it was vital to co-operate with the new rulers for the sake of slowing down the process of Sovietisation, in order to salvage something of Poland's culture, national identity, and European heritage. The poet included these famous sentences in 'A Treatise on Morality':

> An avalanche changes its course
> Depending on the stones it encounters as it forces its way through.
> And, as someone used to say,
> If you can, influence the course.
> Soften its savagery and barbarity,
> For that fortitude is needed.

(Wiersze II, 89)

There was a qualitative difference between the actions of a university official or an editor who joined the Communist Party in order to have more freedom to carry out their work and that of a writer who chose a diplomatic career in order to promote his new government using his personality and the trustworthiness he enjoyed among foreigners. In the diplomatic service after 1945, apart from Putrament and Miłosz, there were other writers, such as Julian Przyboś, Stanisław Jerzy Lec, Jerzy Zagórski, Tadeusz Breza, and Antoni Słonimski, who worked as a director of the Institute of Polish Culture in London.

In an unpublished text from early 1957, Miłosz wrote: 'Representing a country that was turned into the province of a totalitarian foreign state was wrong and degrading, which I feel ashamed of today. To take on a diplomatic position overseas without breaking ties with my country seemed to me, however, the lesser of the two evils' ('Wymarsz z czarnej groty', 1956–1957). Miłosz saw the superiority of 'participation', getting involved, being a presence, over observing from a distance, the stance taken by some writers. There were many factors, starting from his leftist sympathies, which would not allow him to lie low like those who were waiting to see how things panned out, and were prepared to write things not worth publishing. He preferred paying a high price and being active, having an illusory sense of having an influence on the course of the avalanche. In the early 1950s, he exchanged letters with another Polish writer, Melchior Wańkowicz, and in one of them expressed the complexity of his situation and convictions:

> You ask whether I believed or not. Not in Stalinism. But, of course, I believed. I believed that it was possible to do something: because that involves a true and honest ethics, and not just words . . . I felt a sense of usefulness and purpose, and that what I was working on had sense for at least the young generation in Poland, which appreciated me. I was a man of work and discipline . . . Communists—I am talking about true Communists and not rogues—regarded me highly because I wasn't one of them from a political perspective, but they appreciated my sufficiently

puritan life-style and intellectual stand. You, like other Poles, have a purely emotional attitude to communism. In fact, I have never met people as pure as some of the Communists I met. I am definitely and irrevocably against this new faith. It is a great threat to humanity, because dialectical materialism is a lie. But that is another matter. (CM to Wańkowicz, January 1952)

Mother's Grave

My dearest, although I have been sending letters to you at any available opportunity, I have not heard from you for many months now. I cannot understand how you can stay in Wilno for so long while there are possibilities of coming to Poland. I am very concerned by the lack of news from you and the fact that you have done nothing yet about coming here. The longer you leave it, the harder it will be to find somewhere. I want to help you settle down and pass on the business of dealing with my earnings to Andrzej, because it might be possible that we will travel abroad for some time with the diplomatic service. Andrzej ought to work in exporting, administration of ports etc.; a special school preparing just for that will be opening in Gdynia soon. Father will also stay close to the sea in the north or somewhere in the western regions. I am coping quite well generally. We have a flat in Kraków and very often visit Warsaw and Łódź. I implore you to write, send a telegram and hasten your arrival here, because the situation is very urgent. I bite my fingernails with worry about you.

CM to his family, 6 August 1945; repr., *Kwartarnik Artystyczny* 3, 2008

Miłosz sent this urgent letter to his parents from Warsaw in early August 1945. Their situation was fraught with danger, as indeed it was for the majority of people living around Wilno. Once more the role of family carer fell on his younger brother's shoulders. In the spring of 1944, when the Soviet offensive was nearing Wilno, Andrzej took his parents away from the city and hid them on a farm in marshland not far from Szetejnie. With his cousin, he personally managed financial and administrative matters relating to the estate. On one occasion they helped a man escaping from the Germans. It later emerged that he was a commanding officer of Soviet partisans, who consisted mainly of Jews. A written account he gave them, detailing the assistance they proffered, subsequently proved priceless when the Red Army took over Wilno. During one of the round-ups when he showed it to NKVD officers, it saved Andrzej. Using various channels, he managed to obtain documents allowing the family to leave the country. And so it was that Aleksander, Weronika, Andrzej, Grandmother Kunat and a servant, with all their worldly belongings, climbed on a train to take them to Poland. In one wardrobe they took with them, at a massive risk to their own lives, they hid an AK Commander-in-Chief along with his adjutant.

They ended up in the village of Drewnica, east of Gdańsk, where they took over a small farm. The area was deserted, and the ethnic Germans had either fled or had been deported. Among the very few remaining inhabitants was an old peasant woman suffering from typhus. Weronika refused to leave the woman without help, and she herself contracted the illness. The nearest doctor, who was also a German, lived thirteen miles away. Andrzej sped off to collect him in the middle of the night, and by threatening him with a gun forced the doctor to come to Drewnica. The family seemed reassured by the diagnosis, and when Czesław brought Janka to meet his family on 18 November, no one, apart from Weronika, suspected that she had only a short time to live. She was in poor health and despondent. Forty years later the poet would incorporate her simple but meaningful words at the close of a poem: 'It all seems now to have been a dream' ('With Her', *NCP* 463). Miłosz received his mother's blessing to leave, or rather flee, Poland. In his partly biographical novel *Zdobycie władzy,* the mother of the main protagonist urges her son: 'Escape. Don't think about me. You mustn't start a new life here. I don't need anything now. I'll manage all right. Escape while there is still time' (*Seizure of Power* 137).

The couple got back to Warsaw on 22 November and received the awful news that Weronika had died. Miłosz immediately wrote to his father:

My beloved, dearest Father,

. . . I think about Mother as much as about you. I have a guilty con-science that then, on Sunday, I spoke against the idea of calling for a priest, but her temperature wasn't very high and we did not suspect that she had typhus. It's been terribly distressing for me. The doctor, who said that the danger had passed—it's unforgivable. I feel guilty that I did not take Mother's illness seriously enough. When I think about it now, I fear that she was apathetic and unusually for her lost the will to live . . . We all made a big mistake, when death was mentioned—and she kept coming back to it—we put it down to imagination, while she was really in low spirits and resigned to die . . .

I kiss you, my dear, beloved, poor Daddy
Your loving son—Czesiek

He attached a short letter to his grandmother:

> My dearest and most beloved Lisia! In this great sadness of ours please remember that you still have a grandson, who loves you and who will always think about you, and after my return, we will all live together . . .
>
> Your loving Czesław

He also wrote to his brother, Andrzej, from which it emerges that Weronika did not want to leave Szetejnie and move to Poland.

At first Aleksander and Andrzej Miłosz planned to concentrate on farming and, in the summer of 1946, Andrzej reported to his brother that they had sowed all the land they had and were waiting for the crops. Then, a year later, because of a plague of mice, the lack of fertilisers and, moreover, a lack of hands to help them on the farm, they abandoned farming. Aleksander, just as after the First World War, opened a building firm, and again, as can be inferred from Andrzej's letter, his partners cheated him. In the end he found a position as an engineer at the Department of Regeneration at Gdańsk Regional Council. Earlier, Aleksander had moved into a villa in Sopot, at 23 Wybickiego Street. Following his elder son's advice, he had it registered in Czesław's name, as the poet planned to live there with his family after their return from America. The house was haunted because its previous German owners had taken cyanide, but a priest's holy water and incense helped a little, and the inhabitants got used to the sounds of knocking and other noises. To his aunts, Gabriela and Janina, it became a place where people were invited for a game of bridge and homemade liqueur, a small sanctuary of the Old World removed from the new and so very different order.

Miłosz's father could not cope with the loneliness of life after Weronika's death, and tried to conquer his depression by means of alcohol. The only possible salvation was a new relationship, and indeed, at the end of 1948, Aleksander married his second wife, Olga Bochaczewska; together with her adult son, the couple moved to Kraków. His two sons did not take kindly to his decision, not only because of Weronika, but also because they thought he was marrying below his status. Old age was not kind to Aleksander. Czesław's coldness towards him, along with financial problems, which Andrzej always helped him through, dashed his spirits. The former Siberian traveller and hunter died of a heart attack in a grey Communist Kraków on 17 November 1959. A year before his death he sent a card to his son: 'I was very moved when I heard you on the radio and learnt that you are a world-famous writer. It is a great pity that I do not have any of your books' (Aleksander Miłosz to CM, 25 March 1958, Beinecke Archive).

In Miłosz's California home, on a shelf above his desk, stood two photographs of his mother, and on the wall hung a reproduction of a portrait of Gabriela Kunat. In the first of the two, a charming girl looks coquettishly from underneath the brim of her hat. In the second a young mother holds on her lap her small son as they embrace each other and face the camera. In Miłosz's estimation, there was no comparison between the impact his father and mother had on his upbringing. Weronika had an incomparably more significant role, and when she died Miłosz may well have realised that he had entered a new stage of his life, with the snipping of a cord linking him to the past. Did he later sense her presence in his life? Andrzej Miłosz was convinced that their mother was still watching over them. Grandma Lisia told her grandson that something gently stroked her face and that she heard a loudly uttered word, 'Mummy'. And she too had a dream:

> I will tell you about my strange dream, which I had just before her death. I dreamt about a beautiful morning in Szetejnie, lilacs and other flowers were in full blossom and the air was quiet . . . and then I saw in the middle of Niewiaża a boat moving, all covered in bulrushes and water lilies, with no one at the tiller. I peered into it and there she lay in a deep sleep, very young and beautiful, like in a dream, all dressed in lilies and meadow-flowers. I couldn't have enough of looking at her and stopped the boat with all my strength, but although the water was still, the current pulled the boat away from my grip and it went further until it disappeared from my sight. (Józefa Kunat to CM, 15 January 1947, Beinecke Library)

The garden in Szetejnie fell into further neglect. In the poem, 'Grób Matki' (Mother's Grave), which Miłosz wrote in 1949, he talks of how

> we live wavering,
> unsteady, while quickly
> like flies in the light of permanent lamps
> electron passes by electron in space.

The poem concludes with a prayer:

> Help me create ever-enduring love,
> From my persistent dissonance with the world,
> . . .
> A fixed point, which, to spite history
> Divides all that is fluid into good and evil,
> Help me, mother, to strengthen as a human being,
> You who recall my promises from childhood.

> (*Wiersze* II, 65–66)

Rescue

On 4 December 1945, a DC-3 which had seen better times took off with difficulty from the snow-covered Warsaw airport and shook in the air. As every minute passed on the six-hour journey to London, Miłosz and Janka felt an increasing sense of relief: 'We submerged in the white mist and this mist covered our past', the poet wrote in 1948 in a draft of a story, 'Historia Londyńska' (A London Story) (Beinecke Library).

They spent five weeks in the British capital, which was slowly recovering from its war-time devastation, and stayed in the Hotel Esplanade in Warrington Crescent, which was run by a Polish Jew. In his later memoirs, Miłosz wrote how he enjoyed being in London, and that he did not feel any stigma at being a 'Red'. He spent a lot of time in discussions with Karol Estreicher and Antoni Słonimski, who edited the magazine *Nowa Polska* (New Poland), which featured a sketch about Stanisław Witkiewicz written during the occupation. Janka introduced Miłosz to the artist Feliks Topolski, and together they visited his studio under Hungerford Bridge, and also attended an exhibition of paintings by Picasso and Matisse. Looking at Picasso's pictures, Miłosz is said to have given a sigh and said, 'Next to him I always look like a small girl', and indeed, only the Picassos remained in Miłosz's memory:

> One has to realise the charge of passion which sprang from the canvasses. Irony, disgust, mockery, anger are obviously present here too, with so much clarity they try shouting in protest through a shape or color that it is impossible to miss them. It is an attempt to increase ways of expressing an artistic language, an attempt to sing a new tragedy by Sophocles using the language of Hottentots. (*Kontynenty* 77)

Czesław and Janka were looked after by a distinguished writer and activist from the International Pen Club, Margaret Storm Jameson (1891–1986). She had visited Poland in 1945 in the company of Antoni Słonimski and Ksawery Prószyński, and in Kraków held long discussions with Miłosz, whom she was clearly drawn to. In her autobiography, *Journey from the North* (1970), she wrote that 'he was very composed, and, despite that, unusually attractive, with a pale, quite wide face and flat lips—almost like Pushkin's, but much paler—and with a contagious smile' (Jameson 567).

She remembered from that visit, among other things, the young Pole's thorough familiarity with English poetry, his respect for Eliot and his rather cold assessment of the international political situation. Now, having received a classic present from Poland, a bottle of vodka—particularly valuable during this time of austerity in London, when whiskey was a luxury—she invited Miłosz and Janka to dinner, during which they met her husband, the historian, Guy Chapman. The icing on the cake was the opportunity to meet T. S. Eliot, who appeared to Miłosz 'easy to talk to and a charming sexagenarian ... with the appearance of a troubled young man' (*Kontynenty* 97). During the evening, Miłosz was given permission to publish his translation of *The Waste Land* without paying the author a fee. That evening marked the beginning of their relationship.

Miłosz had an equivocal attitude to Eliot's work. He successfully translated 'Gerontion', 'The Hollow Men' and 'Burnt Norton', which he discussed in his *A Treatise on Poetry* and in a piece entitled 'Thoughts on Eliot' (*Prywatne obowiązki* 205–215). Eliot's play *The Cocktail Party* appalled him, however. 'Only a wretch could write something like that and applaud it ... After his last two works I became his enemy', he wrote (CM to Jerzy Turowicz, 4 April 1950), and no doubt he meant it. A context for this strange outburst that might be borne in mind is that in the late 1940s Eliot became the object of a series of crude attacks in the Soviet bloc, which were begun by Alexander Fadeyev, the head of the World Congress of Intellectuals in Defence of Peace (1948), who accused the poet of promoting a 'malicious attack on the intellect and a propaganda of irrationalism'. Famously, Fadeyev declared, 'If jackals could learn to type, if hyenas could use a pen, then their work would most certainly resemble books by the Millers, Eliots, Malrauxs and other Sartres.' In Miłosz's archives there is an unfinished article in which he intended to respond to accusations in Fadeyev's address that he devoted too much time to promoting Eliot to Polish readers:

> Becoming familiar with the works of Eliot was to me, personally, an important warning sign, especially when I followed the development of his work from the purely negative poems, ridiculing capitalist civilisation in the twentieth century, to those in which Eliot appears as a high priest who argues that we should revert to the period before capitalism and the Renaissance, and go back to good old medieval corporatism. (Beinecke Library)

In 1945, of course, such times of passive servitude were hard to imagine.

Despite his reservations about Eliot's politics, Miłosz was happy to relax drinking tea at Faber and Faber, probably informing Eliot about his newest volume, *Rescue*. That collection was the fifth poetry book to appear in the new Poland and was published in an edition with ten times more copies than any of the publications before the war, which must have meant a great deal to Miłosz. His vision of popularizing culture was becoming a reality. The elegantly edited 150-page book contained a cross-section of his work, ranging from *A Poem on Frozen Time*, through *Three Winters*, to poems from the late 1930s and poetry written at the beginning of the occupation, through to 'The World' and 'Voices of Poor People', and lastly poems from Goszyce. The two most recent poems were an addendum to the selection, though, importantly, they articulated clearly the poet's stance. The closing piece, 'In Warsaw', depicts the poet standing amongst the ruins of St John's Cathedral, confronted by the tragedy of the nation. The poet who previously wanted to be free from social and traditional romantic obligations now felt the call to speak for the departed:

> You swore never to be
> A ritual mourner.
> . . .
>
> But the lament of Antigone
> Searching for her brother
> Is indeed beyond the power
> Of endurance. And the heart
> Is a stone in which is enclosed,
> Like an insect, the dark love
> Of a most unhappy land.
> . . .
>
> It's madness to live without joy
> And to repeat to the dead
> Whose part was to be gladness
> Of action in thought and in the flesh, singing, feasts,
> Only the two salvaged words:
> Truth and justice.

('In Warsaw', NCP 75)

The most poignant lines were in 'Dedication', addressed to the poets who fell during the Warsaw Rising, representatives of a world that had passed. The artist, who witnessed the Apocalypse, speaks in the simplest of words, setting out his highest aims: to defy ideological madness, to save truth and so the human soul:

> You whom I could not save
> Listen to me.
> Try to understand this simple speech as I would be ashamed of
>   another.
> I swear, there is in me no wizardry of words.
> I speak to you with silence like a cloud or a tree.
> . . .
>
> What is poetry which does not save
> Nations or people?

A connivance with official lies,
A song of drunkards whose throats will be cut in a moment,
Readings for sophomore girls.

That I wanted good poetry without knowing it,
That I discovered, late, its salutary aim,
In this and only this I find salvation.

(NCP 77)

With perhaps more than a touch of friendly exaggeration, Tadeusz Breza described *Rescue* as 'the Bible for all young people, poetic or not' (*Zaraz po wojnie* 469). The book's reception was not exactly unambiguous, which was made apparent when Przyboś, and not Miłosz, received an annual award from the City Council of Kraków in 1945. Reviews were mixed. Aleksander Rymkiewicz, for example, clearly did not pick up on the poet's irony in 'Songs of Adrian Zieliński', which went beyond the reviewer's intellectual understanding. He saw the distance between the artist and his protagonists as a betrayal: 'The tragedy of our homeland in 1939 and the years that followed was voiced by a detached observer-botanist ... A writer, as a collector of emotions, must stand almost above the nation' (*Tygodnik Warszawski:* 14, 1946). Dominik Horodyński reached a similar conclusion, accusing Miłosz of escapism and an inability to participate in the fate of the nation: 'The cause of this tragic climate is the way you lived through the war. There is not a single word about fighting, heroism or sacrifice.' Curiously, an Anders's Army soldier, Konstanty Jeleński, did not share their sentiments, but rather asserted that Miłosz had reached 'the highest level'. He noted intelligently that 'his poetry strikingly resembles English poetry' and concluded, 'In Miłosz's verse, there is, above all, a vision and a poetic ability to express things which cannot be expressed any other way' (*Salamander:* I, 1946). This review was probably not read by the author. At home, however, no-one was able to appreciate the artistic revolution in *Voices of Poor People* that initiated a new trend in Polish poetry of the twentieth century, which preceded and foretold the poetic achievements of Tadeusz Różewicz and Zbigniew Herbert.

His confident use of poetic personae and irony put Miłosz ahead of his time and so made too great demands on the sensitivities of his readers. He had evidently moved away from lyrical Romanticism, drawing instead from earlier traditions. Miłosz's scornful assessment was that, despite all appearances, 'the models promoted by the authorities lacked authenticity'. 'In Polish literature Romanticism is having a renaissance. Leftist critics ... are not humanists at all, but disguised Romantics'. He recalled English poets such as Eliot, Auden and the young American Karl Shapiro, who were comfortable employing micro-drama, satire or philosophical treatises. And he said that an artist was 'a person who fought against someone or something using a pen as a weapon' (*Kontynenty* 80), because standing up against evil 'is the privilege of every poet' (ibid., 89). Miłosz aspired towards a poetry that was intellectually sober and witty, that refused to shun sarcasm or jest, and that wanted to absorb history, sociology, philosophy and all that would be necessary for humankind.

In the last two letters Miłosz sent to friends on 16 January 1945, just before saying farewell to Europe, he referred to *Rescue*. He asked Tadeusz Breza to contact Czytelnik to send him his author's copies, because when he left Poland the volume was not yet ready. He approached Jerzy Turowicz, the only person he could trust not to censor any of his poems, to oversee the book's editing and correction. It was to him that Miłosz sent his thanks from the boat anchored near Glasgow:

Dear Jerzy,

Quite by chance, just before leaving London, I got a copy of *Rescue*. I am truly grateful and do not have words to thank you enough for all the effort you put into the corrections. We are moored in the Clyde estuary in Scotland and will be shortly sailing off to New York. (CM to Jerzy Turowicz, 16 January 1946)

Chochoły

From the cry of children on the floors of stations beyond time,
From the sadness of the engineer of prison trains,
From the red scars of two wars on the forehead,
I awoke under the bronze of winged monuments,
Under the griffins of a Masonic temple
With the dying ash of a cigar.[3]

Czesław Miłosz, 'The Spirit of the Laws' (*NCP* 97)

The S.S. *Elysia* was a small cargo ship with only a few cabins. It slogged through stormy Atlantic waters for twelve days, and the passengers could only talk about their good luck later when their friends who sailed on another vessel got lost among icebergs. At the docks in New York, Miłosz and Janka were met by Aleksander Hertz, whom they knew from pre-war times at Polish Radio. Whereas Hertz was a great fan of America and its commitment to freedom and entrepreneurship, Miłosz would turn out to be rather less of an enthusiast.

What did the poet really know about the country to which his fate had brought him? Probably very little. From his school days he retained an image of a virgin forest, which, strangely, was missing in what he saw of New York or Washington. Then there was Charlie Chaplin. And Whitman. Maybe stories from Janka's father, as he toiled in a steelworks here. To top everything there was that sense of the absurd he had encountered when at Market Square in Kraków he saw soldiers standing under a portrait of Zhukov, belting out, 'This is America/The famous USA/It is a lovely land/Heaven on Earth.' Had he been sent to an embassy in Paris or Rome, his life would have taken a different course. Perhaps he would have severed links with Warsaw and found a place for himself in a Communist-sympathising but spiritually closer Europe. But here, across the ocean, he encountered a different reality, one utterly alien to him.

If one were to conceive of a scenario to describe his surreal situation, it might have looked like this: a man who only recently had tramped through burnt-out ruins, before whose eyes flashed images of people murdered and dead from exhaustion, had arrived here in a stone gorge, untouched by bullets, upon whose walls was plastered an advertisement for cigarettes four storeys high, depicting a young man from whose lips emerged real smoke. A plane circling the cloudless sky above did not drop bombs, but spelt a word beginning with 'P', which turned out to be not 'peace', but 'Pepsi', while on the ground police cars and ambulances shot past whose alarms sounded almost identical to the anti-aircraft signal used in Warsaw. Here, however, nobody reacted to the wailing sound or buried their heads in their shoulders. He could see cheerful crowds drinking milk in the morning, quickly scoffing a hamburger in a drugstore, before hurrying to work by metro. Everyone was polite, but expressed no interest in the newcomer's story. The questions posed, not by Miłosz, but by another European, Albert Camus, who arrived in New York two months later, were 'whether we find ourselves amongst the craziest or the most sensible people on earth? Is life as easy as they say here, or as idiotic as it seems?' (Camus to J. and M. Gallimard, 20 April 1946). The future author of *The Plague* would not have come up with a comparison made by the Polish poet, who found himself in what seemed like the world of Witkiewicz's prophecy fulfilled, where an animal-like humanity had abandoned its metaphysical dreams:

> The gigantic city itself was an outrage, because it stood there as if nothing had happened—it had not received a single notch from a bomb—and the people in the streets of Manhattan were free from what flowed in me like molten lead. The absurd paperwork that piled up on my desk and the letter lying on top of it, from a camp near Archangelsk, was an outrage. The letter had been received in Poland by relatives of the prisoner and sent to me with a request for a package for him. I had to live

with the image of camps and trainloads of prisoners heading towards them. So orange juice, milk shakes, and a new shirt were outrageous. The constant lying of my colleagues and superiors . . . half-wittedness and innocence. (*NR* 265)

In an unpublished sketch written in 1947, 'Thoughts in a Hotel Lobby', Miłosz acknowledged the development of civilisation and educational facilities in the country where he lived, but also the superficiality of human contact and the lack of a sense of history, both of which weighed on his mind:

> My muscles are tensed to jump . . . Invariably the American advice, 'Relax, just relax'—misses the point. Inside: fury, revolt, sarcasm, flowing down to the end of fingers resting on an armchair. What is it that you want? To go, to burn the world, to roar, to shout abuse—instead of relaxing muscles and mind during afternoon siesta? (Beinecke Library)

Two years later, while delivering a talk to students at Columbia University, he explained how the experience of war affected him, how during his first months in the States he could not rid himself of a feeling that he had 'God's eye, which, as it is presumed, could see through the vanity and void of human desire' ('Odczyt o literaturze', Beinecke Library). These tormented feelings had an impact on his health: 'Czesław suffered a collapse . . . his eyes acquired this miserable, slightly misty expression', Janka told Jerzy Andrzejewski. 'Generally, if someone refuses halva, then there must be something wrong with them' (*Zaraz po wojnie* 48).

Banal small talk during cocktail parties, theatre and cinema audiences who cackled joyfully during tragic scenes, the contact with art limited to comics in a newspaper, those were among his earliest impressions. In one letter he commented:

> The spiritual poverty of millions of the inhabitants of this country is horrifying . . . The only living people—the ability to create art is a sign of living—are the Blacks and the Indians—if we were to take groups of people rather than individuals . . . Americans' lives revolve around listening to the radio, whereas for a normal person being subjected to a two-minute dose of it would make them sick . . . You will tell me that I care too much about art and that I am an incorrigible bureaucrat. I don't care about art. What I mean to say is that it is important what it is an expression of and not what it is like. I am talking about people who live, feel and think, and those who perceive the world with sobriety, for whom life is worth living. These unfortunate American puppets move like *chochoły*, with a depressing inner stupor. (*Zaraz po wojnie* 383)

He ought to have stood on a corner of one of Manhattan's streets and shouted, like Moses, 'Convert! Destroy the golden calf!',[4] but he did nothing as spectacular as that. He would later tell Eliot of his conviction that he had been sent to live among 'figures that resembled straw-covered shrubs', lifeless, with plastic souls—ideas that made their way into the poem 'A Man from Detroit'. It was so critical of America that, on Kroński's advice, he decided not to publish it, so that people in Poland would not presume that he had joined the anti-capitalist campaign.

'Millions of people who care about money. I cared about it little. I was not born into a class that knew how to prize it' (*NR* 264). From his early youth he was contemptuous of 'small town' values and conceded that after the war, 'emotionally I did not condemn the destruction of private shops and farms (this does not mean that I always approved of it intellectually); it even gave me a sadistic pleasure' (*NR* 33). His profound distaste for what he termed 'cow-like existence' led to far-sighted conclusions which he shared with Andrzejewski and Turowicz. He argued that in the United States, the art of brainwashing had reached perfection, and surpassed what the Soviets had achieved: 'The means by which public opinion was moulded in countries such as Poland were child's play compared to the art-form the Americans had developed, and the methods used by security services there are like something dating from the stone age up to the nineteenth century' (*Zaraz po wojnie* 58), whereas in the United States 'the security authorities apply exceptionally subtle methods which are invisible, and each citizen has a *dossier* about them as thick as a theological file' (CM to Jerzy Turowicz, 15 April 1947). A question one might consider is the extent to which he was presenting his opinions for more than one audience, being aware that his correspondence would be censored, and that his anti-American sentiments might sit well and improve his ratings in the records of the perhaps less highly developed but still sufficiently efficient Polish security services.

Tapping ash off his cigar, the editor of *Reader's Digest* put Miłosz straight on one occasion:

> 'You intellectuals have lost. Your aims to change people have proved pointless. We won, because we give them what they want. Our publications are read by millions, and they don't want you and never will'. It was then that I realised that I am a Promethean Romantic who was led to believe that I had a special mission to try 'to transform ordinary people into angels'. The fat chortle of the gentleman with a cigar offended me deeply, because he had pocketed for himself common sense and clarity of judgment. I also realised that, unfortunately, intellectuals and com-

munists shared a Romantic pedigree and that his America was not for me. (*Rok myśliwego* 158)

In small university enclaves and in New York's Greenwich Village, Miłosz began to meet international intellectuals. He valued the opportunity of seeing Thomas Mann; made friends with the novelist and dramatist Thornton Wilder; and while working in the Library of Congress met Saint-John Perse and Dwight Macdonald, who edited a leftist but anti-Stalinist magazine, *politics,* as well as Mary McCarthy, a co-founder of *Partisan Review,* who could be considered the Susan Sontag of her time. He had closer links with the young poets Randall Jarrell and Robert Lowell. Visiting 'a communist' in his Washington flat held no fears for Lowell, who Miłosz would introduce to Polish readers in a report following the meeting: 'I attacked his poetry mainly because it is so similar to mine in *Three Winters*' (*Rok myśliwego* 286).

Miłosz launched himself into an extensive reading programme of American poetry, prose and drama. He rated highly American prose, then poetry, but thought drama was its weakest genre. From delving into American fiction, he deduced that stories produced by Polish prose writers could easily shed half their word count without inflicting any harm. Soon he became a regular cinema-goer, particularly enjoying Alfred Hitchcock's *Notorious,* starring Cary Grant and Ingrid Bergman. His visits to theatres in the States, however, sometimes ended in disappointment. An example was the production of *A Streetcar Named Desire* he saw in Baltimore in January 1950, after which he criticised the author for captivating then shocking the audience with the play's pure brutality: 'I had to drink two bottles of beer after the show in order to wash away the bad taste in my mouth' ('Obyczaje').

His relationship with the Polish émigré community in the United States was incomparably worse than with that in London, and feelings of antipathy were mutual. Intellectually, the poet was totally detached from the older generation, while newcomers such as Kazimierz Wierzyński and Jan Lechoń were locked in a nostalgic vision of pre-war Poland: 'Nothing interests them here; they don't understand and don't try to use their poetic nature to understand things. They treasure memories of the Poland of their youth, which seems highly irritating and false to us. It is incredibly stale and old-fashioned' (*Zaraz po wojnie* 141). He probably regarded the artistic form Julian Tuwim adopted in a similar light. The two poets were very amicable in each other's company, and Tuwim was full of admiration for Miłosz's poetry, as he confessed to Czytelnik's driving force, Jerzy Borejsza:

It has been a long time since I read such entrancingly beautiful poems as in 'The World: A Naïve Poem'. Already in Poland I knew what a self-made and unusual poet he was. But his new poems awakened in me love and a springtime dizziness . . . enchantment, love, fever at being touched by poetry. There is so much lyrical wisdom, knowledge! I have the impression that Miłosz is the foremost poet of contemporary Poland. (Tuwim to Borejsza, 12 December 1949)

Tuwim chose to return to Poland, and from Warsaw sent a letter to Miłosz thanking him for his support; it began with the following phrases: "My good, helpful, polite, noble, decent, friendly, well-wishing, dear, pleasant, beautiful, blessedwith hugepoetictalent, endowedwithunheardofpersonal charm, dear Mr Czesław!' And Tuwim added in the margin: 'Would you be so kind as to inform the editor-in-chief of *The Reader's Encyclopedia,* the book, as they say, v. useful and interesting, that on page 720, between "Mickey Mouse" (sic!) and "Midas" (sic sic!) there is the name of a certain Polish poet missing' (Tuwim to CM, 25 October 1949).

His stay in America 'resembles the afterlife a little', Miłosz reported to Aniela Micińska, explaining that he primarily focused on his work and had hardly any social life as a result of the increasing Cold War rhetoric and actions of both sides. His circle of friends in those years was indeed small, and the atmosphere of distrust and suspicion in the New York consulate and later in the embassy in Washington was not conducive to expanding it. Miłosz stayed on friendly terms with Ksawery Pruszyński (now a lawyer at the 'Red' embassy), but did not find common ground with him. He developed a closer relationship with Maciej Nowicki, an outstanding architect who was then beginning his international career. Together with Le Corbusier and Oscar Niemeyer, Nowicki was the co-creator of the United Nations building. His was an untimely death in a plane crash in 1950.

The closest Polish social networks in New York consisted of small groups of the Jewish intelligentsia who had managed to escape to America at the beginning of the war: these included the psychoanalyst Gustav Bychowski, Aleksander Hertz and Janka's old friend, Aniela Geppner, the daughter of a Warsaw merchant, now married to Lucjan Borowik, whose house 'served us always as a welcome base'. Thanks to the Borowiks, Miłosz became acquainted with Alfred Berlestein, a curator of the Slavonic collection at the New York Public Library, who would help him in organising exhibitions and reading events. Miłosz later wrote a note about him: 'It was he who, one day when I was sitting in the library, . . . came over to me and asked me in a whisper if I knew who the gentleman was who was seated next to me. It was Kerensky, the prime minister of the first post-tsarist Russian government' (*ABC* 68).

Given the few temptations in his social life, the best option seemed to be to concentrate on work, with occasional breaks for holiday trips. Living in the most technologically advanced country in the world, Miłosz was tireless in his quest to discover primeval nature, and, chasing his childhood dreams, journeyed to Maine and Vermont, camped in the most remote places, rode horses, travelled in boats to observe beavers, and followed the tracks of bears and moose. In the wilderness, he looked for something familiar, close to home: the 'America of trees and plants, fragrant with the hay reaped on forest meadows, fitted over me smoothly and I ceased to be a foreigner in her' (*NR* 260–261). And at least these pursuits provided a temporary escape from memories: Europe with its bloody history and politics were set aside when, above the current of the Potomac River, as above the Niewiaża, birdsong rang out.

Before long the naturalist's escapades turned into more formal family outings. On 29 March 1947, in the Washington Garfield Memorial Hospital, after a difficult birth which ended in a caesarean section, the couple's first son, Antoni Oskar Jan, came into the world:

> Why Antoni? Perhaps because I liked the protagonist in *The Moon Rises*, perhaps named after Słonimski, a good Catholic name, better than Baltazar or Hieronim, and of Slavonic names I had had enough … Very light pink skin, blond and blue-eyed. No communication: eats, poos and sleeps and, of course, screams. Strange. (*Zaraz po wojnie* 142)

The boy was healthy and grew very quickly: 'I refer to him as "puppy", a term of endearment. He is very sweet. Pink and smiles a lot. For now he is simply called "Pussy", that is, a kitten' (ibid., 149). By the end of 1947 he had four teeth and had learnt to say 'tiatia' (daddy) and how to fall out of the cot. Janka, instead of writing film reviews, spent endless hours feeding him, changing him and washing nappies. A prevailing theme in letters from that time was Miłosz's complaint about a lack of available childcare, not being able to trust black baby-sitters hired on spec.

'I am curious to know what it is going to be like in the future and who he is. I am dying to discuss Sartre with him, but feel a little shy. Judging by his dignified behaviour, he may be someone special, or perhaps a dolt', he wrote soon after his son's birth to Tadeusz and Zofia Breza. It is hard to assess his fatherly emotions, because, following traditional family rules, Janka predominantly looked after and cared for the baby, while Czesław spent most of his time travelling, giving talks and writing articles. During their free time the family left for Cape Cod in their Chevrolet with its 'Diplomatic Personnel' sticker. Suddenly and unexpectedly, the world around them showed its gentle side: 'On the vast, renewed by spring earth./My home, a second: in it, the beginning of the world' ('Na śpiew ptaka nad brzegami Potomaku', *Wiersze* II, 33).

'A passion for doing something useful'

Straight after their arrival in America, Miłosz started work at the consulate in
New York, and not in Chicago as expected. They rented a small apartment in
Madison Square, but soon had to move to a bigger flat, at 342 West 71st Street.
Meanwhile at the New York consulate Miłosz began as a lowly 'contracted clerk
at the cultural and press office'. Thanks to hard work and drive, he quickly began
to climb the ladder; as early as October 1946, he was promoted to the position of
cultural attaché at the Washington Embassy, and then on 1 April 1948 he was
nominated for the post of second secretary. He was highly praised by his superiors. At the start of 1948 a report arrived in Warsaw, stating that Miłosz

> is an exceptionally suitable employee and is a true expert in matters re-
> lating to culture. He is no ordinary clerk and does not require supervi-
> sion. He is a good communicator and speaker. In political matters, he still
> has to be monitored, due to his poetic ability to digress from concrete
> matters, but he improves each passing day. (Miłosz Personal Archives)

Six months later his bosses maintained that Miłosz possessed 'exceptional, and
brilliant intelligence' as well as 'great ethics and wide political interests', and that
he was 'trustworthy'; 'the results of his work so far have been "very good"', while
'his literary interests do not interfere in his development as an excellent diplomat,
on condition that further practice will further develop his organisational skills.'

A recommendation from the central office to the ambassador, Józef Winiewicz, was that he 'ought not to be burdened with bureaucratic chores ... Let
him create'. Miłosz himself did not just want *to appear* to work; on the contrary,
he was bursting with energy and determination to excel in managing editorial
projects, preparing exhibitions and events. He stood out from the majority of the
staff, who were frightened, busily plotting, writing poison-pen letters, and planning escape. There were very few true Communists; the majority looked simply
for opportunities to flee Poland, like the consul from New York, Jan Galewicz,
who after completing his term of office headed for Uruguay, where he opened his
own business.

In the Department of Culture and Art, Miłosz worked with a composer,
Tadeusz Kassern, who had only just arrived from Poland. At the beginning, as
Miłosz explained to Andrzejewski, he wished to concentrate on 'informing the
country about the literary, artistic and scientific aspects of American life' (*Zaraz po
wojnie* 34), purchasing books for Polish institutions and acting as a liaison officer in
publishing matters. State publishers would take a long time sending ordered books
and periodicals, while gifts in the form of books from America, instead of being

made accessible to readers, were left untouched, gathering dust in storerooms in the National Library. Miłosz for his part kept very busy, and it would be almost impossible to list all the activities he undertook. He organized showings of short documentary films and concerts featuring Chopin's and Szymanowski's music; he took part in conferences for the Commission for International Educational Reconstruction, and invited Polish artists like Tadeusz Brzozowski, Maria Jarema, Jerzy Nowosielski and Tadeusz Kantor to exhibit their art. He sent requests for Polish books and reproductions of works of art, saying that 'only avant-garde art will be of interest here'.

In August 1947, Miłosz took part in a writers' conference at Bread Loaf in Vermont, where he met Robert Frost. In his report on the event, he stressed how he had made 'a great number of literary contacts among others from within the top intellectual circles in New York'. During the Cultural and Scientific Conference for World Peace in March 1949, Miłosz looked after Polish delegates. At the embassy, he collaborated on the publication *Poland Today;* took part in radio programmes about Ignacy Jan Paderewski; interviewed Thornton Wilder and John Dos Passos prior to possible visits by them to Poland; and met with Philip Drury, director of the United Nations Theatre, but due to a lack of translations from Polish could not suggest any plays. At the New York Public Library, Miłosz organized an exhibition of books and photographs which was visited by 20,000 people. He also organised his own poetry-reading event, which took place on 27 April 1946; he was introduced by Manfred Kridl, who had done so much to support his literary career back in Wilno.

Miłosz worked together with groups who wanted to organise a humanitarian action for Poland, and participated in a meeting of the American Jewish Congress to commemorate the third anniversary of the Warsaw Ghetto Rising. In an official report Miłosz wrote: 'I was applauded when I said that the current Polish government was best when it comes to solving the problem of restoring Jewish life in Poland'. An article in the *Boston Globe* on 19 April 1946 reported that Miłosz asserted openly to an audience of over 1,000 that the Red Army did not come to the aid of Poles during the Warsaw Rising strictly for political reasons, and that the Polish government, albeit not a puppet authority, has to co-operate with 'a powerful neighbour'.

He fought for grants for students and scientists independently as well as alongside the Kościuszko Foundation, the Massachusetts Institute of Technology and the Institute for Advanced Studies in Princeton. When his endeavours met with indifference in Poland, he became despondent and critical of the Polish authorities: 'I worked out a detailed plan for providing support to Ernest Lilien, the author and editor of a monumental Polish-English dictionary . . . I can only express my disappointment and regret that although the project was supported by the Embassy in Poland, it has not met with approval' (Embassy Report, August–September 1946). Not losing heart and faith in the common sense of people in power, he re-issued his objectives and proposed:

> 1. Funding, following the Czech example, of a Department of American studies at one of the Polish universities. 2. Setting up and supporting a department at the Ministry of Education, which will provide funding for American students and teachers; and increasing the scholarship or fellowship allowance. 3. Providing support to Polish students visiting USA. 4. Supporting Polish scientists visiting USA. 5. Putting pressure on Polish publishers and editors of cultural, literary and scientific books to send their publications to American libraries and educational establishments. 6. Promoting free exchanges of books between America and Poland . . . 7. Removing the seal 'exchange control' on letters arriving from Poland, which is received here with sniggers and treated like a censorship stamp.

In summing up, he came to a number of bluntly expressed conclusions:

> The Anti-American attitude in Poland is for those of us, living overseas, very uncomfortable when we are trying to build wider cultural links. Why does a Marxist regard some cultures as taboo, sensing demonic elements in them, since . . . the socialist economy is going to take over the world, including English-speaking countries? . . . I would like to turn your attention to the fact that steps need to be taken which would demonstrate the cordial disposition of the Polish nation towards the American nation. One of those steps would be to open a Department of American studies at one of the Polish universities. The tone of the Polish press is particularly aggressive—taking out sentences which express a friendly disposition to America, refusing to celebrate Independence Day . . . A picture of a few small American flags on a wall may have a much better effect than any other propaganda. (Embassy Report, July 1947)

Miłosz made many visits to Smith College in Northampton, Massachusetts, a small town roughly a hundred miles from Boston, where Kridl became a lecturer soon after his arrival in the States, just after the outbreak of war. Both Czesław and Janka visited him there in June 1946, when they admired pictures by Goya, Corot and Picasso in the local gallery. After that Miłosz made subsequent visits on his own. The purpose of one trip was to give a lecture, 'The Inner Experiences of Contemporary European Writers'. In this he introduced poems by Tadeusz Różewicz and spoke out against the marginalisation of countries like Czechoslovakia or Poland in discussions on Western civilisation. Another reason for the visit was to see a new female friend. Jane Zielonko was the daughter of Polish emigrants and grew up in a working-class environment, but rose in social status thanks to her brilliance and hard work. She graduated from Columbia University and got a job at a prestigious institution, Smith College. For a time, she was the partner of Ksawery Pruszyński, but later became Miłosz's lover. What drew him to her was primarily her intelligence, humour and sense of irony.

Jane was one of very few people with whom Miłosz could have honest discussions, and thanks to her he learnt about the unofficial history of the States, a power built on poverty and the slave labour of generations of immigrants. Their American affair was short, because Zielonko left for France after receiving a Fulbright scholarship. After his defection, the poet met up with her again in Paris in 1951. Their friendship was renewed, but mainly in order for the two of them to work on an English version of *The Captive Mind.*

In these early years Miłosz made many trips all over the country, some on his own, and some on which he was accompanied by the artist Wanda Telakowska. A painter and sculptor, she devoted her career to teaching aesthetics. She worked at the Ministry of Culture in Warsaw after the war, and was keen to see high-quality designs applied in industrial production and encouraged the use of folk art motifs. In 1948, she set up a mobile exhibition of fabrics and cottage industry products, which she brought to the States. In May and June she and Miłosz embarked on a road trip to see Santa Fe, Indian villages in Taos and the Grand Canyon, but also visited Los Angeles, which Miłosz dismissively summed up as 'a small hell-hole with no imagination, consisting of palm trees and nothing' (*Zaraz po wojnie* 178). As part of his great efforts to find support for the enterprise, Miłosz approached Henry Miller and Wanda Galska, a California multi-millionaire who owned Le Théâtre des Champs-Élysées in Paris. Telakowska and Miłosz had many meetings with museum and gallery directors as well as entrepreneurs, many of whom expressed an interest in using Polish art designs. According to Miłosz, however, the indolence of Polish bureaucrats meant that a realistic opportunity for Polish design to be made famous worldwide was missed.

Of the many projects Miłosz initiated, the one that could be regarded as his greatest success was establishing the Department of Polish Studies, named after Adam Mickiewicz, at Columbia University.

> Millions of Americans of Polish origin could become a great and political power. At universities they could change to Slavonic Studies, so that they would no longer be just Russian Studies. But what can be expected from collective incompetence? Polish Studies at Columbia proved that . . . Simmons, a professor of Russian, approached me in 1948, I think, . . . with a suggestion that Poland fund a Polish department.

Because he put forward Manfred Kridl ... he could count on my support in the matter. The Polish authorities understood the propaganda
value of the enterprise and got the required (then very high) sum of ten
thousand dollars a year ... There was no Polish Studies department in
America and I created it. And then all hell broke loose—the entire Polish
émigré press in America were up in arms about Communist infiltration ... but the thought that they could have founded a department
themselves never entered their minds. A few years later, the subsidy from
Warsaw ended and the department ceased to exist. (*Rok myśliwego* 178)

In June 1948, an ambassador's report notes Miłosz's private contacts with
Ernest J. Simmons and Roman Jakobson, who ran a department named after
Tomáš Masaryk, which was funded by the Czechoslovak government. The Poles
came up with the idea of setting up a department named after Adam Mickiewicz
to coincide with the 150th anniversary of the poet's birth. In the autumn of that
year, the embassy received two letters from Maria Mickiewicz, the poet's granddaughter, one addressed to General Dwight Eisenhower, who was then President
of Columbia University, and the other to Manfred Kridl with the message: 'I am
convinced that just as over a hundred years ago at the Collège de France, now
from the hall at the Columbia University Polish culture will radiate from the lips
of Mickiewicz, thanks to you' (qtd. in *Mój wileński opiekun* 10).

Kridl's lectures were to begin on 27 September, but plotting against the
project started beforehand. The Polish American Congress issued an official letter
to Eisenhower: "We demand that you, the President and the Columbia University
authorities, reject the donation of $5000, given by Józef Winiewicz, the so-called
representative of the Polish nation, currently controlled by the Soviets ... because
this communist infiltration has ... anti-American tendencies' (Embassy Report, 12
June 1948). Students picketed outside Eisenhower's house and the Philosophy Hall
carrying placards with slogans calling for a boycott of the Department of Slavonic
Studies. Meanwhile, the Polish newspapers in America poured out stories about
'a communist cell at Columbia University, a plot aimed at discrediting Eisenhower', 'Judas dollars from Bierut's lackeys' and a 'poetic glorifier of Bierut['s]
rule—little Miłosz'. Despite all this controversy, or perhaps, paradoxically,
because of it, thirty-five students—a very high number—signed up for the initial lectures. The newly established department produced a book entitled *Adam
Mickiewicz: Poet of Poland,* which was nearly 300 pages long; it was prepared by
Manfred Kridl, Józef Wittlin, and its instigator and mastermind, Miłosz, who
was the most active and demanding editor. His contribution to the book included a historical-biographical introduction and an essay, 'Mickiewicz and
Modern Poetry'. In it he emphasised the wide diversity of genres, forms and

subject matter in Mickiewicz's work and its rootedness in Romanticism as well as eighteenth-century classicism and the European humanist tradition.

At the end of 1954 Miłosz wrote a letter from France to Manfred Kridl, which was later included in *Mój wileński opiekun*. He asked about the department's situation in view of the professor's imminent retirement, and then got straight to the point: 'Would you feel very offended if I were to offer my candidature, as it would have many advantages, because *primo,* Polish poet, *secundo,* liberal, *tertio,* that the political benefits of such an appointment would be high considering the reaction it would evoke in Warsaw?' He added that the objective of his course would be to create a

> counterbalance to the colossal historical and non-literary critical writing which is being done in Poland, which involves the incredible distortion and chipping away at truth with the intention of turning it into a lie. I believe that we agree on this assessment of the situation. Therefore I am certain that you will detect in my letter a passion for doing things that are useful'. (*Mój wileński opiekun* 61)

Kridl sent a warm response: 'It is a v. good idea and which Simmons and I had thought about'. He went on to express a doubt, however: 'Would we manage to break the university rules, all the requirements demanding a PhD, and specialist publications etc.? And would you be happy to be on a pedagogical treadmill?' (ibid., 64). The rules could be broken, and, as to the pedagogical treadmill, the poet got used to it very quickly, though this did not actually come to pass until five years later and on the other side of the American continent.

Miłosz wrote many articles and sketches for Polish readers, which were published in such periodicals as *Twórczość, Odrodzenie* and *Nowiny Literackie,* whose main editor was Iwaszkiewicz. The texts had a common theme: an introduction to the Americans. In them, he explained the importance of Auden and Eliot in European literature, and introduced the work of Robert Lowell. He wrote of his admiration for Faulkner's work, and presented articles about Ernest Hemingway, Norman Mailer and Henry Miller. He shared his impressions of the cinema, noting how the mass production of the Hollywood 'dream factory' also managed to promote the dissemination of moral messages. He translated a great deal, drawing attention to the increasing dullness of Polish poetry by contrasting it with brighter material from elsewhere. He translated Shakespeare's *Othello* and the work of Walt Whitman, Carl Sandburg and black writers. Working from English versions, he introduced Polish readers to the Ecuadorian Jorge Carrera Andrade, the Chilean Pablo Neruda, and the great Spanish poet Federico García Lorca. He had actually met Neruda, and though he did not rate his poetry highly, he thought that poetry such as *Tres cantos materiales* would provide a neat contrast to the turgid social realism which Polish readers were now expected to endure.

Miłosz regularly worked late into the night, and often finished writing around two a.m. No wonder that the next morning when he raced to work and cursed every traffic light, he habitually arrived late. Although he carried out his duties diligently, the hours spent behind his office desk were hard to bear, and he could not wait for lunch breaks—not in order to eat, but to be able to rummage through books at Whyte's Bookshop on Connecticut Avenue.

Open-Source Intelligence

Miłosz translated a vehement declaration made by a participant at the writer's conference he attended at Bread Loaf: 'We do not want tyranny . . . If industry becomes nationalised and everything is concentrated in the hands of the government, where would we find any trace of freedom? The government will be the master of the life and death of its citizens' (*Kontynenty* 143). What was very surprising was that the Polish censor allowed this fragment to be included in his report, which was sent to the Ministry of Foreign Affairs. Very often the documents Miłosz forwarded contained a great deal more than accounts of exhibitions organised by the embassy. Sometimes the poet sent analyses of the political situation in the States, or descriptions of the atmosphere in immigrant groups, with the result that his work was becoming closer to what is termed 'open-source intelligence reporting'.

In one of his first letters to Warsaw, Miłosz described the circles in which he moved, dividing them into (1) Americans he knew; (2) older Polish emigrants in America (whom he described as not very intelligent, with no prospects for political or financial enhancement); (3) a much more interesting group, the second-generation Poles living in America; and lastly, (4) the new emigrants, who 'were hostile to the Polish government', noting, however, that 'there are signs of disagreement within that camp'. In the course of private meetings with friends, he gathered their opinions on and their attitude to the 'new' Poland:

> Julian Tuwim: is enthusiastic about social changes in Poland and is returning to the country. He was a perfect host. The impression I had of him was that he suffered from a serious nervous disposition bordering on persecution mania. He has hardly any contacts with Americans, he hasn't written to American journals and is intimidated by Polish émigré groups. He lives in New York as if on a desert island, and is engrossed in Pushkin.

Józef Wittlin: like all intelligent people in emigrant circles, he is very impressed by Polish literary journals, and their high quality and is very interested in writers working in Poland. He expressed an interest in sending some of his literary work to the country. He is, however, full of doubts and inhibitions. Politically, he is undecided—on the one hand, he was connected until now with the group around Jan Lechoń, on the other, he rates highly the positive achievements at home. He is a person with truly democratic convictions.

———

Manfred Kridl: He defines his position and that of his colleagues from the émigré Polish Democratic Party as being 'wait and see', and his return will depend on the development of the political situation in Poland. He is well disposed to the idea of cultural co-operation with Poland. (Embassy Report, February–March 1946)

It is worth noting Miłosz's guarded honesty, which other embassy staff lacked, preferring instead to manufacture information the authorities wanted to hear. The poet himself admitted that his frankness earned him good standing in Warsaw, where his reliable information was well regarded. His reports written on the basis of information from the *New York Times,* the *New York Herald Tribune* and *Time,* as well as his own observations, definitely provided a more objective image than opinions sent to Europe by American Communists. The Polish attaché looked at the last group sceptically and reported: 'They do not perform any role in the United States, the majority of them are bucolic Communists, whose undefined humanistic and pro-Russian sympathies are based on ignorance about the hard living conditions in the USSR' (Report, August 1946). Using a degree of poetic licence as a shield, he inferred that interest in Poland existed, but there was also 'a certain hostility based on information provided in the press about methods employed that are regarded here as totalitarian' (Report, 1 April–15 May, 1946). Then in the autumn of 1946 he reported bluntly that 'sympathy toward Russia has diminished considerably in intellectual circles', analysing the reasons for that, and stating that 'anti-Soviet' books such as George Orwell's *Animal Farm* had become very popular (Report, 1 August–1 September, 1946).

Miłosz reported in great detail the progress of the left-oriented Cultural and Scientific Conference for World Peace that took place in New York between 25 and 27 March 1949. This was 'the result of the co-operation of Communists and liberals united in the party centred round Henry Wallace, with Einstein and Thomas Mann amongst its sympathisers, the disorganised opposition of the State Department, and protests organised both by anti-Communist factions and

"Trotskyites" disappointed in Stalinism'. He devoted particular attention to Soviet speakers, and told no-one what he really thought about Dmitri Shostakovich, who found himself released for a brief time from the Soviet Union. Miłosz reported that the speech the latter made

> was not met with the excitement with which his every appearance was greeted. His lecture . . . was dry like an essay written by a good pupil. Although he said the right things about formalism and realism (not in his own language, but the language of official Party-speak), he could have achieved more if he gave his speech a personal perspective. He resembled an automaton.

Most secret was a report about Henry Wallace, the former vice-president under Roosevelt from 1941 to 1945, and his chances of being elected president in 1948; his candidacy was supported by the Communists. The Polish Ministry of Foreign Affairs believed that there was a strong possibility of that happening, whereas Miłosz's report claimed quite the opposite. The author pointed out the low rating the Soviet Union had in the States as a result of information about 'the figures Americans received of numbers of people employed in *slave labor camps,* which was between ten and twenty million'. With regard to the gulags, Miłosz said that he believed 'that softening reports is against the objective of picturing the true mood at the present moment'. In his conclusions he added briefly, 'Wallace's chances are very small'. Indeed, he was right; Harry Truman won the election.

Miłosz's political interests and intellectual independence turned his attention away from the journal officially recommended by his superiors, *Masses & Mainstream,* towards milieux which did not meet with the approval of either the Polish or the Soviet embassy. He could not talk openly about his contacts with these unvetted individuals. The New York non-Communist and anti-totalitarian leftist group boycotted the Conference for World Peace by organising an anti-congress, the Congress for Intellectual Freedom, under the leadership of Sidney Hook, a philosopher and former Trotskyist. One of the active members in that effort was Dwight Macdonald, an editor of a niche magazine, *politics,* and previously the creator of *Partisan Review,* which until this day has played a vital role in the intellectual scene in the United States. In the late forties, *Partisan Review* had a critical view of capitalism, but no illusions with regard to criminal activities carried out by the Soviet Union. It was a platform for debates about socialism, and also, for example, the attitudes of intellectuals towards religion. Among contributors were authors such as Arthur Koestler, George Orwell, Jean-Paul Sartre, Albert Camus, Saul Bellow, Mary McCarthy and Nicola Chiaromonte. Macdonald issued his independent journal *politics* in the years 1944–1949, and so contributed to Miłosz's 'political enlightenment'. This monthly (later quarterly) published articles by, among others, Bruno Bettelheim, Max Weber, Karl Jaspers, Ignazio Silone, and Daniel Bell, making it an outstanding intellectual forum, covering a rich array of topics, ranging from the American way of life and mass culture to the predicament of the black community and of homosexuals. It examined the moral and artistic consequences of the war, the use of the atomic bomb, and the stand taken by the Soviet Union towards the Warsaw Rising and the seizure of power in Poland by the Communists. It was through his meeting with Nicola Chiaromonte that Miłosz came across the name of Simone Weil, whose essay on *The Iliad* was published in *politics* in a translation from French by Mary McCarthy. In the Cold War political arena, divided between communism and anti-communism, these small groups of intellectuals who sought a 'third option' were undoubtedly closest to Miłosz. These same intellectuals would help him survive when he found himself in France and labelled as a deserter and a traitor to 'the camp of progress'.

'We are slaves here!'

While discovering so much more about life in the United States, did Miłosz slightly lose sight of Poland, in part because he had to infer what was happening from reading between the lines of the censored press and censored letters? Did he consciously suppress certain knowledge that came to light in order not to think too much about his own situation, which decades later he would recognise as 'perilous, incredible, illogical, immoral, indescribable'? (*Rok myśliwego* 153). If so, his relative calmness was shattered within the space of just a few weeks in 1949.

In late spring that year, after a three-and-a-half-year absence, he decided to spend a holiday in Poland. He travelled on his own, because little Antoni was too small to cross the Atlantic, or perhaps Janka wanted to keep as far as possible from a politically unstable Europe. His plane landed in Paris, and soon after he reached Saint-Dominique 57, where the ambassador of the People's Republic resided amid the splendour of gilt, stucco, marble and mirrors. This enviable position belonged to Jerzy Putrament. It must have been a pleasant stay in many respects. Miłosz found time on 20 May to meet for a meal with Iwaszkiewicz, who was on a visit to France; according to Iwaszkiewicz's notes, the reunion was 'spoilt because with us was some terrible hag from the embassy' (*Dzienniki 1911–55* 293). He also spent an evening with Julia Hartwig, Aniela Micińska and Putrament in 'some existentialists' club where Juliette Greco performed'. Hartwig, who worked at the Paris embassy, mentioned that 'over dinner Putrament utterly idolised him, calling him the greatest Polish poet' (Hartwig, *Topos*). No wonder, then, that in July, when on his return journey Miłosz arrived in Paris to give a talk about Oskar Miłosz, a party was given in his honour on the grounds of the embassy. Some pictures from the event survive, showing Miłosz shining among the stars of the leftist or Communist-sympathising literary firmament—Jules Supervielle, along with Louis Aragon and his wife, Elsa Triolet. In contrast to anti-Communist America, in Paris at the time 'Red' status meant being *'très privilégié':*

> Standing with my glass of vodka at receptions at the Soviet Embassy, I watched how Leftist luminaries of French literature and art minced around [a Soviet] diplomat seizing upon his every word, nodding approval—polite little boys in front of their teacher. The magic unguent of power must have rubbed off upon me, too, a new arrival . . . with my broad non-Western face, but I was ashamed of it. (*NR* 165)

On 24 May the writer reached Warsaw. The contrast was stark. After the greenery of the Luxembourg Gardens, it was as if he were entering a prison inhabited by people steeped in hatred for those who ruled over them, people whose faces expressed fear, and who, on top of that, judged from his smart appearance and Western coat that he must be an officer in the Secret Service. To live in Washington and reflect on the diabolical essence within communism was one thing; to hear at first hand from an old friend, 'We are slaves here', another.

This came in a brief exchange with a friend from Wilno, Irena Oświecimska, whom Miłosz met in Sopot, near Gdańsk. Equally dramatic must have been the conversations with his father and brother, whom he visited. Three months before, between 20 and 23 January 1949, the famous Fourth General Congress of Polish Writers had taken place, during which socialist realism was proclaimed as the new gospel, and the theorist Adam Ważyk lauded some of Poland's older and established writers for their skill in adapting themselves to the artistic demands of the Party. Miłosz was among those whose poetry seemed not to step out of line. He could now witness for himself how Party doctrines were being implemented.

> I was present at conferences of representatives of various artistic disciplines, where for the first time the theory of socialist realism was discussed. The attitude of the audience towards the speakers' rigid, prescriptive agenda was decidedly hostile. Everyone considered socialist realism as a theory enforced from above, leading to lamentable results, as was demonstrated in Russian art . . . Usually, there would be one brave soul, who would lunge

onto the offensive with suppressed sarcasm, which met with silent, but very clear support from the auditorium. The response of the key speakers included direct threats to career paths and future problems for any insubordinate individuals. (*Zniewolony umysł* 33)

In Szczecin, the poet gave a reading at Klub 13 Muz (Club of the Thirteen Muses), and also met Andrzejewski, who had moved there a year earlier, having been allocated accommodation, an eight-room villa 'excellently designed, quite well renovated with a big garden' (*Zaraz po wojnie* 75). The state looked after authors of the 'right' kind of books, and regarded *Ashes and Diamonds* as a perfect example of that. Konstanty Gałczyński and Wiktor Woroszylski lived in the same Szczecin suburbs, completely detached from the socialist reality imposed on the rest of the population. That is how Miłosz reacted to Andrzejewski's novel, commenting on it in his letter: 'It is curious that one is under the spell of the book, conscious as one is at the same time that it has nothing in common with the reality of 1945 ... it is a denial of reality, but whoever wants to write in a Marxist style about the actual present must be prepared for that' (*Zaraz po wojnie* 66). Perhaps good manners made him withhold his open criticism, because he regarded *Ashes and Diamonds* as false from the start, due to Andrzejwski's indifference towards his protagonists, who existed simply as counters within a construct.

The next stage of the trip was Wrocław (formerly the German city known as Breslau), where Miłosz visited Anna Kowalska, who recorded in her diary how he commented a great deal 'about the lack of intelligence in Americans' and how 'he lives in isolation' (*Dzienniki* 127). In Katowice, he was present at a congress of the Union of Polish Fine Art Workers, from which he remembered a deeply symbolic scene in a restaurant, where a drunken Secret Service agent was forcing guests to drink with him, and nobody had the courage to refuse.

Having completed a tour of the country, he returned to the capital. In Stawisko, during a short Sunday visit, he was enchanted by his hosts' two blossoming daughters. Zofia Nałkowska in her diary entry for 1 July writes of an official dinner arranged to honour Martin Andersen Nexø, a Danish Communist writer, and how Iwaszkiewicz, Miłosz and Neruda were in attendance. The upper echelons of power liked mixing with high-ranking artists, and Miłosz could satisfy his ego, conversing with Neruda with the eyes of other guests upon him. It is likely that he was referring to such evenings years later in *Podróżny świata:*

I belonged to high society, among well-dressed people, living in comfortable homes, the elite who ruled Poland. And I participated in a party where there was plenty to drink, and people danced happily in that snug, privileged sphere. We were coming back in the early hours of the morning, it was four o'clock—summer, but the night was cold. And I saw Jeep cars carrying arrested people. The soldiers, the guards[,] were wearing sheepskin coats and the prisoners in jackets with turned-up collars shivered in the cold. (309)

Why did that scene make such a big impression on him, since he had witnessed arrests of Home Army soldiers before? Was it one of those moments relating to the proverbial camel and straw, leaving a grand ball and entering the cold of the 'real world', which was like a slap in the face and which could not be erased from memory? The memory of that false dawn from 1949 may have inspired him to work on a poem which alludes to the opening exchanges of Sophocles's *Antigone*:

> Creon will not build his state
> On our graves. Will not establish
> His rule by the sword.
> Strong is the power of the dead. No-one
> Is safe from it. Even if he surrounded himself
> With an army of spies and a million guards,
> They will reach him.

('Antygona', *Wiersze* II, 153)

If Miłosz had stayed in Poland a few days longer, he would have been able to read an extraordinary article in an issue of *Kuźnica* dated 10 July; it was written by Zbigniew Mitzner, his onetime colleague at *Wolność*, and was very much a sign of the times. In a way, it too was dedicated to the dead, whom Antigone refused to forget. Mitzner made the claim that the Warsaw Rising was started by the leaders of the Home Army *in collaboration with the Germans*, who planned later to join forces against the Soviet Union.

The poet left Warsaw on 4 July and headed for France before flying back to the States. In Paris he had several sessions with Tadeusz 'Tiger' Kroński. The two friends had heated discussions, in which invariably voices were raised. The Miłoszes had renewed their relationship with Kroński and his wife in 1946 on learning that their friends had survived the Warsaw Rising and a German camp before settling after the war in Paris. Kroński and Miłosz exchanged many letters, and could afford to be very open in expressing their political views and convictions, because they were not within the reach of the censors. They found common ground, at least at first, since they shared a mutual distaste at the notion of living an 'unreflective' life, a condition Miłosz assumed was so rife in America. In Tiger's view, *l'homme moyen sensuel*—every non-intellectual human being—had to become a philosophical being, even 'terrorized into it' (*NR* 273) if necessary.

Kroński was a severe critic of Miłosz's work, but always acknowledged his genius. In the poet's eyes his friend radiated great authority, and he was content for a good while to have Tiger as an intellectual patron and father-figure, as Oskar Miłosz had been earlier. At the same time, Miłosz was aware that 'he wanted to have total power over my soul, which he failed to do' (*Zaraz po wojnie* 366). Kroński had no interest in critiquing the present situation, only the reactionary ideology of the pre-war past, which had to be destroyed at all cost so that a utopian vision of the future could be realised; after the interim period of 'compromises' passed, the true 'revolution of humanism' would follow:

> We are not at all interested in politicising the masses, but in forcing everyone, without exception, to participate in cultural life ... we will use Soviet rifle butts to teach people in this country how to think rationally and without alienation ... Polish anti-intellectualism, Romanticism, sentimentalism, xenophobia and Catholicism need to be strangled. (*Zaraz po wojnie* 319)

A rejection of absolute values might also bring about very practical outcomes: 'a poet cannot think in categories of "thou shall not steal", "thou shall not kill"' (ibid., 318).

Miłosz remained under Kroński's influence for almost a decade. In his study of the radical thinker, Aleksander Fiut speculated whether in Kroński's fixed stances Miłosz might have recognised his own

> strongest temptations. The temptation of looking down with contempt at simple bread eaters, who would not exercise their brains. The temptation to consider himself superior by belonging to a privileged group, and having fathomed the secrets of history accessible to only the very few. The temptation to provide an answer to the final aim of human history by unveiling the future utopia. ('W objęciach Tygrysa')

Fiut concluded, however, that what enabled Miłosz to reject these dogmatic pronouncements was 'his compassion for hurt and degraded people' (ibid.). And it appeared that the key moment in which he parted decisively from Kroński's perspectives and ideology was this visit to Poland in 1949, during which he saw with his own eyes 'unspeakable horror'. Significantly, the phrase Miłosz cites in English comes from a speech by Cassandra, from an English translation of Aeschylus's *Oresteia*: 'I see before me unspeakable horror, and yet, it fits true nature, I can do nothing, but speak'. Miłosz found himself in the same situation. This prompted him to write the most sarcastic of all his poems, full of self-loathing: 'For Myself in a Diary for the New Year 1950'.

> If I could help in any way. I have nothing but this pen.
> How treacherous this weapon, even for a skilled hand.

No man will listen to me, Nature will destroy me.
I can hear a voice, though no way of knowing from where and to
    where it calls me.

                                                              (*Wiersze* II, 156)

Having descended into hell, he returned traumatised, physically exhausted, with singed skin. He expressed the state in which he found himself in a poem that was understandably never published, as it could only serve a therapeutic purpose to the author himself. 'Song in Praise of My Epoch' resembled a sinister mantra or litany:

Those who chase
are filled with fear
Those whom they chase
are filled with greater fear
Those who write
are full of fear
Those who are written about
are full of fear
Those who make plans
are full of fear
and those for whom things are planned
are full of fear ...
Big black birds
are full of fear
white lambs
are full of fear

(Beinecke Library)

Among his American friends and acquaintances, Miłosz could not find anyone who could understand his predicament or offer an opinion or helpful advice. The person he did approach was Albert Einstein, probably in the summer of 1950, when, during one of his visits to see the physicist, he felt ready to admit to his dilemma. In Einstein he saw not only a genius and a creator of concepts which confirmed the cosmologic intuitions of Oskar Miłosz, but also a man who might fulfil the role of a good father. Tellingly, Miłosz subsequently signed a letter to him 'very respectfully and with a son's love' (CM to Einstein, 2 February 1951). He wrote affectionately of 'Einstein's white mane ... his soft voice, the serene gestures of his hands in front of an old wooden statuette of the Madonna, everything about him appealed to my father complex, my yearning for a protector and leader' (*NR* 282). The conversation, however, left him unconsoled. The young

Polish writer felt that Einstein was not able to comprehend the scale of the physical and, in particular, the existential crisis he was going through. Einstein tried to tell Miłosz that the torment he was experiencing would not last long and that it would be better for him not to sever links with his homeland. The future author of *The Captive Mind*, who grew to be so acutely aware of the demonic presence in history and the powers that acted against the will of individuals, left the Princeton campus realising that he had to address his crisis alone.

When Miłosz first contacted Einstein back in 1948, he invited the physicist through strictly official channels to take part in the World Congress of Intellectuals in Poland. Einstein refused to travel, but agreed to write an address. The Congress, which was attended by several hundred artists and scientists from forty-six countries, took place between 25 and 28 August 1948 at the University of Wrocław. It was meant to be a masterstroke of propaganda, showcasing how progressive intellectuals were willing to gather under the umbrella of the Soviet Union to demonstrate that Poland was independent in its international policy and the legitimacy of Poland's rights to lands 'regained' in the west. Instead of being a success confirming the amity of Eastern and Western 'comrades', it was a spectacular fiasco, in which all attempts to reach a compromise were torpedoed by the Russians, with Alexander Fadeyev—a man capable of describing Stalin as 'the greatest humanist the world has ever known'—insulting Western culture. Dominique Desanti, a participant at the Congress, recalled how a number of western intellectuals reacted on hearing Fadeyev describe Sartre's resemblance to a hyena writing on a typewriter: 'Picasso pulls off his earphones. Eluard takes them off slowly and begins to scribble something. Vercos and Léger are stunned. At the podium Irena Joliot-Curie and Julian Huxley exchange notes. Borejsza looks like an acrobat stabbed with a stiletto during his show-stopping piece' (qtd. in Bikont 216). The Russians did not allow the delegates to hear Einstein's address, in which he appealed for international control of access to nuclear energy. As the Soviet Union was close to possessing its own nuclear weapons, it was totally unwilling to countenance any constraints. In a secret memo to the authorities, Miłosz reported that his efforts to mediate and prevent the scandal reaching the public domain proved unsuccessful. It became patently obvious from Einstein's response to a letter from the Polish Embassy requesting a favourable comment on the Congress that that was not going to happen. Miłosz found it very hard when later he came face to face with the scientist: 'Utterly embarrassed, I explained that I was not responsible for what had happened in Wrocław and had acted in good faith. Einstein replied: "Of course, I hold no grudge against you"' (Fiut 111).

On his return from Poland, the depth of Miłosz's estrangement from the new Polish status quo left him perplexed as to how he might extricate himself from what he increasingly saw as a distasteful situation. What made matters worse was that Janka, the person closest to him, did not seem to share his anxieties and sensitivities. Whereas he regarded America as a 'de-humanised' world, she, although critical, enjoyed the normality of living every day in security. Especially after the birth of their son, she wanted to keep as far away as possible from Poland and even Europe, which many believed would eventually be overrun by Stalin and the Red Army: 'America almost destroyed the warmth and closeness there was between us, which had survived the long war years. After the birth of Antoni she changed, or I became jealous and we kept arguing, mainly about America' (*Rok myśliwego* 159). Conflicts between them recurred at crucial political moments. In November 1949, Janka tried unsuccessfully to persuade her husband to leave the embassy and not represent Poland after Konstanty Rokossowski, a Soviet officer of Polish origin, became Marshal of the Soviet Union, then Marshal of Poland, and then was appointed as Poland's Defence Minister. She wanted to bring up her child and was hoping for a lifestyle where there would be time to read books, go to the cinema, go on holiday and write letters to friends. For him, life away from multiple complicated stimulants—praise, intrigue, the social and intellectual codes of the literary community—was unimaginable: 'The need to believe in one's own worth . . . was a decisive factor in my serving the Warsaw government after the war at the time of my first stay in America'. It was in Warsaw 'that I existed, especially after the publication of *Rescue* and where I planned my strategy in the continuing battle. This is what it boiled down to: the fact that I was totally unknown in America, a minor clerk in a satellite embassy, who scribbled . . . and translated other poets' works [into Polish]'. In the summer of 1949 he declared:

> I chose to live in the service of Polish poetry
> Even if I were to remain meaningless dust.
>
> ('Traktat Moralny', *Wiersze* II, 115)

—————————

From 1950 onwards, when in Poland demands for compliance with socialist realism grew more and more insistent, Miłosz published three poems in *Nowa Kultura*. They gave the impression that he was prepared to fulfil the directives of the propaganda machine. The truth was that, like any other artist worth their salt, he was unable to write poems to order, on subjects dictated to him, in the service of lies. In effect, he 'became an inner émigré . . . restricted so much that on the chessboard there was no room for manoeuvre' (CM to Melchior Wańkowicz, n.d).

Different solutions other than defection to the United States or a return to Poland occurred to him. He rejected a suggestion by Thornton Wilder that he settle down on a farm, yet the ideas he came up with were not much better, and potentially more perilous. When leafing through *politics,* Miłosz noticed an advertisement for the Hutterite Communities in Paraguay, a religious sect formed in Wrocław in the 1920s, but whose roots went back to the sixteenth century. The group fled the city because they were persecuted by the Nazis and settled down in South America. They were inspired by a vision of early Christianity, and they formed settlements, cleared the jungle, cultivated the soil, bred cattle and built brick houses. There were about five hundred members, and they came from over a dozen countries. Miłosz noted down details of groups that had settled in the States: 'that I almost reconciled myself to the thought that I would work with an axe and a shovel in the Paraguayan forests gives some idea of my despair' (*ABC* 225). He warns of 'the horror' of such a complete absence of hope in 'A Treatise on Morality':

> I cannot offer you any hope for the present,
> Don't wait in vain for a *treuga Dei,*[5]
> Because there's no magic escape route
> From the life that you've been given.
> Let us go in peace, we the simple people,
> For before us lies . . .
> > the 'Heart of Darkness'
> > > > (*Wiersze* II, 100, trans. R. E. Pypłacz)

Dry Flame

> A poet from these times does not show his face
> Because were he to do so people would see it contorted in horror
> > > Czesław Miłosz, 'Two Men in Rome'

The fundamental question posed in 'A Treatise on Morality' was how the soul might be saved from exposure to cynicism, lies which seemed 'natural', like communism, which, like an elemental force, was threatening to overwhelm Europe. The avalanche carries within itself moral catastrophe, the destruction of individual responsibility, the acceptance that evil committed is independent from us and that one ought not to oppose it. War, political changes, weapons of mass destruction, are, in fact, visible manifestations, while longer-term and more dangerous are deeper, darker undercurrent processes at work. Human nature alters. Conscience disappears.

Miłosz's persistent fear after the Second World War and the Holocaust
was that another apocalyptic epoch was at hand. Violence and destruction emanating from its 'heart of darkness', he believed, loomed over the entire human
race. A characteristic of Kroński's thinking and perhaps also of Miłosz's was that
this new nightmare scenario did not wholly exclude the possibility of some ultimately positive outcome. Bewildered, perhaps deluded, the poet wrote:

> Our epoch, one of death,
> Mass annihilation,
> How long it will last, I cannot say,
> Nor can I name the rogues responsible.
> Treasure this time, because, thanks to it,
> The world will be transformed,
> Triggering some slight reservations.

('Traktat moralny', *Wiersze* II, 87)

It was a necessity for humanity's survival that independence of opinion and
moral decency be preserved, and that ideologies, myths, and artificially manufactured beliefs be rejected in order to halt the momentum of the avalanche. The
poet pointed out that for masses of people there might be no choice other than
to collaborate, yet the price paid for collusion would be appalling.

Amongst the more positive features of this blackly ironic poem is its concern to speak out on behalf of ordinary people, its attempt to defend fellow human
beings from the nihilism and cynicism of those asserting power over them. Indeed, 'Traktat moralny' was an act of courage, not only in an artistic sense, but also
in the directness of its commentary on Poland's current political situation. Miłosz
submitted the lengthy poem to the monthly literary magazine, *Twórczość*, in December 1947. Kazimierz Wyka, the editor, read it with considerable apprehension,
because he was certain that it would be savaged by the censors and then used as
a pretext to attack the author as well as the magazine that had published it. Curiously, the copies of *Twórczość*'s fourth issue sent to the censorship office containing Miłosz's poem were returned without any objections. This was astonishing given the politically risqué elements within it, of which the lines below are
an example:

> A gravedigger's life is jolly.
> He buries systems, faiths, schools,
> Smoothing the soil over snugly
> With a pen, a *nagan* or a spade.

('Traktat moralny', *Wiersze* II, 87)

To everyone in Poland in those years, 'nagan', a brand of revolver, was specifically associated with the NKVD. It immediately invoked mental images of the 21,000 Polish officers executed in Katyń, shot in the back of the head with this very weapon. It is hard to fathom how 'A Treatise on Morality' was allowed to be published. One plausible explanation was that the images were breaking acceptable norms, but that their sheer audacity left the small group of decision-makers speechless. It is also possible that the decision to allow its publication was a result of internal tensions within the structures of power, but there is no proof to support this surmise. The poem—or at least the extracts from it that appeared in the Polish press—received hardly any attention. A contributor to the Paris-based émigré publishing house Kultura, Jerzy Stempowski, did not hold back when it came to his assessment of the poem:

> I have in front of me the most outstanding Polish poem written since 1939 ... If anyone wants to find out how Polish writers, during years when they were weighed down by the burden of oppression from one side of the world and the indifference of the other, defied the gloom and isolation, and discovered within themselves powers of resistance—they will find a key to it in 'A Treatise on Morality.' (*Listy 1946–69* 179)

'A Treatise on Morality' came about as a result of the direct influence of Kroński, and some passages were changed according to the latter's instructions, which were more important and inspiring to him than Auden's *New Year Letter* or Karl Shapiro's *Essay on Rime*. The poems which made up Miłosz's collection *Daylight* (1953) reflected Heraclitus's declaration that 'a dry flame is the best and wisest soul' (*NR* 267).

A lyric published in 1945, 'Mid-Twentieth Century Portrait', depicts the ambivalent personality of a supporter of the new power, in which it is possible to recognise the figures of Putrament and Miłosz himself:

> Hidden behind his smile of brotherly regard,
> He despises the newspaper reader, the victim of the dialectic power.
> Says: 'Democracy,' with a wink.
> . . .
> Keeping one hand on Marx's writings, he reads the Bible in private.
> His mocking eye on processions leaving burned-out churches.
> His backdrop: a horseflesh-colored city in ruins.
> In his hand: a memento of a boy 'fascist' killed in the Uprising.
> (*NCP* 88)

A splendid concentration of hints at things, portrayed with Orwellian irony, it juxtaposes the newspeak ('brotherly', 'dialectic', 'fascist') and new cynicism of the

present with painful mementoes from the past. Five years later Miłosz wrote
'You Who Wronged', a poem that would one day grace the Three Crosses monument in Gdańsk:

> You who wronged a simple man
> Bursting into laughter at the crime . . .
>
> Do not feel safe. The poet remembers.
> You can kill one, but another is born.
> The words are written down, the deed, the date.

(NCP 103)

A dialogue between a contemporary artist and the great satirist responsible for
Gulliver's Travels, 'Do Jonathana Swifta', issues a reminder that in today's world it is
not so difficult to encounter debased Yahoos or territories like Laputa ruled over
by theoreticians blind to human suffering. These poems are a reminder and self-
reminder about the artist's ethical duty to uncover lies, to defend the lives and
dignity of human beings, and to expose the guilty.

Finally, 'Child of Europe' captures the cynical self-centredness which is a
product of war and its legacy. The speaker in the poem is not a guilty survivor, but
rather a callous alter ego, who

> Having the choice of our own death and that of a friend,
> We chose his, coldly thinking: let it be done quickly.[6]

(NCP 83)

The poem points out other, more politically conditioned features of the period:
how violence takes on the guise of the good and necessary, and language is merely
another weapon to deploy. Thanks to its irony and persuasive form, the poem
achieves a distinctive power. It is, in fact, startling in uncovering the prophecy
which Miłosz saw many years before in an Orvieto fresco, in which the Antichrist
arrives dressed in the robes of the Saviour. The poem was written in 1946, but it was
not published until seven years later, in *Kultura.* And it is not surprising that in
the end

> The laughter born of the love of truth
> Is now the laughter of the enemies of the people.

(NCP 87)

Slaughterhouse

I have a dream that I found myself in Warsaw in disguise, because I had to say something to someone, which I forgot to do earlier, but I was recognised and now will have to stay forever in this Orwellian city, the one I found in 1950: with bugging devices in the walls, with wild fear in everyone's eyes.

Czesław Miłosz, *Wymarsz z czarnej groty 1956–1957*

Freedom. Why should we value it so highly? Why should it be the greatest happiness for people? I think that freedom is a contradiction of humanity— it is an attribute of the animal state.

Jerzy Putrament to Czesław Miłosz, 15 May 1946

By the late 1940s, Miłosz was finding it difficult to conceal his feelings much longer. Poison-pen letters at the embassy were addressed to his superiors, and at the beginning of February 1950 the ministerial committee decided that 'Miłosz is an individual who ideologically is totally alien. After his last visit to the country he expressed a clearly hostile and slanderous attitude to all aspects of life in Poland. His wife—a fierce enemy of the Soviet Union. To be recalled via Paris' (Pasierski 209). Although the poet did not know it yet, the time for withdrawing from the satanic pact was fast approaching.

In June 1950, the Korean War broke out, resulting in a further deterioration in the international situation. It was a time of returning to bases, and even Putrament was called back and given a different task when the Polish Writers Union elected him as their General Secretary. In the course of his brief time back in Paris, he sent Miłosz a letter on 1 July in which he wrote: 'I heard that you are to be moved to Paris . . . I am happy that you will be coming here, because I have been worried about you a little: whether the splendour of material goods in America has overshadowed poverty in other aspects of life' (*Zaraz po wojnie* 362). The poet was not certain whether Paris was to be merely a short stop on the way to Warsaw, but he read the message very clearly: 'Your loyalty is being questioned. It's time to shorten your lead and give you a close look'. The moment for travelling to Europe could not have been more inopportune: many suspected that the world was on the brink of war, and Janka had just become pregnant. They knew full well that the birth was going to be very complicated, if not dangerous. On 7 July the Polish Ambassador, Winiewicz, sent a note to Warsaw providing information about the contents of Putrament's letter, and in order to prevent Miłosz from defecting in

Paris suggested that he should be transported directly to Warsaw. Miłosz, in response to the message from his friend about a possible recall, sent a note to Kroński, reiterating how dangerous travelling would be to Janka's health; he expressed a wish to work and live in Paris, but only after the baby's delivery. He pleaded for help and advice, but neither came.

On 13 July the Ministry of Foreign Affairs received a letter from the Polish Ambassador in Paris outlining a recommended course of action; it proposed that in order to stop Miłosz from seeking asylum in the United States, they ought to send him to Paris and appoint him cultural attaché there. Should any act of insubordination occur, he could be put on a plane to Warsaw. The date of departure was delayed two weeks at Miłosz's request, which caused the ambassador to become increasingly concerned about the poet's transfer and the feasibility of the operation. The authorities in Poland in the meantime could not make a final decision, and so the head of the ministry, Stefan Wierbłowski, decided to travel himself to America to interview Miłosz. During their talks, Miłosz managed to persuade the minister that he had no intention of defecting, and because of his wife's complicated pregnancy he requested that she be allowed to stay for another four weeks. He, in the meantime, agreed to travel on 28 September to Paris and from there on to Warsaw to be interviewed at the Ministry of Foreign Affairs.

Miłosz arrived in Paris to take up a post at the embassy and was nominated First Secretary for Culture. Political relations with France were very tense. There were frequent extraditions, and the embassy was almost barricaded behind walls and a gate, against which concrete slabs were propped. Some employees never left the building for fear of being dismissed. As for insubordinate employees, they were drugged and then delivered to the airport. The ambassador kept the rest in isolation and for Christmas organised a trip to the mountains, so that nobody was able to visit friends or relations.

The poet had the distinct impression that the post in Paris was a fabrication, but nevertheless he tried to keep occupied. At the end of November, he organised a breakfast for Polish artists and scientists living in Paris who did not want to return to the People's Republic. Their economic situation forced them to accept the invitation despite their hatred for the new regime. The consciousness that he was being watched never left Miłosz for a second. He could only speak openly with Aniela Micińska, who was now living on her own in poverty, but anticipated that she would shortly be given a post as a Polish lecturer in Lyon. They met in cafés, and each time he asked her whether he ought to return to Poland. Aniela, who had learnt much about post-war Poland while working as an interpreter during the Peace Congress in Wrocław, was vehement that it would be folly to go back, but he decided otherwise. According to his version of events, he wanted to take the initiative and demonstrate his loyalty, imagining that it would be

highly unlikely for them to recall a freshly accredited diplomat. He did not realise that his fate had already been decided, and so played *va banque* and nearly
lost his entire stake.

In December Miłosz travelled to London, where he was met by Antoni
Słonimski, who offered him a position starting in April as Director of the Institute of Polish Culture, which was affiliated to the embassy. In order to avoid
Allied-occupied sectors in Germany, Polish diplomats were required to travel
home via Prague, which is what Miłosz did.

> A huge fellow with the face of a hoodlum, wearing the uniform of the
> Czech Security Police, opened the door to the cabin and asked for pass-
> ports. The waiting room was empty. My footsteps echoed back at me . . .
> I took a taxi. The tribe of taxi drivers has a gift for discerning whom one
> can or cannot speak freely to; for half an hour my driver spilled out his
> laments and reproaches against 'them'. I did not answer . . . Colorless
> streets in the twilight. From some building high over the city shone a
> huge red star. (*NR* 150–151)

He arrived in Warsaw on 20 December and a day later reported to the
Ministry, where he was told to surrender his passport. The initial talks did not
indicate that anything was wrong; when he was asked to sign his new Ministry
pass he noticed that in the box for position, it said 'First Secretary of the Embassy of the People's Republic in Paris'. Did he go the same evening to see Jerzy
Zarzycki's *Unvanquished City,* and was he pleased while watching it that he had
refused to promote the film? He may well have gone to see Putrament, who
would later give his account of how he read Miłosz at the time:

> I got the impression that everything in the country is strange to him, if
> not also hostile. That he is deeply detached from us. I did not see any-
> thing alarming in that, but when a few days later Jakub Berman called me,
> he told me that after receiving confidential information they feared that
> Miłosz was planning to defect, and so decided to detain him in the
> country. He asked my opinion on the matter and I replied that there was
> no other option. 'My sentiment precisely', said Berman and rang off.
> (Putrament, *Pół Wieku* 60)

It was Christmastime, and Miłosz spent Boxing Day at Stawisko. The
guests remembered the tense atmosphere, and Iwaszkiewicz making snide and
ironic remarks directed at Miłosz, about him having returned from the big world.
Iwaszkiewicz may well have been half-worried that his protégé was thinking
about an escape and tried to test him. He also drew attention to Miłosz's flirting
with Natalia Modzelewska, the wife of the Minister of Foreign Affairs, who was

rather taken with him. They had met in America when she accompanied her husband to a NATO conference in the autumn of 1947. Miłosz as an embassy employee assisted her during the stay and entertained her. Years later in Kraków, he confessed to his friend and publisher, Jerzy Illg, 'This was the rock bottom of my fall'.

But now in 1950, back at Stawisko, departing guests thanked their hosts and returned to Warsaw, while Miłosz and Natalia visited a small café. There they were spotted by two of the Iwaszkiewiczs' other guests who happened to drop in there. Very quickly Miłosz learned that he would not be allowed to leave Poland. As Zygmunt Modzelewski was not available, because he was recovering after a heart attack, his deputy acted on his behalf. It was he who called in Miłosz to inform him about the decision, which, despite his earlier suspicions, came as a huge shock to the writer. Modzelewska recalled the events years later in her article 'Miłosz in Poland in Winter 1950', which was published in the Polish journal *Kultura*:

> He became mentally unstable, and suffered from bouts of depression, which gradually got worse. I met him every day, because he telephoned me every day and from his voice it was easy to discern that he was close to a nervous breakdown. He needed me, because somehow I managed to turn the conversation to different subjects. After having reported about his latest failures from the previous day, his attention moved on to other things. I was saying goodbye not to a sick man, but to someone who was recovering. Unfortunately that recovery period did not last long and relapses recurred after shorter and shorter periods of time. One day he ended up calling me again after a few hours. I found him in such a state that I had no doubt that his immunity was getting weaker and the moment of his final collapse was imminent. (Modzelewska, *Kultura:* 3, 1981)

The failures the minister's wife alluded to were Miłosz's attempts to retrieve his passport and to leave. He turned for help next to Nina Andrycz, who was related to Micińska and married to the then Polish Premier, Józef Cyrankiewicz. Next, at the suggestion of Kroński, he tried to persuade a woman lauded by the regime as an 'aunt of the revolution' to intercede on his behalf; she was a former friend of Feliks Dzierżyński (1877–1926), the ruthless director of the Soviet Secret Police. After her, he approached the Head of the Cultural Department at the Central Committee of the Polish Workers' Party; and probably many others. All attempts to get his passport retuned came to nothing. The most obvious route to the Minister of Foreign Affairs was blocked, because Modzelewski was not available, and his wife was reluctant to ask him to speak up on Miłosz's behalf.

For the New Year celebrations he refused to go to the Writers' Union ball and chose to spend the evening with Aleksander Wat and Jan Parandowski and his wife. Finally, whether it was fate or providence which intervened, fearing for the poet's sanity and that suicide might cross his mind, Natalia Modzelewska decided to speak to her husband.

—Invite him, said my husband.

Czesław came in the afternoon ... explained his situation, not hiding any of the details known to me, [and] gave honest explanations to Modzelewski's questions. After his departure my husband said:

—Perhaps I will be able to help him.

By a lucky coincidence, he went to see the President, Bolesław Bierut, on other matters, and touched on Miłosz's case and put forward his opinion, which was, in a nutshell, that Miłosz was not a diplomat, but a writer and if he chose to work with the government it would bring benefits, but if he really wanted to stay abroad, there was no point in keeping him by force ...

—Can you vouch that he will return?

Modzelewski replied:

—I think he will. But if he were not to return, I am deeply convinced that he ought to be allowed to go. (Ibid.)

Zygmunt Modzelewski belonged to the so-called ideological Communists. A well-informed anonymous outsider who wrote a piece for *Kultura* in Paris in 1949 or 1950 about the Sovietisation of Poland and the members of the government in 1949–1950 characterised Modzelewski as an orthodox activist who was well respected in Moscow. Modzelewski was of the opinion that during the new state's early years, people in the diplomatic service ought to have 'pre-war' qualities. They also needed to be familiar with Western lifestyle and culture, well-mannered, very intelligent, able to appreciate culture, and well-disposed to people. In Miłosz's opinion Modzelewski was a converted Stalinist, but in a certain way pure, because he did not speak to Bierut about helping him escape, but acted according to genuine convictions.

Natalia Modzelewska recalled her final meeting with Miłosz when she told him that he ought to feel free to act according to his conscience in deciding whether to return to Poland or not. Miłosz modified her account of this encounter by adding how, in a low voice, Modzelewska said to him:

'But please remember that when you decide not to, there is an obligation you have to fulfil.'

'What obligation?', I asked.
'To fight against the executioner of Russia'.

(Podróżny świata 84)

On 11 January Miłosz visited Maria Dąbrowska and was particularly tense that evening, not knowing what to do: of course he wanted to leave, but was not totally convinced about the wisdom of defecting. Two days before, he had signed a contract to do a translation of *Othello;* he even took an advance and discussed getting a flat in Warsaw. The decisive moment for him, really, was a plenary assembly of the Polish Writers' Union in January 1951, specifically, Putrament's speech. It would be better, he thought, to run and cut his ties rather than to become a well-paid author with whom a Party member could play a game of cat and mouse, and, to cap it all, could insist on the mouse writing masterpieces. During the assembly Miłosz listened with a stony face as Putrament appealed for the writers' support of the working masses in fulfilling the six-year plan, and then called on each writer by name and invited them to evaluate their work and the contribution it made. Miłosz spoke, and from the archive notes it emerges that he delivered a knowledgeable address about realism, or rather the lack of it, in contemporary poetry. One participant present at his address said that there was a tragic note and that his was the only 'human voice' that was heard.

As part of the event, there was a literary morning celebration, which took place at the National Theatre, where an anti-American poem by Adam Ważyk, 'The Song about Coca-Cola' was recited and reverberated around the auditorium:

> You enjoyed drinking Coca-Cola.
> You sucked our sugar cane,
> ate our rice fields,
> chewed rubber, gold and platinum,
> you enjoyed drinking your Coca-Cola . . .
>
> We who drink the water of hope
> know where your next wishes lie:
> you marched out of China, you will leave Korea,
> we will curtail your Coca-Cola dream
> we who drink the water of hope.

Miłosz observed how those listening to the readings concentrated hard on identifying the appropriate moment to break into applause, the prompt always a banal political slogan. His own contribution to the proceedings was made with great forethought. He opted for Vachel Lindsay's poem 'Simon Legree', which he had translated himself. It depicts the fate of the villainous slave-owner of *Uncle Tom's Cabin*, the man responsible for the kindly, pious hero's death. It was ideal for a number of reasons, as he wryly notes in *Kontynenty*: 'Legree is an American, and Americans torment black people . . . He ends up in hell, which leads to the conclusion that all capitalists will go to hell' (430). The poem concludes with a folksy, humorous depiction of Legree, sitting alongside Satan, playing poker, throwing dice, supping wine brewed from 'Blood and turpentine'. When Miłosz reached the end, the audience responded with prolonged applause. Putrament remembered it as the best performance of the morning, but for the poet, it was largely a humiliation.

Miłosz headed back to Paris from Warsaw on 15 January 1951, again travelling via Prague. There he stopped over with a friend who saw how agitated he was, pacing the room, appearing as if he wanted to open up, but each time holding back. When he arrived in Paris he immediately fell ill, either as a result of the overwhelming tension or because he was too afraid to go to the Polish Embassy. On 22 January he received a telegram from the United States to inform him of the birth of his second son, Piotr, and saying that if he wanted to see his wife alive, he ought to come instantly. Although he had been assured by someone at the ministry that he would be able to travel to America to see his wife if anything went wrong, that person had no intention of keeping the promise and probably chuckled to himself at the naivete of the poet. It must have been yet another one of those demons Miłosz saw in Poland, 'men corrupted absolutely by absolute power. They turned my loyalty into a subject of mirth, and in Warsaw I felt like a fool who, of his own free will, had walked into a den of bandits armed to the teeth' (*NR* 285). After his defection, in a letter written to someone who considered returning to Poland but could not make a decision, Miłosz wrote:

> I came across astronomical changes since 1949. The atmosphere was very close. The atmosphere resembled that of the war years. Peasants go mad with despair, and in the intellectual world state control is deeply entrenched and it is necessary to be a 100% Stalinist, or not at all. The so-called Marxists are highly depressed. The 'higher circles' are afraid of two things: 1) that in the case of a war, eminent people and intellectuals will be taken away to the Soviet Union, 2) that invasion by an occupying army will cause incredible tensions. Living conditions now are much harder than in 1949.

———

As far as I am concerned, I decided that I am not going back there, despite the fact that I have a lot of money there from royalties, and can be sure of good financial support, and despite the fact that my decision marks the end of my literary career. I simply could not stand that ever-growing totalitarian atmosphere there, and that fear of everyone by everyone. If in order to make the ideal complete, every minute detail dictated by our eastern neighbour has to be implemented here, and if the faint hopes of the Polish Marxists about something better emerging are only an illusion—then one has to take into account the reality of the situation. I spoke to people there, and their hatred is strong. If they think that the suffering of millions of innocent people is a fitting sacrifice in the name of the future, then I do not share that sentiment . . . This monstrous larva will never turn into a butterfly. Polish people in comparison to people in France are deeply unhappy. Whatever may be said about the capitalist world, there are possible changes and new forms and the masses are not as helpless as in the east. Of course, Marxist dialectics is the creation of a genius, but it is evil and turning people into demons. During my recent stay, I came to the conclusion that the most a human can achieve is not to become a demon . . . The Marxist sky, the sky of the future is to me an illusion and for the sake of that fictitious sky, I would not kill anyone. And it is, I believe, a fundamental criterion. Because whether you kill with a word, or by other means, it is all the same. (CM to unknown recipient, n.d.)

In Paris, Miłosz met with Aniela again. They chose a different café, because the poet suspected that they were being watched. They went to a post office, from where he rang the only man who could help him. It was Jerzy Giedroyc, the Editor-in-Chief of *Kultura,* whose offices were located in Maisons-Laffitte, in a suburb of Paris, and who assured him that he would find a refuge and a warm reception there.

On 1 February 1951, Miłosz stepped outside into the rue Dumont d'Urville. Aniela was already waiting in a taxi, which took them straight to Maisons-Laffitte. The same day on Wierbłowski's desk a telegram appeared: 'On 01.02.1951, Miłosz left his apartment with all the belongings he could possibly take and got into a taxi. It seems certain that he has defected' (Archives of the Ministry of Foreign Affairs/Miłosz's Archive).

A Story of One Particular
Suicide Case
1951–1960

'And you are a deserter'

I was convinced that anyone who stood up against the 'laws of History' was doomed to fail, or to put it in other words, the one who broke the pact with Evil, working the other way round, to the advantage of Good . . . Later I discovered that an individual can attain freedom only by acknowledging responsibility for their own past failures.

Czesław Miłosz, *Kontynenty*

'The story I am going to tell can be called a story of one particular suicide case' ('Nie', 1951). This was the opening sentence of an article, emblematically entitled 'No', which Czesław Miłosz published in *Kultura,* a Polish émigré literary magazine edited in Paris. Separation from his homeland, his culture and the readers with whom he shared a common tongue, in Miłosz's eyes, constituted a sentence of solitude and silence, death by his own hand. As it turned out, he was able to sustain his poetic gift, not least because of the huge support he received from *Kultura* and its editor, Jerzy Giedroyc. What he certainly did not anticipate when writing these words was the vitriolic attacks and lies to which he would be subjected from other émigrés in Western Europe and old friends back in Poland.

After walking out of the Polish embassy in Paris, he spent three and a half months in hiding at Maisons-Laffitte. Finally, on 15 May 1951, at a press conference for a Parisian magazine, *Preuves* (Proofs), he officially made an announcement about his defection and his decision to stay in France. Miłosz, the first artist from a 'people's republic' who publicly gave reasons for breaking ties with the new Communist regime, became a media sensation. Earlier he had prepared a statement addressed to fellow citizens back in Poland, in which he defined his political stance and identified the moral rationale behind his decision:

> I am not a reactionary ... My homeland ... ought to belong to the Polish people and not to high officials ... people should not lie. A lie is ... the source of all crime ... The paramount duty of a poet is to tell the truth ... Who knows, perhaps my pen may manage, to a certain degree, to avenge the pain of those Poles or Russians who mourn their closest ones. ('Drodzy Rodacy')

Here he is alluding to the millions of lives brutally cut short in both Poland and the Soviet Union during the recent wartime occupation and subsequent 'liberation' of Europe by the Soviet Union.

Hundreds of copies of his statement were printed by Giedroyc to be sent by post to Polish writers, in the hope that a small number would escape the attention of censors; additionally, it was read on the Voice of America radio station. Hours after defecting, Miłosz appeared on Radio France Internationale, where he met Andrzej Chciuk, who recalled the occasion seven years later:

> I stayed ... to hear and see how W. A. Zbyszewski was going to conduct his interview with Czesław Miłosz, who the previous day cut his links with Warsaw. Zbyszewski, who was working at the Polish Section of French Radio, and a man of impeccable manners, was, like Miłosz, from Wilno, and so could not be malicious or aggressive towards a fellow citizen. Yet there was a noticeable touch of antipathy and a faint tone of contempt in the voice of the 'proper' emigrant during the interview with someone, who until yesterday, was the cultural attaché at the Paris Embassy of the Warsaw government ... What stayed in my memory was the interviewer's nonchalance and aversion, which contrasted with the calm and concentration on Miłosz's face ... I thought to myself then that what awaited Miłosz would be a great deal of unpleasantness and misunderstanding ... [and] also the envy of small-minded people. The poet's face had a tranquil expression, and a conviction about the validity of his decision ... a forerunner of the contemptuous courtesy and supercilious silence he would adopt, which is the best method for dealing with numbskulls. I liked his face then very much. ('Wiadomości Polskie', 7 September 1958)

Supercilious silence and calmness were not always so easy to sustain. In the meantime, the article portraying him appeared in *Preuves*, while *Kultura*, in its

May issue, under the subheading 'My Poetic Credo', included five poems and
'Nie'. Miłosz's inclusion of the poems seems to indicate that he was afraid of
being pigeonholed, and also did not intend to act according to the expectations
of émigré circles. Using the past tense, Miłosz introduced himself:

> I used to be a celebrated Polish poet and a translator ... My name was
> uttered with respect, and the trajectory of my career meant I was certain
> to have a promising future ... I served loyally my people's homeland
> and always endeavoured to fulfil my duties as I understood was right ...
> I was happy that the semi-feudal social structure in Poland had been
> abolished, that young people from working-class backgrounds and vil-
> lages filled university places, and that agricultural reform was carried
> out ... I therefore had every reason to stay in the new Poland that was
> building socialism, and it remained like that until it was decided that I
> would ... be christened. Then, I said 'No'. ('Nie', in *Kultura* 5).

Being 'christened' was code for submitting to ideological orthodoxy, which previously was not compulsory for artists who were not Communists, but who had a
positive attitude to the new system, that is, 'good pagans', as Miłosz called them.
In the post-war period, dialectical materialism *(diamat)* and communism had been
transformed into a quasi-religious system, a New Faith, to which so many desperate, embittered people turned, having been unable to find hope elsewhere. There
were many reasons for accepting 'christening' in the countries which were forcibly
made to adopt 'people's democracy'. The position of a poet there was far more
prestigious than in the West. Being a member of a privileged caste meant not only
enjoying honoraria, a comfortable apartment, and free accommodation and food at
'creative work retreats', but also the sense of being accepted, instead of being confined to the sidelines of society, as artists generally were in the 'free world'. Being
a writer conferred status in the centre of a system in which 'the power of words is
understood' (ibid.).

The price of privilege in the new Poland, however, was high, because
the poet, playwright or novelist had to take on the role of a propagandist, and
yet while they were working away, 'desperate cries for a mug of water arise
from sealed wagons, taking away peasants resisting collectivisation to camps
somewhere by the Arctic Circle' ('Nie'). Miłosz talked about the writers who
convinced themselves that by accepting Evil, they indirectly contributed to
an ultimate Good. He then added: 'I could not bring myself to step over that
threshold. Madness? Perhaps. Suicide, the end of my literary career ... so be it.
If freedom means only understanding necessity, then I, a humble creature, take
the road through which History will pass in the thunder of tanks and flapping
of banners' (ibid.).

In his first public appearance, against all common sense, not only did Miłosz refuse to don the role of apologetic ex-Communist; he instead adopted a somewhat cool attitude towards other émigrés: 'My attitude to Polish political émigrés was, to say the least, ironic: since I was one of those who understood the dynamics of changes taking place in Poland, arguments from minor political factions seemed to me like useless games, and the figures looked like characters in a vaudeville' ('Nie'). This statement met with strong disapproval and provoked an avalanche of articles, which turned into a string of attacks. Mieczysław Grydzewski, who was one of the first to voice his opinion in London, spoke disrespectfully of Miłosz and accused him of arrogance, suggesting that after 'six years of devoted service in captivity' there ought to be 'at least six years of silence' (*Wiadomości* 22, 1951).

It has to be admitted that if it were not for Miłosz's postponed defection, there would be no Paris *Kultura* in which he could have published his work extensively. In June, Piotr Yolles, chief editor of an émigré publication in New York, wrote a balanced assessment of Miłosz's position:

> In my opinion, he should have not written that. He ought to have stayed quiet. He has not found mature words at this point, new immunisations have not started working yet, because the old poison, which will stay for a while yet, is still fighting them. Readers are touched by the openness, great sorrow and tragedy of this Pole and his unhappy love. One would be tempted to welcome this talented, great poet with words which we usually use to say . . . goodbye to those who leave: 'Let freedom be kind to you'. (*Nowy Świat*/'New World', 12 June 1951)

Meanwhile, in August, Aleksander Bregman, who worked for *Dziennik Polski* (Polish Daily) in London, dubbed Miłosz a 'pen mercenary'. The majority of refugees from Soviet-controlled Europe, he asserted, 'are welcomed with open arms', but the least one might demand from apparatchiks and former diplomats who had actually worked for communist regimes was a thorough 'examination of conscience' ('Sprawa Miłosza', 11 August 1951).

This reference to an examination of conscience appeared in response to the July issue of *Kultura*, in which Zygmunt Zaremba and Juliusz Mieroszewski discussed Miłosz's case. In 'Odpowiedź' (A Response), Miłosz answered accusations directed against him and the first fragment of *The Captive Mind*, entitled 'Ketman', which had appeared in *Kultura*. Zaremba, a Polish Socialist Party activist, defended Miłosz from outright condemnation, but disagreed with some statements in 'Nie'. He was critical of Miłosz's motivations, as in his opinion he gave undue emphasis to the issue of the freedom of artists, and perceptively wrote that the poet 'trembles before this new faith, communism. He rejected it, but is still dwarfed by its mighty power' (*Kultura*, 7–8, 1951). Mieroszewski pointed out that the essence of Miłosz's case and the point of view adopted by *Kultura* would soon cause an increasing gulf with adamantly hostile émigrés from London, saying that it was possible to disagree with Miłosz in a number of respects. The deep divisions within the émigré community in Western Europe could not be ignored, and it was thanks to people like Miłosz that it was possible to understand the dramas 'inside the hearts of thousands and tens of thousands of Poles' (Mieroszewski, *Kultura* 7–8). It would take someone with an almost equally solid intellectual background and thorough embedding in political and artistic circles to appreciate fully the sociological and psychological analyses presented in 'Ketman'. Miłosz tended to be least diplomatic when weighing arguments, and appeared to provoke antagonists, accusing them of a lack of preparedness for the challenging intellectual debates which communism prompted. In his view, few outside the country were sufficiently equipped to understand the underlying currents in the Polish political situation and disregarded the deep shifts in consciousness towards the new reality developing there. Those shifts were generally still pro-left, but decidedly anti-Stalinist.

Giedroyc and the group he worked with must have been well disposed to Miłosz to ignore the contemptuous remarks appearing in his statements and his open dissatisfaction at not being able to publish a collection of his poetry. Sergiusz Piasecki, a former Home Army officer, was indignant at the idea that Miłosz was to be given a voice. As a former Communist sympathiser, the poet had been an ardent advocate for the changes which were now taking place in post-war Poland, and therefore was indirectly responsible for the very conditions there which he now abhorred. Piasecki was of the opinion that Miłosz 'was dangerous to the cause of Poland and the cause of the free world fighting Bolshevism' (*Wiadomości*, 44, 1951).

Piasecki's attack may have also been coloured by the fact that he had been for a while the husband of Jadwiga Waszkiewicz, the young Wilno woman wronged by Miłosz. He was not alone in voicing a disparaging attitude. Jan Lechoń, now an émigré poet himself, wrote in a letter to the editor of *Wiadomości*: 'I consider the article about Miłosz, a triumph of the publicist's art ... If Miłosz has an ounce of honesty, he ought to hang himself, or at least work as a labourer to prove that he is with "the common people"' (Lechoń to Grydzewski, 2 December 1951). Ryszard Warga, in a 1952 letter to a London émigré paper, called Miłosz 'an agent of a Bolshevik subversive group in the West' (*Dziennik Polski*, 8).

Most expatriates had no interest in the fate of an obscure poet. Had it not been for political coincidences and the temperament of some participants in this affair, Miłosz might in all probability have returned to his family in Washington and taken up a post at one of the American universities. He desperately wanted to be able to see his newborn second son, and Giedroyc believed that Miłosz would have been best placed in America, where he would be most useful for anti-Soviet propaganda purposes. Even the Polish Ministry of Foreign Affairs would have happily avoided a situation which discredited them publicly. The matter was complicated by the Americans' anxiety about Communist infiltration, by Miłosz's inability to make gestures of humility, and by the tactics employed by Giedroyc, who, on realising that Miłosz's move to America was becoming problematic, decided to use him as much as possible for the benefit of *Kultura*. Mirosław Supruniuk, who researched 'Miłosz's case', believed that it had been intentionally blown out of all proportion by Giedroyc, who recognised a great opportunity for his periodical to take a key position in the lives of expatriate Poles. To some extent it was true, but it would be an over-simplification to attribute the furore solely to the editor and his Machiavellian motivations. The literary contributions Miłosz made undoubtedly resulted in *Kultura*'s profile rising greatly. Giedroyc was genuinely interested in and moved by Miłosz's experiences, and, despite many doubts, behaved loyally towards the poet, even risking a considerable drop in circulation. In the end they did form a relatively good working relationship, albeit difficult at times due to their differences and complicated characters.

Giedroyc sent 'Nie' to an émigré publicist living in London, Juliusz Mieroszewski, who praised it highly. In his reply, he wrote: 'One senses ... more the tragedy of a turn-coat rather than the joyous return of a prodigal son to the "bosom" of western Christian democracy and civilisation. In fact, what pains him is that he is forced to stop believing ... We know nothing of the dramas of that other world' (Mieroszewski to Giedroyc, 2 May 1951). Giedroyc answered: 'Your impression is absolutely correct ... I understood how big the gap between Poland, us and the West has become, and I must admit that I observe and follow the situation very closely'. Neither Giedroyc nor Mieroszewski wanted to fill the journal with the usual nostalgia-laced emigrant fare, Romantic heroism leading to tragedy, soft-focus shots around the good old homestead. The proof of this was in *Kultura*'s fifth issue in 1951, in which, next to Miłosz's statement, a fragment from Witold Gombrowicz's controversial *Trans-Atlantic* appeared. When the defector-poet was labelled a *poputchik*, a name given to writers who sided with the Soviet government in the 1920s, both editors defended him; Mieroszewski criticised Piasecki's use of that insulting attribute, and Giedroyc referred to the Miłosz case as a latter-day 'Dreyfus affair'. In addition, they prepared a statement of support on his behalf to be signed by writers and intellectuals, though, unfortunately, only thirty-three people appended their names, a figure which included the two editors. Consequently, in issue 12, *Kultura* published a piece defining the magazine's attitude to defectors from Poland during Bolesław Bierut's premiership: 'If newly arrived emigrants co-operated actively with the regime, we have the right to expect them to make their cases public. We do not have the right, however, to demand from them degrading gestures of remorse such as occur at Soviet show trials'.

In 1951 nothing seemed to indicate that a new wave of emigration was about to come. Although previously Stanisław Jerzy Lec had left his post as a cultural attaché in Vienna and gone to Israel, it was Miłosz's flight that constituted the first major breaking of ranks within Poland's literary circles. The reaction of those left behind was orchestrated by the government, but also reflected the complex personal feelings of the writers, who displayed such hostility to Miłosz that it deterred any poet from following his example for a long time. Although the news of his 'betrayal' was not officially announced in Poland, it quickly spread among the writing community. Maria Dąbrowska learnt about it in mid-February, and on 3 March Zbigniew Herbert said ironically in a letter to Turowicz that the Literary Society had to abandon its absorbing preoccupation with finding a suitable villa for Miłosz. Others used an array of insults when referring to Miłosz, such as 'enthusiast for fascist Eliot', 'dyed fox', 'deserter', 'yesterday a *Volksdeutsch* [a native German living in Poland], today a traitor, and tomorrow already—an agent'.

At the end of October 1951, a two-day conference took place in Warsaw concerning 'the issue of artistic creativity', attended by Jakub Berman and Deputy Minister for Art and Culture Włodzimierz Sokorski, as well as other prominent writers, among them Jerzy Andrzejewski, Tadeusz Breza, Jan Kott, Jarosław Iwaszkiewicz and Antoni Słonimski. It was turned into a trial *in absentia,* whose aim was to stigmatise Miłosz as a renegade, with a secondary purpose of clearing those who had come into contact with him of any suspicion of ideological contamination. To recall the atmosphere of those times, it is worth quoting fragments of some of the pronouncements.

Jan Kott:

> We have to be honest with ourselves. I have to declare that in our circles we found not only people with small-minded souls, but also one with the soul of a lackey. Czesław Miłosz had the nerve to send many of us a printed epistle, written in the style of an apostolic letter, entitled 'Dear Countrymen'. In it he had the audacity to write that a man should not lie, because a lie is a terrible thing, and a source of all crime. This man . . .

fails to mention that he acquired and used a Lithuanian passport to avoid the fate and misery of the Polish nation . . . he lied, for many years, working in our diplomatic service, lied coming here, lied at our writers' plenum, lied to his superiors, and lied to us until the end. It seems to me that this example of betrayal, this example of cowardice and fear of facing responsibility, when writers in our country face such an arduous, but so commendable role, requires from us a moment of reflection. Not that we would feel sorry for the writer who left us. We do not feel sorry for traitors and never will.

Antoni Słonimski:

Words which reach us today from overseas represent a betrayal of our collective work mission, which involves ever wider masses of the Polish people, threaten our efforts to build factories, universities and hospitals, and incite conflict within our nation. These words are an enemy to every worker and peasant, architect and bricklayer rebuilding our capital city, engineer who designs new factories, party member who fights illiteracy in the countryside. They are on the side of destruction, of hatred, and absolve assassins.

Jarosław Iwaszkiewicz:

Writing is always a struggle. Fighting the environment is hard, but fighting oneself is even harder. We found ourselves in a situation where there is no choice. There is no escape to an ivory tower. There is no escaping to the comfort and peace of our studies. We have to choose between the two. And let the example of Czesław Miłosz be a warning to us all, that wanting to remain in his ivory tower, after crossing the border, he found himself instantly in a neo-Nazi paper alongside Vlasov [a Soviet general who collaborated with the Germans and defected with his troops to join the Nazi army].

It is interesting to note the different writing styles each one of them uses to evoke emotions—from the prosecutorial tone of Kott, through the rhetorical flourishes of Słonimski, who probably did not believe his own words, but felt that for his own security he had to utter them, to Iwaszkiewicz's comment, being really a reflection of the inner struggle played out within himself and which involuntarily revealed his own captivity.

Expressions of hatred poured out on both sides of the Iron Curtain. Curiously, two lampoons criticising Miłosz were published on the same day, 4 November 1951—one by Słonimski and one by Piasecki—in Warsaw and in

London. The continuing hounding of Miłosz in Western-based Polish papers, and the intimidation used in Poland to keep other writers in line, were decried in a letter sent by one of Miłosz's friends to another around this time:

> The last assault in *Wiadomości* made us all depressed ... it is really, and I am saying it with complete conviction, a national crime. Because, who after that will want to flee? ... I do not know whether *Wiadomości* is aware that even if they were handsomely paid, they would do a better service for the Soviets than when they are doing it for free. (Stanisław Vincenz to Józef Czapski, 3 November 1951)

Most painful, certainly, for the poet was the criticism from his home country, such as a short story by Kazimierz Brandys, 'Let Us Forget Him', published in the autumn of 1955, immediately before the political thaw following Stalin's death. Its protagonist is a painter, Weymont, who takes the opportunity of a stay in Vienna to escape to the West. Brandys employs all the necessary elements of a lampoon—a Lithuanian passport which saves Weymont from being arrested; abandoning a woman who loves him; accepting a prospective offer in the West; spitting at his homeland in radio interviews and books—ending with an irrevocable literary failure, the inevitable fate of a deserter. From a safe distance, in a polemical article, 'Reflection on a Closed Circle', Miłosz turned on his detractors: 'They know that above them flows a stream of history, that they have no power to make a mark in their existence and they are looked at with contempt. That is where the psychological intensity comes from, nowhere else ... this attacking of others, to convince each other that their actions come from within themselves' (*Kontynenty* 391).

In the mid-1950s, Marek Skwarnicki, while working at the National Library in Warsaw, came across a heap of copies of Miłosz's *Rescue*, which had been removed from school libraries. The government of the Polish People's Republic wanted to ensure that he really would be forgotten and censored his name, but did not stop there. They removed him from encyclopedias, and even from the list of employees of *Karta* in Wilno, using a retouching technique. After major changes in the Polish Communist regime in October 1956, when it seemed that Miłosz's books would reappear in Poland, it turned out again that in his homeland he was to remain an Orwellian unperson. He was not to be mentioned, and only lies about him were permitted. The poet himself wrote in his 'Letter to Polish Communists': 'People suspect that you are servants of Satan, and if I were you, I would not take the accusation lightly' (*Kultura* 11, 1959).

Rock Bottom

I will have to take advantage of America, because they will not let me in a second time.

Czesław Miłosz to Tadeusz Breza (1948)

Let your mornings be calm and do not let the noisy, enraged man down-stairs scare you. Let there be no door slamming by the enraged man in the evenings. You will, I wish, feel more than just disgust towards me. Say to yourself that he did like us a little, although he was unbearable ... My elec-tric Junona, that is my request, and it contains everything I felt and thought during this year, because, after all, I did feel and reflect under this cover of sarcasm, fury and egoism. I also felt and thought about you all, about how you bear with pride and your best good will this punishment from God.

Czesław Miłosz to Zofia Hertz, 1952

Dear Zygmunt, I only now realised how much I loved you.

Telegram from Czesław Miłosz after
Zygmunt Hertz's death (1979)

The Devil is a prince of lies, and it is important to see that in the decision taken in Paris. Miłosz definitively severed the pact with him, and chose truth. Refer-ring to his decision to seek political asylum many years later, the poet stated that it was determined by the necessity 'to find a place on earth, where I could wear a face and not a mask' (*Zaraz po wojnie* 12). The house where *Kultura* was based became a place where Miłosz discovered how many demons nestled inside him. Observations made by Andrzej Bobkowski at the time offer an insight into the defector's spiritually vulnerable state of mind:

> Crossing over to an opposite side by a man like Miłosz is similar to a religious conversion ... He still can't believe that he stopped believing [in his former faith]. Miłosz from the beginning took the leftist path; the entire shaping of his soul has been Marxist. And today it is a religion like any other ... A moment of losing faith is terrible for any man. (Bob-kowski to Giedroyc, 16 November 1951)

Until now, accounts of Miłosz's life have avoided two weeks in January 1951 which cover the period from when he left Warsaw to his arrival at Maisons-Laffitte. During this period Miłosz was clearly engaged in clandestine contact with Jerzy Giedroyc, Józef Czapski, and Czapski's friend James Burnham, an American political scientist who was also a CIA adviser. Burnham's role was to guarantee the poet a prompt departure to the United States. Sitting in the taxi taking him away from rue Dumont d'Urville, Miłosz could not possibly have imagined that he would not see his family for the next thirty-three months. He arrived at 1 avenue Corneille, where the *Kultura* offices were situated, with two suitcases, 150,000 old French francs and a few cartons of cigarettes, supplies which would diminish astonishingly fast. With him he also carried his diplomatic status, which meant that the inhabitants of the house could have found themselves in trouble for kidnapping him, had the Polish embassy chosen to accuse them of that act. To avoid that, Giedroyc and Czapski contacted the French Ministry of International Affairs, which granted permission for Miłosz to stay at Maisons-Laffitte and provided discreet security in the form of the local police. At Miłosz's request two Polish Secret Service officers visited him and interviewed him in the presence of Jerzy Giedroyc. The latter later reported: 'He was worried that they would press for some revelations or information, but it did not happen. It was a conversation which touched generally on the situation in the People's Republic of Poland and the role of the embassy, but no undue pressure was placed on him' (Jacek Żakowski, *Gazeta Wyborcza*). It is likely that during that meeting, Miłosz officially requested political asylum in France.

Kidnapping or secret assassinations were not something that only happened in books or films, so Miłosz was compelled to stay in hiding. His links with the outside world were limited to correspondence with Janka and, through Jerzy Giedroyc, Józef Czapski and his sister Maria, and Zofia and Zygmunt Hertz. These are the people who constituted his 'family'—almost a monastic commune that was far from being conflict-free, but was totally devoted to *Kultura*. He scarcely ever left the villa, which had been damaged after being occupied by German soldiers. When he went into the surrounding garden, he was always accompanied by Hertz. When guests came to the *Kultura* offices, Miłosz was introduced as Mr Kwiatkowski. He made himself useful round the house by doing the washing up. He soon began to write for the monthly, and undertook translations, but never used his own name. An example of this use of a pseudonym was an article he wrote about Thomas Merton, the American writer and mystic, which was supposedly the work of 'Edouardo Roditi'. The poet slept in the library on a camp bed, wrapped in army blankets which offered inadequate protection from the gnawing cold. Nor did a small coal burner that had a long metal flue running almost to the ceiling generate much heat. The room he occupied had tall shelves filled with books and a solid desk, at which Miłosz wrote.

Habitually, the poet paced the room, chain-smoking and scratching himself nervously, not noticing that it caused bleeding. He felt no sense of relief for having made the right decision; on the contrary, he was terrified, convinced that he had failed by severing himself from the system of thought that was right 'historically', and remorseful at his betrayal of his friends. As Giedroyc said in a letter to Stanisław Vincenz, the poet could not 'shake off his attraction towards Stalinism, like a rabbit towards a snake. Today having read that nasty lampoon by Słonimski ... he delivered an act of contrition very much in the mode of Russian trials, agreeing that all accusations were legitimate and deserved' (Giedroyc to Vincenz, 9 November 1951). Repentance could also be detected in another letter written to Vincenz, in which Miłosz exclaimed:

> How can one get rid of the feeling that one is a traitor and a swine? I live with this problem, and move and sleep and perhaps it will lead to a total catastrophe. Dear God, had I known that it would hit me like this, I would have never done it ... Please tell me what I should do, and whether there is a way out of this moral dilemma. I am slapped in the face by one side and the other, abused by the Americans ... I have sinned because I stood up against compulsion ... its victory in the whole world is inevitable. (CM to Vincenz, n.d. 1951).

From today's perspective, it is hard to imagine how someone so evidently capable of a thorough analysis of an individual's dependence on ideology was himself so steeped in ideology, and how fearful of the Ghost of History whom he had crossed. It could be likened to a serious illness which was destroying his body. He would manage to emerge from that, thanks to desperate, intensive work, and thanks to meeting a wise man, and to love, though convalescence would last a number of years. In the meantime, he was deeply worried about his wife and sons. In a letter to Giedroyc, who was visiting Berlin, Zofia Hertz complained of having passed

> two terrible days with Czesław. I was seriously worried that he would either go mad, or tear us to pieces. After your departure he paced like a lion in a cage until 7 p.m., then sent a telegram to his wife, who again has not written. Later, standing close to me ... he tormented me for four hours. At first he shouted, so I did too, but then calmed down after drinking a litre of wine. However, yesterday it was exactly the same. I literally thought I would go mad, because he walked up and down the hall outside the office and this regular thud of his footsteps drove me to despair. Unfortunately, I could not say anything, as he would have said that he was in a concentration camp. He concluded that his wife is not writing for two reasons, firstly that things have gone wrong in Washington, and then, that on the way there or back, probably along with the children, she had died in a car crash. In his imagination his wife's and children's bodies had already been consigned to the earth, and there was no way of persuading him otherwise.

This morning when I was making myself breakfast before going out to the printers, he came out looking dishevelled and said: 'You see, she has not responded to the telegram. I was right, she is dead, that's it'. I am telling you, *cet homme est dangereux* [this man is dangerous], a religious maniac is nothing compared with him. I said that there was no mail yet. To which he replied that he knew that there would be nothing coming. A few minutes later the mail arrived with a letter from his wife in which she reported that they received her exceptionally well at the State Department, that they changed their attitude and things will be sorted out quickly, and that they rate his lecture and articles as very positive and ask for copyright etc.—Perhaps he will go? What do you think? His reaction was such that he went to bed and slept until my return, that is, 3 p.m. . . . and today he set to work and is a different man. (Z. Hertz to Giedroyc, n.d.)

There was something very close to Miłosz's experiences in Goszyce back in 1945 in this emotional torment. Neurotic, bristly, and in pain, he saw in his hosts a group of surviving remnants of pre-war right-wing sympathisers about to disappear into obscurity: 'There is in the world a very clear and sharp division between people of the right and the left . . . and there is no common ground. All Polish emigration is right-wing . . . I suffer greatly from my links with so stark a rightist periodical as *Kultura*', he wrote to Vincenz on 17 September 1951, and was equally critical of the inhabitants of Maisons-Laffitte. He felt thrown into an abyss, humiliated. Now fate threw him together with others who had failed, towards whom until recently he had derisory feelings, and who would disappear into oblivion.

For me it was reaching rock bottom, simply because I had nowhere to go to. My hurt pride could, to a great extent, manifest itself in rudeness towards my hosts and furious sarcastic attacks on them. In my arguments with them there were mainly provocations on my part and playing ignorant to tease the 'reactionaries'. Our mentalities were alien also due to Giedroyc's, Zofia's and Zygmunt's living in pre-war Poland, from which they were slowly breaking away. (*Rok myśliwego* 312)

It was really the Hertzes, and not Czapski or, locked in his office, the imperious, inaccessible Giedroyc, with whom Miłosz formed intellectual ties and who took upon themselves the pain of his bouts of depression. He would later talk of them as 'witnesses, helpers, midwives, participants, rabble-rousers, feeders, callers, healers, tamers of wild animals' (qtd. in Gorczyńska, 'Portrety paryskie' 196). Zofia was energetic, assertive, cold and not good at befriending beasts—taming them was altogether another matter. Zygmunt was the opposite, 'a buzzing bumble-bee in search of the sweetness of life', 'a glutton, a gourmet, enjoying his drink, and above all a chatterbox'. He was the gentlest and warmest among the not-so-easy-to-live-with inhabitants of Maisons-Laffitte, and someone who for Miłosz embodied calm, common sense, 'humor, kindliness, skeptical democratic belief' (*ABC* 306). Zygmunt would thrust a hundred francs into his pocket to cover the costs of a ticket into Paris, a packet of cigarettes and a glass of red wine. His reactions were often much more astute and appropriate than might seem at first: 'Cześ, think before you sound off, or better still don't speak—just write' (*Zaczynając od moich ulic* 435). Hertz, who had worked since September 1939 as a representative of a Belgian company, Solvay, could easily have had a lucrative business career after the war. Instead he chose the thankless role of Jack-of-all-trades, including packing the magazine, piling it on a cart and taking it to the post office himself, and helping his wife, who would not leave *Kultura*. And so, for many years this ironic, intelligent, sometimes spiteful, but nevertheless philanthropic friend would continue to devote his life to supporting others, looking after consecutive arrivals from Poland. And the first and perhaps most difficult person he ever had to care for was Miłosz, who, having moved out to the house in the rue Corneille, admitted:

> I tried your patience very hard, without doubt . . . I am grateful to you, Zygmunt, who in a harsh but friendly way spurred me to stay active. You made sure that I wrote and did the dishes. Perhaps you were not tough enough with me. You radiate kindness, and I kept myself warm round this kindness, when I was very lonely. You know what hardship I went through during the time I spent in Maisons-Laffitte, and let it be, in part at least, an excuse and my apology for my egocentric behaviour . . . I ask you to remain my friendly giant and when you talk about me, talk of a pig who had human feelings. (Qtd. in Grochowska 202)

James Burnham worked as a consultant for the CIA, and in post-war Europe arranged gatherings of scientists and writers from different countries who openly opposed communism. From their first encounter with him in Washington, Czapski and Giedroyc seriously considered the possibility of Miłosz's escape, and tried to prepare for it by promising that he could be smuggled to the United States. The evidence for that is an extensive correspondence between Giedroyc, Czapski and Burnham, kept in the Archives of the Literary Institute in Paris, where Miłosz is referred to as 'M'. Czapski provided a brief account of the writer leaving Poland, and informed the CIA man that 'he is staying here . . . hoping to get a visa in his consular passport, as usual, but not through the Polish Embassy. I have tried your embassy. Impossible. A reply from Washington said that "the gentleman is not interesting enough(?) and that the visa has to be issued in America"'. Czapski also stressed the usefulness of Miłosz in anti-Communist propaganda, stressing that 'getting him out' would be a matter of great importance to the Americans. Miłosz could potentially become the first intellectual and writer of that calibre to become a fugitive from the Soviet bloc. Then, in a final dramatic plea,

> I implore you to give us instructions as to what I should do with M. For now, he is staying at his post in Paris, but he is besieged and hunted . . . No one better than M could explain to all those comrades on their journey, and others, what Stalin's regime offers after five years, even to a defiant nation like ours. I particularly think about Einstein, who was on very friendly terms with M. Would you be able to request an instant visa for M? (Czapski to Burnham, 31 January 1951, Instytut Literacki Archive)

In a letter to Einstein dated 2 February 1951, Miłosz wrote:

> My friends here contacted the US Embassy, but the answer was negative. I consider it unwise from a political point of view . . . not to mention purely human matters . . . I turn to you in the key moment of my life. I do not know what your competences are, but your name is respected by everyone. I believe that your intervention on my behalf to the President may prove successful. I am a father of two sons born in America. I have never been a member of a Communist party . . . or any other. (Einstein Archives)

On 6 February Einstein replied that only the State Department could intervene and that any action he took would only worsen the situation. To the suggestion that Einstein should intervene with the State Department came a reply from Christian Gauss, who stated that 'the situation will be very difficult taking into consideration *tensions*'. By this he most likely meant a conflict between the superpowers, though equally he could have been alluding to the political situation in the States dominated by 'Red hysteria' as a result of the activities of Senator Joseph McCarthy. For these reasons, despite his good intentions, Gauss did not take any action himself, but turned to an acquaintance, an assistant to the Secretary of State. To Einstein, Gauss wrote: 'As I suspect, the obstacle here is the McCarran Act and not the stand of the State Department on this matter, but I do not lose hope' (Gauss to Einstein, 7 March 1951).

The Internal Security Act, issued in 1950, was also referred to as the McCarran Act, which was to prevent 'Red' infiltration by, among other things, disallowing the issuing of citizenship to, and even entry to the States by, persons suspected of Communist activity who were either current or former members of Communist parties. In March 1952, a year after Miłosz's opting for 'freedom', an article entitled 'The McCarran Curtain' appeared in *Life* magazine that discussed absurd situations which arose as a result of strict adherence to stipulations in the act. Miłosz's case was cited, as were those of Graham Greene, who was denied a visa for a long time, and Arthur Koestler, who was allowed entry thanks to special permission issued by Congress.

Snippets of information gathered from different sources regarding the issue of Miłosz's struggle to obtain an American visa indicate that there were at least three decisive factors. The first was the status of the man himself, an ex-diplomat from Poland during the Bierut period, as well as the fact (mentioned by Burnham in one of his letters) that Miłosz had had leftist leanings in the past. American bureaucrats at the Paris Embassy could easily dig back into his past in Wilno by means of information provided by the Polish authorities or other Polish émigrés. To them, leftist sympathies were no different from a commitment to the Communist cause, and that was reason enough to refuse him entry to the States. This decision was firmly adhered to despite numerous articles about Miłosz in the American press. In December 1951, for example, articles referring to his case were published in the *New York Times* and the *New Leader*, where the writer's 'issue' was branded 'a stupidity, tragic in consequence'. Constant pressure was applied by Burnham and by many institutions, such as the International Rescue Committee, the American Civil Liberties Union, the National Catholic Welfare Conference, and especially the American Committee for Cultural Freedom (ACCF). In January 1952, the latter published an open letter to the visa section in the State Department with signatures from, among others, Sydney Hook, W. H. Auden and Arthur Koestler. An ACCF activist, Sidney Hook was also one of the founders of the Congress for Cultural Freedom operating in Europe, secretly financed by the CIA; he made great efforts on Miłosz's behalf by publishing his essays and inviting him to conferences and talks. It is easy to see the paradox, pointed out by Sarah Miller, who carried out research in the Washington Archives into 'Miłosz's case'. One CIA department, dedicated to the fight against communism, blocked Miłosz from coming to the States, while another at the very same time used him in the Congress for Cultural Freedom campaign. The second factor was that the quota for admitting Polish emigrants had been reached and the American officials failed to recognise that Miłosz's was a special case, requiring a special approach. Initially, in February 1951, the clerical staff in the American Embassy in Paris were not even planning to talk to Miłosz. At the beginning of March, Józef Czapski wrote to Burnham that following his intervention, he had at last received visa application forms for Miłosz to complete, and for the first time felt that there was the prospect of a happy outcome. The forms were submitted, probably by Czapski, on 13 April 1951. From correspondence in the Beinecke Library, it can be seen that Miłosz considered applying for a visa from the Lithuanian quota, and that, if that failed, to try for a Canadian visa with the hope of moving from Canada to the States.

A third factor was the Polish émigré community's attitude to Miłosz. In August 1951 Burnham underlined the fact that 'his fellow countrymen were the principal source of Miłosz's woes, those outside the country, that is. You must understand that it is difficult to ignore a condemnatory report written by a "friend from the West"' (Burnham to Czapski, 10 August 1951). This came as no surprise to Miłosz's friends, who had had personal dealings with influential émigrés. Within the 'Polish little hell', there were scores of unhappy souls willing to discredit the poet in the eyes of the American authorities, sometimes as a result of their own despair at being banned from returning to their homeland. Some must have been convinced of Miłosz's culpability and the danger he might pose, while others were driven by pure envy. 'Poles in the States are furious and issue endless denunciations. The more Miłosz's position is highlighted in the international press, the greater the fury', reported Giedroyc to Bobkowski on 8 September 1951. Two months later he wrote that 'we have been told by the American embassy that Miłosz has not been granted a visa because of a huge number of denunciations and interventions from émigrés'. Months later, in a note to another supporter, he conceded that despite all their best efforts, 'so far Grydzewski and Piasecki are stronger' (Giedroyc to Jerzy Stempkowski, 18 February 1952).

Amongst the other high-profile figures Czapski petitioned for a positive reference on Miłosz's behalf was General Władysław Anders, whose conduct throughout the Second World War had earned him huge respect. Anders's reply was prompt and courteous but negative. Contacts were made by Alfred Berlstein with Stanisław Mikołajczyk, the former Prime Minister for Poland's Government-in-Exile, and feelers were put out towards the Vatican, yet, like all other attempts, to no avail.

In the end Miłosz decided to remain in France and bring his family there, which initiated a lengthy, painful quarrel with Janka. The hatred and contempt he had encountered from fellow Poles left deep marks, triggering bouts of despair, self-pity and intense resentment towards those responsible for his separation from his family. After the first year of 'freedom', he confessed to Vincenz: 'I will never forget ... what it means to be a hounded animal ... my wife and the children would have died of hunger, had it not been for the Americans. I despise the Polish émigrés and cannot help it'. In a subsequent letter he found a possible way out for himself. Having heard that Tadeusz Borowski, the brilliant author of *This Way to the Gas, Ladies and Gentlemen*, had committed suicide in Warsaw 'by turning the gas knob', he concluded that 'sooner or later I will have to end my life' (CM to Vincenz, n.d. 1952). A quarter of a century later Vincenz recalled those days to Adam Michnik: 'We agreed to meet in the Latin Quarter ... It was a small, cosy Bulgarian place. We sat down, Miłosz ordered wine and said: "I wanted to invite you to this place. I used to come here every day in the early fifties, each time thinking that I would commit suicide that day"' (Michnik, *In Memoriam*, 185).

'The enemy of order—humankind'

> A person living in a Western country doesn't even realise that millions of his fellow men ... live in a world which to them is as equally fantastical as the world of the inhabitants on Mars.
>
> Czesław Miłosz, *The Captive Mind*

In order not to kill himself, he sought any argument that could dissuade him from such an act, although the most important and hardest to pinpoint was something deep within him. Faith and piety? To be more precise, it was the belief that the world was not based on a void, that there was a higher authority which did not allow anything to occur by chance:

> Painful, and a consequence of pressure from within, *The Captive Mind* originated in a prayer. Had it not been for the piety of a child brought up in the Catholic faith and able to pray in adulthood, I would not have coped, I would have perished ... On the verge of a prayer, with deep concentration, I was haunted at rare moments in important moments in my life by a kind of intuitive clairvoyance, when for a split second my future appeared before me ... I believed that I have a place in God's agenda and I asked for ability to fulfil the tasks awaiting me. (*Rok myśliwego* 108)

Besides the fear, despair, accusations and self-accusations, traces of peace and belief endured, which were absent during quarrels with the Hertzes or Giedroyc and from the despondent letters to Janka. He remained capable of sobriety, distance, insight, *claritas*, as Karl Jaspers noted, recognising in *The Captive Mind* 'a vision ... endowed with superhuman purity' (247). If he were to fight 'the Russian executioner', the whispering, lying Antichrist, if he were to find explanations, then there was only one possible way to do it. He sat for hours at his desk in Maisons-Laffitte, while excitedly Giedroyc confided to his trusted correspondents that his guest 'is finishing writing a book ... which will be a sensation throughout the world ... one of the most important blows to the Warsaw regime' (Giedroyc to Vincenz, 17 September 1951).

Miłosz did the bulk of the writing probably over ten months. In winter 1951, a version of the text was sent to Jane Zielonko, who was to translate it into

English, and to André Prudhommeaux, who would translate it into French. Whether it was due to waiting for the translations to be finished or the need for Giedroyc to find funds, the Polish edition came out a little over a year after the book was finished, at the end of February or the beginning of March 1953, as the third volume in Kultura's Library, just behind editions of Gombrowicz's *Trans-Atlantic* and Orwell's *Nineteen Eighty-Four*. Simultaneously, editions appeared in France, England, America and Germany.

The book was written for Western readers, to give them an insight into the intellectual and social changes that had occurred in the 'social democratic' countries of Eastern and Central Europe. Miłosz drew on Witkacy's book *Voracity* and his vision of the clash between the West and the East, in which the former appeared passive and inert in the face of the ideological advantage its opponent had gained. In promoting an *instant* world-view, Communist propaganda was as effective as the pills concocted by a Mongolian philosopher, Murti-Bing. Miłosz depicted international intellectual and artistic circles haunted by a void, and thus susceptible to a 'new faith' which would allow them to find social justification for their existence, but also detach themselves from down-to-earth, 'materialistic' people. An intellectual, after all, was a friend of humanity, not as it is but as it 'ought to be'. Having lived through the war and the full horrors of Nazi occupation in a way his French and especially his English counterparts had not, a Central European intellectual feels that only dialectical materialism, by illuminating history and reality, seems to lessen the pain that the camps and crematoria have left them with. Subsequently, Western European civilisation and democracy, Miłosz argued, had been deeply damaged, and now could offer only 'freedom from', not 'freedom to'. He was convinced that citizens of the Eastern bloc do not miss capitalism and believe that 'the means of production ought to belong to the state, which planned economic growth and allocated national income for health, education, science and art'. What distresses them, however, is that the New Faith imposed on them cannot satisfy their spiritual needs.

Trembling before Soviet might which would shortly take over the continent, incapable of completely shedding their old mentality and democratic habits, and subjected to continuous control, intellectuals could save themselves only by acting, adopting a mask, and surviving through pretence. The name Miłosz gave this strategy for coping was Ketman, a word taken from a book by Arthur de Gobineau, a French diplomat and writer, which referred to a strategy widely used in Moslem culture. It enabled people to conceal their true convictions while displaying seeming adherence to current religious practices by performing all the required rituals. It produced a de facto school of hypocrisy, which ensured the safety of those who were part of a minority. Adapting this

notion to the Central European situation, Miłosz referred to numerous manifestations of Ketman. Among these there was a national Ketman, in which contempt
for Russia was masked by loud enthusiasm for 'socialism', 'revolutionary purity'
('Stalin is a murderous usurper, and after the final victory, it will be possible to return to true revolutionary values') and 'professional work' (manifesting orthodoxy,
endeavouring to do something useful within one's abilities). There was also a form
he termed 'sceptic Ketman', the idea that humanity has been overtaken by madness, which one needs to survive with a clear conscience, while externally adhering
to 'correct' attitudes. And finally there was 'metaphysical Ketman' (Who knows
whether 'acts of God are not taking place' by means of the barbarians, and whether
the Soviets' actions might not wake humanity from its religious lethargy?).

> He who practices Ketman lies. But would he be less dishonest if he
> could speak the truth? . . . A poet muses over what he would write if
> he were not bound by his political responsibilities, but could he realise
> his visions if he were at liberty to do so? Ketman brings comfort, fos-
> tering dreams of what might be, and even the enclosing fence affords
> the solace of reverie . . . Fear of freedom is nothing more than fear of the
> void . . . Perhaps it is better for him to breed a full-grown Ketman, to
> submit to pressure and thus feel that he *is*, than to take a chance on the
> wisdom of past ages which maintains that man is a creature of God.
> (*Captive Mind* 80–81)

Miłosz analysed this fear of the void, this inability to find metaphysical certainty
and to understand how the 'New Faith' tempts souls, taking as his examples four
Polish writers whose identity he hid under pseudonyms, but who were easily recognisable to Polish readers. He himself had decided to fight for his liberty: 'But
suppose one should live without Ketman, to challenge fate, to say: "If I lose, I
shall not pity myself."' On the chessboard of dialectical materialism and historic
necessity, there was a disruptive presence, 'the enemy of order—humankind'. In
them, despite exposure to constant propaganda which resembled religious in-
doctrination, human beings retain the need to see truth expressed, the capacity
for love, care and tenderness, like that Polish family Miłosz glimpsed lost in the
crowd at a Soviet railway station. 'Now I am homeless—a just punishment. But
perhaps I was born so that the "Eternal Slaves" might speak through my lips.
Why should I spare myself?' (ibid., 250). He ended by cutting ties with Tiger.
'My friend accepts naked terror, whatever name he may choose to give it. We
have parted ways. Whether the side on which I find myself is the future victor
or the future victim is not the issue here' (ibid.).

   The Captive Mind was well received by circles not enchanted by ideas of a
Communist utopia. In an essay, which was used as an introduction to the French

and German editions, one of the most outstanding European philosophers, Karl Jaspers, remarked how 'the captivity of the mind'

> was shown in its core ... We observe how humanity changes in totally new circumstances—when forced to live in mistrust of everyone else, in perpetual mutual vigilance ... in a merciless struggle between people wearing masks, in performing parts, which, in the end become our second nature. Is it a new human being? No, it is a human being any one of us could become in these circumstances ... A reader of this book can question the certainty of being faithful to his or her humanity. (*Zniewolony umysł* 293–294)

Albert Einstein congratulated the author, saying that *The Captive Mind* was 'a very good contribution to our knowledge and understanding of the situation faced by the Eastern European intelligentsia' and that up until then, he had not come across a publication 'which would provide a deeper psychological picture' (Einstein to CM, 12 July 1953), while Dwight Macdonald told the readers of the *New Yorker* that 'apart from Hannah Arendt's *Roots of Totalitarianism* ... I do not know of a more subtle study of the totalitarian mindset' (14 November 1953). Peter Viereck, in the *New York Times Book Review*, described Miłosz as a 'great contemporary poet' and 'a hero of the Polish resistance' during the occupation, and there were other fine reviews by Nicola Chiaromonte in *Partisan Review* and by Heinrich Böll in the German press. Initiating what would be an important friendship for the poet, Thomas Merton wrote to Miłosz on 6 December 1958, admitting that *The Captive Mind* made 'most other books on the present state of man look abjectly foolish'. 'I find it especially important for myself', he added, 'in my position as a monk, a priest and a writer ... the inspiration of much thought, meditation and prayer' (*Striving towards Being* 3). For Juliusz Mieroszewski, 'when it comes to inner or spiritual mechanics, then Miłosz explains things far better and more deeply than Koestler' (Mieroszewski to Giedroyc, 9 March 1953). Gombrowicz, the biggest name on Kultura's list, described the book as 'excellent' and predicted that it would spark 'strong international repercussions' (Gombrowicz to Giedroyc, 21 April 1953). Even Lechoń admitted that while reading the book, he felt fewer unequivocal emotions than usual

> towards this Miłosz who is so very unPolish. It is a masterpiece of a psychological analysis, which is not a psychoanalysis, and a style none of our writers possess—here economy of language makes an impression of a hidden richness. But while reading it through, my heart grows cold, there is admiration for Miłosz, and at the same time almost pity—or

fear of him. This intellect is razor sharp, but also as cold and cruel as a razor. (*Dzienniki*, 13 May 1956)

The Captive Mind also reached readers in Poland, albeit through different methods, the most spectacular, but least effective, involved it being dropped from balloons. Maria Dąbrowska noted the shock the book caused Andrzejewski and how harmful it was to Putrament's colleagues in the Party, while Tadeusz Kwiatkowski recalled how 'Miłosz was regarded in the intelligentsia and literary circles as the voice of our secret thoughts' (*Panopticum* 148).

The assessment of *The Captive Mind* by émigrés changed greatly following the easing of censorship and better access to news from Poland after the June 1956 Rising in Poznań, suppressed on the orders of Konstantin Rokossowski, the Soviet-appointed Defence Minister, at the cost of around sixty lives. Readers appreciated the extent to which the book demonised the role of ideology and attacked Stalinism and socialist realism. When Andrzej Walicki, the author of *The Captive Mind Years Later* (1993), was visiting Paris in 1961, Giedroyc asked him to what extent Miłosz's analysis accorded with the reality in Poland:

> My wife and I gave an identical response ... we consider the book to be a thorough, splendid analysis of matters very familiar to us, which we understood and had experienced personally ... Miłosz saw the most important feature of totalitarian communism ... mighty and ubiquitous ideological pressure, which was to be used to create 'a new man' and a new, totally controlled world. I consider this diagnosis analogous to Orwell's vision and later confirmed by Solzhenitsyn ... Miłosz was mistaken in his assumption that this totalitarian project would become a success. (Walicki 29)

When the turn of historic events luckily was contrary to the writer's predictions, 'a generation of young Poles, the generation of Solidarity, celebrated Miłosz as a great exposer of the totalitarian system' (ibid., 309–310).

Miłosz found allies in a circle of intellectuals and activists who, having had leftist leanings in the 1930s and a fascination with communism, realised that Stalin's regime had committed countless crimes against humanity. The non-Communist left was represented by Arthur Koestler, the author of *Darkness at Noon*, who, together with Burnham, was part of a think-tank responsible for organising an anti-Communist congress in June 1950 in West Berlin. The founding committee included, among others, Bertrand Russell, André Gide, Albert Camus, John Dos Passos, Karl Jaspers and Herman Broch. Subsequently, Miłosz became one of the keenest contributors to their activities, co-organising meetings and conferences on their behalf. Having financial backing from the American Federation of Labor, the Congress for Cultural Freedom was the most serious attempt at resistance to Soviet ideological expansion. Miłosz summed up the growth of the organisation thus:

> After the convention in Berlin, it was decided that Paris should be the center's headquarters. *Le Congrès* was the work of minds which had passed through Marxism, revisionism, Trotskyism; the only such minds, it turned out, [who] understood the danger of the Stalin system because they were the only ones who knew what was going on there. In short, it was mostly Jewish intellectuals from New York who founded the Congress. (*ABC* 87)

The administration was supervised by Michael Josselson, one of very few people, if not the only one, who knew that some of the Congress's funding came from the CIA. Pierre Grémion, a researcher into its history, claimed that the inclusion of a Polish poet in the West played a key role in the development of the institution.

Giedroyc's papers record how De Rougemont and Silone organised a press conference for Miłosz in Paris on 21 March 1951, and soon after he was invited to publish fragments of *The Captive Mind,* a translation of 'Nie' and 'Poetry and Dialectics' in *Preuves,* a French magazine funded by the Congress. A few months later he took part in a conference organised by the Secretariat where they discussed the attitude of intellectuals towards communism. Miłosz became one of the most active contributors to their activities and co-organised meetings and conferences on their behalf in Europe. In Paris interest in and fascination with communism was increasing. By publishing chapters of *The Captive Mind, Preuves* could demonstrate to its readers 'that it was not a paper used by the Americans for anti-Communist propaganda, but a serious monthly' (Rita Gombrowicz 74).

During the 1950s Miłosz developed a strong bond with Albert Camus, who had himself been brutally criticised in the first half of the decade, mainly by *Les Temps Modernes,* jauntily edited by Jean-Paul Sartre, a writer enchanted by orthodox Stalinism. After Simone de Beauvoir published *Mandarins,* which was partly a lampoon directed at Camus, Miłosz sent him a letter on 24 October 1954 as a sign of solidarity and recognition: 'I am not looking for a master in you, but for someone who could in part justify my existence'. It was with great joy that three years later, on 29 October 1957, he learnt from a BBC broadcast of Camus's reaction the moment he heard about being awarded a Nobel Prize: 'Now I am going into hiding for three weeks, so no one can find me' (BBC article, Beinecke Library).

Camus, in turn, supported Miłosz's books, in particular *The Issa Valley,* which was put out by Gallimard, his own publisher. Even more importantly, Camus displayed understanding and a friendly disposition towards the isolated Polish writer, which at the time were priceless gifts:

> He was one of very few Western intellectuals who shook my hand when, in 1951, I left Stalinist Poland. Others avoided me as if I had a contagious disease or was a sinner . . . To the right—no common language. To the left—total misunderstanding. My political knowledge preceded every-thing by a number of years, that is, the events in 1956. In such a trying situation, friendship warms and offers a minimum of safety, without which we are exposed to the temptations of nihilism. (CM, *Preuves,* April 1960, qtd. in Grémion 145)

For Miłosz, these must have been years of repeated prayers for hope, strength, recovery and the ability to touch the world and regain all his senses. Ideological contamination had a far greater impact on him than on any of his Polish col-leagues, many of whom wrote prescriptive pieces of literature for the new regime, and then quickly and happily forgot them.

Exorcisms

> My memory of seeing Czesław Miłosz for the first time at a lecture on American literature in Paris, around 1950, was how very young he looked, almost boyish. After the lecture, we went with him and Aniela Micińska to a café . . . our conversation moved on to devil creatures in Lithuanian and Hutsul folklore and their disappearance under the pressure of civilisa-tion. We walked out of the café; it was dark outside and Miłosz finished the conversation with his slow Lithuanian accent, saying that little devilish creatures have perished and there is now only one Monstrous Devil instead.
>
> Andrzej Vincenz

> I have the need of and seek the company of professors; there was Oskar Miłosz, Einstein and now, there is you.
>
> Czesław Miłosz to Stanisław Vincenz (1951)

There are exceptional moments—crossing-points carrying meaning and opening the future—in Miłosz's biography. One such occasion was a New Year's Eve in Goszyce, and the beginning of a story about two opposing views of patriotism, about desperate cynicism and loyalty without illusions. Equally unusual was the moment when Miłosz, an artist given to temptation, like Adrian Leverkühn, the protagonist in Thomas Mann's *Dr Faustus,* met Stanisław Vincenz, a Socratic philosopher. Konstanty Jeleński devoted the last essay of his life to this encounter, because he recognised that the meeting of the Poet and the Wise Man was a story line for a great novel.

When Giedroyc gave up hope of having a peaceful relationship with his guest at Laffitte and that Miłosz would make a speedy recovery from the trauma following his defection, he decided to turn for help to Stanisław Vincenz, an able-bodied sexagenarian and an expert in Hutsul culture, who, thanks to his great erudition and his many memories of the southeast corner of Poland, where he grew up, carried around in his head a vast knowledge of Homeric verse and Polish, Ukrainian, Armenian, Roma and Hungarian folktales, which transformed him into an outstanding authority on Eastern European culture.

From a family of French descent, Stanisław Vincenz (1888–1971), the son of a Galician oil producer, graduated from Lwów University, having also studied law, biology, Sanskrit and psychology in Vienna. It was there that he obtained his PhD, examining the influence of Hegel on Feuerbach, before going on to teach himself Russian and translate Dostoyevsky. He served as a soldier in Piłsudski's army in Kiev, and in 1939 became a prisoner of the NKVD. After being freed, he escaped to Hungary and then found a home in Grenoble, which from time to time he left for a family retreat in the small village of La Combe-de-Lancey, at the foot of the Alps, accompanied by his wife, Irena, and his children, Barbara and Andrzej. The old stone cottage, where water had to be drawn from a well, and where there were only tomatoes and polenta bread to eat, catered for many visitors, and sometimes sheets had to be torn in two to accommodate guests. Vincenz, 'tall, heavy built, with a huge round head and a pair of unusual blue eyes, was a friend to everyone. He was visited by the old, children, men, women, everyone . . . to tell him what happened to them or that nothing happened. Everyone sat for a while to be listened to, noticed and loved' (Hersch 257). Miłosz visited La Combe for the first time in late summer 1951, then returned a few times to see Vincenz there as well as in Grenoble, attracted by the radiance generated by this man. Despite the ailments his host suffered from, the poet recognised in his eyes a 'horse of a good breed', which, occasionally, felt the need to kick and stand on his hind legs.

Reading the letters exchanged between them in the early 1950s, one becomes a witness to a lengthy, moving and painful process, which might most aptly be termed exorcisms. After all, the Devil is not only the Prince of Lies, but also of the spirit, and brings despair, takes away hope and pushes one towards death. Miłosz wrote to Vincenz in the autumn of 1951 of how he had 'lost the will to live'. He confessed to his guilt at breaking away from his nation, and to his intellectual helplessness in the face of dialectical materialism, which he could only oppose with disgust:

I only live by intellectual passion, not being able to accept just anything. I would have suffered there and am suffering here and long for something unattainable—a city of sunshine, where everyone would have the joy of common effort and intellectual passion and freedom to discuss things, which is something that Marx or anarchists had in mind. Diamat is a tank . . . I feel like a fly which wants to stand up against that tank . . . By thinking I become unwell, nauseous and physically drained . . . I can't do anything, because my writing is never an act of desperation and I never burden readers with my dark state of mind. For writing I need peace and emotional balance. (CM to Vincenz, December 1951)

———

I think that I truly deserve what had happened to me and that I will pay even more, because I stood up against the historical Zeus. I suspect that sometimes this Zeus is the Zeus *tout court* . . . one ought to accept and share a nation's fate—and here both are the same. Why do you accuse me of being saturated with Diamat, when for me it is a problem of the homeland? (CM to Vincenz, late 1951)

Miłosz struggled with his uprooted state, and so Vincenz's goal was to create a home for him, to make him realise that being in one's homeland did not necessitate being physically present within borders of a country, and that history is not constituted from an assembly of iron rules, but springs from individuals' memories. Vincenz did not try to talk to the Tempter in his language, an abstract speech full of syllogisms. Instead he recounted a story late into the night in the stone cottage as if to teach Miłosz of the need to enter into the heart of stone to find earth's power. He employed a treatment which allowed the poet's pained 'I' to detach itself, patiently explaining, 'You escaped to find your true fate and your inner freedom' (Vincenz to CM, 5 November 1951). Vincenz made him experience the world by touching it with foot and hand, tasting things, humbly taking in its limitless forms, and so prised him away from human madness and Satan's murmured whispers. Vincenz's son called these beautiful wanderings a 'therapy of hope',

practised in the course of walks and excursions in which my father showed him [Miłosz] hope in a tangible form, a spotted beetle, juniper bushes shooting towards the sky . . . in a pastel pink sunset over Saint Eynard on the other side of Izer, or in magnificent chestnuts in La Combe itself . . . All that was like a paper symbol of something else, this or that abstraction, but having the right to its own existence, because it was created by the same Creator, and had the same rights to exist as a human being . . . I had a feeling that after those Parises, Warsaws and

Washingtons, the former village child brought up in Lithuania enjoyed with my father these beetles, cows, wild mushrooms, found unexpectedly in a French forest. (Andrzej Vincenz, from a lecture delivered at Catholic University of Lublin, c.17 October 1987)

Although the therapy did not seem to bear immediate results, gradually it diffused anti-toxins throughout the body. When after a number of years Miłosz could sum up the lesson of hope offered to him by Stanisław Vincenz, he said that it was a counterbalance to fear and the absurd 'whose true names were probably ungodliness and nihilism' (*Zaczynając od moich ulic* 325), and an inability to see anything else apart from 'I', which impoverished the imagination. Nihilism was also 'the feeling that the home country, heavenly and earthly, is lost. Our homeland is what we love. Is it possible to love Heaven devoid of our imaginings about it, or the Earth, whose space turns into abstraction?' (ibid.) Our memory, giving us the sensation that our hand 'which is holding a pen is also the hand of a Byelorussian peasant setting light to a twig during an All Souls festivity, an Indian killed by Cortes . . . and all those who passed on became not just dust to us superior, still living beings, but next to us' (ibid., 308). This enabled one to find a home in any given corner of the world, wrote Miłosz in *A Treatise on Poetry*. But the first sign of hope was a 'recovery poem', 'Mittelbergheim', written in September 1951 and dedicated to Vincenz.

> Wine sleeps in casks of Rhine oak.
> I am wakened by the bell of a chapel in the vineyards
> Of Mittelbergheim. I hear a small spring
> Trickling into a well in the yard, a clatter
> Of sabots in the street. Tobacco drying
> Under the eaves, and ploughs and wooden wheels
> And mountain slopes and autumn are with me.
>
> I keep my eyes closed. Do not rush me,
> You, fire, power, might, for it is too early.
> I have lived through many years and, as in this half-dream,
> I felt I was attaining the moving frontier
> Beyond which color and sound come true
> And the things of this earth are united.
> Do not yet force me to open my lips.
> Let me trust and believe I will attain.
> Let me linger here in Mittelbergheim.
>
> I know I should. They are with me,
> Autumn and wooden wheels and tobacco hung

Under the eaves. Here and everywhere
Is my homeland, wherever I turn
And in whatever language I would hear
The song of a child, the conversation of lovers.
Happier than anyone, I am to receive
A glance, a smile, a star, silk creased
At the knee. Serene, beholding,
I am to walk on hills in the soft glow of day
Over waters, cities, roads, human customs.

Fire, power, might, you who hold me
In the palm of your hand whose furrows
Are like immense gorges combed
By southern wind. You who grant certainty
In the hour of fear, in the week of doubt,
It is too early, let the wine mature,
Let the travelers sleep in Mittelbergheim.

                                                                                    (*NCP* 104)

Daughter of Prophets

I am writing using a typewriter, as I am afraid of writing by hand, because
Jeanne said that my handwriting reveals my psychological illness, so this is
safer.

                                                                 Czesław Miłosz to Stanisław Vincenz

'I would very much like for God the Father to be like Stanisław Vincenz. I would
feel safe everywhere and not only in his house, where I slept better than anywhere else' the philosopher Jeanne Hersch said many years later (qtd. in Andrzej
Vincenz, 'Nie ma wolności'). She had visited the stone cottage in La Combe,
thanks to Czesław Miłosz. Their mutual intellectual fascination quickly turned
into a stormy relationship, which the poet treated, despite all the respect he had
for his lover, as in part functional. It served as another antidote to his depression: 'I cannot exist without Jeanne for this simple reason, that I need her as a
garde-malade, or like a child who is afraid to be left in a dark room', he explained
to Vincenz. 'I have been alone for only a few days and I am already in a terrible
state. How can I explain such things to normal people? Isn't it fantastic and incredible? But that's how it is. I cannot be alone. Things keep happening inside me
which I have no control over' (CM to Vincenz, 4 May 1953). Initially the affair

really brought calm and support, but it soon turned into another battle of minds. Miłosz confided his feelings about Jeanne to his mentor:

> She elevated to the level of moral duty my abandonment of my wife and children for the sake of a literary career which threatened to become a complete fiasco if I did not do that. I am not saying that my friends in Warsaw were wrong in saying that I would end up committing suicide if I were to break ties with Warsaw. I am not denying that Jeanne wasn't right. But it is difficult to exist in the reach of those extended claws and have to listen to her hissing, 'you will perish', alongside the feeling of being a leper and rejected by the world. (CM to Vincenz, probably 1954)

A year older than him, slim, not very tall, with dark hair and olive skin—almost Indian features—she was not a beauty, but that was not what Miłosz was looking for then. He needed a partner with whom he could engage in discussions, someone quick-witted and strong-willed who could take him in hand, and Jeanne did not lack those attributes. She was a descendant of Polish Jews—her father had emigrated from Wilno to Switzerland at the beginning of the century—and, like Hannah Arendt, was a student of Karl Jaspers (1883–1969), the renowned philosopher, who was a professor at the University of Geneva. At the Congress for Cultural Freedom in Brussels in 1950 she made friends with Giedroyc and Czapski, who later introduced her to Miłosz. He later tried to sketch a complicated portrait of an individual whom he regarded as 'slightly unearthly', worthy of belonging to 'a lineage of prophets' by the purity of her soul and passion.

On 20 March 1952 Miłosz moved with Jeanne into the Trianon Hotel, on rue de Vaugirard, in the heart of the Latin Quarter, next to Boulevard Saint Michel and the Luxembourg Gardens. In June they travelled together south to the Dordogne, an area so beautiful and graceful that the poet wrote later that people chose to live there, 'moved by a Platonic recollection of Paradise' (*NR* 293). They stayed in a small town called Montpon-on-Isle, west of Bordeaux, at a small hotel where 600 francs covered accommodation and meals at the Golden Cockerel Inn in the town square. Swimming and kayaking did the poet a lot of good, as he reported to Vincenz: 'I am a calm pig, because I weigh thirteen stones, the first time in my life I have had so much fat on me, whereas I ought to be just over 11 stone' (CM to Vincenz, 1952). Life flowed past like a sleepy river. History never quite reached there; the greatest event was an angling competition, and 'the local police station represented the state and had absolutely nothing to do, so the policemen filled their time growing roses . . . On Sundays in the square an orchestra played, consisting of a chemist, a joiner, a teacher and a post-office worker' (Miłosz, BBC talk, 14 January 1956). Permission to stay in France had to be renewed every month in the mayor's office, and the poet wrote about the clerk, a descendant of generations of bureaucrats:

> He spent a long time looking at instructions, trying to work out what to do when there were problems with my papers. In the end he pushed away files of documents, stamped my papers and said, 'I have no idea what it is about, but anyone who sees this stamp will not understand anything anyway and in the end that's what it's all about'. ('Rivière')

Departing from Paris was not meant to be a holiday, but an escape from the noise of the big city, from reading Polish papers at the editorial offices of *Kultura,* and from the daily brooding over the past; all this provided favourable conditions for writing a new book. In May, Hersch came across an announcement of a newly established prize, the Prix Littéraire Européen, awarded by Centre Européen de la Culture in Geneva and funded by an association of book clubs, Communauté Européenne des Guildes et Clubs du Livre. The requirements were that the entry must be an unpublished book, written in one of the western European languages, and be sent to the committee before 1 October 1952. The prize was 10,000 Swiss francs and royalties from the sales of the winning book. It was only recently that Miłosz had explained to Jeanne that he ought to free himself from obsessively going over the past, perhaps by incorporating it into a work of fiction. She responded by placing a newspaper clipping referring to the literary prize in front of him, and promising that she would translate his book into French. Hersch's insistence combined with the thought of a looming deadline energised him, and he immediately imposed a rigorous regime on himself to ensure the writing progressed rapidly. He spent the summer months in Montpon, mainly in his room in the Golden Well hotel, working seven or eight hours each day, avoiding wine from the local vineyards of St Emilion, because on a hot day a glass would make him sleepy. Only in the evenings did he find time to swim. Later he remembered those days, when filling up page after page held at bay his self-preoccupation:

> I was drawn to people who kept appearing on paper by the touch of my pen. There were more and more of them, they demanded to be heard; unique characters, not doubles of the author, were developing as their existence demanded ... It probably isn't a good book, I was saying to myself, but through it I fulfil, at least in part, what I promised the people who had died. If I can learn, if I am capable of recalling from memory faces and gestures of those that were not a copy of me, it means that I can do it in future and in prose, not poetry only, and fulfil my duty, which runs in line with my ambition (we are not noble spirits only), so that they are

almost one. (unfinished manuscript, on *The Seizure of Power*, Beinecke Library)

Every day, when he finished another short chapter, he read it out to Jeanne, who immediately began to translate it. This way, *The Seizure of Power* was written in three months, a micro-account of the birth of the People's Republic of Poland, encompassing the period between the Warsaw Rising in August 1944 and the Stalinist post-war era. Its tone is aptly expressed in a quotation from the prophet Jeremiah which was clearly meant to be used as an epigraph, but in the end was left out. It survived with the manuscript of the novel in the Beinecke Library Archive: 'From a prophet to a pontiff—everyone pays homage to a lie. Prophets and priests alike, all practice deceit. They dress the wound of my people as though it were not serious. "Peace, peace", they say when there is no peace' (Jeremiah 8:10). The book is written in a simple, direct style, with short sentences, often semi-sentences, which perhaps reveal haste and dislike for the extended process of novel-writing. Overall it is more of a successful practice piece than a great achievement. What is noticeable, however, is how gradually the author becomes more confident and fluent, although always, as with *The Issa Valley* later on, he finds it easier to write a description than to convey a protagonist's thoughts or provide convincing dialogue.

After the book was finished, Miłosz and Hersch spent a few days by the sea at Sanary in Provence, and then, having visited the Vincenz family, returned to Paris. By that time French jurors in different countries were making the initial selection for the Prix Littéraire Européen from over 350 entries. During a meeting in Geneva, on 24 March 1953, the top prize was awarded to two winners, a German writer, Werner Warsinski, and Czesław Miłosz. At the time, 5,000 francs was a substantial sum of money, and the winner could rely on receiving royalties from subsequent editions. In the autumn of 1953, *The Seizure of Power* came out in Switzerland, France and Germany, and, in the following years, in Great Britain, the United States and Spain, thus bringing Miłosz the beginnings of financial security.

Early in April, while visiting Switzerland to receive the award, Miłosz became acquainted with a new intellectual-artistic circle whose members included Denis de Rougemont (a poet), Jean-Paul de Dadelsen (a painter and sculptor), Robert Hainard (an author of books about ecology and the philosophy of nature), and Helen Naef (a translator of Jaspers's work into French). The latter's house in Mont-sur-Rolle by the banks of Leman would be recalled in *Native Realm*. Together with Jeanne Hersch, they went to Basel to pay Karl Jaspers a visit. The philosopher, who had just finished reading a German translation of *The Captive Mind*, was 'very moved by the book', and 'the conversation went really well', as Miłosz noted in a report on the visit to Giedroyc.

The first readers of both the French translation and the Polish original of *The Seizure of Power* had divided opinions and, so to speak, balanced each other out. The warmest reception of the book came from Stanisław Vincenz and Konstanty Jeleński. The latter asserted:

> Naturally, I was sceptical (because I do not believe in the possibility of a 'social novel'). I still have some reservations ... But in your case, poetry, combined with intelligence, saves the case ... You are an exceptional literary phenomenon: one of the first contemporary lyrical poets writing a philosophical essay of such calibre as *The Captive Mind* and then a novel you cannot be ashamed of. (Jeleński to CM, 22 September 1953)

A writer and psychologist, Manes Sperber, pointed out the author's inability to render the feelings of the insurgents and his fascination with the world of victors. Czapski made similar observations, stating that the 'vision of this world ... is after all *un peu* CLICHÉ, the underground army, the Jews, the stupidity of landlords and the iron wisdom of the Bolsheviks (where, as in Koestler, it is possible to sense a restrained admiration)' (Czapski to CM, 8 November 1952). A lot of attention was paid to the book by Bolesław Taborski, a representative of young intellectual circles in London, who, in contrast to the older émigrés, was convinced that Miłosz needed to be taken very seriously. He appreciated that the poet had taken on such an important issue and drew attention to the book's economy of language and its skill in presenting a Marxist way of looking at the world, which leaves us with a choice between two possibilities, 'reactionary capitalism and inhuman communism' (Taborski, *Merkuriusz*).

The poet regarded Gombrowicz's critique as the most accurate, when in 1954 he wrote about *The Captive Mind, The Seizure of Power* and *Daylight:*

> Miłosz allowed History to dictate not only the theme, but also some certain stances, which I would call the stance of a converted man. Does he rebel? Yes, he does, but using means which the opponent will accept. It looks like he believed in communism, but that he is now a crushed intellectual and stood up to fight the final heroic battle as a crushed intellectual ... Being afraid of cliché and denying himself any luxury, he, Miłosz, who is loyal and dependable towards his brothers in crisis, wants to be poor like them. But such an intention in the artist does not accord with the nature of his actions, because art is a luxury, a freedom, a playing, a dreaming and might. Art is born not out of poverty but from riches, and it comes into existence not when things are down, but when they are up. Art has in itself something triumphant, even when it wrings its hands in despair. A man who will refuse to become

poor will respond to Marxism with a different kind of art, reflecting the unexpected richness of life. Has Miłosz managed to make the final effort to come out of the dialectics that fettered him? (Gombrowicz, *Dziennik* 150–151)

Miłosz later wrote about Jeanne Hersch, the translator of *The Seizure of Power:*

> She was for me a pretty good instructor in mental climbing and I felt really uplifted whenever she said, *'De nouveau tu as oublié d'être bête'*, which, in loose translation, meant, 'You have forgotten again how to be stupid'. She existed on the border of philosophy and theology . . . I appreciated in her her piety, because she really was a priestess of transcendence or a voice subjugated to a calling from high above. And in the name of that I was and am prepared to forgive her faults. (*Rok myśliwego* 325)

These faults were not minor, reinforced by her passionate temperament. She constantly generated cascades of words and was unable to accept moderation in anything, which applied to love too.

> She used to provoke such rows that we could not stay in Geneva and that was really the reason for our return to Paris. I am a humble man who wants an intellectual partner, but what Jeanne wants I don't really know. If she wants to break up my family, it's not going to happen. In fact I looked at her with horror, as if a devil got into her and muddled her mind. She wants to save my soul and my genius, but it strangely coincides with her interests. (CM to Vincenz, n.d. 1953)

Having now secured financial stability, Miłosz finally applied for visas to bring Janka and his sons over to France. The love-stricken Jeanne desperately fought to keep their relationship going, dissuading Miłosz from going to America, and suffering at the news that his family had arrived, unable to accept the fact that he was not going to abandon them. She was totally devoted to him and at the same time possessive, and so at some point lost, when the man she had dominated decided to free himself by living separately. It was probably during that time that the poet lived in rented rooms, including Denfert-Rochereau 83, which forty years before was occupied by the Society of Polish Artists in Paris, one of whose not-so-active members was Oskar Miłosz.

But the separation from Hersch was neither easy nor quick. In May 1953, Miłosz took stock: 'Setting up a family life on the European continent is nerve-racking. I can exist only with a *garde-malade,* while Janka's and the children's presence multiplies my levels of anxiety. I have this physical sensation of crumbling and altering that I can do nothing about'. He tried to describe to Vincenz the causes of his paralysing fear. Even after Janka's arrival, it would not be easy for him to cut all contacts with Jeanne, although he tried. Writing to Giedroyc from Geneva, where he attended a conference in 1953, he said that it was essential 'for both parties to be happy and everything free of complications' (CM to Giedroyc, ca. 2–12 September 1953).

When Jeanne found herself alone and rejected, though unable to abandon hope, her situation was far more difficult. She turned to Vincenz, a wise 'rabbi', for help, an assessment of the situation, a decision, which, best of all, might result in her lover returning. Even in mid-June 1954, the inhabitants of La Combe had to calm Jeanne down after her outbursts of despair and jealousy. In the end the relationship between the philosopher and the poet finally developed into a friendship in their old age, when in their eighties they spent a holiday together in Guadeloupe. As in the past, she was principled, and embittered by the stupidity that lorded it over our civilisation, while he was still sensuous, living in a bubble, and composing in his head a poem about her. After her death on 5 June 2000, he wrote down everything that he had learnt from her, a list worth quoting in full and memorising:

1. That the mind is God's great gift and one ought to trust in its capacity to learn about the world.

2. Those who undermined trust in the mind were wrong in claiming that it was dependent on class war, libido and will power.

3. That we ought to be aware that we are locked within the sphere of our experiences, and should not interpret reality according to our dreams and figments of our imagination.

4. That truthfulness is a proof of freedom, and deceit reveals a state of captivity.

5. That the right attitude to existence is respect. It is vital then to avoid the company of people who degrade existence with sarcasm, and condone nothingness.

6. That even though it might prompt accusations of arrogance, intellectual life follows strict hierarchical rules.

7. That the habit of twentieth-century intellectuals was mindless blabber.

8. That in the hierarchy of human activities, art takes a higher position than philosophy, but bad philosophy can spoil art.

9. That there is objective truth, which means that out of two opposing statements only one is true and the other false,

apart from exceptional cases when accepting the opposites is
acceptable.

10. That independent of the fates of different religions, we ought to
keep 'philosophical faith', that is, belief in transcendence, as an
important feature of our humanity.

11. That time excludes and condemns to oblivion only those products
of our minds and hands which will prove useless in building the
great edifice of civilisation, which is humanity's continuous task.

And one more conviction, most important, which became for Miłosz in his fifties and later a source of hope in his perpetual struggle with *delectatio morosa*, his
dwelling on sins and misdeeds:

12. That in life one ought not succumb to despair over past mistakes
and sins, because the past is not a closed chapter and becomes
meaningful through our later acts. (*O podróżach w czasie* 159)

'Beyond tears'

I am scared of us falling into their hands.
Janina Miłosz to her husband, n.d.

Janka's interventions with the State Department ... were destined to be
fruitless, and her outburst must have been absolutely incomprehensible for
the bureaucrats when she shouted out: 'You'll regret it, because he's going to
win the Nobel Prize'.
Czesław Miłosz, *ABC* 32

Although she found it hard to stay calm in the circumstances, Janka wrote a
letter to Miłosz on 12 March 1951:

Sometimes I regret deeply that I did not stop you from going. But when
I remember your attacks directed at me—then what argument could I
use to stop you? You would blame me for it for the rest of your life. Now
we have to suffer. You must realise how naïve were your expectations.
Tough. I beg you for one thing—if you love us—be calm and patient.

She was left without support just after the birth of their second son and at
the end of her tether; she was terrified by her husband's situation, fearing that
he might be kidnapped, taken to Poland and imprisoned, particularly given the

times, when political cases brought to trial often ended with death sentences. She wanted Miłosz to lie low, get a visa and come to the United States, and, if that was not possible, to settle down in England, because France, to her mind, was too close to Moscow. She did not want to risk her sons' lives and kept warning him: 'There will be a second wave of hatred directed at you and they will rub their hands when they hear that we settled there. Because there, they can get to us easily' (Janka to CM, 3 November 1952).

At first Janka could not even imagine going back to Europe. On 9 February she asked for political asylum and began organising her life in the States. She was helped by friends, among them the Borowiks and Thornton Wilder, who appeared to be very sympathetic. But all she had to rely on was a mere handful of friends, and when Czapski met her again during one of his trips to the States, he found her very lonely, unwell and exhausted. She had no sources of income; any savings they had were disappearing quickly, and she could not undertake any work, having two young children to look after. She received limited help from humanitarian organisations such as the International Rescue Committee, which sent her a monthly cheque for the meagre sum of thirty-five to fifty dollars, while the rent for her flat in Washington was one hundred dollars. In the end she moved to the small provincial town of York, Pennsylvania. An old friend, Ignacy Święcicki, was beginning a new chapter in his life there. He had been a pupil at a gymnasium in Wilno, then studied in Warsaw, and when the war started reached the western front and served as a pilot in England. After the war, he emigrated to the States. There he met a colleague of Miłosz's from the embassy, Anna Giebułtowicz, who agreed to become his wife. About a week after the wedding, Janka joined them in York with Antoni and Piotr, sharing the cost of the rent, and experiencing the good and bad aspects that come with two different families living daily under one roof.

She certainly was not a good house-mate, as she was exhausted by her situation, and so could be sarcastic, short-tempered and difficult to please, not making any effort to be a good friend to Anna, but rather, on the contrary, being somewhat condescending. Her ever-hostile presence brought a great deal of disruption to the life of the childless middle-aged couple. Separation from her husband, bringing up children on her own, and the uncertainty of the family's fate drove Janka to despair. Piotr grew quickly and seemed to resemble his father, 'delicate, friendly, but short-tempered'. He used to steal the limelight and was adored by everyone, leaving Antoni in the shadows. Despite that, the older brother was well disposed towards him and even said one day, 'Didn't we get the best baby from God?' (Janka to CM, 2 September 1951).

The life of the four and then five year-old Antoni was much harder than Piotr's. Janka wrote to Czesław: 'Today I got out your big photographs, because he [Antoni] said that he forgot what you looked like. This is totally heart-breaking for me. "O yes, this is our Daddy", he shouted out. When it started to rain, I had to reassure him that you are indoors like us and you will not get cold' (Janka to CM, 2 May 1951). Another time Janka described Antoni as a slightly anaemic, very sensitive, intelligent and musically talented little boy who could spend hours listening to Beethoven, and who was developing much faster spiritually than physically. At school he demonstrated his individuality, which made him stand out from his peers.

Janka made frequent trips to Washington to enlist support for their cause with different institutions, and stood in queues for hours at the State Department, where her dealings with the American immigration officers bore a striking resemblance to scenes from Franz Kafka's novel *The Trial*. She had to put up a fight on two fronts, urging Czesław to act, while at the same time trying to lessen his stress: 'There is no need for you to feel hurt or humiliated when it comes to the visa, because there is no point and it makes life difficult' (Janka to CM, 15 August 1951). From his letters it appears that he lost heart over making further efforts to obtain a U.S. visa. He was in all probability offended by the Americans' suspicious attitude towards him, and also, when things quieted down, afraid of losing his poetic gift in exile: 'The University of Chicago wants to employ you for a year . . . apparently they are keen and serious about it. Would you take it? . . . Do you think that twelve to fifteen hours a week would stop you from writing? In my view, delivering pieces of writing on demand with short deadlines is more likely to destroy you' (Janka to CM, 7 November 1952). After she had applied for a French visa at his request, she was still hoping that matters would turn out differently and that they might be able to remain in America. She went on to plead with her husband to request an interview with the American consul in Paris, to be calm, not to argue, and in the end to be honest: 'Everyone here thinks that while I am killing myself here, you sit there feeling bruised and offended, not moving a finger' (Janka to CM, 30 November 1952). The principal problem, however, did not lie in Miłosz's fiery temperament or his dislike of dealing with bureaucrats. The disagreement harked back to the late forties, when Janka accepted America as the best option, since it placed them at a healthy distance from war-stricken Europe, and was a country in which they would feel safe and at home: 'My whole fight is for the children not to become *étrangers*, and I do not see protecting them from that outcome as a great sacrifice.' By contrast, he wanted their children to be brought up in closer proximity to Poland and its affairs, and blamed her for Americanising them, fearing that, being brought up there, they would never develop 'intellectual passion'. In addition, he clearly felt better in France, where his writing was gaining greater recognition and benefiting from a small but nevertheless supportive environment.

Each pictured the move to the other side of the world as a painful sacrifice, which was the source of the long, intense impasse which ruined their relationship. To Vincenz, Miłosz depicted his reading of the problem thus:

I have pleaded and used threats, urging my wife to come here, but with no success . . . I forbade her to make any further attempts to get an American visa, because I could not stand all that begging, trying to get permission to be admitted there. I explained that I would be able to earn a living from writing here, but not there. All to no avail. I learnt and still do about her new efforts to get a visa for me without my consent or knowledge. In the end she put in an application for a French visa . . . After receiving this award [Prix Littéraire Européen for *The Seizure of Power*] I got a letter from her, most of which was about an American visa. This prize, it seems, is partly confirmation that I have left America, a sign that my fate is here. I replied that if she wants to, she can stay in America and I will send them money each month. That's our situation. And when I think about Antoni my eyes well up and I can't understand anything. If she were happy there [it would be different], but no, she suffers and struggles with two small children. This insistence on America has a manic dimension—is she mad or am I an idiot, I ask myself sometimes. In her opinion Europe is the end, death, plague, but I can't think about it, because if I were to do that, I couldn't exist or write, and it is all in God's hands anyway. And her every letter shatters what is my unstable confidence, reminds me about these things, makes me wonder whether I am really a lunatic and a family destroyer. (CM to Vincenz, 14 April 1953)

Things got to the point of being on a knife-edge when in a June issue of the *New York Herald Tribune* the Miłoszes' stalemate was referred to in a letter from the American Committee for Cultural Freedom. He was furious and gave Janka an ultimatum either to join him or prepare for the marriage to end. In response, he received a telegram saying that she and the children would arrive in France in mid-July. This was followed up with a long and moving letter from her which indicates that he had revealed his relationship with Jeanne Hersch, and also how painful the breakup would be for Jeanne and the sacrifice it would mean. Her reply:

I love you . . . We have hurt each other and now we have to forgive. It is wrong that you introduced an emotional element from a third party. You shouldn't have done it and now write to me about the 'tragedy' my arrival is going to be to someone else . . . Czesław, I expect us to create a strong and stable home for our children, that there will be no things on the side or tragedies. If my arrival is a tragedy for her, then you ought to take the blame. For me a situation where one party is unfaithful would be a death blow. It would break me and destroy me . . . But you kept saying in your letters that you loved me and the children, and this is the base I hope to build on . . . I am very tired and a letter such as this, in such a harsh tone, takes away what courage I have. 'I take half the blame . . . and you take the other half . . . Is that clear?'

My heart hurts so much and I can barely move. I would like to have enough strength to cope with it all, but will I? I only want to sleep. I hardly sleep at night . . . You don't know yet what it means to bring up children . . . A father's role is difficult and you have to take it on. Learn it. This is not something you drop when you get tired. I count on you to share this burden with me. Say to yourself, as I do, that we must make reuniting our family a success . . . it's not worth the half-hearted effort . . . Admit to yourself some of your traits: egoism, crazy egoism (I have arguments and proofs that you can make someone suffer in order to be happy yourself, the latest example being Jeanne Hersch) . . . It is not a reason not to share your fate, our fate, no, but yes I will share it, I made my mind up a long time ago. ('Materiały do mojej biografii')

They had reached a critical point. Towards the end of his life, he would admit that 'it felt as if it was the end of the marriage, a spiritual separation, since I observed how alien to her my inner torment was' (ibid.). But what of her feelings? She did not leave behind any memoirs, and we will never learn how much love remained in her, and how much what drove her was the need to give their children a home. Did he stay with her out of a sense of duty? Did she come to terms with that and tolerate later infidelities? Who can assess, encompass and pass judgment on the multiplicity of emotions uniting two people, in which indifference and attachment, cruelty and tenderness, co-exist; the separations and returns that follow may puzzle even them. The fact is that we are looking at the situation from the outside, and are incapable of understanding it. Ultimately, they stayed together, and, when all the suffering eased, chose to cement their relationship by getting married at last.

Janka had not been able to get a divorce in 1943, because Eugeniusz Cękalski was then in London. There were a number of occasions when she and Miłosz agreed on a date, but the wedding took place much later. A certificate exists for the marriage of Czesław Miłosz and Anna Dłuska at the Church of the Ascension of St Mary in Paris, which is located in rue Saint Honoré 263 bis. A document can be seen there stating that Augustyn Gałęzowski, the priest conducting the service, saw a civil marriage certificate from a magistrate's court in Warsaw, dated 1 January 1944. The witnesses present were Władysław

Szynakiewicz, also a priest in that parish, who frequently was asked to serve as a witness, and Anastazja Marecka, who lived in Gentilly. The marriage certificate is dated 13 January 1956.

'Enough of this lethargy and fighting'

I need Warsaw magazines, *Nowa Kultura, Twórczość, Myśl Filozoficzna*. I can't function without keeping in contact with the country. I also need a Polish first reading book for Antek.

Czesław Miłosz to Jerzy Giedroyc (14 September 1953)

We will try to get the book.

Jerzy Giedroyc to Czesław Miłosz (16 September 1953)

Janka set off for France thinking that she might be making the biggest mistake of her life, not knowing how changed, how close or distant, Miłosz might prove to be. One of her friends drove her to Canada, where she could take a much cheaper liner from Quebec which had been chartered by students going on a holiday. On 12 July she and the boys arrived in Le Havre, where Miłosz was waiting; from there the four of them travelled to Bons, a village situated on the French side of Lake Leman.

Miłosz rented accommodation for them in a house belonging to a Miss Charmot: three rooms and a kitchen, with one heater for the entire building, which in the autumn they were to find was by no means ideal. Until then it was not a major issue. Above all, Janka wanted a peaceful village life and to enjoy nature in the surrounding area, which for Czesław was 'absolutely heavenly. It consisted of a landscape of gentle slopes, covered with forests, and fifty metres up a path from which you could see Leman' (CM to Vincenz, 18 July 1953). He let Giedroyc know, with a hint of satisfaction, that

> after all the kerfuffle with shifting trunks, crates, chests, bundles and general luggage, as if it was a move from Mars to the Moon, I have set-tled with the family here, where we have comfortable accommodation in a beautiful area and I hope that the low rent will recompense for the financial burden created by the travelling costs . . . I begin a new chapter in life and perhaps I ought to grow a beard the better to fulfil my new role as *pater familias*. The children like to stay close to me and are very sweet. Toni said that he likes it *awfully* here. As to the younger one, he is sharp and more phlegmatic. (CM to Giedroyc, July 1953)

To Vincenz he wrote a letter that was more preoccupied with himself and his fairly complicated emotions, as if after a long run he could stop at last, though he was not sure yet whether the pause would suit him:

> I am concerned about a number of things, such as the fact that Janka is completely absorbed in looking after the children and always tired, and not very competent in running the household. I have the burden of making sure that we have enough to eat, relying on the meagre financial means available. I am confined within the four walls of my room to express my reactions to the world outside, because the world she belongs to is at present the children's room or the world of plants, a more vegetative sense of existence than mine. There are some definitely good points in that for me, but at the same time it brings loneliness. And, as you know, the two women are like fire and water: stormy arguments with Jeanne, being at each other's throats with shouting and swearing when discussing principles . . . and suddenly a totally different situation, where my explosions, hatred, despair etc., cannot find an object to be directed at. The final period with Jeanne was very hard, my nerves couldn't cope any longer, and so I think that I am now more normal. (CM to Vincenz, 18 July 1953)

Along with more familiar activities, such as participating in the annual Rencontres Internationales conference in Geneva, during which he discussed philosophical and literary issues, he engaged in family life, doing the shopping, taking his wife and children to see *Kultura*'s new premises, reciting serious and light children's poetry to his boys, watching a 'movie' Antoni made of *Treasure Island* (recorded music played to moving pictures on a revolving tape). He made sure that his older son obtained a copy of *Elementarz,* the first reading book used in Polish schools, because little Antoni was about to start school. There he was at the top of his class and recited with his fellow pupils: 'Our forefathers, the Gauls, had blond hair and blue eyes'. During breaks, the children would sing, to the tune of 'La Marseillaise': 'Allons pisser sur le gazon,/Pour ennuyer les coccinelles,/Allons pisser sur le gazon/Pour ennuyer les papillons' (Let's wee on the lawn to annoy the ladybirds/let's wee on the lawn to annoy the butterflies). When the first cold spell came, the writer started looking for a new place to rent that would be warmer and closer to Paris. At the end of October they moved to a new house belonging to a farmer, M. Benier. It was at Place de Bergeries 4, in a small town, Brie-Comte-Robert, which was proud of its castle ruins—where the boys looked for bullet shells and rusting German helmets—and also of its ugly cathedral, and which was an hour's bus ride away from the Bastille Square. With eight bedrooms, a garage and a garden, the property was far too big, at least for Janka, who was getting weaker as a result of her deteriorating health. It had central heating, which required carrying coal from the cellar to the boiler room, thus giving the poet an opportunity to improve his physical condition, which was needed because of the long hours he spent sitting at his desk. In time, they acquired a piano for Toni, as he was usually called, along with a tortoise called Joachim, a dog, Dico, and a cat which ate the goldfish. The first thing that had to be done was to have good clear-out, followed by cleaning and renovation work.

Not long ago Miłosz had borrowed a hundred francs from Hertz to buy cigarettes. Now here he was, with enough funds to rent a house. However, he was still far from having financial stability and lived from one publication to another. 'Always when they ran out of money, Janka used to go to Czesław and say, "Czesiu, lay a golden egg". And then, reluctantly, Miłosz set to write an essay for someone, who would pay him a larger sum of money', said the editor of *Kultura*, who himself would pay very little. More important as sources of funds were honoraria from *Preuves*, articles written for the BBC, and a German edition of *The Seizure of Power*, though these barely covered the costs of the most basic things. At times Janka felt uneasy going to the local shop, where they were given credit, because the debt they had amassed was getting out of hand. Whenever he went to Paris, Czesław had in his pocket only enough cash for his bus fare and a glass of wine. It reminded him of his student times, but it was not a happy memory:

> Anyone who has experienced poverty knows. Knows the fear, what will happen tomorrow, where will I find money for dinner? I can't buy cigarettes. Worse than the shortage of material things is the feeling of degradation and exclusion. There, where everyone is poor, it is reasonably easy to cope with poverty. It is harder when every restaurant you pass reminds you that everyone can go there except you, because it is too expensive. I feel shy crossing the threshold of a plush hotel, and from the eyes of the porters and waiters, I can guess that they know the paltry amount of cash I have in my pocket, and even paying for a cup of coffee amounts to a big problem, while for others it is nothing. ('Pieniądze', Beinecke Library Archive)

Uncertain about tomorrow, fighting with editors and, what is more, seeing Janka unhappy and isolated by having so little French, he felt guilty for forcing the family to leave America. Yet, there were some cloudless times too, like a holiday in 1955, when he was given a down payment for a French edition of *The Issa Valley*, and they could afford to go to the Ile d'Oléron on the Atlantic Ocean, close to La Rochelle, where Toni began to learn to swim. In September that year the writer took part in a conference in Milan on the future of freedom, organised by the Congress for Cultural Freedom to mark its fifth anniversary. Here he met

Dwight Macdonald, and later joined an international group of friends, including Nicola Chiaromonte and his wife, Miriam Rosenthal Chiaromonte, to spend a few days in the seaside village of Boca di Magra, near Carrara:

> The sheer pleasure of swimming, lying about on marble slabs, and going for a swim again. My reflection on this now: during my stay there, I had a feeling that time should always be like those moments of happiness in the marble inlet, but at the same time I experienced sorrow that that is not how it is, because my familiar pangs of conscience gnaw at me from inside. (*ABC* 64–65)

A year later the Miłosz family visited Italy again, for a longer period this time, spending time in the Aosta valley in the western Alps. Their companions on the trip were their American friends Mac and Sheba Goodman, who perhaps covered the cost of the holiday.

———————

'People in the West like to live in the heaven of exalted expressions about spirituality and freedom, but hardly ever ask the question as to whether someone has enough money for dinner. Not many people cared for my humble body, so their kindness is even more dear to me today' (*NR* 326), drily commented Miłosz in later years. Though he had entered the circles of the intellectual elite of contemporary Europe, he still remained a poor emigrant, putting a brave face on things, and looking for help in America. He spent time sitting in the Paris branch of the International Rescue Committee, a humanitarian organisation which exists to this day. Sheba Goodman, who worked there, sometimes received Polish applicants who were hoping to find, if not someone who understood their problems as Central European emigrants, at least a measure of generosity.

Miłosz clearly stood out from this crowd, because he got on good terms with the Goodmans and became a frequent guest in their beautiful apartment, which had a 'bar behind which Mac liked to celebrate. Their house was open, warm, welcoming, and they very often gave parties and dinners. And in a sense this house was my refuge' (*Rok myśliwego* 317). Sheba's husband was a legal adviser at the American embassy for the oil industry and, thanks to the very high exchange rate of the dollar, his salary meant that they could afford a comfortable life in France, which was a new experience for two left-wing New Yorkers from poor Jewish emigrant families. Mac, unfulfilled as a poet, used his work hours at the embassy to polish a translation of Paul Valéry's *The Sea Cemetery* and his own poems, two of which Miłosz translated into Polish and published in *Kultura*. Many guests milled through the living room in the avenue du General Leclerc.

Miłosz met there, among others, Bertram Wolfe, a historian who specialised in the subject of communism, the Indian philosopher Raja Rao, and the editor-in-chief of *Partisan Review,* William Philips.

> Friendship with the Goodmans continued after Janka's arrival with the children, when we lived in Brie-Comte-Robert. The arrival of their long car outside was received each time by Toni and little Piotr with so much joy, despite their frequent visits, as if it were a family festivity, because, after all, we did not have any other family. (*Rok myśliwego* 318)

Far more complicated were relations with Hannah Benzion, a Czech Jew and an immigrant, who had survived the war on a farm in the Dordogne, and who now managed the French branch of Interrescue.

> My acquaintance with Hannah ... started on the wrong footing. I did not make a good impression, as she told me later. I was sombre, shy, aloof, which was enough to raise suspicions. Then gradually, after the arrival of the family, Hannah's doubts turned into love for us, especially towards the children, but a fanatical love in its exclusivity. (*Rok myśliwego* 319)

What Miłosz discreetly omitted to mention was that this fanatical devotion had at its heart Hannah Benzion's unfulfilled desire for the writer. She belonged, in Hertz's description, to the type of intellectual who is full of energy and curiosity about the world, absorbing everything that had anything to do with culture. Immersed in European leftist history, and a onetime friend of Trotsky's, she introduced Miłosz to Alfred Rosmer, co-founder of the French Communist Party, later 'a renegade', a historian of revolutionary movements, and author of *Moscow under Lenin* and many books on Trotskyism. Among the other notables he met through her were the philosopher and painter Pierre Klossowski, and Simone Weil's mother. Salomea Weil told him a beautiful anecdote about Albert Camus, how the writer, having received the Nobel Prize, rang her doorbell and told her that 'he must go to Simone's room to think' (*Podróżny świata* 248).

Hannah's possessiveness expressed itself in attempting to dissuade Miłosz and his family from going to America towards the end of the fifties, and in long letters analysing how Antoni and Piotr were being brought up, as well as how Janka's total concentration on the welfare of the family allowed no space in her world for anyone else. However, it was Hannah who helped them get their next house by introducing them to her rich friends Muriel and Joseph Buttinger. Muriel, née Gardiner, had inherited a fortune from American meat moguls and was by profession a psychiatrist and a student of psychoanalysis. In the 1930s in Vienna, she married Joseph, a socialist and subsequently an expert and a writer on Vietnam, with whom she collaborated in anti-fascist underground activities.

After the outbreak of the Second World War, they managed to travel back to the United States, and in the fifties often visited Paris, where they entertained leading artists and writers, such as Stephen Spender. Miłosz owed a debt of gratitude to them not just for enabling him to obtain a grant from the American New-Land Foundation to write *Native Realm,* but also for providing an interest-free loan to buy a house. The Miłosz family were looking for a new base outside Paris, which was far too dear. Hannah Benzion suggested Montgeron, on the outskirts of the capital, with access to the city by electric train to the Gare de Lyon. It also had an excellent school for Toni. She found a spacious house in a big garden at number 10, avenue de la Grange. Thanks to the $21,000 loan generously provided by the Buttingers, the family ended their stay in Brie in July 1957.

> The black River Jerres bursts its banks each spring and for the rest of the summer there is lush green grass on the sodden meadows. When Mick- iewicz, the Polish Romantic poet, spent a holiday here in 1853, he could look at these meadows and gentle slopes on the other side, but certainly without the red roof-tops: it resembles the landscape where people went horse-riding near Kaunas, and the valley of my Niewiaża. (Unpublished sketch, Beinecke Library Archive)

Miłosz is describing here the area round Soisy-sur-Seine, Étiolles and the Sénart Forest, a mirror image of his childhood landscape, which he would miss in Cali- fornia. Janka loved the setting too: 'An excellent place, a splendid place, a place that cannot be compared to anywhere else, a place where you are in a won- derful village close to civilisation . . . that is Montgeron' (CM and JM to Aniela Micińska, 29 August 1957). Despite complaining about having too many things to do, the poet quickly settled down; he mowed lawns with fervour and nailed bird boxes for the blue tits to the cedars in the garden. Before long, after con- suming a few bottles of red wine, guests from Poland would be sleeping there on a borrowed ottoman from *Kultura.*

Apart from vacations and shorter trips, like the wonderful week in Por- tofino, where they met Aleksander Wat and Gustaw Herling-Grudziński in April 1960, Miłosz spent long spells in his study, writing more articles, which Janka later typed out on a Smith Corona with a Polish keyboard. However, he did travel a lot in August 1957, to the Collège de l'Europe Libre in Strasbourg to give a talk, and to London, where Stefan Kisielewski tried to talk him into writing a follow-up to *The Captive Mind.* A year later he ran classes in Jugendburg Gemen, Germany, where in the evenings he enjoyed the company of international stu- dents, sitting at a long table in an inn, singing songs. In 1959 there was a similarly convivial atmosphere in Berne, where Vincenz's seventieth birthday celebrations were held, and later in Brussels, when Miłosz was a guest at a conference organised by the Imre Nagy Institute of Social Sciences on the third anniversary of the tragic events in Hungary.[1] In 1960 he visited Germany twice, in January to give a lecture in Cologne, and in June in Berlin, on the tenth anniversary Congress for Cultural Freedom, where he met Robert Oppenheimer, 'the father of the atom bomb'. In 1960 he also travelled to Copenhagen to discuss welfare states and literature. Invitations such as these, as well as ones to many other cultural and literary events, made it apparent that Miłosz was now receiving and enjoying considerable recognition in European literary circles.

'To be able to earn a living through writing'

A writer's situation in exile is hopeless. You must say to yourself that you will not manage to cope financially by writing alone. The only person who manages that and with a great deal of effort is Miłosz.

Jerzy Giedroyc to Teodor Parnicki (1955)

'I have so much work to do that I have changed into a bear sucking not a paw, but a pipe all day long, and I hardly ever go into town, that is, Paris, these days. In fact, it takes a lot of perseverance sitting at a desk to be able to earn a living through writing' (CM to Andrzejewski, 12 March 1958). At the end of the 1950s, as a memento, Miłosz placed on his desk a Polish-French dictionary from 1866, which had 'inscribed on its title page by its previous owner' the Latin word *Laboremus*, 'We work'.

One major fruit of his labours was *Kontynenty* (Continents), which Kultura published. This was a collection of articles, poems and translations from 1945 to 1957, and constituted a response to accusations from fellow émigrés who had regarded him as merely a Communist stooge. It was a very well-written volume which brought together an extensive selection of work composed in America and France. It included translations of Milton and Oskar Miłosz; articles devoted to Witold Gombrowicz and Dwight Macdonald; an extensive study of Józef Czechowicz's poetry; notes on translations of Shakespeare and Heraclitus; and short pieces on Simone de Beauvoir's *Mandarins* and about Warsaw writers in the wake of the political 'thaw' following Stalin's death. Much of *Kontynenty* was about a quest for common ground which could link people belonging to different political camps, and about decline in the Western world, whose inhabitants 'do not want to live'. Since in Europe 'notions of the sacred and the tragedy of existence' still survive, it might yet save America from its spiritual void. Yet the book presented only a small selection of Miłosz's writing from those years, when he was one of the most important authors published by Kultura, not just because of the quality of his published writing, but also since he was often prepared to take on requests from Giedroyc. He produced, for example, a column, 'Notes on Literature', in which he discussed works by Gombrowicz, but also other books which were less interesting to the poet. Like it or not, he took on the role of theatre critic and, more surprisingly, music critic and wrote monthly reports on festivals in Paris organised by the Congress for Cultural Freedom; on works of the twentieth century in 1952; and on the International Festival of Drama (1955), during which he could barely endure seeing through to its close a performance of a drama by his former mentor, Iwaszkiewicz.

For *Kultura,* he wrote pieces on Boris Pasternak, the winner of the Nobel Prize for Literature in 1958; on the annual conference of the Pen Club in London, which he had attended in 1956; and on the history of the Polish publishing house Pax. The latter commission was indicative of how Polish remained very much at the forefront of his mind, as were articles on Joseph Conrad's father (Apollo Nałęcz-Korzeniowski), on literary life in occupied Poland and on the state of contemporary Polish writing.

There were two texts which particularly stood out from this substantial array of works, whose focus lay in a different direction. In February 1955, Miłosz went to West Germany, to a camp in Valka near Nuremberg which was set up for those caught escaping the Eastern bloc countries. He described the distaste the German authorities displayed towards potential asylum seekers, and the help-lessness and the precarious fate of individuals who challenged the politics of their home countries. His exchanges with detainees there were very upsetting for Miłosz. A related task which he found painful to undertake was a piece entitled 'Brognart', which was included in *Prywatne obowiązki* (Private Obligations). This was the story of an eighteen year-old Frenchman who was in Poland at the outbreak of the war; he was arrested by the Soviets and sent to a camp, where he died after twelve years behind wire. His family, after seeking help from every possible institution and authority, could do nothing to save him. Brognart's story was shrouded in silence, and was regarded with embarrassment by journalists and intellectuals who were familiar with the circumstances in which people perished in the Soviet Union, but who were keen not to inflict damage on the pro-Soviet front. A victim perishing in Algiers at the hands of 'French imperialism' was one thing, and a legitimate subject for protest. For pro-Communist French writers and intellectuals, however, the fate of millions of political prisoners incarcerated in the gulags was off limits, as, after all, only a maniac, an émigré or a reactionary would get excited about that.

A consequence of *The Captive Mind*'s success was that Miłosz was labelled a 'political writer', though he experienced unease at being so defined and 'placed'. This may be the reason he delayed finishing 'Brognart', which can be found, however, in Bogdana Carpenter and Madeline G. Levine's valuable selection of his essays, *To Begin Where I Am* (2002). What he did pay close attention to was the political scene in Poland, especially the post-war political and social changes. He wrote an analysis of Polish anti-Semitism and about tensions between national minorities, both of which sprang in part from the easing of the Communist terror. Following the Soviet intervention in Hungary in 1956, he published a selection of essays devoted to the Hungarians' plight, addressed to intellectuals in the West and to Pablo Picasso, who in 1953 succumbed to pressure to create a portrait of Stalin. Deliberately echoing Zola, Miłosz began: 'I accuse you, Mr Picasso, and not only you, but all the Western artists and intellectuals, of allowing yourselves to be caught in a trap of words. During this time of terror and suffering, all of you, people who have freedom of choice, choose pure conformity' ('Lettre à Picasso', in *Preuves*, June 1956).

Giedroyc confided to Józef Mackiewicz in a letter that, 'unfortunately, the writers' situation is getting worse ... Miłosz ... is struggling, and I don't know how he would cope if it wasn't for the BBC' (27 September 1959). Miłosz's articles for the Polish Section of the BBC became one of his most important sources of income in the second half of the 1950s. Unlike other exiled writers, Miłosz refused to work for Radio Free Europe. Miłosz's contract with the BBC for a series of talks was the result of efforts by Zdzisław Broncel, a poet and journalist. Miłosz coped very well with his new brief, and his *Letters from France* continued after he left Europe. In order to encourage Zbigniew Herbert to seek out similar income-generating opportunities, Miłosz provided him the following simple instructions: 'You take any news item from the press, elaborate on it, place it against a particular background, and that's it' (CM to Zbigniew Herbert, n.d. 1960). However, he was rather underplaying the extensiveness of the knowledge he possessed and his gift for seeing links between seemingly unrelated subjects, which was one of his special skills. A series of about two hundred copies of his submissions survive, each typed script roughly five pages long, which Miłosz sent to London each week, and which chronicle the intellectual and political life of the time. Alongside pieces on the Polish October and the Hungarian Rising in 1956, de Gaulle and Khrushchev, Sartre and Camus, cartoons and Maria Callas, Miłosz devoted time to Ingmar Bergman's *The Seventh Seal* (1957), an analysis of Nabokov's *Lolita* as a pornographic novel, and a protest against Genet as 'the most nihilist living writer' (March 1960, Beinecke Library Archive). Miłosz's piece about the Qumran manuscripts, more commonly referred to as the Dead Sea Scrolls, ended with words that appeared to be prophetic: 'Nothing disappears. Who knows, maybe even such a tiny and transient thing as a "word", read out once on the radio?' (n.d. 1956, Beinecke Library Archive).

When one looks at the sales figures of the Kultura Library, they paint a pretty sorry picture of Polish émigré intellectual life. Miłosz contributed many publications which were popular among readers, and though Giedroyc was of the opinion that Miłosz's books sold well, in reality sales were only relatively good. *Światło dzienne* (Daylight), his 1953 poetry collection, cost 350 francs, the price more or less of five packets of Gauloises. A thousand copies were printed, but four years later, in 1957, 320 remained unsold. His best-selling book was *The Captive Mind*; out of 2,000 copies, only 283 remained in 1957; 1,000 copies of *The Seizure of Power* were printed, which sold out in two years. It took two years for the reduced print run for *The Issa Valley* (600 copies) to sell out. As is customary, a number of complimentary review copies of every publication had to be set aside—as gifts, in effect. Little wonder that Kultura's founder at times talked of émigré publishing as a species of charitable work.

Les grands seigneurs

We entered onto a merciless chessboard of black and white fields, on which we and all that surrounds us are expected to move within these two constricting colours. We have no choice but to do that, and it sometimes drives us to despair.

Andrzej Bobkowski to Jerzy Giedroyc (1951)

You have too little contempt, worse even—too little scorn towards certain phenomena. In all this Marxism, there is something seriously stupid (and in Marxists), although here and there it can be useful—but the subject matter is poor, and the people unexceptional, and in today's intellectuals I detect a degree of shyness towards this blatant rubbish. That doesn't apply to you—but you would not have to fight so many things if you were more proficient in scorn.

Witold Gombrowicz to Czesław Miłosz (1953)

Miłosz's intellectual and spiritual hunger reached beyond the black and white chessboard of Communism and anti-Communism, and he must have found it unbearable when Jerzy Giedroyc sought to use him to perform consecutive, incredibly urgent and important tasks. There was a clash between the man of action and the complex artist, who would not give in one moment, but the next would succumb to pressing requests or demands. Miłosz reflected on the 'difference between a writer, who lives for his obsessions, and a politician. The latter had an instrumental attitude to literature and would publish a devil, if it suited his strategy. Giedroyc's was not a literary strategy, but political, albeit of a higher level, and not dependent on instant gratification' *(O podróżach w czasie)*.

Their relationship can be viewed as the story of a painful separation. Giedroyc later commented, 'There was never a decent bond between us' (*Auto-biografia* 175). When Miłosz moved out of Kultura's headquarters, he left a letter at Maisons-Laffitte asking for friendship:

Dear Jerzy,

Now that I am moving out of Maisons-Laffitte, I would like to write a few words—as I find it easier to write than to speak . . . I have a debt of gratitude to you for helping me out in such a difficult time in my life, and I wouldn't have written a book if it wasn't for you. I also feel grateful that you stood by me despite all the unpleasantness you suffered as a result. My feelings for you are those one has for a right and kind person. Also, when I observed you and looked at your hurt pride, which you conceal, and so much warmth and kindness behind your silent compo-sure, I sometimes felt a deep sadness that I could not get through that 'protective layer' and become your close friend . . . Undoubtedly I was in an extremely difficult situation this year. I missed my wife and children so much that sometimes it reached a point of complete internal torture, so that when I came to breakfast I was like a man who can't see day-light, not to mention people . . . I projected my dislike of émigré Poles onto you, which was very unfair . . . Even if I was blind, I still observed everything carefully with my third eye and made a careful mental note, and when your controlled anger seemed at its highest, I wanted to come near you and say: 'Dear Jerzy, I can perfectly understand you, let's drop these masks and be friends'. Let this letter help you realise that, to a certain degree, you had a 'Miłosz issue' and I had a 'Giedroyc issue', and you have a special place in my heart where you are a man carrying the burden of loneliness and solitary stubbornness.

  Please remember that I can see that deep down you are a very warm person with so much love to give—and you, dear Jerzy, know that de-spite my sarcasm and irony, I seek that in people only, and before that I go down on my knees.

I kiss both your cheeks. (CM to Giedroyc, 20 March 1952)

In the difficult year 1951, Giedroyc was fascinated by Miłosz, or at least by his situation, thanks to which Kultura found itself regarding the writer's opinions on the 'New Faith' as aptly reflecting changes in the mentality of Polish society. For years Giedroyc steadfastly defended Miłosz from accusations of selfishness.

Over time, however, he became increasingly less patient, perhaps not being able to fathom the writer's mixed emotions—Miłosz's sense of guilt, the duality of his feelings, and the difference between a literary persona, created by the writer in essays and books, and a lost man in his letters and on a personal level: 'I can't stand this duality, "Hamletising", let's be frank, his cowardice . . . He wants to be a prophet, a master, and play this card in his books. If he could only pick up the courage and "reveal" in his writing all his cowardice and helplessness, he would be a much happier man' (Giedroyc to Vincenz, 27 March 1954).

For a long time Miłosz was afraid of being labelled 'reactionary', and probably in conversations with representatives of the Congress for Cultural Freedom or guests from Poland stressed his autonomy and independence from *Kultura*. Forging a strong personal relationship with Miłosz was not one of Giedroyc's priorities, and may have not been something he would anyway have sought to do. Whereas the writer felt at ease with Czapski, Hertz and Jeleński, he avoided the editor, who, in turn, tended to limit their contacts to current matters relating to the monthly magazine. He had a similar attitude to other contributors which was tinged with arrogance. This manifested itself in his response to readers' requests to provide a list of co-editors of *Kultura*. It read as follows: Editor, Jerzy Giedroyc, Editor Giedroyc Jerzy, J. Giedroyc, Giedroyc Jerzy, Jerzy and other members of the team' (*Kultura*, 3, 1955). Gradually, despite similarities in their thinking, a shared antipathy to intellectual stagnation, a shared commitment to the concept of Poland as a multinational entity, there was an ever-increasing gap between them, although at the outset their collaboration had looked promising. An example of Miłosz's admiration for the editor was expressed in a letter in 1952:

> Your Highness, History shows slowly, but surely, that you are splendid . . . over the course of last year you acquired or adopted Gombrowicz, Wittlin, Straszewicz, Parnicki and Miłosz, Hertz, Iwańska and who else . . . Straszewicz and Parnicki are a living proof that even if you found yourself in a desert where there would be only one latrine with a note saying, 'The key is with the concierge', then you would get that key. I do not intend to be ironic, I sincerely congratulate you. (CM to Giedroyc, n.d. 1952)

In their exchange of letters over the years—and by Giedroyc's death the number had risen to 1,000—Giedroyc detailed the various ways in which Miłosz could make himself useful for Kultura, while Miłosz tried to influence those ideas. Giedroyc made endless suggestions which would make use of the writer's skills: from analysing radio propaganda addressed to Poles, to, soon after the fall of the Soviet Union, taking up the post of Ambassador for the Polish Republic in

Vilnius (formerly Wilno). In the 1960s he imagined Miłosz in a role later undertaken by Ryszard Kapuściński, writing

> a book about Africa, mainly about different nationalities, intellectual elites,
> aspirations, a matter of urgency. You have always displayed an unhealthy
> affinity with Negroes . . . All your traits . . . (in my opinion) would be in
> your favour. We are talking about a book that would be local—friendly,
> anti-colonial, and specifically with an air of misty leftist leanings which
> are your forte. (Giedroyc to CM, 8 December 1960)

Miłosz, who for years loyally fulfilled all kinds of requests and assignments, including trying to find funds for *Kultura* in America, had a different idea
about his contributions to the magazine. At the beginning of 1954 he suggested
releasing special issues, one devoted to the subject of the Jews, another to the
Warsaw Uprising (1 August 1944). Giedroyc, who rejected the idea, regarded this
as a purely intellectual approach, whereas Miłosz was reluctant to use *Kultura* as
a medium solely for political views. A good example of that would be a dispute in
1959 regarding the setting up of a literary competition in the West on the subject of Milicja (police) and Polish Secret Service crimes carried out in Poland.
This was advertised by *Kultura* in response to a competition in Poland which
sought to glorify the work of various government agencies in the Polish People's
Republic. To Giedroyc, the competition would be an oppositional act, a counter
to propagandist lies. Miłosz believed that Kultura ought to avoid being seen
as simply an anti-Communist publishing house, because it would diminish the
long-term position of its literary magazine. Giedroyc, finding himself in circumstances dictated by history, felt compelled to serve as an ambassador for Polish
culture, but did not relinquish his political aims and ambitions. Miłosz wanted
the monthly to become strictly an intellectual medium, working on establishing a
basis for the education of new generations of readers who would not be nostalgic
about the pre-war Polish cultural scene—'literature is a blessing, because it encompasses everything and will express everything using its own language' (CM
to Giedroyc, 6 May 1961). The editor, however, had a different perspective on
these matters, and clear blue water opened up between him and the writer in the
1960s, and, to a certain extent, between the poet and politics, or social changes
in Poland. Giedroyc tried, unsuccessfully, to persuade Miłosz to write an article
condemning the repression of student dissent throughout Poland in March 1968,
and was surprised by his refusal, despite the writer's explanation: 'My worth to
Kultura and to its readers lies in my development specifically as a writer, far removed from the infection everyone is affected by . . . I am outside it and that's
where my strength lies' (CM to Giedroyc, 10 June 1968).

Miłosz, having reached the age of sixty, decided that he could no longer expend his energy on short-term projects and had to fight for the greater goals referred to in his letter to Czapski:

> Doesn't this Jerzy understand that at a certain point in life the fear that one has not fulfilled one's potential comes into play, and that hours diverted to writing articles or essays merely exacerbate that sense of guilt? And what can I offer him apart from poems, which he neither understands, nor appreciates, nor honours? ... How could we explain to Giedroyc that I am not playing at being 'a professor', or 'opportunistic', or 'softening', but that our generosity sometimes ends because our task [as poets] is to join two words or two colours, and we will not have a second life to carry it out. (CM to Czapski, 6 April 1967)

This letter was written in April 1967 and, later on, affirms:

> I have this strong sense that life is very short and I should not write articles, reviews, essays, which I did so wastefully for many years. Here in Vence, Gombrowicz had a go at me for my laziness, which is masked by putting fingers in too many pies. I was conscious of that without him pointing it out to me, and I do not slight his advice. He is a wise man. (Ibid.)

Before the war he and Gombrowicz ran into each other from time to time, but when the poet moved west, they struck up a good rapport from the start. In 1953 Miłosz named Gombrowicz as the only writer in exile who counted in Poland, and to help promote his friend's work asked Camus for assistance in finding a theatre which would be interested in putting on *The Wedding*. Gombrowicz praised 'Ketman' as an outstanding piece of work, but after *The Seizure of Power* won the Prix Européen, he sighed, but then recognised Miłosz's worth and merits: 'Why did I not receive the award, and why am I not sleeping on money like Miłosz! ... If, however, I were to give the prize, I would definitely give it to him, because of his talent and the fact that the book is very timely, and also because I feel a close affinity to him' (Gombrowicz to Giedroyc, 11 May 1953). A year later, he added that 'Miłosz and I are the only two people in exile who could be understood on the other side' (Gombrowicz to J. Giedroyc, 28 June 1954).

A few months before his death, Gombrowicz received a letter from California in which Miłosz bemoaned the parlous state of their native culture: 'The situation in Poland is terrible, on a deeper level than the politics, because thinking and language are hitting rock bottom: they are harking back to the mistiness of old Slavonic ... it looks as if we could be the last Polish writers'

(CM to Gombrowicz, 17 January 1969). In *Kultura* they discussed the current dire state of Polish poetry and the effects of the regime's insistence on socialist realist models. Gombrowicz said that almost no-one in Poland liked such poetry because it presented a fabricated reality, a false world. 'The moment poets stopped seeing a physical human being, and turned to abstractions, nothing could stop them from falling down into the abyss of the absurd' ('Przeciw poetom', *Kultura*, 10, 1951). Although some *Kultura* readers might have been stunned by these assertions, Miłosz was in full agreement.

Gombrowicz's hope was that the poet might be freed from viewing communism as the principal problem of modern times. In his view, Miłosz should not preoccupy himself solely with the political and social situation in the East, but seek to 'impose on the West his own distinct experience from there' and his 'own new knowledge about the world' (*Dziennik 1953–1958*, 23–31).

———————

In spring 1967 Miłosz and his family spent a long holiday in Europe. For over a month they stayed at La Capricorne, a villa near Saint-Paul-de-Vence belonging to English women friends, and from there were able to visit Gombrowicz easily. There was a strong mutual respect and affection between the two writers, and what was particularly interesting was that Janka and Gombrowicz got on really well. Their views coincided on many issues, and they had a similar sense of humour. Miłosz must have been pleased seeing this, and remarked to Aniela Micińska, 'To Janka, Warsaw writers are psychological gelatine' (13 August 1967). At a later date he noted what Gombrowicz said 'about Janka and me: "I cannot fathom how such a clever woman puts up with an idiot like him". And he was right there' (*Rok myśliwego* 286).

The two writers did not wrestle with, but rather supported each other. Gombrowicz said of Miłosz: 'He is one of the very few who understands me and where I am most vulnerable . . . I know that our exchanges are serious, razor-sharp, tense and . . . involve no mutual back-slapping . . . we are both like soldiers in trenches, reckless and tragic' (Gombrowicz, *Dziennik 1953–1958*, 323–324). The last letter Miłosz received from him had to be written by his wife, Rita, though Gombrowicz managed to write at the bottom of the page: 'I am going down-hill very fast. Kind regards. W.G.' (Gombrowicz to CM, 28 May 1969).

News of Gombrowicz's death reached Miłosz while he was camping in the Rocky Mountains. He wrote immediately:

> I admired him. To be with him was like entering a building of light and transparent architecture . . . Compared with him, I was twisting and

winding, not so much possessing as possessed by powers outside my control. But while in Vence . . . his example gave me hope that I would manage to bring order in my territory, as he did, truly *un grand seigneur*. (*Zaczynając od moich ulic* 429–430)

'To you, sweetheart, I cannot say hello'

Both you and I sinned: by having no faith. And I also imagined that things will not be any different. And yet the nation proved to be wiser and more intelligent, not only than I was (which is not difficult), but even than strong-headed and big-headed Miłek.

Jarosław Iwaszkiewicz to Konstanty Jeleński (1957)

It is not hard to realise what a price Miłosz had to pay for defying Stalinist orthodoxy, the lie, and submission to subjugation. It is easy to dwell on the latter, happier years of his life, when he was constantly honoured. From 1951 until he was awarded the Nobel Prize in 1980, he had a small readership, and could count on the fingers of one hand the number of articles written about him. *Native Realm* did not receive a single Polish review, and for a long time, absolutely nothing about his work appeared in newspapers and magazines. How different after the Nobel announcement, when he, like the newly elected Pope John Paul II, 'could give Poland a good name world-wide', as Artur Międzyrzecki averred in a piece entitled 'Poetycka Sprawiedliwość' (Poetic Justice) (*Twórczość*, 6, 1981).

For almost three decades after his defection from Poland in 1951, Miłosz was a writer who had resigned himself to the fact that he had failed and would be forgotten. This realisation was hardest to bear when in America he was labelled a political scientist, a university lecturer and, at best, the translator of Zbigniew Herbert's poetry. In France, after 1956, when writers from Poland began to travel to the West during the brief 'thaw', there were possibilities of communication between Poland and the émigrés, and his feelings of isolation were soothed by the renewal of some personal contacts. Conversations over a glass of wine did sometimes occur in Brie-Comte-Robert and Montgeron, 'despite Janka's quiet protests about them and their bad influence on the children. To an outsider not able to grasp the sense of them, these discussions sounded absurd, and the flashes of humour in them bordered on the macabre' (*Rok myśliwego* 35). Toni Miłosz used to remember references to a black angel called Putrament, whose ghost appeared over a table blocking his father's way to the fatherland. In fact, for the boys, born in America and now growing up and being educated in France, Poland must have seemed a mysterious zone, marked by clouds of cigarette smoke, the clinking of wine glasses, and endless arguments running into the night. In spite of Janka's lack of enthusiasm for them, these visits took place, and the bridge between the home country and Miłosz was no longer limited to newspapers read in the Polish Library on Paris's Isle St Louis.

After the turbulent political events of the mid-1950s, a number of famous Polish writers came to Paris, including Jerzy Andrzejewski, Jarosław Iwaszkie-wicz, Stanisław Kisielewski and Irena Sławińska. One visitor, the playwright and Catholic activist Jerzy Zawieyski, remembered that among the subjects he and Miłosz touched on during their long discussions were religion and the nation-alistic tendencies in the Polish Church. Zawieyski sensed that Miłosz had re-turned to religion, and wondered whether that changed him and how. There was no clear proof that this conviction was confirmed by any sources of information. Could Miłosz, who was usually discreet in these matters, have admitted some-thing? Could it be that his Church wedding, which he certainly did not mention to his friends, might be interpreted as a turning point in the poet's life? Perhaps another indication that can lead us to believe that was the mention of priests in his correspondence. Could he be receiving religious teaching in private and meeting with a 'spiritual guardian'? Undoubtedly he was very interested in reli-gious thought and had been almost his entire life. He explained to Nela Micińska: 'The only discipline from which one can draw a great deal is theology . . . where would a poet be without theology?' (CM and JM letters to A. Micińska and J. Ulatowski, 29 November 1959).

In September 1957 another visitor to the house in Montgeron was Janusz Odrowąż-Pieniążek, later the director of the Museum of Literature in Warsaw, who made Miłosz's day when he mentioned a circle of literary lights from the younger generation (Andrzej Biernacki, Zdzisław Najder, Zbigniew Herbert and Leopold Tyrmand) and their admiration for his work. Pieniążek told the poet how Tyrmand had transcribed the 'Treatise on Morality' onto tissue paper, and then passed it on from reader to reader. Miłosz read the poems the guest brought with him and listened with eagerness to the latest gossip from Warsaw, and so the visit went on until very late and the guest ended up sleeping on a sofa, cov-ered by the host's sheepskin coat. The two men's conversation was interrupted the next morning by Janka asking her husband in a theatrical tone, 'Are you not working today, Czesław?', after which the poet retreated to his study. During fur-ther visits, Pieniążek remembered Janka taking her husband to task, and Miłosz watering the garden, or sitting in his study with a map of the Duchy of Lithuania on the wall, with his pipe and Virginia tobacco at hand, saying emphatically that he could not get used to the 'trimmed' version of Poland. He later introduced the writer to a group of students from Poland who met in the Old Navy Café, which was frequented by Andrzej Wat, Olga Scherer, Jan Lebenstein and Herbert.

During the thaw, which followed Stalin's death and the events in October 1956, the Communist authorities adopted a new strategy towards the émigrés, using radio broadcasts by intellectuals still in Poland to lure back certain higher-profile figures with promises of position and opportunities to be published. At the beginning of 1957 offers of publication appeared. Państwowy Instytut Wydawniczy (PIW), the state publishers, planned to release all of Miłosz's work. Another literary publisher, Wydawnictwo Literackie, wanted to print *The Issa Valley* and a selection of poems, but as the thaw lasted only a brief time before hard-line Communist policies were re-introduced, these publishing plans came to nothing. Whether on their own initiative or in the role of unofficial emissaries, some friends in Poland contacted Miłosz to suggest that he return to the country, but the poet had no intention of going back. What were his motives for the refusal? Janka's determination to remain in the West was a major factor, along with his reservations about the political situation and his own personal security in Poland. Memories of his ill treatment, and the suspicion that the Communist regime's dependence on the Soviet Union was increasing, all served as deterrents.

Jerzy Andrzejewski wrote to Miłosz in the autumn of 1957, confirming many of the poet's worst fears: 'You must be tormented by your situation, but you did not lose face, and that is most important. It is a good thing that you are not here' (Andrzejewski to CM, 18 October 1957). When in 1959 Andrzejewski spent a few months in Paris thanks to a Ford Foundation stipend, their friendship was renewed, and they spent a lot of time walking round the Latin Quarter, slipping into galleries, and having long discussions over wine. To his surprise and delight, Andrzejewski was invited for Christmas Eve, the most important evening in the Polish festive calendar. It was very touching to be included in the family celebration, and he later praised the warm and homely atmosphere created by the hosts and their children and the poignancy of seeing Miłosz singing Polish carols, with tears welling up in his eyes. From these meetings with Andrzejewski, Miłosz discovered that one could still love a friend despite the many differences between them: 'Those contacts gave me a feeling of brotherhood in weakness, in frailty' (CM to Thomas Merton, 8 July 1960, *Striving towards Being* 86).

However, it was much harder for him to extend this fraternal love to the master of his youth, Jarosław Iwaszkiewicz. Iwaszkiewicz had not played a prominent role in the hate campaign in Poland and had not really been appalled by the poet's 'desertion'. All archival materials point to the fact that he did not adopt the public stand against Miłosz demanded by the authorities, although he believed in propagandist lies. In private, however, he condemned Miłosz for 'wriggling out of the role' of contributing to the country's cultural and social development, because abandoning this responsibility was an act of treachery. Iwaskiewicz was clearly envious of the younger poet, who now lived in the cradle of culture, enjoying the (Mont)-Parnassian life, free of the hard fate still suffered by fellow Poles.

Iwaszkiewicz's own situation can hardly be described as grim, as the authorities allowed him to travel abroad often. In 1955 he attended an international theatre festival, during which his play *Summer in Nohant* was performed. The play turned out to be so poor that the audience left in large numbers after the first half. Some stayed until the end to meet in the foyer of the Théâtre Sarah Bernhardt. Spotting Miłosz among those gathered, Iwaszkiewicz walked hurriedly and nervously past, saying, 'To you, sweetheart, I cannot say hello' (*Rok myśliwego* 194). He later regretted the comment and having treated Miłosz like a traitor. The two writers did not speak to each other for another ten years, until Iwaszkiewicz came to Paris again, bringing with him his protégé's old manuscripts. During their encounter in the Hôtel de Suède, Miłosz showed no emotion at seeing him, and even avoided making eye contact. Pointedly, he did not disclose either his address or telephone number. Iwaszkiewicz commented that Miłosz had changed from being a very beautiful, warm man to a hostile person with a cold manner, an unforgiving gaze and a harsh tone in his voice. However, it took only another few months before Miłosz's bitterness and anger eased and he sent a card to Iwaszkiewicz as a gesture of reconciliation. The two men rekindled their earlier warm relations and dedicated some of their work to each other.

Through the good offices of Tadek Byrski and his wife, Zbigniew Herbert became acquainted with Miłosz in 1958, introduced as a promising young poet and dramatist. Herbert was invited to meet Miłosz in Montgeron in May of that year when he arrived in Paris as a visiting scholar. As well as there being a significant age disparity between them - thirteen years - the two had a very different outlook on various matters and historical events. Herbert had a much more positive attitude to developments in Poland in the 1920s and 1930s, and experienced the war and occupation of the country during his teenage years, and so was more emotionally invested and actively engaged in political developments; he saw action with the underground resistance movement, and following the Soviets' capture and annexation of Ukraine in 1944 was expelled from his native city, Lwów, along with the rest of its Polish population. He never accepted the post-war reality.

Despite the differences between them, the beginning of the acquaintance was entirely positive. Herbert, who stayed in Montgeron, enjoyed the company of the Miłoszes greatly, and to his second letter after the visit he attached one of his most beautiful poems, 'Elegy of Fortinbras', which he dedicated to the older poet. In the spring of 1959, Miłosz invited Herbert for a bouillabaisse in a café near Odéon, but could not have foreseen the irony that a decade later, during a dinner where again bouillabaisse would be served, Herbert would shout at Miłosz, accusing him of treachery and of lacking patriotic feelings.

The time in Montgeron initiated an important friendship, as their correspondence reveals. They both drank Herbert's favourite Beaujolais, and Miłosz, noticing in his younger friend worrying symptoms, commented out of concern that 'it is possible to live without drink. Beware', and warning him that 'getting drunk in the evenings on red wine will not solve all one's inner problems' (CM to Zbigniew Herbert, 30 January 1964). Most importantly, Miłosz enabled Herbert to achieve international fame when he translated his poems into English and sought publishing opportunities for them. He served as a poetic guide for Herbert, who would later repeatedly acknowledge the artistic debt he and other poets of that generation owed to Miłosz. The poets had some common ground: above all, the pursuit of clarity, and a desire to capture the existence and physicality of real objects—a tree as an entity and not the notion of it. They also shared a bias against art that navel-gazed. The subject of poetry could not only be, as Herbert expressed it, 'a small broken soul feeling great pity for itself'; art ought to 'comfort or at the least show solidarity with people and not invent new distress and horrors' (Herbert to CM, 10 December 1965). As he wrote to Miłosz, when values such as 'selflessness, ability to contemplate, a vision of lost Paradise, bravery, goodness, empathy, mixture of despair and humour' are absent, then poetry becomes a game, preoccupying the artist only (Herbert to CM, 17 February 1966).

Eternal Moment

The Greeks believed that in Hades the shadows of the dead come to life for a moment, but only when they taste fresh blood. Similarly, we can bring our past to life, only when we nourish it with our own blood, our faith, in a struggle only specific to us.

Czesław Miłosz, from an article for the BBC (1955)

Poetry 'is a voice and a voice only, a voice like a flame in a lamp that flickers and dies' (Zbigniew Herbert to Aleksander Wat, 2 February 1966). In the 1950s Miłosz had struggled to regain that bright light. Whereas he could write essays with ease, the melody of the verse was silent, as if the Ghost of History had struck him. It was as if he had lost his place on earth; indeed, he had. He knew too well that stanzas would not come from trembling, but had to come from light, from the most painful 'yes', a 'yes' uttered to the world.

Writing to Vincenz circa 1954, as so often, he lamented his misjudgements: 'With regard to poetry . . . I destroyed it, that is, I destroyed the only thing of any value in my existence'. Certainly he wrote very few poems in the first years of his emigration, primarily because of the pressures on him to elaborate in detail, and to justify again and again, the reasons that forced him to sever his links with the Communist regime and its lies. Faced with accusers and his own doubts, he spoke directly, not through a poetic persona. His poem 'Pożegnanie' (Farewell) was an address to an actual person, but was also talking about the country where the writer would love to live and be able to say

> clouds above Warsaw belong to me
> And the clouds blowing over the Polish countryside,
> Their shadows moving over a tapestry of corn
>
> (*Wiersze* II, 25)

Doubly in the opening lines, he reiterates, 'ciebie nie zapomnę' (I will not forget you), adding that the calling of a poet is bound up with remembering, and with speaking truth on behalf of those compelled to stay silent.

The volume *Daylight*, published in 1953, incorporated poems written earlier, between 1945 and 1950. In the preface Miłosz wrote that 'the title has a double meaning: there are a number of poems which I could not publish in Poland, and additionally, poetry is a matter of day-time rather than night' (Beinecke Archive). The poems 'To Jonathan Swift', 'Child of Europe', 'The Spirit of the Law' and 'You Who Wronged', as well as 'Warsaw Faust' and 'On the Death of Tadeusz Borowski',[2] all lent the book a decisive tone and an engaged stance, fighting for the light of hope in the darkness of the times. The book also included the cycle 'The World', and ended with 'Mittelbergheim'. While still in Bons, Miłosz wrote 'A Notebook: Bons beside the Shores of Leman', a lyric pulsating with the intensity of the world, Existence with the capital 'E', a contemplation of what ought to satisfy human desire. Here stagnation is replaced by a foaming wave of time, from whose current a man has the right to lift an 'eternal moment' and say yes:

> Artists crave being, a communion with the divine promise inside creation. For them, processions of armies, social struggles, the chaos of dying regimes and emergent political systems simply happen on the outside. For others, those battles and that chaos are reality itself. As for me, whatever I accomplished that was worthwhile was due precisely to the clash of these two attitudes'. (*NR* 294)

The 'Leman' poem contains the germ of Miłosz's *magnum opus* from 1956, *A Treatise on Poetry*. Recapitulating the journey he had taken in the previous ten years in search of poetry, he outlines its shape in the poem "Preface":

First, plain speech in the mother tongue.
Hearing it you should be able to see,
As if in a flash of summer lightning,
Apple trees, a river, the bend of a road.

And it should contain more than images.
Singsong lured it into being,
Melody, a daydream. Defenseless,
It was bypassed by the dry, sharp world.

. . .

Poetry, seasoned with satire, clowning,
Jokes, still knows how to please.
Then its excellence is much admired.
But serious combat, where life is at stake,
Is fought in prose. It was not always so.

And our regret has remained unconfessed.
Novels and essays serve but will not last.
One clear stanza can take more weight
Than a whole wagon of elaborate prose.

('Preface', *NCP*, 109)

Miłosz argued that poetry can fight for the highest causes; by representing, in condensed form, the history of contemporary Polish poetry and pointing out its weaknesses, poetry leads the reader to the core philosophical challenges of the times. This is achieved without depriving stanzas of their purely poetic power. The first part of *A Treatise on Poetry* depicts parochial Kraków at the turn of the twentieth century. Amidst its silent, suffering masses emigrating to escape stark poverty, and the looming shadows cast by the coming slaughter, above the sounds of a pianola, an 'ethereal' song emerges, separated from the 'sad affairs of earth', forbidding itself everything that is not poetic enough, and creating in the reader a schizophrenic division between sensual corporeality, gender and the subconscious, and bathed with a fragile, starlit spirituality. Miłosz creates a series of micro-images with a skill he prided himself on in earlier poems, but which he here elevates to the highest point and enriches by moving tenderness. Here is how the Kraków of 1918 is encapsulated in a few verses:

That day fades. Someone has lit the candles.
On Oleandry field the locks of the carbines
Don't click anymore, the plain is empty.

The aesthetes in infantry boots have departed.
Their hair has been swept from the barber's floor.
Fog and smell of smoke hang about the place.

And she, she wears a lilac-colored veil.
By candlelight she puts her fingers to the keys
And while the doctor fills glasses with liqueur
She sings an air that seems to come from nowhere:

The laughter in cafés
Echoes about a hero's grave.

(*NCP* 115)

What the second part of *A Treatise* evokes before our eyes is Warsaw, free
for a while after gaining its independence from Russia in 1918, and glimpses of
the talented Polish poets of the period, particularly from Skamander: 'There had
never been such a Pléiade!/Yet something in their speech was flawed,/A flaw of
harmony' (ibid., 119). The poem captures the futurist illusions of the avant-garde,
Gałczyński, Czechowicz, Ważyk, the inter-war world of poetry which whirled
for a time away from nothingness, only to disappear into thin air soon after and
proclaim with certainty that the route to pure beauty is a barren path, since 'we
need to speak gracelessly and roughly' (ibid., 125):

Where wind carries the smell of the crematorium
And a bell in the village tolls the Angelus
The Spirit of History is out walking.

(Ibid., 128)

The third part of *A Treatise* deals with the German occupation of 1939–1945, with
the young poets of Warsaw, the tragedy of the ghetto, and smoke coming from
the fires of the Rising covering the Warsaw sky. These struggles are presented as
doomed to a tragic futility, because on Poland's eastern borders rises the dawn of
Historic Necessity:

A poet has already recognised the walker,
An inferior god to whom time and the fate
Of one-day-long kingdoms is submitted.
His face is the size of ten moons. He wears
About his neck a chain of severed heads.
Who does not acknowledge him begins to
                        mumble.
Whoever bows to him attracts his scorn.

(Ibid.)

Is the Spirit of History the same as the Spirit of the Earth? Are the laws of History equally as determined and irreversible as the laws of biology when there is nothing else except the compulsion to survive within the species, the pendulum of reproduction and decay, and where everything else is an illusion?

> With what word to reach into the future,
> With what word to defend human happiness—
>
> (Ibid., 130)

particularly when faced with the power of diamat, which tears the matter of the world: 'The golden house of *is* collapses and the word *becoming* ascends'. No idealistic averting of the eyes or cynical resignation towards events can bring salvation. And when the morning star, the symbol of hope, the eternal spirit elevating us above death and above the fate of animals, seems to be waning,

> In a dream the mind visits two sharp edges.
> Woe to the unearthly, the radiant ones.
> While storming heaven, they neglect the Earth
> With its joy and warmth and animal strength.
> Woe to the reasonable, the heavy-minded.
> Their lies will extinguish the morning star,
> A gift more durable than Nature is, or Death.
>
> (NCP 130)

'The whole history of Europe, from the French Revolution onwards, is seen as a struggle between *être* and *devenir,* between *esse,* a static sense of existence, and becoming, a struggle which has its political equivalents. My principal argument here is that we cannot get stuck in the *esse* state, by digging in our heels and shouting "No!" to change', explained Miłosz (*Rozmowy polskie* 588). If, however—in life and in art—neither 'reactive' Existence nor passivity of thinking and submission to changes imposed by Communists are acceptable, then it is necessary to look for an escape route. It is historicity: History perceived not as a collection of deterministic laws, but as a continuity of human existence, in which memory places us above an indifferent and extremely cruel nature, a symphony of murder, into whose chain we are genetically linked. This is the theme of the fourth and last part of *A Treatise.* Identifying with those who died, filling them with our own blood, we stand where time and eternity intersect:

> Yesterday a snake crossed the road at dusk.
> Crushed by a tire, it writhed on the asphalt.
> We are both the snake and the wheel.
> There are two dimensions. Here is the unattainable

Truth of being, here, at the edge of lasting
and not lasting. Where the parallel lines intersect,
Time lifted above time by time.

(NCP 143)

'Historicity then can be a weapon ... against nothingness' (Rozmowy polskie 589).
This liberating conclusion generates an important poetic task:

I want not poetry, but a new diction,
Because only it might allow us to express
A new tenderness and save us from a law
That is not our law, from necessity
Which is not ours, even if we take its name.

(NCP 144)

This gesture of reaching out to help, motivated by tender emotion, makes this part of the poem powerful and also presents us with a portent of Miłosz's poetry to come, in which the voice steeped in great ideas will abate, allowing more prominence to human whispers.

A Treatise on Poetry was published in *Kultura*, and later in book form in 1957, winning the periodical's Literary Award for that year. In the poet's eyes, however, a higher accolade came in the form of a congratulatory letter from Warsaw sent by 'Tiger' Kroński, whose strong presence fills the close of *Native Realm*; for Miłosz 'there could have been no better crown of laurel' (*NR* 296). Other opinions were also deeply positive. 'What riches!', exclaimed Jeleński. 'I felt very moved by it' (letter to Giedroyc, 13 June 1956). '*Treatise* is wonderful. I, an old prose writer, not sensitive to poetry, am left breathless when reading aloud the stanzas' (Czesław Straszewicz to Giedroyc, 8 July 1956). Andrzej Bobkowski wrote: 'Although I detest poetry, I read with despair the whole of *A Treatise on Poetry* and found it a real gem' (Bobkowski to Giedroyc, 4 March 1957), while Aleksander Wat crossed the t's and dotted the i's, saying, 'This is a peak that our poetry has not reached for over one hundred years' (Wat to Czapski, 24 March 1963). More important than the praise was that the poem proved that Miłosz had triumphantly regained his voice and could now declare, 'I am beginning to see an outline of some lands' (CM to Vincenz, n.d. 1956).

The publication of *A Treatise on Poetry* prompted a new type of verse to emerge from his pen, as can be seen in the volume *King Popiel and Other Poems*. In these poems we find the old Miłosz. He reflected that 'it would have been better if I had not turned to political issues. Unfortunately, taking into account historical events, it was difficult to avoid such self-restraint. All my latest poetry, however, in which I am a faithful chronicler of our times, adheres to the rule "I see, I describe", nothing else' (*Rok myśliwego* 61).

A Place on Earth

There is too much talk about what poetry ought to be and too little
about what it is. It is primarily a contradiction to nihilism. Like an
apple in a Dutch painting, there is a stanza in Mickiewicz's *Sir Thaddeus,
or the Last Lithuanian Foray: A Nobleman's Tale from the Years of
1811 and 1812 in Twelve Books of Verse*, because it refers to something
that is particular. An author of rhyming introductory articles can be a
fairly good poet for a while, because he uses his observations as resources,
but he has to shout much louder . . . because this is the price for moving
away into a desert of ideas. One real tree, one real droplet of dew,
are enough to destroy him and reduce him to nothingness.

Czesław Miłosz, *Poetry and Dialectics* (1951)

In 1955 Miłosz was informing BBC listeners about the road the French poet
Pierre Emmanuel had to take after breaking away from communism, about how
much effort it cost to rediscover the gravity of most common words: 'because
doctrines which lead to paradise on earth, constantly pushed into a distant future,
direct our eyes away from the earth, sensual things around us' (BBC talk, 19 November 1955, Beinecke Library Archive). While forming these observations he
was clearly aware that he was also talking about his own experience. Around this
same period, Toni, Miłosz's eldest boy, related a curious but not entirely funny
story to Konstanty Jeleński, which unconsciously sheds insight into where his
father might have been going wrong:

> I will write a short story about cows grazing on a meadow. They are
> grazing and grazing and here comes Daddy. He is coming up to a cow
> and the cow runs from him up in the air. And it circles over Daddy and
> plops a huge pile on top of him. Daddy keeps running away and the cow
> keeps following him. It hovers and hovers . . . and again drops a pile on
> top of him. And why is this cow so bad towards Daddy? It's because he
> doesn't like cows. He only likes the word 'cow'. (Note, 29 March 1956, in
> Iwaszkiewicz, *Dzienniki 1956–1963*, 61)

In order to be able to write *A Treatise on Poetry* the poet then had to come down
to earth again, or, as Thomas Merton said, rediscover his 'younger earthy and
cosmic self' totally different from his 'later political self' (Merton to CM, 21
May 1959, *Striving towards Being* 37).

The route towards this rediscovery was opened up by *The Issa Valley*, which
Miłosz started to write in the autumn of 1953 and finished in the middle of the
following year. He later affirmed that 'it pulled me away from abstraction' (*Rok*

myśliwego 194). As in *The Seizure of Power,* the writer composed the narrative in short chapters, moving away from linear chronology, and, like a painter, laying down patch after patch of colour. The material he chose and the episodes he selected produced much more satisfying results than those he achieved in his first attempt at writing a novel. *The Issa Valley* was a beautiful, poetic story, written in a lucid style, where, in accordance with rules of dramatic composition, he gave up autobiography, and suspended, as it were, the status of the main protagonist, Thomas. Skilfully, rather like D. H. Lawrence in *Sons and Lovers,* he shifted, sometimes seamlessly, to and fro between the protagonist's perspective and the narrator's commentary, in order to capture finally, at a deeper level, the emotional, intellectual and sensuous essence of childhood. He searched for a ritual, and his imagination hovered over an image of the river. He moves away from the Niewiaża and the imaginary Veza, opting instead for Issa, the name of a famous Japanese poet, but also a signifier replete with charm and mystery, whose central snake-like 's's recall a river's meandering.

In one of the early pages we read how

> the Issa Valley has the distinction of being inhabited by an unusually large number of devils ... The peasant farmers along the Issa used to place, by the entrance to their cottages, a bowl of milk for the water snakes, which were not afraid of humans. In time, the inhabitants became fervent Catholics and the presence of devils made them recall the struggle being waged for dominion over the human soul. (*Issa* 4)

The initial intention was to produce a story 'about devils and werewolves', but it became an account or evocation of a boy growing up in a secret garden, whose sacral power had not yet been blighted by nothingness. Humankind is never completely lonely there, because each and every individual is observed by divine and diabolic and perhaps also other, older divine Powers. There are human dramas unfolding around Thomas, and the metaphysical fabric of the world is revealed. *The Issa Valley* is, after all, a deeply religious book, because it confronts us with the basic questions about antinomies of good and evil, mercy and sin, trust and despair. The boy becomes more aware of the world around him, and discovers crime and extreme hopelessness, understanding that like Magdalena, a rejected lover, 'it takes a fairly desperate person to swallow rat poison, a surrendering to one's own thoughts so complete as to make one oblivious to everything but one's fate' (*Issa* 36). Could one believe, then, that given the misery and tragedy caused, a cardinal sin will be forgiven? And if her former lover, the priest Peiksva, committed such a grievous sin, could absolutions given by him to others be valid? And does anyone accompany us when we fall? Does God exist, and could we rebel against him, like Dominic, who perhaps is a future revolutionary, but for now is a disillusioned blasphemer who tortures animals and desecrates holy bread, in vain waiting for the thunder which obliterates everything, and which could be a sign of the Father's just severity?

Kultura published the novel in extracts and in 1955 as a book. A year later a second edition came out, published in London by Oficyna Poetòw i Malarzy (Printing House of Poets and Painters), illustrated by Jan Lebenstein, along with a French translation by Jeanne Hersch, for whom work on the book was 'something unimaginable', reliving sensual experiences—smells, images, sounds. The book was filled with vocabulary relating to farming, hunting, ornithology and weaving. 'Sometimes at two in the morning I had this sensation that pages from dictionaries were dancing around me' (Hersch, 'O przekładach'). According to Miłosz, the novel did not receive positive reviews in France: 'I remember seeing my picture, in *L'Express,* if I am correct, with a note underneath: "La métaphysique est facile". It implied that touching on social and political matters is difficult and commendable in an author, but writing about metaphysics is escapism' (*Rok myśliwego* 324). Polish reviewers' comments, however, could be turned into an anthology of rapture.

Thanks to the political thaw and censorship easing its grip on literary texts, Irena Sławińska was able to review Miłosz's novel: 'When words turn quiet, something lingers like a melody—very simple and pure, rising on two strings. One plays children's and common folk songs, while the other has overtones of the mature and bitter wisdom of the poet. Both . . . lead to a celebration of the world's beauty and human greatness' (*Tygodnik Powszechny* 16). Jan Błoński pointed out that the writer 'does not "look" at the beauty of things, but pounces on it, like a dog on game' (*Przegląd Kulturalny* 24).

The second half of the 1950s was for Miłosz a time of closing chapters, making subconscious preparations, gathering strength for the next stage in his life. In the story about Thomas he reached back to beginnings, to be reborn as a poet. In *A Treatise on Poetry* he summed up his artistic journey, not annulling his contradictions, but rather overcoming them. Having finished the narrative poem, he began to work on an intellectual autobiography, in which he attempted to grasp his identity, define his position towards the West, and, above all, say farewell to the temptations and fascinations of youth, the tall shadow of Kroński, and the perpetual sense of guilt. As late as 1957, Stanisław Vincenz talked to Ryszard Matuszewski about Miłosz, noting how 'he still reproaches himself and explains the reasons for breaking ties with Poland. Six years have passed and he is still upset about it' (Matuszewski 182). When a year later Miłosz finished his next book, *Native Realm,* Vincenz, having read an appendix to the book, 'La Combe', said with a sigh of relief that this was a final 'abandonment and relinquishing of Stalinism' (Vincenz to Giedroyc, 18 October 1958).

Miłosz described in the introduction to *Native Realm* how the idea for it occurred to him in 1953, in the house of Helena Naef on the banks of Lake Leman, when he looked at the red flowers painted on furniture which 'served generations of Swiss peasants'. He then felt pain at his inability to explain to his hosts the fate of the 'inferior' part of the European continent, stuck between Asia and the West, a zone called Central or Eastern Europe, and at the same time his own uncertain status. Supposedly he was a European, but from 'poor relations', torn between envy, the need to be accepted and contempt. Having toughened up in his émigré life, he could now say that much about himself, or rather that he was a European from the eastern marches who was born in a place situated outside the frame of most maps, on the verge of modern times. His childhood was marked by explosions of shrapnel; his studies took place in a town which was a lost echo of the Italian Baroque in the northern forests. He travelled to Paris and Asia, grappled with questions of religion, lived through the horrors of the Nazi occupation, and finally confronted the greatest challenge of the epoch, communism, and had to find in himself the strength to stand up to it.

The writer delved frequently into his biography, translating notes about the past into a skillful, masterful construct. Here we are reading not simply an accumulation of memories, but a fluent series of narratives, ordered story lines and imagery full of tangible details. The author of this book was a fully matured artist, who, as he had hoped in Vence, took on the task of 'putting things in order in his land'.

The decision to write a book based on events from his own life came at a price. As to the opinions of its readers, there was a clear divide between those who simply recognised it as an outstanding piece of work, based on the merits of its artistic structure, and those who had been personally involved either with Miłosz or in the events described by him in the text. Among the latter group was Józef Łobodowski, who accused the author of conducting a Hamlet-like search for a 'personal alibi' and holding a false conviction that 'to partake in contemporary history was only possible by succumbing to the Marxist experience'. He particularly disliked the persistent mythologisation of Kroński. 'Tiger? Rather a very intelligent and very unhappy kitten, whose dream it was to deceive a powerful, spiteful and mighty monkey' (Łobodowski, *Orzeł Biały-Syrena*).

The person who seemed most affected by the book was Iwaszkiewicz, who was mortified at being absent from the story line and even more so by the openness with which the writer referred to his relationship with his homeland, which he then abandoned. In his diaries, he railed at how the conceited and chaotic soul of little Czesław takes delight in intellectual snobbery ... All these manoeuvres were designed to exemplify the extraordinariness of his personality and the extraordinariness of his situation in Europe. Behind it all lay a very ordinary need to present himself as whiter than white ... All the tedious collection of reasons to prove that he was not cut out to live in Poland. Nor was he fit to live in America or anywhere else, in fact. He is an albatross after all. It is an example of extreme haughtiness and contempt towards human beings ... 'a devilish book'. (*Dzienniki* 1956–1963, 442)

It is hard to believe that he had been reading the same book as Maria Dąbrowska, who started on *Native Realm* one evening and found herself unable to put it down:

For the first time I am spellbound by Miłosz. It is his first autobiography, so to say, historiosophical and a little apologetical. But it would be almost impossible to detach oneself further ... and then find oneself and give an explanation to all one's complexes. Because this was written to solve complexes, and there are masses of them. But how finely it is all written. I cannot even express to what extent it appeals to me and where its singularity or specific greatness lies. It is Miłosz's masterpiece. (Dąbrowska 155)

At the end of a shattering decade, Miłosz regained his spiritual strength and now stood firmly on the ground and was far from thinking that his act of defecting was really the story of a suicide. At long last he was free and could write:

The classic result of all sudden raptures and reversals is the rumination on one's own worthlessness and the desire to punish oneself, known as *delectatio morosa.* I would never have been cured of it had it not been for the beauty of the earth ... After a few years of groping in the dark, my foot once again touched solid ground, and I regained ability to live in the present, in a 'now' within which past and future, both stronger than all possible apocalypses, mingle and mutually enrich each other. (*NR* 293–294)

In July 1959, Miłosz took great pleasure in informing Stanisław Vincenz of an approach recently made to him: 'I have received an offer of a Visiting Lectureship at one of the American universities, but I refused it because it would mean that I would have to pack and leave everything I am working on at the moment, which I cannot afford to do' (CM to Vincenz, 18 July 1959). The prestigious University of California repeated its offer the following year, and the writer was fully aware then that opportunities in France were diminishing and that his contacts with Poland were becoming increasingly limited, and so he faced a choice between the status of a 'pilgrim on the Parisian pavements or writing for French readers' (CM to Weintraub, 21 March 1959).

He had enough strength in him not to feel afraid of the aridity of America, and to make a decision which a few years ago would have seemed unimaginable. 'There is a new trend among the French intellectuals to earn good money from lecturing at American universities, and I don't think I ought to avoid it, but try it. I hope that being there I would be able to create a *modus vivendi,* which would enable me to stash some cash giving lectures' (CM to Wat, 18 September 1960). Despite the fact that the political atmosphere had improved considerably, and although the university exercised its influence, visa problems resurfaced again, and it seemed for a while that he might not be able to leave. Miłosz went to Copenhagen, and Janka embarked on a project to renovate the kitchen; then, at the end of September, a letter arrived from the American embassy, 'and there was hardly any time at all to get ready to leave' (CM to Weintraub, 3 December 1960). After their past experiences, there was no thought of travelling separately. Knowing that they might not be able to come back to France, the whole family packed their suitcases at the beginning of October and rushed to Paris. This time they crossed the ocean by plane, not by boat.

The Magic Mountain
1961–1980

Grizzly Peak

In the mid-1970s Czesław Miłosz wrote this poem:

> I don't remember exactly when Budberg died, it was either two years
>   ago or three
> The same with Chen. Whether last year or the one before.
> Soon after our arrival, Budberg, gently pensive,
> Said that in the beginning it is hard to get accustomed,
> For here there is no spring or summer, no winter or fall.
>
> 'I kept dreaming of snow and birch forests.
> Where so little changes you hardly notice how time goes by.
> This is, you will see, a magic mountain.'
> . . .
>
> I sensed Budberg was right and I rebelled.
> So I won't have power, won't save the world?
> Fame will pass me by, no tiara, no crown?
> Did I then train myself, myself the Unique,
> To compose stanzas for gulls and sea haze,
> To listen to the foghorns blaring down below?
> Until it passed. What passed? Life.
> Now I am not ashamed of my defeat.
> One murky island with its barking seals
> Or a parched desert is enough
> To make us say: yes, *oui, si.*
> 'Even asleep we partake in the becoming of the world'.

Endurance comes only from enduring.
With a flick of the wrist I fashioned an invisible rope,
And climbed it and it held me.

('A Magic Mountain', *NCP* 335–336)

In 'A Magic Mountain', the poet encapsulates many experiences from two long American decades. In order to picture these years, it is necessary to slow the pace, and expand or dilute this story to present somehow the taste of this Californian monotony. In California, Miłosz found himself in a space which existed somehow outside of time when glimpsed from the customary European rhythm of the seasons so familiar to the boy born by the River Niewiaża. He settled down in a place which reminded him of a desert island, with all the symbolic connotations that location involves—a site where character is tested, a place of alienation, a landscape difficult to read and understand.

Having landed in San Francisco on the evening of 9 September 1960, Miłosz and his family headed for Berkeley, a town spread over hills across the bay from San Francisco. The following morning, the newly-appointed Visiting Lecturer at the University of California delivered his first lecture, and straight after that a seminar on neo-Romantic Polish poetry from the late nineteenth and early twentieth century. The modern campus, which covered a wide area, appeared too splendid and somewhat unreal, with its substantial white buildings amongst the green eucalyptus, pine and larch trees, the Italian-style campanile, sports stadium, numerous swimming pools and, above all, a huge library and well-stocked bookshops which provided an intellectual feast for nearly 30,000 students. What added to his disorientation was the fact that California was so distant from the eastern side of the continent with which he was familiar, and that the *New York Times* arrived in Berkeley by train after a three-day delay.

In his first letters to friends, he appreciated the fact that America had changed in the ten years he had been away. He declared that 'everything is too big, too opulent, they are too concerned about themselves to care for anything outside their comfort zone'. Still recovering from jet lag, he kept waking up at three in the morning, staring at the dazzling panoramic view of the stretch of San Francisco Bay down below, having seen 'nothing like that in Europe: shining neon lights on a wonderful night, . . . and when at dawn they go out and it gets light, a great number of white bones appear above the blue bay . . . the white buildings' (CM to A. Wat, 15 October 1960).

For the first few days the family stayed with the Dean of Slavonic Studies, Frank Whitefield, and his wife, Celina, who came from Warsaw. Celina had been deported from Warsaw to a German camp after the Warsaw Rising in 1944 and then, via London and New York, came to San Francisco, where she met Frank, a polyglot, linguist and historian working at the university. He had previously worked at Columbia University and had met Manfred Kridl, probably through Celina, and was keen to strengthen the Polish Department at Berkeley. He was looking for a suitable replacement for a colleague due to retire, and decided to bring Miłosz to the States. Victor Weintraub, Professor at the Slavonic Studies Department at Harvard, played an important role here, because on his post-war visits to Europe he met Miłosz. A photograph exists of Weintraub and Miłosz with Zdzisław Broncel preparing to take part in a discussion for the BBC. From Miłosz's letters to Weintraub it appears that the idea of working on the other side of the Atlantic came about during a meeting in Paris in 1958, and the kindly disposed professor became an invaluable American connection who followed developments at Berkeley, but also looked for opportunities elsewhere, including Indiana University in Bloomington. Initially, Miłosz was too preoccupied in Paris and did not seriously consider this option, but a year later, he realised that by continuing in the current vein there he would be relegated to the position of a writer on demand: 'If I were to write in French and about popular subjects, I would have to conform to trends here . . . an American campus does not appear too scary, and if I can devote more time to lectures about Polish literature rather than analysing municipal elections in France, then who knows, this option might be more tempting?' (CM to Weintraub, 29 March 1959). In his next letter he added: 'I am very grateful to you for being so supportive. You are in an advantageous position being able to monitor the situation there' (CM to Weintraub, 23 April 1959). Halfway through 1960 Miłosz received another invitation and accepted the post in Berkeley.

The family's first place of residence was rented accommodation in an apartment at 2601 Ridge Road. The apartment was beautifully and richly decorated in oriental style with the latest fittings, which impressed the poet, who described them in detail to Giedroyc. By July 1961, they could afford to rent a house at 820 Euclid Avenue, which was further away from the campus, but higher on Grizzly Peak, and soon they had a secondhand Dodge sitting in the garage. Their circle of friends was very small, but they met acquaintances from their time in Montgeron, Artur and Rosa Mandel. 'We met them again in Berkeley . . . we could relate to them better than to American or non-Jewish Poles. Artur was from Bielsko, and from a German cultural background, while Rosa was born near Żywiec. America, Poland, anti-Semitism, Judaism, Christianity, socialism, Thomas Mann and other Manns, the German colony in Berkeley, these were the subjects of our discussions' (Rok myśliwego 88). The Mandels took them for trips in their car, showing them, among other sites, the vineyards of the Napa valley.

Artur instructed Miłosz on the history of the Franks, and later translated into German his *History of Polish Literature.*

In June 1962, having been granted American citizenship and having achieved financial stability by holding a permanent post at the university, Miłosz could afford to buy a house. A plot on Grizzly Peak Boulevard 978 was close to the top of a hill overlooking Berkeley, on a steep slope. Straight through the gate from the street, there was a narrow path sloping down towards an area shaded by pine and redwood trees, as if leading to a magic forest. Often mysterious rustling could be heard there, accompanied by birdsong and, from time to time, the lightning flash of squirrels leaping from branch to branch and glimpses of shy deer. The house itself was not large. It had two floors and a sloping roof, and a front room whose main feature was the fireplace, which had a stone surround the size of a 'hearth of primitive people'. The front entry was hidden in the shade, and the other side of the house opened onto a verandah and a brightly sunlit, scorched garden whose air was filled with the perfume of herbs, and from which there was an unobstructed panoramic view of Berkeley and San Francisco. The poet's study was situated next to the main entry, and visitors heading for the knocker on the front door could see the poet's head bent over his desk. On light-coloured walls with thickly laid and textured plaster hung a copy of Aunt Gabriela's portrait; dark wood shelves were filled to the brim with books and files, and on the desk, which stood by another larger window, stood a compact line of dictionaries. As years went by, many objects—birds made of wood and clay, a soft teddy bear and, intriguingly, a Miss Piggy—found their home among the books. The house's layout could be seen as symbolic: dark at the front and, hidden behind it, bright spaces. This perhaps reflected the couple's characters, the Bacchic Czesław and the Apollonian Janka, who sought in life light and clarity in a metaphysical and a physical sense, as well as the warmth of the sun.

The family took holidays more often in America than they had in the Old World. Their first destination was Lake Tahoe, on the California-Nevada border, surrounded by forests; but later they enjoyed camping holidays in Oregon, Washington State and British Columbia in Canada, where less bright, more northern sunlight lit up landscapes which reminded him of Lithuania. After travelling more than a thousand miles, they went up as far as Vancouver, pitching their tents on the banks of the Athabasca, where they encountered moose, brown bears and pumas. Their clapped-out Volvo took them in 1974 to a Slavonic conference in Banff, Alberta. After that, Janka admitted to one of her friends that a woman her age should not have to start the day clambering out of a tent onto wet grass.

Czesław spent the first months preparing classes, while Janka was simply pleased to be back in America. The boys initially had problems settling down and integrating, but found themselves in a more egalitarian and open environment than in France, in a society where almost everyone had an emigrant background. The boys became trilingual and felt closer to American or French culture than Polish. They grew and developed different interests. While Antoni was curious to know more about the history of religion, anthropology and music, what fascinated him most were the sciences and electronics. Describing his sons in 1965, Miłosz remarked that

> Toni has a big ginger-coloured beard and resembles a portrait of a German Romantic. He is so engrossed by the deepest areas of metaphysics ... that neither cars nor girls interest him, only highly spiritual matters. Piotr is a tall man of Apollonian beauty with a blond mane of hair, who is oblivious to his physical attributes and reads Pascal. (CM to Zbigniew Herbert, 15 July 1965)

A mere three years later, the situation had changed dramatically. Toni became a husband and a father, and entered the Pharmacy Department at medical school in San Francisco, where he also completed his doctoral studies before becoming a lecturer at the University of California in Santa Cruz, and then finally a programmer of computer systems.

Piotr's fate was more unusual. In the summer of 1967 he went to Alaska for the first time, working as a carrier for a trapper. After a morning wash in a lake, they would set off to hunt moose, and often encountered wolves. In later years as a student of anthropology, he went on an expedition to South America, where he met diamond smugglers. In 1974 he travelled back again to America's far north, where he took on a well-paid job as a tanker driver at a pipeline construction site. The job demanded great psychological strength to cope with the inhospitable weather conditions and the solitude. In letters to his friends in Paris, Miłosz wrote of his younger son's wanderings, which must have struck him as not so dissimilar from his own father's:

> The edge of the Arctic Ocean was like the Moon. It was dark twenty-four hours a day and it got a little lighter for one hour, around noon, with temperatures below 50 F, and nothing, not one tree. Even snow is scarce, because it is dry, with only strong winds ... Piotr became a hero there because he put out a fire which could have blown up the whole of Pump No. 1. (CM to Giedroyc, 23 December 1974)

Unfortunately, it was soon to become apparent that this hazardous expedition had effects that would totally transform the whole family's life.

Settling Accounts on Two Fronts

I would like to show you my workroom. From the chaos it generates, it would be very easy to deduce that I choke with greed and if I could, I would stretch a day to make it longer than twenty-four hours. Books in four different languages lie spread open on the couch and on the shelves, proofs of willingness to do more than realistically possible. There is an enormous table covered with notes, manuscripts from under which peer pipes, dirty glasses, pencils, cigars, newspaper cuttings, ash trays, bags with dried fruit, volumes of poetry and on the floor columns of folders that would not fit anywhere anymore.

Czesław Miłosz, 'I should have written' (ca. 1963)

Only now do I discern the thread joining the various phases of and influences on my mind's progress: Catholicism, Stanisław Brzozowski, Oskar Miłosz, Hegelianism (in the person of my friend, Tadeusz Juliusz Kroński), Swedenborg, Simone Weil, Shestov, Blake. That thread is my anthropo-centrism and my bias against Nature. The succession of influences forms a pattern that begins with my interest in Manichaeism, first stirred by my readings in Church history, and ends with my course on Manichaeism at Berkeley.

Czesław Miłosz, *The Land of Ulro*, 159–160

Providing a progress report after three weeks in his post, Miłosz informed Jerzy Giedroyc that

giving lectures is not as painful as I had expected. I do not have to write them. Notes in Polish and dividing the material into section bullet points suffice. I have the feeling that the students like me very much . . . There are only a few of them, but not one or two as Janka likes to tease. They are very few, because they signed up for different courses when it was not certain whether I would come . . . I do not get the impression that I am talking to a wall, and the interaction is generally good. So far I have received a cordial reception, which I find touching, and an official carrying out a kind of appraisal congratulated me after one lecture. What else can I add? I feel like a cow that joined the ballet. (CM to Giedoyc, 29 October 1960)

Having earned a Master of Law degree from Wilno University after transferring from Polish Literature studies, Miłosz was initially frightened at the prospect of being a teacher. After only two months, however, his career took a positive turn when he was offered full-time employment and tenure, which was an unprecedented occurrence given his lack of professional teaching experience. And thus Dwinelle Hall, the home of the Department of Slavic Languages and Literature, became the place where for twenty years the poet would carry out his duties—in room number 5405, with its metal desk, small blackboard, and chairs with green plastic covers. Within eight months he was promoted and given the title Professor of Slavic Languages and Literatures, and that is when he admitted to Merton, 'for the first time in my life I feel a "useful member of society"' (30 May 1961, *Striving towards Being* 115).

Wacław Lednicki, Miłosz's predecessor in the post, introduced a requirement for all students in the department to take courses not only in Russian language and literature, but also in other Slavonic literatures. As a result, when Miłosz was discussing the Renaissance poet Jan Kochanowski and Mickiewicz's *Forefathers' Eve,* the lecture theatre had more students than usual, although generally Polish studies did not excite much interest. Miłosz combatted this state of affairs by introducing to his courses exotic plays and novels which reflected wider historical and social contexts, so that Polish culture could be recognised as an integral part of European and world civilisation, something students of emigrant descent, most of whose parents were American farmers and workers, were generally not attuned to. In the early 1960s, both recent and distant European history had registered very little on the American consciousness, with the consequence that Professor Miłosz was obliged to forewarn students during the initial classes that he would be dealing

> with the present and not the past. By the present, I mean the current state of the world and humankind, which has been subjected to violent changes with regard to customs, morals and beliefs. The changes taking place on the planet are fascinating. There is a strong correlation between minor developments in a distant, parochial country and political movements on a global scale. (CM course notebook on 'Polish Culture', Beinecke Library Archive)

The professor also talked of the exceptionally painful history of Poland, a small country in Europe. Though it currently seemed calm on the surface, the disturbing issues affecting its people also affected human lives everywhere. The approach to teaching Miłosz employed was interdisciplinary:

> So far I have talked very little about literature and a lot about history, politics, and so on . . . and now predominantly about the Aryan race. For the older students I have a seminar on contemporary poetry . . . I was sweating hard when I tried to explain about Wyspiański, but we killed ourselves laughing reading Tadeusz Boy-Żeleński's *Small Words.*

Among my students there are a few dumb ones, but also many quick-witted and extremely intelligent characters, heading for careers in Slavic subjects. (CM to Wat, after 15 October 1960)

There was a good deal of language switching in tutorials, because apart from English, some students knew Polish, Russian or French, and Miłosz's history of literature course also involved a blending of philosophy, history and anthropology. In order to avoid repeating himself in the first semesters, he ran courses on contemporary prose, as well as on Tadeusz Różewicz and Polish drama, which he combined with weeks on Brecht and the theatre of the absurd. He offered sessions on film and on the art of translating poetry. The variety of subjects and material with which he was engaged gave him immense pleasure, because he could combine his academic work with his passions as a writer, translator and essayist.

No-one was bored in his seminars. According to one of his first students, Richard Lourie, the professor grabbed their attention mostly by the fact that he was not a theoretician, but a witness to and participant in European history. Mimi McKay, his student in the late seventies, remembered how 'each course began with a lesson in history. In Contemporary Polish Poetry and Fiction, he said, "This course will deal with much history, a field in which Americans show a great lack of understanding". My marginal note shows how accurate he was; I wrote: "Get a good map of Europe"' (McKay, *Partisan Review* 96). Another student wrote that Miłosz began lectures by posing a question and then considered all the variant answers, throwing in minor digressions, which was scary for the less-experienced students. He valued independent thinking and boldness, and 'emanated an inexhaustible fascination with the world around him' (Vołyńska-Bogert, *Tydzień Polski*). And Linda Gregg saw in him 'the physical and spiritual vitality of a warrior . . . as if his war had not ended yet, and he was still ready for action' (Gregg, *Ironwood*). From his correspondence it is clear that in the 1970s he had found his calling. 'I always found my jobs a torture and a bore until now . . . Lecturing about Polish literature has much more meaning and sense', he confessed to Vincenz after the first academic year (CM, 22 May 1961). To Andrzejewski he explained:

I was never interested in politics, only, let's say, meta-politics . . . but *The Captive Mind* was enough to pigeon-hole me, something which I will never be able to shed. Coming here was an attempt to forget about it and I am very happy at Berkeley for that reason. I am a professor of Polish literature and a poet, and this is what I always ought to have been. (CM to Andrzejewski, 15 August 1962)

Teaching not only provided financial stability, but also allowed him time to do his own writing. Preparing as stimulating seminars as he could manage had other positive aspects, fulfilling his need for social interaction, reinforcing a sense of the importance of his work, and lifting his spirits, which had already been bruised by his anonymity as a poet in this faraway land. To Błoński in the mid-1970s, he wrote: 'You speak about my poems, but here they are as incomprehensible as if they were written in Chinese. And on top of that I have had this strong sense of solitude for over twenty years. So now addressing a big audience is like living in hope that I can offer something to people' (CM to Błoński, 8 December 1974). Miłosz enjoyed performing. One of his friends, Aleksander Schenker, a major player in Polish studies in the United States, and formerly Professor of Slavic Studies at Yale, noted how 'engaging with an audience excited him. He wanted to be liked and to know that he was liked. The performing skills helped him in his seminars during which . . . he was first to laugh at his own sayings and comments, and in this way lightened the atmosphere' (Schenker, *In Memoriam*, 162–163). His former student Rimma Volyńska-Bogert recalled perfectly the dramatic but not comical atmosphere he conjured during lectures dealing with evil in Slavonic literatures, which were held in the Biology Department:

> Hanging on the walls there were glass showcases with specimens of different human and animal body parts and different organs. In one at the end there was an embryo. When I stood in front of it I felt a sharp pain, which made me wonder whether the scenery for that lecture was chosen on purpose. A huge table dominated the middle of the room. Behind this table covered in test tubes and other laboratory equipment, like Faustus, the professor stood with his bushy eyebrows and piercing eyes. He was talking about the Russians taking over Lithuania, about the inevitable iniquity that followed . . . 'And then I saw the devil doing his work', the professor managed to say when suddenly roller blinds on the nearest window went up with a mighty crash. Everyone turned to look at the blinds, which became still again, and we were all struck by the feeling that we were not on our own in the room. We sense[d] the physical presence of his subject in the lecture theatre'. (Volyńska-Bogert, 'Sceny')

The lectures whose subjects dealt with more than just Polish literature drew the biggest attendances and earned him popularity. Courses about Manichaeism, which he introduced as part of his remit, had a particular personal significance, of course, and, as he also explained to his students, enabled him 'to show the essence of the situation of contemporary humanity' (Notebook, Beinecke Library Archive). It was similar with lectures on Dostoyevsky, whose work the poet taught in the early sixties. He later explained: 'Whereas normally I had fifteen students attending Polish courses, with Dostoyevsky I instantly got a hundred and fifty' (CM, in Zmarz-Koczanowicz's film *A Magic Mountain*). Students later said that when Miłosz spoke with his Slavic accent, they had an impression that they were listening to Ivan Karamazov himself. A surviving reading list encourages students to read *Poor Folk, The Double, Notes from the Underground, Crime and Punishment, The Idiot* and *Demons* and, among others, Mikhail Bakhtin and Nikolai Berdyaev, which demonstrates how demanding and also illuminating the classes must have been. In other courses Miłosz concentrated on selected plots in Dostoyevsky's work, such as 'The Grand Inquisitor', giving his hearers an insight into core twentieth-century concerns. To them he was not only a lecturer, but a sage whose sessions were enriched by his own experiences and the ethical perspectives he drew attention to.

While exploring Dostoyevsky's *Brothers Karamazov* in 1979, Miłosz risked being unpopular when he referred to the subject of hell and the necessity to choose good even when the majority chooses evil. For him Satan was a real presence. One student, Lillian Vallee, a future translator, especially remembered that address: 'Miłosz was giving a lecture about Dostoyevsky, and a black dog with a red band began to jump on him and bark. Miłosz did not budge: in the corner of his mouth a smile began to appear and with an accent resembling Transylvanian he said: "Sometimes a dog takes on the form of a devil"' (Vallee, 'The Exile in California').

When in 1978 Miłosz retired, the University of California awarded him a Berkeley Citation, the equivalent of a PhD, *honoris causa*, a gesture that must have left him delighted and very moved. In the laudatory speech, Hugh McLean, Dean of the Humanities Department, complimented him on looking so well, 'especially in this gown. Nobody would have thought that Czesław Miłosz reached retirement age this year. And while his looks are great, his achievements are even greater' (McLean, 'Odznaczenie').

In the early years at Berkeley, Miłosz made the decision to collate the notes he prepared for his lectures on the history of Polish literature into book form. Unlike Julian Krzyżanowski's tome with the same title, his book was to be free from messianic-nationalistic interpretations. In a private letter, years before, he dismissed one of Krzyżanowski's other books, *Polish Romantic Literature*, as 'a collection of entirely banal pieces, which are there to reinforce forever *la Pologne martyre*' (CM to Błoński, n.d.1952). Miłosz drew up an outline plan of the book in winter 1964–65 and began dictating it to one of his students, Catherine S. Leach, later the translator of *Native Realm*. In 1969 *The History of Polish Literature* was published in New York by Macmillan.

'For me it was a hobby and fun, dictating for a few hours, once a week,' Miłosz remarked, but the book's readers would have been impressed by the sheer amount of work that he must have done in his first years as a lecturer. Although a clever pupil in an excellent school and a faithful reader of Polish poetry, Miłosz was definitely not a historian of literature then, but now, in nearly six hundred pages, he skillfully wove together literature dating back from Latin monuments of the Middle Ages to contemporary works, introducing readers to hundreds of characters and works. His book provides a thorough, in-depth account of the historical and cultural backgrounds to the texts; introduces authors in an insightful and concise manner, avoiding the cold detachment of a researcher; and does not shy away from expressing strong opinions and asking pertinent questions as to whether a particular work could possess resonances for today's readers. He delves deeply into works of the Renaissance and Baroque periods, focusing on the religious contexts and the importance of the Reformation. He is sceptical about the displays of Romanticism in intellectual life during the partition period in Polish history, but also about modernity as initiated by Młoda Polska (neo-Romanticism). Miłosz carries out re-evaluations which are summarised in this extract from the introduction:

> Romanticism was regarded as the heart of Polish literature . . . and an inseparable ingredient within it was Roman Catholicism. In reality, however, this truism is relatively new . . . the sixteenth- and seventeenth-century 'golden age' shaped Polish literature, and nearly half my work is devoted to the remarkable literary phenomena of these periods, which occurred long before Romanticism. Poland of the 'golden age' was in the main a Protestant country, 'a paradise for heretics'. And despite the later victories of the counter-reformation, the legacy of intellectual rebelliousness was never lost . . . Dichotomy can be regarded as a more or less constant feature of Polish literature, namely emotional moralism, most clearly fed by a strong input of Christian ethics that coexists with anti-clericalism and extreme skepticism towards any dogmas (religious or political). (*A History of Polish Literature* 11)

Miłosz presents not simply a history of Polish literature, but an in-depth examination of what really engages him, how people in those times wrote and thought. Though distant historically, their language is close to us now, as one contemporary researcher has written.[1]

Perhaps there were few professors for whom lecturing at the university was so closely tied to their daily regimen. For many years the poet stuck to a daily routine: an early rise, a walk, writing, going to the campus and, on his return, having a glass of vodka, and then working again until late in the evening in his cigarette smoke–filled office, not treating his work as a chore, but as a safe form of existence and a way to develop.

Preparing for courses on Dostoyevsky enabled him to analyse Polish attitudes to Russia, and subsequently ensured the Russian writer's prominent place in *The Land of Ulro* where he features as one of the authors who most affected

Miłosz's spiritual stance. Having discovered intellectual links between the author of *The Brothers Karamazov* and Emanuel Swedenborg, whose work was very familiar to him, he published an essay on the subject in *Slavic Review* and earned himself a reputation as a renowned critic among Russian literature scholars. In a later study, he argued that many of the psychological illnesses, complexes and inner tensions that have become so prevalent in the twentieth century are anticipated in Dostoyevsky's fiction.

Essays written in English on Dostoyevsky, Pasternak, Shestov, Simone Weil, Brzozowski and Witkacy which reflect his passion and careful research appeared in a collection entitled *The Emperor of the Earth: Modes of Eccentric Visions,* published by the University of California Press in 1977. Miłosz's articles about Russian or French literature were always written in Polish, and then later, with the help of students like Richard Lourie or Lillian Vallee, translated into English. During those years Kultura, in Paris, remained his main publisher, though in the mid-1960s two London-based publishing houses, Kontynenty and Oficyna Poetów i Malarzy, also brought out his work. The latter, which was run by Czesław and Krystyna Bednarczyk, accepted a dozen poems and two articles in their quarterly and, more importantly, decided to publish a 150-page volume entitled *Wiersze* (Poems) in 1967. Not even Giedroyc was prepared to publish the full range of Miłosz's literary output to date, mainly for financial reasons, but also because poetry did not feature highly on his publishing agenda. He was, however, prepared to put into print works which from his point of view were very risky, such as Miłosz's study of Tadeusz Brzozowski, entitled *A Man among Scorpions* (1962).

During his first decade in California, Miłosz fought battles on two fronts: one against America in *Visions from San Francisco Bay,* and the other with contemporaneous Polish culture. In *Settling Accounts on Two Fronts,* a piece written in 1964, he examines the fragmentation in Polish intellectual life as a result of the 1772, 1793 and 1795 partitions, and how that prompted the creation of compensating myths, as well as a passion for political justice and restitution, whatever the human costs. In his view, the obsession with nationalism, heroism and martyrdom post-partition meant that too many writers neglected larger metaphysical questions.

As in the preceding decades, he was prone to bouts of intense irritation with the Polish temperament, mixed with feelings of responsibility and brief surges of tenderness, such as during one of his visits to Vancouver: 'I threw myself into Czaykowski's and Busz's arms when I saw their children and heard their Polish chatter. I was overcome with emotion towards everything Polish, which reflects the other side of the coin' (CM to Herbert, 14 September 1967). This battle with antithetical emotions is revealed in his letters to Andrzejewski, where he talks of his desire to detach myself from a small geographical strip of land, from a community I feel was imposed on me. My situation is, after all, different from those Poles who suffer longing for their native soil. I have no family associations with Poland . . . and the paradox is that I am an émigré, one of those who became a Marxist writer by a reflex-reaction . . . I wish for that Poland to be gone once and for all and to bring those thirty million out of the thatch-roofed houses. (CM to Andrzejewski, 14 September 1962)

Five years later he wondered, 'Isn't really my most essential and unsolved complex, my detestation of this notion of orthodox "Polishness", generated in the bucolic works of literature which presented the world as an idyllic place, and ignored the ugliness of History?' (CM to Andrzejewski, 25 January 1967). Berkeley was gradually becoming the centre of his intellectual scene, and he was defining his place in the social processes that were taking place there, and *not* in socialist Poland. Literary culture in Poland he saw as diminished and second-rate as a result of Bierut's and then Gomułka's years in power; whatever legitimacy they might have claimed had been totally undermined by the disgraceful acts initiated on their watch, of which the suppression of student protests and anti-Jewish campaign of March 1968 were amongst the most recent. Writing to Jerzy Turowicz, a key figure in the Kraków-based Catholic journal *Tygodnik Powszechny*, Miłosz explained:

When they named me 'an enemy of the People's Republic of Poland', I was not an enemy then, but I have become one now . . . Since Polish political emigrants, the ones from the time of the Second World War, either die out or love the Republic of Poland for strangling the Jewish infection, it is time for a few more determined people to take the course I took in order to lead the way to a resurgence in Polish literature. And although Gombrowicz is dead, the centre of gravity is clearly shifting, and today's [Polish] literature is created in the West just as it was in the nineteenth century. (CM to Turowicz, 17 October 1969)

In *Private Obligations,* a collection of essays which took its title from an article, 'Private Obligations towards Polish Literature', Miłosz authoritatively states, 'I must make some elementary statements. I was not born in Poland, I was not brought up in Poland, I do not live in Poland, but I write in Polish' (*Prywatne obowiązki* 104), and that when learning the language in his childhood, he 'was not aware that Polish was a language of people who were defeated, downtrodden, and prone to martyrdom and slavery complexes' (ibid., 100). At the same time he acknowledges the existence of very strong ties that cannot be broken:

> My relationships with foreigners are too shallow . . . with Poles a small
> sign is enough, and I begin to recall everything that is within them,
> because it is not within them only, outside of me, it is within me too, as
> the part of *le moi haïssable* [the hateful me]. Their behaviour irritates me,
> because it reveals propensities which I endeavour to suppress in myself.
> (Ibid., 107)

Elsewhere in the collection he identifies what he regards as a worrying facet
of Polish culture, the way Sienkiewicz's *Trilogy* is treated so reverentially: 'If
a nation chooses a somewhat childish story as their *Iliad,* doesn't it pay a high
price? Does it not suggest a Peter Pan–like condition of not wanting to grow
up?' (*Prywatne obowiązki* 147). He lamented, for example, the way that at times
the complexity of Polish-Russian relations had been reduced in nationalist mythology to the dialectics of victim and executioner.

In the second half of the 1970s, Miłosz's interests underwent a reconfiguration, though behind the changes one detects older anxieties and preoccupations.
Once more his correspondence sheds considerable light on his priorities, which
are revealed here as his seeking still to become a less peripheral cultural figure,
more engaged and 'useful', something the award of the Nobel Prize would make
easier to achieve:

> I am only concerned with what I have to say to people. Although I
> struggled desperately with my own life among strangers, I suddenly re-
> alised that I was completely powerless and that I didn't have anything
> to say to them. The breakdown to which I am a witness accelerates and
> I cannot help feeling a growing sense of disgust towards all this civilisa-
> tion, this pseudo-art, pseudo-thinking and pseudo-religion. And indeed,
> my despair signifies a deep religious crisis. I have translated the whole
> of *The Book of Psalms* . . . to apply my poetic skills to make myself most
> useful to people. (CM to Czapski, 19 June 1978)

Among the tasks he set himself were translations of the works of Kabir, a
fifteenth-century Indian poet and thinker; a piece of gnostic apocrypha *(Hymn
of the Pearl);* and translations into Polish of ten books from the Bible. In order to
undertake that, he learnt Greek and Hebrew, with the aim of finding a language
capable of making the holy text sound clear to a contemporary reader, while at
the same time retaining its sacred tone. The kind of clarity he sought existed in
the late fifteenth-century Puławski Psalm, which captured the vigour and energy
in the Polish language, and the richness of its rhymes. His translation of the
Book of Ecclesiastes was published for the first time in *Tygodnik Powszechny* in
1979, followed by the Book of Wisdom, Psalms and the Book of Job, his choices

closely connected with the pain in his personal life at the end of the 1970s: 'I saw many deeds done under the sun. And it is all but futility, chasing the wind' (*Księgi biblijne*/'Books of the Bible', 438).

When other methods of coming to terms with failures, disappointments and loneliness failed, Miłosz saw in the Bible a potentially verifying source. It is interesting that in the sixties and seventies he had attempted several times to write a novel, only to abandon it because 'each time it turned out to be a Kafkaesque story about a man imprisoned on an island, where there are towns, but no passersby, and inside the houses, he can see through the windows stuffed animals with shiny buttons for eyes' (*Ulro* 50). Maybe a genuine impulse was lacking, as it had been when he wrote *The Seizure of Power* to a tight deadline. Perhaps Californian reality seemed too amorphous for him, too detached from history and culture, and so he slipped into hallucinatory prose and unconvincing, unnatural fantasy. The Bible clearly helped him capture something pivotal to him, and also provided an antidote to the world of 'pseudo-thinking' which surrounded him and filled him with dread. Like his poem 'Readings', the Gospel, when read in Greek, issues a reminder that

> There were plenty of people whom the text calls
> *Daimonizomenoi*, that is, the demonized
> Or, if you prefer, the bedeviled (as for 'the possessed'
> It's no more than the whim of a dictionary).
> Convulsions, foam at the mouth, the gnashing of teeth
> Were not considered signs of talent.
>
> ('Readings', *NCP* 262)

Wilderness

> I did not choose California. Fate brought me here.
> What else could draw a northerner to such a scorched wilderness?
> Czesław Miłosz, *Separate Notebooks* (1977–1979)

> This feeling of being mute! Here in the West I am mute, and I have to struggle with my inner contradictions, because I am here and it is only, only there that I can communicate with people simply through monosyllables, and it is not through a common knowledge about things, but from the same way of thinking.
> Czesław Miłosz to Aleksander Wat (1960)

> You are separated in your ivory tower from all the smaller and greater
> intrigues, and so not directly involved in an argument with Przyboś, and
> unable to hear conversations between Kotts and the little Pawels ...
> Then why complain about not being in this country; away from the
> small and grey Vistula River, which gulps down the sewage from San-
> domierz; ... arguments with a herd of whores, who haggle with the cli-
> ents, the state, over a price, and among themselves fight for that client's
> favours, pretending that it isn't so ... Thank God you are in America
> and have peace and quiet. (Zygmunt Hertz to Miłosz, 18 May 1962)

Miłosz, however, wanted something more than just 'blessed peace', even though
living at a remove from Władysław Gomułka's and later Edward Gierek's Poland, as well as from the literary 'vanity fair', enabled him to concentrate fully
on the work in hand and probably even prolonged his days. At the same time,
throughout the 1960s and 1970s he experienced extended spells of alienation
within the university environment. It was not because people were not friendly
or well-disposed towards him, but because of a disparity between his passions
and the interests of his colleagues. To Miłosz's great joy, the acclaimed Polish
philosopher Leszek Kołakowski spent the 1969–70 academic year in Berkeley,
and the latter recalled how the poet repeatedly engaged in animated discussions
with him on fundamental subjects such as God, the afterlife and the origins
of evil. Miłosz's fellow professors in Slavic studies were not the kind of people
willing to get engrossed by those sorts of subjects, or possibly Miłosz simply
formed the impression that they would not.

During those years he found it extremely difficult to socialise with people
there. He was demanding, impatient, and prone to lose his temper very quickly.
Here he was in this country, where he could express his opinions without difficulty,
and yet wrongly assumed that nobody would understand him. His mind was occupied with 'damned problems', which, here under the Californian sky, appeared
almost unreal, belonging to different times, different places and different modes of
thinking. Like one of Dostoyevsky's characters, he felt deracinated, transplanted
into a civilisation where normality meant listening to the Rolling Stones, smoking
marijuana, being preoccupied with social revolution and protests against the war
in Vietnam. Robert Hass, the poet, recalled a friend of his saying that when she
went to the house on Grizzly Peak to visit Toni Miłosz, she felt as if vibrant,
brightly coloured California had simply vanished and that she had suddenly
stepped into the interior of a European art-house movie, shot in a grim, dim light.

The words that Miłosz seems most often to have associated with California
were 'desert' and 'emptiness'. His America was like something in an Edward Hopper
canvas, an immense expanse against which human figures and homesteads dis-

appear, a country of lonely and lost people. The vast landscapes of America underlined the insignificance of humanity's existence, the fragility of its achievements in the face of the permanence of the ocean, mountains and desert. Nature there was 'inhuman', a wild, brutal environment which left our familiar, 'homely' world looking vulnerable and exposed. The first Californian settlers had already experienced that, trudging through snow-covered mountain passes, killing one another, discovering the frailty of humanity when struck by hunger and fear. In a letter from mid-1964, Miłosz describes an expedition to Death Valley he and young Piotr undertook over Easter 1964:

> We were walking together and when we neared the lights of the village where we were staying, I felt a sudden enlightenment . . . this is the essence of America; a camp, a place to eat and rest overnight, towns which are not real, which can be deserted any day and then there is nothing . . . And this, in turn, gives a specific perspective on human civilisation in general . . . In Europe this nihilist lining is providentially covered over by *son et lumière*. (CM and JM to Aniela Micińska, n.d, summer 1964)

> In Death Valley salt gleams from a dried-up lake bed.
> Defend, defend yourself, says the tick-tock of the blood.
> From the futility of solid rock, no wisdom.
>
> ('City without a Name', *NCP* 215)

America in Miłosz's eyes revealed the tragedy of human existence and uncovered its transience: here a rock was real, and the 'deathly ocean', from which it was possible to shield oneself only through work and thought, strengthening what was artificial, and thus un-natural.

A native poet who confronted this expanse was Robinson Jeffers, who, in Carmel, a small town lying on the coast of the Pacific Ocean, built a stone tower to watch the waves constantly lapping the beach, an eagle waiting for prey, and the cold light of the stars. All through the sixties, Miłosz thought a great deal about Jeffers and translated his work, seeing in him an ally in the struggle to find poetry's meaning and free it from an aesthetic cage. A loner who talked about the 'dehumanisation of thought', Jeffers wrote poems 'dedicated to the contention that nature should be held in religious veneration', seeing it as 'perfectly beautiful', 'perfectly innocent' and 'perfectly cruel' (*Visions* 88).[2] Everything in it was caught up in an eternal cycle of disintegration and renewal, in which the individual counted for nothing. Miłosz, in the opening of his splendid poem inspired by fellow feeling for the poet, evokes a vision of domesticated rural order ('homespun linen', 'birches and firs' with 'feminine names', 'orchards'), which he set against the vast 'void' and 'the nakedness of the elements' in America:

Above your head no face, neither the sun's nor the moon's,
only the throbbing of galaxies, the immutable
violence of new beginnings, of new destruction.

     . . . Basalt and granite.
Above them, a bird of prey. The only beauty.

What have I to do with you? From footpaths in the orchards,
from an untaught choir and shimmers of a monstrance,
from flower beds of rue, hills by the rivers, books
in which a zealous Lithuanian announced brotherhood, I come.
Oh, consolations of mortals, futile creeds.

And yet you did not know what I know. The earth teaches
More than does the nakedness of elements. No one with impunity
gives to himself the eyes of a god. So brave, in a void,
you offered sacrifices to demons . . .

Better to carve suns and moons on the joints of crosses
as was done in my district. To birches and firs
give feminine names. To implore protection
against the mute and treacherous might
than to proclaim, as you did, an inhuman thing.

         ('To Robinson Jeffers', *NCP* 252–253)

From his standpoint in California, 'the land of most complete alienation' (CM
to Jeleński, n.d. early 1960s), Miłosz repeatedly castigates America to his correspondents as a 'country without history', a place of 'spiritual poverty', 'where
the only entertainment of the locals is to stare at passing cars for hours on end,
drinking or shooting from their cars at road signs they pass by' (CM to Skwarnicki, 27 August 1964).

  Though it certainly is not apparent from the quotations above, in reality
Miłosz harboured complex feelings towards the land of his latest exile, best
reflected in his attitude to the students' revolt in the 1960s, which saw great
changes in moral attitudes that he followed as a citizen, a lecturer and a father.
Though he describes his older son as an 'irritating and often stupid adolescent',
he also admits to being 'completely under his spell', and that through him, he
gets 'an insight into the very young America' (CM to Thomas Merton, 31 December 1964, *Striving towards Being* 161).

  A great part of his first decade in Berkeley was overshadowed by student
unrest, which began with protests against the discrimination black people faced

in the streets neighbouring the campus. Picket lines in defence of citizens' rights turned in the autumn of 1964 into mass protests, most notably by the Free Speech Movement, which galvanised thousands of students to demand the right to hold political demonstrations on campus. He gave Giedroyc his mixed impressions of this movement, the members of which he sums up, somewhat simplistically, as 'beatnik, individualistic', inspired by 'zen philosophy' and 'peyote', who believe in 'freedom for all', and are in 'revolt against the older generation'. They are simultaneously 'sarcastic' and 'surprisingly idealistic, craving warmth, a commodity lacking in this society' (CM to Giedroyc, December 1964).

Regular confrontations occurred on and around the campus from 1966 onwards as hostility amongst the young towards the United States' actions in Vietnam gained an increasing momentum. The hours Miłosz spent on the campus increased substantially because of the number of meetings and informal gatherings being organised. When the university authorities brought in the police, many student demonstrators ended up being arrested and brutally beaten with batons, which prompted a large number of the academic staff to sign resolutions in defence of the protesters to help secure their release. In a letter to Aleksander Wat, he was keen to explain how his reading of student activism had changed:

My stand is different from what it was two years ago, because

1) although not formally, I support what is, in essence, opposition to crimes of homicide and

2) in European universities police would not be allowed onto the university grounds

3) there are no other protests against [Lyndon] Johnson outside universities ... The horrors of Vietnam can only be interpreted by reading reports from American pilots (who are unaware that what they write about is, in European eyes, an atrocity that almost puts Hitlerism in the shade). Deep in my heart I believed that crimes committed in the twentieth century (Stalin, Hitler) would be overshadowed by what comes after them. So, for two days I honoured the strikes by cancelling lectures and putting my career on the line, but risking rather little, because should the new chancellor ... wish to sack people like me, they would quickly destroy the university. Of course, I was the only one in that Department [to take this line], because the others are not political animals. (CM to Wat, 5 December 1966)

By 1969 and 1970, it had become increasingly problematic for Miłosz to display his solidarity with the students on campus, over which police helicopters circled continually and a thick cloud of tear gas hovered. Young people more and more often voiced hatred towards their own country, and developed a fascination with Chinese and Cuban communism, and with the October Revolution and Stalin, which, to his mind, demonstrated total, woeful historical ignorance. Among the incidents he recounts was one in which groups of 'black protesters armed with clubs burst into classrooms, chased out the professors and students, demolished furniture and burnt down an auditorium for 1,000 people' (CM to Giedroyc, 30 January 1969). On other occasions there was an arson attack on the library, and an explosion which damaged a line supplying electricity to the university, including a laboratory where Miłosz lectured.

Although he knew from experience how revolutionary movements end, even after these episodes Miłosz did not want simply to reject the activists and their aims, but rather tried to identify the underlying factors behind the violence and the possible outcomes. Inclined towards historical fatalism, he was terrified by the escalation in violence, which he imagined could lead to the collapse of the state, or at least to a division of American society into two antagonistic groups: a continent of, on the one hand, labourers with hair cropped short, 'broad-shouldered hunks' from the farming states, and 'white-collar workers' from Wall Street, and, on the other, an island of politicised, long-haired hippies who, to the astonishment of the professor, would come barefoot to classes, and were sometimes barely clad as they arrived to participate in elections to the student council. Miłosz did not hesitate to expel an agitator from his class, and was brave enough to confront a crowd who were blocking Sather Gate. When he scathingly denounced them as 'the spoilt children of the bourgeoisie', 'it was as if they were struck by lightning ... and they made way for me' (Interview, *A Magic Mountain*). The outburst earned the students' respect.

Addressing a department meeting, he strongly defended the very concept of a university. While walking across the campus in a gas mask, it occurred to him that California had become a laboratory in which it might be possible to see processes at work determining the future shape of civilisation. At the end of what proved to be a tumultuous decade, he collected his observations of his experiences on the West Coast in *Visions from San Francisco Bay* (1969), a book of superbly written essays, which he saw as a continuation of the biographical and philosophical reflections initiated in *The Captive Mind* and *Native Realm*.

It cannot be stressed too strongly that, in his eyes, California offered an epiphany of anti-sense, which undermined humanist and cultural faith and values.

Starting from the tension between humans and their non-human environment, the poet looks from a wider perspective and asks whether our propensity to see symbols in nature is only a delusion, or reflects some archetypal truth, some memory of the species. Ultimately, he regarded the place as occupied by a demonic presence, one devoid of heartening European ideologies, in which a Christian must arrive at a terrible conclusion about the hidden resources of evil within humanity. Faced with this predicament, he concludes that 'only God can save me, because in ascending to Him, I rise above myself, and my true essence is not in me, but above me. Like a spider, I am climbing a thread, and that thread beyond any doubt mine alone, is fastened at the point I came from and at the point where Thou resides addressing me as Thou' (*Visions* 74). Throughout the collection, he returns repeatedly to what he had spoken of in 'The World' as the 'sharp rock' (*NCP* 48) of faith: 'We are either born pious, or impious, and I would be glad were I able to number myself among the former' (*Visions* 33). Though the home of multiple religions, America, like ancient Rome in decline, paradoxically seemed to be losing all sense of reverence. As a result, the various churches were desperately searching for an accommodation with modernity, and so jettisoned the notion of sin at the first opportunity. Is it really possible still to talk about 'sin' in a society where everything is permitted, including, for example, pornography and sadism, as long as they are presented in a tasteful, artistic form? Consider the case of humanity's 'avant-garde', represented by the beatniks and later the hippies. They loathed people from small towns and farms because of their conservatism and small-mindedness and felt superior to them and their 'square', mundane lives. By means of narcotics they sought to achieve higher levels of consciousness, rather than an existence tied to what they viewed as the inhuman struggle to accumulate material things. They rejected what they saw as the outmoded virtues of the pioneers who built America, especially perseverance and the Protestant work ethic.

Miłosz recognised the prospects facing a society that does not believe in anything. In response to the questions 'What did I learn in America and what did I find most precious there?', his answer took the form of 'three sets of pros and cons: for the so-called average man, against the arrogance of intellectuals; for the Biblical tradition, against the search for individual or collective nirvana; for science and technology, against dreams of primeval innocence' (*Visions* 218). The heady, excitable days in Wilno and Warsaw were long past, but he could still be capable of making lightning judgements and adopting binarist positions. Reading *Visions from San Francisco Bay* three decades later and pointing out how ahead of its time it was in comparison with Jean Baudrillard's famous essay, *America*, Marek Zaleski demonstrates how Miłosz the European, despite everything, 'defends

America from decadent Europe' and 'glorifies American democracy', because 'it saved America from European nihilism, its fierce hatred for existence, which ended up producing two sinister political utopias', fascism and communism. 'A secret of Miłosz's power lies in the fact that while his thoughts are brave and modern, at the same time he has no anxiety about appearing dated' (Zaleski, *Gazeta Wyborcza*).

Letters to Oneself

I was courageous. Industrious. Nearly a model of virtue.
But that is good for nothing.
Please, Doctor, I feel a pain.
Not here. No, not here. Even I don't know.
Maybe it's too many islands and continents,
unpronounced words, bazaars, wooden flutes,
Or too much drinking to the mirror, without beauty,
though one was to be a kind of archangel
or a Saint George, over there, on St. George Street.

'I Sleep a Lot', *NCP* 207

Not long after he started work in Berkeley, Miłosz confided to Jerzy Giedroyc: 'No one writes to me. It is as if I ceased to exist, and perhaps I am becoming more and more sceptical about writing and publishing in Polish' (CM to Giedroyc, 16 December 1961). A decade later, in another note to *Kultura*'s editor, he wrote, 'I have just celebrated my sixtieth birthday. No-one except those closest to me remembered it' (CM to Giedroyc, 1 July 1971). Five years further on, he wrote to another friend, 'My sixty-fifth birthday was doleful . . . it was as if I did not exist' (CM to Jeleński, 7 July 1976). Twenty-six years later, in one of his many late biographical pieces, he discloses poignantly, but self-pityingly, how 'during my isolated time as an émigré, there were months when I wondered whether it would be worth writing to myself, just to find something in the letter box' (*Rok myśliwego* 92).

In Berkeley he was brave and industrious and endeavoured to find happiness, but missed the warmth and directness between people he had known in the years in Lithuania and Poland. At the university, he was highly regarded for his lectures on Dostoyevsky and Manichaeism, but in the daily life of the gigantic institution his was a peripheral position without any administrative responsibilities or any expectations that he would produce 'scholarly' articles on a regular basis. His colleagues in and beyond the Department of Slavic Languages and Literature were neither interested in him nor in Polish poetry, and many of them responded to the award of the Nobel Prize with astonishment. And three years earlier, when in 1976 he reached his 'doleful' sixty-fifth birthday, nobody picked up on an idea mooted by Aleksander Schenker that the occasion might be marked with a *Festschrift*.

Departmental gossip held no appeal for him, and he was bored by cocktail parties and chit-chat about trivial matters. On social occasions he would get drunk very early on and invite guests to participate in a game Gombrowicz devised, which he passed off as a venerable Polish tradition; this involved lying on the floor and creating a tangle of bodies. He appears to have had a strong compulsion to try to hit on women students. As this most certainly did not meet with Janka's approval, she quickly put an end to his partying. Often she endeavoured to instruct him in good manners and the correct code of behaviour, telling him off as if he were a little boy when he had had too much to drink or ate too quickly or did not sit properly at the table. It is possible that she did not realise that these social failings were indicative of a core sensuality within him and a hunger for intense, 'naked' sensations, unrestrained by conventions.

Witnessing such scenes was embarrassing for the family, and parties at the house on Grizzly Peak soon ceased. What replaced them were long sessions devoted to translating his poetry, to which he invited a select number of students. There were also occasional sorties with his old classmate from Wilno, Stanisław Kownacki (see *ABC* 167–172), and, equally rarely, the appearance of visitors from Poland.

What lay behind Miłosz's acutely negative pronouncements about the United States was in part a frustration at the lack of an audience for his poetry there, despite the fact that the country contained a huge population of people of Polish descent. The older generation of American Poles he regarded as culturally deficient, and besides, they knew little or nothing about him, because they did not read *Kultura* and the poetry he published in it. Though this section of the population included intellectuals, the majority of them were of Jewish origin and small in number, and for most of them Julian Tuwim was the only important Polish poet worth knowing. By far the largest number of people of Polish extraction were labourers, descendants of illiterate peasants, many of whom arrived from Galicia to escape acute poverty. Initially Miłosz had difficulty understanding how, after toiling away each day, they put aside every spare dollar towards the education of their children, not to enable them to study Polish and Polish culture, but to help them acquire proficiency and qualifications in technical subjects to ensure that they would have a better-paid career. This kind of behaviour

led him to declare in one of his letters that 'the Polish community in America ...
is utterly beyond hope. As a policy, I maintain no contact with them' (CM to
Skwarnicki, 3 October 1964). It was not until the 1970s that the poet softened his
opinions, after a visit to Alliance College in Cambridge Springs, near Buffalo,
following a conversation with its president. This revealed rather more about the
first generation of better-off Poles.

> The conversation was in English, because, though he knows Polish, he
> is ashamed because he speaks the dialect of peasants, and so is afraid
> that he will speak incorrectly. I tried to persuade him to open a centre
> for Polish Ethnic Studies, to study the social history of the Polish
> immigration ... He began to talk about his father, how he used to
> leave early each morning as if he were looking for a job. His wife
> made him a sandwich, but it was obvious that, because there was no
> work, he wandered around ... looking for shoes for her, and could not
> bring himself to eat the sandwich, because there were hungry children
> at home. And about all the discrimination directed towards people
> with Slavonic names, though his father used to get jobs because he
> spoke German. Around Poznań all the supervisors were German.
> And then I felt terribly sorry for all of them. (CM to Skwarnicki, 3
> October 1964)

Perhaps after that he grasped how much contempt and hatred lurked within
classic 'Polish jokes', such as the one about the Polish pencil having an eraser at
both ends. They contained vicious propaganda which needed to be resisted.

Unknown to the Polish emigrant community living in America, one of the
most outstanding of their number wrote these bitter words, which suggest that
important lessons were being learned:

> Faithful mother tongue,
> I have been serving you.
> Every night, I used to set before you little bowls of colors
> ...
> This lasted many years.
> You were my native land; I lacked any other.
> ...
> Now, I confess my doubt.
> There are moments when it seems to me I have squandered my life.
> ...
> Faithful mother tongue,
> perhaps after all it's I who must try to save you.

So I will continue to set before you little bowls of colors
bright and pure if possible,
for what is needed in misfortune is a little order and beauty.

('My Faithful Mother Tongue', *NCP* 245–246)

Dated 'Berkeley 1968', the poem carries the imprint of events in Poland that year, but also reflects the preceding period in California, when Miłosz had the impression that having written the poems in his native tongue, he might as well have thrown them in the Pacific or hidden them in birds' nests. He wrote, published, edited and then faced a void. Soon after arriving in the States, he had complained to a friend back home, 'It seems that these books of mine in *Kultura* are expressly there so that nobody would print even a line about them. I'd have preferred it if someone attacked them and criticised them—but no, nothing' (CM to Andrzejewski, 16 August 1962). Just over a decade later, he voiced his frustrations again, this time in a letter to the magazine's editor: 'Because my book, *Private Obligations,* did not get a single review . . . psychologically it would be difficult for me to write further articles in Polish' (CM to J. Giedroyc, 1 August 1973). Even in the autumn of 1979, when his candidature for the Nobel Prize was close to reaching its positive outcome, he felt like a miser who sleeps on a mattress filled with money; because no-one knows about it, the mattress will end up in a rubbish dump.

When the poet and essayist Marek Skwarnicki[3] visited the States in 1964, Miłosz took the trouble to copy out by hand in a notebook about seventy of his poems and translations, so it could be taken to Poland and circulated to his friends and acquaintances. The motive for doing this is obvious, and expressed wryly in a note he subsequently wrote: 'I begin to doubt more and more whether my existence is not just the existence of a ghost at a spiritualist séance . . . who cannot tell whether his knocking is picked up by anyone' (CM to Skwarnicki, 1 May 1970). He was a professor, best known as the author of *The Captive Mind*, but his finest work was unread by the audience he desired most in Poland.

In those years, he was an extremely lonely man whose number of friends with intellectual ties living in America was very small. His contacts there consisted primarily of Thomas Merton, Aleksander Wat and Leszek Kołakowski, who were resident in Berkeley only for short periods. An important new addition to this limited circle was Aleksander Schenker, a linguist born in Kraków and now working at Yale University, whom Miłosz met in 1968 at a poetry reading he gave in New York. Schenker soon after was invited to Berkeley to give lectures during the 1969–70 academic year, and remembered especially Janka's warm attitude towards him and Czesław's insatiable hunger for readers. He needed feedback, or, as he described it, intellectual ping-pong, and prevailed on Schenker to read his poems before they went into print, albeit not with any intention of taking any criticism on board. Like any other writer, Miłosz craved those priceless words of encouragement, 'What you are doing is very good'.

It was to Schenker that Miłosz was indebted when in 1976 a beautiful volume of his work appeared, ten years after the London publication of *Wiersze*. The publisher was Michigan Slavic Publications at the University of Michigan at Ann Arbor, which in 1977 awarded the poet an honorary doctorate. The director of the publishing house was a friend of Schenker's, a Czech specialist, Ladislav Matejka. Schenker recalled the warm response he received to the suggestion of a new Polish edition of Miłosz's work. Matejka, however,

> demanded an introduction in English, because this would be the only way to receive funding for the project ... An additional incentive was the hope that an English introduction might be a decisive factor during the deliberations of the Nobel Committee, because Miłosz's name was frequently mentioned in that context. Because there was no one who would be prepared to write such an introduction, I succumbed to Miłosz's persuasion and undertook the task. (Schenker, *Zeszyty Literackie*)

In his introduction, or rather extensive study, Schenker made it very clear to readers that Miłosz was not just one of the most important figures in twentieth-century Polish literature, but also one of the world's most outstanding living poets.

A question that might be asked is how this Dionysian character, filled with vitality and desire, managed to cope with the approach of old age. In 1981 he reported to Konstanty Jeleński that the results of medical tests he recently undertook showed that his testosterone level stood at 755, whereas men over fifty could usually expect on average 300. Jeleński, conscious that Eros was a major source of poetic vigour and inspiration in Miłosz, had years earlier warned his friend openly, 'You succumb to moral precepts too much ... You have at least ten years ahead of you in which you can enjoy love and girls. After all, the campus is a natural environment for you' (Jeleński to CM, 23 December 1965). With his warrior posture and his unexpectedly soft and melodic voice, Miłosz was attractive to women. As he travelled extensively alone, he could well have had a number of affairs between the mid-1960s and the early 1980s, although he kept them secret and each time struggled with his guilt. Obviously he sought erotic fulfillment, but also warmth in the company of happy young women, a need not unconnected to his difficulties in forging stronger bonds with his own sons. It was not until the late

1970s and early 1980s that he had a relationship which did become known to his friends.

He tried love, but more often than not alcohol and emptiness were his companions. Along with different types of vodka, gin and California wine, he had a particular fondness for bourbon, though drinking never provided inspiration for his work. On the contrary, work required an early-morning start, clarity of mind and awareness. An evening drink of bourbon could be a treat and act as company when he was writing letters, and, more than anything, serve as a stay against fear. And there was plenty of that in his room overlooking the ocean, as he battled feelings of failure—the fact, as he saw it, that he had become less and less known in Poland, and never discovered in America. Amongst his recurring dreams was one about being in Warsaw, trapped in a house where a search was being carried out by German or Russian soldiers who were 'gradually working their way up to me' (*Visions* 198). Another, more Kafkaesque nightmare involved a 'small guillotine working in a room resembling a hairdresser's'; although he and his companions in the dream begin as witnesses, at some point they are beckoned towards the deadly device, 'and we walk up in a stupor, realising that it has to happen to us' (*Prywatne obowiązki* 233). Though products of his experiences of two world wars, to the 'Lithuanian bear' in the house at Grizzly Peak, these may well have seemed intimations of his own mortality.

An American in Paris

Dear Czesław—the only solution for you would be to come to Europe for the whole summer. There are crowds milling around here and lots of people asking about you . . . If you do not come, you will rust completely.

Zygmunt Hertz to Czesław Miłosz (1961)

'Finally I got the so-called green card with a photograph, a document legalising my status in the States, and now I can leave the country for up to one year . . . Because I will be free one semester, the trip to Europe for a longer period of time at the beginning of next summer is becoming real' (CM to Jerzy Giedroyc, October 1962). And indeed, thanks to a sabbatical, the Miłosz family were able to take a long holiday and stay in England, France, Switzerland and Italy from June 1963 until January 1964.

It was then that the family, now sure of their future in America, sold the house in Montgeron and bought a Volkswagen Beetle, which would serve them for many years to come, and proved its reliability during their grand tour of Italy. They stopped over at Stanisław and Irena Vincenz's place in Grenoble, then

headed for Lucca, Florence, San Gimignano, Siena, Rome, Assisi—according
to the poet, the longest and most affecting experience in the whole of their
journey—then continued on to Arezzo, Ravenna, Venice, Padua and Verona.
They spent two weeks in the company of Nicola Chiaromonte and Mary Mc-
Carthy, which enabled the poet to share with them his opinion on the current
state of Western civilisation and his firm conviction that 'the end of the world
was imminent' (Mary McCarthy to Hannah Arendt, 28 December 1963). The
poet got to Rome for the opening of the Second Vatican Council, and there
he ran into one of *Tygodnik Powszechny*'s top correspondents, Jerzy Turowicz,
who was working there. In Turowicz's company, discussions were held late into
the night about Simone Weil, Thomism, Swedenborg and Blake, sipping brandy
and grappa. After the Miłoszes' return to Paris, they heard in Maisons-Laffitte
the terrible news about the assassination of John F. Kennedy. Something they
retained in their memories were the tasteless Italian adverts they saw, which took
advantage of the president's popularity to advertise 'Kennedy' washing machines.

Although it would be hard to imagine a more beautiful trip, Miłosz told
Zbigniew Herbert about the 'melancholy' of Italy, with its 'ashes of fine art' (CM
to Herbert, 18 October 1963). Europe did not merely disappoint him; he found it
horrible. It seemed small and lacking in ideals, thirsty only for peace and pros-
perity. Subsequent visits to Europe—and there were several in the next two
decades—helped him remain balanced and provided injections of hope. They
reminded him that he was not just a scholar at Berkeley, but a poet, and that his
voice, despite impediments, reached the intelligent young in Poland; he pointed
out in a 1976 letter to Lillian Vallee that a new generation who knew and understood his books was emerging, thereby bringing to an end traditional Polish
stupidity (CM to Vallee, 27 September 1976). The most important location for
the dissemination of his work was Paris, to which friends from Poland travelled
to meet him, the best of them understanding him almost without words.

Whenever possible, he preferred travelling to Europe on his own. He felt
rejuvenated rediscovering what he referred to as his 'Roma blood' (CM to Turowicz, 6 November 1965). At international literary conferences, he captivated his
audiences, such as in 1965, when he participated in the Biennale de Poésie in
Knokke-le-Zoute, where he met, among others, Artur Międzyrzecki, Vasko Popa
and Pierre Emmanuel. On the journey back to California, he travelled through
London to meet his publishers, the Bednarczyks, with whom he had developed
a 'warm friendship' (CM to A. Wat, 27 September 1965).

In March 1967 the Congress of Poets, organised by Jeleński and held in
Paris, was devoted to translations of Polish poetry. Miłosz and his wife arrived
together, and in the course of that visit Janka saw Andrzejewski for the last time.
'Already' by that time, Miłosz observed painfully, 'she was suffering from acute
depression' (*Zaraz po wojnie* 24). They spent a few months in Europe, meeting

Gombrowicz in St Paul-de-Vence, keeping up the cordial relationship with Herbert and, while in London, seeing the Bednarczyks, who showed him the first copies of his *Poems*.

In subsequent years Miłosz travelled to a number of places, including Amsterdam in 1971, where he and Janka visited the Rijksmuseum, admiring especially 'the Dutch artists from seventeenth century, probably the best art (to hell with the Impressionists, the beginnings of the plague!)' (CM to Andrzejewski, 2 July 1971). They also visited Lourdes in the mid-1970s, about which the poet wrote: 'In no way did it confirm the unfavourable stories that I had heard about its over-commercialisation. It was the most poetic place in the world I have ever seen, poetic on a higher level, different from twentieth-century poetry' (CM to Vallee, 27 September 1976).

From Paris in 1978 he made a telephone call to Andrzejewski in which he talked with bitterness about his wife's illness and the difficulties of old age. On 5 October 1979, soon after returning to America, Miłosz received the shattering news of Zygmunt Hertz's death. Hertz's correspondence gives an ironic but accurate glimpse of what the repeated Parisian visits meant to Miłosz, and how they helped lift his spirits:

> So Czesław arrived here ... What is important is that 1) he became convinced that he is not an unknown writer, but a known one. There was a gathering of about twenty people in Cluny ... they knew his verses by heart, asked questions such as what, how and why. It went on for a number of hours. 2) Sadzik wants to publish *A Treatise on Poetry* with Janka's illustrations ... 3) in the light of that and because of the interest shown in him, France no longer stinks. (Hertz to Jeleński, 9 July 1975)

Miłosz considered himself very lucky to have befriended Konstanty Jeleński, who was an insightful reader of his poetry and one of the most persevering individuals in promoting it. Initially he did not trust Jeleński, and felt suspicious of his flexibility and refined 'Parisian' intellect, but over time learnt to appreciate how 'consistent, just, faithful, wise' he had proved to be:

> All these years I have had only one reader, him. My prose enjoyed Polish and non-Polish readership, but I was only reluctantly accepted as a poet, even by those who recognised my talent. For example, I did not expect Zygmunt Hertz to judge my poems, because he was not capable of appreciating them. He considered *The Issa Valley* to be my best piece of work and always gave me this advice: 'Czesław, write for people!' Poems were not so much for people in his mind, not to mention essays ... The only confirmation of the quality of my work I found in letters from Jeleński. (*Rok myśliwego* 92)

Jeleński wrote numerous critical articles, beginning in 1945 with a piece on the collection *Ocalenie* ('Rescue') in *Salamander*, a monthly issued by the First Polish Armoured Division,[4] through to an extensive essay, 'The Poet and Nature', in 1968. Jeleński's analysis of the work left him increasingly convinced about its worth and how highly Miłosz should be ranked, as is conveyed in a comment in a letter from the late 1960s: 'You are the only Polish writer who has a vision, moral courage, a feeling for reality' and 'lives as a free man' (Jeleński to CM, 1 August 1969).

Another supportive presence was Józef Sadzik, one of those unusual priests who combined deep faith with empathy, understanding and tolerance. He was a man totally at ease with and open to the contemporary world and art, and commissioned from the Polish Jewish sculptor Alina Szapocznikowa a figure of Jesus and stained-glass windows depicting the Apocalypse from Jan Lebenstein to be placed in the Pallottine Centre on the rue Surcouf in Paris. Miłosz was enchanted by this exceptional priest, experiencing 'a physical sense of joy, the joy eyes express', on seeing his friend, and a greater 'appreciation of existence' (*Rok myśliwego* 94). Sadzik, who came from near Kraków, was a fine scholar of theology and philosophy, and so an ideal companion with whom Miłosz could discuss the issue of faith. Sadzik wrote the introduction to *The Land of Ulro* and was an initiator and persevering assistant when it came to the poet's translations of biblical texts. Additionally, he acted as a trusted confidant, with whom Miłosz could talk about his painful family experiences, and one of those few people in his life whose higher moral ground he acknowledged and revered.

Józef Sadzik died on 26 June 1980, soon after delivering Miłosz's translation of the Book of Job to the publishers. Fifteen years later the poet recalled:

I begged you when you died to help me change my life, and although I do not know ... what was your contribution, I reflect on how much my life has changed. I missed you, because I could confess to you alone, not hiding anything over what happened to me during those years. Stand by me, let your presence protect me and support me. ('I oto, drogi', *Nasza Rodzina* 7–8, 1995)

Second Space

In 1950, in Warsaw, I said to a friend of mine, 'In ten years I shall write on God, but not earlier'. Perhaps by 'writing' I meant pronouncing His name. A detour, a long detour, is necessary.

Czesław Miłosz, letter to Thomas Merton (1960),
in *Striving towards Being* 93

I have considered for a long time how to reach to the heart of intellectual events in Europe in the twentieth century, which Nietzsche predicted,
talking about 'the death of God'.

Czesław Miłosz, letter to Nela Micińska (1962)

In one of the final letters he sent to Józef Sadzik, Miłosz wrote that Catholicism lay at the core of his thinking and his poetry, which continued to retain an
apocalyptic dimension. His return to America in 1960 coincided with a phase
of intense self-scrutiny, reflection and reform within the Catholic Church initiated by Pope John XXIII, which Miłosz followed with great interest. Pope John
was keen that his pontificate should see the Church more actively promoting
the rights of the 'oppressed', particularly 'workers, women and children', countering the widespread commodification of human beings, and placing far greater
emphasis on the need for reconciliation and dialogue with other faiths (John
XXIII, *Mater et Magistra,* 8, 18, 20–21). While many aspects of this reformist
pope's agenda met with Miłosz's approval, the latter felt anxieties too that post–
Vatican II certain fundamental elements of traditional Catholic theology were
being jettisoned because of a 'craze to acknowledge the world, to adapt to it'
(Haven, *Czesław Miłosz: Conversations* 125).

   As a result of what he regarded as this shying away from harder, less palat-
able metaphysical truths about the actuality of sin, judgement, heaven and hell,
young Americans seemed progressively to be regarding religion simply as a set
of rules for conduct. If this were to continue, the world that God left must inevitably collapse:

> I did not expect to live in such an unusual moment.
> When the God of thunders and of rocky heights,
> the Lord of hosts, Kyrios Sabaoth
> would humble people to the quick,
> allowing them to act whatever way they wished,
> leaving to them conclusions, saying nothing.
> It was a spectacle that was indeed unlike
> the agelong cycle of royal tragedies.
> Roads on concrete pillars, cities of glass and cast iron,
> airfields larger than tribal dominions
> suddenly ran short of their essence and disintegrated.
>   . . .
>
> People, afflicted with an incomprehensible distress,
> were throwing off their clothes on the piazzas so that nakedness might
>   call for judgment.

But in vain they were longing after horror, pity, and anger.
Neither work nor leisure
Was justified,
nor the face, nor the hair nor the loins
nor any existence.

('Oeconomia Divina', *NCP* 263)

While the 1940s and 1950s were a time in Miłosz's life focused on politics, philosophy and history, in the two following decades he was more preoccupied with matters relating to theology, religion and God. From this it can be seen that his friendships with Sadzik and Merton were not matters of chance. Writing to Turowicz in 1962, he explained that religion did not interest him as a bulwark against communism. Instead he hoped that the new generations would be able to nurture a deep, intellectual faith, and that the task of *Tygodnik Powszechny* should be to prevent the 'quite primitive Voltairean tendencies of the progressive Polish intelligentsia'. An issue which concerned him was the weakness of the language used in translations of religious works. 'While we can boast a rich tradition in the translations of literary and rationalist texts, the language feels like pulp when it comes to religious writings' (CM to Turowicz, 21 November 1962).

A major issue of concern to him in the reforms introduced by the Second Vatican Council was the alteration made to the liturgy, which was no longer to be in Latin, but in each of the different national languages used throughout the world. Like many older Catholics, Miłosz was deeply emotionally attached to Latin, which served to underline the universality of the Church; everyone, including exiles, could feel 'at home' in the mass, using the same familiar words. Miłosz feared that the Polish language was not capable of bearing the *sacrum*. It is worth remembering that the poet witnessed the outcomes of these changes not in deeply conservative Poland, but in ultra-liberal California, where Catholics were just one group among scores of other faiths or religious groups; where he noted with despair the reluctance of priests to refer any longer to sins of human nature and to the devil; and where some parish priests, in their keenness to foster 'togetherness', ended up mounting services which seemed more like jolly scout gatherings, complete with sing-alongs to the accompaniment of a guitar. These changes he regarded as symptomatic of a more general decline, a thinning down in the religious imagination caused by the development of science and the advance of a more materialistic, more facile way of life.

For Miłosz a religious experience was something more intimately bound up with the essence of an individual. This was reflected in his collection of essays *Ogród nauk* (The Garden of Science), published in the 1970s. 'Saligia'[5] includes a reminder of the existence of the seven deadly sins, a gesture of protest against 'progressive' convictions about the innate good nature of humanity and the failure to reiterate the crucial importance of the concept of free will. An essay titled 'About Hell' reminds us of the visions of Dante, Milton and Swedenborg, presenting them as works which 'offer a foretaste of something that is Inexpressible' (*Ogród nauk* 117). He felt that this sense of 'other', non-physical spaces was disappearing from the contemporary consciousness, as is reflected in the opening poem in the last collection published during the poet's lifetime:

> Have we really lost faith in that other space?
> Have they vanished forever, both Heaven and Hell?
>
> . . .
>
> Let us weep, lament the enormity of the loss.
> Let us smear our faces with coal, loosen our hair.
>
> Let us implore that it be returned to us,
> That second space.
>
> ('Second Space', *SS* 3)

A very important prose publication, *The Land of Ulro*, published in 1977, is an essay about the decline of the artistic and religious imagination and the evisceration of the human world, reducing it to a scientific, one-dimensional picture alien to 'human' ways of seeing. In some ways this might be seen as a continuation of *The Captive Mind*, since the totalitarianisms of the twentieth century are rooted in 'nineteenth-century science, vulgarised and turned into pseudo-evangelism for the masses' (*Ulro* 11). Józef Sadzik, who wrote the introduction, described Miłosz as an artist who wanted something more than literature 'only', posing the most basic question, framed by Martin Heidegger, who was horrified by the disappearance of God: Why, really, is there Something, rather than Nothing? Miłosz, himself at the height of his skills as an essayist, began his reasoning thus:

> Who was I? Who am I now, years later, here on Grizzly Peak, in my study overlooking the Pacific? I have long deferred the telling of certain spiritual adventures, alluding to them until now only discreetly and grudgingly. Until I noticed that it was getting late—in the history of our shrinking Earth, in the history of a life—and that it was time to overcome my long-abiding distrust of the reader. (*Ulro* 3)

Not worried any more about being unmasked, accused of being a religious fanatic, he declared his conviction 'in the existence of human nature':

In the literature of the mid- and late twentieth century, no one would presume to challenge the laws of physics, biology, psychology, sociology, and so on; they are flatly taken for granted. But if as a result of continual reduction man was no longer king but some subspecies of anthropoidal ape; if he was stripped of Eden, of Heaven and Hell, of good and evil, now defined as the product of social determinants, then was he not ripe for the ultimate reduction, for his metamorphosis into a planetary society of two-legged insects? (*Ulro* 157)

Looking for the reasons as to how we arrived at this state of things, Miłosz went back to the end of the eighteenth century and the consequences of the rationalist Newtonian revolution in science, which resulted in 'the division of the world of scientific laws (cold, indifferent to our values) and the [human] spiritual world'. The position of humanity was downgraded. No longer an inhabitant of a garden given to him by God, or a blessed possessor of an immortal soul, the human being came to be seen as just another creature in a world ruled by a mechanical logic. The struggle against the dehumanisation of the world has been lost, though artists and visionaries have engaged in that fight and are the true heroes of Miłosz's book, 'worthy of admiration, even if their efforts ended in failure' (*Ulro* 269). The central protagonist, who it is not difficult to identify, is Oskar Miłosz, and while many of the essays' themes and threads originate in his work, they also encompass the ideas of Goethe, who waged a 'thirty-year war against Newton', along with those of Swedenborg, Blake, Mickiewicz, and latterly Simone Weil and Lev Shestov. Dostoyevsky is an important presence too, as well as Samuel Beckett, who inhabited Blake's *Land of Ulro*, 'where a man is reduced to a supererogatory number, worse, where he becomes as much for himself, in his own eyes, in his own mind' (*Ulro* 122). This charmed circle of artists and thinkers provides the sources and becomes the subjects of Miłosz's internal intellectual ruminations, which will preoccupy him until the end of his life. He does not present himself as a mystic in a direct line of succession leading back to Swedenborg, Blake and Oskar Miłosz. On the contrary, he states clearly that he is incapable of reliving their visions or possessing the certainty they had that they were in contact with an otherworldly order, and, significantly, he reserves judgement about their truth.

The final part of *The Land of Ulro* attempts a prognosis for our civilisation and contains a personal admission. Unfortunately, the precise nature of the prognosis is not very clear. Rather, it is an expression of a longing for social forms different from secular, nihilistic Western culture, though he does not elaborate on what those ideal forms should be. But what is important is Miłosz's presentation of himself as, above all, a person with a deeply religious sensibility. He does not try to prove to us that God exists. While he concedes that atheism may be more honest and a more demanding position to adopt, it is contrary to his profound need for faith, even if it is constantly beset by waves of doubt. Miłosz's faith is an act of will, driven by the convictions that 'it is not for me to live my life without constantly offering prayers to God', that 'I will not survive without God's help', that only God's grace can lead him to good. Miłosz sought help in prayers and in different translations of the Bible, because he was frequently subject to bouts of revulsion towards himself and his failings. While still in France he wrote to Merton: 'There are people of good grain and of bad grain ... I mean physical inability of total opening towards the others, of altruism, of charity for instance, which does not exclude short moments of good intentions' (CM to Merton, 16 July 1959, *Striving towards Being* 47). Two years later he carried out a more thorough exercise in vivisection:

> What is repentance? There are nights when I am oppressed by a feeling of guilt because of two or three lines which seem to me artistically bad: my wounded self-love. Other nights, a remembrance of all my deeds which prove that I am inferior by nature to the vast majority of human beings: is it repentence? Or just a wounded ambition, just like in the case of not-quite-good lines? I know that 'le moi est haïssable', that only renouncing to it can one attain purity. But I am even unable to confess ... I impose upon myself that going to church (since 1953) ... My constant problem: I believe, with a part of myself ... in the Incarnation, the Resurrection and the Resurrection of the body. I cannot believe in the immortality of the soul. (CM to Merton, 30 May 1961, *Striving towards Being* 117, 118.)

In 1991 the poet said: 'I ought to be asked whether I believe that the four Gospels are truthful. My answer to this is "yes". Do I believe in the absurdity that Jesus rose from the dead? ... My answer is "yes", and so I refute the omnipotence of death' ('Gdyby to można było powiedzieć'). Five years before that, in reply to Aleksander Fiut's question about what the most important thing in life was, he replied with one word: 'Redemption' (Author's interview with Fiut, November 2005).

Prisoners of Ulro

'Contemporary poet'
Imprisoned in Hell says that Hell does not exist.

Czesław Miłosz, 'Sentences'

I carry within me the whole of Różewicz's hell.

Czesław Miłosz in a letter to Aniela Micińska

I consider the Fellini-Antonioni line immoral. They are supposed to be satires on alienation and inauthenticity which are fashionable in intellectual circles, but behind that fig leaf lie unreality and a satire on the whole world, and any satire on the whole world which degrades life is immoral. They are in complete contrast to Ingmar Bergman, a Shakespearean artist, who, surprisingly, did not succumb to this fashionable sickness and accepts the brutality of the world . . . The idea is not about showing sin in order to explain that somewhere behind a curtain some *deus ex machina* is at work, but in order not to degrade *Being,* even in its tangible and earthly forms. That is why I don't care for the theatre of Beckett or Ionesco. (CM to Turowicz, 21 November 1962)

Miłosz sent these comments to Jerzy Turowicz, who was staying in Rome to observe sessions of the Second Vatican Council, but who always found time to go to the cinema. Judgements like these recur in the poet's writing and talks. Because he wrote about the clash between Goethe and Blake, then for many years he attacked artists whom he considered to be exponents of art which paid homage to the dictates of Ulro. Up until the time of 'Treatise on Theology' in 2002, he fought with those he regarded as 'the fraudsters of my time'. This was now a culture where it was

> permitted to shriek in the tongue of dwarfs and demons
> But pure and generous words were forbidden
> Under so stiff a penalty that whoever dared to pronounce one
> Considered himself a lost man.
>
> ('A Task', *NCP* 259)

His objections should not be interpreted as outright rejections, because he usually recognised the artistic significance of his antagonists, as, for example, in that 'most honest writer' in the declining West, Samuel Beckett, whose plays display most fully his 'realization of man's new metaphysical condition, summarized by a single word: *NO.* No voice reaching from the cosmos, no good and evil, no fulfillment of the promise, no Kingdom' (*Ulro* 240).

The opening night of *Waiting for Godot* in Paris took place in the Théâtre de Babylone on 3 January 1953. Miłosz saw the play soon after, and, looking at the audience, who were killing themselves laughing, realised that despair presented in the form of clowning promotes indifference, and that Beckett's characters were totally void of free will. He likened the play to an embryo, an offspring of 'the spirit of determinism, that comes from a conviction that human beings are powerless, that they exist in the prison of the external necessity'. The clapping of the audience, he added bitterly, demonstrated that 'cruelty is . . . a way of providing thrills, and a substitute for eroticism' (BBC talk, 2 May 1957). More important, however, were the larger changes taking place in civilisation: the increasing tendency to reduce human beings to a number in the epoch which brought us the gas chambers and the crematoria.

> That voice of protest we hear in ourselves when we learn of places where human beings torture other human beings resounds in a void and has no justification other than itself. While the millions of men, women and children who died in the years 1939–1945 are still being mourned, it is difficult to think about the tendency, stronger every day, to equate human beings with flies or cockroaches; we may assume that some properly sublime goal could provide reasons for exterminating flies, while those who were left in peace would remain perfectly indifferent. (*The Witness of Poetry* 52)

To characterise the author of *Waiting for Godot* as a callous scoffer at humankind does Beckett a massive disservice. Miłosz himself admitted that Beckett was an artist who heroically rejected illusions, in contrast to Eliot, who fled barrenness to seek shelter in religion. Beckett was a writer 'full of such great pity that he could hardly bear it', and what he presents on stage is 'the utter reduction of human beings, which makes us value even more small, disinterested gestures of goodness, which are indicative of our shared humanity' (*Prywatne obowiązki* 10–12). Whether remembered or, as Wordsworth has it, 'unremembered', these 'little, nameless . . . acts / Of kindness and of love' ('Tintern Abbey', 34–35) instil 'hope, the state of mind which Weil refers to as *l'attente de Dieu* [waiting for God]'. Miłosz watched *Endgame*, *Krapp's Last Tape* and *Happy Days*, recognising in them forewarnings of the end of civilisation, but always countering their desolate image of the human condition with his own trust in the possibility of hope:

> Evil grows and develops, which is understandable, because it has logic and probability on its side, as well as, of course, power. Completely mysterious, however, is how small grains of kindness remain immune . . . It is possible to draw from this certain important conclusions; despite the complex interdependence that exists on earth, human beings have a stake in what might be referred to as a higher metaphysical bond and, thanks to that, are potentially capable of miracles. (CM, 'Gdyby to można było powiedzieć')

Beckett, he avers,

> is like a man who sidles up to a hunchback and begins to needle him: 'Hunchback, you're a hunchback; you'd rather not be reminded of it, but I shall see to it that you are reminded'. As for me, I know I am

a hunchback; I make no pretense to the contrary; that is, I know full well the poverty of my human existence. Yes, there are times I felt like howling, ramming my head against the wall, but from sheer exhaustion of will, from sheer necessity, I buckled down and went to work. (*Ulro* 243)

To Krzysztof Myszkowski, he wrote: 'I regard Beckett very highly and feel strongly that I must do everything to defend myself from him' (CM to Krzysztof Myszkowski, 8 August 1993), and although the quarrel was not as serious, he could have employed the same words in relation to the English poet Philip Larkin, whom he addressed in this poem:

> I learned to live with my despair,
> And suddenly Philip Larkin's there,
> Explaining why all life is hateful.
> I don't see why I should be grateful.
> It's hard enough to draw a breath
> Without his hectoring about nothingness.
>
> My dear Larkin, I understand
> That death will not miss anyone.
> But this is not a decent theme
> For either an elegy or an ode.

('Against the Poetry of Philip Larkin', *NCP* 718)

In his old age he tended to be keener in revealing his own feelings, and when writing *Rok myśliwego* (A Year of the Hunter) and some of the poems from the collection *To* (It), he admitted that there was a lot of Beckett's utter despair and Larkin's deep melancholy in himself—their feelings of hopelessness, and being condemned to loneliness. Despondency arises from the fact that there is no room for communication with another person, not to mention any sign of the existence of a higher order. Larkin can be unflinching in his portrayal of characters with no hope at all, like the speaker in 'Aubade', sensing in the dawn 'Unresting death, a whole day nearer now' (*Collected Poems*, 208).

The two very different personalities of Miłosz and Larkin are well captured in a letter written in the 1990s to Stanisław Barańczak, who had translated Larkin's poetry into Polish:

Both Dickinson's and Larkin's volumes are first-class. But ... I feel slightly sorry that your largesse contrasts with my fanaticism. I don't like Larkin, although I admit he is superb. He worries me a lot. Does the mastery of this poetry mean that a truly contemporary poet must 'sit among jokers' and reduce the human condition to its bare bones? I think that, as in Beckett, the power lies in the bareness of despair, the absence of any consolation. (CM to Barańczak, 21 March 1990)

Contradictory awarenesses in Miłosz took him much deeper than Larkin's consistency, and they allowed him to capture more of human fate—its drama, loftiness and miraculous potential. 'The shallowness of Larkin's thinking is what I abhor most . . . His poems are about being in the most common forms of hell, like the eternity of Svidrigailov's smoky baths in *Crime and Punishment*', he explained in another letter.

Yet a few months later, after having re-read Barańczak's translations, he noticed in Larkin's work a metaphysical element fitting for this period when the religious imagination was on the wane: 'the great poets of the past . . . belong, regardless of their language, to a certain *episteme*, from which we are separated . . . It turns out that most effective works of the new religious imagination seem based on a *via negativa* and Larkin, an agnostic, shakes readers to the core' (CM to Barańczak, 24 June 1992).

Because of the frequency with which dark moods seemed about to overwhelm him, Miłosz felt compelled to maintain a mask, a smile, and to say little. By contrast, American poets had leave to suffer depression and receive psychiatric treatment, their hopelessness finding safe limits and a degree of acceptance. As an émigré, he was convinced that his position might be far more precarious than theirs, and so he maintained a very correct exterior even when he sensed how close he was to breaking. Years later he reflected how, in fear of a dark surge of irresponsibility and madness, 'I forced myself to be very disciplined, exact, precise, punctual so that I could easily have been taken for the perfect baker, scientist or businessman'. He recalled how 'Lowell ended up in a clinic from time to time and I could not stop thinking that if he got fifteen lashes on bare skin, he would recover very quickly' (*Rok myśliwego* 28). Subsequently, he apologised for the remark in a late poem:

I had no right to talk of you that way,
Robert. An émigré's envy
Must have prompted me to mock
Your long depressions, weeks of terror

. . .

and beneath my anger was the vanity,
unjustifiable, of the humiliated.

('To Robert Lowell', *NCP* 722)

A similar story involved his contacts with the best-known poet from California, Allen Ginsberg. Co-creator of 'beatnik' culture, Ginsberg did not recite his poems, but rather shouted them out, and sometimes sang them to the accompaniment of a mouth organ. Ginsberg was an embodiment of a freedom Miłosz never could afford, although the America of 'emancipation', drugs and sexual freedoms was not unattractive to him. He kept his distance, however, usually with a full glass of bourbon in his hand rather than a joint of marijuana. Once again, he picked up the courage to confess only as he neared the end of his life:

> Allen, you good man, great poet of the murderous century, who persisting in folly attained wisdom.
>
> I confess to you, my life was not as I would have liked it to be.
> . . .
>
> And I lived in the America of Moloch, short-haired, clean-shaven, tying neckties and drinking bourbon before the TV set every evening.
>
> Diabolic dwarfs of temptations somersaulted in me, I was aware of their presence and I shrugged: It will pass together with life.
>
> Dread was lurking close, I had to pretend it was never there and that I was united with others in a blessed normalcy.
>
> ('To Allen Ginsberg', *NCP* 611)

'Perhaps only my reverence will save me'

What is pronounced strengthens itself.
What is not pronounced tends to nonexistence.
                              Czesław Miłosz, 'Reading the Japanese
                                          Poet Issa' (*NCP* 350)

I work a lot, seeking to express everything that poetry can encompass, and I think that I am making progress, so there is hope that by the age of eighty, I will begin to write quite well.
                              Czesław Miłosz to Jerzy Turowicz (1967)

Early on in his time in Berkeley, Miłosz described to Jan Błoński the gradual, often arduous process of composition: 'In order to write poems, I have to sleep a lot and make notes of what comes . . . But greed gets in the way, to read, understand, or do something. It is simply a technical difficulty for me, poems form very slowly, they vegetate, so in my drawer there are a lot of drafts, lines I keep getting back to' (CM to Błoński, 3 April 1963). The act of finding the right order of words, and words of the right order, was never for Miłosz a form of torture, but a source of strength and great joy. This was what Renata Gorczyńska concluded in the late 1970s—that he was a writer for whom the prospect of awards and the wider recognition that was so much a part of literary life mattered less than the creative process itself. He himself came to the conclusion that 'no-one overcome by doubt puts words on paper or paints on canvas; the doubt may come five minutes afterwards' (*Rodzinna Europa* 306).

In his first two decades in California he wrote five volumes—*King Popiel and Other Poems* (1962), *Bobo's Metamorphosis* (1965), *City without a Name* (1969), *From the Rising of the Sun* (1974) and also *Hymn of the Pearl* (1982), which included poems written mainly before he received the Nobel Prize—and over time his poetry freed itself totally from political and social implications. In 'It Was Winter', the poem which opens *Bobo's Metamorphosis,* we encounter from the outset his full interaction with the new Californian world, which is experienced with such intensity that its charge is almost sexual:

> And here I am walking the eternal earth.
> Tiny, leaning on a stick.
> I pass a volcanic park, lie down at a spring,
> Not knowing how to express what is always and everywhere:
> The earth I cling to is so solid
> Under my breast and belly that I feel grateful
>
> (*NCP* 192)

In his dreams on Grizzly Peak, California and Lithuania met. His vision is filled with 'straw-coloured' mountains, eucalyptus trees, seals' barking, brassy grass, the concrete surface of highways, the 'prickly lights' of the docks before him; and at the same time from the depths of his memories landscapes surrounding Wilno surface: green forests, horse-drawn carriages on sandy dirt roads. He liked to return to the past, not driven by nostalgia, but seeking roots, having the need to create an internal compass, orientate space around a central point, which still remained his native land, the places where he grew up, and the city of his youth, 'a city without a name', wiped away by fading memories and history.

Miłosz's goal was to step beyond aesthetics to enter Reality. 'My destiny is not about writing poems, but seeking gaps, whether in poetry or prose, it does not matter which' (CM to Skwarnicki, 5 June 1970). From the very beginning of 'Ars Poetica?', a poem which encapsulates many of his key goals, he declares how he is on a quest for a 'more spacious form/... free from the claims of poetry or prose' (*NCP* 240). What he seeks is a poetry which repudiates poetics, reaching out instead for a deeper understanding with the reader than aesthetic conventions could provide. For him, the poet is an instrument played upon by an external agency, a *daimonion* who prompts his words and work, and whose origins may be evil. Receptive equally to agents of dark and light, his soul offers open house to spirits, the 'invisible guests' which 'come in and out at will' (ibid., 241). From this it is apparent that he diverges from the position on literature and morality taken by Simone Weil, who argued that

> imaginary evil is romantic and varied; true evil is gloomy, monotonous, barren, boring. Imaginary good is boring; real good is always new, marvelous, intoxicating. Therefore 'imaginative literature' is either boring or immoral (or a mixture of both). It only escapes this alternative if in some way it passes over to the side of reality through the power of art—and only genius can do that. (Weil, *Gravity and Grace* 70)

The origins of *The Separate Notebooks* (1977–1979) can be seen in the everyday practices of the poet. For years Miłosz used hard-cover notebooks with un-lined paper, writing poems, and jotting down first attempts, sentences, quotations, ideas. Then poems followed on numbered pages; recollected fragments celebrating the hard-working, maternal line of the family; autobiographical comments next to lines about dramatic events in Krasnogruda, then flashes of memories from his childhood in Wilno; memories of Aunt Gabriela; notes about Schopenhauer, about language and culture—all part of this 'delightful and dangerous thing, which does not have a name and which is called Life' (*Osobny zeszyt*, in *Wiersze* III, 241). Rather than an ensemble consisting of different elements, what Miłosz constructs is something artistically and notionally coherent from which

> An old man, contemptuous, black-hearted,
> Amazed that he was twenty such a short time ago,
> Speaks.
>   Though he would rather understand than speak.
>   ('A Mirrored Gallery', *NCP* 362)

At a festival in Montreal in 1967, Miłosz clarified some of his ideas about poetry and what he acknowledged was its spiritual function:

> Poems are always written against death . . . Poetry is contemplation. It is untrue to say that contemplation, guiding a man towards eternal truth, . . . turns him away from his earthly duties. The object of contem-

plation is the whole of human reality, which, subjected to perpetual
necessities of love and death, is not subjected, however, to the right of
perpetual recurrence. It is there always, each year, month, new and un-
named. (*Zaczynając od moich ulic* 474–475)

The key to contemplation is therefore the realisation that there is nothing banal,
nothing obvious, in the human world surrounding us. Rather, it is often a site of
wonders, as the following lyric, written in Berkeley in 1966, exemplifies:

When the moon rises and women in flowery dresses are strolling,
I am struck by their eyes, eyelashes, and the whole arrangement of
      the world.
It seems to me that from such a strong mutual attraction
The ultimate truth should issue at last.

('When the Moon', NCP 222)

In his poetry during the California years there is a strong pull towards glorifying
existence and its varied manifestations accessible to our senses. This can be illustrated by another extract from *The Separate Notebooks*:

Waiting indefinitely. Every day and in every hour, hungry. A spasm
in the throat, staring at the face of every woman passing in the street.
Wanting not her but all the earth. Inhaling, with dilated nostrils, the
smells of the bakery, of roasting coffee, wet vegetables. In thought de-
vouring every dish and drinking every drink. Preparing myself for absolute possession. (*NCP* 374)

Here we see the poet in self-characterising mode, awed, Dionysian, sensual. Elsewhere he can be heard extolling life in hymns: 'O sun, o stars . . . holy, holy, holy
is our being beneath the heaven and the day and our endless communion' ('The
Year', *NCP* 213).

Miłosz also wrote poems directly addressing the notion of faith through
daily experience. One of the first of these is 'Discussion for Easter 1620', in which a
man from the Polish gentry is engaged in an argument with the Tempter, who has
hidden in a confessional, and who points out the man's sins and spiritual poverty,
and tells him of the emptiness awaiting him after death. Although the sinner's
unwavering hope for redemption does not have any substantiation apart from a
'childish' faith, his naivete and sinning are neither covered up nor elevated, which
makes the reader both inclined to smile and deeply moved while reading the
poem.

Over these years Miłosz developed the highest degree of poetic mastery
of a wide variety of forms and gained confidence in using any register of speech

and emotions. Writing in a more voluminous form meant moving away from defined genres. The extended verse acts like a net in which an optimum amount of Reality can be caught. These longer lines are borrowed from Whitman and from biblical verse: 'How strongly I felt the Whitmanesque temptation . . . to encompass everything, include everything in one poem . . . It took me years searching for a new form outside traditional syllabic versification, nothing else would encourage me to undertake a translation of David's Psalms' (*Ogród nauk* 250). In the 1960s and 1970s Miłosz composed gradually longer and longer poems, sometimes joining together earlier works, which were originally intended to be separate pieces, as if only a multiplicity of parts, points of view, characters and languages could bear what he wanted to convey. By bringing into co-presence the quick and the dead, Miłosz sought to annul time, which destroys us.

Miłosz's lyrical poems became like symphonic pieces in which the sounds of different instruments were skilfully orchestrated, and clarity and sublimity achieved. He could combine in such poems as 'A Treatise on Poetry' both the most personal grief and the important philosophical and social issues of the time. One of his finest, most impressive poems is 'From the Rising of the Sun', written in 1974. The title alludes to the psalm sung during vespers which he remembered from childhood ('Where the sun rises and where it sets, let the world say praises to God'), before darker memories intrude, including the bitter thought that he will not return to his native river, and also the feeling of time passing away. The man stands in a window overlooking the Pacific, and at the same time in a cell in a monastery and on the tiled floor of an atrium, both now and long ago, hoping to attain a competency in words: 'In each thing, there ought to be a word./ But, there isn't. And so what of my calling?' The 'thing itself' eludes definition, and so can be approached only by circling around it, and by multiple means—combining lyrical language and narrative, a first-person monologue and a commentary from a chorus, a fragment of a book read in childhood and a song with a university lecture; and employing Polish, Lithuanian and Latin.

The poetic persona attempts to understand his fate, a past of departures, abandonments, and periods in exile, contrasting his discontinuities with the relative stability of generations of his forefathers who managed their land in Kiejdany. Why could he not have enjoyed a different destiny, with a manor house set in peaceful countryside where he could go hunting? He, however, was fated to run, to flee to distant lands, where he hears the voice of the Spirit of Emptiness, who shows him frailty, defeat and oblivion instead of eternal fame, which reminds him of the price of pride, cruelty, loneliness, knowledge of one's own evil and of the times. Finally there is only a bitter 'Lenten Song':

I ran a long time on the earth
And shouldered through a fiery gulf.
I judged others, judged their worth,
Knowing nothing of myself.

. . .

My face perhaps was honest clay.
And now it fades away.
The light shuddered and went out,
Leaving self-love in the dark.

                                                              (*NCP* 299–300)

The final section of 'From the Rising of the Sun' is a point to which so much of
Miłosz's poetry seems to lead.

Perhaps only my reverence will save me.

. . .

And if the city, there below, was consumed by fire
Together with the cities of all continents,
I would not say with my mouth of ashes that it was unjust.
For we lived under the Judgment, unaware.

Which Judgment began in the year one thousand seven hundred
    fifty-seven.

Though not for certain, perhaps in some other year.
It shall come to completion in the sixth millennium, or next Tuesday.
The demiurge's workshop will suddenly be stilled. Unimaginable
    silence.
And the form of every single grain will be restored in glory.
I was judged for my despair because I was unable to understand this.

                                                              (*NCP* 330–331)

'One of the greatest poets of our time, if not the greatest'

I can't think that there's any poet in America that has not read Miłosz.
                                                    Helen Vendler (1999)

To celebrate Miłosz's eighty-fifth birthday in 1996, Leonard Nathan, by then a
Professor Emeritus at UC Berkeley, contributed a piece to *Tygodnik Powszechny*
which gave a slant on Miłosz's achievement from an American perspective. Five

years before, Nathan, who was also a translator of Wat's and Świrszczyńska's poetry, had co-authored an enlightening analysis of Miłosz's thought and its influences, *The Poet's Work*.

> He is an example of . . . a philosophical poet . . . We do not have poet-philosophers. We have lyrical poets preoccupied with their shoes, pants, hands, hearts . . . He acquired a gift of giving meaning to things which are a threat to our equanimity, the things we cannot cope with in any other way except by ignoring them or turning our backs on them. (Nathan, *Tygodnik Powszechny* 26)

For the first thirteen years of his time in California, Miłosz was completely unknown in America, while in Britain at around the same time he might have registered on the radar solely as the translator of *Zbigniew Herbert: Selected Poems* (1968) and as the editor of *Post-War Polish Poetry* (first published 1965, reissued 1970), in the popular Penguin Modern European Poets series. After the first collection of Miłosz's poetry in English came out in 1973, his visibility gradually increased. Following the breakthrough that came with the Nobel award and the publication of *Collected Poems* in 1988, nearly thirty years after his arrival in Berkeley, American readers benefitted from fuller access to his work and an appreciation of its scale. It is worth noting that the first article devoted to Miłosz written in English, by Zbigniew Folejewski, appeared in winter 1969 in *Books Abroad*.

In order to find a place in American cultural life, Miłosz himself nurtured translators and critics of his works among his students, though for a long period he made no attempt to write for the American public, since he regarded Poles as his sole readers. His language was far from being clear or easy to translate, and his poetry relied strongly on its melody, shades of Polish stylistics, and elements from his private history. Much of that, after all, was intimately linked to a country and a culture which only really aroused any international curiosity with the election of Karol Wojtyła as Pope in 1978, followed by the emergence of Solidarity two years later. In a letter to Thomas Merton, Miłosz explained, 'Not only do I not attempt to translate my poetry but I am unable to write prose in any other tongue than my own. I suspect a sort of psychological obstacle or a tendency to self-protection' (17 January 1959, *Striving towards Being* 8–9). He may well have been afraid of drowning in the ocean of American culture, and harboured a continuing unease at the popularity *The Captive Mind* had earned him. Susan Sontag belonged to the generation which learned about Miłosz from his essay on Ketman, and remembered how, in the 1950s and 1960s, *The Captive Mind* was not only a famous piece of writing in America, but also something that had been picked up 'by very reactionary right wing groups', becoming 'a kind of jewel in the crown' for those engaged in 'anticommunist hysteria' (Sontag, interview in *A Magic Mountain*).

It was with this background story that he began his literary life in Berkeley, and for the first few years, led by feelings of futility, apprehension and pride, did virtually nothing to advance his poetic reputation in the States. The situation was different, however, in relation to Polish poetry more generally, where Miłosz took on the role of ambassador. Among the courses he offered in 1961 was a tutorial in translation, which included the analysis of translations. Miłosz handpicked the more able students, whom he invited to work closely with him. Although he had a high level of proficiency in English, it was not enough to discern all its stylistic nuances, and he needed help from native speakers familiar with American idiomatic expressions. Richard Lourie was the first student with whom Miłosz began translation work. 'He had written some nonsense on an exam and instead of simply giving him a bad grade, I invited him in for a conversation in order to explain why he was mistaken. That was the beginning of our friendship' (*ABC* 183–184). A beatnik, though not a hippie, Lourie, who would go on to have a career as a prose writer, screenwriter and translator, remembered visits to the house on Grizzly Peak, where they sat side by side and argued,

> working out, line by line, his poetry and the poetry of Aleksander Wat and others. One day, we were translating a poem and Czeslaw looked at it and said: 'No, it's too smooth; we'll have to roughen it up'. It came as an absolute revelation to me that something can be too smooth and then could be consciously, deliberately, roughened up. (Lourie, *Partisan Review* 98)

In the first few years Miłosz extended the group of students who translated poems with him to include Lawrence Davis, Catherine S. Leach, and Louis Iribarne, who would go on to translate *The Issa Valley*. Foremost among his helpers, however, was a lecturer and a colleague from Berkeley, the poet Peter Dale Scott, who served for a number of years in Warsaw as Secretary to the Canadian embassy and who learnt Polish in part from volumes of Zbigniew Herbert's poetry. Herbert owed his introduction to an English-speaking readership to a collaboration between Miłosz and Scott, who then went to work on Miłosz's poems with the author.

During that period, so deeply entrenched in Scott's memory, Miłosz sent an update to Giedroyc on his recent activities:

> Until now I have spent years writing, reading and translating Polish poetry into English. I already have quite a collection of poems by Wat, Herbert, Różewicz, Czechowicz, Staff, Tuwim and Słonimski in English. Polish poetry is rated really highly and is outstanding when compared to Anglophone verse. Many are of the opinion these days that it is first rate, and I have made a small contribution [to its reputation]

by publishing [Miron] Białoszewski and 'Elegy of Fortinbras' by Herbert and I plan to add more translations, firstly by publishing in literary
magazines and later in an anthology. (CM to Giedroyc, 30 July 1962)

Publication of Miłosz's aforementioned *Post-War Polish Poetry* became possible
thanks to the assistance of Thomas Merton, who, having read the typescript, commented on the 'irony, depth, refinement, intelligence and passion' in 'this new
wonderful poetry', and introduced it with an enthusiastic recommendation to his
publisher, Doubleday. The book had about 150 pages, and began with poems by Leopold Staff, Antoni Słonimski and Jarosław Iwaszkiewicz, but gave the most generous representation to Aleksander Wat, Tadeusz Różewicz, Miron Białoszewski,
Adam Ważyk and Zbigniew Herbert; the fact that Miłosz incorporated only six
of his own poems, yet included eleven of Różewicz's and eighteen of Herbert's,
tells us something of his generosity of spirit.

    In his introduction Miłosz stressed the distinctiveness and quality of Polish
poetry, which he contrasted with the literature of the West. An indication of this
artistry lies in the use of irony, he explained, because 'elegant scepticism and the will
to defend the basic human values of man's existence are not one and the same thing'
(*Post-War Polish Poetry* 9). The previous year Miłosz had reported to Jarosław Iwaszkiewicz how 'Polish poetry introduces a tone which is lacking in American poetry
and readers or listeners of my translations are crazy about it' (CM to Iwaszkiewicz,
21 July 1964). Though there may have been a touch of exaggeration in Miłosz's asser-
tion, the published anthology received very favourable reviews. Babette Deutsch in
Book Review affirmed that 'the poems speak in a way that comfort and encourage
us: with openness, anger, irony and tenderness, manifesting together with shame
the greatness of which people are capable' (qtd. In 'American Critics on Miłosz's
Post-War Poetry', *Kultura* 7–8, 1965). Al Alvarez, one of the most popular critics of
his generation, came to the conclusion in the *New York Review of Books* that the
best Polish poets,

> Miłosz himself, Tadeusz Różewicz and Zbigniew Herbert, who seems
> to be one of the best European poets, perfected the style, in which under
> the most intimate experiences one can detect a political tension. They
> are great ironists, separate, very intelligent and open to emotions ...
> This extraordinary achievement, and Miłosz's translations, are equally
> excellent and accomplished. (Alvarez, 'East is East', 11 November 1965)

That is how Polish poetry began to be read in the West, as part of a literature capable of exploring and exposing the historical baggage from the twentieth century.
    In the blurb he wrote for the dust cover of the anthology, Thomas Merton
drew attention to Miłosz's 'A Poor Christian Looks at the Ghetto', but also wrote
that 'Herbert stands out in the collection and ranks as one of the most important

poets of our times'. In a letter following the publication of *Zbigniew Herbert: Selected Poems*, Miłosz noted, not without mixed feelings, that his and Peter Dale Scott's 'translations, I dare to claim, brought him fame in the English-speaking world' (CM to Giedroyc, 10 June 1968). Though he would not have been human had he not suffered a pang or two that it was not his poems that were the focus of widespread acclaim, on the other hand, he must have been gratified that, thanks to his labours, the outstanding quality of Polish poetry was at last being recognised globally. To poets in their mid-thirties in the mid-1960s, like Mark Strand and Charles Simic in America, and Ted Hughes in England, not to mention emerging young writers elsewhere in the English-speaking world, the discovery of contemporary Polish, Czech, Hungarian, Yugoslavian and Russian poetry opened up a rich seam of possibilities in terms of subject, form and technique. Robert Hass recalled how his contemporaries often reached for Herbert and Miłosz as an antidote to Frank O'Hara, because 'Polish poetry contains a great deal of sobriety, irony, a sense of intricate history . . . and that was something which gave literature force . . . It roused me, inspired, taught me to be vigilant, intelligent, sensitive towards history, which one might get entangled in' (Hass, interview in *A Magic Mountain*), unaware that thirty years later young Polish poets would reach for O'Hara in order to escape the influence of Miłosz and Herbert.

It was in the 1980s, perhaps, that Miłosz wearied of playing the role of middle-man, something he mentioned with irritation to one of his correspondents:

> I was invited to New York to take part in a symposium . . . about translations. I am not going . . . Why the hell do I always have to perform in someone else's skin, my whole life, simply because at some point I happened to play the part of a transplant doctor, or a stamp collector? (CM to Artur Międzyrzecki, 26 January 1973)

He wanted to concentrate more on his own poetry, given that *From the Rising of the Sun* was about to appear. In another letter around this time, Miłosz wrote: 'He forced me to do it . . . Rexroth, so I did my own volume. Obviously, it is not as if I felt indifferent about fame, only that . . . when reading my poems in English at poetry readings, I felt as if I cheated, because you know the difference between translation and the original' (CM to Błoński, 8 February 1975). Błoński wrote in reply:

> I not only understand perfectly well that you don't want to translate, write papers and so on, but I was always surprised that you put so much effort into it . . . I like Herbert a lot and am full of admiration for him, just to give an example, but you being Herbert's translator is something odd, as if a horse carried a fowl and the fowl received all the applause . . . Whether in the form of poetry or prose, your most deeply personal

expressions are what is required most and I can understand that they don't always come easily. In any case, your displeasure at these professor-translator preoccupations I interpret as a sign of strength. (Błoński to CM, 15 February 1975)

The picture of Kenneth Rexroth forcing the author of *Visions of San Francisco Bay* to translate and publish his own poems seems somewhat implausible. Nevertheless, the Californian Rexroth, one of the most colourful figures in American poetry and an active member of California's literary environment, played an important role in the publication of Miłosz's *Selected Poems* by the Seabury Press of New York in 1973. It is curious, or rather symbolic, that the go-between was Oskar Miłosz, whose poems Rexroth translated into English in the 1950s. When, in turn, Czesław translated *Ars Magna* and *Les Arcanes* and wrote an essay about his relative, later published in *The Noble Traveller*, he sent it to Rexroth, who, Miłosz reports,

> was very complimentary and said that it was a perfect example of an introductory text ... Rexroth appreciated highly my translations of the Polish poetry ... I told him once: 'I am very surprised that you hold my translations in such high esteem, because my knowledge of English is limited and I rely on the help of my students'. He told me in the end: 'If someone has a good ear for one language, they will have a good ear for all'. (CM interview in *A Magic Mountain*)

And indeed, in Rexroth's introduction to *Selected Poems* we read that Miłosz's poetry 'transgressed language barriers and is equal in translation to those few truly important poems written today in English and French'.

Later reviews of Miłosz's translated works were somewhat more sceptical, though it was often stressed that the strength of his poetry, even in translations that were far from perfect, still rang through. The selection of just over fifty poems, mostly taken from *Rescue* and *Daylight*, along with some published in California, met with an enthusiastic reception from judicious readers. 'He is regarded in poetic circles as critical for American poetry', quoted Miłosz about himself in a letter to Giedroyc in October 1974, informing him also about a trip to the East Coast in the autumn of 1974 to take part in poetry readings at Yale, New York and Stony Brook.

We should, however, get things into perspective. Until the Nobel Prize changed things forever, his readings were attended only by relatively small groups. When Rexroth and Ferlinghetti invited him to a poetry festival in San Francisco in 1979, 'almost everyone asked: Who is he?' (Ferlinghetti, *Tygodnik Powszechny*). Of course, when Miłosz chose the path of an émigré in the game known as 'literary life', he suddenly had to start anew and compete with thirty-year-old Americans in finding publishers and readers. Neither did it help to be anchored in San Francisco, which, despite its artistic circles, could still be seen as parochial when set against the mighty Manhattan cultural centres. Gradually, however, first thanks to *Post-War Polish Poetry* and then his own Seabury Press collection, he began to be recognised by young American poets, who increasingly signed up for his lectures. The sign of Miłosz's acceptance by New York's establishment was a Guggenheim Fellowship, awarded to outstanding scientists and artists, with which he was honoured in 1976.

In the second half of the 1970s, Lillian Vallee became his student and his translator. She worked with him on the essays in *The Emperor of the Earth* (1977), and then *Bells in Winter* (1978), which was published by the Ecco Press, bringing together just under thirty poems from different periods in his career, from 'Encounter', written in his youth, to 'From the Rising of the Sun'. Jane Hirshfield, a California poet, remembered the moment when 'I opened the book and felt that I am dealing with a great poet … who moves my heart and causes me to begin to think, feel and hear more deeply'. Robert Pinsky experienced a similar sense of awe. The year 1978 proved an important turning point, since the publication of Miłosz's new book fortunately coincided with the award of the Neustadt International Prize for Literature. This was a highly prestigious prize, but despite that, Miłosz initially seemed to take it in his stride: 'Brodsky is a member of the jury for the literature prize … *World Literature.* He put forward my candidature (without consulting me) … The award is presented in February. $10,000 … I am not especially greedy. Benefits are not great—nobody knows about it' (CM to Giedroyc, 4 October 1977). Truth be told, no letter exists in which Miłosz admits that he deserved any award.

Thanks to his growing fame and authority, Joseph Brodsky had a decisive voice in the jury's deliberations, and in April 1978, during the award ceremony in Norman, Oklahoma, he spoke emphatically: 'I can claim without a shadow of a doubt that Czesław Miłosz is one of the greatest poets of our times, if not the greatest … Before us we have someone so strong-minded and unbending, … so fervent that, in my mind, he [can] only be compared to biblical characters, most of all Job' (Brodsky, rptd. in *Tygodnik Powszechny*). In a private letter to his old editor, Miłosz expressed his feelings as follows:

> To end up with a title of international writer by writing poems in Polish
> is most peculiar … and something I hardly believe. I would like to stress
> how much I owe to American poets for their tolerance, and also to
> Joseph Brodsky, who promoted me with such determination. Gener-
> ally, only those who come from either Poland or Russia fully appreciate

poetry and also my poetry. To be brief, this new volume, published soon after the Neustadt (but printed before the award) . . . and a great review of my poems in the *Times Literary Supplement*, and then the poetry reading event in the Guggenheim Museum in New York, which included a book signing—these are extraordinary, bearing in mind that I am neither Jack the Ripper nor have I violated any sad old granny. (CM to Giedroyc, 14 October 1978)

The author of the *Times Literary Supplement* review, entitled 'The Naming of Hell', was Louis Iribarne, who wrote that in contrast to many American poets—for example, Lowell—Miłosz's 'waste land' is 'hellishly real', and therefore metaphor 'seems a luxury' and 'poetical self-pity, immoral' (*TLS*, 25 August 1978). Experience of historical events, moral engagement and distance from the 'I' were the main features which drew American readers to Miłosz. The poet's search was for a new way, different from the modernist tradition of Eliot and from the style in which Ferlinghetti and O'Hara wrote. The eminent poet and critic Robert Pinsky said that the obscure emigrant had gradually become 'perhaps the most important living American poet. When I ask twenty-year-old poets . . . no other name is mentioned as often as this one, whom many of them respect, despite the difficulty they have in pronouncing it'. (Pinsky, *Tygodnik Powszechny*).

Pinsky himself was instrumental in the growing extraordinary popularity of Miłosz, as he was a member of the Grizzly Peak Collective, a new group of translators formed between 1980 and 1981, taking their name from the Miłosz family home. Renata Gorczyńska lived there, making recordings of conversations with the poet to assist Pinsky and Robert Hass. Hass also remembered that during early meetings of the young literary circles in San Francisco, Miłosz looked like a warrior, which perfectly suited the romantic legend of the Berkeley loner, author of *The Captive Mind*. Now Hass had the opportunity to meet him almost every day, when in the evenings, after hours of working in air dense with cigarette smoke, Miłosz looked in on the summerhouse to check on the translators' progress and how his poetry was changed in Pinsky's or Hass's hands. He would look over first drafts, examine the rhythm of the verse, and give details of the clothing his cousin wore, and whether the rock he remembered from childhood was granite or chalk. Hass, thirty years Miłosz's junior, was amazed to witness Miłosz's vigour and insatiable inquisitiveness.

One outcome of the Grizzly Peak Collective's efforts was *The Separate Notebooks*, which came out in 1984. It was a more than two-hundred-page selection of poems, including, among others, 'The World', which created a great deal of interest. *The Separate Notebooks* inspired many writers with its mixing of forms.

Later, in 1988, came the *Collected Poems, 1931–1987*. According to Bogdana Carpenter, these books and an earlier volume of essays, *The Witness of Poetry* (1983), lectures given by Miłosz at Harvard in 1981–1982, transformed 'Miłosz's career as a poet in America. Publishing his poetry crowned his fame . . . lectures . . . evoked amongst the critics and poets a broad and lively discussion about the essence of poetry and particularly about its relationship with history'. It was only then that the 'full impact' of 'his presence in the American poetic landscape' made itself felt, and he 'became a voice which had to be taken very seriously' (Carpenter, *Teksty*). Following the award of the Nobel Prize, Paul Zweig wrote in the *New York Times Book Review*: 'It is a shame to admit that the greatest of the poets living in our country writes in Polish'.

In the eighties the American perception of Miłosz's poetry began to change. The political and historical contexts and the often-used image of the poet as witness were no longer the only ways into an interpretation of the work. Critics discovered religious and philosophical perspectives, resulting in books by Donald Davie and by Leonard Nathan and Arthur Quinn, as well as many articles by Helen Vendler. This change of focus meant that as well as capturing the ethical qualities of the work, the author's 'mystical view of the world' was examined. The critic and historian Robert Faggen noted not just that, but also that the Polish poet 'has an almost burlesque sense of humor: on the one hand, he is deeply serious, and on the other terribly ironic, almost as the silent movies could be. He is like Charlie Chaplin' (Faggen, *Tygodnik Powszechny*). It needs to be added that it is this complexity, this limitless artistic and intellectual wealth, that makes it impossible to imitate Miłosz, especially as he has a completely different historical and cultural background. That is why he was able to present to American writers new perspectives and possibilities, but he did not create anything which would resemble a 'school of poetry'. This opinion was shared by Hass, Faggen, Sontag and especially Helen Vendler, who said openly that

> American poets will not learn from his work any direct lesson . . . scenes at which he looked with horror will not be seen that way by a child of a young parochial imperium. Americans do not carry in them a thousand years of history[,] and their culture, secularized from the beginning, will not be capable of appreciating the breakup of the European religious community. ('Z okruchów, świat jest doskonały')

Retaining his distinctiveness and uniqueness, Miłosz endured what had been a long, arduous journey over three decades in the United States. Starting out as an emigrant who had repeatedly been refused entry, he became a highly-respected member of the country's intellectual elite, and was received and decorated by two presidents, Ronald Reagan in 1983 and George H. W. Bush in 1989.

A symbolic confirmation of that journey was an international literary festival devoted to his work, which took place at Claremont McKenna College in California on 24–27 April 1998. It was attended by a galaxy of American and Polish poets and a large group of critics, students and friends of Czesław Miłosz. Seamus Heaney, the Nobel Prize winner in 1995, said these beautiful words about Miłosz: 'Miłosz occupies his place in ... world poetry because he fulfils the appetite for seriousness and joy, which the word "poetry"' awakens in every language ... Miłosz restores the child's eternity at the water's edge and equally he expresses the dismay of the adult that his name is "writ on water"' (Heaney, *Partisan Review* 23).

Job

And God said to Satan: 'Very well, then, everything he has is in your hands, but on the man himself do not lay a finger'.

The Book of Job

In the last ten years if only it had been just the misery of a body struck by illness, but no, also a degrading of the spirit, whose control slips away daily, until it hides in some unknown place, perhaps in a tear as the only sign of consciousness in a moment of agony.

Czesław Miłosz, *Rok myśliwego* (A Year of the Hunter)

Close to the time when Heaney was giving his speech in Claremont, Miłosz referred to himself, with more than a touch of self-irony, as 'a master of defeated despair'. A few years before that he wrote to Giedroyc:

Piotr's illness is not something recent, it goes back to at least 1977, when he came back from Alaska all confused. At the construction of the oil pipeline for two and a half years there was nothing but ice and heavy drinking each day. From then on life became extraordinarily hard, what with Janka's illness and his. The diagnosis of *manic depression* meant alternating cycles of dejection and euphoria and aggression, something similar to Zbigniew Herbert's condition, but more severe. I sent him twice to a clinic in France and also supported him financially, because he was unable to work ... This time his attack of madness was more severe than at any time before, and there is a question whether the depression phase will return, or acute paranoia will persist. He threatened the neighbours and the police found with him five guns, including one automatic plus two revolvers. (CM to Giedroyc, 18 August 1993)

On reading this story in August 1993, the editor must have not only sympathised with Miłosz, but also felt astounded that he was learning about it only at this point in time. Miłosz kept the mental illness of his younger son a complete secret from his European friends, and probably confided only in Father Józef Sadzik. The nightmare it brought coincided with Janka's illness, which had left her bedridden for two years. In the summer of 1978, when he was enjoying great international successes as a Polish poet, Miłosz wrote to Czapski:

> My life is very hard, and it is not due to the bulk of work I had to do and duties I have to perform. I managed to combine lecturing and caring for Janka. But it all came to me at once: the sufferings of the innocent, which I find very hard to cope with. Old age, because sixty-seven is exactly that, and my inability to come to terms with that and to endure self-denial, while the world around moves in its beauty, in its everlasting youth. Finally coming to the more or less clear and sad realisation of what is happening in the Church in America and in Europe. I was a recipient of many tributes; in 1977 an honorary degree from the University of Michigan with much celebration, in 1978 I was awarded the Neustadt Prize with an equally ceremonial event, television etc., and I only bow and smile like a puppet, maintain a mask, while inside me there is suffering and great distress. I can't say whether there are any people who would know what I feel and realise how much it costs to press this button, to shut away the pain, when I begin a lecture or a talk. I am not writing it just to complain. It is because I never knew that old age can be so full of crazy complications, so far from peace. (CM to Czapski, 19 June 1978)

Then he added with bitter sadness: 'I have run out of faith, hope, love. After all, I did something in life, as much as one man can achieve, which may not seem a lot. I was burdened with illnesses. While others had happiness, I had great work to keep my equilibrium' (ibid.). Now the work appeared to be more jealous and possessive than ever before, and the poet, if it is permissible to speculate on what he may have felt, had the impression that those closest to him had had to pay for his gift. One glimpses this in the poem 'Before Majesty', written in 1978:

> It is bitter to praise God in misfortune,
> Thinking that He did not act, though He could have.
>
> The angel of Jehovah did not touch the eyelids
> Of a man whose hand I hold,
> I, a passive witness of this suffering for no cause.

Unanswered is our prayer, both his and mine.
Unanswered is my request: strike me
and in exchange give him an ordinary life.

(NCP 355)

Intelligent, a bright spark and full of charm, Piotr was, like his parents, acutely sensitive, but he lacked the protective shield that Miłosz possessed, the kind of strength which allowed his father to combat depression and despair. His problems began early in life, but it was not until his second trip to Alaska that he had a sudden breakdown. It was a place where even men who were stronger psychologically than him often could not cope. When he returned he suffered from persecution complex, and compiled a list of enemies that could very easily have turned into a list of victims. He suffered from paranoia and was filled with hatred towards the surrounding world. On one occasion, he opened fire from a motel window at an imaginary opponent, and was sent to prison. When he felt better, he desperately tried to rid himself of the illness, to study, work and write. His state of health stabilised in the mid-1990s, but before then he and his parents underwent a level of distress and pain which is hard to imagine. The hardest moment came when the son saw in his father an enemy, threatened him and compiled lists of absurd grievances against him. It would have been a traumatic experience for any parent, let alone Miłosz, who, with his guilt complex, reproached himself for not being an attentive father, for not devoting time to his sons, believing that the fate imposed on him had an impact on his whole family. He felt that Piotr's illness was the devil's punishment, which he deserved for his pride and his devotion to poetry. 'Why do I always have to pretend to be a tower of strength when I am not? Why do I pay such a high price for the so-called gift(?), as if I were Dante or someone comparable? . . . Why do human beings need to suffer?' he asked in a letter to Konstanty Jeleński of 9 July 1976. As he confessed in a letter to Lillian Vallee, he was burdened with 'a terrible guilt about my existence, partly justified, partly pathological. To go through life with it and, what is worse, to start a family, is, in my opinion, unbearable and a crime. I thought that old age would be free from the Furies, but unfortunately not. Only for short moments the torment is eased by an *I don't care*'. (n.d. 1978). He implored:

Forsake me, dark spirit.
Don't say that you are the truth of my being
And that my whole life was only about concealing evil.

('Odstąp ode mnie', Wiersze III, 213)

In another letter to Lillian Vallee, in May 1977, perhaps thinking about these bitter lines, he wrote:

> On Good Friday I composed probably the most tragic poem in my whole
> career . . . all bitter sorrows and pangs of guilt from the whole hard year.
> Then went with Janka to Hawaii for ten days . . . The misery of the years
> gone by, and the only expression of kindness on my part was to nurse
> Janka and drive her everywhere, because in the last few months she
> became disabled. Making a few steps with a walking stick gives her
> a great deal of pain and the sensation of burning in her feet. (CM to
> L. Vallee, 27 May 1977)

Half-paralysed, Janka, after a few months of putting up with increasing pain,
which they presumed was arthritic, underwent tests soon after their return. The
results brought shattering news, a de facto death sentence, because the diagnosis
was ALS (amyotrophic lateral sclerosis), the incurable condition sometimes
known as motor neurone disease. In August, after additional consultations, it
turned out that the previous diagnosis was wrong and that the cause of the paralysis was a benign tumour in the spine which had to be removed. The operation
was a success, but further complications and surgical operations extended her
stay in various hospitals and physiotherapy centres until the beginning of the following year. When she finally returned home, she had to take strong painkillers,
learn to walk again, and come to terms with the fact that she would now never be
physically active. The illness and suffering renewed and strengthened her bouts
of depression. On New Year's Day 1978, Miłosz reported to Jerzy Andrzejewski:
'She is in a state of constant depression and this stands in the way of her physical
recovery. Various complications after the operation hit her very hard psychologically. 1977 was a year of great misery, which only spared my professional work'
(CM to Andrzejewski, 1 January 1978). At the bottom of the letter his wife managed
to scribble this painful note: 'Things are bad, but perhaps will improve. Janka'.
Half a year later she wrote: 'Life is hard and difficult for me. I don't want to
complain and cry, but at the moment I cannot bring myself to be cheerful or
even cling to hope, but I'd better not whinge too much' (CM to Andrzejewski,
28 June 1978). In *A Year of the Hunter*, Miłosz recalls this cruel and terrible phase
in his life:

> The sight of daily undeserved suffering, of appalling tragedy, witnessing
> the humiliating way the body deteriorates. With an image in my
> memory of the beautiful and laughing Janka, I had to look at this pitiful
> wrecked human body, its vulnerability, passivity and dependency on the
> hands that lift it, take it to the toilet, feed it. Shattering, unbearable,
> but numbing because routine . . . In the first phase of the illness, when
> the paralysis moved up more and more from her feet, there was shock
> in Janka's voice: 'Who is doing it? Who needs it?' And indeed—who

was doing it?—A mind that is conscious of its sliding into darkness, of forgotten dates, names, events; that high level of intelligence, which is still strong enough to submit to paranoia and worry over the children's fate. (*Rok myśliwego* 53)

During the ten years of her illness there were better and worse periods, but Janka never recovered, could barely walk, and was burdened by the pain of her body, but perhaps more by that of her mind: by the fear that nestled inside her which dated back to the war years, and which finally, after decades of suppressing it, overtook her. She was worried about her sons and about her husband and she was afraid of being left alone. She used to cry, 'Don't go, don't go', whenever Czesław was leaving to give seminars at the university, where he had managed to stay on after his retirement. The cost of medical treatment and physiotherapy were, after all, astronomical. Visiting friends could come and stay as long as the painkillers worked. There was not enough money to keep carers or cooks, so Miłosz was now learning to cook. He divided his time between lectures and housework, finding it hard not to be able to travel and gain new experiences. He was realising what had been secretly encoded in his fate:

Situations in our lives have a tendency to repeat themselves, as in a dream. And I am a small boy again and am leading my old grandmother Miłosz, who is moaning and crying and cannot walk by herself, because she feels dizzy and apart from that is preoccupied thinking about her unhappy son . . . How could I know, that I was acting out my fate that would come true many years later, but, in place of my grandmother, it would be my wife and instead of Witold Miłosz, my son? It did not even enter my mind when I met Janka. Perhaps there were signs of that then, and later, when her poorly leg did not allow her to keep up with me. I had to force myself to slow down, because it was in my blood to race around like a dog with my tongue hanging out, looking round everywhere and leaving my scent everywhere. And now, I can measure my maturity by the patience I acquired. It is sometimes difficult, because Janka is in a lot of pain and when she is better she begins to nag. And I indeed remained that boy from Wilno and feel the way I did then, and only perhaps patience is what I learnt in my long life. Looking at her purely physiological state, I think it is slowly improving, but the problems with her nervous system and nerve centres which control the pain have not improved. We are now trying a special massage treatment. When it comes to Piotr, however, it looks as if he is recovering from his affliction, and perhaps my prayers in Lourdes will be heard. And if they are not going to be heard, so be it. (CM letter to L. Vallee, 23 October 1978)

In short intervals between his chores, he found it easiest to translate the Psalms, for example. An intensive reading of the Bible acquired much deeper meaning for him, which he wrote about to Lillian Vallee at the beginning of 1977:

> Do let not my bursts of melancholy put you off and please remember that I need warmth and light, and your letters provide just those. My dejection is not caused entirely by my inherent predispositions to bouts of depression. The whole of 1976 was a year of a real and profound grief . . . I am making attempts to shake it off by doing a translation of Ecclesiastes and now working on the Gospel according to St Mark, and have plans to teach myself Hebrew. You know in *Tygodnik Powszechny* there is a column called 'I think about my life', which I always find very moving and then think about my own life. If I could do something for those people who write about their experiences, I would leave them the Bible written in nice Polish, at least as much as I could manage to, that would be something. (CM to Lillian Vallee, 5 January 1977)

In his work he did not look for success, but sought spiritual support to provide the justification of his existence, an opportunity to consider himself useful to his fellow men. What he felt when reading line after line of the Book of Job will remain a mystery, although in the introduction to the translation he provided more than a hint:

> To evade: hide the feeling of pain, one's own and others', through philosophy, in essay writing. That is a much easier option, and with twisted fate, which, for personal reasons, I did not touch on here, the temptation [towards obfuscation] is understandable. To put it in other words, the one who wears a professor's gown and mortarboard has to give proofs of his mental dexterity—just give him a title, and he will send off a geyser of brilliant arguments, knowing, at the same time, that it is all pretence, a purely agreed role, and the truer man inside him is the silent man. The one at the podium is like an actor: and although he is close to tears, he has to block the route to his own grief, and this duality leaves its mark . . . which means we learn to speak as if nothing happened. Yet, it is better to say nothing about the Book of Job, because speaking just for the sake of it would be useless. (*Księgi biblijne* 285)

Janina Miłosz died on 17 April 1986. During a funeral mass in Latin at St Mary Magdalen Church, Czesław read, among others, Psalm 139, which he had translated himself. Afterwards Janka was buried at Sunset View Cemetery. Toni later described his mother as a strong but very sensitive person, intelligent, principled, sometimes too demanding, who, without fail, could distinguish between the good and the bad. Renata Gorczyńska, who met her during this most difficult time, noticed Janka's total devotion to her children, but also her distance and unwillingness to open up. Her stiffness seemed like a psychological corset— necessary to protect her from the world, from fear?—which she also tried to impose on her irrepressible husband (Gorczyńska, interviewed by the author, 2005). For a while their marriage had been like the paradise which is accessible to us in life. And later, when the moment passed? Perhaps the most honest and insightful portrait of their union was camouflaged in a story written soon after their arrival in California, and which was abandoned by the author. There his protagonist writes of a relationship 'which survived many tests', though one that

> was not free from intemperate conflicts, because our minds and charac-
> ters were incompatible. I accepted her absolute superiority in everything
> where practical thinking and decisiveness were required, sometimes
> feeling like a small boy caught raiding the larder or breaking neighbours'
> windows. She could not reproach herself for many things and did not
> have to, unlike me. ('Na swój los', Beinecke Library Archive)

Miłosz's final farewell to his deeply loyal wife includes these delicately balanced lines:

> I loved her, without knowing who she really was.
> I inflicted pain on, her chasing my illusion.
> I betrayed her with women, though faithful to her only.
> We lived through much happiness and unhappiness,
> Separations, miraculous rescues.
>
> ('On Parting with My Wife, Janina', *NCP* 469)

In October 1979, Czesław Miłosz already knew that the fantastic hope that had sustained Janka over the previous three decades was about to come true, and that the Nobel Prize for Literature was close to being within his grasp. He then wrote a letter to Józef Sadzik, confessing to the priest about his repeated supplication in his prayers for the restoration of Piotr's sanity in exchange for the honour of the Nobel Prize. Whoever listened to this prayer decided otherwise.

NINE

The Nobel and the Poet's Later Years
1980–2004

Remembering the Wounds

I remember the morning he was awarded the Nobel Prize. I got a call
from the *New York Times:*
'Tell us . . . what are his hobbies?'
'Hobbies? Poets don't have hobbies, they have obsessions'.
'No, no, hob-by, do you understand? Come on, he must have a hobby!'
'Oh yes, yes. He has a hobby; he has been translating the Old Testament
into Polish'.
Deadly silence . . . receiver put down . . .

Leonard Nathan, in *The Magic Mountain:
An American Portrait of Czesław Miłosz,*
dir. Maria Zmarz-Koczanowicz

At the Nobel Prize ceremony in Stockholm in December 1980, Czesław Miłosz's
acceptance speech began with the following words:

> My presence here, on this platform, should be an argument for all those
> who praise life's God-given, marvelously complex unpredictability. In
> my school years I used to read volumes of a series then published in
> Poland, *The Library of the Nobel Laureates*. I remember the shape of the
> letters and the color of the paper. I imagined then that the Nobel laure-
> ates were writers, namely persons who write thick works in prose, and

even when I learned that there were also poets among them, for a long time I could not get rid of that notion. (*Nobel Lecture* 11)

This astonishing achievement resulted from his determination to remain faithful to his native tongue, to retain his artistic individuality, and to resist conforming to the expectations of the international market. Miłosz compared himself to the youngest brother from a folktale who chose the least rewarding road to his destination, a decision that sprang from instinct, coincidence or fate rather than reason. Worldwide recognition had finally materialised during the most testing period in his life. One can only imagine his thrill and enormous satisfaction at hearing Lars Gyllensten, the Secretary of the Swedish Academy, announcing that a Lithuanian-born Polish poet had won the prize, a man whose work was 'insightful and uncompromising in its portrayal of the threat humanity faced in a world full of violent conflicts'.[1]

It is hard to find entirely credible Miłosz's own account of a call he received at 4:00 a.m. on 9 October 1980; after a Swedish journalist woke him to break the news that he had been awarded the Nobel Prize, he calmly replied: 'It can't be true' and went back to sleep, as he recalled for the documentary film, *The Magic Mountain* (2000). What he did during those early hours will never be known, but one thing is certain: his doubts vanished a few hours later, when he saw crowds of journalists jostling in the garden outside his house, as well as television cameras focusing on his front door. Here was clear proof that a new chapter in his life had begun.

The University of California's Department of Slavic Studies helped him organise a press conference. At this, Ira Michael Heyman, the university chancellor, spoke with great satisfaction of how the university's first ever Nobel Prize for Literature had 'generated great excitement', adding, 'In an era of scientific power, Professor Miłosz's poetry reaffirms the subtle force of spirit and beauty in human creativity'.[2] When questioned about his political opinions, Miłosz replied sardonically that 'a Nobel Prize winner does not necessarily have to be intelligent'. When pressed with the inevitable question as to who his favourite writer was, after a pause he remembered Flaubert. Finally, he caused roars of laughter when he claimed that with the prize money of over $200,000, he intended to buy a farm and grow marijuana (*Rozmowy polskie 2*, 705).

The press conference did not last long, because the poet was not willing to miss his scheduled class on Dostoyevsky. Miłosz's reluctance to break with his daily routine by calling off the lecture was one of the first indications that he was less concerned with the issue of his privacy than with maintaining the patterns of life to which he was accustomed. After so many years of solitude and discipline, he had no intention of becoming enmeshed in the frenetic international literary scene, or of allowing the Nobel Prize to become a 'kiss of death'.

While readily accepting invitations to readings, lectures and conferences, he shunned the very idea of 'media' celebrity, and becoming a public performer was utterly alien to him. This led to numerous instances of misunderstandings during his subsequent visit to Poland. Immediately after receiving the prize, he explained to a Polish journalist that he generally tried avoiding the press, 'who would like to turn me into a political writer in order to accuse the Swedish Academy of being politically motivated in making the award. Gyllensten explained how it all happened. The decision over the prize had already been made in May, and, besides, I had been a prospective candidate for many years' (*Rozmowy polskie 2* 714). A common misconception in circulation for a long time was that the Nobel Prize had not been awarded to the writer, but rather to Poland itself in recognition of the achievements of Solidarity. The actual sequence of events, however, demonstrates that this was not the case. Although the official vote took place in October, the Swedish Academy had come to its decision well before August 1980, as documentation held by the Polish Secret Service archives testifies. From the beginning of August their agents had been monitoring the literary scene meticulously. It was determined to divert attention from the fact that Poland's most celebrated poet, who lived in exile and was banned from visiting his homeland, had just scooped up the most prestigious literary award available. A Secret Service employee working on what was imaginatively called Operacja 'Poeta' (Operation Poet) refers in one of his reports to a letter supporting Miłosz's candidacy submitted to the Swedish Academy by the Polish Pen Club in February 1980: 'In mid-July, Władysław Bartoszewski received information from Stockholm which indicated that according to unofficial reports circulating in the capital, Miłosz had been earmarked to receive the award for literature' (qtd. in Bereś, 'Operacja "Poeta"').

It is also worth pointing out that for many years Jerzy Giedroyc had been promoting Miłosz's candidature for the prize, along with the poet's other admirers in Paris's *Kultura* circles. Though there was no question about the artistic merits of Miłosz's writing, it needed to be brought to the attention of the jury of the Swedish Academy. It was due to such efforts that one of the academicians would later reveal that 'his name was put forward in the early 1970s', adding, 'I have read his poetry and everything written about him in French, English and German. Many of us have been and are fascinated by Miłosz and his work'.[3]

As far back as 1958, Giedroyc, *Kultura*'s editor, had written to a friend that 'things are now at a more favourable juncture for Poland and so I would like to take this opportunity to put forward [for the Nobel Prize] Miłosz's name' (Giedroyc to Andrzej Bobkowski, 17 January 1958). Fifteen years later, after putting together his *Selected Poems* in English, Miłosz began to feature among the group of potential candidates to receive the award, but joined a small circle of serious contenders only in 1978. In spring 1977, Giedroyc initiated what proved to be an affectionate correspondence between writer and publisher:

> Because of your latest successes, it would be worth considering putting forward your candidature for the Nobel Prize . . . The first soundings from Sweden have been rather positive. In any case, we need to try to make the most of the favourable connections we have with Katarzyna Gruber,[4] who works at the Nobel Library, and establish whether they have a collection of all your works there. I can send you any missing books, so that you could quickly fill in the gap. In addition, I'll need a comprehensive note from you in English, including your biography and a list of your entire works. This will be a means to display all your peacock tail feathers. No need to feel uncomfortable about it, because I will present the piece as all my own work. Try to think of anyone else we could engage in the process. (Giedroyc to CM, 8 March 1977)

In reply, Miłosz commented:

> With regard to the Nobel Prize, I don't feel greedy about it. I am not sure whether even thinking about it is good for our spirits, because it destroys our peace of mind. However, if one of my friends in Poland were to receive it, I would feel upset, because I would most likely interpret it as a rejection, an inevitable consequence of my status as an émigré. (CM to Giedroyc, 19 March 1977)

This prompted Giedroyc to respond that he appreciated that he was not 'hungry' about gaining this particular form of recognition. 'Nevertheless, I believe that it is important to put forward your candidature' (Giedroyc to CM, 25 March 1977).

An important contributor to the campaign was Katarzyna Gruber, a Polish émigré who was responsible for the Slavonic collections in the Nobel Library, which she regularly enhanced with the co-operation of the Jagiellonian Library in Kraków, the Institute of Literary Studies in Warsaw, and the Kultura publishing house in Paris. She collected every publication written by and about Miłosz in French and English that had appeared in relation to the Neustadt Prize, as well as in *Kultura* and *World Literature Today in the US*. It was thanks to her efforts and Giedroyc's perseverance in monitoring the situation that the members of the Nobel jury were able to familiarise themselves with Miłosz's works. During this same period in Poland, an informal committee started lobbying on his behalf, as Konstanty Jeleński informed Miłosz: 'We had a meeting with Leszek Kołakowski and [Roman] Zimand with the aim of supporting your candidacy for the Prize. An action plan was drawn up and various roles were assigned among us' (Jeleński to CM, 16 October 1977).

The year 1979 saw Miłosz on the threshold of success, with fifteen poems and two essays translated into Swedish by Gruber, amongst others. Importantly, the writer and translator Artur Lundkvist, a member of the Swedish Academy since 1968, wrote an essay on Miłosz's work in which he declared that 'the more one immerses oneself in this poetry, the more apparent is its unique character' (qtd. in *Literatura na Świecie*, 6, 1981). That year, however, the prize was awarded instead to the Greek poet Odiseas Elitis. Brushing aside this setback, Giedroyc forwarded a letter to Miłosz saying that he remained hopeful about his prospects, and the following year their shared dream came true.

On 5 December 1980 Miłosz and his son Toni met up with Giedroyc in Stockholm. Three days later Miłosz delivered the first of his lectures at the Library of the Swedish Academy, and the next day spoke at the Polish Institute in Stockholm. Although he might not have been aware of it at the time, his insistence on sporting a Solidarity badge on the lapels of his tailcoat and jacket at both events provoked considerable interest from the KGB and the Polish intelligence service. The Soviet Embassy in Sweden sent a letter of complaint to the Polish Embassy, stressing how damaging Miłosz's lecture at the Polish Institute had been from a political perspective, not least because of an allusion he had made to the three Baltic states, Estonia, Latvia and Lithuania, which the Soviet Union had annexed in 1940 under the terms of the Molotov-Ribbentrop Pact. What particularly infuriated them was the Polish ambassador's failure to object to Miłosz's comments.

The official ceremony at which King Carl Gustaf XVI of Sweden presented the Nobel Prizes took place on 10 December. In his laudatory presentation address, Lars Gyllensten stressed the extent to which

> disruption and breaking up have marked Miłosz's life from the very beginning. In both an outward and an inward sense he is an exiled writer—a stranger for whom the physical exile is really a reflection of a metaphysical or even religious exile applying to humanity in general. The world that Miłosz depicts in his poetry and prose, works and essays is the world in which man lives after having been driven out of paradise. But the paradise from which he has been banished is not any bleating idyll, but a genuine Old Testament Eden for better or worse, with the Serpent as a rival for supremacy. Destructive and treacherous forces are mingled with the good and creative ones—both are equally true and present.[5]

Miłosz began his lecture describing how one of his favourite childhood texts, Selma Lagerlöf's *Wonderful Adventures of Nils*, helped shape his sense of the poet's vocation, which involves adopting a 'double vision', viewing the world from a wide perspective, yet also in detail and with exactitude. He then proceeded to relate this early insight to those of his adult masters, Oskar Miłosz and Simone Weil, before dwelling on memory and tragic history by referring to the Ribbentrop-Molotov Pact, the Katyń massacre and the Warsaw Rising.[6] Amongst the many factors which had intensified Miłosz's hostility towards the new Communist regime in Poland had been the appointment of the Polish-born Soviet marshal Konstanty Rokossowski as Minister of Defence in November 1949, in order to ensure 'Poland's reliability in the looming international conflict'. Five years earlier Rokossowski had been the very commander who had delayed the Soviet advance on Warsaw, thereby enabling the Nazis to crush the Warsaw Rising and subsequently raze the city to the ground.[7]

A masterpiece of the genre, his Nobel speech covers an extraordinary range of topics, demonstrating his acute alertness to the weighty burdens borne by those living through the contemporary era. The perspective he offers on the twentieth century is that of an inhabitant of 'the other Europe', whose destiny it was 'to descend into "the heart of darkness"', to experience life at first-hand under totalitarian movements whose victims run into millions. What these 'evil forces' set out to sever were the 'bonds that exist between people organically . . . sustained by family, religion, neighborhood', customs, language traditions, 'parochial attachments and loyalties', passed on from generation to generation:

> It is good to be born in a small country where Nature was on a human scale, where various languages and religions cohabited for centuries. I have in mind Lithuania, a country of myths and of poetry. My family already in the sixteenth-century spoke Polish, just as many families in Finland spoke Swedish, and in Ireland, English; so I am a Polish, not a Lithuanian, poet. But the landscapes and perhaps the spirits of Lithuania have never abandoned me . . . Only when teaching in America did I fully realize how much I had absorbed from the thick walls of our ancient university, from formulas of Roman law learned by heart, from the history and literature of old Poland, both of which surprise young Americans by their specific features: an indulgent anarchy, a humor disarming fierce quarrels, a sense of organic community, a mistrust of any centralized authority.
>
> A poet who grew up in such a world should have been a seeker for reality through contemplation. A patriarchal order should have been dear to him, a sound of bells, an isolation from pressures and the persistent demands of his fellow men, the silence of a cloister cell. If books were to linger on a table, then they should be those which deal with the most incomprehensible quality of God-created things, namely, being, the *esse*. But suddenly all this is negated by the demoniac doings of History, which acquires the traits of a bloodthirsty Deity . . . Reality calls

for a name, for words, but it is unbearable, and if it is touched, if it draws very close, the poet's mouth cannot even utter a complaint of Job: all art proves to be nothing compared with action. Yet, to embrace reality in such a manner that it is preserved in all its old tangle of good and evil, of despair and hope, is possible only thanks to a distance, only by soaring *above* it—but this in turn seems then a moral treason. (*Nobel Lecture* 11)

Miłosz focuses specifically on the fate of artists in Central and Eastern Europe, who, unable to accept the official lies, choose exile and gain freedom, though their stories seem to hold little interest for anyone in the West, where civilisation has entered a phase of indifference, as if Nietzsche's prediction of European nihilism had come true: '"The eye of a nihilist"—he wrote in 1887—"is unfaithful to his memories: it allows them to drop, to lose their leaves . . . And what he does not do for himself, he also does not do for the whole past of mankind: he lets it drop"' (*Nobel Lecture* 12). But the essence of humanity *is* memory, and the poet's role lies in maintaining the link with the dead, in rejecting the lie, in respecting a reality hidden within a code of a higher order: 'Like all my contemporaries I have felt the pull of despair, of impending doom, and reproached myself for succumbing to a nihilistic temptation. Yet on a deeper level, I believe, my poetry remained sane and, in a dark age, expressed a longing for the Kingdom of Peace and Justice' (*Nobel Lecture* 14).

A year later, in a series of six lectures delivered at Harvard, Miłosz expanded upon much of the material in the Nobel speech, when, at the invitation of the university authorities, he took up the prestigious post of Charles Eliot Norton Professor of Poetry. These lectures demonstrated again the ease with which in his scholarship he could encompass geopolitics, economy, contemporary science, sociology and theology, and saw him increasingly donning the mantle of a Central European poet. 'If there is any hope left for the European continent', he argued in his introduction to a Polish edition of the lectures, 'it lies in the potential of countries between Germany and Russia which have been artificially held back' (*Świadectwo poezji* 8). In the first lecture, 'Starting from My Europe', he describes the terrible legacy left by the pillaging of the east of the continent, and how a writer's survival depended on his or her ability to cope with 'every kind of pessimism, sarcasm, bitterness, doubt' (*The Witness of Poetry* 14). Not only those living under Soviet occupation, but globally, people were continually confronted with a reductive, materialist interpretation of the world. The issue was whether measures might be taken to protect the human imagination, since it was a matter of urgency equal to the fight to save endangered species. What was necessary to achieve this was a spiritual reawakening. Drawing inspiration from Oskar Miłosz's writings, he hopes that what will emerge in the twenty-first century is a radical turning-away from the *Weltanschauung* marked principally by biology, and this will result from a newly acquired historical conscious-ness. Instead of ... presenting a man through those traits that link him to higher forms in the evolutionary chain, other of his aspects will be stressed: the exceptionality, strangeness and loneliness of that creature mysterious to itself, a being incessantly transcending its own limits. Humanity will increasingly be turning back to itself, increasingly con-templating its entire past, searching for a key to its own enigma, and penetrating, through empathy, the souls of bygone generations and of whole civilisations. (*The Witness of Poetry* 110)

Miłosz goes on to define his convictions about the distinctiveness of the Polish poetic tradition represented by Tadeusz Różewicz, Aleksander Wat, Zbigniew Herbert, Miron Białoszewski and Anna Świrszczyńska, a cluster of writers who felt compelled to create aesthetic strategies to address extreme experiences, and to establish common ground with the reader, infusing history with a profound sense of the personal.

During his short visit to Stockholm, along with numerous official speeches and readings, Miłosz found time for less formal gatherings, often with audiences which included many who had fled Poland following the repression of anti-government student protests in March 1968.[8] High on the list of those invited were his brother, Andrzej, with his wife; attendees also included Jerzy Giedroyc and Zofia Hertz, the co-founder of the Literary Institute in Paris; Irena Sławińska, a Lithuanian-born literary historian; Jane Zielonko, translator of *The Captive Mind;* Mirosław Chojecki, an underground publisher who worked with Giedroyc at *Kultura* and was a member of Poland's anti-Communist opposition; Stanisław Barańczak, a poet, literary critic and highly respected translator into Polish of contemporary British and American poetry; and lastly, Stefan Kisielewski, a writer, composer and politician, with whom Miłosz, for the benefit of press photog-raphers, took part in a 'making ugly faces' competition.

Once the official ceremonies in Sweden ended, Miłosz travelled to Rome for a private audience with Pope John Paul II, and then on to Paris, where in the church of Saint Pierre du Gros Cailou he read to an audience of 1,200 people. Amongst the other contributors to the event, which involved readings and dis-cussions, were well-known names from the Polish literary scene. The champagne flowed, and Miłosz signed hundreds of autographs. According to one of those in attendance, however, he did not appear to be at all triumphant or, indeed, in the best of moods:

I was shocked then, as were other younger émigrés present in the large basement of the church ... by the cold irony, almost fury, with which he treated the overflowing public. 'Today you are proud of me', he was saying, 'but when I needed your help, you accused me of communism and you informed on me at the U.S. Embassy'. (Grudzińska-Gross 67)

Aptly, the title of a long interview given to Jerzy Turowicz for *Tygodnik Powszechny* during this Paris visit was 'Remembering the Wounds'. Previously, that same periodical had published 'The Wormwood Star' and 'The Song', which were amongst the most bitter poems he ever wrote.[9]

At this very juncture, as Chapter 8 has revealed, Miłosz was struggling with heart-rending circumstances at home and feelings of intense loneliness. One year later, he confessed in a letter to a friend his feelings on being awarded honorary doctorates:

> A subtitle to one of Adolf Rudnicki's short stories applies to my situation now, 'Everyone gets what they care about least'. I have many griefs and they concern me more than 'successes'... After a while one gets good at it, as Lech Wałęsa used to say to me. I learned similarly how to give talks and readings and bow, but remain uninvolved, as if a mannequin was performing for me. (CM to Zofia Hertz, 8 October 1981)

'This crown keeps slipping over my ears'

In Berkeley, Czesław sometimes showed his friends a three-panel cartoon from a Warsaw newspaper: first panel, a man walking along while reading a book, with another, sinister figure lurking around the corner; middle panel, the hidden figure leaps from the shadows to stab the walking man in the back; in the final panel, the killer walks away from the bleeding corpse, reading the stolen book, with its cover now visible: 'Miłosz: Poems'. From the poet displaying this little artifact, those characteristic barks of laughter—skeptical, but undeniably pleased.

Robert Pinsky, 'A Poet Worthy of Protest',
New York Times, 26 August 2004

To understand the momentous changes that occurred in Poland in the 1980s which enabled Miłosz to return, and which subsequently led to the collapse of Soviet hegemony in much of Central and Eastern Europe, an appropriate point in time to begin might be Saturday, 12 December 1970. On that day the state-run radio station in Warsaw announced some substantial increases in food prices in the week before Christmas: 'flour rose by 16 per cent, sugar by 14 per cent and meat by 17 per cent' (Ascherson 100–101). On Monday, 14 December, around three thousand workers from Gdańsk's Lenin Shipyard headed for the Communist Party HQ to demand that the planned price rises be rescinded. After a junior official there ordered them to return to work, disturbances broke out in the city on such a scale that the local police (the *milicja*) were unable to cope. The next day, Tuesday, 15 December, the unrest intensified, with both the Communist Party building and the Gdańsk railway station being burnt to the ground. Demonstrations also broke out in the neighbouring port of Gdynia, and protests started spreading to other parts of the country.

After learning of these developments and news that shipyard workers in Gdańsk had called a general strike for Wednesday, 16 December, Władysław Gomułka, the First Secretary of the PZPR, Poland's ruling Communist Party, decided it was time to put an end to what he regarded as 'counter-revolutionary' activity. A state of emergency was declared along the Baltic coastal area, and police and army units were ordered to fire on protesters, which they duly did. It is impossible to establish exactly how many people perished on the streets of Gdańsk and Gdynia, since those responsible for the state-authorised killings customarily concealed the evidence by burying the dead secretly at night:

> The more the authorities attempted to suppress the memory of the December dead in subsequent years, the more fiercely the people of the coast remembered. Forced underground, the myth of the martyrs grew in the fertile subsoil of the national conscience. To the shipyard workers ... the Poles murdered by Poles, workers murdered by a 'Workers' State', became the symbol for their accumulated grievances. (Garton Ash 14)

Four days later, Gomułka was ousted from his post as First Secretary and replaced by Edward Gierek, who put forward a Five-Year Plan to boost the economy by pouring money into a few heavy industries such as steel and shipbuilding. At the same time he sought to raise living standards and increase access to a wider range of consumer goods. 'What was unique about Gierek's "great leap forward" was its scale', Garton Ash notes, but also 'the breathtaking incompetence with which it was executed' (17). For the next five and a half years prices were kept artificially pegged down. In June 1976, however, having learnt nothing from recent history, the government announced without warning a massive hike in food prices of around 60 percent, which triggered nationwide strikes and demonstrations that far exceeded those of December 1970, and quickly forced the government to re-consider their decision. Though they caved in, the authorities were determined that those workers who had taken part in the strikes in certain areas should be taught a lesson. Two thousand people from Radom and two hundred from the Ursus tractor plant in Warsaw were arrested, and many were then subjected to heavy beatings by being forced 'to run the gauntlet between files of policemen armed with batons'. In addition, 'special summary courts sentenced many workers from Radom and Ursus to gaol terms' (Ascherson 114).

As his epilogue to the second edition of *The History of Polish Literature* (537–540) testifies, Miłosz followed the unfolding crisis attentively, in particular a momentous development of September 1976 when a group of distinguished young intellectuals founded KOR (the Workers' Defence Committee), initially in order to defend the rights of Radom and Warsaw strikers persecuted in the wake of the June unrest. Amongst its founding members and leading lights were Jacek Kuroń and Adam Michnik, both of whom had experienced spells in prison for their activities, and Jerzy Andrzejewski, Miłosz's close friend; the latter had quitted the Communist Party shortly after the brutal suppression of the Poznań Uprising of 1956, in which fifty-three people were killed and several hundred wounded for protesting about the country's dire economic situation. Within a short period of time, KOR managed to mobilise increasing numbers of intellectuals in dissident activity, thereby fostering the growth of 'an opposition counter-culture without parallel in the Soviet bloc' (Garton Ash 20). Despite 'constant harassment' (*HPL* 537) by the secret police, through the industry and ingenuity of friends and the underground press, sections of the Polish public were at last able to access the latest literature, as well as banned works such as Orwell's *Animal Farm* and Miłosz's writings.[10]

A precursor of Solidarity, KOR maintained excellent relations with progressive elements in the Catholic hierarchy, particularly with the Polish Primate, Cardinal Wyszyński. One of those responsible for that bridge-building between socialism and the Church was Tadeusz Mazowiecki, who in late August 1989 would become Poland's Prime Minister, the first non-Communist to hold that post since 1939.

What hugely lifted spirits in Poland and transformed the political situation was the election of Kraków's charismatic archbishop, Karol Wojtyła, as Pope in October 1978. In an instant, the country became the subject of massive international media coverage, from which the Communist government hoped to benefit (Ascherson 124). The cameras and microphones were out in force when Pope John Paul II, the first non-Italian in four centuries to become head of the Church, returned to his homeland on an eight-day apostolic visit in early June 1979. Hundreds of thousands turned out to hear and see him in Victory Square, Warsaw, on Saturday, 2 June, the day before Pentecost Sunday. His homily was entirely fitting for a feast day celebrating the mission to disseminate love, truth and forgiveness its founder assigned to the Church, though John Paul's words included a subtext which many in the square would have picked up on. Three times he reminded his audience that for the past thousand years Christianity had been integral to Polish cultural identity, a vast stretch of time in comparison to the relatively brief period in which an external power had imposed its ideology on their country:

It is therefore impossible without Christ to understand the history of the Polish nation—this great *thousand-year-old* community—that is so profoundly decisive for me and each one of us. If we reject this key to understanding our *nation*, we lay ourselves open to a substantial misunderstanding. We no longer understand ourselves. It is impossible without Christ to understand this nation with its past so full of splendor and also of terrible difficulties. It is impossible to understand this city, Warsaw, the capital of Poland, that undertook in 1944 *an unequal battle against the aggressor, a battle in which it was abandoned by the allied powers,* a battle in which it was buried under its own ruins. (John Paul II, Homily, 2 June 1979)

The allusion to 'an unequal battle against the aggressor' which left Warsaw ruined in 1944 might at first be read as referring to the Nazis' suppression of the Warsaw Rising, though it might equally apply to the relationship between the Poles and the Soviets, who passively looked on from the east bank of the Vistula, enabling the Germans to pound the insurgents into submission. When the Pope talked of 'the allied powers' abandoning Poland, he certainly might have been thinking both of the limited support the Americans and British gave to the Rising itself and to their limited efforts to resist Soviet expansionism at the conferences at Tehran, Yalta and Potsdam. Sixteen times in his address John Paul referred to 'the nation', and towards the end tellingly affirmed that 'there can be no just Europe without *the independence of Poland* marked on its map'. He followed that up by mentioning concepts fundamentally associated with social democracy, 'the rights of man', 'the inviolable rights of the people', and 'freedom', fully aware that such rights and freedoms were in scarce supply in the Communist-controlled 'People's Republic of Poland'. Amongst the millions of Poles inspired and emboldened by John Paul II's words and triumphal visit was a former Lenin Shipyard worker in Gdańsk, Lech Wałęsa, who had been placed under arrest several times in the late 1970s, once for 'distributing clandestine copies of *The Captive Mind*' (Craig 181), Miłosz's exposé of Stalinist ideology.

When in July 1980, because of the parlous state of Poland's economy, the Communist government tried to increase food prices once more, civil unrest spread rapidly yet again. In Gdańsk the following month, the sacking of Anna Walentynowicz, a popular trade union activist, prompted major strikes along the entire length of Poland's Baltic coast. Such was the 'maturity and self-discipline' (Miłosz, *Los Angeles Times*, 12 October 1980) of the strikers, the quality of their leaders, and their extensive popular support throughout the nation that Gierek's government were compelled to concede to their demands, which included legal recognition of independent, self-governing trade unions, a thing unheard of in

the Soviet bloc. When, in September, Solidarity (Solidarność) was officially registered as one of these unions, it gained ten million members within the space of
fifteen months.

Amongst the first tasks the union set itself was the construction of a monument to commemorate those killed during strikes in Gdańsk ten years earlier.
In a sign of the esteem in which Miłosz was held, lines from his poem 'You Who
Wronged' were inscribed on the monument's plinth, as well as a line from his recent translation of the Psalms, 'The Lord will give strength unto his people' (Psalm
29:11). On 17 June 1981, during a visit to Gdańsk to meet Solidarity officials and
shipyard workers, Miłosz saw the Three Crosses monument for himself, but also a
vast banner unfurled especially for the occasion which read, 'The People will give
Strength unto their Poet' (Wroe, in *Conversations,* ed. Haven, 199).[11]

A former student of Miłosz's at Berkeley who was of Lithuanian descent,
the American writer and translator Richard Lourie, recalled a visit to Poland in
November 1980:

> I arrived at the Lenin Shipyard in Gdańsk, for one reason, because at that
> time it was the most interesting place to be on earth. I walked up to a
> worker dressed in a blue, stained overall and asked him how was it that
> in a country where Miłosz's poems were proscribed, a monument to
> the murdered shipyard workers bears a line from the poem 'You Who
> Wronged'. 'He was banned, but we always knew Miłosz', the worker re-
> plied. This response could have impressed or terrified Karl Marx. On my
> return from this Polish trip, Miłosz was lecturing at Harvard and living
> in Cambridge, where I went to meet him. As soon as he opened the door,
> he hugged me warmly and asked: 'How are things in Poland?' For an
> instant I felt as if I was being grilled at a viva. 'No sign of hostility there',
> I replied. He smiled. I knew I had passed. (Lourie, 'Mój Miłosz', 2001)

The story about Polish shipyard workers' familiarity with Miłosz's verse
may sound a little unreal today, but then many unusual, delightful things occurred
during Solidarity's euphoric early days, when ten million people participated in
the protest movement, and all-night queues were as common a sight outside
bookshops as outside butchers' shops. Despite censorship and tight border controls, Miłosz's books found their way into the country during his émigré years,
from 1951 onwards.[12]

Amongst the many who employed a range of strategies for getting audio
tapes of Miłosz's poetry recordings to Poland was his close friend Zygmunt Hertz.
From a letter written in 1965, it appears that one such courier was none other
than Cardinal Wyszyński, who carried two tapes into the country from Rome and
had one forwarded to the Catholic University of Lublin and the other to Jerzy

Turowicz, the editor of a leading Catholic weekly (Hertz to CM, 10 June 1965). The following year Polish sportsmen smuggled copies of *Kultura* in their luggage with the aim of selling them on the black market. Hertz reported back to Miłosz that the issue containing 'A Treatise on Poetry' fetched the highest price in Warsaw (Hertz to CM, 31 January 1966). Two years earlier, Zbigniew Herbert sent an encouraging letter to Miłosz saying, 'Young people look up to you as if you were a star. Really, Czesław, you are shaping the face of Polish poetry, and neither bans nor borders have any effect' (Herbert to CM, February 1964).

Many of his Polish readers recall the furtive means by which they gained access to his books: a copy lent by a professor, just for a day; a version written out by hand; an edition which had survived by magic in a second-hand bookshop or a public library. Krzysztof Czyżewski, years later a curator of Miłosz's heritage in Krasnogruda, recalls one such moment of discovery:

It was 1977, or perhaps the beginning of 1978 ... I was in my first year studying Polish literature at the Adam Mickiewicz University in Poznań. Slowly, we got used to reading books printed by underground presses, copied, on bad-quality paper, bound with whatever was available, which caused eye-strain because of how dense the print was for economic reasons. To us they were real treasures ... We attended clandestine university meetings in private homes. One particular evening, Ryszard Krynicki came to a flat owned by Jacek Kubiak, a leader of a student underground organisation. Instead of reading his own poems, he started talking about a Polish émigré poet whose name many of us heard for the first time. He reverentially held a book in his hands, from which he read a number of poems which left us all transfixed. We waited impatiently for the moment each one of us could touch the book and turn the pages. It was a beautiful volume, bound in green linen with golden letters printed on the cover: *Czesław Miłosz: Poetical Works*. (Czyżewski, 'Linia powrotu' 376)

Czyżewski's senior by ten years, Adam Michnik had long been aware of Miłosz's work and achievement, and owned one of Miłosz's early collections, *Daylight* (1953). He and his close friends were members of the first post-war generation of Polish intellectuals, who did not regard émigré writing as anachronistic, but rather cherished the cultural values it embodied. Michnik was also one of those who determined that NOWA, a Warsaw-based underground publisher, should circulate Miłosz's books. That may well have been partly prompted by his 1976 meeting with the author in Paris:

After the third bottle of wine, I began reciting Miłosz's poems from memory, without a break. I knew a good few of them. And suddenly, I saw, to my amazement, tears flowing down the poet's cheeks. Embarrassed, I stopped . . . and then heard him speak in a tremulous voice: 'I never expected young people in Poland to know my poems by heart. I thought I was *persona non grata*'. (Michnik, 'A Free Mind', 186)

Miłosz struggled to find an explanation as to why his fellow countrymen were so drawn to his work and so often alluded to his name indirectly, by referring to him as 'the author of *Three Winters*'.

Regularly during the Communist era both writers and arts administrators in Poland found themselves not just at odds with the censors, but uncertain as to what might be allowed. Occasionally, it was possible to discern micro-signs of tensions within the government, which resulted in censorship guidelines being subtly relaxed. An example of this was when permission was granted to stage *As You Like It* using Miłosz's translation; the mere fact that his name appeared on the posters was enough to feed rumours that he was returning to Poland. In 1974, the Polish Pen Club received confirmation that they would be allowed to award Miłosz a prize for his translations of Polish poetry into English. The poet himself had mixed feelings on how to react, as his correspondence reveals: 'What the heck is happening? Have I ceased to be the devil incarnate? I appreciate that it was a great effort on the part of the Pen Club [who] only give awards for translations, and this is an honour not to be sniffed at' (CM to Giedroyc, 28 January 1974). A year later, in a meditative letter to another friend, he speculated whether in Poland some 'collective instinct' might be at work, a need to identify someone capable of performing 'a national role'. In his view, currently 'very few' writers would be up to the task of fulfilling people's massive expectations (CM to Jan Błoński, n.d. 1975).

On 5 June 1981, during his first visit in thirty years, Miłosz had the opportunity to experience in person the huge esteem in which he and his literary contribution were held. Though the Polish Communist government no longer felt able to prohibit his return, it tried to neutralise its effect by making conciliatory gestures. Senior officials, including the Minister for Culture, Józef Tejchma, belatedly sent Miłosz congratulatory telegrams on his Nobel award. His arrival that month in Warsaw generated intense emotion, coming as it did at a time of great anxiety and immense loss. In recent weeks, on 13 May, an attempt on the life of Pope John Paul II had been made in Rome, followed a fortnight later by the death of Stanisław Wyszyński, the revered Polish Primate. This period saw considerable restlessness within the country, not least because of constant friction between the government and Solidarity, whose leaders and members were blissfully unaware that the Communist authorities had already earmarked large numbers of them for internment.

In such a climate, people's expectations of the poet, or rather *the* Poet, were high. Miłosz's journey around Poland resembled a pilgrimage, and he was received like a prophet whose visitation might have an impact comparable to one by John Paul II. Elżbieta Morawiec in *Życie Literackie* spoke of him as 'a constant presence for the faithful', while Jan Tarnau proclaimed in *Więź*, 'When we have Wojtyła, Wałęsa and Miłosz, we should be able to feel stronger psychologically'.

The main ostensible purpose for his visit was to receive an honorary doctorate from the Catholic University of Lublin. In order to avoid an official welcome at Warsaw airport, he had considered travelling by car through Germany. In the end, however, he opted to fly to Warsaw. Among the reception party to greet him on 5 June was a former colleague from Polish Radio in Wilno (Vilnius), Tadeusz Byrski. Catching sight of him at the airport, Miłosz found it impossible to contain his emotions, and shouted out his name, 'Tadeusz!'. Crowds awaited him with flowers, cheers and traditional Polish-Lithuanian songs. In an impromptu speech, he expressed his gratitude to Poland's workers, 'who can read, think for themselves and lift the Polish economy' (*Rozmowy polskie 2*, 724). The next day, 6 June, met by more applauding, effusive crowds, he attended a cocktail party in his honour given by the Minister of Culture in Warsaw's magnificent Łazienki Palace. He was also invited to a private viewing of Andrzej Wajda's film *Man of Iron* (1981), which won the Palme d'Or at Cannes that year and a nomination as the best foreign language film at the Oscars in 1982. The film opens with an actress (played by Maja Komorowska) reading a poem into a microphone at a radio station; it turns out to be 'Hope', from Miłosz's sequence 'The World':

> Hope is with you when you believe
> The earth is not a dream but living flesh,
> That sight, touch, and hearing do not lie,
> That all things you have ever seen here
> Are like a garden looked at from a gate.
>
> You cannot enter. But you're sure it's there.
> Could we but look more clearly and wisely
> We might discover somewhere in the garden
> A strange new flower and an unnamed star.
>
> Some people say that we should not trust our eyes,
> That there is nothing, just a seeming,
> There are the ones who have no hope.
> They think the moment we turn away,
> The world, behind our backs, ceases to exist,
> As if snatched up by the hand of thieves

(*NCP* 49)

No sooner has she finished than a brief exchange occurs as to whether the censor will spot that the poem is by Miłosz, and so ban it.

That same evening, at Stodoła, a student club, fifteen hundred young people turned out to meet him, many of whom had obtained invitation tickets on the black market. Monitoring the event, Miłosz and anyone with whom he came into contact was Marat, a secret police agent, who filed an immediate report to his superiors in the Urząd Bezpieczeństwa (Department of Security):

> Representatives of a youth discussion group tried to turn the meeting into a political demonstration and goad Miłosz into delivering an ideo-logical speech . . . They got nowhere with this strategy as Miłosz treated the gathering as a strictly literary event . . . he categorically refused to pick up the baton, and without further ado began reading his poems . . . Digressions in the course of the reading made him come across as an old poet, who had experienced a lot of hardship in his life, and who was happy to have the opportunity to present his poems in Polish. However, he does not feel he has a special vocation to become a 'national prophet' or politician. Despite . . . requests that he clarify his position on Russia, on living conditions in Poland, emigration and similar concerns, he sought to maintain that the subject of the evening was a 'private matter', 'a talk by a poet about his poems'. In answer to a direct question as to whether he did the right thing in going into exile, he replied: 'I lived through so much that it should have finished me off. Because I survived, it shows that it helped' was the joke with which he ended his reply. 'I had no intention of setting an example to anyone else. I am rather like "Stupid Johnny" in the fairy tale, who went for the least sensible option. The fact that it worked out well for me does not prove a thing'. (Bereś, 'Operacja "Poeta"')

Tensions in the hall were intense. On the one hand, there were the understand-able expectations of the audience; on the other, there was the writer himself, who was disinclined to take on the role of political guru, or indeed to pander to the bi-narist mind-set of many Poles who viewed the United States as indisputably 'the good guys'. Not attuned to contemporary Polish ways of thinking, he was cautious and keen to avoid provoking the authorities, remembering all too well the repres-sive Poland of the late 1940s and the 1950s. As he subsequently acknowledged, the passionate atmosphere in the room seemed to him almost overwhelming, leaving him with the impression that an uprising might break out any second. The audi-ence and Miłosz were both right up to a point in their reading of the event, and doubtless many participants left feeling it all might have gone better.

The following day, during a meeting with the members of the NOWA publishing house the mood improved. Seeing samizdat copies of his work for the first time, Miłosz was deeply touched. He remarked that writing poems was a far less demanding task than publishing and distributing them, to which one of the printers replied, 'No, that's not true, because we did try to write like you, but failed' (Bereś, 'Operacja "Poeta"').

One of the trip's most momentous dates was 8 June, when Miłosz was readmitted as a member of the Polish Literary Society (Związek Literatów Polskich), having been expelled in 1951 following his defection. He visited an exhibition devoted to his work in the Museum of Literature, met a group of alumni from his old school, and visited two of Poland's foremost publishing houses, Państwowy Instytut Wydawniczy and Czytelnik. Not surprisingly, the seventy-year-old was by this time very tired and was not looking forward to further engagements. A newspaper reporter who had been hoping to get an interview recalled how, sitting in his brother's flat, Miłosz looked 'utterly exhausted ... And apart from that he does not hide the fact that he has no time for journalists. The very first words directed at me were: "God, how I dislike it when they write about me"' (Zielińska, *Kurier Polski*, 8 June 1981). Without doubt, the person who revelled most in the warmth and attention that greeted the poet was his brother, Andrzej, not just because he was not the one being constantly placed in the limelight, but also because he had a more lively, robust, open temperament. For him, it must have been an exceptionally happy time, a kind of recompense for all the years of living as a brother of '*that* Miłosz'. Having graduated with a sociology degree and worked as a journalist for Radio Polonia, in 1951 Andrzej suddenly found himself in a terrible dilemma. Maintaining an official distance from his brother would have guaranteed him peace for a while, but he refused to take that route. As a result, he was blacklisted, lost his job, and for a long period was unable to obtain any other employment. Eventually, he managed to get into a film editing company, where he worked on translations and credits, and later completed courses on screenwriting and filmmaking, which enabled him to work alongside his boss, Jerzy Bednarczyk, on the first-ever Polish documentary about Israel, *Between the Mediterranean and the Red Sea*. In the repressive, anti-Semitic aftermath of 1968, this friendship with Bednarczyk and his refusal to denounce him cost Andrzej his job once more. He put this latest setback behind him, however, by setting off with Grażyna, his second wife, on expeditions to the Caucasus and Georgia, both parts of the Soviet Union, where they made documentaries. In this way, Andrzej was able to enjoy two of the great passions in his life—travelling, which he had inherited from his father, and filmmaking. His career in documentary filmmaking reached its zenith in 1980, when, with a team from Telewizja Polska, he set off for Berkeley to record a documentary about his brother. That was the first time in decades that they could communicate 'legitimately', though, not surprisingly, there had been 'unofficial' encounters between the two brothers before, mostly in France.

Never leaving his brother's side, dashing here and there, shirt-sleeves turned up, Andrzej was kept constantly busy during Czesław's triumphant progress through Poland. From Warsaw they set off together on a tour of Poland, starting with Kraków, where a conference devoted to Miłosz's work was being held at the Jagiellonian University. There, too, Jerzy Turowicz and staff from Tygodnik Powszechny, and two publishing houses, Znak and Wydawnictwo Literackie, eagerly awaited his arrival. Miłosz ended up complaining to journalists that much of the time it felt like being under permanent siege: 'I am not able to go for a walk in the city. It was only around midnight or one o'clock in the morning that I could finally wander around Kraków, so I don't know what it is going to be like later' (*Rozmowy polskie 2*, 748).

By 10 June the brothers were in Lublin, where Miłosz received an honorary doctorate from KUL (the Catholic University of Lublin); Irena Sławińska gave a laudatory address. A recital of his poems followed, delivered by a cluster of leading Polish actors, including Gustaw Holoubek, Krzysztof Kolberger and Daniel Olbrychski. Especially poignant was the point in the celebrations when a letter from Cardinal Stefan Wyszyński was read aloud; he had written it expressly for the occasion, not long before his death:

> On a lonely journey through history, the poet carries himself, perhaps hurt at times, but always a representative figure from the twentieth century, who has experienced much and refuses to become a slave to any philosophical school, social programme, or prison architecture, or to impudent rulers who become crueller and crueller ... The main purpose of his suffering is to save human freedom ... In his struggle to navigate his lonely way through time, the man called Czesław Miłosz is supported by a vision of God made Man, a spirit which is in every man saved from captivity. (Qtd. in *Kultura* 7–8, 1981)

Densely packed with quotations from the Psalms and Miłosz's own works, the Cardinal's eulogy raised the tone very high—so high that the poet clearly experienced feelings of disquiet as he stood there dressed in his graduation gown. Subsequently, in an address, Miłosz endeavoured to clarify his attitude to the Catholic Church:

> I became a medium, a voice from a certain specific civilisation, which, due to its Christian origins, set a sharp divide between good and evil. Nonetheless ... I feel a duty to declare that I am not a Catholic poet. Those who use this epithet in relation to literature often categorise others as non-Catholic, which in my view is a questionable practice which clashes with the meaning of the word *katholikos,* which means universal ... By

imposing categorisation, what brings people together can be easily
missed ... Often a believer finds non-believers among those close to
him and vice versa ... And I think that both groups belong to the same
family of thinkers, if they join together in respecting the great mystery
of the world and human existence ... Whatever label they give themselves, they are all humanity's friends, because the respect they have for
the world and mankind sets them in stark contrast to those ... con-
temptible, self-satisfied believers in theories and doctrines who imagine
there are explanations for everything. I would be very happy if my books
were of service to people devout in the broadest sense of the word. And
if I have followed in the footsteps of religious writers such as Simone
Weil and Lev Shestov, and if I have translated the Bible, it is not without
a hidden intention. I wanted to demonstrate that these spiritual writers
and texts are not the sole preserve of professional Catholics. (*Zaczynając
od moich ulic* 497–498)

Those few days in Lublin were dramatic at the time, but also anticipated future
controversy. There the poet had been feted and honoured from the grave by one
of the two most illustrious figures in the post-war Polish Catholic Church. A
quarter of a century later, the same Church's 'professional Catholics' sought to
prevent Miłosz's entombment in Skałka, one of the most famous churches in
Kraków, where other giants of Polish culture were buried. The accusation they
levelled against him was that he had had negative attitudes towards the Faith, the
Bible and, of course, Poland itself.

The warmth of his reception at the Catholic University of Lublin had already
provided ample evidence of how much Miłosz's literary endeavours were prized
there and throughout the country. Further recognition came the very next day,
when he met and was photographed standing side by side with Lech Wałęsa, the
leader of Solidarity, the first-ever free trade union in Soviet-controlled Eastern
Europe. Miłosz can be seen sporting two Solidarity emblems, and Wałęsa, as always, a badge depicting the Madonna of Częstochowa. Both had broad smiles on
their faces, which grew even wider when one of the hosts mistakenly welcomed
'Czesław Wałęsa'. Of Miłosz, Wałęsa declared, 'He was there before our movement, before me. And we really regarded his writing as an inspiration'. Turning
to the poet, he added, 'I think I went to prison twice for what you wrote!' In response, Miłosz said: 'I am conscious as a human being of the debt I owe to Lech
Wałęsa and to the workers of Poland. My contribution is negligible compared to
theirs' (*Rozmowy polskie* 2, 737–738).

Beforehand an exchange between the two was recorded in the office of the
university, and reads almost like a playscript:

Czesław Miłosz: Please believe me, I am a massive admirer of you as a leader.

Lech Wałęsa: I began to admire you much earlier. I learned to regard you as someone to emulate. It is I who am more indebted to you. Perhaps all of us are . . . it is difficult to estimate people's contribution to this situation today, which could have been very different.

CM: Regardless of that, if the so-called co-operation between intellectuals and workers is so important, there is no need for intellectuals to exaggerate their role.

Andrzej Miłosz: Wait a moment—for this meeting, there has to be a bigger badge. [He attaches a larger Solidarity badge to his brother's lapel.]

CM: Why? It was a small badge, but very pretty. What was wrong with that?

LW: You don't seem to be familiar with all the additional tricks of the trade.

CM: I am not familiar with them and do not want to be . . . I never in my life imagined myself in this kind of role. Yesterday in a speech I remarked that this coat was too big for me.

LW: Really, you know, you can get used to it. At first I had problems, but now they can do what they like as long as it doesn't hurt.

CM: . . . I used to write all sorts of things, better and worse. Now they dig deep into everything, and, because of my name, publish it. I end up being ashamed, I blush, and my ears burn. I have to swallow it all now.

LW: Yes, but that's life. And probably they interpret certain things in a way you never meant or intended.

CM: Exactly. I personally feel humble in the company of people of action. I am a pen-pusher. I sit in my room, write something, and I never imagined that they would be read aloud in public. Some time ago, fifteen people constituted an audience to me. Yesterday at that evening event, when the actors were reading my poems, I found it very moving.

LW: But that has already happened before. You know that once they even arrested me for your writing.

CM: Yes, but all that is too great a responsibility. This crown keeps slipping over my ears; it is much too big. (*Rozmowy polskie* 2, 733–734)

After this meeting, Miłosz recalled his absolute conviction that in due course Wałęsa would perform 'a pivotal role in Polish twentieth-century history, one of equivalent importance to that of Kościuszko' (CM to Barańczak, n.d.). They would have a second encounter on 17 June in Gdańsk, when Miłosz placed a wreath at the Three Crosses monument, dedicated to the forty-two shipyard workers killed in Gdynia during the strikes of December 1970. Their workmates and local people gathered in great numbers that day to hear the distinguished visitor's address:

> If you were a political movement striving for power, the world's attitude to you would have been such as it is to many movements involved in a temporary struggle for power. But there would be this one factor missing, which is why you have attracted the attention of people from different countries, nations and races. They [those other movements] would not have had your hope. (Miłosz, qtd. in Archive of the Shipyard Monument Committee, 17 June 1981)

Carved into the monument were verses from Psalm 29, translated by Miłosz: 'The Lord will give strength unto his people. The Lord will give his people blessing for peace', as well as the following lines from 'You Who Wronged':

> You who wronged a simple man
> Bursting into laughter at the crime . . .
> You can kill one, but another is born.
> The words are written down, the deed, the date.
>
> (*NCP* 103)

Here at this place, where so much blood had been spilled, the choice could not have been more fitting.

Reflecting, many years later, on those heady days of his return visit to Poland, he dwelt on how

> I tried to manage this tricky situation as best I could, when I found myself, after the award of the Nobel Prize, thrown into a role I had never anticipated. Until recently, I kept a badge someone bought at a market which depicted four sacred symbols for Poland: a bishop's mitre, which represented Cardinal Wyszyński; keys, the Pope; electric tools, Wałęsa; and a book, Miłosz. (*Rozmowy polskie* 543)

And it is true that he tried to maintain the pretence about the private nature of his visit, although, hardly surprisingly, the crowds of people at each consecutive event anticipated quite the opposite, waiting expectantly for each emphatic, unambiguous, 'engaged' word. And when those words did not materialise, they

quoted bracing patriotic verses which he had not written. To all too many, unfortunately, 'he gave the impression of a man who was arrogant, off-putting, and
lacking in empathy' (Illg 53).

His inner conflict, however, involved something more than his status as a
poet; rather, it was a matter of what his responsibility should be with regard to
the nation's spiritual well-being. As Communist power lessened, it seemed to
Miłosz, there was the danger of the re-emergence of nationalistic, right-wing
tendencies. To what extent was he correct in claiming that? Today perhaps, in the
wake of the many painful experiences the new Polish Republic has lived through,
we might be more inclined to agree with him than we were in 1981. Certainly what
dictated his attitude then was a deep resentment towards the bombastic nationalism of pre-war Poland.

Less than a year after the Three Crosses monument in Gdańsk was unveiled,
the Polish Premier, General Wojciech Jaruzelski, imposed martial law throughout
Poland on 13 December 1981 in an attempt to crush Solidarity and stave off a
possible Soviet invasion. Writing in the American press, Miłosz predicted that
Solidarity still had a major contribution to make to Poland's future:

> I do not think ... that democratic movements in Eastern Europe, where
> Solidarity is a driving force, will prove to be a passing phenomenon. On
> the contrary, whether they operate openly or in secret, their presence
> will last longer than all the twentieth-century juntas put together.
> (Miłosz, 'It Is a Grave Responsibility to Kill Hope', *New York Times*, 18
> December 1981)

Despite the internment of its leaders, including its president, Lech Wałęsa,
and the brutal treatment meted out to thousands of its imprisoned members, the
union continued functioning underground. In the United States, Miłosz, Susan
Sontag, Joseph Brodsky, Stanisław Barańczak and Tomas Venclova immediately
formed a committee to agitate on Solidarity's behalf; it called for a boycott of all
'transactions, economic and other' (*New York Review of Books*, 21 January 1982) with
Poland, until all internees were freed. On the last day of January 1982, the U.S.
Department of Information broadcast worldwide by satellite a ninety-minute
film, entitled *Let Poland Be Poland*, which featured contributions from, among
others, Ronald Reagan, Margaret Thatcher, Orson Welles, Frank Sinatra, Paul
McCartney and Miłosz himself.

Over the next few years, throughout Europe and America, coverage of the
Polish crisis remained intense. Between 13 December 1981 and March 1985, according
to the Polish Helsinki Committee, 'at least seventy-eight people lost their lives as
a result of the use of force by members of the police and security forces' (Garton
Ash 367). Amongst the vilest of these killings was the murder on 19 October 1984

of the pro-Solidarity priest Father Jerzy Popiełuszko by three agents of the Służba Bezpieczeństwa (the Polish Security Service). Although the regime succeeded in weakening Solidarity, they were unable to initiate the kind of economic recovery that might have won over some of the Polish people. Instead, as a Solidarity report from 1985 made clear, the country was plunging into a worsening crisis, with foreign debt increasing, wages stagnating, food shortages and levels of pollution spiraling, and standards of health care declining (Garton Ash 369).

The only way forward economically and politically, the government came to realise, was some kind of accommodation with the opposition, and so in September 1986 they issued an amnesty for political prisoners. In a secret document from 1987, Mieczysław Rakowski, a leading figure on the Party's Central Committee and from September 1988 to January 1990 Poland's Premier, conceded that Solidarity represented 'a lasting element on the country's political map' (qtd. in Garton Ash 369). And so it was that eight years after the signing of the Gdańsk accords, Lech Wałęsa was formally invited for talks by General Czesław Kiszczak, the Interior Minister, on 31 August 1988, which led directly to the 'Round Table' talks. Between 6 February and 4 April 1989 members of the Communist Party and the Solidarity opposition, together with representatives of the Catholic Church, met in the Vice-Regal Palace, now the Presidential Palace, to discuss the future constitutional shape of Poland. The key features of the agreement they signed on 4 April saw the introduction of the post of elected President, the creation of a Senate, and the formal legalisation of free, independent trade unions. Exactly two months later, elections resulted in Solidarity candidates winning 99 of the 100 seats in the new Senate and all of the 161 seats they could contest in the lower house, or Sejm. After protracted discussions within Poland—and between Rakowski and Mikhail Gorbachev[13]—on 24 August 1989, former Solidarity internee Tadeusz Mazowiecki became Poland's Prime Minister, an early signal of the epic changes that would fundamentally transform swathes of Central and Eastern Europe and bring the USSR to an end. In the coming months, Communist-run regimes were toppled successively in Hungary, East Germany, Bulgaria, Czechoslovakia and Romania.

Overjoyed by these developments, Miłosz returned to Poland in 1989, and thereafter during the 1990s regularly spent his summers there before finally settling permanently in Kraków in his last years. Equally momentous was the visit he made to the country of his birth in 1991, which he had last seen in 1939; it was a trip that filled the pages of his next collection, *Facing the River* (1995). What made the journey possible was Lithuania's secession from the Soviet Union, which was formally recognised in September 1991. That independence was not won without bloodshed, however, since the Soviet government had sent in troops in January of that year who fired on protesters, killing eleven and injuring hundreds in Vilnius (formerly Wilno). In an acknowledgement of his major contribution to its own and world literature, the newly independent state bestowed on the eighty year-old Miłosz the title of honorary citizen.[14]

Heloise

No, you never 'pretend'. Your pessimism is plain to see, except that it is the pessimism of a man born to experience happiness and life; it is the pessimism of a man who is physically strong and brave.

Konstanty A. Jeleński in a letter to CM (1979)

When you were here last, you told me that you were afraid of your youth, and also mentioned that for the first time in your life you were happy. That is a youthful way of thinking. They are those experiences of happiness for which you have to pay so dearly.

Józef Czapski in a letter to CM (1984)

'*Unattainable Earth* is about Ewa and enchantment, if you do not believe in love. This enchantment revived me after the solitary struggle reflected in *Hymn of the Pearl*' (CM to Jadwiga Waszkiewicz, 20 July 1985).[15] Miłosz shared these confidences with one of his earliest loves, having again met someone whose presence made his heart race and who rescued him from indifference and grey depression. Published in 1986, and the work of a man in his seventies, *Unattainable Earth* is an exceptionally sensuous collection, another great gulp of fresh air in which the poet opens his arms to the temporal world to embrace as much joy as possible.

In a note to another friend in the winter of 1979, Miłosz described his encounter with the woman who before long would assume the role of muse: 'We had a very pleasant young lady for a week-long visit, who came from New York, and works for the newspaper *Nowy Dziennik*. This is the new generation . . . which reveres me as if I were a living legend' (CM to Jeleński, 21 November 1979). A Polish émigré publication, *Nowy Dziennik,* had hit upon the idea of issuing a series of books about distinguished Poles living in America. And given the fact that he had just been awarded the Neustadt Prize, Miłosz was an ideal subject with which to open this venture. One of those involved in the project was Ewa, a thirty-five year-old journalist and recent arrival in the States who held a degree in Polish studies. It was she, rather than her boss, who decided to approach Miłosz.

They had initially met briefly in the autumn of 1978, in New York, where Miłosz was giving a reading at the Guggenheim Museum. Following the event, she was one of the party who joined him and the other speakers at a French

restaurant he had chosen for its relaxed, informal atmosphere. It would take another twelve months, however, before Ewa was able to overcome all the obstacles
preventing her from flying to Berkeley to conduct the necessary interviews. These
were recorded interviews at the university, because Janka objected to any discussion
of *The Issa Valley*, because she regarded it as too autobiographical and in places
'pornographic'.[16] A second phase of recordings took place in September 1980, when
Robert Hass and Robert Pinsky joined Miłosz in what they termed a 'translation
collective'. Following the announcement that he had been awarded the Nobel
Prize, the poet appointed Ewa as his secretary in order to help deal with the
avalanche of letters which arrived on a daily basis. Early on, when they started
travelling together, they visited Paris, where Ewa was introduced to the team
from *Kultura*. Jeleński was very taken with Ewa and happy to see the effect she
had on Miłosz; he even suggested to his friend that he ought to leave Janka,
whose health was actually improving at that time. After Miłosz's visit to Poland in the summer of 1981, Ewa accompanied him to Corsica, where they met
Jeanne Hersch. It was as if Miłosz had an intense need to talk about Ewa with
women with whom he had had strong ties in the past. Some years later, when
new sources of suffering became interwoven with the old, he wrote to one of his
oldest friends about Jeanne, Janka and Ewa:

> Jeanne could never get over the fact that I did not want to divorce
> Janka and marry her. And, let's be frank, I lost Ewa for exactly the same
> reason, as I am absolutely incapable of leaving my wife, who, physically
> and mentally, is a ninety-five year-old. And what loving woman will put
> up with a double life? (CM to Jadwiga Waszkiewicz, 24 June 1984)

As his letters make plain, what Jeleński wanted above all for his friend was personal contentment, which in turn would generate artistic fulfilment. So much,
though, bound Miłosz and Janka together. The solemnity he attached to his
marriage vows would not allow him to abandon his life companion, particularly
given her very infirm and vulnerable state.[17] The relationship with Ewa lasted
only three years but was full of passion and inspiring experiences. Both were
aware that inevitably it would have to end, but by journeying the world together
from America to Europe and Japan they maintained their bond and created a
justification for its existence:

> This relationship lasted three years and was very happy. It ended in May,
> leaving me in a stupor . . . Of course, I would have never thought of myself,
> at the age of seventy to seventy-three, as a Romeo. Most of my school
> friends are old codgers now. And now, I find things difficult, because this
> 'pride in my body' was like a dam protecting me from waves of nihilistic

feelings. When you write to me about your revulsion towards people, I understand that perfectly. It is perhaps intensified by hereditary factors, that burden of fear *(angoisse)*. Genetically, I was wonderfully endowed, having incredible vitality, which enabled me to deal with fundamental obstacles in that other, neurotic aspect of my nature, which inflicted so many miseries. That other part could only be overcome by great effort. So, whereas the relationship I am referring to occurred when my vitality was at its zenith, loneliness condemns me to stare into the mirror of psychological illnesses of those closest to me, which is not healthy for me. (CM to Jadwiga Waszkiewicz, 24 June 1984)

In April he had composed a farewell poem, 'To Heloise', which he had no intention of publishing. It expresses pain, and deals with destiny and the curse of a jealous daemon. At the same time its speaker voices the man's pride and conviction that his lost love will never again experience such emotional intensity. Hers will be a journey not to a different life, but to a state which will be almost deathly:

This is farewell, my Heloise, after three years of great good fortune.
I should not be too much concerned with life, or death,
or any experiences . . .

But, Heloise, it was I who was to blame,
For childish greed, for the childish hope
That it is possible to commit yourself to someone magnanimously
And blow a horn and shout and dance in celebration.
It's a delusion, Heloise, because we are paralysed by fear,
Which demands forgiveness and is forgiven . . .

(Unpublished typescript, Beinecke Library Archive)

The enchantment and exhilaration Jeleński felt on reading *Unattainable Earth* sprang from the fact that it was engendered

under the sign of . . . Ewa, fastened (from *The Garden of Earthly Delights to Seventy-Year-Old Poet*) with a clasp of her jewel . . . It is so strange, however, that . . . [Ewa] left at the time when his collection was being readied for the publisher, as if it and the time of love were predestined to endure for a thousand days and a hundred and seventy pages. (Jeleński to CM, 30 June 1984)

Towards the end of his life Miłosz said that his poems were born not from despair, but, on the contrary, from phases when he was able to draw deep breaths and take in the world. What revitalised the creative impulse was excitement, libido, Eros, the chance to join in a 'chase with the hounds for the unattainable meaning of the world' ('Winter', *NCP* 420). *Unattainable Earth* is charged with this passionate energy, which differentiates it so markedly from the bitterness of *Hymn of the Pearl*, written only two years before. At the book's outset, we find ourselves standing in front of Hieronymus Bosch's triptych in the Prado. 'I' the poetic persona, 'I' the man, born under the sign of Cancer, is led by women towards

> the room where *The Garden of Earthly Delights*
> Had been prepared for me. So that I run to its waters
> And immerse myself in them and recognize myself.
>
> ...
>
> I was old but my nostrils craved new scents
> And through my five senses I received a share in the earth
> Of those who led me, our sisters and lovers.
>
> ('Summer', *NCP* 401)

'I', Adam, is contemplating Eve, the Temptress and Mother, who simultaneously embodies the prehistoric wisdom of Sophia and the sensuality of Lilith. The division of human beings into male and female engenders a perpetual search for one another, since only through the joining of their bodies can a paradisal unity occur, bringing with it a sense of security and of God's presence. In this collection Miłosz and his readers pursue something deeper than culture, something encoded in nakedness, in skin—something primal.

> We are untouched by death and time, children, myself with Eve, in a kindergarten, in a sandbox, in a bed, embracing each other, making love, saying the words of eternal avowals and eternal delights ... To absorb with your eyes the inside of a flower shop, to hear the voices of people, to feel on your tongue the taste of just-drunk coffee. Passing the windows of apartments, I invent stories, similar to my own, a lifted elbow, the combing of hair before a mirror. I multiplied myself and came to inhabit every one of them separately, thus my impermanence has no power over me. ('The Hooks of a Corset', *NCP* 408)

Miłosz was a man of acute sensibilities, who experienced the world with such an intensity, remembering every detail of a morning when boulevards were sprayed with water, the shade of an iris, the smell of food. And he retained these sensations in his memory as if he were a witness sent to earth, who would acknowledge many years later: 'Wherever I am, at whatever place on earth, I hide from people the conviction that I'm not from here. It's as if I'd been sent, to extract as many colors, tastes, sounds, smells, to experience everything that is a man's share, to transpose what was felt into a magical register and carry it there, from whence I came' ('Wherever', *NCP* 687).

As in his earlier volumes, Miłosz assumes here that the limitless riches of actuality can be accessed only through a multiplicity of forms, and he is therefore at ease combining poems, sketches, prose commentaries, translations, a letter from Czapski, a cluster of quotations from the eleventh-century *Corpus Hermeticum*—all of which fit perfectly into place with Baudelaire writing about Constantin Guys. And although Miłosz is operating at a far remove from classical poetic forms, he instils this collage with existential meaning. By this means, he strives to escape the deceptions of conventional life and attain a greater closeness to truth in the everyday, truth which is intimately bound up with the body:

> What will poetry be like in the future? That is a question I think about, but about which I will never know. I know that it is possible, because I am familiar with those brief moments when my pen almost brought it into being, only for it to vanish in that selfsame moment. The rhythms of bodies—the heart-beat, sweat, menstrual blood, sperm and its stickiness, the stance while relieving oneself, the movement of the bowels, these will always co-exist with elevated needs of the soul. ('W Głąb Drzewa', *Wiersze* IV, 32)

Under Ewa's influence, he developed 'some kind of empathy towards personal human affairs, which I had problems with in the past' (CM to Aniela Micińska, 17 July 1984). And indeed *Unattainable Earth* displays a range of emotional responses which in earlier works had no voice, a commonplace, almost timeless joy derived from being 'simply alive among the living' ('Epigraf', *Wiersze* IV, 136). This is reflected in the poem 'At Noon', which recalls the pleasure of chatting together on a terrace, next to Jeanne and Ewa:

> At a mountain inn, high above the bulky green of chestnuts,
> The three of us were sitting next to an Italian family
> Under the tiered levels of pine forests.
> Nearby a little girl pumped water from a well.
> The air was huge with the voice of swallows.
> Ooo, I heard a singing in me, ooo.
> What a noon, no other like it will recur,
> Now when I am sitting next to her and her
> While the stages of past life come together
> And a jug of wine stands on a checkered tablecloth.
> The granite rocks of the island were washed by the sea.
> The three of us were one self-delighting thought
> And the resinous scent of Corsican summer was with us.
>
> (*NCP* 426)

The deep satisfactions of a physical relationship with the world wins out here, as if Stanisław Vincenz's advice had come back to him, although on this occasion it did not have to be deployed to escape something phantasmal. At last we discover in Miłosz's verse a man who 'runs and runs' ('Meaning', *NCP* 569) constantly throughout the world, but who can now stop for a while and come to terms with himself. This occurs when a relationship with another individual allows him to accept his own imperfections, when the sight of a neck leant forward, a glimpse of a nose, the shape of an eye, creates a feeling of great *tendresse*. Of this the poet wrote: 'I prefer this word to the Polish equivalent. When I feel a lump in my throat, because the person I look at is so fragile, vulnerable, mortal, that then is *tendresse*' ('Anka', *Wiersze* IV, 95).

Unattainable Earth is a collection so dense, so rich in meaning, that, if read carefully, it offers invaluable insights into Miłosz's poetic and intellectual world. It can be seen as a gift he received from a particular woman, whose beneficent influence he acknowledged when writing to a friend:

> The change within me has very little to do with the Nobel Prize or my return trip to Poland ... Although I never signed the pact, like old Faust, I grew to despise all the wisdom that comes from books, and treasure instead relationships between people, loves and friendships ... And although there were misogynistic strains within me, I have almost converted to feminism, so much do I enjoy the company of women, that special aura that comes from talking to them and sharing wine. Although a little late in the day, I think it has humanised me in some way. (CM to Jeleński, 30 July 1981)

'I will haunt you with my strange love'

> Recently Brodsky gave an evening reading at our place. Our relationship is extremely good and the triumvirate (+Venclova) is continuing.
>
> CM to Giedroyc (1980)

Miłosz was in his late seventies when history produced yet another great change. Suddenly the Berlin Wall began to crumble and, much faster than anyone could have anticipated, the Soviet Empire collapsed. To a certain extent, he was able to remain at peace with himself, to adopt a sceptical tolerance and to ease down a little when it came to the pace of life.

At Yale

We were drinking vodka together, Brodsky, Venclova
With his beautiful Swedish girl, myself, Richard,
Near the Art Gallery, at the end of the century
Which woke up as if from a heavy slumber
And asked, in stupefaction: 'What was that?
How could we? A conjunction of planets?
Or spots on the sun?'

                                        —For history
Is no more comprehensible. Our species
Is not ruled by any reasonable law.
The boundaries of its nature are unknown.
It is not the same as I, you, a single human.

—Thus mankind returns to its beloved pastimes
During the break. Taste and touch
Are dear to it. Cookbooks,
Recipes for perfect sex, rules
Lowering cholesterol, methods
Of quickly losing weight—that's what it needs.
. . .
Are we that? Does it apply to us? Yes and no.

—For, visited by dictators' dreams,
Don't we soar above them who are light-headed
And unwilling to think of the punishment that awaits
All those who are too much in love with life?

                                                    (*NCP* 516)

The 1980s and 1990s were a period when, through his writing, Miłosz developed
a kind of international poetics, as his time was often taken up with translation
and attendance at conferences and symposia. At the periphery of his life, he experiences fulfilment, recognition, success. There is no need for further struggle,
for proving anything or competing with anyone. He can sustain friendships, relax
sipping vodka with Richard Lourie, Joseph Brodsky, Tomas Venclova, and also
Seamus Heaney. The latter would later recall:

> Miłosz's achievements made me so insecure that I avoided meeting him,
> but when Robert Hass and Robert Pinsky introduced us in Berkeley in
> the early eighties, I immediately felt overcome by a sense of peace . . .
> We were both Catholics, and we suddenly began to exchange stories

about our school days spent amongst habits and birettas . . . I left . . .
with a renewed sense of the man's poetic vision, his fortitude, the scope
of his intellectual life and spiritual experiences. (Heaney, 'Mój Miłosz',
in *Tygodnik Powszechny* 26)

Another member of Miłosz's circle was Stanisław Barańczak, a New Wave poet,
whom he tried to help get out of Poland to take up a post waiting for him at
Harvard. What undoubtedly had a decisive impact on the Communist authorities granting Barańczak a passport[18] was the intervention of Cardinal Wyszyński
at Miłosz's request. Subsequently the older poet sent an invitation to Barańczak
to come to Stockholm as his 'personal guest'. Miłosz was always warm and caring
towards Barańczak and interested in where his poetic journey would take him;
in addition, he also greatly admired the latter's skills as a translator. Miłosz treasured close friendships, as Irena Grudzińska-Gross observed: 'Friendship was
for him most of all the virtue of mutual well-wishing, support and attention. The
word *friend* was used by him often' (Grudzińska-Gross 66).

Amongst the most enduring bonds was with Joseph Brodsky, one of the
greatest poets of the second half of the twentieth century. When he was still
in his early twenties, Brodsky had been sentenced by the Soviet authorities to
internal exile for being a 'parasite', and had his citizenship revoked. Intense international pressure prompted his release in 1972, enabling him to move to the
United States. Learning of his arrival, Miłosz welcomed him and wished him
courage, keen to demonstrate that exile does not necessarily have to mean defeat.
He dictated a letter in Russian and sent it to the University of Michigan, where
Brodsky had begun working.

> I think that you are very worried, like all of us from our part of Europe,
> brought up on the myth that the life of a writer ends if he abandons
> his native country. But it is only a myth, understandable in countries
> where the civilisation long remained a rural civilisation, in which 'the
> soil' played a great role. Everything depends on the man and his internal
> health . . . What else can I say? The first months of exile are very hard.
> They shouldn't be taken as a measure of what is to come. With time you
> will see that perspectives change. (Qtd. in Grudzińska-Gross 2)

Miłosz also planned to invite Brodsky to California to deliver a number of lectures and suggested that it might be a useful exercise if the Russian translated some
poems from *Wiersze,* his 1967 collection published by Oficyna Poetów i Malarzy.
Brodsky replied two weeks later, closing with a famous sentence, 'As for the first
part of your letter, my own is so short just because of what you wrote in yours'
(Grudzińska-Gross 4–5). The note contained crossed-out words and was not very

well written. What Brodsky is saying here to Miłosz is 'I understand and I am already working; let's not talk about emigration and suffering' (Grudzińska-Gross 5). As Miłosz had been compelled to years earlier, Brodsky imposed on himself a discipline which saved him from despair. This exchange of letters marked the beginning of their friendship, surprising in that it brought together two great artists neither of whom possessed a temperament conducive to compromises. It was Brodsky's arrogance, spiritual aristocracy and absolute belief in his talent that especially impressed Miłosz.

At the outset, the chemistry between the two may not have always been good, judging from a remark Miłosz made subsequently to Giedroyc:

> Brodsky was here for an evening reading and I delivered the introduction. He was very pleasant, good mannered, approachable, warm, completely unlike the same man . . . three years ago, when only I could tolerate his behaviour. So civilisation has a positive effect after all, because when he arrived in America he emanated barbarity and conceit. (CM to Giedroyc, 9 March 1976)

That the relationship flourished can mainly be attributed to the fact that the Russian poet was full of admiration for Miłosz's work, and was prepared to admit to its superiority over his own. Brodsky declared on one occasion that certain 'pages from *A Treatise on Poetry* devoted to the Spirit of History contain the greatest poetic utterance I have ever known. Looking at it from an intellectual point of view, they border on the inconceivable' (Gorczyńska 107). Miłosz felt a strong affinity with Brodsky, who was thirty years his junior, treating him as a kindly elder brother might, and never regarding him as a rival; this was especially true after 1980, when he gained his place in the elite Nobel club, and came to feel above all that. When Brodsky became a member in 1987, Miłosz sent a witty telegram remarking that 'Polish-Russian relations have returned to normal' (qtd. in Gorczyńska 107). They were both devotees of a classical style, convinced about the importance of hierarchy, to which the world of art has to submit. A conversation between them recorded in 1989 shows how many artistic views they held in common, such as their positive attitude towards realism. Miłosz observes how 'after all the . . . abuse heaped on the term "realism", it takes some courage to even use the word. But what strikes me is how relatively little of the reality of our century has been captured in words. And so, to me, the true measure of literary worth is the presence of objective reality in poems and novels' (*Rozmowy polskie* 2, 378). Over two wonderful decades they met in New York and then Kraków, translated each other's poems, wrote about each other, and, as Miłosz was wont to say, established an international brotherhood, a poetic lodge, which was ended by Brodsky's untimely death from a heart attack in January 1996.

Between poets of that high calibre it is perhaps unusual to witness such deep affection. With Tomas Venclova, they constituted a triumvirate, bringing together Lithuania, Poland and Russia. Their fates had intertwined years previously, when Venclova brought Miłosz to Brodsky's attention during a visit to Leningrad. When Brodsky asked him whether Herbert was the greatest living Polish poet, Venclova answered that there was someone whose work occupied an even higher plane, Miłosz. Venclova had come across Miłosz's poems for the first time in the literary periodical *Naujoji Romuva* while browsing in his father's library. Subsequently, in a conversation with Miłosz in America, Brodsky described Lithuania as the best nation in the Soviet Empire, and went on to mention young Tomas, the son of Antanas Venclova, who composed the words to the Lithuanian Socialist Soviet Republic's national anthem.

Miłosz was among the leading international literary figures who campaigned to enable Tomas Venclova to leave the Soviet Union in 1977, writing letters on his behalf and telephoning him to underline their support. His poetry had been suppressed by the authorities because of his involvement in dissident activity, not least because of his founding role in Lithuania's Helsinki group, which monitored human rights' abuses. On learning from Brodsky of Venclova's release and arrival in Paris, Miłosz spoke of his 'great joy' (CM to Lillian Vallee, 2 February 1977). Before leaving Paris en route to the United States, Venclova sent a warm, appreciative letter to Miłosz and all his 'known and unknown friends': 'I wrote to you a number of times (I imagine that all of it was noted in the KGB archives) ... Your works opened up the greatest experiences ever. I am really happy and forever indebted to you for dragging me out of that mire' (Venclova to CM, 27 January 1977). Miłosz hoped that Venclova would become a lecturer and then take over his post in Berkeley. Although that never happened, they met numerous times in America, Vilnius and Kraków, remaining the best of friends, and providing an illustration, which Miłosz often cited, that Polish-Lithuanian understanding was possible.

Two years after Lithuania became an independent state following the disintegration of the USSR, Miłosz revisited his native realm for the first time in over fifty years. He yearned to recapture the country in which he had grown up, the Lithuania whose distinctive Polish elite had once had such pride in its autonomous status within Poland. This was the land he came to know and love as a young child when he travelled from village to village with his mother. In the intervening years, his motherland had been crushed and occupied by Soviet Russia. Miłosz was pained seeing the area in which Szetejnie once nestled, a place dotted with small holdings and private orchards, now given over to a monotonous plain of collective farms.

Back in 1968, this deep yearning to re-discover 'his native land' had caused a rift with Zbigniew Herbert, whose opinions on patriotism and racial inequality, not to mention his adulation of the West, conflicted with Miłosz's. The simmering tensions came to a climax one evening during Herbert's visit to Berkeley in early July 1968, when they met in the home of Bogdana and John Carpenter. After having consumed far too much wine, Herbert launched into a sudden, vicious tirade against the man who had done so much to promote his poetry worldwide. He charged Miłosz with a lack of patriotism, and castigated him for hiding behind a Lithuanian passport during the Nazi occupation and for his negative attitude towards the Home Army (Armia Krajowa), which was loyal to the London-based Polish Government-in-Exile. Herbert's outburst gave an early indication of the serious psychological instability that plagued his later life, and which, when combined with alcohol, triggered uncontrollable aggression. The attack left Miłosz utterly dumbfounded, so much so that Janka took the initiative, insisting that they leave immediately, which they did. The incident revealed a darker side to Herbert, who struggled to live with his mentor's superiority and greater success as an artist.

Following the incident in Berkeley, their relationship never regained its previous warmth and closeness, though Miłosz did accept Herbert's apology. Signs that Herbert was keen to repair the breach can be seen in a note from late December 1968:

> Forgive me for not keeping in touch for so long. Whether you like it or not, I will haunt you with my strange love until the end of my life and then some time afterwards . . . I am now preoccupied with everyday things; I write and cheat my anxieties. I read three of your beautiful poems in *Kultura*. It perked me up a bit. You must understand certain things, which I am unable to communicate to you, because of the lump in my throat. Please be generous to me and forgiving. (Herbert to CM, December 1968, in *Korespondencja* 99)

Not long afterwards, in a significant act of trust, Herbert confided to Miłosz his difficulties with the Polish Secret Service (the Urząd Bezpieczeństwa), whose officers had embarked—unsuccessfully—on a sustained attempt to recruit him as an informer. This too failed to restore relations. In a letter to Aleksander Schenker seven years later, supporting Miłosz's candidacy for the Neustadt Prize, Herbert confessed that he had

> little contact with Miłosz to speak of. Our friendship ended many years ago, following an argument on fundamental principles while we were under the influence of drink. Perhaps it was my fault, but to be truthful, I detest salon communists and socialists. Despite differences of opinion, I still regard him as the pre-eminent poet writing in Polish. (Herbert to Schenker, 12 June 1975)

There was something of a thaw in their chilly relationship in the 1980s, however. When martial law adversely affected basic food supplies in Poland, Miłosz sent parcels from America to his sick friend and in 1988 accepted the Bruno Schulz Award on Herbert's behalf. Two years later, after coming across new poems by Miłosz in *Zeszyty Literackie*, Herbert wrote enthusiastically about them to the author, describing himself as 'your pupil' (Herbert to CM, 9 May 1990, *Korespondencja* 126).

During the 1990s, the far right in Poland repeatedly disseminated 'rational' and 'objective'—that is, essentialist—arguments about the concept of national identity. As part of this polemic, they frequently dubbed Herbert 'the truly Polish poet', in order to differentiate him from the 'non-Polish' Miłosz.

The Dragon

Time-tempered ferocity, but with tolerance increased all-embracing doubt. He sat in the darkness in front of the puppet theatre and watched the chases, prayers, puff and subservience, while recognizing his own stupidity.

Czesław Miłosz, *Road-Side Dog*

In the publisher's office we referred to him—after Durrell's description of Cavafy—as an 'Old Poet of this City'. It was not true, strictly speaking, because he was never old. A witness from a bygone era, he talked, asked questions, and sought answers that were relevant to the present day. He truly occupied the present at all times.

Adam Boniecki, 'To nic, że czasem nie wie'

Zbigniew Herbert's accusations were not the only attacks that Miłosz encountered in the new Poland, when history, 'the second name of which is Annihilation' ('Why', *NCP 584*), suddenly revealed its kind face, at least for a while. Inevitably, there were squabbles and disagreements after the Round Table accords, before relief and exhilaration prevailed. At this particular historical juncture, opinions on Miłosz's value and worth divided Poland in two. His admirers turned him into a cult figure. In 1994 he was awarded Poland's highest honour when he became a member of the Order of the White Eagle. Four years later he received one of Poland's most prestigious literary awards, the Nike, for *Road-Side Dog*. When in 2001 he celebrated his ninetieth birthday, a festive event was organised in Kraków during which his son and granddaughter gave out birthday cake to the people of the city, well-wishers left cards, and an orchestra performed underneath his window.

In some people's minds, however, Miłosz was not 'ours', although it was difficult to determine to whom he really belonged—Lithuania? the Jews? the

Communists? Or was he the creation of *Gazeta Wyborcza* and its demonic editor-in-chief, Adam Michnik? When in 1993 he was granted honorary citizenship of Kraków, there were those who declared that he did not deserve the title because he was a Lithuanian. After he suggested during one public debate that Poland's Communist system actually had a benign influence on the dissemination of literature because the arts were made so accessible to all and so heavily subsidised, it was eagerly jumped upon by critics as a sign that he was willing to glorify oppression by the Reds. A mere seven years after his death, in 2011, when the Polish Parliament (the Sejm) announced the establishment of a Year of Czesław Miłosz, there were voices declaring that he was undeserving of such an honour.

Nevertheless, though occasional conflicts surfaced or re-surfaced, Miłosz entered a good phase in his life from the late 1980s onwards, and was pleased at the recognition afforded his work during what turned out to be a very creative period. In the autumn of 1989, on his second trip to Poland, he received a doctorate *honoris causa* at Kraków's Jagiellonian University. Four years later he bought a flat in Kraków, at number 6 Bogusławskiego, where initially Miłosz and Carol, his second wife, spent summer and autumn before returning to Berkeley for the winter months. After suffering a stroke in 2000, he settled for good in Kraków in order to be close to Wawel (the Royal Castle), and over time Turowicz's and Wisława Szymborska's intimate city came to replace Wilno, the city of his youth.

In the United States he was one of twelve people to be awarded the National Medal of Arts in 1989, and that same year he received an honorary PhD from Harvard. Helen Vendler commented later on the radiance his face displayed, which she attributed to joy 'that Poland opened its doors for him'. The 'sombre exile' whom she remembered from 1981 and 1982, when he lectured at Harvard, 'had become a happy Miłosz, who could return home . . . I can imagine the suffering and loneliness that emigration caused him' (Vendler, in *Czesław Miłosz: In Memoriam*, 65).

The Round Table Agreement of April 1989, which initiated the move towards the democratisation of politics in Poland and formally legalised free trade unions, undoubtedly contributed greatly to Miłosz's raised spirits, since it freed him to travel back there whenever he wished. An even greater factor in his well-being was the presence in his life of Carol Thigpen, a senior academic at Emory University in Atlanta, Georgia, whom he married in 1992. Thirty years his junior, slim, blond, with a throaty, infectious laugh, she would become a constant joy to him and was referred to by him as a 'gift', the source of a new lease of life. Born on 5 April 1944 in Florida, Thigpen came from a family who had settled in the American South; she held a doctorate in humanities and the history of education. In 1982 Miłosz accepted her invitation to give a reading at Emory. Subsequently, she relished re-telling the story about how she lost her car keys while collecting him from the airport. When, cuttingly, Miłosz enquired how often

that happened, she replied, 'Only when I am with handsome men'. The happy
punch line to the anecdote was: 'And would you believe it? He bought it'. She
found herself greatly moved by his poetry and attracted by his blue eyes.

The following year Miłosz returned to Atlanta for a literary festival and, in
the end, as Carol put it 'so we, you know, enjoyed each other' (Thigpen, speaking
in *The Magic Mountain*). The emotional bond between them grew, which necessitated considerable patience and devotion on her part, not only because Janka was
still alive, but also because he was with 'Ewa', who, as it happened, was her friend.
Despite the substantial differences between them in terms of culture, life experiences
and mind-set—for example, her American roots and Protestant upbringing, and her
lack of any connection with Poland and its literature, a world which was essential
to Miłosz—they had several core features in common. Carol had similarly spent
her childhood on a country farm, living with grandparents in Tarborough, North
Carolina. As writers, they enjoyed a similar daily routine, starting with a morning
coffee, followed by mid-morning work, and ending with reading newspapers in the
evening. They also gained pleasure from discussing their opinions on various topics,
especially religion, about which they frequently talked at length.

Jerzy Illg, a friend of Miłosz's and a leading publisher in Kraków, recalled
witnessing a telling, emblematic scene between them:

> Czesław rises from the sofa in order to get a book from a shelf. As he
> walks through the hall, without his walking stick, he loses balance a
> little. The door is ajar, so I can see Carol's hand supporting him, and how
> gently, but firmly, she steadies him by holding on to his jacket. The ges-
> ture said everything. (Illg, 'Carol Thigpen-Miłosz', *Gazeta w Krakowie*,
> 9 August 2002)

In a filmed interview from 1999, Miłosz paid tribute to Carol's many qualities
and spoke of his extreme good fortune in having her at his side: 'She is a brave
fighter for my rights, not to mention her easy personality. She is always in a good
mood, which counterbalances my depression. And this way I experience moments of relief' (*The Magic Mountain*). In her presence he mellowed, developing
an easier, friendlier, more tolerant disposition towards others. Increasingly he
also enjoyed company, which brought out his strong sense of humour. At times
mischievousness or glee would just erupt within him.

Whenever Richard Lourie visited the flat in Kraków, there would always
be 'coffee, pastries, absorbing conversations, a relaxed, convivial atmosphere.
Then, when we were saying goodbye, warm embraces'. On one occasion he was
already by the door when Miłosz called out: 'I turned round. He wanted to say
something pleasant that came to mind before I left. But he couldn't utter a single
word, it was so funny. "Richard", he said in his strong, pronounced Slavonic ac-

cent, "it is a shame I am not gay'" (Lourie, in *In Memoriam* 110). And there was that deep, spontaneous laughter, which all who met him must have remembered, and which Irena Grudzińska-Gross characterised as

> profoundly infectious . . . it cordially pulled in the people who were within its range. It expressed in a primordial way Miłosz's attitude to life, which he found wonderful, although somewhat ridiculous . . . There was nothing ironic, sardonic or bitter in his laughter; rather it expressed his appetite and vitality. It was healthy, approving, and wise. (Grudzińska-Gross 269–270)

Certainly the most important facet of his personality was his gift for tender love, which buoyed up and prolonged his life.

As he moved into and through his nineties, it seemed as if Miłosz would live forever. Although he now used a walking stick and was losing his hearing, he remained extremely strong. An authority who was revered but sometimes feared, he acted as a watchful guardian of Polish literature, giving interviews, participating in radio and television programmes, and appearing in documentaries and public discussions. He prepared dozens of lectures, co-organised seminars on American and Polish poetry, and even funded and awarded a literary prize in his name. Repeatedly he urged people to remember poets who had died and to read the work of the new generation of writers, whose books he discovered and promoted.

Over the summer and autumn of 2000, he expended considerable energy travelling first to Vienna to deliver a lecture, then to New York to attend his granddaughter's wedding, and next to Paris to attend Jerzy Giedroyc's funeral, before heading to Sweden and Lithuania for meetings and events prior to a trip to Frankfurt for the book fair, whose spotlight that year was on Polish literature.

Most days, however, were still taken up with reading and writing. His secretary, Agnieszka Kosińska, recollected how he loved the safe anchorage of his desk, on which his favourite computer, a Mac, sat; arrayed beside it were

> a faulty printer, a telephone complete with answerphone, and a black desk lamp which refused to stay upright, and regularly collapsed onto the piles of papers . . . a green notebook, a blood-pressure monitor in a box, literary journals, daily newspapers, flowers in a vase—Carol always saw to those—and writing implements . . . a pencil with red and blue at either end to make corrections. Always in his hand there was either a pen, a magnifying glass or glasses. (Kosińska, *Rozmowy o Miłoszu*)

Of all the prose works and books he wrote and edited during that period, the most important is *Road-Side Dog* (1997), which Leszek Kołakowski interpreted, perhaps not entirely seriously, as embodying Miłosz's metaphysics, in which

nothing in the world has one meaning, and what is more, behind anything that exists and happens, there is an underlying opposite and evil
force. Under the cover of existence, nothingness creeps, and nothingness
feeds on existence; from beneath a cloud of evil[,] goodness shines, and
evil latches onto goodness and follows in its footsteps. It is similar to
truthfulness and deception, comedy and tragedy, faith and despair, identity and distortion, spring and autumn, Thursday and Friday, suffering
and enchantment, dream and earth, things that passed and things which
never existed. (Kołakowski 176)

Miłosz reveals himself in this book as very modern in a real and philosophical
sense. He presents 'truth' as something we cannot grasp, but only get close to.
Every section of the book contains particle clouds, myriads of thoughts engaging
with, complementing and contradicting one another: 'To believe you are magnificent. And gradually to discover that you are not magnificent. Enough labor
for one human life' (*RD* 60).

Miłosz continued to publish extensively to the end of his days, particularly
collections of essays and letters. *Legendy nowoczesności* (1996) consisted of recovered essays from the war years, while *Życie na wyspach* (1997) explored the invasion
of mass culture and how to resist its tyrannous materialism: 'I won't hide the hatred I feel towards the "civilisation" promoted by the cinema, television and colour
magazines, in short to how money enslaves the mind'. Miłosz was unwavering in
his scepticism towards deconstruction and postmodernism, which were increasingly dictating the agenda in university humanities departments at the time. He
describes himself as existing on 'a university island', isolated from 'postmodern
ills' and those faddish 'new research subjects' which constantly evoke the names of
Foucault, Lacan or Derrida. Too often, he declares, the debilitating effect of that
trio insinuates its way into poetry and prose, 'often ignoring the rules governing
good writing, which are not unrelated to common sense' (*Życie na wyspach* 93).

A number of other publications from the mid-1990s are particularly worth
noting. Not least of these was *Jakiego to gościa mieliśmy* (1996), a study of the life
and poetry of Anna Świrszczyńska. By writing this book for a Polish audience
and collaborating with Leonard Nathan on translations of her poetry (*Talking to
My Body*) for an anglophone one, Miłosz sought to rescue her remarkable work
from obscurity and to extend her readership. Such acts of homage and tenderness
were a characteristic feature of Miłosz's latter years.[19]

Twelve of her lyrics were incorporated by Miłosz in a widely read international anthology he compiled, entitled *A Book of Luminous Things* (1996) in its
English version. This set out to enable contemporary readers to encounter poems
created in very different epochs and cultures from their own, reaching as far back
as the contemplative Chinese and Japanese traditions. He reiterates in his intro-

duction that the three main criteria that determined his choice were whether the poems were 'short, clear, readable', and that his purpose was 'to undermine the widely-held opinion that poetry is a misty domain eluding understanding' (xv). What he wanted was a 'book of revelations', consisting of poems describing nature and objects which encapsulated a particular sensation, such as the feel of a woman's skin, or which engaged with people's emotions and dilemmas.

Throughout the 1990s Miłosz dominated the Polish literary and intellectual scene because of the scale of his talent, the extent of his knowledge, the incomparable level of his productivity, and also perhaps his innumerable media appearances. Those of us working on radio, television, newspapers and literary journals struggled to keep up with him, and used to say jokingly that he wrote books much faster than we managed to read them. It can be said that he was too demanding, especially in a post-Communist era of speed and superficiality, when there was no time for seriousness, concentration, and the 'attentiveness' he expected. More and more he failed to keep up with the present, and though he was revered and adored, one suspects that his work was never fully read and thought through. While he expected a discussion and an exchange of opinions, more often than not the programmes in which he appeared and the reviews he garnered ended up being complimentary, 'polite', and lacking in rigour. The media were preoccupied with other things, and so, as often happens in the lives of great writers, a spell in 'purgatory' began, and other writers' voices managed to be heard.

A reconfiguration in poetic language was under way in Poland, which saw a moving away from the preoccupations and forms Miłosz had strenuously cultivated and supported in his own writing and valued in those he translated. Initially, certain American influences, which came to be dubbed O'Harism,[20] became popular; and then this in turn was followed by a phase in which language itself provided both the subject and the impetus for the poetry. One of the most prominent of the young poets associated with this latter trend, Marcin Świetlicki, commented ironically on Miłosz and his influence in the early 1990s, comparing him to a dragon:

> Czesław Miłosz belongs to the Last of the Scary Poetical Monsters, whom you either kneel before or ignore. Luckily he is quite a harmless Dragon, lives far away, and does not feed on human flesh . . . I do not admit to having any closer relationship with his work, but it is very nice to know that he exists. (Świetlicki, 'Smok', *Tygodnik Powszechny* 26, 1991)

Subsequently, this kind of playful indifference gave way to sarcastic, reductive and hostile responses to Miłosz's work from other poets in their thirties, which came as no surprise, though the poet, naturally, was deeply hurt. The difference between the new wave and the old master related to the poet's status. He was an artist whose poetry did not automatically resort to irony. He pointed to the art's limitations and failures, but also believed that a poem could fulfil the highest aims. Świetlicki's generation, and those who came after, could not possibly maintain such a position. Their poetry centred on the private and the subjective, was modest in its ambitions when it addressed wider social questions, and rarely embraced current events.

There are also other dimensions to Miłosz's writings which it is impossible to overlook when reading them these days: his shock and horror at the human propensity for limitless evil, his alarm at the increasing apathy towards religion amongst later generations, and his indignation at the general compliance with stupidity. Stefan Chwin, in an obituary, highlighted the differences between his contemporaries and Miłosz:

> For him the Holocaust was a shock, whose painful outcome was *Rescue*. For us a holocaust, the murder of a million people in Rwanda and Cambodia and ethnic cleansing in the Balkans or a massacre of thousands of Iraqi soldiers in deserts near Baghdad are simply 'normal things' which happen in the world . . . That beauty had to contest with atrocity in the world was to him a constant source of frustration. We learned to live with this frustration. We escape from the cruelty into a virtual and narcotic world, knowing full well that it is not possible to change the world. He belonged to an era of utopia and hope. We belong to the world without utopia, in which, at the most, hope takes on the form of aspiring to reach other states of consciousness He carried with him wounds that could not be healed and he left a beautiful trace of those wounds in his poems. He was not capable of writing grotesque or derisive verse, or manic word-play, which for us is as natural as the air we breathe. (Chwin, *Rzeczpospolita*, 21–22 August 2004)

Should we then pause to reflect on Miłosz's warning that 'whoever considers as normal the order of things in which the strong triumph, and the weak fail, and life ends with death, accepts the devil's rule'? (*SS* 57).

Provinces

'What is poetry which does not save / Nations or people?' ('Dedication') you write. I am not sure whether your poems will ever 'save me', but they are certainly healing, consolatory, a support for the lame.

Konstanty A. Jeleński to CM (1980)

It is a powerful and dark spirit, which, with surprising determination, transforms itself into brightness.

Stefan Chwin, *Tygodnik Powszechny* (2001)

Erin Gilbert, the daughter of Rondi Gilbert and Antoni Miłosz, remembered an occasion when she attended a reading with her grandfather: 'He sat beside me, was quiet and appeared to be listening attentively'. As they were leaving, however, 'he whispered happily, "I have just finished a poem"' (qtd. in *The Magic Mountain*). Throughout the last twenty years of his life Czesław Miłosz wrote poems regularly, lines, images and sentences often coming to him in dreams, which he would then transcribe into his notebook, to be worked on later. After *Unattainable Earth* came *Chronicles* (1987), then *Provinces* (1991), *Facing the River* (1995), *This* (2000) and finally *Second Space* (2004).

It was *Chronicles* that seemed to initiate a new phase in his poetical work, one somehow difficult to define, since he began composing many interrelated, compact, controlled, transparent verses, which captured tiny epiphanic moments in his life, such as, for example, childhood memories of a smithy. On its threshold a little boy and an eighty year-old man stand together and

> I stare and stare. It seems I was called for this:
> To glorify things just because they are.
>
> ('Blacksmith Shop', *NCP* 503)

Although these poems represent additional proof of the author's artistry with verse, they do not move the reader with such force as 'Voices of Poor People', 'A Treatise on Poetry' and 'From the Rising of the Sun' had done. It is as if the poet has grown comfortable in his mastery of poetic technique, happy to strike an intimate note, and unwilling to break from the conventional and wide-ranging forms to which he will return at the end of his career. There are numerous poems which delve deeply into memory, and at least one outstanding volume, *This* (2000), which opened up new perspectives in the interpretation of Miłosz's poetry.

> If I could at last tell you what is in me,
> if I could shout: people! I have lied by pretending it was not there,
> It was there, day and night.
> . . .
> Writing has been for me a protective strategy
> Of erasing traces. No one likes
> A man who reaches for the forbidden.
>
> I asked help of rivers in which I used to swim, lakes
> With a footbridge over the rushes, a valley
> Where an echo of singing had twilight for its companion.
> And I confess my ecstatic praise of being
> Might just have been exercises in the high style.
> Underneath was this, which I do not attempt to name.

This. Which is like the thoughts of a homeless man walking in an alien city in freezing weather.

And like the moment when a tracked-down Jew glimpses the heavy helmets of the German police approaching.

The moment when the crown prince goes for the first time down to the city and sees the truth of the world: misery, sickness, age, and death.

Or the immobile face of someone who has just understood that he's been abandoned forever.

Or the irrevocable verdict of the doctor.

This. Which signifies knocking against a stone wall and knowing that the wall will not yield to any imploration.

('This', *NCP* 663–664)

Miłosz in this volume from 2000 probed deeply entrenched areas of consciousness, exposing again the dark background to his assiduousness and sensual vitality, and, above all, his profound sense of vocation. In his old age the writer was on the verge of opening up, and despite the uplifting force of many of these new poems, there remained a certain reluctance to confront the causes of his pessimism and his fears over the situation in the world, which demonstrates how much these were embedded in his psyche. It is no coincidence that in *Alphabet* he turns to Robert Frost, whom he met in the 1940s:

> To think at one and the same time about that poetry and the biography concealed behind it is to descend into a bottomless well. No one will learn about Frost's own wounds and tragedies by reading his poetry; he left no clues. An appalling chain of misfortunes, numerous deaths in the family, madness, suicides, and silence about this . . . The worst part of all this is that in concerning oneself with him one is menaced by a sense of one's own particular existence. If the borders of one's personality are so fluid that we do not truly know who we are and are constantly trying on different changes of costume, how did Frost manage? It is impossible to grasp who he really was, aside from his unswerving striving towards his goal of fame in order to exact revenge for his own defeats in life. ('Frost', *ABC* 125)

Unlike Frost, he was less consistent in covering his tracks, and not just when it came to his personal life. Miłosz said at one time that the most appropriate way to express some of his feelings would be to let out an unarticulated scream: 'I wanted to shout, but at the same time I knew that it would be ineffective.

Feeling guilty for not shouting' (*Rok myśliwego* 132). What burdened him was his acute awareness of the fragility of the body, of loneliness and of death, which ought to make all preoccupations and passions irrelevant. And perhaps other factors. Brutishness? The cow-like state? The vegetative aspect of existence? A world devoid of meaning, which we attempt to remedy by imposing one or attempting to fashion one? 'To give a meaning, any, only to get out of this bovine, perfectly indifferent, inert reality, without aims, strivings, affirmation, negation, like an incarnated nothingness. Religions! Ideologies! Desires! Hatreds! Come to cover with your multicoloured fabric this blind thing, deprived of even a name' ('Tropics', *RD* 41).

Others question Miłosz's attempts to confront our responsibility for others, the demand that we should be useful, and the necessity for literature to provide a degree of spiritual fortification, because

> If there is no God
> Not everything is permitted to man.
> He is still his brother's keeper
> And he is not permitted to sadden his brother
> By saying that there is no God.
>
> ('If There Is No God', *S&LP* 254)

There was in him 'a good boy', as he acknowledged, one 'who was granted special gifts with which to expose and obliterate limitations in human behaviour'. As a consequence, it became necessary 'to find ways to appear to be like others' ('Epigraf', *Wiersze* IV, 136). In his later years he confessed that

> the good boy inside me was God-fearing, industrious, prejudiced, conservative, always taking the side of authority and opposing anarchy. To delve into my psychological core and baggage in order to attain power, I had no gift for that ... My books are full of respect for conventional virtues and, though that role was never intentional, I could sometimes be considered a moralist. I was deeply ashamed of my lack of virtue, and was reluctant to say, 'Yes, I admit to that, that's what I am like and that's it'. This lack of virtue had its origin from a clash in my relationship with collective entities ... and could be described as excessive individualism. (*Rok myśliwego* 258)

And would it not be appropriate also to suggest that there was a touch of beautiful naivete and perhaps pride as well? 'I do not feel authorized / to reveal a truth too cruel for the human heart' ('Zone of Silence', *NCP* 707), he wrote, as if not recognising that the human heart—though not his—grew so desensitised that no truth exists that is beyond compassion.

One of the major themes in the late poems was old age, that 'province' of life which we enter without 'the option of turning back'. Old age often surprised his ageing body, though his mind remained lofty, one could almost say divine. The poet retained his intense joy, his sensuality, his appetite for sight, touch and taste, the pleasure of staring at women's thighs in mini-skirts, or of biting into roast lamb and cloves of garlic. But often old age brings with it that calming sense of being 'past', of taking a breather after a long struggle, of taking the opportunity to casually say 'goodnight' and let others chase and strive. And standing at the threshold, the poet can say to himself:

> Forget the suffering
> You caused others.
> Forget the suffering
> Others caused you.
> The waters run and run,
> Springs sparkle and are done,
> You walk the earth you are forgetting.

('Forget', NCP 674)

From this perspective, it is easy to recognise an element of the grotesque in the latter stages of human life, while at the same time Miłosz's poems affect the reader powerfully through their grasp of the commonality of suffering. Whereas Miłosz's work began with depicting a young man looking down on the stupidity of the 'monkeys' around him, in its concluding phase it is marked by profound compassion:

> In the ninth decade of my life, the feeling which rises in me is pity, useless. A multitude, an immense number of faces, shapes, fates of particular beings, and a sort of merging with them from inside, but at the same time my awareness that I will not find anymore the means to offer a home in my poems to these guests of mine, for it is too late. I think also that, could I start anew, every poem of mine would have been a biography or a portrait of a particular person, or, in fact, a lament over his or her destiny. ('Pity', *RD* 106)

More and more the author of *Road-Side Dog* delves into the lives of others, recollecting how in his youth 'I did not expect that I would be one day so fascinated by people, by their everyday existence in time, by that day, by that year' ('In a Buggy at Dusk', *NCP* 489). It is fitting to point out that these intriguing people were primarily women. They appear as sensuous-erotic creations in the poetry, but also as something else, because, as Miłosz pointed out, the gender of poetry 'is feminine' ('Poetry's Sex', *RD* 35). And in his subconscious he anticipated that his death would be announced by a feminine figure.

In 2001 Miłosz composed *Treatise on Theology*, because, in the words of its introduction, he 'was searching for a language which could be used to talk about religion. The accepted language was conventional and devotional, and formed a barrier, because the language of theology seemed to be . . . overly verbose' (*Tygodnik Powszechny* 47, 2001). The poet endeavoured to write in a simple and accessible language, and, not having much time left, he cut corners to attain his aim, which was redemption. He wanted 'to write a theological treatise / to redeem himself from the sin of pride' (*SS* 48). The work represents the culmination of Miłosz's reflections on religion, a recurring concern over the previous three decades. It challenged ideas of the universe as without meaning, and went on to explore disparities between the poet and his co-religionists. The Polish Catholic faithful cultivated the concept of a national religion; for him, their faith did not promote peace, but rather sowed perpetual doubt. The re-energising of spirituality worldwide necessitated an escape not just from the dryness of theology, but also from the reductive childish pieties perpetuated in Catholic tradition; 'it will not do to prattle on about soft little Jesus in the hay of His manger' (*SS* 50).

One of the most marked features of the treatise is the tension between love of self and something he acquired towards the end of his life, his status as a 'parishioner', feeling 'warmth among people at prayer' (*SS* 63) before the altar, united by their shared sinfulness, suffering and fear. Miłosz identifies pride, which 'sees at its core the sin of desire' (*SS* 58), as the force that destroyed Creation's original unity, and as the cause of evil and death. Even before Adam and Eve rebelled against their Creator, there was one who pitted 'no' against God's 'yes', when 'an angel of great beauty and strength turned against the incomprehensible Unity, for he uttered the word "I", which meant separation' ('We Have Read in the Catechism', *SS* 54). Only by cultivating the Blakean values of 'compassion, pity, understanding' (*SS* 58) can humankind hope to remedy their fallen, 'alien' state, poem number fifteen ('Religion Comes') suggests.

Was Miłosz's aim in *Treatise* to help believers, or those, like himself, who oscillated every day between belief and unbelief? Increasingly during his final years he turned towards the Church, or more exactly the figure of Pope John Paul II. Despite certain reservations and a feeling of distance, he regarded the Pope as the embodiment of moral probity and purity, in a world where sinners are beset on all sides by 'senselessness, crime and television' (*Rok myśliwego* 38).

Miłosz longed for an authority he could trust, an example to emulate. Watching coverage of the Pope praying in Jerusalem beside the Wailing Wall in late March 2000, he was profoundly moved and immediately telephoned a former editor of *Tygodnik Powszechny* and close contact of the Pope, Marek Skwarnicki, with a prediction that 'he will be canonised the moment after his death' (Skwarnicki, *Mój Miłosz* 181). At this very period he was composing an ode to mark

Pope John Paul II's eightieth birthday, which was published soon after on the front page of Poland's biggest-selling newspaper:

> Shepherd given us when the gods depart!
> In the fog above the cities the Golden Calf shines,
> The defenseless crowds race to offer the sacrifice
> Of their own children to the bloody screens of Moloch.
>   . . .
>
> You are with us and will be with us henceforth.
> When the forces of chaos raise their voice
> And the owners of truth lock themselves in churches
> And only the doubters remain faithful,
> Your portrait in our homes every day remind us
> How much one man can accomplish and how sainthood works.
>
> ('Ode for the Eightieth Birthday of
Pope John Paul II', NCP 709–710)

A portrait of the Pope was displayed in his house in Berkeley, alongside one taken with the poet himself. Their first meeting had taken place not long after Miłosz received the Nobel Prize; John Paul had sent him a congratulatory telegram on that occasion. In the 1980s Miłosz attended several symposia at the papal residence of Castel Gandolfo, and in June 1986, while visiting Rome, he was invited for a private audience, also attended by Jerzy Turowicz. In his archive, *Tygodnik Powszechny*'s editor left notes about this encounter, which speak of the cordiality of the Pope's reception and mention his familiarity with Miłosz's works, specifically referring to *The Issa Valley* and *Six Letters in Verse*. The poet declared that

> all my thinking has a religious aspect and in that sense my poetry is religious. However, when it comes to Christianity, it is still a matter of 'yes' and 'no'. In a private conversation about *Six Letters in Verse*, John Paul II remarked that 'you always make one step forward, then one step back', to which I replied, 'Is it possible to write religious poetry any other way at the present time?' (*Rok myśliwego* 34)

A decade later he was enchanted by the Pope's *Letter to Artists*, commenting that on reading it 'our heart tells us that each of his words rings true, despite it being truth in terms of millennia, and not a short moment in time. We would like the twenty-first century to bring confirmation of the truth he speaks of in the form of uplifting and pure works' (*O podróżach w czasie* 78).

On 2 April 2004 Miłosz sent the Pope a letter with an unusual request:

> Holy Father, age changes our perspective on things and when I was young for a poet to request a papal blessing was deemed an impropriety.

And this, in fact, is my great concern, because in the last few years I wrote poems in which I consciously adhered to Catholic orthodoxy, but I am not sure whether I was successful in achieving that. I, therefore, ask for your words confirming my pursuit of our common goal. Let's hope Christ's promise of Resurrection comes true.

John Paul's reply arrived two weeks later:

Dear Sir,
I read your letter of 2 April with great emotion, or rather I read it several times. In those few words rich and multiple matter was compressed. You write that the subject of your concern was whether your work 'adhered to Catholic orthodoxy'. I am convinced that this intention is of decisive significance. In this sense, I am happy to confirm your words about our 'pursuing a common goal'. From the bottom of my heart, I also would like to wish that the promise Christ gave to the whole of humankind through his Resurrection comes true for you. I wish God's blessings on you, your life and work.

Four months later the Pope cited these very words in a telegram sent before Czesław Miłosz's funeral. It was read out at the Holy Mass in Kraków's Mariacki Church on 27 August 2004. From there, the funeral procession was to proceed to Skałka, a crypt belonging to the monastery of the Pauline fathers, where others of great merit already lay. Miłosz was to be interred in a grey granite sarcophagus with the inscription *'Bene Quiescas'* (Sleep Well), along with a quotation from his own translation of Wisdom, chapter 6: 'A dbałość o naukę jest miłość' ('And the concern for learning is love'), which his family had chosen. Fittingly, Miłosz's body was laid to rest in close proximity to many of Poland's major artists: Stanisław Wyspiański, Jacek Malczewski, Adam Asnyk and Karol Szymanowski.

––––––––––

Treatise on Theology was published in *Second Space* along with the lyric 'Father Severinus', whose subject struggles with the question of faith, and 'Apprentice', which pays further homage to his master, Oskar Miłosz, as does one of the very last poems Czesław ever wrote, from 22 December 2003. 'Goodness' bears a poignant message about *storge*, the Greek word 'describing the kind of love parents have for their children' (*SS* 73), an unconditional love without illusions about its object, and which in Miłosz's mind was repeatedly associated with pain. In its more positive manifestation, one feels 'as if time had turned back and the paths / Of the heavenly garden shone anew' (*S&LP* 325).

Light springs from everywhere, continually, in these late lyrics, and, as the end of the journey approached, the wanderer wanted

> only one, most precious thing:
> To see, purely and simply, without name,
> Without expectations, fears, or hopes,
> At the edge where there is no I or not-I.
>
> ('This Only', *NCP* 460)

For so much of his life and poetic career, he had treasured the luminous as giving relief from the darkness which beset the world: 'What remains of life? Only light' ('Notatnik: Brzegi Lemanu', *Wiersze* II, 162), he admitted: 'I love the light too, perhaps the light only' ('City without a Name', *NCP* 218). He conceived of resurrection as that instant when we are again woven from condensed light.

> Light off metal shaken,
> Lucid dew of heaven,
> Bless each and every one
> To whom the earth is given.
>
> Its essence was always hidden
> Behind a distant curtain.
> We chased it all our lives
> Bidden and unbidden.
>
> Knowing the hunt would end,
> That then what had been rent
> Would be at last made whole:
> Poor body and the soul.
>
> ('Rays of Dazzling Light', *NCP* 745)

'One bright point'

> If I should accede one day to Heaven, it must be there as it is here, except that I will be rid of my dull senses and my heavy bones.
>
> Changed into pure seeing, I will absorb, as before, the proportions of human bodies, the color of irises, a Paris street in June at dawn, all of it incomprehensible, incomprehensible the multitude of visible things.
>
> 'An Honest Description of Myself with a Glass of Whiskey
> at an Airport, Let Us Say, in Minneapolis' (*NCP* 679)

Miłosz's eyesight gradually deteriorated in the final years, and those who visited him at the apartment in Bogusławskiego often found him sitting in front of a special projector which cast enlarged pages onto a screen. On his computer he used enlarged page view, and for readings he used to take copies of his poems printed in larger font sizes. In the spring of 1998, he wrote to Giedroyc: 'I have written a second volume of the *ABC* and it will be the last book I will write myself, because of my sight loss' (CM to Giedroyc, 4 April 1998). After that he dictated articles and poems, although for a long time he still made entries in his notebook.

The untimely death of Carol Miłosz was a tragedy that could not have been anticipated, as she was so much younger, and physically very fit and so full of joy. She was meant to see him off on his last journey and after his death become his literary executor. When in late May 2002 she began to feel unwell, she flew to California to undergo tests for what at first appeared to be anaemia (Kosińska, *Miłosz w Krakowie* 276). Her condition, which was diagnosed as a form of blood cancer, worsened very quickly, and she died there on 16 August. Her husband, who was becoming very weak himself, boarded his final flight to America and managed to say goodbye to his wife in a hospital in San Francisco, whose cold, sterile corridors found their way into the lament 'Orpheus and Eurydice', which was composed soon after. Beneath pale strip-lighting, walking past silent electronic dogs before entering an elevator that descends hundreds of floors, the poetic persona enters the Underworld, armed only with a lyre and memories of the wife he has lost:

> He remembered her words: 'You are a good man.'
> He did not quite believe it. Lyric poets
> Usually have—as he knew—cold hearts.
> It is like a medical condition. Perfection in art
> Is given in exchange for such an affliction.
>
> Only her love warmed him, humanized him . . .
> He could not fail her now, when she was dead
>
> (*SS* 99)

The song he carries with him is a challenge to 'the abyss / That buries all of sound in silence'. In it, however, he extols his love, not for Eurydice, but for the beauty of existence, reiterating that 'he composed his words always against death' (*SS* 100). When he stands face to face with Persephone, the goddess's words are curious, but compelling: 'I don't know . . . whether you loved her or not, / Yet you have come here to rescue her' (*SS* 100). The journey upwards and away from the underworld ends as myth and human experience dictate it must:

. . . behind him on the path was no one.

Sun. And sky. And in the sky white clouds.
Only now everything cried to him, Eurydice!
How will I live without you, my consoling one!
But there was a fragrant scent of herbs, the low humming of bees,
And he fell asleep with his cheek on the sun-warmed earth.

(*SS* 102)

That closing image is beautifully apposite, imbued with the knowledge that the 'sun-warmed earth' can yield at best a brief, uncertain solace.

A month later, on 21 September 2002, the poet's brother, Andrzej, died, prompting Czesław to write this farewell note:

You were a very brave man, but I was primarily struck by your kindness, which saved you in many difficult situations, because everywhere you went there were people indebted to you in some way . . . You were a Christian who never invoked your faith to justify your actions in defence of your fellow men. You were one of the very few who never displayed a concern for yourself, but always looked to others' welfare. Your life was a race, in the literal sense of the word, because almost until the end you liked to run every day, but also figuratively, as you were engaged in a never-ending optimistic struggle. Farewell, Andrzej, and I hope that you will continue to run among heaven's meadows. (*O podróżach w czasie* 255)

Miłosz outlived many of his friends, attending successively the funerals of Herbert (d. 1998), Turowicz (d. 1999) and Giedroyc (d. 2000). It may have seemed as if some force had decided to deprive him of everything that was most important and closest to him, consigning him, like Job, to the depths of pain. The speaker of 'Prayer' offers up what is at times a bitter, bewildered address to his Maker:

I made a plea and You deigned to answer it,
So that I could see how unreasonable it was.

But when out of pity for others I begged a miracle,
The sky and the earth were silent, as always.

. . .

Now You are closing down my five senses, slowly,
And I am an old man lying in darkness.

(*NCP* 742)

He must have felt like the last pawn on a chessboard, making calculations, looking back over and over again at his spent and mis-spent life:

> What interests me most in all of this is the difference between our image of ourselves and our image in others' eyes ... A lucky guy. The sort for whom everything goes smoothly. Incredibly crafty. Self-indulgent. Loves money. Not an iota of patriotic feeling. Indifferent to the fatherland, which he has traded in for a suitcase. Effete. An aesthete, who cares about art, not people. Venal. Impolitic (he wrote *The Captive Mind*). Immoral in his personal life, (he exploits women). Contemptuous. Arrogant. And so forth.
>
> This characterisation was usually supported with a list of my shameful deeds. What is most striking is that it is the image of a strong, shrewd man, whereas I know my own weakness and I am inclined to consider myself, rather, as a tangle of reflexes, a drunken child in the fog. ('Hatred', *ABC* 136–137)

How did he assess his own life? Sometimes he imagined the past as already out of reach, closed and indifferent. He returned to it with increasing regularity, asking visiting friends what they thought about his decisions, wondering whether a piece of work he wrote was worth the price those close to him paid. 'So often your verses helped us, gave us hope and strength, filled us with joy and enchantment', he heard in reply. Did it bring him consolation, though? The most important question concerned his sense of fate. Was it accidental or the work of supernatural forces that led him, shielded him, saved him, gave him good health and long-lasting youth? And because of his commitment to so possessive a vocation, was he deprived of the tranquil, loving closeness of family life? He dwelt on these questions many times in his writings, such as in the piece pointedly entitled 'After Traveling': 'How strange life is! How incomprehensible! ... I had intentions, motivations. I made decisions, performed acts. Yet from here that man seems so irrational and absurd. As if he did not act, but was activated by forces that made use of him' (*NCP* 672). Amidst the questioning and self-reproach, there were pleas for forgiveness.

> I woke up in the middle of the night, and experienced a feeling of happiness so intense and perfect that in all my life I had only felt its premonition. And there was no reason for it. It didn't obliterate consciousness; the past which I carried was there, together with my grief. And it was suddenly included, was a necessary part of the whole. As if a voice were repeating: 'You can stop worrying now; everything happened just as it had to. You did what was assigned to you, and you are not required anymore to think of what happened long ago'. The peace I felt was a closing of accounts and was connected with the thought of death. The happiness on this side was like an announcement of the other side.

I realized that this was an undeserved gift and I could not grasp by what grace it was bestowed on me. ('Awakened', *NCP* 693)

That he was fully conscious that death was approaching can be seen from the dedication to Jerzy Illg in his copy of *Second Space:* 'To the ferryman of Charon's boat' (CM to Illg, 9 July 2002). Despite that apprehension, he still worked on. He had a bust of Carol's set up in his work-room, and talked at length to Toni, who was caring for him. He received guests while lying in bed with an oxygen apparatus beside him and while nurses were changing shifts. One visitor remembered visiting him in June 2004:

> He was weak and lay in bed. I sat next to him and held his hand. Every few minutes he would wake up and ask me to talk to him about Italian poets, Siena, and the screenplay to the melodrama *Campo de' Fiori,* which young Federico Fellini wrote in 1943. He wondered whether he could have met Pavese, and asked me what I thought about the poems of Quasimodo and *The First Man* by Camus. When I paused, because I thought he had fallen asleep, he spoke again with his eyes closed: 'Do please continue'. When I finished, he said in a strong, ringing voice: 'What a shame that I can't share your enthusiasm'. (Mikołajewski, in *Czesław Miłosz: In Memoriam* 103).

His heart grew weaker, and the moments when he lost consciousness became more frequent. In May, he was taken to his regularly visited clinic, where he dictated his last notes to his secretary:

> *26 May.* A stay in hospital considerably changes our perceptions. Firstly, attention is focused entirely on our body. The body seems to be detached from us, and its contortions sometimes happen independently, as if the muscles were acting on their own volition, which is not pleasant to behold. Also, there are long journeys through some magical continents in scorching weather and getting back from them requires will-power and time. These emotions are accompanied by a strong sense of empathy for lives imagined and remembered. It could be said that a stay in hospital offers a great experience in sympathy or compassion. That is why I decided to dictate this after regaining consciousness, in order to ease the suffering of others, that is all the patients who are not informed about medical procedures they are subjected to or their purpose. They are under the impression that they are in the hands of monstrous spiders, who do as they like with them. It is vitally important for the medical professionals to tell patients everything that they intend to do with them and why. This is a message from the other shore, but it is very

important. I believe that delivering it from the shore of consciousness is a rare achievement. Generally, being in hospital resembles something of a journey in which we take on a different form. So we take on the form of a grasshopper or some other insect and suffer its suffering. The world we visit is incoherent. It resembles a warehouse of broken toys, where parts do not fit and we are haunted by deficiency . . .

23 June. Giving up on movement brings ease, but at the same time it is demoralising, because with it comes an acceptance of this state of lethargy. The will degenerates, because it is awaiting the inevitable. And it all happens while the mind's condition is lucid, which makes for an interesting predicament. Dead body weight with a clarity of mind is, in fact, a hellish combination, invented only to cut proud man down to size. It is one of many forms of humiliation. ('Notes dictated in hospital', 2004, Miłosz Archive, Kraków)

Even at the last, he tried to do something useful, to describe his own dying to help others cross over the threshold. He wanted to get to the other side not from a hospital bed, but from his own home. He died in Kraków, the last city in his life, in the apartment in Bogusławskiego Street, on 14 August 2004 at 11:10 a.m. At the forefront of his mind perhaps was the hope of being reunited with his beloved mother, Weronika:

You were my beginning and again I am with you, here, where I learned the four quarters of the globe.

Below, behind the trees, the River's quarter; to the back, behind the buildings, the quarter of the Forest; to the right, the quarter of the
  Holy
Ford; to the left, the quarter of the Smithy and the Ferry.
. . .

Garlands of oak leaves, the ave-bell calling for the May service, I
  wanted
to be good and not to walk among the sinners.

But now when I try to remember how it was, there is only a pit, and it's so dark, I cannot understand a thing.

All we know is that sin exists and punishment exists, whatever philosophers would like us to believe.

If only my work were of use to people and of more weight than is my evil.

You alone, wise and just, would know how to calm me, explaining that I did as much as I could.

That the gate of the Black Garden closes, peace, peace, what is finished is finished.

('In Szetejnie', *NCP* 640, 642)

CHRONOLOGY

CZESŁAW MIŁOSZ'S LIFE	CONTEMPORANEOUS POLITICAL AND HISTORICAL EVENTS
1911 Born 30 JUNE, Szctejnie, Lithuania, to Aleksander and Weronika Miłosz, on an estate belonging to her family.	
1913 Miłosz family in Krasnoyarsk, Siberia, where Aleksander was working on a tsarist government contract.	
1914 AUG: Aleksander conscripted into Russian Imperial Army. The whole family returns briefly to the estate in Szetejnie.	1 AUG: Outbreak of First World War.
1915 Weronika, CM and maternal grand-mother seek safety in Wilno. After the Germans seize Wilno in November, CM and his mother head for Alek-sander's detachment at the front.	
1917 SEPT: Birth of Andrzej Miłosz. Threat from advancing German Army results in Poles in Lithuania retreating east to Dorpat, Estonia. CM meets his paternal grandmother, Stanisława Miłosz, whose reading from story-books has a lasting impact on his imagination.	15 MAR: Tsar Nicholas II abdicates. 2–6 APR: U.S. Congress summoned to consider President Woodrow Wilson's proposal to declare war on Germany. 16 APR: Lenin returns to Russia. 7 OCT: Bolshevik Revolution. Winter Palace in St Petersburg captured. 5 DEC: Russia signs armistice; 3.7 million Russian dead.
1918 MAR: The family returns via Latvia to family estate in Lithuania.	3 MAR: Treaty of Brest-Litovsk ratified between Russia and Germany–Austria Hungary. Russia transfers Russian Poland to Germany and accepts independence of Ukraine. 23 MAR: Lithuania declares independence from Russia. 16 JULY: Tsar Nicholas and family executed. 6 NOV: Austria-Hungary and Germany accept defeat. Poland declares itself a republic. DEC: Poland occupies Poznań (formerly Posen).

(continued)

1919   Education at home, reading books in family library.

APR: Attempted coup to incorporate Lithuania into Poland thwarted by Lithuanian nationalists.

Aleksander Miłosz proclaimed a persona non grata and banned from entering the country, thereby blocking all access to the Miłosz family's estates.

FEB: Estonia invaded by Red Army.

APR: Wilno seized by Poles.

7 MAY: Allies impose massive war reparations on Germany.

28 JUNE: Treaty of Versailles signed in Hall of Mirrors.

1920   SPRING: Weronika Miłosz moves to Wilno to join her husband. Family becomes dispersed again due to Russian-Polish war. Weronika heads back to Szetejnie with her sons.

JAN: League of Nations comes into existence (U.S. and China do not join).

War breaks out between Poland and Bolshevik Russia.

8 MAY: Poles and Ukrainians retake Kiev from the Bolsheviks.

12 JULY: Red Army advances for a second time closer to Wilno. Soviets sign treaty with Lithuanians giving the latter control of the city, while at the same time attempting to incite a revolt which would enable them to seize power in Lithuania.

27 JULY: Red Army enters Polish territory.

14–16 AUG: In what comes to be called 'the miracle on the Vistula', Poles under Józef Piłsudski defeat five Russian armies as they approach Warsaw. Lithuania briefly regains military control in Wilno.

9 OCT: Poland annexes Wilno.

1921   Threats from local Lithuanians compel Miłoszes to move to an apartment in Wilno.

CM passes examinations enabling him to attend the King Sigismund Augustus Boys' State Gymnasium, 1.

18 MAR: Polish-Russian frontiers agreed at Treaty of Riga.

6 DEC: British Government and Dail Eireann representatives sign treaty which establishes Irish Free State.

1922   Poland's Head of State, Józef Piłsudski, visits Gymnasium in April.

9 OCT: In Middle Lithuania (area around Wilno), a breakaway group in Parliament consisting of Poles, Lithuanians, Jews and Byelorussians pass a decree which formally unites them with Poland.

28 OCT: Italian fascists march on Rome. Mussolini heads government consisting of liberals, nationalists and fascists.

30 DEC: USSR comes into existence.

CZESŁAW MIŁOSZ'S LIFE	CONTEMPORANEOUS POLITICAL AND HISTORICAL EVENTS
1923	8 NOV: Beer Hall or Munich Putsch. Adolf Hitler's Nazi Party attempts to seize control of the government in Bavaria.
1924	21 JAN: Death of Vladimir Lenin.
	APR: Hitler handed five-year sentence for involvement in putsch. Writes *Mein Kampf* while in prison.
	4 MAY: German election results: Social Democrats 100 seats; Communists 62; for first time in its history, Nazi Party wins 32 seats.
	7 DEC: German election results: Social Democrats 131 seats; Communists 54; Nazi Party down to 14, a loss of 18 seats. Hitler released from prison.
1925 Aleksander travels to Brazil in search of economic boost for family, but quickly returns.	3 JAN: Mussolini becomes Italian dictator. 16 JAN: Leon Trotsky ousted from Revolutionary Military Council in USSR.
1926 DEC: Aleksander accepts engineering post as manager in the Roads Department at Suwałki's Regional Office. JULY / AUGUST 1926 (or possibly 1927): CM holidays in Krasnogruda, where he becomes besotted with his Aunt Gabriela.	12–14 MAY: With several regiments behind him, Piłsudski marches on Warsaw and wrests power from the President and government. He later becomes Minister for Defence. 19 OCT: Joseph Stalin increasingly controls reins of power in USSR, isolating political enemies such as Trotsky before expelling them from the Politburo.
1927	14 NOV: Trotsky expelled from Soviet Communist Party.
1928 Breakthrough in CM's writing after joining PET.	20 MAY: German election results enhance position of Social Democrats (153 seats), Communists (54), Nazis (12 seats).
1929 MAY: Final school exams. OCT: CM enters Law School at Wilno University. Joins student Vagabonds' Club.	24–29 OCT: Wall Street Crash triggers worldwide economic depression.
1930 CM's poems published in student magazine, *Alma Mater Vilnensis*. Joins Żagary, the Intellectuals' Club, and Scholars' Circle, whose chair is Manfred Kridl. NOV: CM meets the poet Jarosław Iwaszkiewicz at a reading in Wilno.	14 SEPT: German election results: Social Democrats down to 143 seats, while Nazi Party gains 95, giving it a total of 107, which makes it second biggest party in the Reichstag.

(continued)

CZESŁAW MIŁOSZ'S LIFE	CONTEMPORANEOUS POLITICAL AND HISTORICAL EVENTS
1931 JAN: CM visits Warsaw for the first time, staying with Iwaszkiewicz.	21 MAR: Austria and Germany plan to create a customs union.
APR: First edition of the monthly literary supplement *Żagary* appears.	15 JUNE: Poland-USSR Treaty of Friendship and Commerce signed.
MAY: Travels across Europe to see Paris Colonial Exhibition. Meets Oskar Miłosz for the first time; achieves instant rapport.	
CM's relationship begins with Jadwiga Waszkiewicz.	
NOV: Anti-Semitic attacks by right-wing group, Młodzież Wszechpolska, on students at Wilno University. Targeting also of Jewish shops and a synagogue. CM and Teodor Bujnicki defend Jewish students.	
DEC: CM files an application to transfer to Department of Law at Warsaw University, but stays for only one semester.	
1932 MAR: Contacts Władysław Sebyła, editor of *ZET,* by letter, hoping to publish in the journal.	25 JAN: Poland-USSR non-aggression pact.
	24 APR: Nazis become largest party in Reichstag.
	31 JULY: Nazis win 230 seats, Social Democrats 133, Communists 89.
	6 NOV: New German elections held because of deadlock; Nazis win 192 seats, Social Democrats 121, Communists 100.
	8 NOV: F. D. Roosevelt (Democrat) wins U.S. presidential election.
	19 NOV: Hindenburg invites Hitler to create coalition government, but the latter is unable to do so.
1933 5 FEB: CM reads at anti-racist 'Poetry of Protest' event in Wilno.	30 JAN: Hitler sworn in as German Chancellor.
	27 FEB: Reichstag fire. Nazis curtail civil rights and press freedom, blaming Communists for the blaze.
	23 MAR: In Germany, act is passed giving Hitler dictatorial powers until 1937.

CZESŁAW MIŁOSZ'S LIFE	CONTEMPORANEOUS POLITICAL AND HISTORICAL EVENTS
1934 Graduates from Wilno University. Żagary breaks up as a poetic group. CM wins a scholarship to Paris to study for one year. Frequent meetings with Oskar Miłosz. Visits shelter for unemployed Poles in Levallois-Perret.	MAY–JULY: Nazi regime suppresses trade unions, then all other political parties.
1935 JUNE: CM attends International Congress for the Defense of Culture in Paris. Ends his relationship with Jadwiga Waszkiewicz. DEC: Returns to Wilno.	JUL–AUG: The People's Front in Europe emerges, strategically supported by Stalin, with the aim of encouraging those opposed to growth of right-wing groups to abandon neutrality and align themselves against fascism.
1936 JAN: *A Letter to Defenders of Culture*, an appeal against fascism, published. Works on literary programmes for Polish Radio in Wilno, acting as secretary to Tadeusz Byrski. *Trzy Zimy/Three Winters* (poetry) published by the Union of Polish Writers, CM paying for printing costs.	MAR: In contravention of Versailles Agreement, German troops re-occupy the Rhineland. MAY: Formation of Popular Front government in France, a coalition of leftist parties. JULY: Beginning of Spanish Civil War, in which General Francisco Franco receives military support from Germany and Italy, while Soviet Union supports the elected leftist coalition government.
1937 Dismissed from Polish Radio in Wilno because of his leftist views. APR: Trip to Italy. SUMMER: Moves permanently to Warsaw. WINTER: Meets Janina (Janka) Cękalska at the radio station.	APR: Guernica, in northern Spain's Basque country bombed by Luftwaffe. JUNE: Stalin initiates army purge in USSR, executing a number of leading generals in the Red Army.
1938 AUG: Visit to Kaunas (Kowno), where he becomes acquainted with literary circle around *Naujoji Romuva*.	12 MAR: Anschluss. Austria becomes a state in the German Reich, following plebiscite on 10 Mar. 29–30 SEPT: Munich Conference. British and French prime ministers accede to Hitler's demands that Germany be allowed to occupy the Sudetenland in Czechoslovakia, on condition that the other Czechoslovak borders are respected. 9–10 NOV: Kristallnacht. In Germany, Jewish business properties and homes attacked, with over 90 Jews killed.

(continued)

1939   MAR: Oskar Miłosz dies.

JULY: CM ill with severe flu, recuperates at his parents' home in Głębokie. The rest of the summer spent in eastern Poland with Janka.

I SEPT: Invasion of Poland.

4 SEPT: Evacuation of Polish Radio's Warsaw HQ, which heads for Lublin, then Lwów. At outbreak of war, Janka is with her family outside Warsaw, so does not leave with radio staff.

9 SEPT: Poet and CM's friend, Józef Czechowicz, dies during the Nazi bombing of Lublin.

17 SEPT: En route to Lwów, CM encounters Soviet Army. To avoid capture, flees to Romania.

Arranges permission to go to Lithuania; travels through Soviet territories to Wilno.

15 MAR: Czechoslovakia's thirty years of independence end as German troops occupy Bohemia, Moravia and Slovakia.

26–29 MAR: After Franco's forces capture Barcelona and Madrid, forces of the Spanish Republican government surrender.

31 MAR: Britain and France guarantee to aid Poland in the event of it being subjected to attack, in the hope that this will deter a Nazi invasion.

18 APR: USSR proposes a joint military alliance with Britain and France, which British PM Neville Chamberlain rejects on I May. Winston Churchill, no longer a minister, repeatedly argues for just such a pact. Joseph Davies, U.S. Ambassador in Moscow, suggests to his counterpart in London, Joseph Kennedy, that he can 'tell Chamberlain from me that if they are not careful they will drive Stalin into Hitler's arms'.

23 AUG: Molotov-Ribbentrop Pact. Soviet Union and Nazi Germany sign secret protocols allowing for partition of Poland.

I SEPT: Nazi invasion of Poland, leading to outbreak of Second World War.

4 SEPT: Polish government personnel leave Warsaw.

17 SEPT: Soviet invasion and occupation of eastern Poland.

Soviet secret police (NKVD) arrest and imprison tens of thousands of Polish officers.

Polish government flees to Romania with the idea of creating a government-in-exile in Paris.

1940   Leaves Lithuania on perilous journey to reach Warsaw to rejoin Janka.

Works at the Warsaw University Library to save books.

SEPT: Publishes, under pseudonym, *Poems,* a 28-page booklet.

10–11 APR: German forces march into Denmark and invade Norway.

10 MAY: Winston Churchill becomes British PM.

10–14 MAY: German forces occupy Holland, Belgium, and Luxembourg.

	CZESŁAW MIŁOSZ'S LIFE	CONTEMPORANEOUS POLITICAL AND HISTORICAL EVENTS

CZESŁAW MIŁOSZ'S LIFE

MAY: Execution of over 20,000 Polish officers in Katyń on Stalin's orders. (When in 1941, following German invasion of USSR, Polish General Władysław Anders requests that these officers be allowed to join the army he is creating, he is told first that they had escaped to Manchuria, and then subsequently that they were executed by the Germans in MAY 1941.)

15 JUNE: Red Army invades Lithuania, and, after rigging election results, incorporates it within the Soviet Union.

17 JUNE: Free French leader General Charles de Gaulle escapes to Britain.

22 JUNE: France's new Prime Minister, Marshal Pétain, signs armistice with Germany, and in July becomes President of Vichy France.

10 JULY–31: Oct: Battle of Britain. Royal Air Force loses 915 planes, German Luftwaffe 1,733 planes.

1941

22 JUNE: Nazi Germany invades the Soviet Union (Operation Barbarossa).

8 SEPT: Siege of Leningrad by German forces (lasts until January 1944).

7–8 DEC: Japanese air force attacks U.S. naval base at Pearl Harbour, then attacks U.S. possessions in the Pacific.

8 DEC: U.S. and Britain declare war on Japan.

1942   CM edits for underground press the anthology *Invincible Song: Polish Poetry of War Time*, and publishes his translation of Jacques Maritain's 'A travers le désastre'.

Attends clandestine philosophy seminars.

20 JAN: At Wannsee Conference, 15 Nazi leaders meet to determine what form 'the final solution of the Jewish Question' should take. Plans to deport Jews to Madagascar abandoned in favour of a Europe-wide roundup and internment in labour camps designed to exterminate large numbers through 'natural diminution'.

27 MAY: Assassination in Prague of Reichs-Protektor Reinhard Heydrich, one of the architects of the Final Solution.

(continued)

CZESŁAW MIŁOSZ'S LIFE	CONTEMPORANEOUS POLITICAL AND HISTORICAL EVENTS
	10 JUNE: In revenge for Heydrich's killing, Nazis raze the village of Lidice in Czechoslovakia, killing 173 men and 52 women.
	17–21 JUNE: Washington Conference: Roosevelt and Churchill meet to review war strategy.
	23 OCT–4 NOV: British 8th Army defeats Germans at Battle of El Alamein, Egypt.
1943 With his brother Andrzej, finds hiding places in Warsaw and financially supports two Jewish families. Composes the sequence 'The World: A Naïve Poem', plus 'Voices of Poor People' and 'Campo dei Fiori'.	31 JAN: Germans, under General von Paulus, surrender at Stalingrad, after Red Army encircles them.
	19 APR–16 MAY: Rising in the Warsaw Ghetto. Over 28 days, 40,000 Jews killed or deported to concentration camps.
	25 APR: Soviet Union breaks off diplomatic relations with Polish Government-in-Exile, accusing latter of falsely blaming USSR for Katyń massacre after mass graves discovered near Smolensk by Germans.
	11 MAY: Washington Conference. Roosevelt and Churchill decide on strategy, including sequence for the invasion of Italy, starting with Sicily.
	4 JULY: General Sikorski, Head of Polish Government-in-Exile, dies in plane crash near Gibraltar.
	4–20 JULY: Germans attack Kursk salient, in what becomes biggest tank battle in history. Soviet counter-attack results in end to any further German advances on eastern front of USSR.
	12 AUG: Roosevelt and Churchill meet in U.S. and discuss co-operation in development of atom bomb.
	3 SEPT: Italy surrenders to Allies. Germans capture Rome.
1944 OCT: After the defeat of the Warsaw Rising, CM and Janka escape to southern Poland, to Goszyce, staying with Jerzy Turowicz, future editor of *Tygodnik Powszechny*.	17 JAN–18 MAY: Monte Cassino, Italy. Long battle to oust German defenders from strategic location on hilltop monastery. Fourth attack, led by Polish troops, succeeds. Allied troops able to advance through Italy.

CZESŁAW MIŁOSZ'S LIFE	CONTEMPORANEOUS POLITICAL AND HISTORICAL EVENTS
	6 JUNE: D-Day. Allied landings in Normandy, beginning of liberation of France and western Europe.
	22 JULY: Soviet Army enters Lublin, where a Communist-headed Polish government is established, in opposition to the London-based Government-in-Exile.
	The nearby Majdanek concentration camp discovered, which the Germans hurriedly attempted to demolish, though gas chambers remained intact.
	1 AUG–2 OCT: Warsaw Rising, led by General 'Bor' Komorowski of the Armia Krajowa, loyal to London-based Polish Government-in-Exile. Soviets block supplies from the western Allies. Subsequently Germans drive the population of Warsaw out of the city before systematically destroying it.
	6 and 18 OCT: Soviet Army moves successively into Hungary and Czechoslovakia.
	7 NOV: Roosevelt re-elected as U.S. President.
1945 CM joins Writers' Union. FEB: Appointed a regular contributor to *Dziennik Polski*. Translates Blake, Milton, Wordsworth and Browning. Death of his mother, Weronika, near Gdańsk. Enters Polish Diplomatic Service. Publishes *Ocalenie/Rescue* (poetry) to acclaim. DEC: Meets T. S. Eliot while staying in London, before setting off for America. Appointed cultural attaché at Polish embassy in New York.	27 JAN: Soviet forces enter Auschwitz concentration camp. 4–11 FEB: Yalta Conference. Roosevelt, Churchill and Stalin agree on a Provisional Government of National Unity for Poland, in which Communists and non-Communists would be represented. The Soviet Union's annexation of eastern areas of Poland accepted as a fait accompli by America and Britain, and, in compensation for those losses, Poles from these regions are to be resettled in territories stripped from Germany. 12 APR: Roosevelt dies. Harry S. Truman, the Vice-President, assumes U.S. presidency. 30 APR: Suicide of Hitler and his wife, Eva Braun, in the Chancellor's Berlin bunker. 7 MAY: Germany surrenders. Thereafter, the west of the country is divided into British, French and U.S. zones.

(continued)

CZESŁAW MIŁOSZ'S LIFE	CONTEMPORANEOUS POLITICAL AND HISTORICAL EVENTS
	6 AUG: U.S. drops atom bomb on Hiroshima.
	9 AUG: A second bomb is dropped on Nagasaki, leading to Japanese surrender 14 August.
1946 Diplomatic service appointment in Washington, D.C.	30 SEPT: Verdicts in Nuremberg trials of Nazi prisoners announced. Amongst the 10 leading officials condemned to death are von Ribbentrop and Hermann Goering, who, on 15 Oct, commits suicide before he can be executed.
1947 Birth of first son, Antoni.	JUNE: U.S. President Truman appoints General George Marshall as Secretary of State. The Marshall Plan provides $13 billion in aid to help rebuild Europe after the war. Stalin blocks Eastern European countries from applying for aid.
1948 'Treatise on Morality' appears in *Twórczość*.	Polish United Workers Party (PZPR) founded.
	25 JULY: Allies mount the Berlin Airlift, following Soviet blockade of the city.
1949 Visits Poland briefly.	
1950 Appointed to post of First Secretary in Polish embassy, Paris. His family remains in the U.S. On visit to Warsaw, because his loyalty to the regime is doubted, Miłosz's passport is confiscated.	9 JAN: Senator Joseph McCarthy claims that over 200 Communists are working in U.S. State Department.
	25 JUNE: Korean War. North Korea invades South Korea.
	JULY: UN responds by sending military forces from sixteen member states, though most troops are from the U.S.
1951 1 FEB: Seeks political asylum in France, and receives great support from Jerzy Giedroyc, Józef Czapski, and Zofia and Zygmunt Hertz, staying in Maisons-Lafitte, home of the Polish émigré press, Kultura.	6 DEC: Proposal from West and East Germany to involve UN in organising free elections in Germany blocked by Stalin.
Begins multiple attempts to gain an American visa to rejoin family in U.S. Birth of second son, Piotr.	
MAY: His work begins to appear in *Kultura,* starting with his article 'Nie'. Meets Stanisław Vincenz.	

	CZESŁAW MIŁOSZ'S LIFE	CONTEMPORANEOUS POLITICAL AND HISTORICAL EVENTS
1952	Develops friendship with Albert Camus, one of his few French intellectual supporters. Meets and begins relationship with Jeanne Hersch.	15 JAN: Treaty proposal from U.S., Britain and France that Austria become an independent state, which USSR rejects in AUGUST. 20 NOV: Bolesław Bierut, for previous five years Polish President, elected Polish PM.
1953	Publishes *The Captive Mind* (non-fiction). MAR: Awarded Prix Littéraire Européen (European Literary Prize) for *The Seizure of Power* (novel). 12 JULY: Janka and the children arrive in France.	5 MAR: Death of Stalin. 12 SEPT: Nikita Khrushchev becomes First Secretary of the Communist Party in USSR. 26 SEPT: Cardinal Stefan Wyszyński placed under house arrest, which lasts for next three years.
1954		30 JULY: U.S. Senate sets up a committee to investigate Senator McCarthy's activities. In DECEMBER its findings are announced and he is censured.
1955	Publishes *The Issa Valley* (fiction). SEPT: Attends 'The Future of Freedom' conference, which was organised by the Congress for Cultural Freedom.	5, 9 MAY: End of Allied occupation of West Germany, which joins NATO. 14 MAY: Warsaw Pact established, with its command HQ in Moscow.
1956	13 JAN: Janka and CM marry in a church in Paris.	25 FEB: Khrushchev denounces Stalin for 'despotism' and promoting the 'cult of personality' at closed session of Twentieth Communist Party Conference. He points out how, in the late 1930s, 98 out of 139 Central Committee members were arrested and shot. The speech is made public on 18 MAR. 28 JUNE: Uprising in Poznań violently suppressed, on instructions from Polish Minister of Defence, Rokossowski; 60 killed, over 200 wounded. 24 OCT–DEC: Hungarian Uprising. Imre Nagy forms government which includes non-Communists. Khrushchev agrees to Soviet Army withdrawal on 28 OCTOBER, then after Nagy introduces liberalisation and announces Hungary will leave Warsaw Pact, USSR invades on 4 Nov with 1,000 tanks. An estimated 4,000 Hungarians killed resisting invasion.

(continued)

CZESŁAW MIŁOSZ'S LIFE	CONTEMPORANEOUS POLITICAL AND HISTORICAL EVENTS
	5 NOV: Britain and France invade Egypt to seize control of the Suez Canal, which its President, Gamal Abdel Nasser, had nationalised. U.S. pressure leads to the withdrawal of British and French forces.
	2 DEC: Fidel and Raul Castro and Che Guevara land on east coast of Cuba to launch guerrilla campaign against the country's head of state, General Batista.
1957 The family buys a house in Montgeron. Publishes *Traktat poetycki / A Poetical Treatise* (poetry).	6 FEB: Decolonisation. Gold Coast becomes first African country to gain independence from Britain; renames itself Ghana.
	25 MAR: Treaty of Rome establishing the European Economic Community (EEC) signed by Belgium, France, Germany, Italy, Luxembourg and Holland.
	OCT: USSR launches first satellite, Sputnik 1.
1958	14–15 SEPT: Historic meeting between German Chancellor Konrad Adenauer and French PM Charles de Gaulle.
1959 Death of Aleksander Miłosz. Publishes *Letter to Polish Communists*. Publishes *Rodzinna Europa / Native Realm* (memoir).	1 JAN: President Batista flees from Cuba. Fidel Castro becomes Prime Minister.
1960 Offered post at UC Berkeley; appointed a Visiting Lecturer in the Department of Slavic Languages and Literature. 9 SEPT: Arrives in San Francisco.	1 MAY: USSR downs a U-2 spy plane flying over the Urals, capturing the pilot, Gary Powers.
	7 MAY: Leonid Brezhnev becomes President of USSR.
	16–19 MAY: Paris Summit. Khrushchev clashes with U.S., British and French leaders (Eisenhower, Macmillan and de Gaulle), citing U-2 incident.
	SEPT: Khrushchev addresses UN on issues of decolonisation and disarmament.
	8 NOV: John F. Kennedy wins U.S. presidential election.
1961 Promoted to Professor of Slavic Languages and Literature at UC Berkeley.	12 APR: Yuri Gagarin of USSR becomes first human being to orbit the earth.
	17–18 AUG: Berlin Wall erected by East Germany.

	CZESŁAW MIŁOSZ'S LIFE	CONTEMPORANEOUS POLITICAL AND HISTORICAL EVENTS
1962	JUNE: Granted green card. His aunt, Gabriela Kunat, dies in Sopot. Family takes a trip to Europe, including visits to France, Switzerland and Italy. Publishes *King Popiel and Other Poems* (poetry)	22–28 OCT: Cuban Missile Crisis, following U.S. discovery that USSR is supplying nuclear missiles in Cuba. World on brink of nuclear war before Khrushchev withdraws missiles. President Kennedy's prestige increases amongst western Allies.
1963		22 JAN: De Gaulle and Adenauer sign Franco-German treaty to increase co-operation. 29 JAN: Britain denied entry to EEC. 23–27 JUN: President Kennedy's visit to West Germany; includes famous 'Ich bin ein Berliner' address. 28 AUG: Martin Luther King Jr. leads civil rights demonstration in Washington; 'I have a dream' speech. 22 NOV: Assassination of President Kennedy.
1964		5 OCT: Martin Luther King Jr. wins Nobel Peace Prize. 15 OCT: Leonid Brezhnev replaces Khrushchev as First Secretary in USSR. 3 NOV: Lyndon Johnson (Democrat) elected U.S. President.
1965	Edits and publishes *Postwar Polish Poetry* (anthology). Publishes *Bobo's Metamorphosis* (poetry).	7 FEB: U.S. planes begin bombing North Vietnam. 21 MAR: Martin Luther King Jr. organises Selma-to-Montgomery march.
1966		2 APR: Disturbances in Saigon, where protesters call for end of military rule. 6, 11 JULY: 50 captured U.S. airmen paraded in Hanoi. USSR increases aid to North Vietnam. 13 DEC: U.S. raid on Hanoi kills more than 100 civilians.
1967	London's Oficyna Poetów i Malarzy publishes CM's *Wiersze (Poems)*.	5–10 JUNE: Six-Day War between Israel and Arab states, who are supported by USSR. 21 OCT: Protests against Vietnam War in Washington, London and other cities.

(continued)

CZESŁAW MIŁOSZ'S LIFE	CONTEMPORANEOUS POLITICAL AND HISTORICAL EVENTS

1968   *Native Realm* published in U.S.
Publishes *City without a Name* (poetry).

4 JAN: U.S. troop numbers in Vietnam reach 486,000.

5 JAN: Alexander Dubcek becomes First Secretary of Czechoslovakia Communist Party.

8 MAR: Student protests brutally repressed in Poland.

16 MAR: My Lai massacre in Vietnam. Over 100 civilians killed by U.S. troops.

4 APR: Assassination of Martin Luther King Jr.

14, 17 MAY: Dubcek initiates a programme of liberalising measures called the Prague Spring. Andrei Kosygin, Prime Minister of USSR, visits Prague for talks.

5 JUNE: Assassination of Robert Kennedy.

3 AUG: During visit to Bratislava, Leonid Brezhnev, the Soviet leader, announces what comes to be called the Brezhnev Doctrine, which asserts the right of the USSR to intervene in any Communist state if the Party's monopoly of power is under threat.

20 AUG: Invasion of Czechoslovakia by Warsaw Pact countries.

5 NOV: Richard Nixon (Republican) elected U.S. President.

1969   Publishes *The History of Polish Literature* (non-fiction) and *Visions from San Francisco Bay* (essays).

16 JAN: In protest against the military occupation of Czechoslovakia by USSR, a student, Jan Palach, burns himself to death in Prague.

JUNE-SEPT: 55,000 U.S. troops withdrawn from Vietnam.

20 JUL: Neil Armstrong, Buzz Aldrin, land the lunar module, Eagle, on the moon.

3 NOV: Nixon promises complete withdrawal of U.S. troops from Vietnam.

17 NOV: Strategic Arms Limitation Talks between U.S. and USSR begin in Helsinki.

1970   CM becomes U.S. citizen.

APR: President Nixon authorises bombing of Cambodia.

CZESŁAW MIŁOSZ'S LIFE	CONTEMPORANEOUS POLITICAL AND HISTORICAL EVENTS
	MAY: Shooting of four unarmed students at Kent State University by Ohio National Guard.
	12 DEC: Polish government announces steep food price increases.
	16 DEC: Killing of strikers in Gdańsk, Gdynia and Szczccin shipyards by Polish government forces.
	Władysław Gomułka resigns as First Secretary of PZPR (Polish United Workers' Party), replaced by Edward Gierek.
1971	10 MAR: Jews in USSR demand right to emigrate.
	31 MAR: U.S. Lieutenant William Calley imprisoned for role in My Lai massacre in Vietnam.
1972	21–27 FEB: President Nixon's trip to China.
	4 APR: Winner of Nobel Prize for Literature, Aleksander Solzhenitsyn, denied visa by USSR to attend ceremony in Stockholm.
	7 NOV: Richard Nixon re-elected as U.S. President.
1973	*Selected Poems* published by Seabury Press in New York.	1 JAN: Britain, Ireland and Denmark join European Community.
	8 JAN: Watergate break-in trials open.
	27 JAN: Vietnam cease-fire agreement signed in Paris.
	25 JUNE: Nixon's involvement in Watergate break-in revealed to Senate committee.
	SEPT: General Pinochet mounts coup in Chile, ousting the elected President Allende.
1974	*From the Rising of the Sun* (poems) published.	13 FEB: Aleksander Solzhenitsyn deported from USSR.
	9 AUG: President Nixon resigns.
1975	11 FEB: Margaret Thatcher elected leader of British Conservative Party.
1976	24 JUNE: Strikes in Radom and Ursus in response to government's increase in food prices.

(continued)

	CZESŁAW MIŁOSZ'S LIFE	CONTEMPORANEOUS POLITICAL AND HISTORICAL EVENTS

SEPT: Founding of KOR (Workers' Defence Committee). Key members include Adam Michnik and Jacek Kuron.

OCT: During presidential debate, U.S. President Gerald Ford claims that 'there is no Soviet domination in Eastern Europe'.

NOV: Jimmy Carter (Democrat) wins U.S. presidential election.

1977   *Utwory Poetickie* published by Slavic Dept., University of Michigan.

Publishes *Ziemia Ulro / The Land of Ulro* (non-fiction).

Awarded Honorary Doctorate by University of Michigan. Miłosz among the leading international literary figures who campaign to enable Lithuanian poet Tomas Venclova to leave the Soviet Union in 1977.

1978   CM winner of Neustadt International Prize for Literature.

On retirement made Professor Emeritus at Berkeley.

Publishes *Bells in Winter* (poetry).

16 OCT: Karol Wojtyła of Kraków elected Pope; he becomes John Paul II.

1979   Publishes *The Separate Notebooks 1977–79* (poems and prose).

The Book of Ecclesiastes published for the first time in *Tygodnik Powszechny*, followed by *The Book of Wisdom, Psalms*, and *The Book of Job*.

4 MAY: Margaret Thatcher becomes British Prime Minister.

2–10 JUNE: John Paul II's triumphant visit to Poland.

1980   DEC: CM winner of Nobel Prize for Literature.

Receives congratulatory telegram from Pope John Paul II.

14–31 AUG: Strikes in shipyards of Gdańsk and along Baltic coast lead to emergence of Solidarity, first independent trade union in the Soviet bloc.

4 NOV: Ronald Reagan (Republican) elected U.S. President.

DEC: Three Crosses Monument in Gdańsk unveiled, dedicated to murdered shipyard workers of 1970.

1981   JUNE: CM's first visit to Poland since 1951.

Visits Three Crosses Monument in Gdańsk.

9 FEB: General Jaruzelski becomes Polish PM.

27 MAR: Solidarity branded 'counter-revolutionary' by USSR.

CM readmitted as member of Polish Literary Society (Związek Literatów Polskich).

13 MAY: Assassination attempt on Pope John Paul II in Rome.

23 JULY: Polish government reduces rations and increases food prices.

4 NOV: Crisis discussions involving General Jaruzelski, Lech Wałęsa, and Cardinal Glemp.

13 DEC: General Jaruzelski, head of Polish Communist government, imposes martial law, banning Solidarity.

1982   Publishes *Hymn o Perle / Hymn of the Pearl* (poetry) and *Visions from San Francisco Bay*, trans. Richard Lourie (prose).
Delivers Norton Lectures at Harvard University.
Meets Carol Thigpen.

31 JAN: U.S. Department of Information film *Let Poland Be Poland* broadcast worldwide.

1 MAY: Solidarity supporters protest against martial law.

10 OCT: U.S. imposes trade sanctions on Poland.

19 DEC: Martial law in Poland ends.

1983   Publishes *The Witness of Poetry* (non-fiction).

23 FEB: President Reagan puts forward idea of "Star Wars" missile defence system.

5 OCT: Nobel Peace Prize awarded to Lech Wałęsa.

1984   Publishes *Nieobjęta ziemia / Unattainable Earth* (poetry).
The Separate Notebooks, trans. Robert Hass and Robert Pinsky (poetry and prose).

19 OCT: Murder of pro-Solidarity priest Father Jerzy Popiełuszko by four Secret Service agents.

1985   Publishes *Bells in Winter* (poetry).

11 MAR: Mikhail Gorbachev becomes First Secretary of the USSR Communist Party. Stresses need for greater openness, *glasnost*.

1986   Private audience with Pope John Paul II, in Rome.
Death of his first wife, Janina.

APR: Chernobyl nuclear disaster near Kiev in Ukraine.

SEPT: Amnesty for political prisoners in Poland.

11 OCT: Arms limitation discussions in Reykjavik end without agreement.

1987   *Chronicles.*

15–17 SEPT: U.S.-USSR agreement on getting rid of intermediate-range nuclear weapons.

(continued)

CZESŁAW MIŁOSZ'S LIFE	CONTEMPORANEOUS POLITICAL AND HISTORICAL EVENTS
1988 *Collected Poems 1931–1987* published.	8 FEB: USSR announces decision to withdraw troops from Afghanistan from MAY onwards.
	31 AUG: Talks between Lech Wałęsa and Interior Minister General Kiszczak about resolving Polish crisis.
	1 OCT: Gorbachev elected President of USSR.
	8 NOV: George H. W. Bush (Republican) wins U.S. presidential election.
1989 Awarded Honorary Doctorate by Harvard University. Return visit to Poland.	FEB–5 APR: Round Table Talks between Polish Communist government and the Opposition.
	FEB: Vaclav Havel imprisoned in Czechoslovakia.
	4 JUNE: Sweeping victory for Solidarity in elections.
	24 AUG: Tadeusz Mazowiecki becomes Polish Prime Minister, first non-Communist PM since war.
	In Baltic states, 50th anniversary of Molotov-Ribbentrop Pact marked by protest of 2 million citizens.
	9 NOV: Berlin Wall falls.
	10 DEC: 'Velvet Revolution' in Czecho-slovakia. First new government without Communist majority takes office. On 29 DECEMBER Vaclav Havel elected President.
	22–25 DEC: Romanian dictator Nicolai Ceausescu overthrown.
1990 *Rok myśliwego* published.	FEB: USSR Communist Party Central Committee opts to end its political monopoly.
	11 MAR: Lithuania declares its independence from USSR.
	4, 8 MAY: Latvia and Estonia declare their independence from USSR.
	3 OCT: Reunification of Germany.
	9 DEC: Lech Wałęsa elected Polish President.

	CZESŁAW MIŁOSZ'S LIFE	CONTEMPORANEOUS POLITICAL AND HISTORICAL EVENTS
1991	*Provinces* (poetry). Visit to Lithuania for first time since 1939.	JAN: Soviet troops invade Lithuania, killing 13 civilians. JUNE: Boris Yeltsin becomes President of the new Russian Federation. SEPT: Soviet Union recognises Lithuanian independence.
1992	Marries Carol Thigpen.	
1993	Moves to Kraków for good.	1 JAN: Czechoslovakia splits to become the Czech Republic and Slovakia. 7 APR: After Bosnia and Herzegovina declare independence, Bosnian Serbs fire on Sarajevo. Bosnian War continues till 1995.
1995	Publishes *Facing the River* (poetry).	JULY: Following Bosnian Serbs' capture of Srebrenica, a so-called UN safe haven, over 7,000 Bosnian Muslim men and boys are massacred.
1997	Publishes *Striving towards Being: The Letters of Thomas Merton and Czesław Miłosz*, ed. Robert Faggen.	
1998	Publishes *Road-Side Dog*, trans. Czesław Miłosz and Robert Hass. *Ogród nauk* (Garden of Science). *Zaraz po wojnie* (Straight after the War). Death of Zbigniew Herbert.	5 MAR: Fighting breaks out in Kosovo, where Serbs attack ethnic Albanians. 10 APR: Good Friday Agreement signed in Belfast, Northern Ireland.
1999	Death of Jerzy Turowicz.	MAR: Peace talks over Kosovo fail, resulting in NATO air strikes being carried out on Belgrade.
2000	Death of Jerzy Giedroyc. *Magic Mountain* (documentary). Publishes *This* (poetry).	NOV: George W. Bush elected U.S. President after protracted dispute over election results.
2001	*To Begin Where I Am: Selected Essays*, trans. and ed. Bogdana Carpenter and Madeline G. Levine. Publishes *Rok myśliwego* (A Year of the Hunter).	11 SEPT: Attack on World Trade Center and Pentagon by Islamist extremists. OCT: U.S. and British governments attack Taliban regime and Al Qaeda in Afghanistan.
2002	Publishes *Druga przestrzeń / Second Space* (poetry).	13 MAY: U.S. and Russian Federation agreement to destroy two-thirds of nuclear weapons.

(continued)

CZESŁAW MIŁOSZ'S LIFE	CONTEMPORANEOUS POLITICAL AND HISTORICAL EVENTS
Miłosz's ABC, trans. Madeline G. Levine (prose). Death of Carol, his second wife.	26 OCT: Chechen rebels kill 116 hostages in Moscow theatre.
2003 Publishes *New and Collected Poems 1931–2001*, trans. Robert Hass.	19 MAR: Invasion of Iraq by U.S. and UK–led coalition.
2004 Publishes *O podróżach w czasie* (About Journeys through Time). 14 AUG: Miłosz dies in Kraków.	NOV–26 DEC: Disputed election result in Ukraine. Eventually Viktor Yushchenko declared PM, defeating Viktor Yanukovych, who supported closer ties with Russia.
2006 *Zaczynając od moich ulic* (Beginning with My Streets).	
2011 *Selected and Last Poems, 1931–2004*, selected by Robert Hass and Anthony Miłosz.	Polish Parliament (Sejm) announces establishment of a Year of Czesław Miłosz.

Many of the exact dates in the above chronology are drawn from *Chronology of the Twentieth Century*, ed. Philip Waller and John Rowett (Oxford: Helicon, 1995).

NOTES

Introduction

1. Joseph Brodsky, 'Presentation of Czesław Miłosz to the [Neustadt Award] Jury', *World Literature Today* 3 (1978), p. 364.

2. Nobel Prize in Literature 1980, press release, Swedish Academy, Nobelprize.org., 26 January 2011, http://nobelprize.org/nobel_prizes/literature/laureates/1980/press.html.

3. Seamus Heaney, 'In Gratitude for All the Gifts', *The Guardian*, Saturday, 11 September 2004. In an interview with Dennis Manning and Robert Hedin, in *The Southern Review* 21 (January 1983), p. 103, Miłosz comments that 'every poetry is directed against death—against death of the individual, against the power of death'.

4. 'Britain and America continued to regard the Polish Government in London as their first and staunchest ally; whilst the Russians, having severed diplomatic relations, began to smear the Polish leaders publicly as "reactionaries" and "Fascist collaborators" . . . In the first of the meetings of "The Big Three", held at Tehran at the end of November 1943, it was agreed that post-war Europe would be divided into "zones of influence"—Western and Southern Europe for the Anglo-Americans, and Eastern Europe for the Russians. This implied that Poland would fall under Soviet occupation and control. It was agreed that the post-war Polish-Soviet frontier should follow the line once put forward in 1920 . . . Few cared to notice that the Curzon line was essentially the same as the Nazi-Soviet Demarcation Line of 1939 . . . Stalin persuaded the Allied Powers to adopt the Russian imperial view of Poland's national territory. At this stage, the Polish Government [in London] was not even informed of these crucial decisions, which had been made over its head. They were to be told of the *fait accompli* at a moment more convenient for the Allies. A lamentable precedent was set for future Allied decisions on the Polish Question at Yalta and Potsdam' (Norman Davies, *Heart of Europe: The Past in Poland's Present*, p. 65).

5. Norman Davies, *Rising '44: The Battle for Warsaw*, p. 516.

6. In June 1956, Rokossowski gave the orders which resulted in the quelling of the Poznan Rising, in which an estimated seventy-four protesters perished.

7. Miłosz likens the simplistic, materialistic 'philosophy of life' communism expects people to swallow to the 'Murt-Bing' tablets which appear in Witkiewicz's 1932 novel *Insatiability*, which create instant feelings of serenity and happiness. See *The Captive Mind* 3–7.

8. The phrase comes from a review by Terrence des Pres, which Cavanagh cites on p. 243.

9. 'Warsaw Ghetto Uprising', https://www.britannica.com/.

10. In an interview with Ayyappa K. Paniker, 'Dialogue with Czesław Miłosz', in *Czesław Miłosz: Conversations*, ed. Cynthia L. Haven (Jackson: University Press of Mississippi, 2006), p. 33, the poet avers that 'there is free will and there is no free will'.

11. Czesław Miłosz, 'Speaking of a Mammal', in *To Begin Where I Am*, p. 216.

12. 'Footfalls echo in the memory': T. S. Eliot, 'Burnt Norton', from *Four Quartets*, in *The Collected Poems and Plays of T. S. Eliot* (London: Faber and Faber, 1969), p. 171.

13. Miłosz's mother died from typhus in 1945. In *Native Realm*, p. 65, Miłosz pays tribute to his mother as a woman of depth: 'Under the surface was stubbornness, gravity, and the strong conviction that suffering is sent by God and that it should be borne cheerfully'.

14. It is interesting to note the poems he dedicates to American writers, such as 'To Robinson Jeffers' (*NCP* 252), 'To Allen Ginsberg' (611), and 'To Robert Lowell' (722), and his enduring appreciation of Walt Whitman to which Clare Cavanagh refers (*Lyric Poetry* 244–246).

1. The Garden of Eden

1. W. H. Auden, *Collected Shorter Poems, 1927–1957*, p. 145.

2. Adam Mickiewicz (1798–1855) is Poland's national poet. In Kenneth Mackenzie's 1966 translation of *Pan Tadeusz,* the narrator refers to how the Madonna

> didst heal me with a miracle
> For when my weeping mother sought Thy power,
> I raised my dying eyes, and in that hour
> My strength returned (2)

The image of Our Lady of Ostrabrama, once located above one of the city's gates, has been situated in a nearby chapel since the 1670s. In a Russian attack in 1655 most of the city was burned, though the painting of the Madonna survived unscathed. After Wilno was seized by the Swedes in 1702, legend has it that the Madonna intervened, enabling the Lithuanians to counterattack and drive out the enemy. In the final poem of 'Treatise on Theology' (*SS* 64), Miłosz alludes to the Virgin's role as Protector in Poland's national mythology (Eds.).

3. The individual executed for his assassination, Dmitri Bogrov, was a police agent who was given access by the police to the Kiev Opera House, where Stolypin was attending a performance. Richard Cavendish in *History Today,* 61:9, September 2011, points out that investigations into the murder were halted 'on Tsar Nicholas's orders' (Eds.).

4. In this respect his upbringing was not dissimilar to that of John Clare and Thomas Hardy among the English poets, Patrick Kavanagh and Seamus Heaney among the Irish (Eds.).

5. Gucio is mysteriously changed into Bobo in the English translation of *Gucio Zaczarowany* (Eds.).

6. This is the church where his grandfather, Zygmunt, was later buried.

7. Interestingly, in Lithuanian 'kunas' means 'body'.

8. 'Lis' is the Polish word for 'fox' (Eds.).

9. The Sapiehas were an extremely wealthy and influential Lithuanian family from the early sixteenth century onwards. The first major figure in the dynasty, Andrzej Sapieha (1539–1621), held the post of Deputy Cup-bearer to the Lithuanian king. Much of the family fortune was created, however, by Lew Sapieha (1557–1633), who rose to be Court Chancellor and Great Hetman of Lithuania (Eds.).

10. 'Litwo! Ojczyzno moja!' is the opening line of Adam Mickiewicz's great epic, *Pan Tadeusz.*

2. The Young Man and the Mysteries

1. Amongst the fictional Dr Mucholapski's qualities that Miłosz must have warmed to, Franaszek notes, were his 'deep commitment to science and his contempt for people who lacked passion' (67).

2. Henryk Sienkiewicz's intensely patriotic novel *With Fire and Sword* is set during the Polish-Lithuanian Commonwealth, a period viewed with intense nostalgia given that at the time of its publication, 1884, Poland remained partitioned (Eds.).

3. Andrzej Franaszek identifies all three in the Polish text of his biography (pp. 87, 767), and how one of them, Mieczysław Kotarbiński, subsequently became a very good friend to Miłosz (Eds.).

4. Kline's translation appears at http://www.poetryintranslation.com/PITBR/French/DuBellay Poems.htm.

3. Black Ariel

1. Many years later, Sukiennicki's wife, a lawyer, defended a friend of Miłosz's who was tried for political offences.

2. In Poland now, as in Polish-controlled Middle Lithuania then, 100 groszy make up one złoty.

3. During the 1930s, Stalin set out to eliminate anyone in the Soviet leadership, the Communist Party or the military who was suspected of 'disloyalty'. It has proved impossible to establish the exact number of Soviet citizens who were arrested and sent to the gulags, though estimates suggest that by 1936 there could have been as many 5 million prisoners (https://www.britannica.com/place/Gulag). The terrible, inhuman conditions in the camps resulted in the deaths of a high proportion of those detained (Eds.).

4. For an account of the events from a Jewish source, see http://www.jta.org/1931/12/04/archive /two-jews-arrested-in-vilna-on-suspicion-of-having-killed-national-democratic-student-waclawski (Eds.).

5. This was a nationwide student organisation, founded in Kraków in 1859, which gave considerable support to less-well-off students in the form of scholarships and grants, and by setting up affordable canteens. The group was also committed to extending education to the working-class population.

6. Aleksander Fiut (1945–) is a leading academic at the Jagiellonian University in Kraków, who, from the early 1980s onwards, conducted a series of interviews with Miłosz, as part of an advanced research project. This resulted in two subsequent publications in English, *Conversations with Czesław Miłosz* (New York: Harcourt, 1987) and *The Eternal Moment: The Poetry of Czeslaw Milosz* (Berkeley: University of California Press, 1990).

7. 'Konrad's Cell' is located in the Basilian Monastery in Wilno (Vilnius), and named after the protagonist in Adam Mickiewicz's poem, *Dziady* [Forefather's Eve]. Mickiewicz was imprisoned in the monastery from 1823–1824 for agitating against the continuing partition of Poland. In part III of Mickiewicz's poem, Konrad too is imprisoned by the occupying Russians. As a location for a literary event, therefore, it carried considerable resonance.

8. Skamander was a band of young Polish poets who joined forces in 1918 with the aim of developing a new poetic idiom which more accurately captured the world in the twentieth century. Its founder was Julian Tuwim, and amongst the other poets linked to the group or sympathetic to its goals were Kazimierz Wierzyński, Antoni Słonimski, Maria Pawlikowska-Jasnorzewska and Boleslaw Leśmian, the latter often rated as one of Poland's foremost lyric poets of all time. https://www .britannica.com/topic/Skamander-Polish-literary-group.

9. Miłosz was absent from some of these early meetings, but later voiced his conviction that *he* had suggested the name Żagary, which 'Bujnicki accepted enthusiastically'.

10. 'My days are shaped by the number of pages I have read from Brzozowski, who inspires me and impregnates me' (CM to Iwaszkiewicz, 18 March 1931).

11. Miłosz is no doubt referring to sin, redemption, heaven and hell.

4. The Country of the First Emigration

1. Suprematism was an abstract art movement, founded by Kazimir Malevich in Russia shortly before the First World War. Signature features of suprematist painting were repeated geometrical forms and a limited palette of colors. Malevich's contemporaries included the Russian Formalists, 'a highly influential group of literary critics', who 'opposed the idea that language is a simple, transparent vehicle for communication' (http://www.theartstory.org/movement-suprematism.htm).

2. William Carlos Williams, 'Landscape with the Fall of Icarus', *Selected Poems*, p. 238.

3. Miguel Mañara (1627–1679) was born into a rich family, inherited his father's fortune and became mayor of Seville. Following his wife's death in 1661, he underwent a spiritual crisis and became an ascetic. He returned to Seville and joined the Brotherhood of the Holy Charity, where he was responsible for setting up a hospital and hospice for the poor. In July 1985 Pope John Paul II initiated the process that may lead to his beatification.

4. Wanda Wasilewska (1905–1964) was a Polish-born Communist political activist whose activities included the composition of propaganda pieces aimed at Polish children. During the war she became a Soviet citizen, and was on three occasions awarded the Stalin Prize for Literature, in 1943, 1946 and 1952.

5. Coincidentally, it was also the birthplace of Stefan Wyszyński, the popular and highly respected cardinal who led the Polish Catholic Church during the difficult post-war years.

6. Jacques Maritain (1882–1973) was a French philosopher who was brought up in the Protestant faith, but, after a period as an agnostic, converted to Catholicism in his mid-twenties. The core themes in his work, which would have had considerable appeal to Miłosz, include 'the contentions that science, philosophy, poetry and mysticism are among many legitimate ways of knowing reality', that 'the individual person transcends the political community', and that 'people holding different beliefs must cooperate in the formation and maintenance of salutary political institutions'. https://www.britannica.com/biography/Jacques-Maritain (Eds.).

5. Voices of Poor People

1. Bradley Lightbody, 'Invasion of Poland', http://www.bbc.co.uk/history/worldwars/wwtwo/invasion_poland_01.shtml.

2. Miłosz recalled dropping a piece of paper with obscenities written on it into the ballot box.

3. Miłosz knew the poet's father in Wilno. Andrzej Franaszek, in *Miłosz: Biografia*, p. 807, speculates that the poet may even have attended Baczyński's wedding in June 1942, at which his close friend Andrzejewski was a witness (Eds.).

4. According to 'Nazi racial laws, he was a *Mischling* and she deserved immediate removal from the face of the earth' (*NR* 243).

5. Stanisław Ignacy Witkiewicz (1885–1939), often known as Witkacy, was one of Poland's foremost artists in the pre-war period. A poet, dramatist, painter, photographer, art theorist and philosopher, he was described by Jan Kott as a man whose work was characterised by 'stunning clarity and acute vision' and likened to George Orwell. In Jeziory, in the Polish Ukraine, he committed suicide on 18 September 1939 on learning of the Soviet invasion of eastern Poland (Eds.).

6. The Warsaw Rising represented an attempt by the Armia Krajowa to seize control of the Polish capital from the retreating Germans. The Polish Government-in-Exile in London were keen to prevent Warsaw falling into the hands of the advancing Red Army (Eds.).

7. The Areopagus was situated on the Acropolis in Athens, and often functioned as the location where judgment on serious crimes was passed (Eds.).

6. *In Partibus Daemonis*

1. Many readers will recall Szpilman as the subject of Roman Polanski's award-winning film *The Pianist*. It won the Palme d'Or at Cannes in 2002, as well as three Oscars, including Best Director for Kraków-born Polanski and Best Actor for Adrien Brody (Eds.).

2. *Popiół i Diament* (Ashes and Diamonds), which in 1958 was made into a cinema classic by Andrzej Wajda (Eds.).

3. *Chochoły* is 'the straw wrapping tied around shrubs to protect them from winter frost' (Eds.).

4. An allusion to Exodus 32: 1–36.

5. Literally, 'the truce of God', a period when warfare was officially suspended in medieval times.

6. In translating 'Byle się spełnilo' as 'Let it be done quickly', Jan Darowski may well be recalling the famous lines from Shakespeare's *Macbeth*, act 1, scene 7: 'If it were done when 'tis done, then 'twere well / It were done quickly' (Eds.).

7. A Story of One Particular Suicide Case

1. On 23 October, students in Budapest took part in a march commemorating the Hungarian revolt of 1848 against the Austrian occupation of their country. Within days, the numbers of protesters had swelled to over 200,000. Their principal demands were that Hungary should again be an independent nation and that Soviet troops leave. Although for a short while the troops were withdrawn, on 4 November they returned, along with a 1,000 tanks which, within a week, crushed the Rising, killing and wounding around 5,000 Hungarian civilians (Eds.).

2. Borowski committed suicide in 1951, at the age of twenty-eight, deeply affected by his experiences in Auschwitz and Dachau, and disillusioned, like Miłosz, with the post-war Communist regime and the injustice and inhuman treatment of people it perpetuated (Eds.).

8. The Magic Mountain

1. T. Walas, 'Czesław Miłosz jako historyk literatury polskiej', *Dekada Literacka* 11, 1994.

2. Cf. Miłosz's comment towards the close of *The Land of Ulro* that 'Nature (which equals Necessity), though cruel in our eyes, is innocent' (257).

3. Skwarnicki (1930–2013), who had moved to Kraków in 1958 to work for *Tygodnik Powszechny*, would in later years become a close companion to Pope John Paul II (Eds).

4. The soldiers of the First Polish Armoured Division served the London-based Polish Government-in- Exile, and were commanded by General Stanislaw Maczek. They took part in the Battle for Normandy in August 1944 and were attached to the First Canadian Army.

5. Saligia is an acronym drawn from ecclesiastical Latin, for the seven deadly sins: *superbia, avaritia, luxuria, invidia, gula, ira,* and *acedia* (pride, avarice, lust, envy, gluttony, anger, and sloth).

9. The Nobel and the Poet's Later Years

1. http://www.nobelprize.org/nobel_prizes/literature/laureates/1980/presentation-speech.html.

2. Ira Michael Heyman, press statement, 9 October 1980, Chancellor's Office, UC Berkeley.

3. Lars Gyllensten, qtd. in *Express Wieczorny,* 5 December 1980.

4. Katarzyna Gruber (1922–) is an author who translated Miłosz's poetry into Swedish. From 1971 to 1988 she worked at the Nobel Library in Stockholm, with responsibility for its Slavonic collection, regularly adding thousands of banned Polish books (Eds.).

5. http://www.nobelprize.org/nobel_prizes/literature/laureates/1980/presentation-speech.html.

6. The Katyń forest, in what is now Belarus, was the site of the mass killing of over four thousand unarmed Polish officers in April 1940, carried out on Stalin's orders. Amongst the victims who 'now repose in a mass grave', Miłosz informed his audience in his Nobel Lecture, were two of his friends and fellow poets, Wladysław Sebyła and Lech Piwowar (Eds.).

7. See Michael Parker, 'Past Master', 826.

8. An initial trigger for the Polish student protests in spring 1968 was when a production of Adam Mickiewicz's *Forefathers' Eve* at the Teatr Narodowy in Warsaw, directed by Kazimierz Dejmek, was halted on government orders, probably as a result of pressure from the Soviet ambassador in Poland. Dating from the 1830s, it is a play which captures the 'suffering and humiliation' Poles experienced under partition, and, in Neal Ascherson's words, offers a 'devastating' critique of 'Russians . . . police states and . . . censorship' ('The Polish March: Students, Workers and 1968'). Following the last performance on 30 January 1968, several hundred students set off on a march to the Mickiewicz monument calling for an end to censorship; towards the end of the demonstration, police moved in, wielding batons, arresting

and fining protesters. Almost exactly a month later an extraordinary gathering of the Warsaw members of the Polish Writers Union, including Jerzy Andrzejewski, Stefan Kisielewski, and Leszek Kołakowski, passed a resolution criticising the decision to stop the play's run.

When, on Friday, 8 March, a mass meeting organised by Warsaw University students was held to protest the suppression of cultural freedom under the Communist regime, condemn the expulsion from the university of Adam Michnik and Henryk Szlajfer, and voice support of the writers' resolution, they came under attack from armed police and 'bus-loads of Party-organised thugs' (Ascherson, *The Polish August* 92). Street clashes continued over successive days and weeks, and resulted in over 1.200 students being arrested and a number of university staff including Kołakowski and Zygmunt Bauman, a sociology professor, being sacked. Albeit on a lesser scale, there was similar unrest in Kraków, where several academics were beaten up by police. In a key moment in Andrzej Wajda's film *Man of Iron*, the point is underlined that the failure of workers to come to the aid of students and intellectuals in March 1968 resulted in the latter declining to support workers' protests on the Baltic coast in 1970 (Eds.).

9. The title comes from Apocalypse 8:10–11: 'there fell a great star from heaven, burning like a torch, and it fell on the third part of the rivers, and upon the fountain of waters. The name of the star is called Wormwood; and many people died of the waters, because they were made bitter'. Significantly, the star is alluded to in Dostoyevsky's *The Idiot*, book 2, chapter 10 (see notes to *The Separate Notebooks* 211) (Eds.).

10. For an invaluable account of how the Polish censors were thwarted, see Jerzy Illg, 'An Invisible Rope: Miłosz's Underground Publication', *Partisan Review* 1 (1999): 14–18.

11. The preceding pages of historical contextualisation, starting from 'To understand the momentous changes . . .', have been added by Michael Parker.

12. In 1970, Miłosz sent a postcard to Zygmunt Hertz from Poland, Maine, commenting wryly that it was the only Poland he could go to then.

13. 'Reportedly crucial in determining both the Party's and Moscow's attitude was a telephone conversation between Gorbachev and the new Polish Party leader, Rakowski, on 22 August' (Timothy Garton Ash, *We the People*, 41).

14. The preceding pages of historical contextualisation, starting from 'Less than a year after the Three Crosses monument . . .', have been added by Michael Parker.

15. In the biography, Ewa is referred to by her first name only, in order to maintain her privacy (Eds.).

16. Ewa, in conversation with the author, 2005.

17. See Chapter 8, pp. 411–414 and the poem 'On Parting with My Wife, Janina', *NCP*, p. 469 (Eds.).

18. In contrast to the West, where every citizen was entitled to a passport, which they then retained, in the Polish People's Republic applications to go abroad were regularly refused. Those fortunate enough to be given a passport would immediately have to surrender it to the police on their return home (Eds.).

19. Three years earlier, in 1993, Czesław had translated Oskar Miłosz's *Storge* into Polish and written an introduction.

20. A member of the New York school of poets, Frank O'Hara (1926–1966) was deeply influenced by contemporary visual artists, particularly Jackson Pollock, and French Symbolist and Russian poets (Eds.).

BIBLIOGRAPHY

WORKS BY CZESŁAW MIŁOSZ

Books and Essays in English Translations

The Captive Mind. First published 1953 by Secker and Warburg. Reprint, London: Penguin, 1985.

The Seizure of Power. Translated by Celina Wieniewska. First published 1955 as *The Usurpers* by Faber. Reprint, London: Sphere, 1985.

Native Realm. Translated by Catherine S. Leach. First published 1968 by Doubleday US. Reprint, London: Sidgwick and Jackson, 1981.

The Invincible Song: A Clandestine Anthology. Ed. Czesław Miłosz. First published 1942. Ann Arbor: Michigan Slavic Publications, 1981.

The Issa Valley. Translated by Louis Iribarne. First published 1981 by Sidgwick and Jackson. Reprint, London: Sphere, 1984.

Visions from San Francisco Bay. Translated by Richard Lourie. New York: Farrar, Straus and Giroux, 1982.

The Witness of Poetry. Cambridge, MA: Harvard University Press, 1983.

The Land of Ulro. Translated by Louis Iribarne. New York: Farrar, Straus and Giroux, 1984.

The Separate Notebooks. Translated by Robert Hass and Robert Pinsky, with Czesław Miłosz and Renata Gorczyńska. New York: Ecco, 1984.

The Collected Poems, 1931–1987. London: Penguin, 1988.

*Beginning with My Streets: Essays and Recollections. Translated by Madeline G. Levine. New York: Farrar, Straus and Giroux, 1991.

*A Year of the Hunter. Translated by Madeline G. Levine. New York: Farrar, Straus and Giroux, 1994.

Striving towards Being: The Letters of Thomas Merton and Czesław Miłosz. Edited by Robert Faggen. New York: Farrar, Straus and Giroux, 1997.

Road-Side Dog. Translated by Czesław Miłosz and Robert Hass. New York: Farrar, Straus and Giroux, 1998.

Miłosz's ABC. Translated by Madeline G. Levine. New York: Farrar, Straus and Giroux, 2002.

*Quotations in the biography from the asterisked texts are translated by Aleksandra Parker from the Polish originals, and are not from these published English translations.

To Begin Where I Am: Selected Essays. Translated and edited by Bogdana Carpenter and Madeline G. Levine. New York: Farrar, Straus and Giroux, 2002.

New and Collected Poems, 1931–2001. Translated by Robert Hass. New York: Ecco, 2003.

Second Space. Translated by Czesław Miłosz and Robert Hass. New York: Ecco, 2004.

Legends of Modernity: Essays and Letters from Occupied Poland. Translated by Madeline G. Levine. New York: Farrar, Straus and Giroux, 2006.

Selected and Last Poems, 1931–2004. Selected by Robert Hass and Anthony Miłosz. New York: Ecco, 2011.

Translations into English by Miłosz of Other Writers' Works

Miłosz, Czesław, comp. and trans. *A Book of Luminous Things: An International Anthology of Poetry.* Orlando, FL: Harcourt, 1996.

Świr, Anna. *Talking to My Body.* Translated with Leonard Nathan. Washington, DC: Copper Canyon Press, 1996.

Books and Essays in Polish

These following works include some previously untranslated poems.

Pieśń niepodległa: poezja polska czasu wojny (Invincible Song: Polish Wartime Poetry). Oficyna Polska, 1942.

Kolorowym atramentem (With Coloured Ink). *Przekrój* 1 and 2 (1945).

Kontynenty. Paris, 1958.

'O wstydzie i agresji' (On Shame and Aggression). *Kultura* 7–8 (1962).

Trzy Zimy: Głosy o wierszach (Three Winters: Reflections on the Poems). London, 1987.

Świadectwo poezji (The Witness of Poetry). Paris, 1993.

Ogród nauk (Garden of Science). Kraków, 1998.

Zaraz po wojnie (Straight after the War). Kraków, 1998.

Zniewolony umysł (The Captive Mind). Kraków, 1999.

Rok myśliwego (A Year of the Hunter). Kraków, 2001.

Wiersze I. Kraków: Znak, 2001.

Wiersze II. Kraków: Znak, 2002.

Przygody młodego umysłu (Adventures of a Young Mind). Kraków, 2003.

Wiersze III. Kraków: Znak, 2003.

O podróżach w czasie (About Journeys through Time). Kraków, 2004.

Wiersze IV. Kraków: Znak, 2004.

Mój wileński opiekun: Listy do Manfreda Kridla (My Wilno Guardian: Letters to Manfred Kridl). Toruń, 2005.

Rozmowy polskie 1979–1998. Kraków, 2006.

Zaczynając od moich ulic (Beginning with My Streets). Kraków, 2006.

Wiersze V. Kraków: Znak, 2009.

Rozmowy polskie 1999–2004. Kraków, 2010.

Wiersze wszystkie. Kraków: Znak, 2011.

Unpublished Sketches

'Sea Is My Destination'. Film scenario. Circa 1938. Beinecke Library Archive.

'Odczyt o literaturze'. 1949. Beinecke Library Archive.

'Ze wszystkich możliwych pobudek do pisania'. Circa 1951. Beinecke Library Archive.

'Rivière'. 1952. Beinecke Library Archive.

Untitled manuscript, on the composition of *The Seizure of Power.* 1953 or 1954. Beinecke Library Archive.

'Pieniądze'. Circa 1953–1954. Beinecke Library Archive.

'Wymarsz z czarnej groty'. 1956–1957. Beinecke Library Archive.

'Materiały do mojej biografii'. Undated. Miłosz Archive, Kraków.

Articles and Occasional Pieces (English, French and Polish)

'List do obrońców kultury' (Letters to the Defenders of Culture). *Poprostu,* 20 January 1936.

'Prawie zmierzch bogów' (Almost the Dusk of Gods). *Kurier Wileński,* 13 March 1938.

'Obrona rzeczy nieuznanych' (Defense of Unknown Things). *Kurier Poranny,* 9 October 1938.

'Na "Fantazym"'. *Odrodzenie* 33 (1945).

'Na skraju Warszawy'. *Przekrój* 16 (1945).

'Obyczaje'. *Zeszyty Wrocławskie* 1–2 (1950).

'Nie'. *Kultura* 5 (1951).

'L'interlocuteur fraternel'. *Preuves* (April 1960).

'Poet of Exile'. *Los Angeles Times,* 12 October 1980; reprinted in Haven, *Czesław Miłosz: Conversations,* 5.

The Nobel Lecture, delivered 5 December 1980, published in *New York Review of Books,* 5 March 1981, 11–15.

'It Is a Grave Responsibility to Kill Hope'. *New York Times,* 18 December 1981.

'Prolog'. *Pamiętnik Teatralny* 1–2 (1981).

'The Polish Crisis: Three Statements', by Czesław Miłosz, Joseph Brodsky, Susan Sontag, Stanisław Barańczak, Tomas Venclova, et al. *New York Review of Books,* 21 January 1982. http://www.nybooks.com/articles/archives/1982/jan/21/the-polish-crisis-three-statements/.

'Poszukiwania: Wybór publicystyki rozproszonej 1931–1983'. Warsaw, 1985.

'I oto, drogi'. *Nasza Rodzina* 7–8 (1995).

'A Dialogue about a City'. In Venclova, *Winter Dialogue*, 97.

Kontynenty. Kraków, 1999.

Szukanie ojczyzny. Kraków: Znak, 2001.

Interviews

Rzepińska, Maria. *Poeta o Malarstwie. Rozmowa z Czesławem Miłoszem* (The Poet on Painting: An Interview with Czesław Miłosz). *Przegląd Artystyczny* 1 (1946).

Simpson, Mona. 'A Talk with Czesław Miłosz'. *California Living Magazine,* 4 January 1981, 15–16; reprinted in Haven, *Czesław Miłosz: Conversations,* 7–11.

Conversation. Czesław Miłosz with Helen Vendler, Lannan Foundation video, 26 March, 1998. https://podcast.lannan.org/2010/04/26/czeslaw-milosz-with-helen-vendler-conversation-26-march-1998-video.

The Magic Mountain: An American Portrait of Czesław Miłosz. Directed by Maria Zmarz-Koczanowicz, 2001.

Podróżny świata (A World Traveller). Interview with Renata Gorczyńska. Kraków, 2002.

Czesław Miłosz Autoportret (Self-Portrait). Interview with Aleksander Fiut. Kraków, 2003.

SECONDARY MATERIAL

Alvarez, A. 'East Is East'. *New York Review of Books,* 11 November 1965.

Andrzejewski, Jerzy. *Gra z cieniem.* Warsaw, 1987.

———. *Z dnia na dzień.* Warsaw, 1988.

Ascherson, Neal. *The Polish August.* Harmondsworth: Penguin, 1981.

———. 'The Polish March: Students, Workers and 1968'. 6 March 2008. https://www.opendemocracy.net/article/globalisation/the_polish_march_students_workers_and_1968.

Auden, W. H. *Collected Shorter Poems, 1927–1957.* London: Faber, 1969.

Barańczak, Stanisław. 'Searching for the Real'. In *Breathing under Water and Other East European Essays.* Cambridge, MA: Harvard University Press, 1990.

Bereś, Stanisław. *Ostatnia wileńska plejada. Szkice o poezji kręgu Żagarów.* Warsaw, 1990.

Bereś, Witold. 'Operacja "Poeta": Wybór Dokumentów'. *Gazeta Wyborcza,* 148 (26 June 2004): 13.

Bikont, Anna, and Joanna Szczęsna. *Lawina i kamienie: Pisarze wobec komunizmu.* Warsaw, 2006.

———. 'Onieśmielenie Wisławy Szymborskiej'. *Gazeta Wyborcza,* 17 January 2004.

Błoński, Jan. 'Biedni Polacy patrzą na getto'. *Tygodnik Powszechny* 2 (1987).

———. Review of Miłosz, *Dolina Issy. Przegląd Kulturalny* 24 (1957).

Bond, Edward. Introduction to *The Fool* and *We Come to the River*. London: Methuen, 1982.

Boniecki, Adam. 'To nic, że czasem nie wie'. In Gromek-Illg, *Czesław Miłosz: In Memoriam.*

Breza, Tadeusz. *Nelly. O kolegach i o sobie*. Warsaw, 1983.

Brodsky, Joseph. 'Presentation of Czesław Miłosz to the [Neustadt Award] Jury'. *World Literature Today* 3 (1978): 364.

———. 'Wytrwałość bólu'. *Tygodnik Powszechny* 26 (1996).

Bujnicki, Teodor. *Szkice wileńskie*. Kraków, 2002.

Byrski, Tadeusz. *Teatr-radio. Wspomnienia*. Warsaw, 1976.

Carpenter, Bogdana. 'Recepcja poezji Czesława Miłosza w Ameryce'. In *Teksty* II, 3–4 (2001).

Cavanagh, Clare. *Lyric Poetry and Modern Politics*. New Haven, CT: Yale University Press, 2010.

Craig, Mary. *The Crystal Spirit: Lech Wałęsa and His Poland*. London: Coronet, 1986.

Czyżewski, Karol. 'Linia powrotu'. In *Żagary. Środowisko kulturowe grupy literackiej*. Kraków, 2009.

Dąbrowska, Maria. *Dziennik 1915–65*. Vol. 4. Warsaw, 2009.

Davies, Norman. *Heart of Europe: The Past in Poland's Present*. Oxford: Oxford University Press, 2001.

———. *Rising '44: The Battle for Warsaw*. London: Macmillan, 2004.

Dunin-Horkawicz, Janusz. *Co było a nie jest . . . czyli kilka lat młodości mojej w Wilnie*. Łódź, 1990.

Eisler, Jerzy. 'March 1968 in Poland'. In *1968: The World Transformed,* edited by Carol Fink, Philipp Gassert and Detlef Junker. Copublished by the German Historical Institute, Washington, DC / Cambridge: Cambridge University Press, 1998, 237–252.

Eliot, T. S. *The Poems of T. S. Eliot*. Edited by Christopher Ricks and Jim McCue. London: Faber, 2015.

Fałtynowicz, Zbigniew. *Wieczorem wiatr. Czesław Miłosz i Suwalszczyzna*. Gdańsk, 2006.

Fiut, Aleksander. 'W Objęciach Tygrysa'. *Teksty II,* 3–4 (2001): 160–170.

———. Interview. In *Czesław Miłosz: Autoportret przekorny* (A Contrary Self-Portrait). Kraków, 2003.

Folejewski, Zbigniew. *Kilka Wspomnień o Żagarach*. *Poezja* 5–6 (1981).

Garton Ash, Timothy. *The Polish Revolution: Solidarity*. 3rd ed. New Haven, CT: Yale University Press, 1999.

———. *We the People: The Revolution of '89 Witnessed in Warsaw, Budapest, Berlin and Prague*. Harmondsworth: Penguin, 1999.

Giedroyc, Jerzy, and Czesław Miłosz. *Listy 1952–1963*. Edited and introduced by Marek Kornat. Warsaw, 2008.

Gilbert, Martin. *A History of the Twentieth Century: 1933–1951.* London: HarperCollins, 1998.

Gombrowicz, Rita. *Gombrowicz w Europie: Świadectwa i dokumenty 1963–1969.* Kraków, 2002.

Gombrowicz, Witold. *Dziennik 1953–1958.* Kraków, 2009.

Gorczyńska, Renata. *'Jestem z Wilna' i inne adresy.* Kraków, 2003.

———. *Portrety paryskie.* Kraków, 1999.

Grémion, Pierre. *Konspiracja wolności. Kongres Wolności Kultury w Paryżu (1950–75).* Warsaw, 2004.

Grochowska, Magdalena. *Jerzy Giedroyc, do Polski ze snu.* Warsaw, 2009.

Gromek-Illg, Joanna, ed. *Czesław Miłosz: In Memoriam.* Kraków: Znak, 2004.

Grudzińska-Gross, Irena. *Czesław Miłosz and Joseph Brodsky: Fellowship of Poets.* New Haven, CT: Yale University Press, 2009.

Grydzewski, Mieczysław. 'Silva rerum'. *Wiadomości* 22 (1951).

Hartwig, Julia. Interview with Wojciech Kass. *Topos* 3–4 (2004).

Hass, Robert. *Twentieth Century Pleasures: Prose on Poetry.* New York: Ecco, 2002.

Haven, Cynthia L., ed. *Czesław Miłosz: Conversations.* Jackson: University Press of Mississippi, 2006.

———. *An Invisible Rope: Portraits of Czesław Miłosz.* Athens: Ohio University Press, 2011.

Heaney, Seamus. *A Giant at My Shoulder.* RTE Radio, 25 August 1999.

———. 'In Gratitude for All the Gifts'. *The Guardian,* 11 September 2004.

———. 'Mój Miłosz'. *Tygodnik Powszechny* 26 (2001). www.tygodnik.com/apokryf/16/mojmilosz.html.

———. *Opened Ground: Poems 1966–1996.* London: Faber, 1998.

———. 'Secular and Millennial Miłosz'. In *Finders, Keepers: Selected Prose, 1971–2001.* London: Faber, 2002.

Herling-Grudziński, Gustaw. 'Granice poezji'. *Pion* 8 (1939).

Hernik-Spalińska, Jagoda. *Wileńskie Środy Literackie 1927–1939.* Warsaw, 1998.

Hersch, Jeanne. 'O przekładach'. *Zeszyty Literackie* 36 (Fall 1991).

———. *O Stanisławie Vincenzie.* Warsaw, 1983.

Homer. *The Iliad.* Translated by E. V. Rieu. Harmondsworth: Penguin, 1963.

Illg, Jerzy. 'Carol Thigpen-Miłosz (1944–2002)'. *Gazeta w Krakowie,* 9 August 2002.

———. *Mój Znak.* Kraków, 2009.

Iwaszkiewicz, Jarosław. *Dzienniki 1911–1955.* Edited by A. R. Papiescy. Warsaw, 2007.

———. *Dzienniki 1956–1963.* Edited by A. R. Papiescy. Warsaw, 2010.

———. *Portrety na marginesach.* Warsaw, 2004.

Jameson, Margaret Storm. *Journey from the North: An Autobiography.* New York, 1970.

Janta, Aleksander. *Nic własnego nikomu.* Warsaw, 1977.

Jasienica, Paweł. *Pamiętnik.* Warsaw, 1993.

Jędrychowska, Anna. *Zygzakiem i po prostu.* Warsaw, 1965.

John Paul II. Homily delivered on Victory Square, Warsaw, 2 June 1979. Libreria Editrice Vaticana, https://w2.vatican.va/content/john-paul-ii/en/homilies/1979/documents /hf_jp-ii_hom_19790602_polonia-varsavia.html, accessed 4 June 2016.

Judt, Tony. 'Captive Minds'. *New York Review of Books,* 30 September 2010. http://www .nybooks.com/articles/2010/09/30/captive-minds/, accessed 17 October 2016.

Keliuotis, Juozas. *Mano autobiografija atsiminimai.* Vilnius, 2003.

Kisielewski, Stefan. 'Bramy arsenału'. In Czesław Miłosz, ed., *Trzy Zimy: Głosy o wierszach.* London, 1987.

Kołakowski, Leszek. *Wśród znajomych. O różnych ludziach.* Kraków, 2004.

Korabiewicz, Wacław. *Pokusy.* Warsaw, 1986.

Kornacki, Jerzy. *Rachunek pamięci.* Warsaw, 1957.

Kosińska, Agnieszka. *Miłosz w Krakowie.* Kraków, 2015.

———. *Rozmowy o Miłoszu.* Warsaw, 2010.

Kott, Jan. 'Sprawa książki'. *Odrodzenie* 17 (1945).

Kowalska, Anna. *Dzienniki 1927–1969.* Warsaw, 2008.

Kurtzweil, Edith. 'The Captive Mind'. *Partisan Review* 66, no. 1 (1999): 55–60.

Kwiatkowski, Maciej. *Wrzesień 1939 w warszawskiej rozgłośni Polskiego Radia.* Warsaw, 1984.

Kwiatkowski, Tadeusz. *Panopticum.* Kraków, 1995.

Lechoń, Jan. *Dziennik.* London, 1967.

Łobodowski, Józef. 'Rodzinna Mitologia'. *Orzeł Biały-Syrena* (London) 46 (1960).

Lottman, Herbert. *Albert Camus: A Biography.* London: Picador, 1981.

Lourie, Richard. Interview. *Writers in Motion,* Jagiellonian University, Kraków Writers Festival, 17 July 2013. https://www.youtube.com/watch?v=8waIYFewS3A.

———. 'My Miłosz' (Mój Miłosz). *Tygodnik Powszechny* 26 (2001). www.tygodnik .com/apokryf/16/mojmilosz.html.

———. 'The Teacher and His Students'. *Partisan Review* 16, no. 1 (1999): 97–99.

MacNeice, Louis. *Selected Poems.* London: Faber, 1988.

Mann, Thomas. *Death in Venice, Tristan* and *Tonio Kröger.* Translated by H. T. Lowe-Porter. 1928. Reprint, Harmondsworth: Penguin, 1975.

Maritain, Jacques. *Sztuka i mądrość* (Art and Wisdom). Translated by K. K. Górski. Warsaw, 2001.

Marx, Jan. *Z Jerzym Putramentem rozmawiał. . . . Poezja* 5–6 (1981).

Matuszewski, Ryszard. 'Moje Spotkania z Miłoszem'. Kraków, 2004.

McLean, Hugh. 'Odznaczenie Czesława Miłosza'. *Kultura* 9 (1978).

Merwin, W. S. 'Remembering Czesław Miłosz'. In Haven, *An Invisible Rope*, 74–79.

Michnik, Adam. 'A Free Mind'. In Gromek-Illg, *Czesław Miłosz: In Memoriam*.

Mickiewicz, Adam. *Pan Tadeusz*. Translated by Kenneth Mackenzie. London: Dent, 1966.

Mieroszewski, Juliusz. 'List z wyspy'. *Kultura* 7–8 (1951).

Mikołajewski, Jarosław. 'Rzeka, góra, drzewo'. In Gromek-Illg, *Czesław Miłosz: In Memoriam*, 99–105.

Mikonis, Anna. *Życie filmowe Wilna w okresie międzywojennym 1919–39*. *Kwartalnik Filmowy* 44 (2003): 211–227.

Miłosz, Andrzej. 'Autobiografia'. *Jaćwież* 14 (2001).

———. 'O starszym bracie'. *Tygodnik Powszechny* 26 (2001).

Modzelewska, Natalia. 'Miłosz w Polsce na przełomie 1950–51'. *Kultura* 3 (1981).

Parker, Michael. 'Past Master': Czesław Milosz and His Impact on Seamus Heaney's Poetry'. *Textual Practice* 27, no. 5 (2013): 825–850.

Pasierski, Emil. 'Gamma i Omega.' Doctoral diss., University of Wrocław, 2009.

Piasecki, Sergiusz. *Człowiek przemieniony w wilka*. Wrocław, 2000.

Pinsky, Robert. 'A Poet Worthy of Protest'. *New York Times*, 26 August 2004. http://www.nytimes.com/2004/08/26/opinion/a-poet-worthy-of-protest.html?ref=topics&_r=1.

———. 'Rodzaj skupienia'. *Tygodnik Powszechny* 26 (1996).

Pollak, Seweryn. 'Apokalipsa w cuglach'. *Nowa Kwadryga* 3 (1937).

Przybylski, Richard. 'O młodszym bracie'. In Czesław Miłosz, ed., *Trzy Zimy: Głosy o wierszach*. London, 1987.

Putrament, Jerzy. *Pół wieku: Młodość*. Warsaw, 1969.

Rzepińska, Maria. 'Poeta o malarstwie: Rozmowa z Czesławem Miłoszem'. *Przegląd Artystyczny* 1 (1946).

Schenker, Aleksander. 'Wędrowiec'. In Gromek-Illg, *Czesław Miłosz: In Memoriam*.

Scott, Peter Dale. 'A Difficult Inspirational Giant'. In Haven, *An Invisible Rope*, 65–79.

Sławińska, Irena. 'To jest daleki kraj'. *Tygodnik Powszechny* 16 (1956).

Słonimski, Antoni. 'Heretyk na ambonie' (A Heretic at the Lectern). Warsaw, 1934.

Stempowski, Jerzy. *Listy 1946–69*. Warsaw, 1998.

Stomma, Stanisław. *Trudne Lekcje Historii*. Kraków, 1998.

Sukiennicki, Wiktor. *Legenda i rzeczywistość. Wspomnienia i uwagi o dwudziestu latach Uniwersytetu Stefana Batorego w Wilnie*. Paris, 1967.

'Susan Sontag Provokes Debate on Communism'. *New York Times*, 27 February 1982, https://www.nytimes.com/books/00/03/12/specials/sontag-communism.html.

Synoradzka, Anna. *Andrzejewski*. Kraków, 1997.

Szczepańska, Danuta. *W Goszycach*. Kraków, 2004.

Szymańska, Irena. *Miałam dar zachwytu. Wspomnienia wydawcy*. Warsaw, 2001.

Taborski, Bolesław. 'Na tropach "rewolucji"'. *Merkuriusz* (London) 3 (1955).

Tarnowska, Beata. 'Pieśni trampów. Poezja i wierszopisarstwo z kvęgu Akademick-iego Klubu Włóczęgów Wileńskich'. In *Poezja i poeci w Wilnie lat 1920–1940*, ed. T. Bujnickiego and K. Biedrzyckiego. Kraków, 2003, 117–136.

Toporowski, Marian. *Strop. Wspomnienie warszawskie*. Warsaw, 1970.

Urbanowicz, Bohdan. *Gimnazjum im. Króla Zygmunta Augusta w Wilnie*. Bydgoszcz, 1999.

Vallee, Lillian. 'The Exile in California'. In *Periphery: Journal of Polish Affairs* 4–5 (1998–1999).

Venclova, Tomas. *Winter Dialogue*. Evanston, IL: Northwestern University Press, 1997.

Vendler, Helen. 'Kim był dla mnie Czesław Miłosz?' In Gromek-Illg, *Czesław Miłosz: In Memoriam*, 64–71.

———. *The Music of What Happens: Poems, Poets, Critics*. Cambridge, MA: Harvard University Press, 1988.

———. 'Understanding "The World"'. *Partisan Review* 66, no. 1 (1999): 129–135.

———. 'Z okruchów, świat jest doskonały'. In *Poznawanie Miłosza*, ed. Aleksander Fiut. Kraków, 2000.

Vincenz, Andrzej. 'Nie ma wolności bez prawdy'. *Tygodnik Powszechny* 30 (2000).

———. 'Stanisław Vincenz and Czesław Miłosz'. Lecture delivered at the Catholic University of Lublin, circa 15–17 October 1987.

Vołyńska-Bogert, Rimma. 'Sceny z życia uniwersyteckiego w Berkeley'. *Tydzień Polski* 13–14 (December 1980).

Walicki, Andrzej. *Zniewolony umysł po latach*. Warsaw, 1993.

Weil, Simone. *Gravity and Grace*. London: Routledge, 2002.

Williams, William Carlos. *Selected Poems*. Edited by Charles Tomlinson. New York: New Directions.

Wordsworth, William. 'Lines Composed a Few Miles above Tintern Abbey'. In *Poetical Works*, ed. Ernest de Selincourt. London: Oxford University Press, 1967.

Wroe, Nicholas. 'Czesław Miłosz, a Century's Witness'. *The Guardian*, 10 November 2001; reprinted in Haven, *Czesław Miłosz: Conversations*, 99–208.

Wyszyński, Stefan. 'Do świadków promocji doktorskiej Laureata Nagrody Nobla Czesława Miłosza'. *Kultura* 7–8 (1981).

Zagórski, Jerzy. 'W Żagarach in trochę potem'. *Poezja* 5–6 (1981).

Żakowski, Jacek. 'Bo to jest rodzaj zakonu' (interview with Jerzy Giedroyc). *Gazeta Wyborcza*, 12 October 2000.

Zaleski, Marek. *Przygoda drugiej awangardy*. Wrocław, 2000.

Zaremba, Z. 'Wobec nowego uchodźcy'. *Kultura* 7–8 (1951).

Żebrowski, Marek. 'Bukareszt w ambasadzie'. *Zeszyty Historyczne* (Paris) 171 (2010).

Zmarz-Koczanowicz, Maria, dir. *The Magic Mountain: An American Portrait of Czesław Miłosz*, 2001.

ARCHIVAL MATERIALS

Czesław Miłosz's archival materials are primarily kept in two places: (1) at Yale University in the United States, listed as Czesław Miłosz Papers (GEN MSS 661) and Beinecke Rare Book and Manuscript Library; and (2) in the poet's personal archives held in his home in Kraków. Quotations from Miłosz's works, letters, and documents were drawn from the archives of Kultura in Paris, Literary Institute in Maisons-Laffitte (Archiwum Instytutu Literackiego); the Museum of Literature in Warsaw; and archive collections of Antoni Bohdziewicz (Warsaw); Jerzy W. Borejsza (Warsaw); Tadeusz Bujnicki (Kraków); the Polish Ministry of Foreign Affairs (Warsaw); Jerzy Turowicz (Kraków); University of Stefan Batory (the Central State Archive of Lithuania, Vilnius); Warsaw University, Bohdan Tadeusz Urbanowicz; the Institute of Arts, PAN (Warsaw); Maria and Edmund Wierciński, in the Institute of Arts PAN (Warsaw); and the Institute of the National Remembrance (BU MSW II 30313: "Czesław Miłosz's Nobel Prize").

Czesław Miłosz Correspondence in Book Publications

Giedroyc, Jerzy, and Czesław Miłosz. *Listy 1952–1963*. Edited and introduced by Marek Kornat. Warsaw, 2008. A further selection of correspondence was published in 2011, which Andrzej Franaszek drew upon from the Archives of the Literary Institute, Paris.

Herbert, Zbigniew, and Czesław Miłosz. *Korespondencja*. Edited by Barbara Toruńczyk, notes by Maciej Tabor and Barbara Toruńczyk. Warsaw, 2006.

Merton, Thomas, and Czesław Miłosz. *Listy*. Translated by Maria Tarnowska. Kraków, 1991.

Miłosz, Czesław. Letters to Aleksander Wat. In Aleksander Wat, *Korespondencja*. Selected and edited, notes and prologue by Alina Kowalczykowa. Warsaw, 2005.

———. *My Guardian from Wilno: Letters to Manfred Kridl (1946–1955)*. Introduction and notes by Andrzej Karcz. Toruń, 2005.

Miłosz, Czesław, and Jarosław Iwaszkiewicz. *Double Portrait*. Selected by Barbara Toruńczyk and Robert Papieski. Warsaw, 2011. The full correspondence was not published when Franaszek's book was being written and so drew upon the collections Letters of Czesław Miłosz to Jarosław Iwaszkiewicz, Library of the Institute of Literary Research, PAN, and Letters of Czesław Miłosz to Jarosław Iwaszkiewicz, Museum of Anna and Jarosław Iwaszkiewicz in Stawisko.

Miłosz, Czesław, and Konstanty A. Jeleński. *Korespondencja*. Edited by Barbara Toruńczyk and Radosław Romaniuk. Warsaw, 2011. This correspondence was not published when Franaszek's book was being written, so *Miłosz: Biografia* quotes from the archives of the Beinecke Library.

Miłosz, Czesław, and Ola Wat. *Letters about What Is Most Important*. Vol. 1. Collected by Barbara Toruńczyk. Warsaw, 2009.

Correspondence of Czesław Miłosz: Publications in Periodicals

Miłosz, Czesław. Letters to Zbigniew Fałtynowicz. *Jaćwież* 27–28 (2004).

———. Letters to Artur Międzyrzecki. *Kwartalnik Artystyczny* 3 (2007).

———. Letters to Krzysztof Myszkowski. *Kwartalnik Artystyczny* 3 (2005).

———. Letters to the Family. *Kwartalnik Artystyczny* 3 (2008).

Miłosz, Czesław, and Witold Gombrowicz. *Korespondencja.* Edited by Jerzy Jarzębski and Ryszard Nycz. *Teksty II*, 1–2, 1992.

'They Could Have Had My Scalp'. Letters of Czesław Miłosz to Józef Witlin. Edited by Barbara Toruńczyk. *Gazeta Wyborcza*, 30 June–1 July 2001.

Ziółkowska, Aleksandra. 'Wańkowicz and Miłosz in the Light of Their Correspondence'. *Twórczość* 10 (1981).

Correspondence of Czesław Miłosz: Archive Collections

Letters to Jerzy Andrzejewski, 1957–1979. Jerzy Andrzejewski Archives, Museum of Literature, Warsaw.

Letters to Stanisław Barańczak. Stanisław Barańczak Archives.

Letter to Jan Błoński. Jagiellonian University, Kraków.

Letters to Albert Einstein. The Albert Einstein Archives at the Hebrew University of Jerusalem.

Letters to Aniela Micińska and Jan Ulatowski. Emigration Archives, the University of Nicholas Copernicus in Toruń, Jan Ulatowski Archives.

Letters to Bolesław, Halina, Aniela, and Anna Miciński. Manuscript Department, National Library, Warsaw.

Letters to Władysław Sebyła. Museum of Literature, Warsaw.

Letters to Jerzy Turowicz. Jerzy Turowicz Archives, Kraków.

Letters to Victor Weintraub, 1959–1987. Jagiellonian University, Kraków.

Other Correspondence

Anders, Gen. Władysław. Letter to J. Czapski, 29 October 1951. Polish Institute and General Sikorski Museum, London.

Arendt, Hannah, and Karl Jaspers. *Briefwechsel 1926–1969.* Munich, 1993.

Arendt, Hannah, and Mary McCarthy. *Between Friends: The Correspondence of Hannah Arendt and Mary McCarthy, 1949–1975.* Edited by Carol Brightman. New York, 1995.

Błoński, Jan, and Sławomir Mrożek. *Listy 1963–1996.* Kraków, 2004.

Czechowicz, Józef. *Listy.* Collected and edited by Tadeusz Kłak. Lublin, 1997.

Giedroyc, Jerzy, and Andrzej Bobkowski. *Listy 1946–1961.* Selected, edited, and introduced by Jan Zieliński. Warsaw, 1997.

Giedroyc, Jerzy, and Witold Gombrowicz. *Listy 1950–1969*. Selected and edited by Andrzej Kowalczyk. Warsaw, 1993.

Giedroyc, Jerzy, and Konstanty A. Jeleński. *Listy 1950–1987*. Collected, edited, and introduced by Wojciech Karpiński. Warsaw, 1995.

Giedroyc, Jerzy, and Juliusz Mieroszewski. *Listy 1949–1956*. Parts 1 and 2. Collected and introduced by Krzysztof Pomian, notes and index by Jacek Krawczyk and Krzysztof Pomian. Warsaw, 1999.

Giedroyc, Jerzy, and Jerzy Stempowski. *Listy 1946–1969*. Parts 1 and 2. Edited and introduced by Andrzej Stanisław Kowalczyk. Warsaw, 1998.

Giedroyc, Jerzy, and Melchior Wańkowicz. *Listy 1945–1963*. Selected and introduced by Aleksandra Ziółkowska-Boehm, notes by Aleksandra Ziółkowska-Boehm and Jacek Krawczyk. Warsaw, 2000.

Grydzewski, Mieczysław, and Jan Lechoń. *Listy 1923–1956*. Edited and introduced by Beata Dorosz. Warsaw, 2006.

Herbert, Zbigniew, and Aleksander Schenker. Letter dated 12 June 1975. Archives of A. Schenker.

Hertz, Zygmunt. *Listy do Czesława Miłosza, 1952–1979*. Selected and edited by Renata Gorczyńska. Paris, 1992.

Iwaszkiewicz, Jarosław. *Listy do córek*. Introduction by Maria Iwaszkiewicz and Teresa Markowska. Edited by Anna Romaniu and Radosław Romaniuk. Warsaw, 2009.

Karpiński, Wojciech. 'Głosy z Beinecke I' [Voices from the Beinecke]. *Zeszyty Literackie* 66 (1999).

Miciński, Bolesław, and Jerzy Stempowski. *Listy*. Edited by Maria Micińska, Jarosław Klejnocki, and Andrzej Stanisław Kowalczyk. Warsaw, 1995.

Stempowski, Jerzy. *Listy z ziemi berneńskiej*. London, 1974.

Vincenz, Stanisław. Letter to Józef Czapski, 3 November 1951. Józef and Maria Czapski Archive from Maisons-Laffitte, National Museum, Kraków.

Miłosz incorporates comments from interviews in the documentary film *The Magic Mountain: An American Portrait of Czesław Miłosz*, screenplay by Andrzej Franaszek and Jerzy Illg, directed by Maria Zmarz-Koczanowicz, produced by the film studio Largo, Agencja Produkcji Filmowej, Telewizja Polska Programme 1, 2000.

ACKNOWLEDGEMENTS

When I began to read through the vast array of materials in the Czesław Miłosz archive at the Beinecke Library over ten years ago, I often entertained doubts about whether I would manage to produce a book dedicated to the poet. Never for a moment did I imagine that such a book when it was completed would be translated into English and published in America, let alone by Harvard University Press. I must admit to having been truly pleased by that development, as I believe Miłosz would have been too: in so many poems, essays and books, he endeavoured to convey to American readers the experiences in Europe that shaped his world-view, and to provide them with a sense of some of the places and cultures deeply marked by key events in twentieth-century history.

This publication would never have appeared, had it not been for the good-will and commitment of a number of people. I would like to take this opportunity to thank John Kulka of Harvard University Press, my Polish publisher, Jerzy Illg, Ewa Ledóchowicz, Helen Vendler, Adam Zagajewski and for his knowledge and continuing support Anthony Miłosz. I must also recognise the efforts of Luke Ingram, Percy Stubbs, and Lauren Rogoff at The Wylie Agency. I would especially like to express my gratitude to Aleksandra and Michael Parker, the translators and editors of the book. They performed a service much greater than any I have a right to expect from a pair of translators—they provided additional contextual information in the book in exactly those places where English-language readers were likely to encounter difficulties. They are also responsible for the in-troduction, a helpful chronology and useful maps, and they produced the whole book on an unforgiving schedule, moved by a love for Miłosz and his work.

Andrzej Franaszek

In our role as translators and editors, we would like to express our thanks to all those who provided assistance and support in the preparation of this book. The appro-priate place to begin is with Andrzej Franaszek, whose detailed research makes this biography such a rewarding read. We would like to endorse wholeheartedly Andrzej's thanks to John Kulka and Jerzy Illg, the driving forces behind the project. We also thank the staff at Harvard University Press, especially Joy Deng and Kate Brick, and Barb Goodhouse and Melody Negron at Westchester Pub-lishing Services. During the preparatory phase of the project, James McGeever, who is based in Lithuania, provided us with a steady stream of useful material on Miłosz and his homeland, and when it came to preparing the finished manuscript, Niall Munro of Oxford Brookes University proved a solid and supportive friend.

Without the hard work of Marta Zabłocka of the Znak Press, Kraków, we would not have the maps, and without the help of Barbara Baj Wojtowicz and Jolanta Lebioda of Oxford University's Taylor Institute (Slavonic Studies) we would not have had access to so many editions in Polish of Miłosz's works. We are grateful also to Eric Falci, who organised our visit to Berkeley in 2015, which included an excursion to the poet's home on the 'Magic Mountain'. He could have provided us with no more fitting a guide than Robert Hass, foremost among many outstanding translators who enabled Miłosz's poems to reach an audience worldwide. Thanks go equally to Aleksander Fiut, who arranged and provided a tour of the Miłoszes' apartment in Kraków. Last though not least, it is appropriate to mention two further names, without whose encouragement, we might never have taken on this difficult, but rewarding task—Seamus Heaney and Helen Vendler. Their unerringly perceptive analyses of Miłosz's poetry served as an inspiration to us, as to so many others.

Aleksandra and Michael Parker

ILLUSTRATION CREDITS

1. Weronika Miłosz (née Kunat) and Aleksander Miłosz, the poet's parents. Andrzej and Czesław Miłosz Family Archive, National Library of Poland, Warsaw.

2. Aleksander Miłosz *(fifth from left)* on board the ship of the explorer Fridtjöf Nansen *(centre)* in 1913. Fridtjof Nansen Photo Archive, National Library of Norway, Oslo. (nansen / 3f201)

3. In Szejtenie: Weronika Miłosz *(left)*, baby Czesław *(centre)* in the nurse's arms. Andrzej and Czesław Miłosz Family Archive, National Library of Poland, Warsaw.

4. Weronika with the two year-old Czesław. Andrzej and Czesław Miłosz Family Archive, National Library of Poland, Warsaw.

5. Czesław, aged two. Czesław Miłosz Papers. Series VII, Family Photographs. Beinecke Rare Book and Manuscript Library, Yale University.

6. Stanisława Miłosz, CM's paternal grandmother, with Czesław *(left)* and his brother, Andrzej *(right)*. Czesław Miłosz Papers. Series VII, Family Photographs. Beinecke Rare Book and Manuscript Library, Yale University.

7. Jozefa Kunat, CM's maternal grandmother, with her daughter, Weronika (Milosz). Czesław Miłosz Papers. Series VII, Family Photographs. Beinecke Rare Book and Manuscript Library, Yale University.

8. Czesław at the start of his time at the King Sigismund Augustus Boys' State Gymnasium. Andrzej and Czesław Miłosz Family Archive, National Library of Poland, Warsaw.

9. Czesław's Aunt Gabriela. Andrzej and Czesław Miłosz Family Archive, National Library of Poland, Warsaw.

10. Czesław *(back row, far left)* towards the end of his time at the Gymnasium. Leopold Chomski is in the front row, third from left. Andrzej and Czesław Miłosz Family Archive, National Library of Poland, Warsaw.

11. A view of Wilno (Vilnius) from Castle Hill, 1912. Sergei Mikhailovich Prokudin-Gorskii Collection. Library of Congress, Prints and Photographs Division, Washington, DC. (LC-USZ62-94002)

12. Members of PET. Czesław is in the back row, centre. Stanisław Stomma.

13. Czesław smoking in the Café Rudnicki, Wilno. Andrzej and Czesław Miłosz Family Archive, National Library of Poland, Warsaw.

14. Czesław Miłosz in the 1930s. Andrzej and Czesław Miłosz Family Archive, National Library of Poland, Warsaw.

15. Oskar Milosz. Photograph by Pierre Choumoff. © Collections de la Bibliothèque Littéraire Jacques Doucet, Paris (Chancellerie des Universités de Paris), 2016.

16. Jadwiga Waszkiewicz with Czesław Miłosz on the Barcie estate, on the outskirts of Wilno. Władysław Tomaszewicz. Family Archive of Ewa Tomaszewicz.

17. Janina (Janka) Cękalska's identity card, 1935. Andrzej and Czesław Miłosz Family Archive, National Library of Poland, Warsaw.

18. Czesław Miłosz, 1942. Andrzej and Czesław Miłosz Family Archive, National Library of Poland, Warsaw.

19. A group of Jews being led away by German soldiers during the Warsaw Ghetto Rising, 1943. Photograph from Jürgen Stroop Report to Heinrich Himmler, May 1943. Buyenlarge Archive / UIG / Bridgeman Images.

20. General Dwight D. Eisenhower surveys Warsaw's Old Town in ruins after the conclusion of the war, 1946. Library of Congress, Prints and Photographs Division, Washington, DC. (LC-DIG-ppmsca-19261)

21. Czesław Miłosz *(standing)* in the Polish Embassy, Washington, DC. Janka is seated on the sofa *(second from right)*. Andrzej and Czesław Miłosz Family Archive, National Library of Poland, Warsaw.

22. Poster for a talk on the 1943 Ghetto Rising, during Milosz's time as cultural attaché in the Polish Consulate, New York, 1946. Andrzej and Czesław Miłosz Family Archive, National Library of Poland, Warsaw.

23. Czesław Miłosz *(centre)* with Jozefa Winiewicz, the Polish Ambassador's wife, and Natalia Modzelewska, the Foreign Minister's wife, in Club Cairo, Washington, DC, 1947. Czesław Miłosz Papers. Series VII, Family Photographs. Beinecke Rare Book and Manuscript Library, Yale University.

24. Andrzej and Czesław Miłosz in Sopot, on the Baltic Coast, 1949. Andrzej and Czesław Miłosz Family Archive, National Library of Poland, Warsaw.

25. Janka in the United States in the late 1940s. Andrzej and Czesław Miłosz Family Archive, National Library of Poland, Warsaw.

26. Czesław Milosz relaxing in Rehoboth Beach, Delaware. Andrzej and Czesław Miłosz Family Archive, National Library of Poland, Warsaw.

27. Kultura's main office and its staff: Jerzy Giedroyc, James Burnham, Zygmunt Hertz, Józef Czapski, Zofia Hertz, Maria Czapski, Czesław Miłosz, 1951. Archives of the Literary Institute, Paris.

28. Janina Miłosz with her sons, Antoni *(standing, left)* and Piotr *(sitting, right)*. Andrzej and Czesław Miłosz Family Archive, National Library of Poland, Warsaw.

29. The Milosz family at Montgeron, near Paris, 1957. Photograph by Janusz Odrowąż-Pieniążek.

30. Manuscript of the poem 'From the Rising of the Sun'. Czesław Miłosz Papers. Series II, Writings. Beinecke Rare Book and Manuscript Library, Yale University.

31. Piotr, Janina, and Czesław Milosz, with Zbigniew Herbert, on board a ship taking them to America. Photograph by Tony Milosz, 8 January 1964. Andrzej and Czesław Miłosz Family Archive, National Library of Poland, Warsaw.

32. Witold Gombrowicz with Czesław Miłosz, Vence, May 1967. Photograph by Oswaldo Malura / Rita Gombrowicz Archive / Fotonova / East News.

33. Czesław Miłosz at the University of California, Berkeley in 1980, holding a copy of *Utwory poetyckie*. Photograph by Andrzej Miłosz. Andrzej and Czesław Miłosz Family Archive, National Library of Poland, Warsaw.

34. Czesław Miłosz receiving the Nobel Prize for Literature from King Carl Gustaf XVI of Sweden, 10 December 1980. Photograph by Jerzy Undro / PAP.

35. Antoni and Czesław Miłosz visiting Zuzela, the birthplace of Janina Miłosz (née Dłuska) in 1981. Photograph by Andrzej Miłosz. Andrzej and Czesław Miłosz Family Archive, National Library of Poland, Warsaw.

36. Lech Wałęsa, addressing crowds following attacks on Solidarity members in Bydgoszcz, 21 March 1981. Forum / Bridgeman Images.

37. Lech Wałęsa and Czesław Miłosz, during the poet's return visit to Poland, June 1981. Photograph by Maciej Billewicz / PAP.

38. Czesław Miłosz addressing staff at NOWA, an underground publishing house, June 1981. Adam Michnik is seated at the front left of the photo. Photograph by Tomasz Michalak / FOTONOVA.

39. Czesław Miłosz and Carol Thigpen on holiday in Yugoslavia, 1985. Photograph by Andrzej Miłosz. Andrzej and Czesław Miłosz Family Archive, National Library of Poland, Warsaw.

40. Czesław Miłosz in his homeland, beside the River Niewiaża, Lithuania. Photograph by Andrzej Miłosz. Andrzej and Czesław Miłosz Family Archive, National Library of Poland, Warsaw.

41. Czesław and Carol Miłosz in the composer Zbigniew Preisner's house, October 2001. Anna Włoch.